A-Z WEST SU...

C000225659

CONTENTS

REFERENCE

Motorway	M23		Cycleway (selected)	🚲
Primary Route	A23		Fire Station	■
A Road	A259		Hospital	Ⓗ
B Road	B2135		House Numbers (A & B Roads only)	13 8
Dual Carriageway			Information Centre	🇮
One-way Street			National Grid Reference	^{5}60
Traffic flow on A Roads is also indicated by a heavy line on the driver's left.			Park & Ride	Hop Oast P+R
Road Under Construction			Police Station	▲
Opening dates are correct at the time of publication.			Post Office	★
Proposed Road			Safety Camera with Speed Limit	㉚
Restricted Access			Fixed cameras and long term road works cameras. Symbols do not indicate camera direction.	
Pedestrianized Road			Toilet:	
Track & Footpath			without facilities for the Disabled	▽
Residential Walkway			with facilities for the Disabled	▽
Railway	Station / Heritage Station / Level Crossing / Tunnel		Disabled use only	▽
Built-up Area	PARK RD		Viewpoint	🔆 ✳
Local Authority Boundary			Educational Establishment	▢
National Park Boundary			Hospital or Healthcare Building	▢
Posttown Boundary			Industrial Building	▢
Postcode Boundary (within Posttown)			Leisure or Recreational Facility	▢
Map Continuation	80 / Large Scale City Centre 172		Place of Interest	▢
			Public Building	▢
Car Park (selected)	🅿		Shopping Centre or Market	▢
Church or Chapel	†		Other Selected Buildings	▢

SCALE

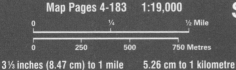

Map Pages 4-183	1:19,000	Map Page 172	1:9,500
0 ¼ ½ Mile		0 ⅛ ¼ Mile	
0 250 500 750 Metres		0 100 200 300 400 Metres	
3⅓ inches (8.47 cm) to 1 mile	5.26 cm to 1 kilometre	6⅔ inches (16.94 cm) to 1 mile	10.52 cm to 1 kilometre

Copyright of Geographers' A-Z Map Company Limited

Fairfield Road, Borough Green, Sevenoaks, Kent TN15 8PP
Telephone: 01732 781000 (Enquiries & Trade Sales)
01732 783422 (Retail Sales)

www.az.co.uk
Copyright © Geographers' A-Z Map Co. Ltd.
Edition 2 2013

 Ordnance Survey®

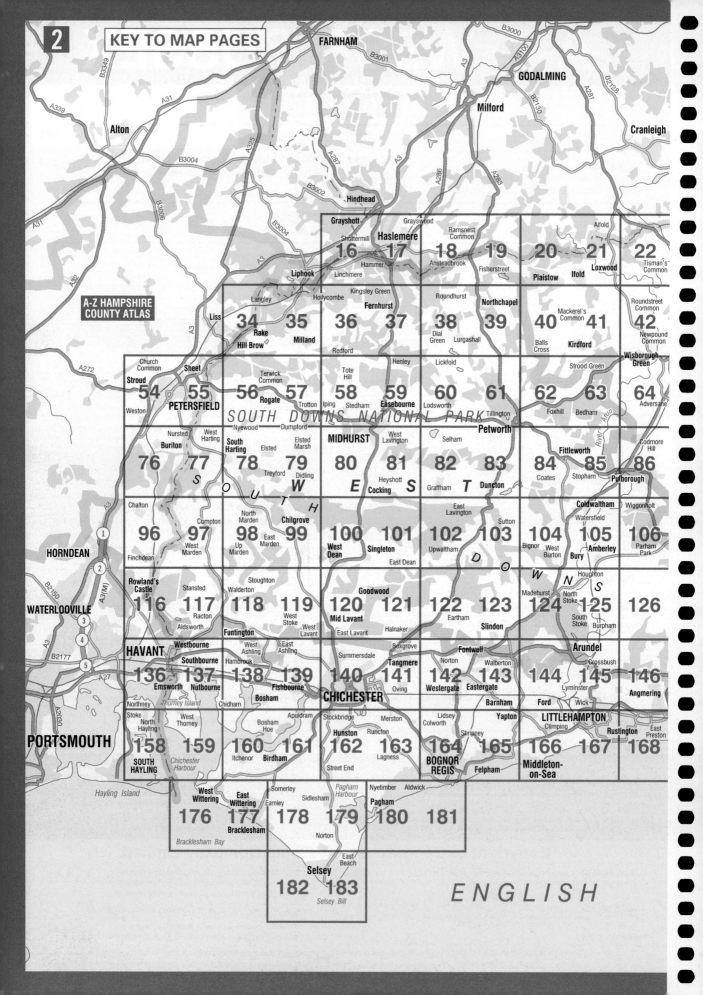

KEY TO MAP PAGES

2

A-Z HAMPSHIRE COUNTY ATLAS

FARNHAM

GODALMING

Milford

Cranleigh

Alton

Alfold

Grayshott
Grayswood
Ramsnest Common
Loxwood
Tisman's Common

Hindhead

Shottermill
Haslemere
Ansteadbrook
Fisherstreet
Plaistow
Ifold

16 **17** **18** **19** **20** **21** **22**

Hammer
Linchmere

Liphook

Kingsley Green

Roundhurst
Northchapel
Mackerel's Common
Roundstreet Common

Langley
Hollycombe
Fernhurst

Liss

34 **35** **36** **37** **38** **39** **40** **41** **42**

Rake
Milland
Dial Green
Lurgashall
Balls Cross
Kirdford
Newpound Common

Hill Brow
Redford

Henley
Lickfold
Strood Green
Wisborough Green

Church Common
Sheet
Terwick Common
Tote Hill
Stroud
Weston

54 **55** **56** **57** **58** **59** **60** **61** **62** **63** **64**

PETERSFIELD
Rogate
Trotton
Iping
Stedham
Easebourne
Lodsworth
Foxhill
Bedham
Adversane

SOUTH DOWNS NATIONAL PARK
Tillington

Nyewood
Dumpford
Petworth

Nursted
West Harting
West Lavington
Selham
Fittleworth
Codmore Hill

Buriton
South Harting
Elsted
Elsted Marsh
MIDHURST

76 **77** **78** **79** **80** **81** **82** **83** **84** **85** **86**

S
Treyford
Didling
Heyshott
Graffham
Dunton
Coates
Stopham
Pulborough

O
W
E
S
T
Cocking

Chalton
North Marden
Chilgrove
East Lavington
Sutton
Coldwaltham
Wiggonholt

Compton
East Marden
Watersfield
Parham Park

96 **97** **98** **99** **100** **101** **102** **103** **104** **105** **106**

Finchdean
West Marden
Up Marden
West Dean
Singleton
Upwaltham
Bignor
West Burton
Bury
Amberley

East Dean
D
O
W
N
S

HORNDEAN

Rowland's Castle
Stansted
Stoughton
Walderton
Goodwood
East Lavant
Madehurst
North Stoke
Houghton

116 **117** **118** **119** **120** **121** **122** **123** **124** **125** **126**

WATERLOOVILLE
Racton
Aldsworth
Funtington
West Stoke
West Lavant
Mid Lavant
Halnaker
Eartham
Slindon
South Stoke
Burpham

Westbourne
West Ashling
East Ashling
Summersdale
Boxgrove
Norton
Fontwell
Walberton
Arundel
Crossbush

HAVANT
Southbourne
Hambrook
Tangmere

136 **137** **138** **139** **140** **141** **142** **143** **144** **145** **146**

Emsworth
Nutbourne
Fishbourne
CHICHESTER
Oving
Westergate
Eastergate
Lyminster
Wick
Angmering

Northney
Thorney Island
Chidham
Bosham
Ford

Stoke
North Hayling
West Thorney
Apuldram
Stockbridge
Merston
Runcton
Lidsey
Colworth
Yapton
LITTLEHAMPTON
Climping
Rustington
East Preston

158 **159** **160** **161** **162** **163** **164** **165** **166** **167** **168**

PORTSMOUTH
SOUTH HAYLING
Chichester Harbour
Itchenor
Birdham
Hunston
Lagness
BOGNOR REGIS
Felpham
Middleton-on-Sea

Bosham Hoe
Street End

Hayling Island
West Wittering
East Wittering
Somerley
Earnley
Sidlesham
Pagham Harbour
Nyetimber
Aldwick
Pagham

176 **177** **178** **179** **180** **181**

Bracklesham
Norton

Bracklesham Bay
East Beach

Selsey

182 **183**

Selsey Bill

E N G L I S H

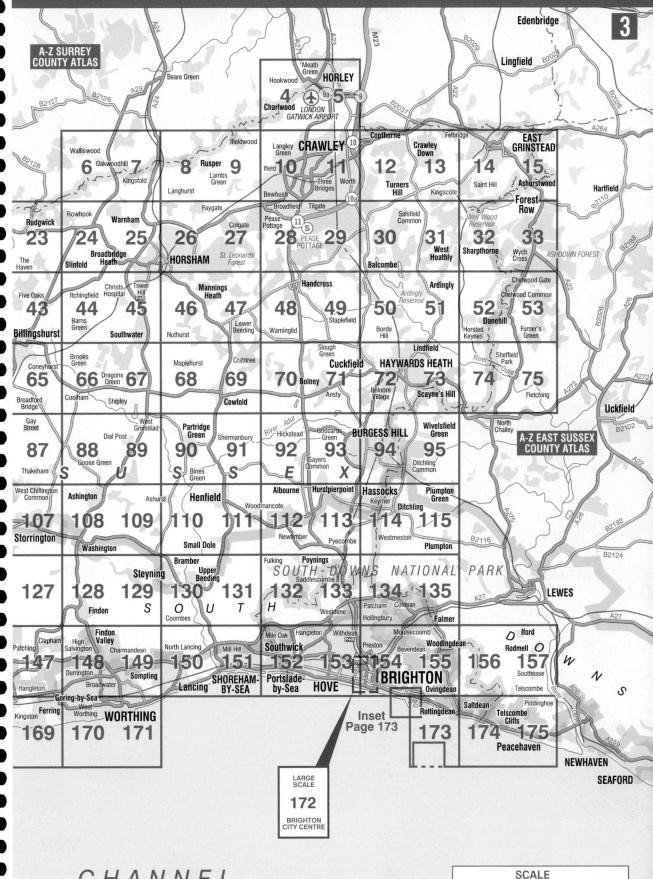

3

A-Z SURREY COUNTY ATLAS

Edenbridge
Lingfield
Beare Green
Meath Green
Hookwood
HORLEY
Charlwood
LONDON GATWICK AIRPORT
4 — **5**
9a 9

Felbridge
Copthorne
CRAWLEY
Crawley Down
EAST GRINSTEAD
Langley Green
Ifield
Ashurstwood
Hartfield
6 **7** **8** Rusper **9** **10** **11** **12** Turners Hill **13** **14** Saint Hill **15**
Walliswood
Oakwoodhill
Kingsfold
Lambs Green
Langhurst
Worth
Bewbush
Three Bridges
Kingscote
Forest Row

Walliswood 10a
Faygate
Broadfield
Tilgate
Selsfield Common
Weir Wood Reservoir
ASHDOWN FOREST
Wych Cross

Rudgwick Rowhook Warnham Colgate Pease Pottage Balcombe West Hoathly Sharpthorne
23 **24** **25** **26** **27** **28** **29** **30** **31** **32** **33**
The Haven
Slinfold
Broadbridge Heath
HORSHAM
St. Leonards Forest
PEASE POTTAGE

Five Oaks Itchingfield Christs Hospital Tower Hill Mannings Heath Handcross Ardingly Chelwood Gate
43 **44** **45** **46** **47** **48** **49** **50** **51** **52** **53**
Billingshurst Barns Green Southwater Nuthurst Lower Beeding Warninglid Staplefield Borde Hill Ardingly Reservoir Horsted Keynes Danehill Furner's Green
Chelwood Common

Coneyhurst Brooks Green Maplehurst Crabtree Slough Green Cuckfield Lindfield Sheffield Park River Ouse
65 **66** **67** **68** **69** **70** **71** **72** **73** **74** **75**
Broadford Bridge Coolham Dragons Green Shipley Cowfold Bolney Ansty HAYWARDS HEATH Bolnore Village Scayne's Hill Fletching
Uckfield

A-Z EAST SUSSEX COUNTY ATLAS

Gay Street West Grinstead Partridge Green Shermanbury River Adur Hickstead Goddards Green BURGESS HILL Wivelsfield Green North Chailey
87 **88** **89** **90** **91** **92** **93** **94** **95**
Thakeham Dial Post Bines Green Sayers Common Ditchling Common
Goose Green

West Chiltington Common Ashington Ashurst Henfield Woodmancote Albourne Hurstpierpoint Hassocks Plumpton Green
107 **108** **109** **110** **111** **112** **113** **114** **115**
Storrington Washington Small Dole Newtimber Pyecombe Keymer Ditchling Westmeston Plumpton

Bramber Fulking Poynings
Steyning Upper Beeding Saddlescombe SOUTH DOWNS NATIONAL PARK Patcham Coldean LEWES
127 **128** **129** **130** **131** **132** **133** **134** **135**
Findon Coombes Westdene Hollingbury Falmer
Mile Oak Hangleton Withdean Moulsecoomb

Clapham Findon Valley High Salvington Charmandean North Lancing Mill Hill Hangleton Preston Bevendean Woodingdean Iford Rodmell
147 **148** **149** **150** **151** **152** **153** **154** **155** **156** **157**
Patching Durrington Sompting Southwick BRIGHTON Ovingdean Southease Telscombe
Hangleton Broadwater Lancing SHOREHAM-BY-SEA Portslade-by-Sea HOVE Rottingdean Saltdean Piddinghoe

Goring-by-Sea West Worthing Telscombe Cliffs
Ferring Kingston **WORTHING** Inset Page 173 Peacehaven
169 **170** **171** **173** **174** **175**
NEWHAVEN
SEAFORD

LARGE SCALE
172
BRIGHTON CITY CENTRE

C H A N N E L

SCALE
0 1 2 3 4 5 Miles
0 1 2 3 4 5 6 Kilometres
West Sussex County Boundary
National Park Boundary

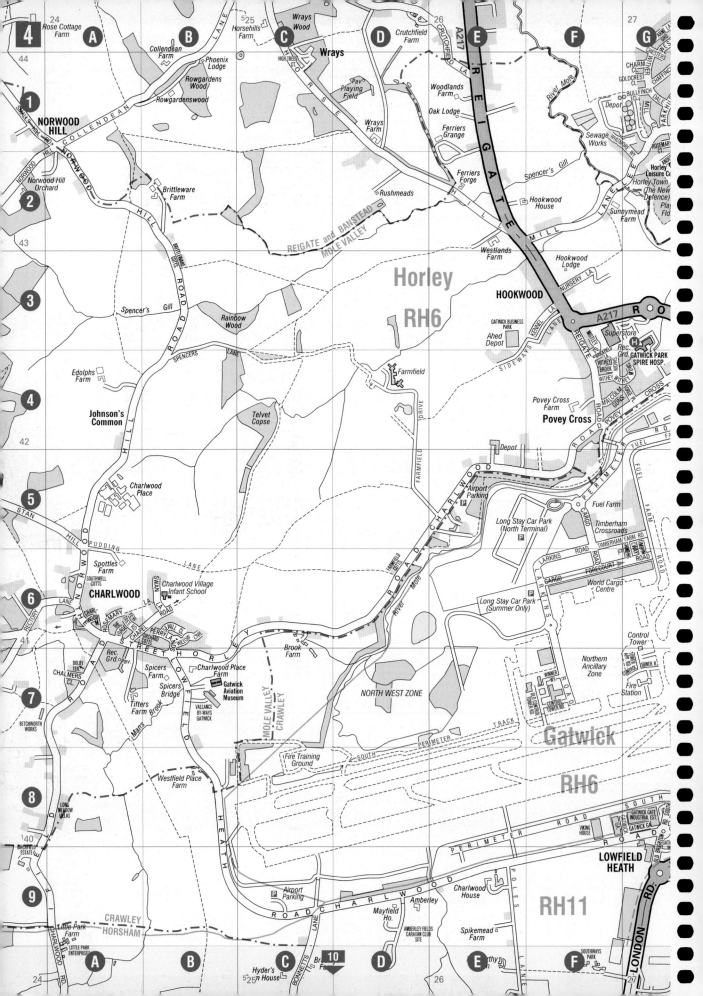

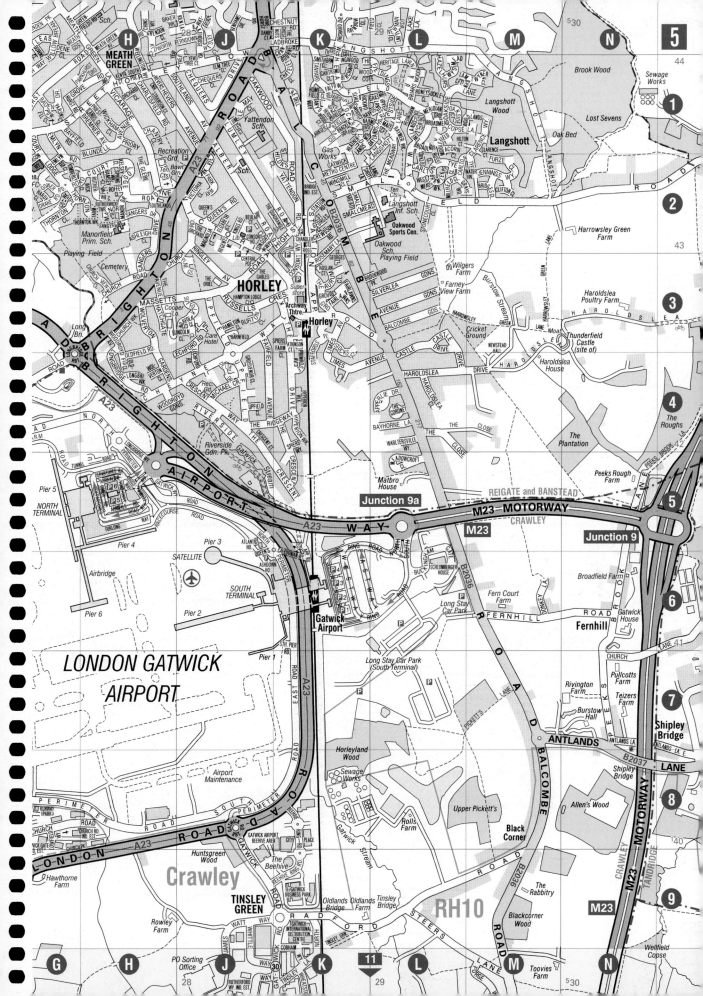

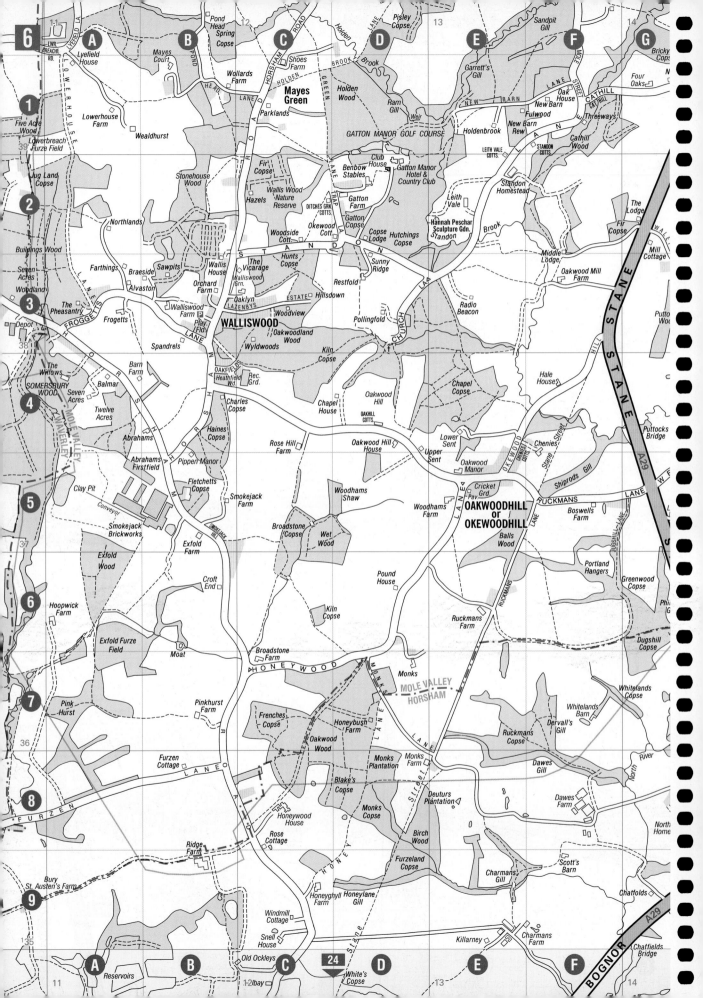

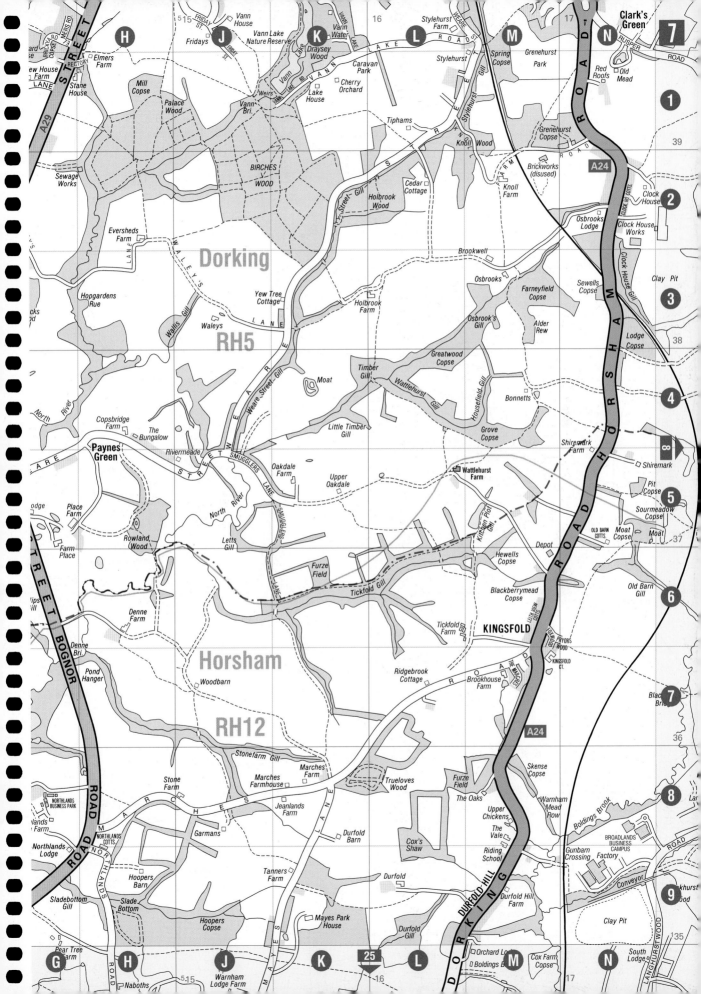

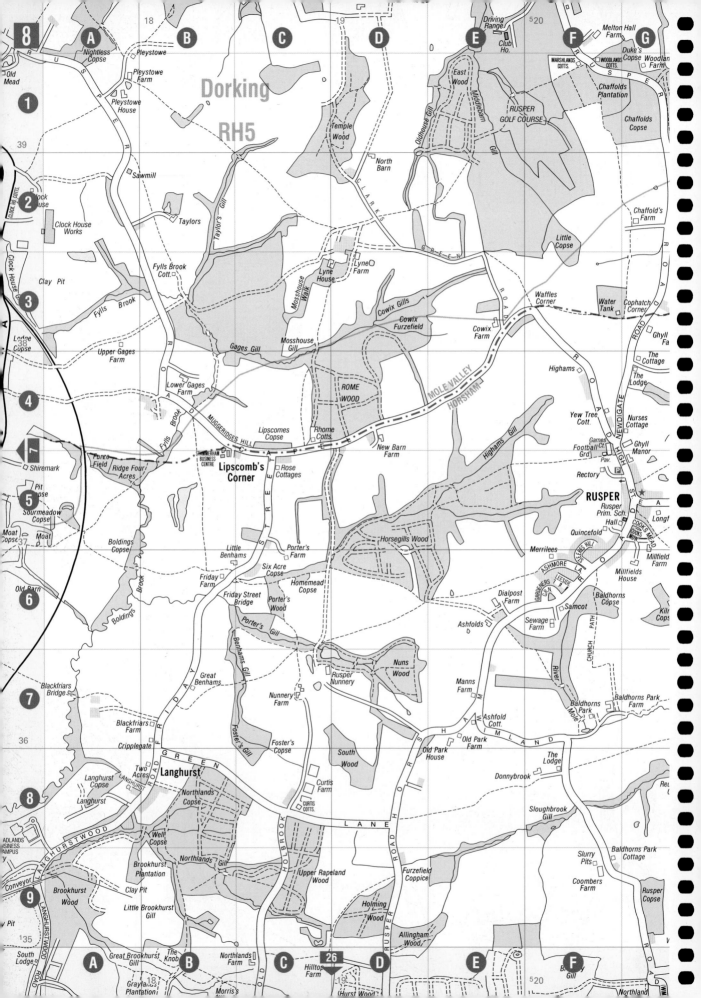

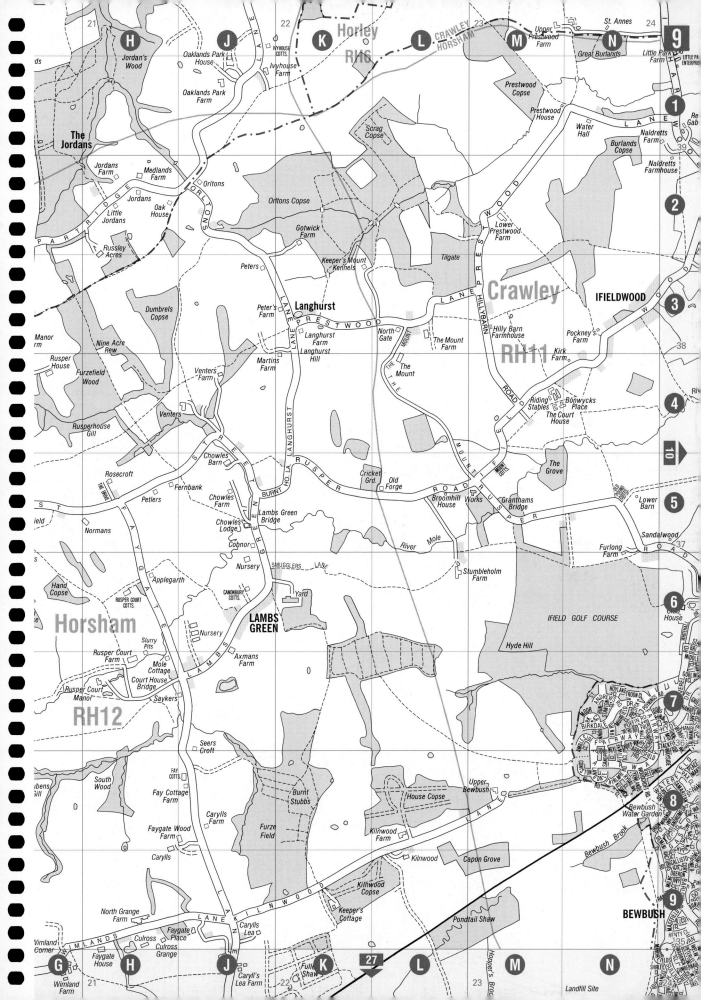

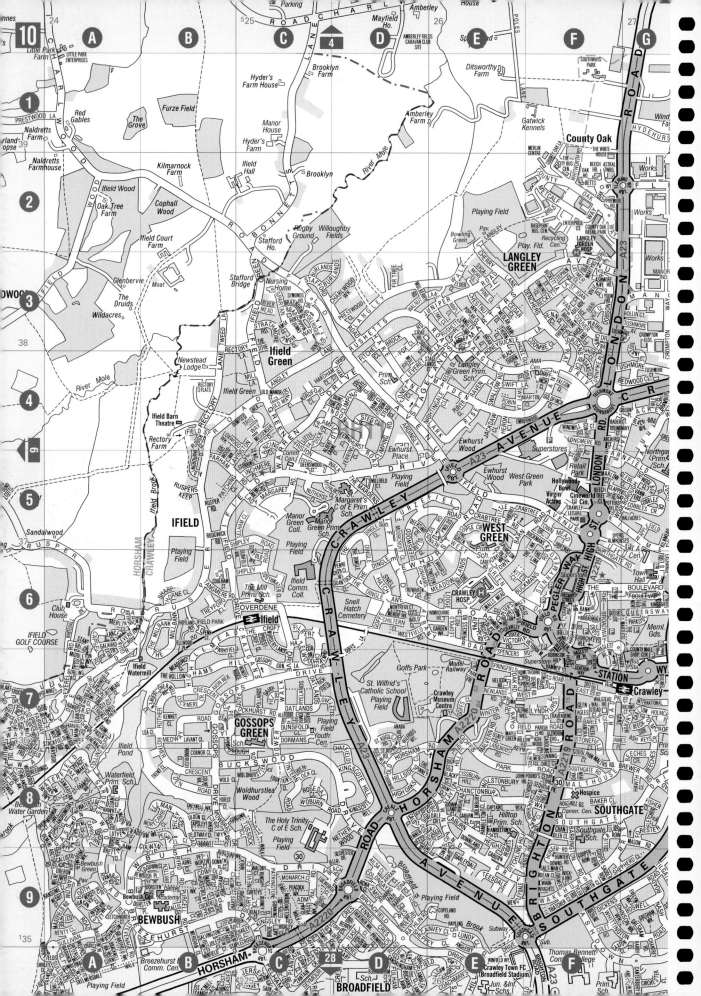

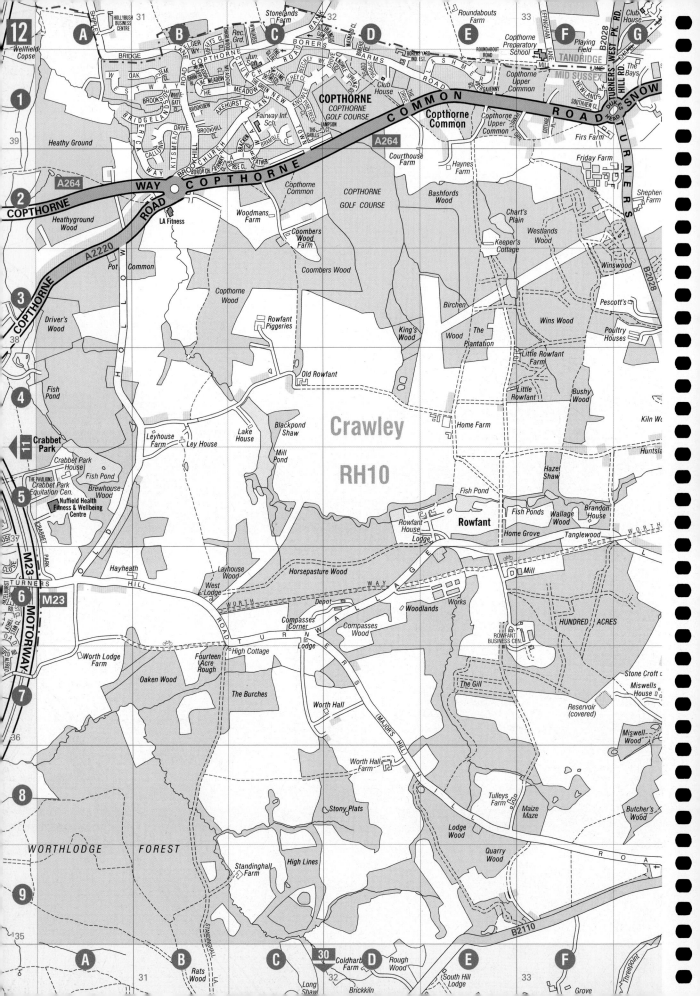

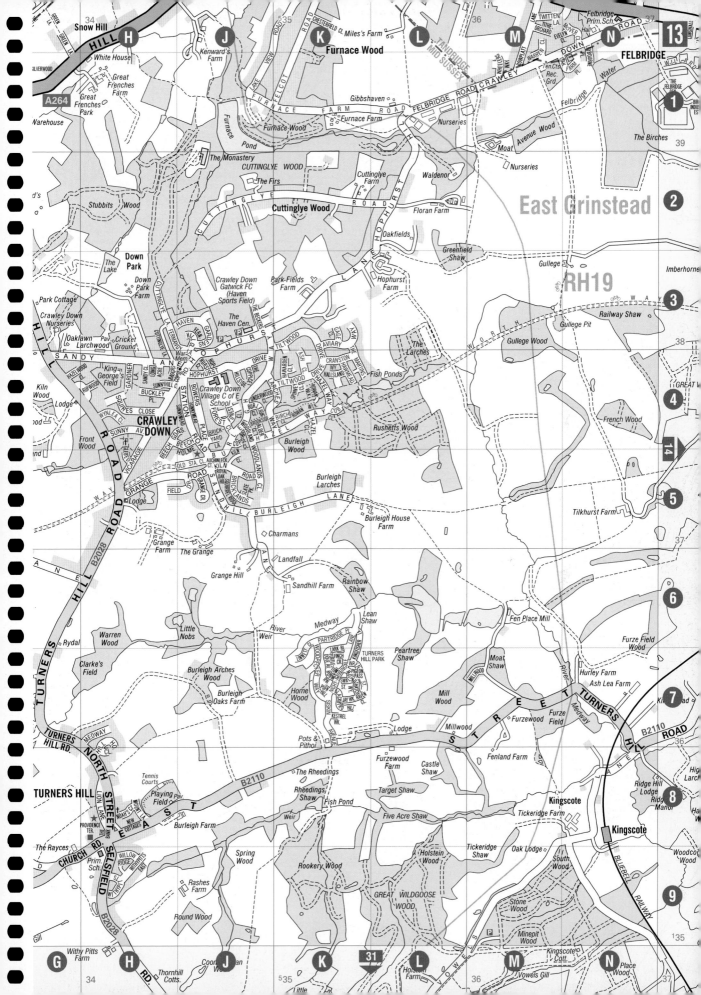

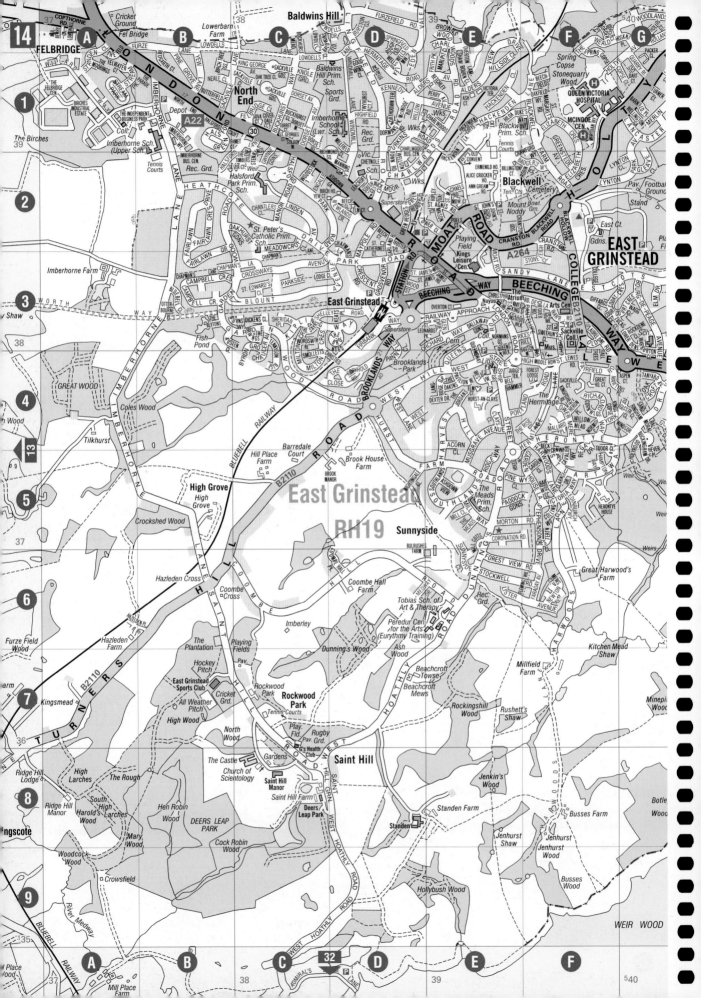

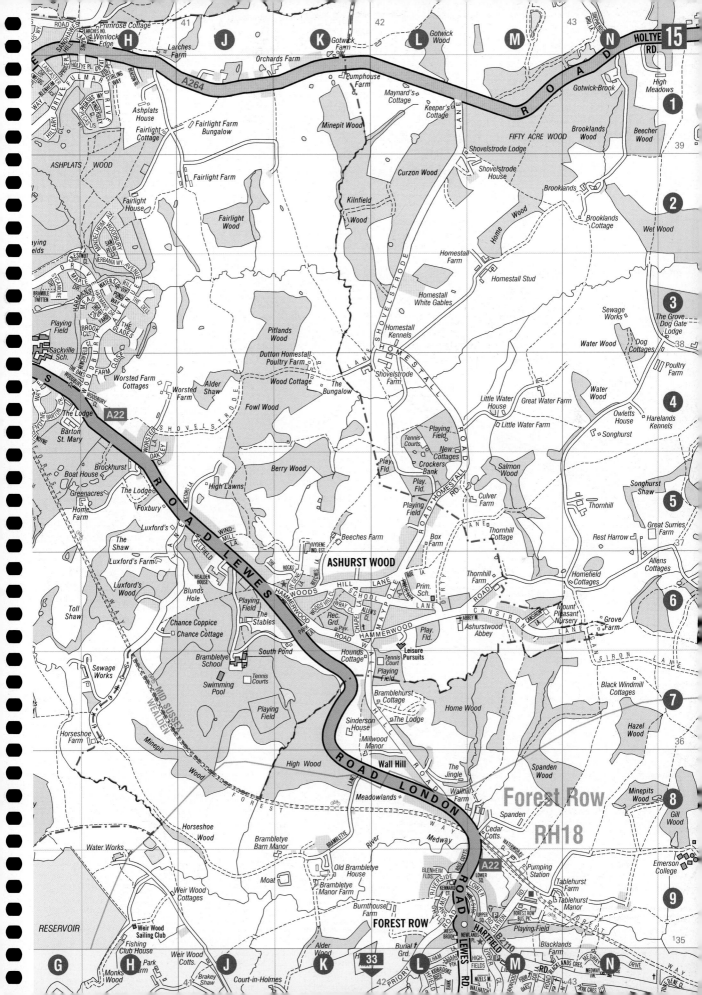

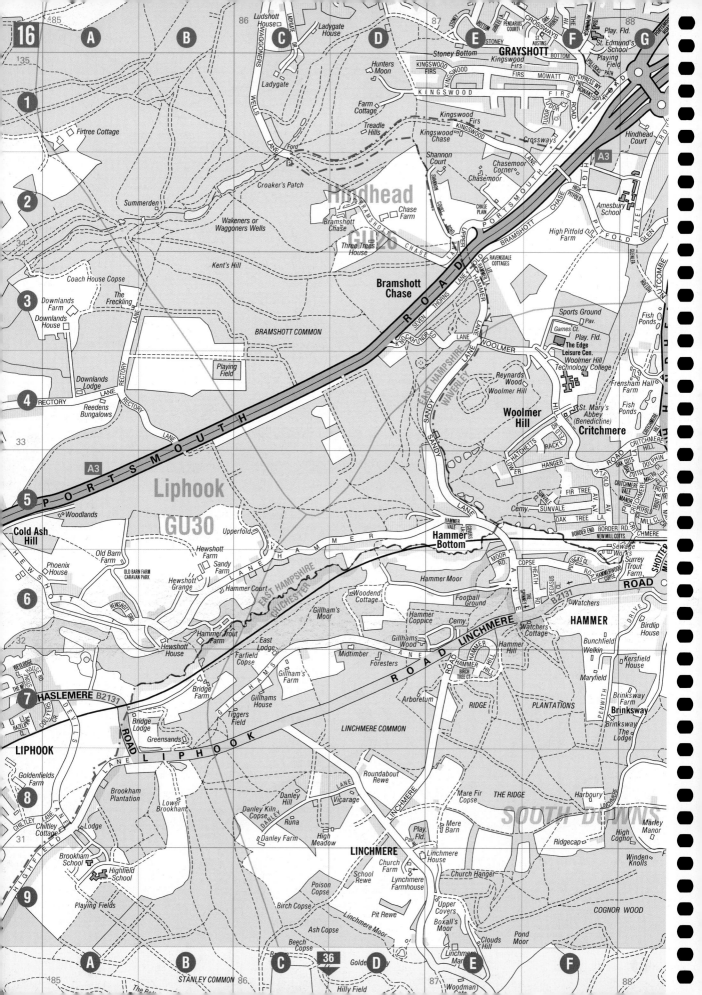

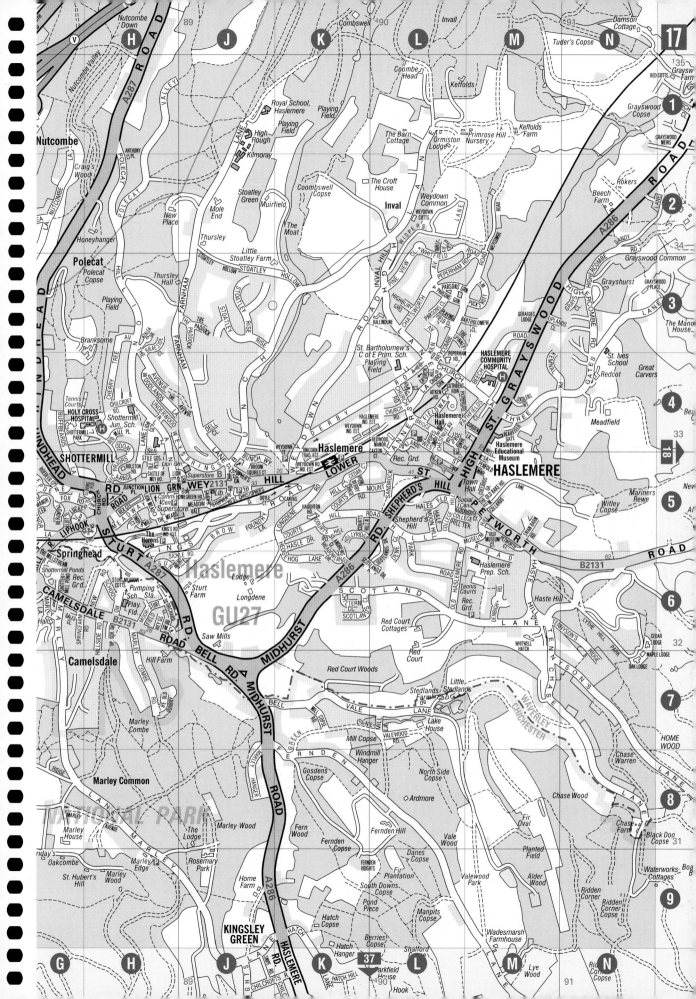

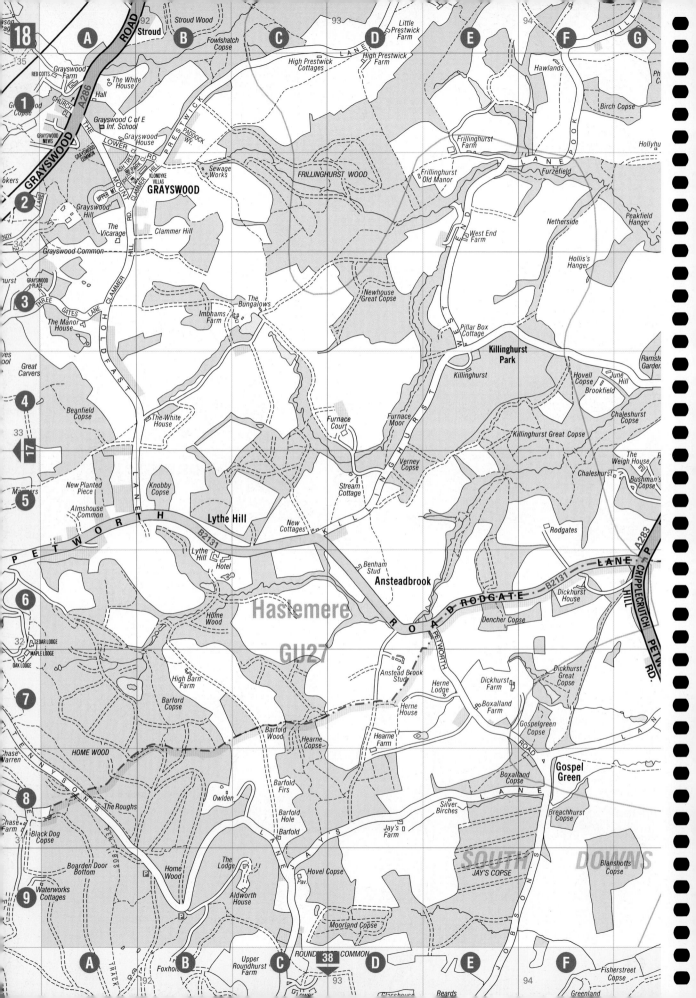

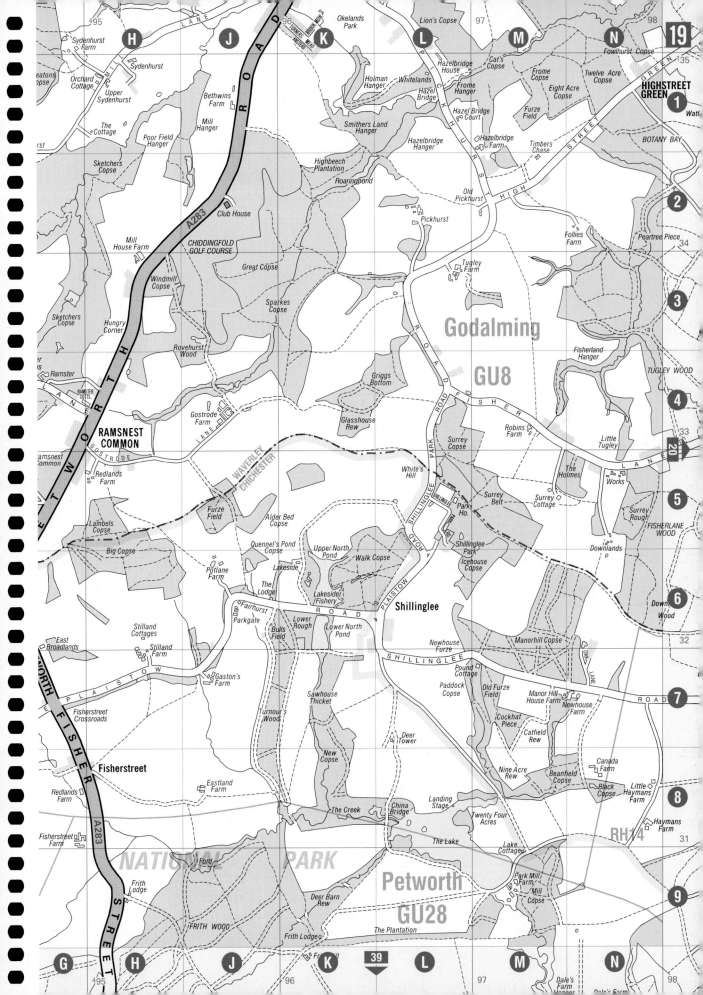

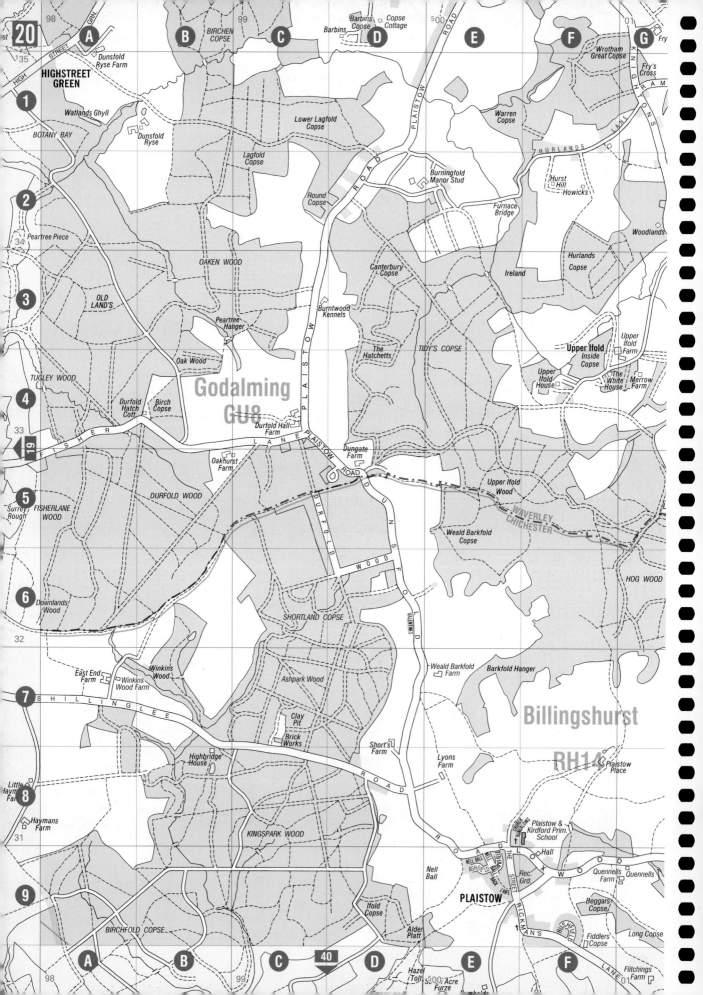

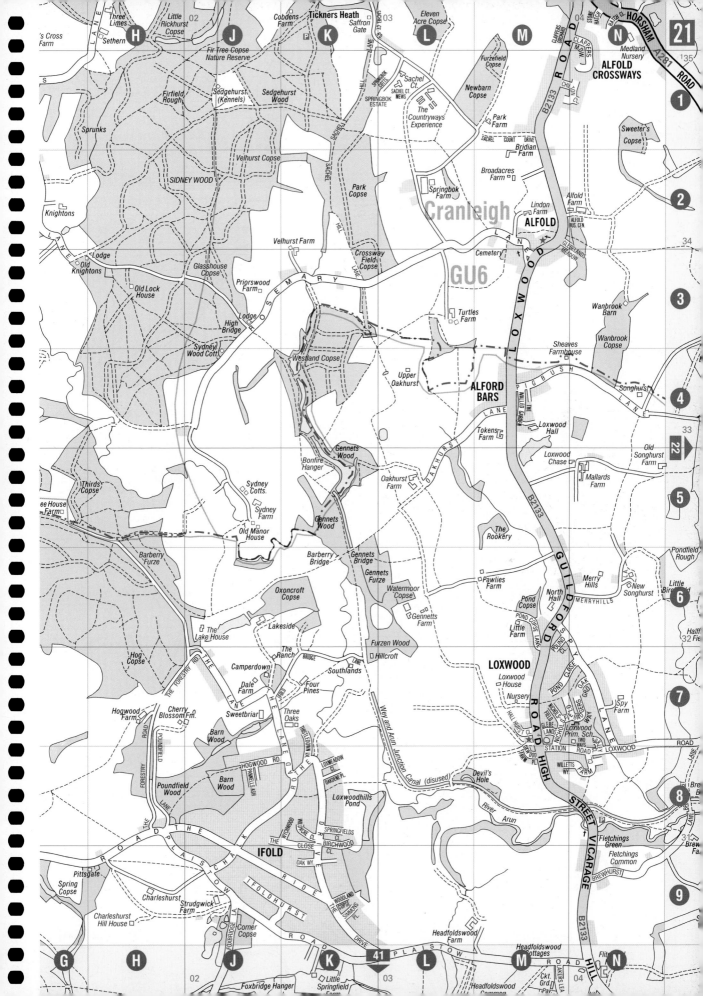

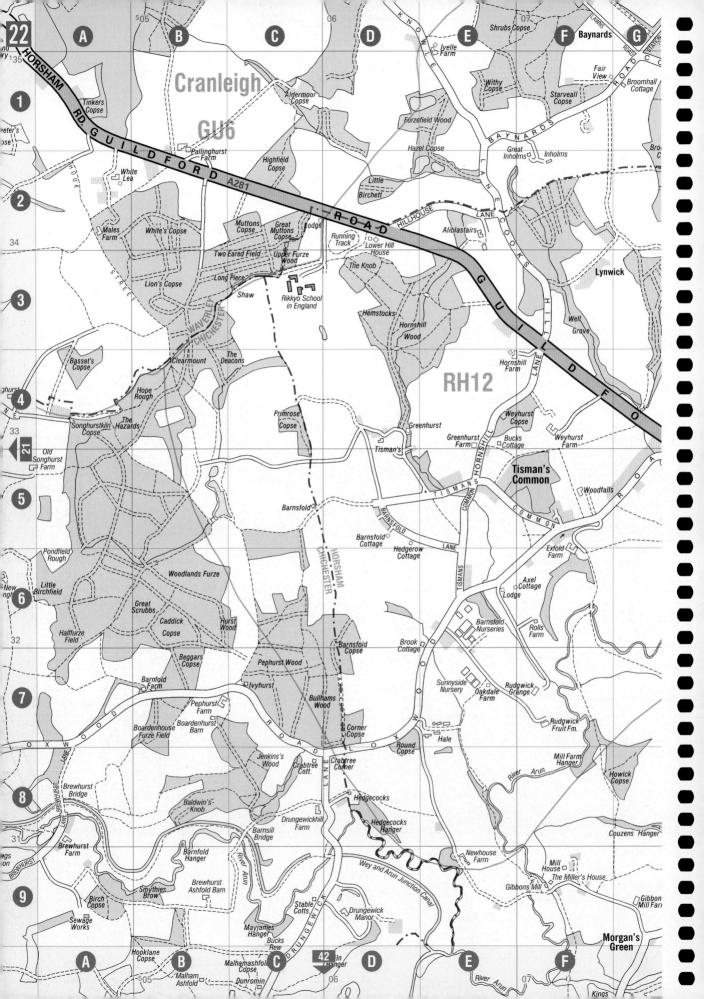

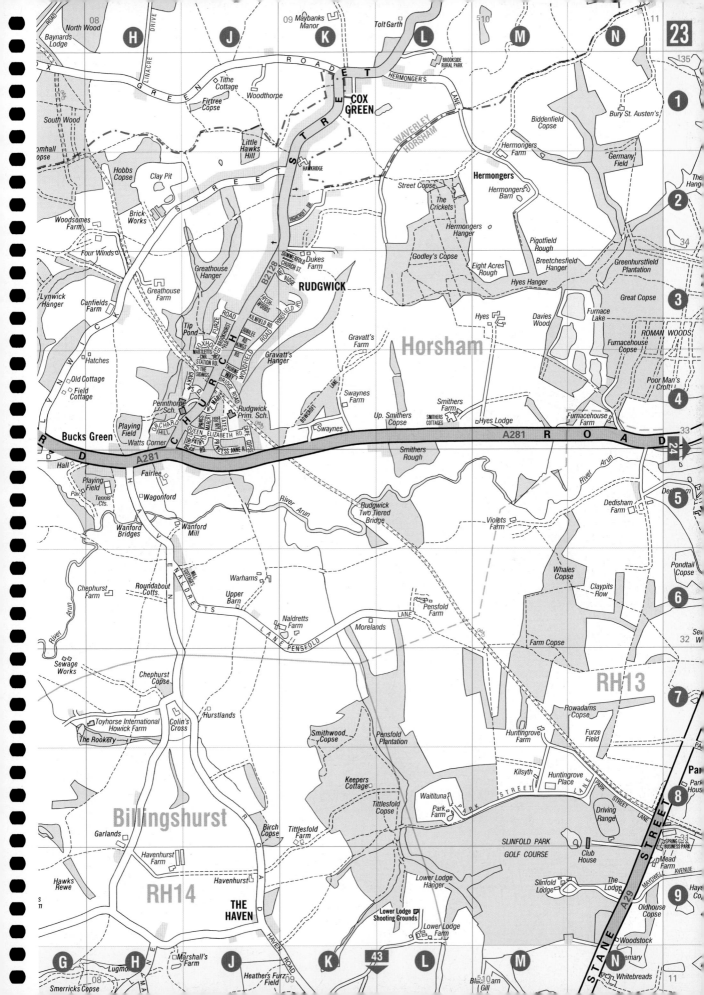

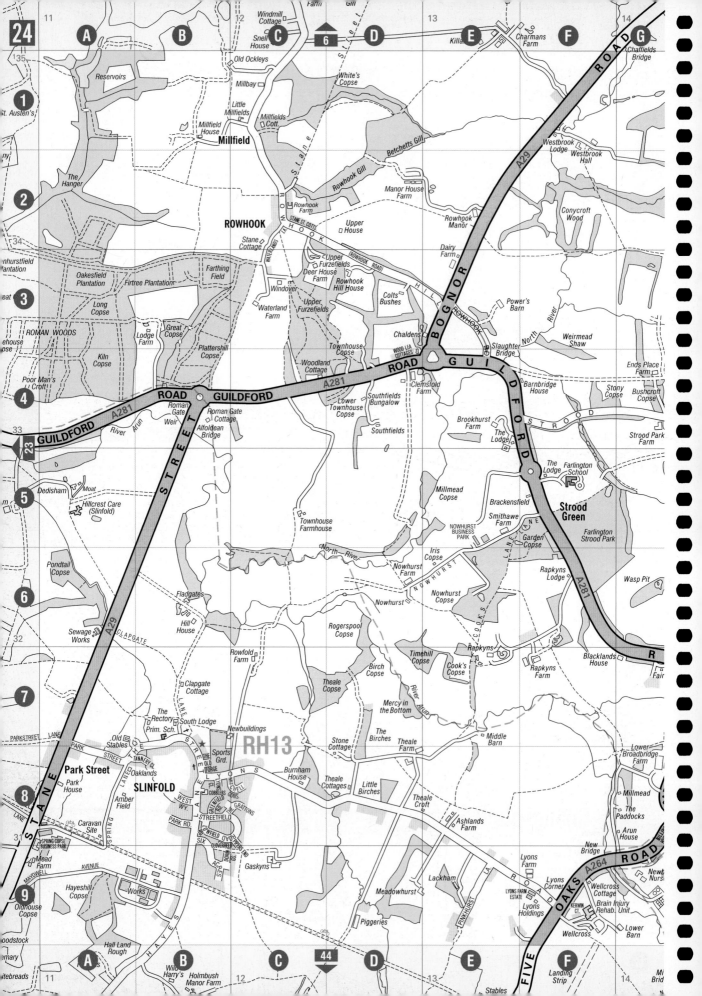

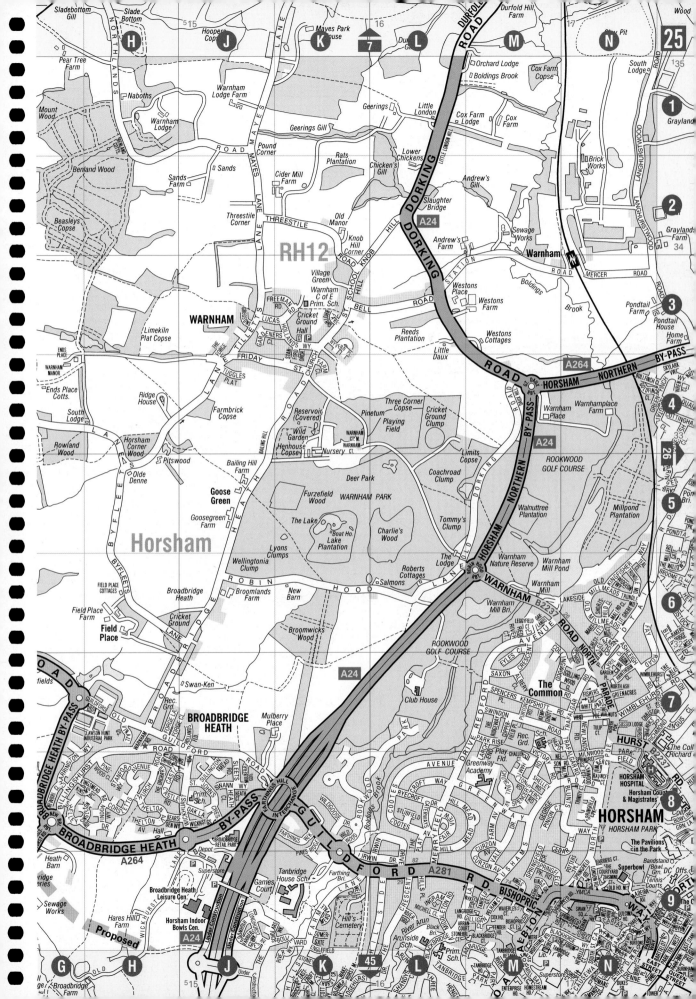

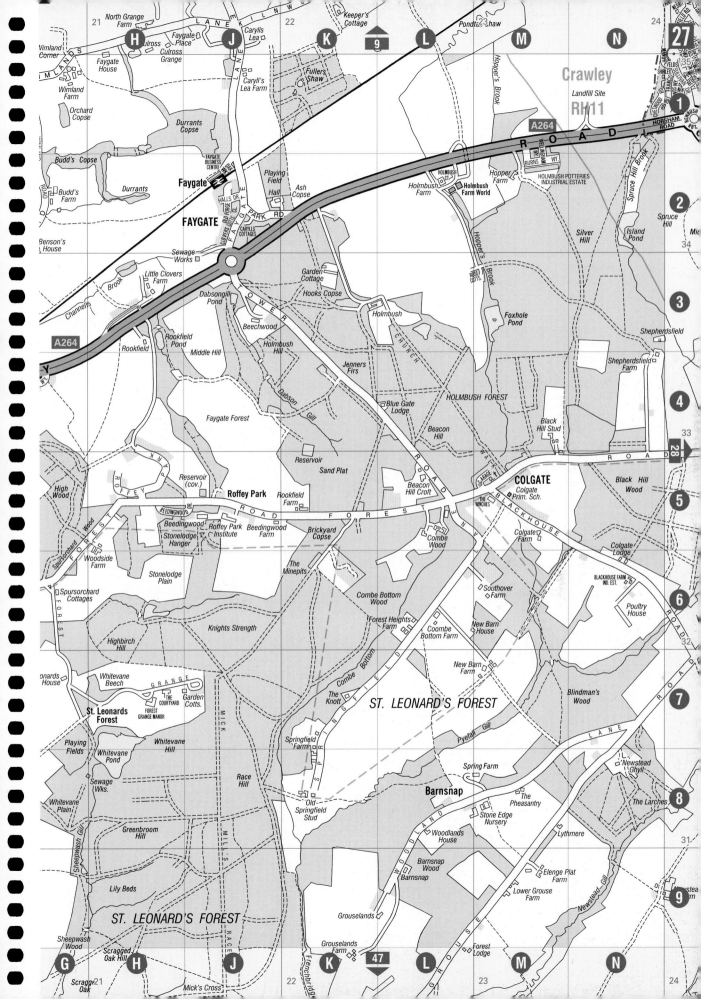

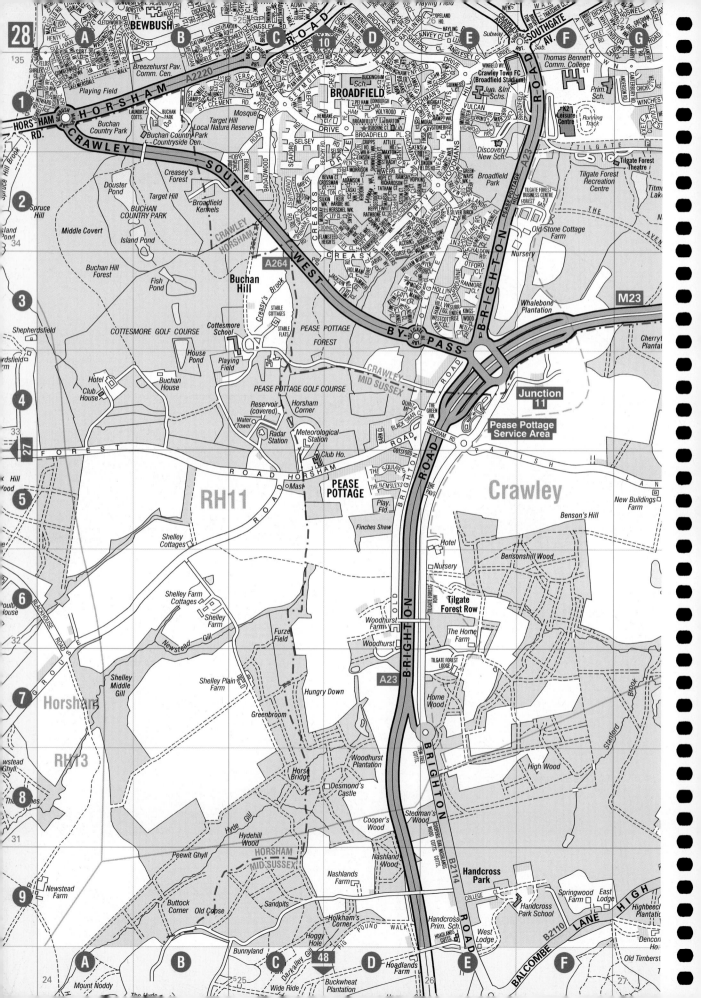

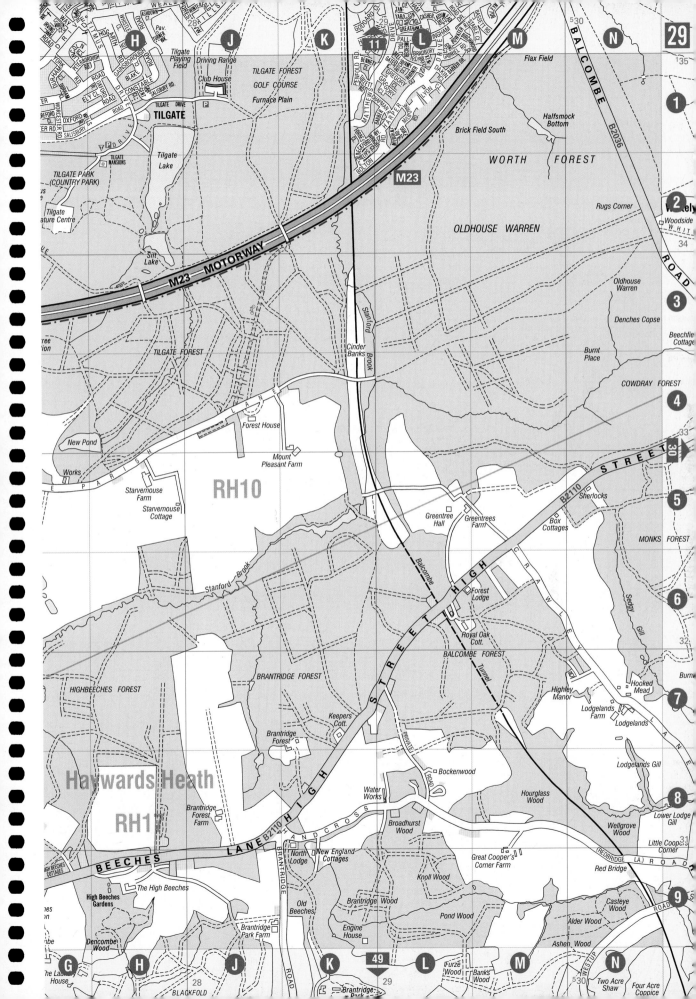

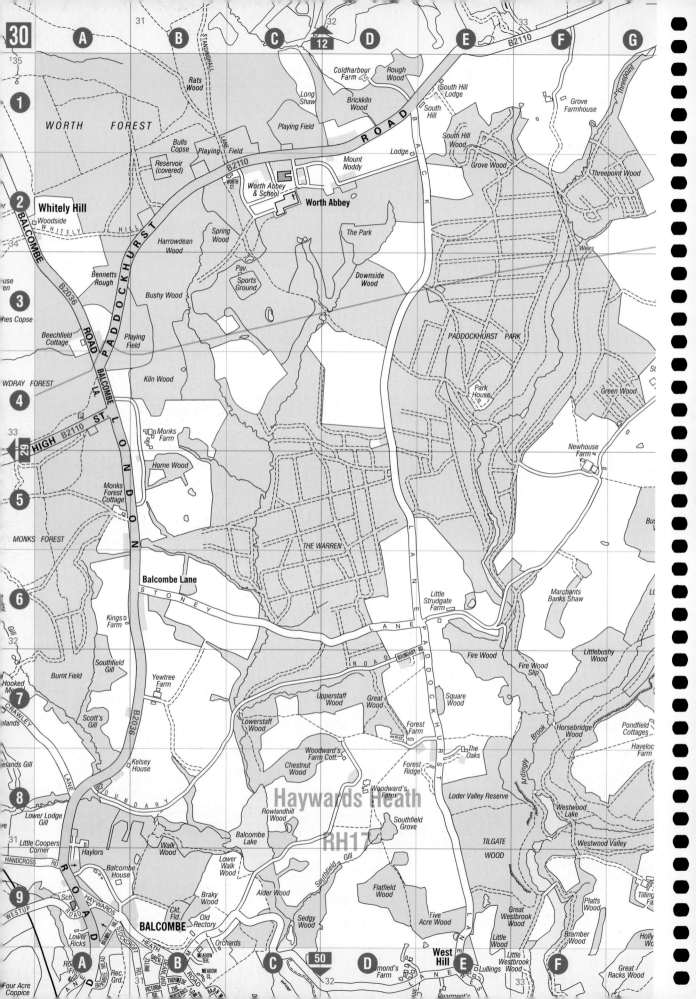

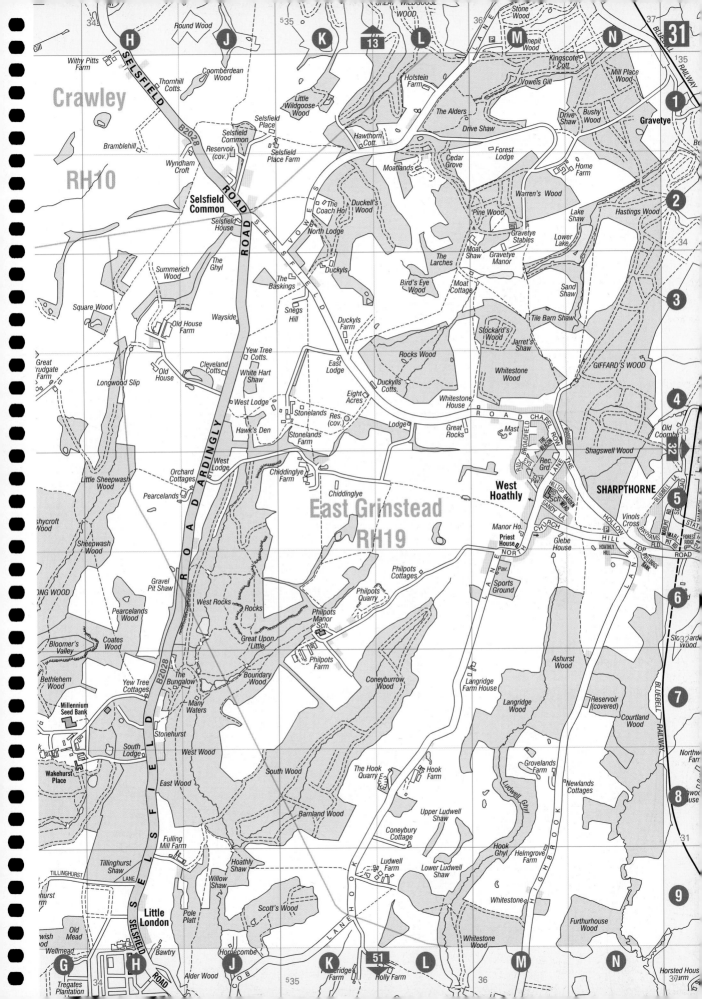

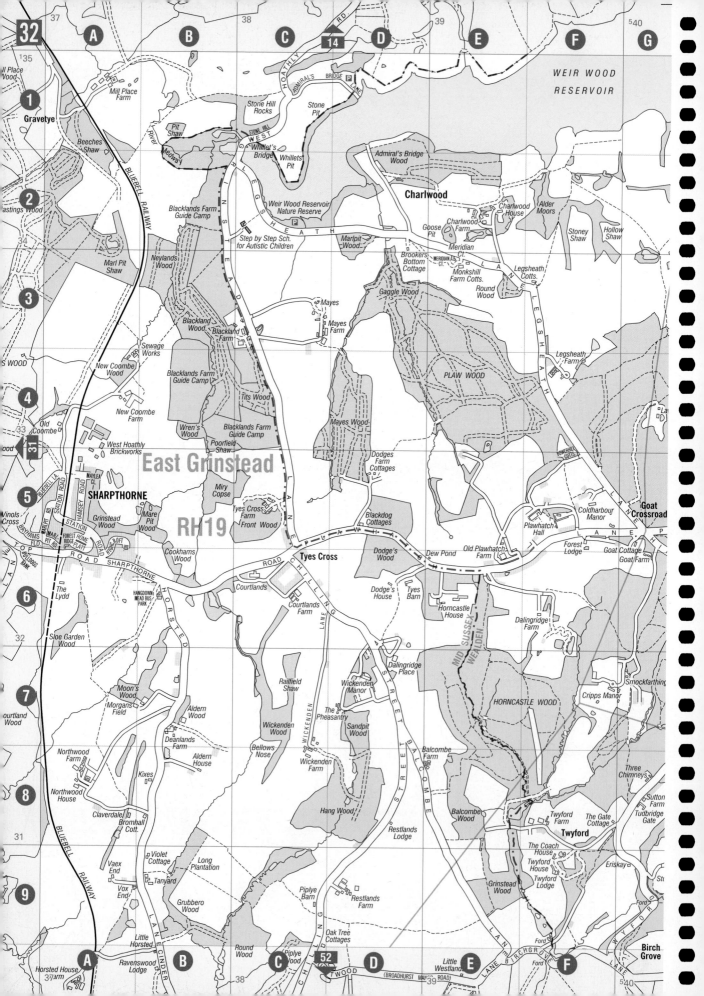

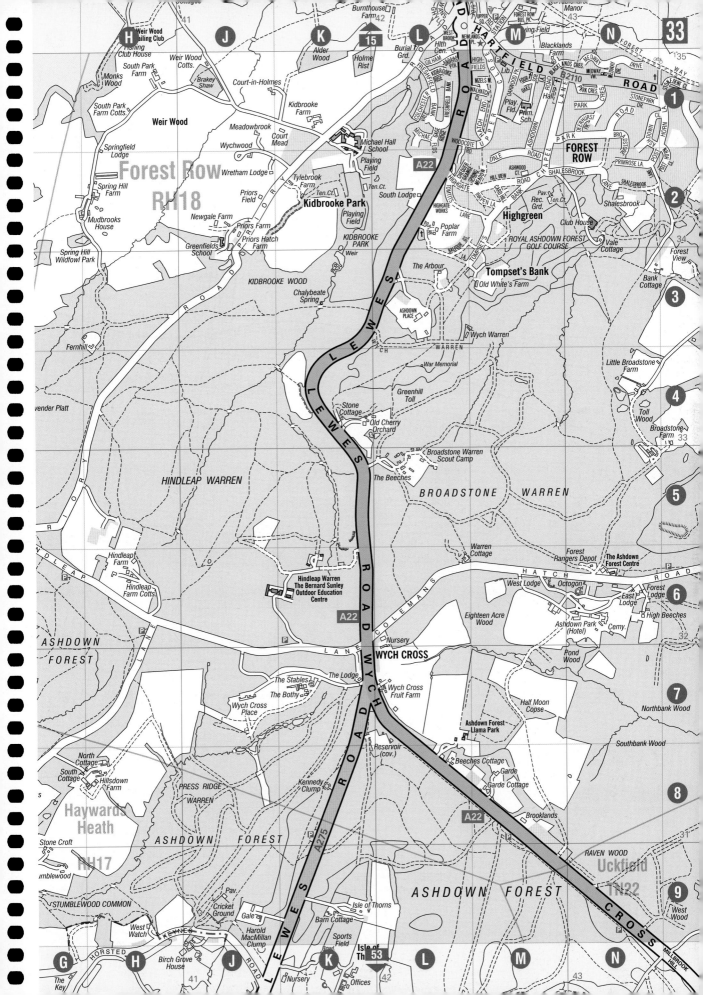

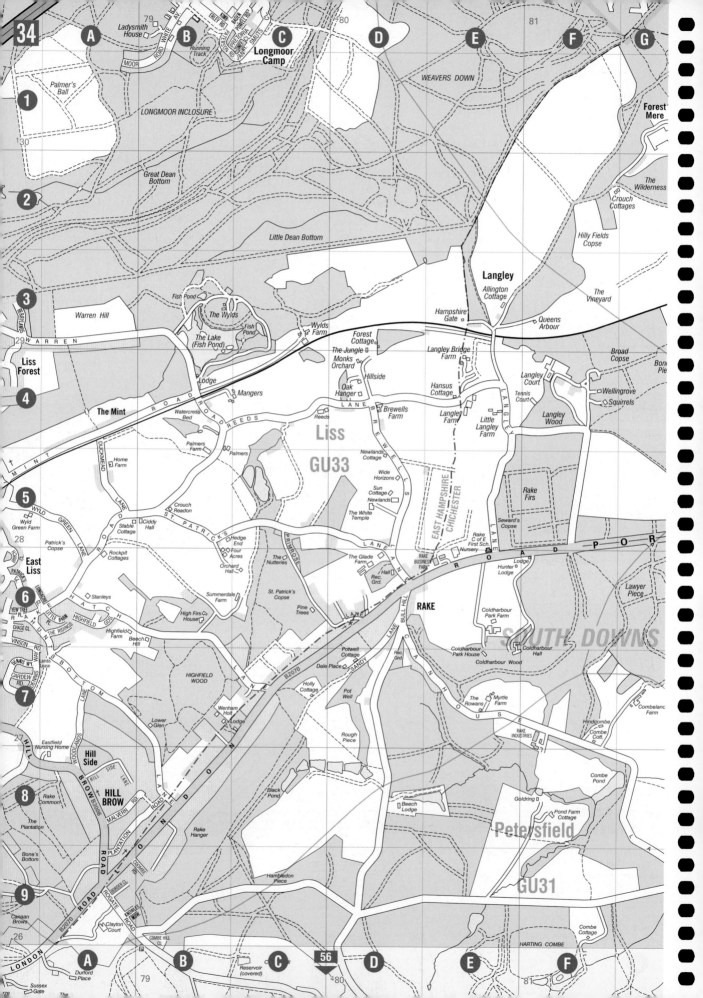

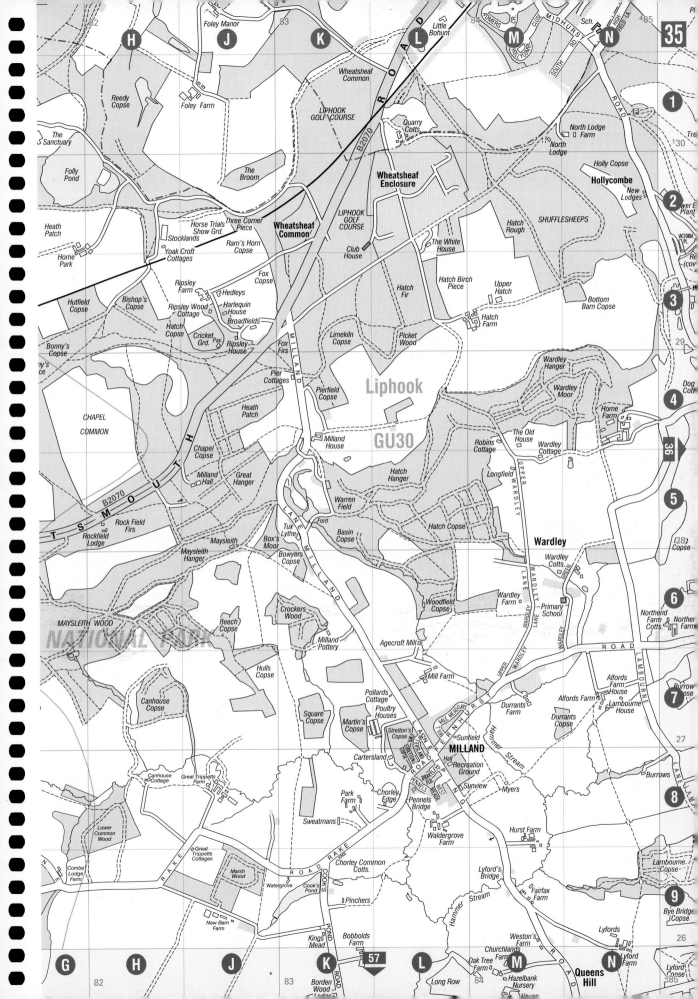

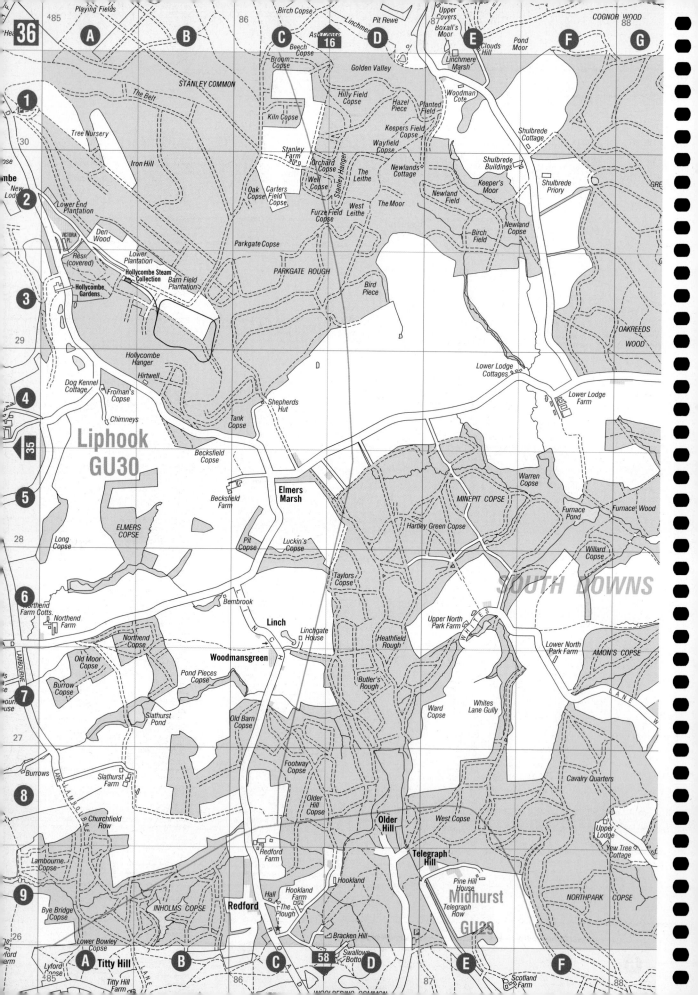

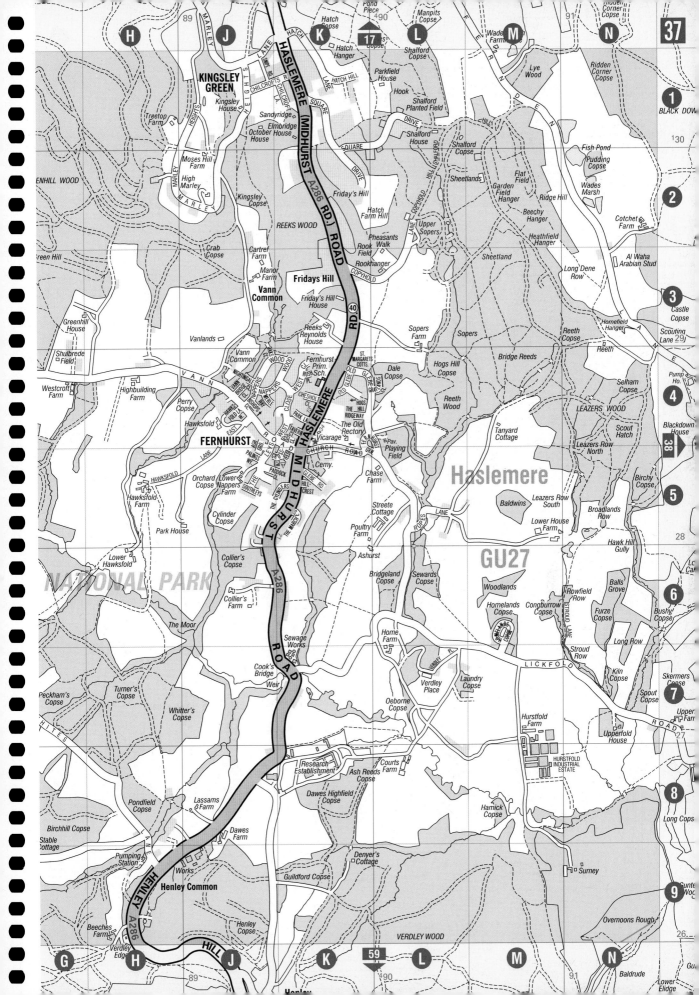

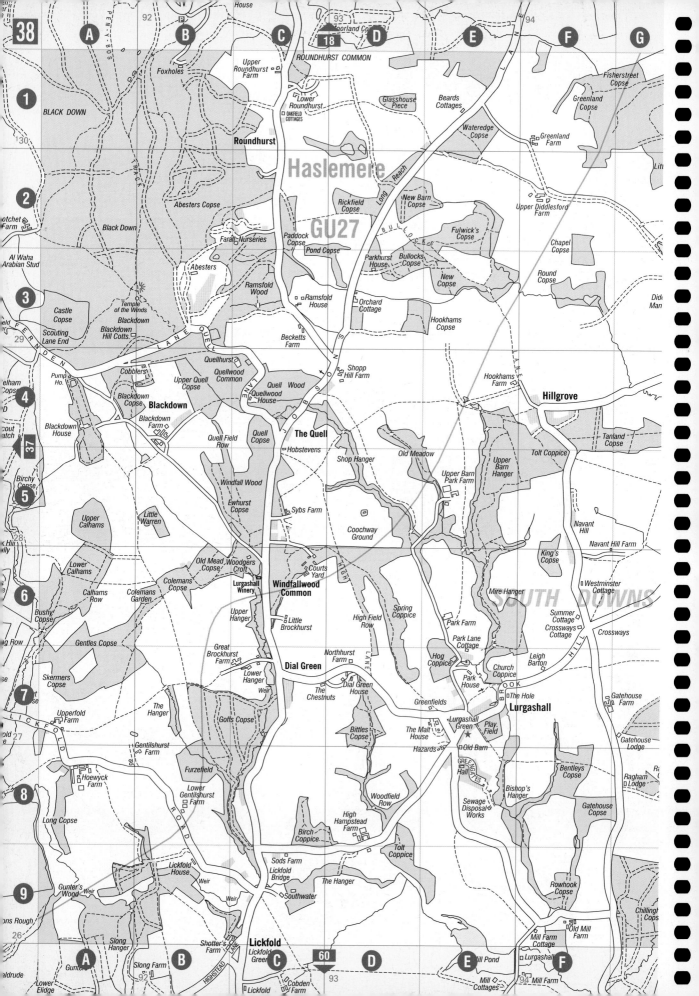

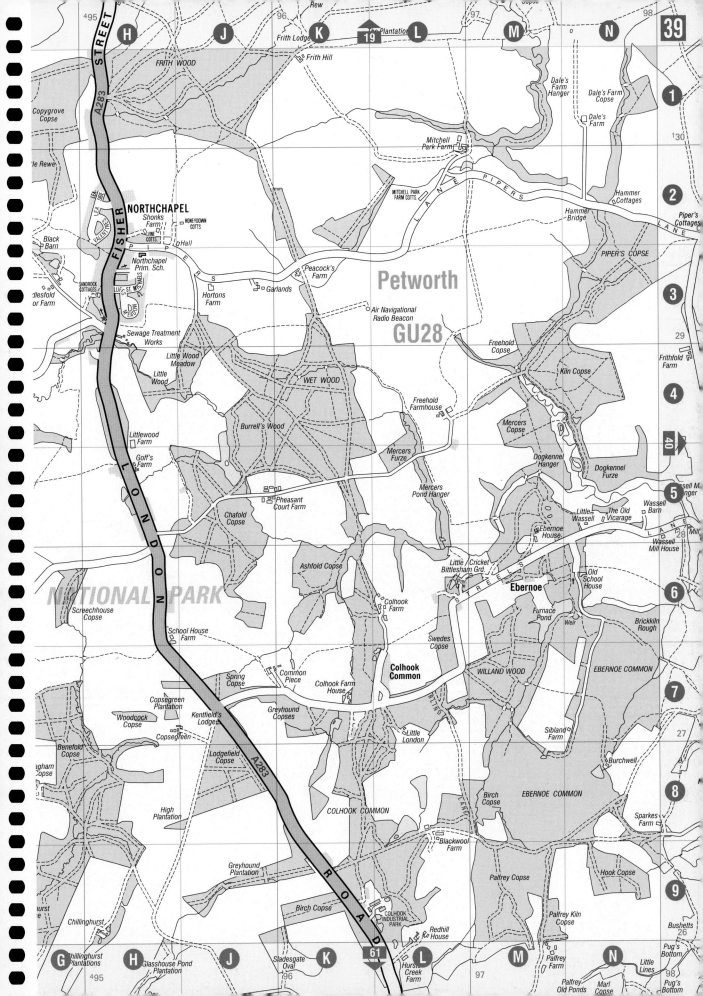

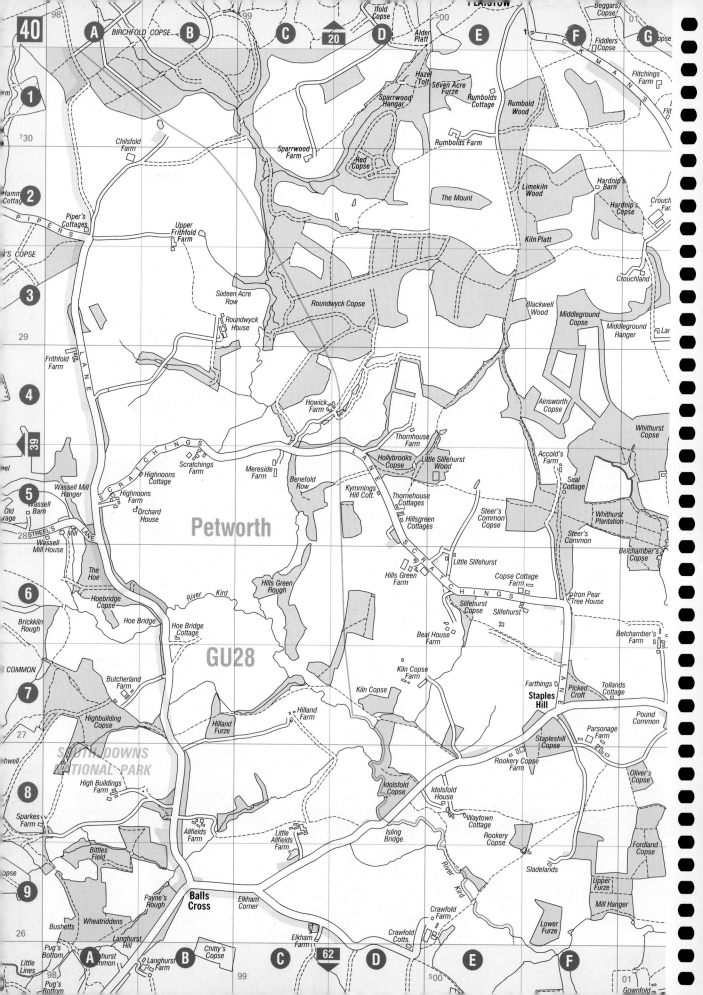

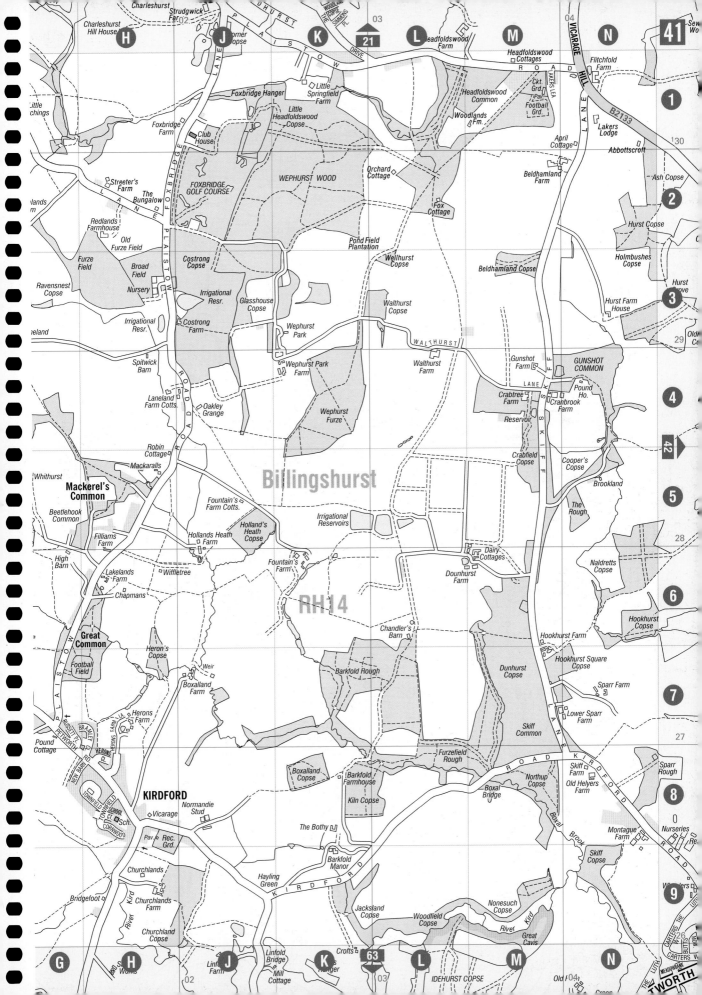

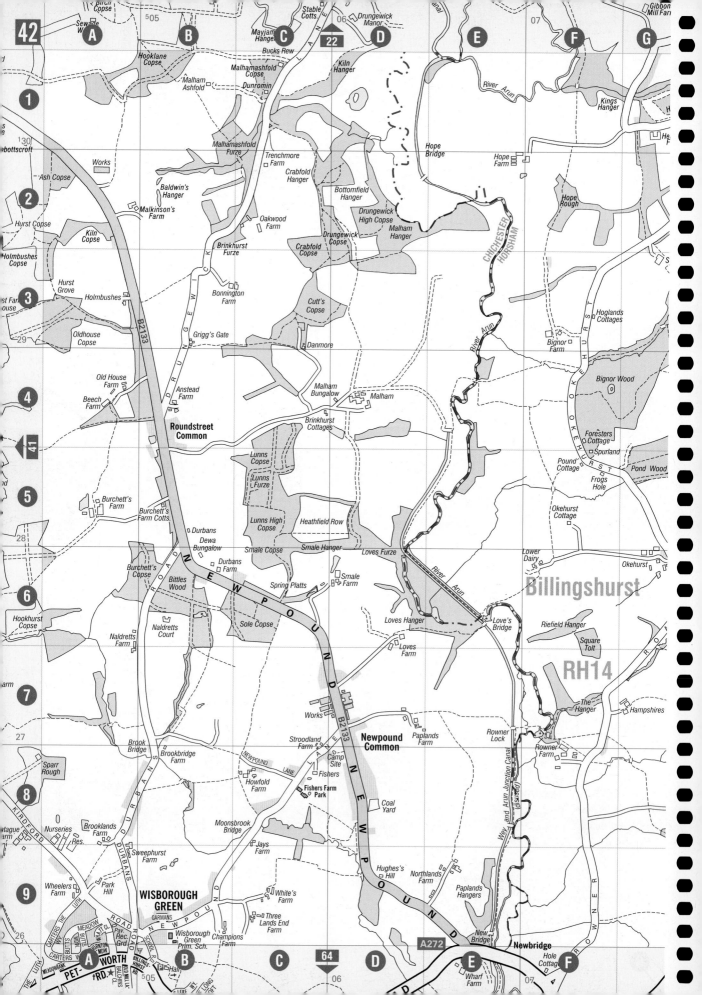

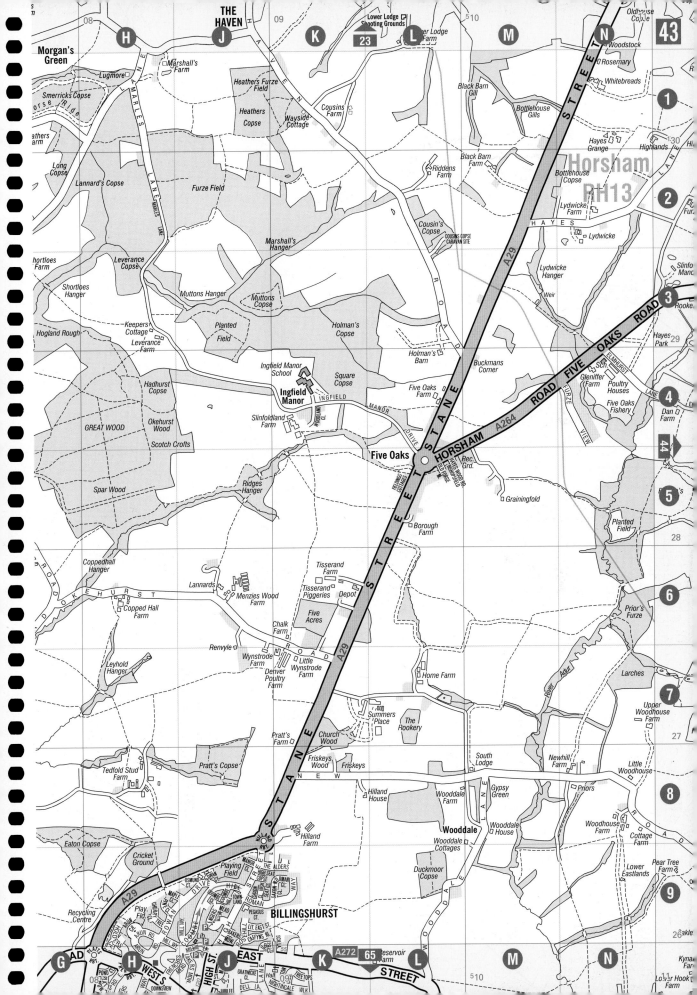

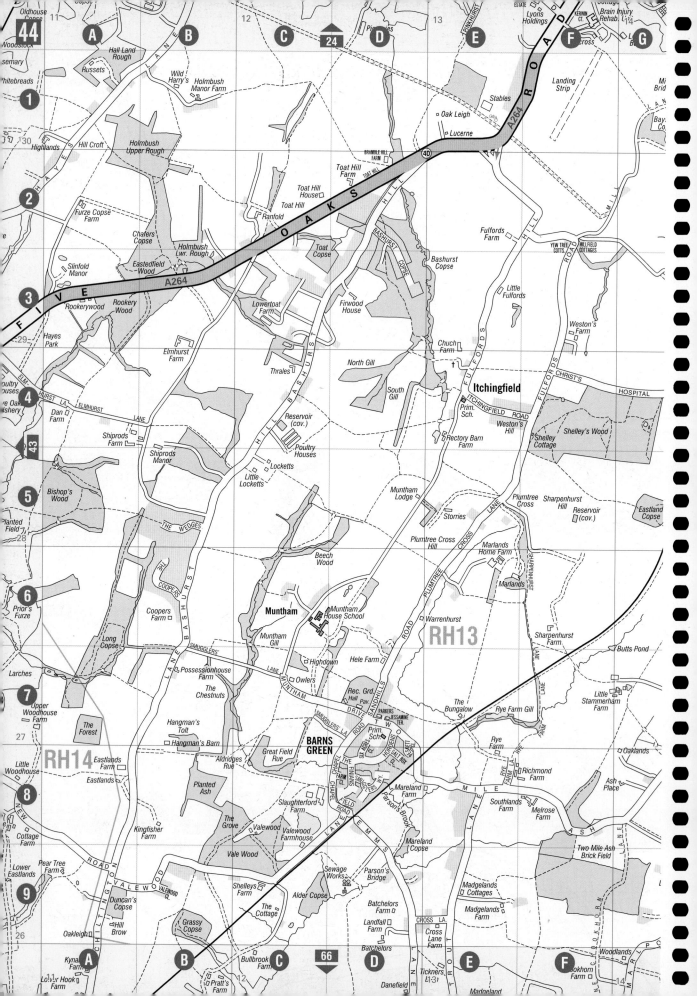

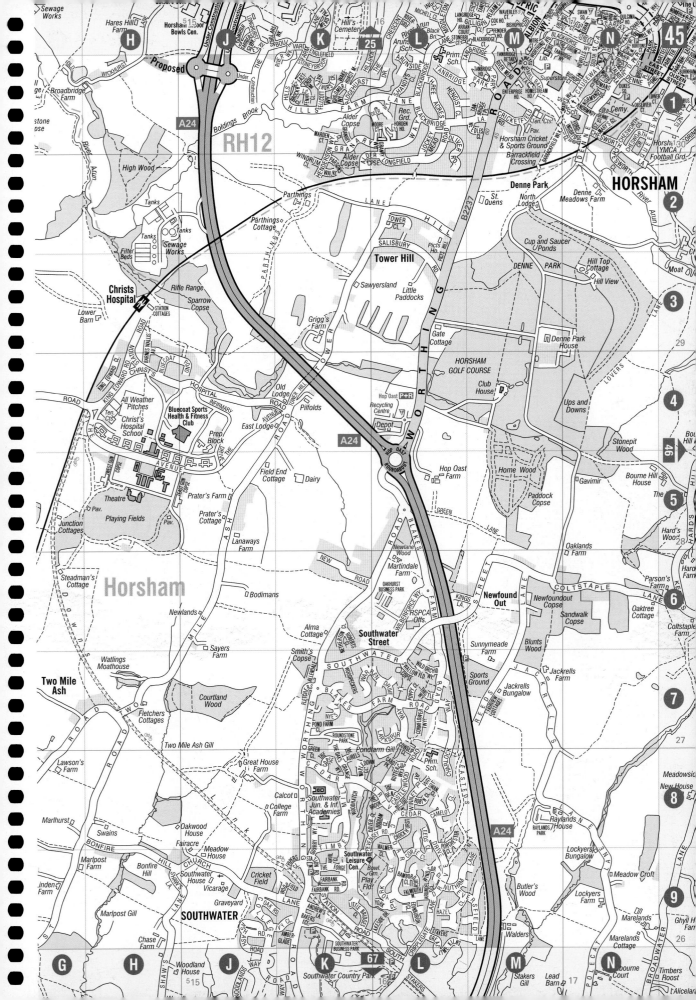

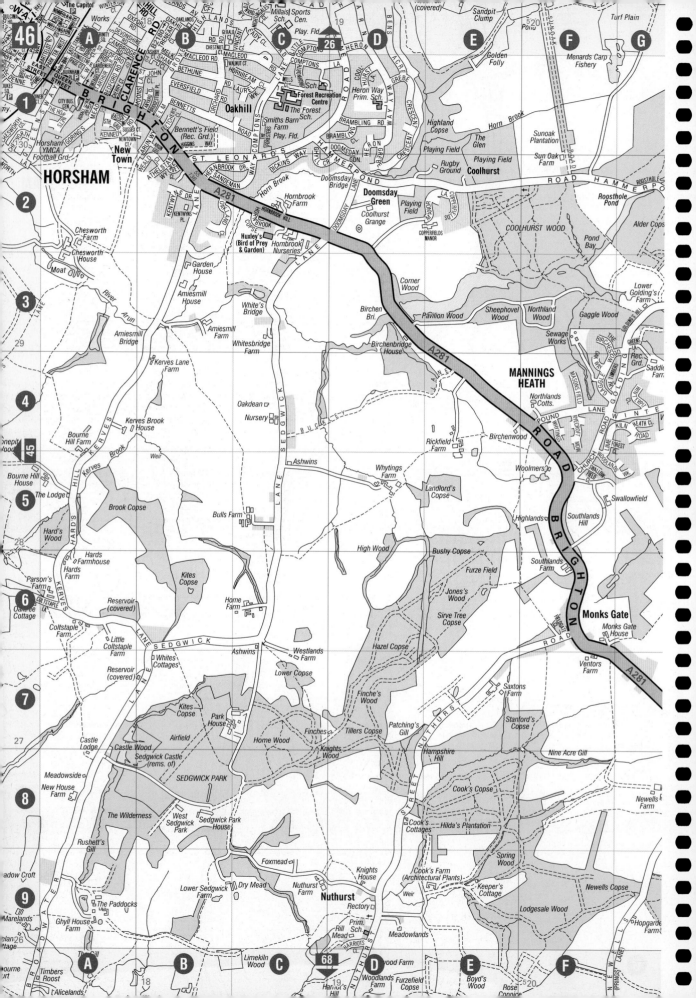

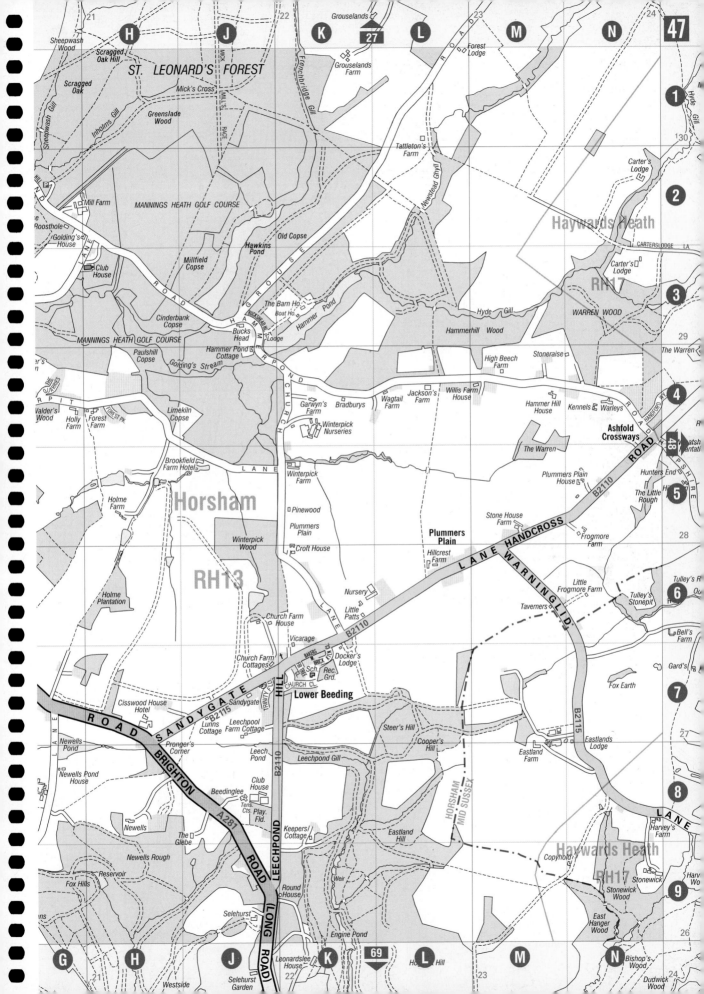

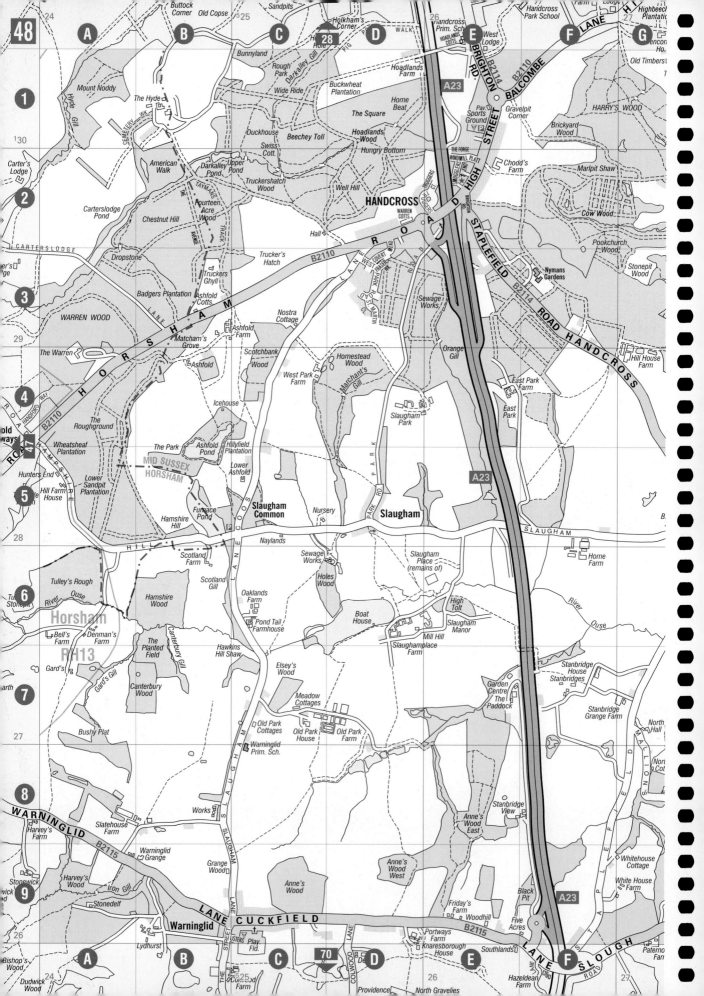

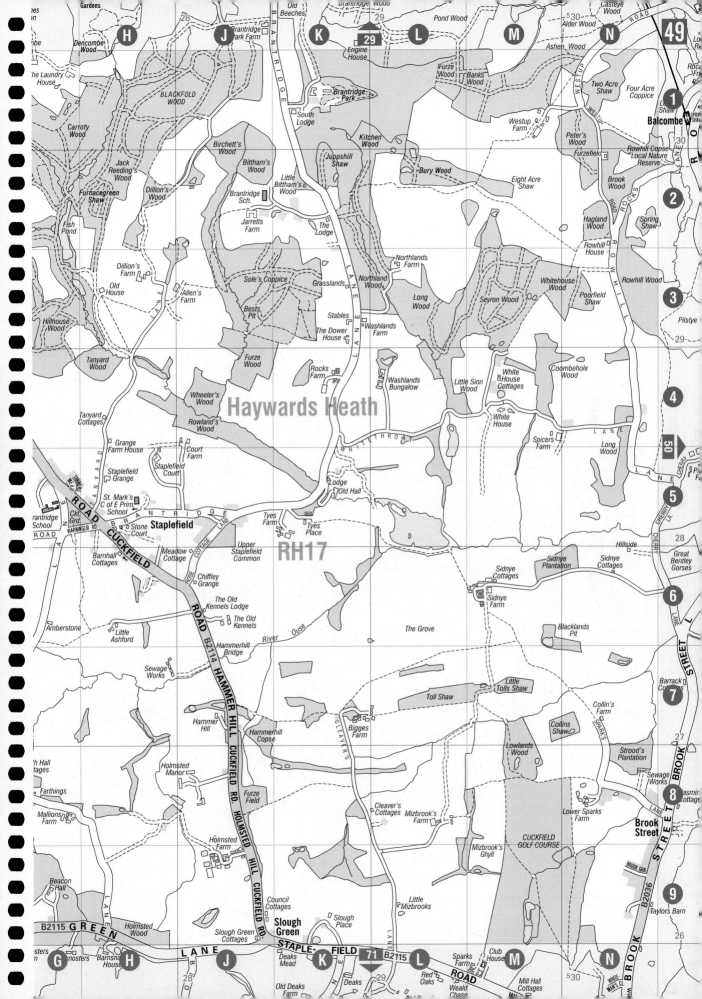

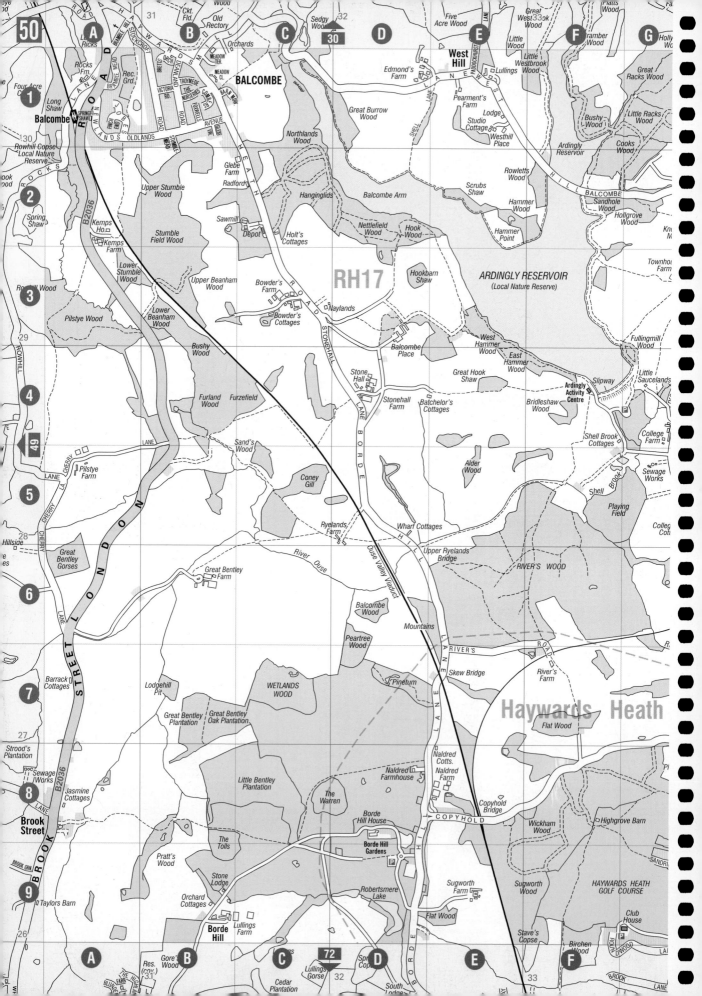

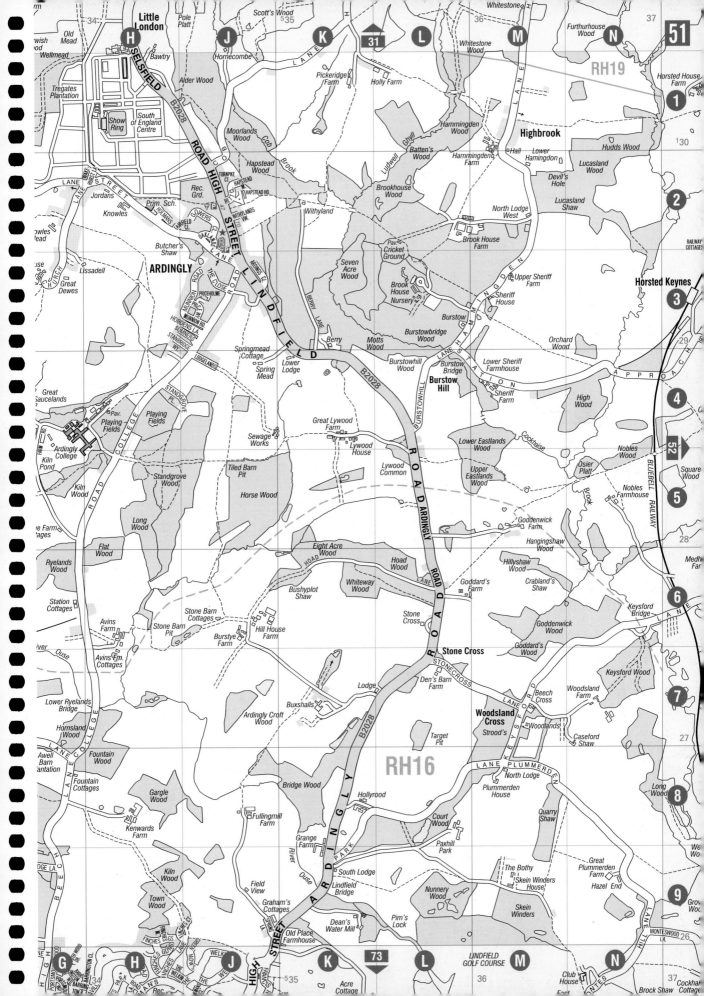

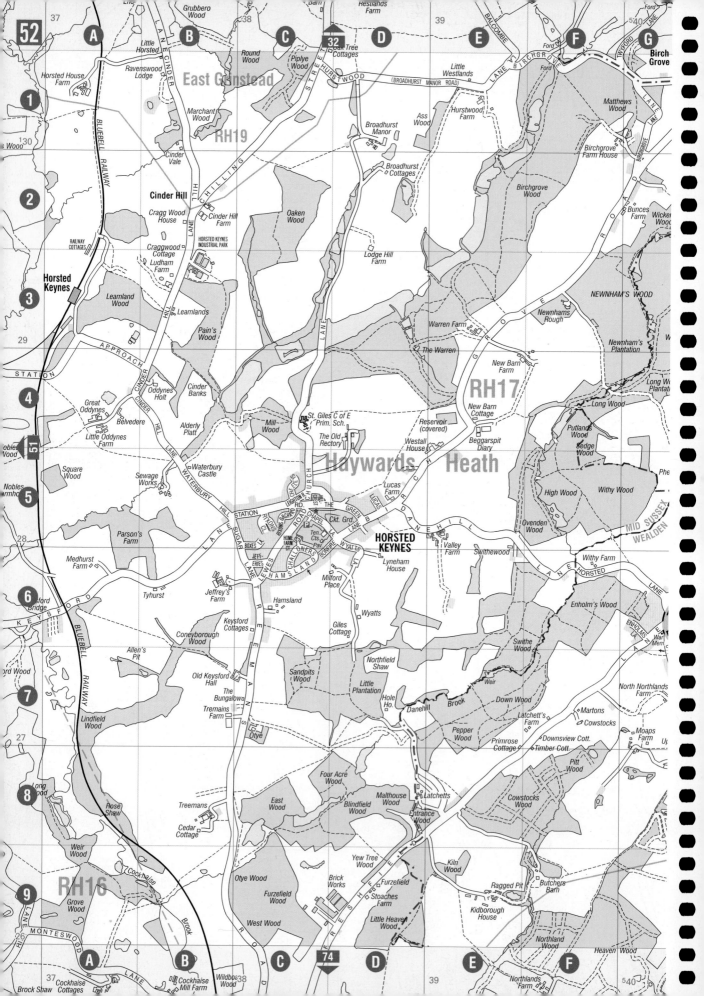

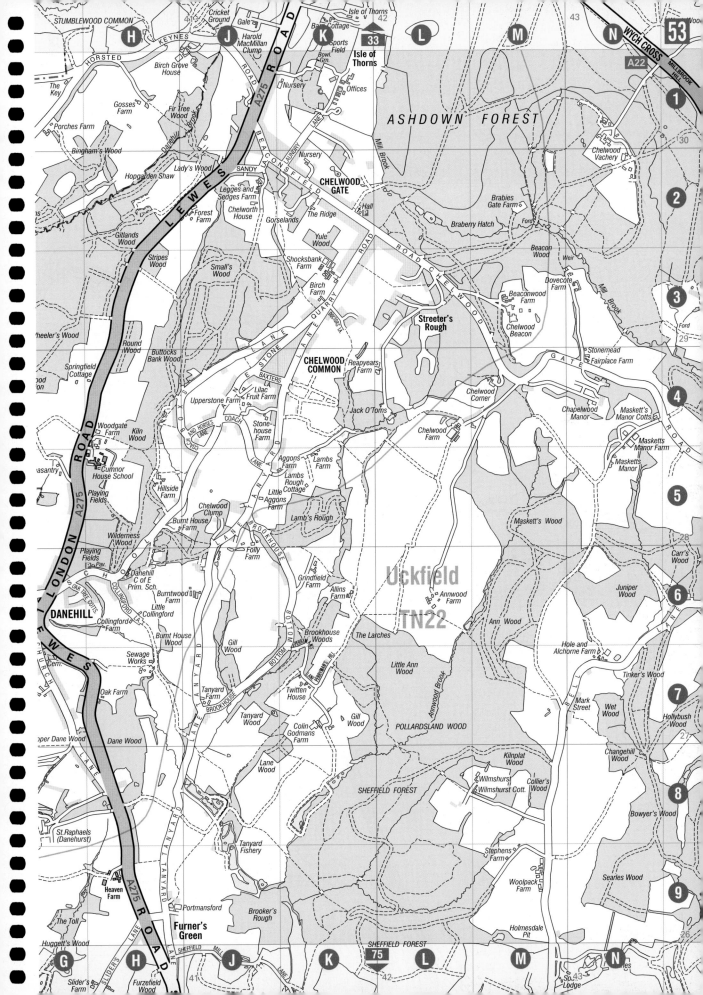

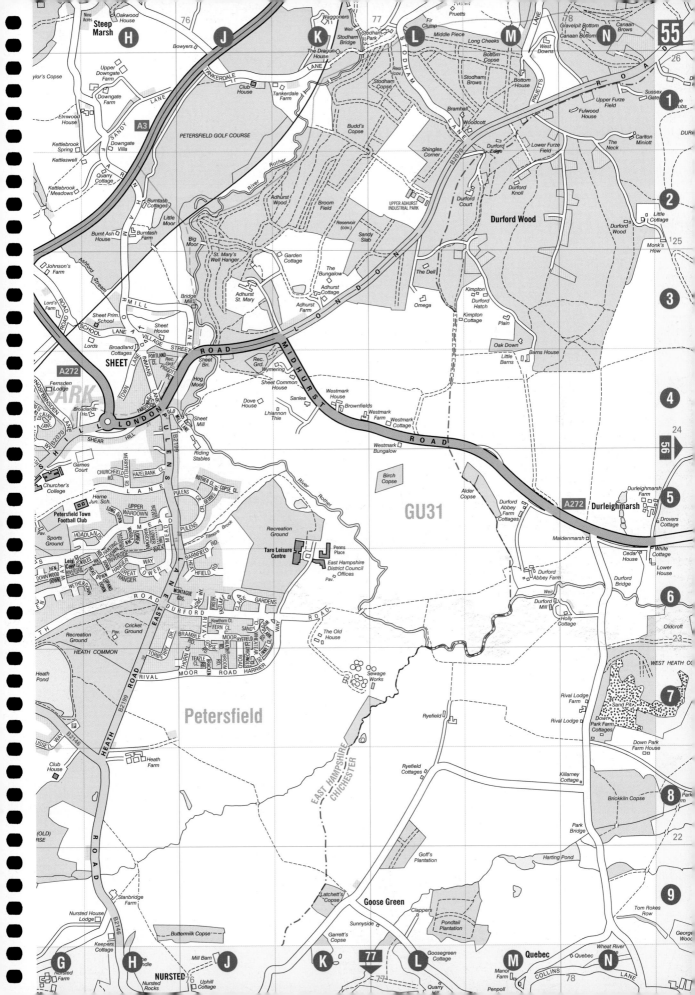

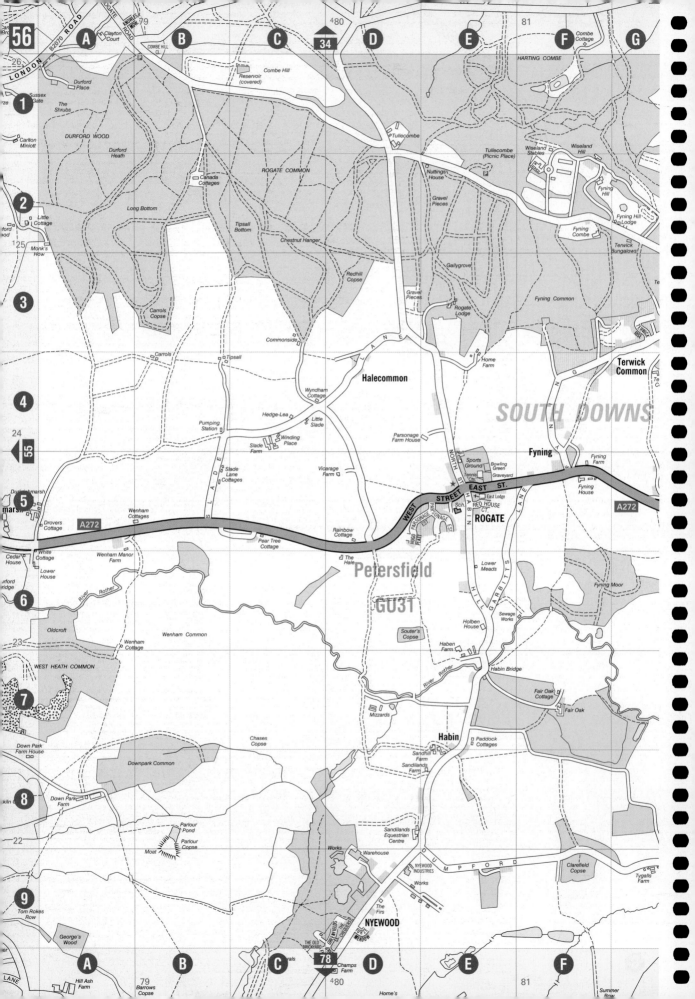

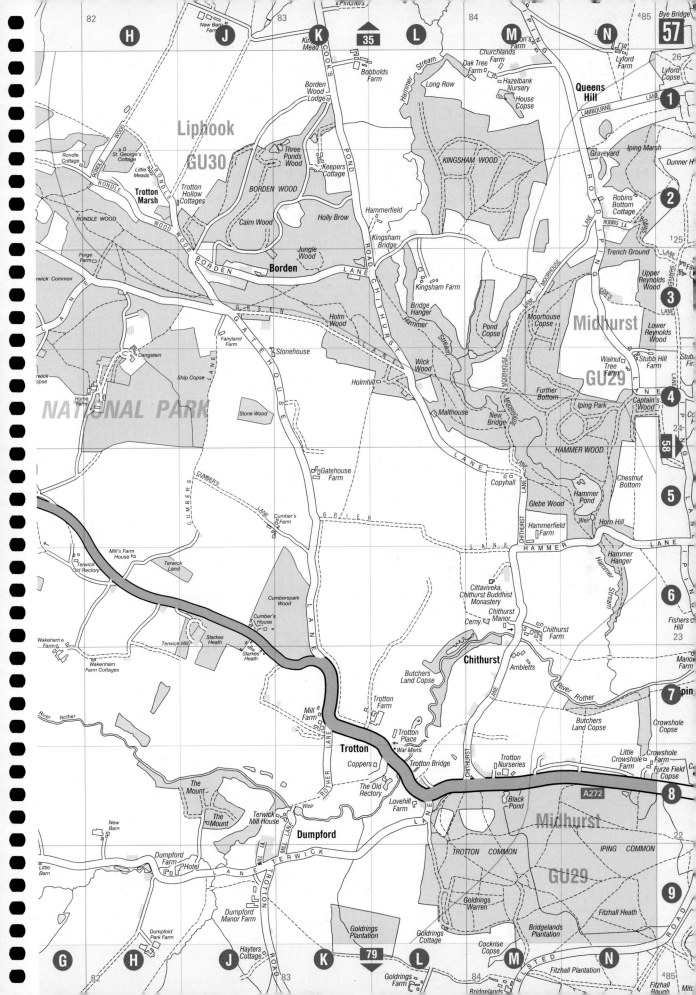

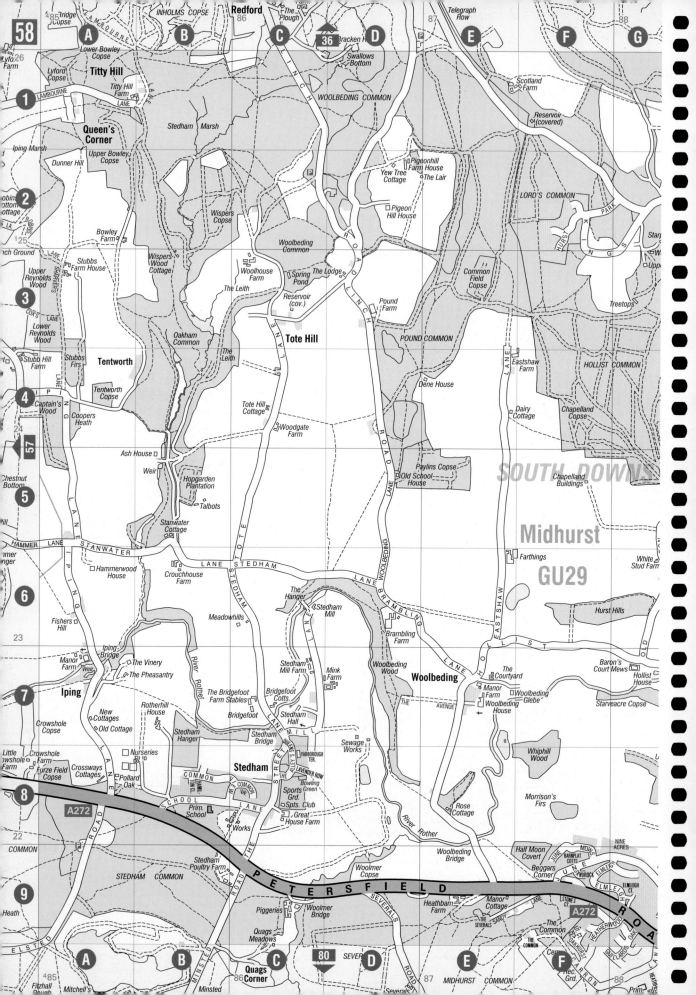

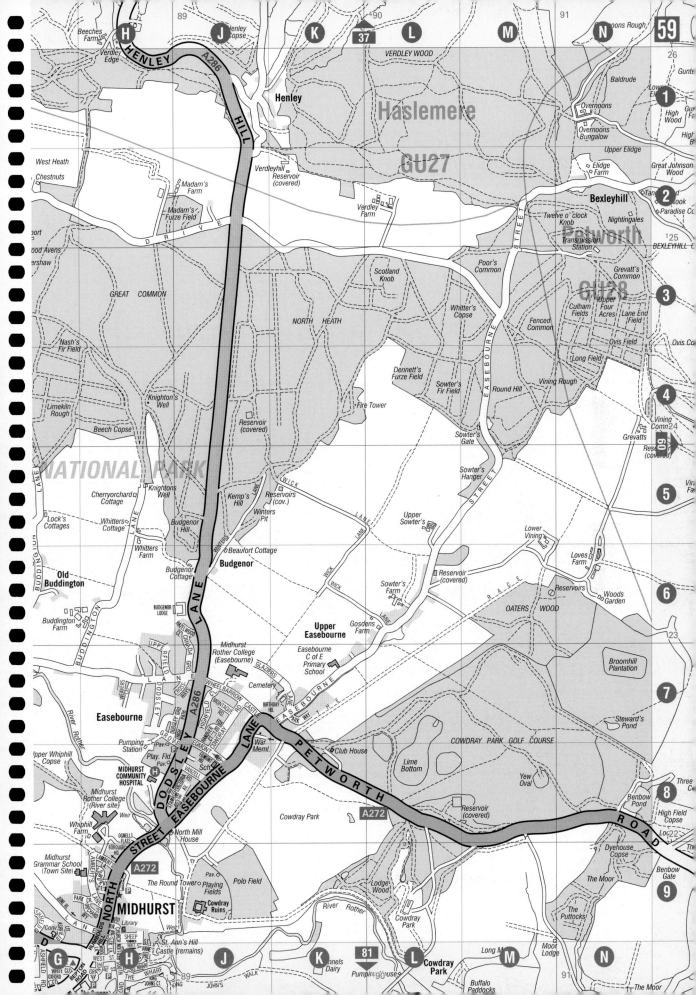

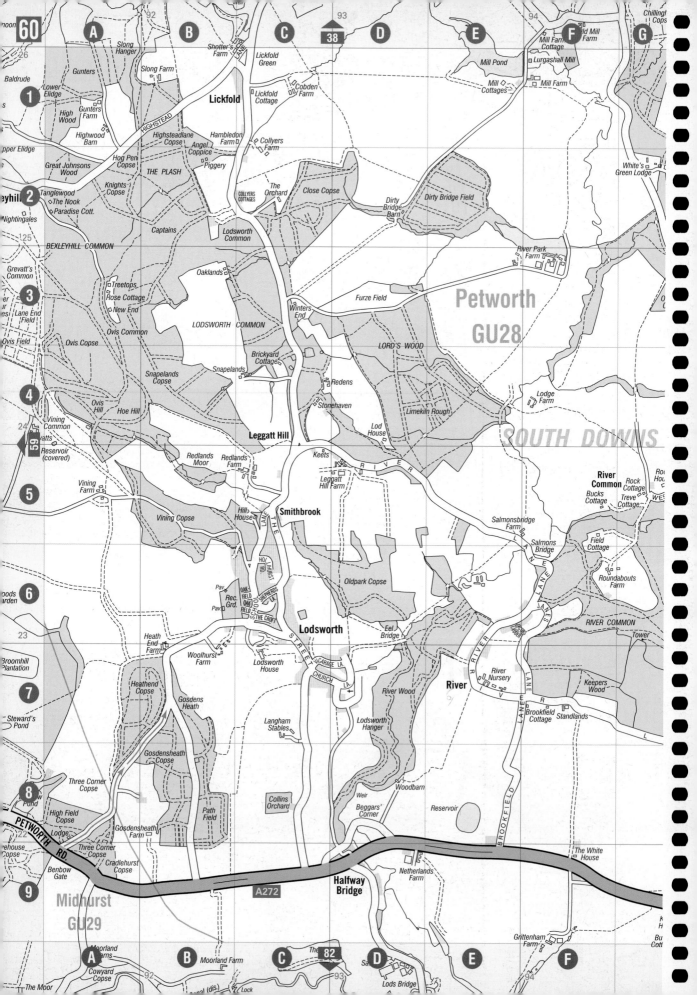

A   B   C   D   E   F   G
38

1

Baldrude
Lower Elidge
High Wood
Gunters
Gunters Farm
Slong Hanger
Slong Farm
HIGHSTEAD
Highstead Lane Copse
Shotter's Farm
Lickfold Green
Lickfold Cottage
Cobden Farm
Well
Mill Pond
Mill Farm Cottage
Old Mill Farm
Chillingham Copse
Lurgashall Mill
Mill Farm
Mill Cottages

Highwood Barn
Upper Elidge
Lickfold

2
eyhill
Tanglewood
The Nook
Paradise Cott.
Nightingales
Great Johnsons Wood
Hog Pen Copse
THE PLASH
Knights Copse
Captains
Hambledon Farm
Angel Coppice
Piggery
Collyers Cottages
The Orchard
Close Copse
Collyers Farm
Dirty Bridge Barn
Dirty Bridge Field
White's Green Lodge
125

3
Grevatt's Common
Lane End Field
Ovis Field
Ovis Copse
Treetops
Rose Cottage
New End
Ovis Common
BEXLEYHILL COMMON
Lodsworth Common
Oaklands
LODSWORTH COMMON
Winters End
Furze Field
Petworth GU28
River Park Farm

4
24
59
Vining Common
Watts
Reservoir (covered)
Ovis Hill
Hoe Hill
Snapelands Copse
Snapelands
Brickyard Cottage
Redens
Stonehaven
LORD'S WOOD
Limekiln Rough
Lod House
Lodge Farm
SOUTH DOWNS

5
Vining Farm
Vining Copse
Redlands Moor
Redlands Farm
Hill House
Leggatt Hill
Keets
Leggatt Hill Farm
THE LANE
RIVER
Salmonsbridge Farm
Salmons Bridge
River Common
Rock Cottage
Treve Cottage
Field Cottage
Rou House
WEST

6
oods arden
Rec. Grd.
Pav.
Pav.
OAK FIELD
OAK FIELD
OAK FIELD
SHEPHERDS LA.
HOLHURST RD.
THE CROFT
Smithbrook
Oldpark Copse
Eel Bridge
LANE
JAMES
LANE
RIVER COMMON
Roundabouts Farm
Tower

7
23
Broomhill Plantation
Heath End Farm
Woolhurst Farm
Heathend Copse
Gosdens Heath
Lodsworth
Lodsworth House
VICARAGE LA.
STREET
CHURCH LA.
Langham Stables
River Wood
Lodsworth Hanger
River
River Nursery
Keepers Wood
Brookfield Cottage
Standlands

8
Steward's Pond
Pond
High Field Copse
Gosdensheath Copse
Three Corner Copse
Path Field
Collins Orchard
Weir
Beggars' Corner
Woodbarn
Reservoir
BROOKFIELD LANE
The White House

9
22
PETWORTH RD.
ehouse opse
Lodge
Gosdensheath Farm
Three Corner Copse
Cradlehurst Copse
Benbow Gate
A272
Halfway Bridge
Netherlands Farm
Grittenham Farm
Bu Cott

Midhurst GU29

A   B   C   D   E   F
82

The Moor
Moorland Barns
Coxward Copse
Moorland Farm
The
Sa
Lods Bridge
Canal (dis)
Lock
92   93   94
26   92   93   94

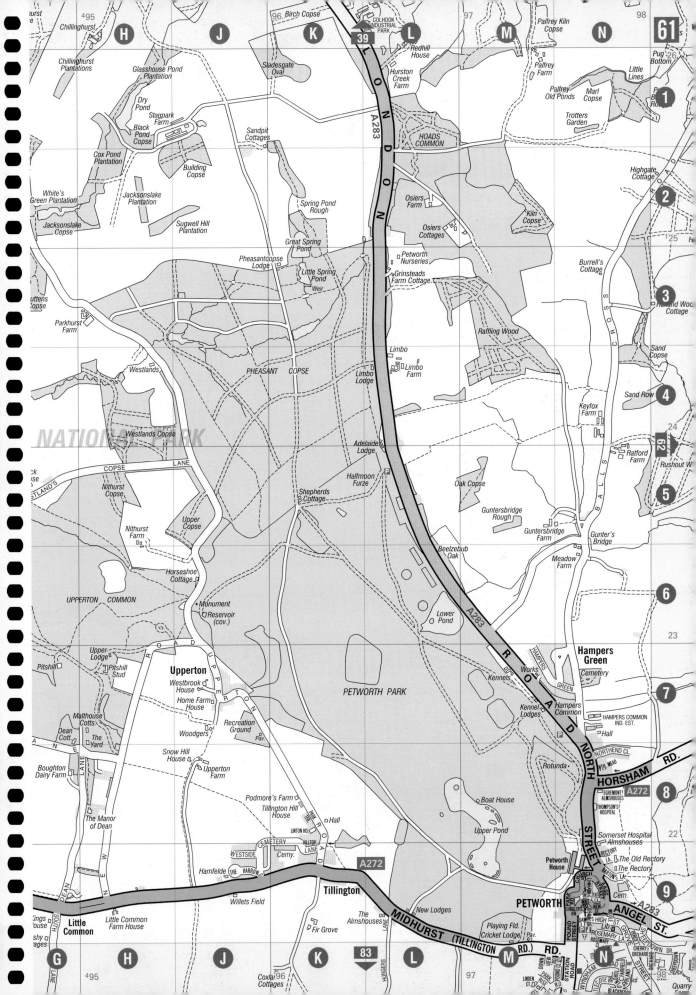

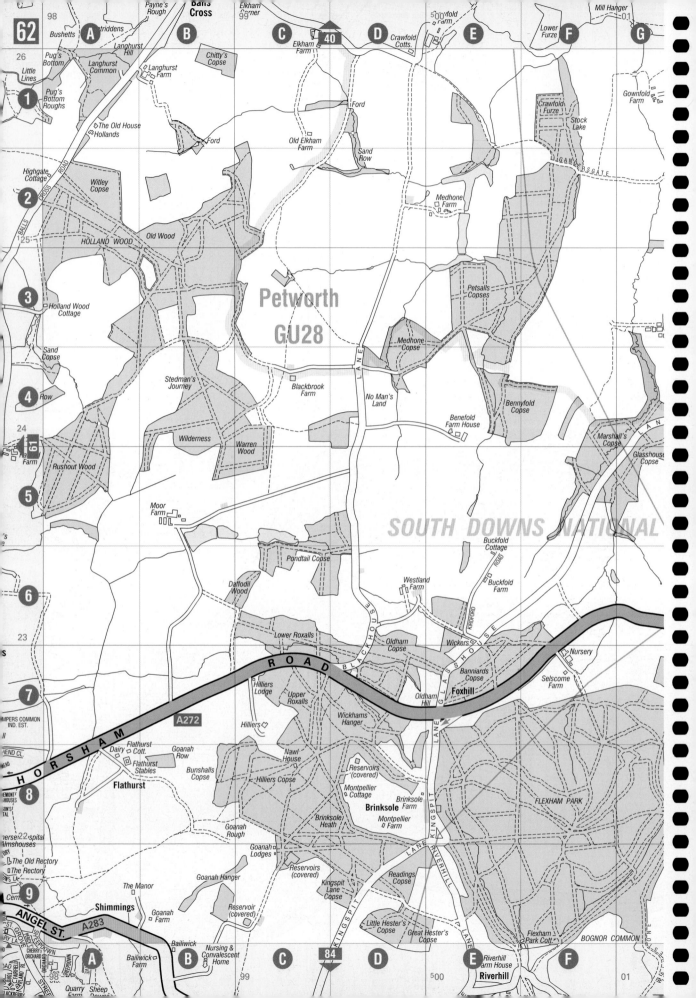

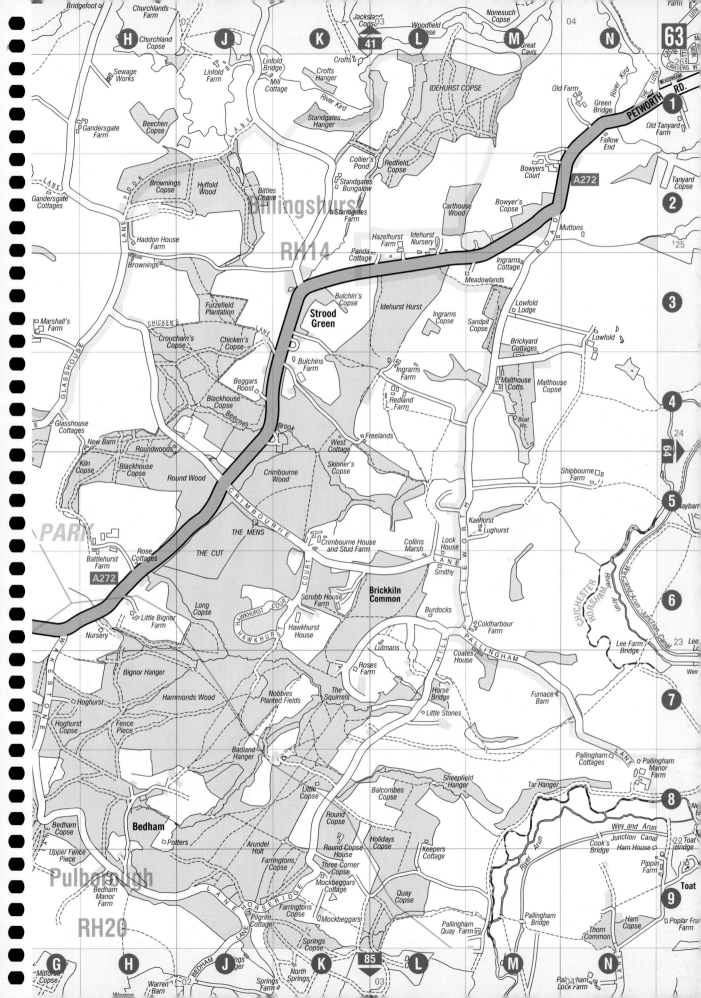

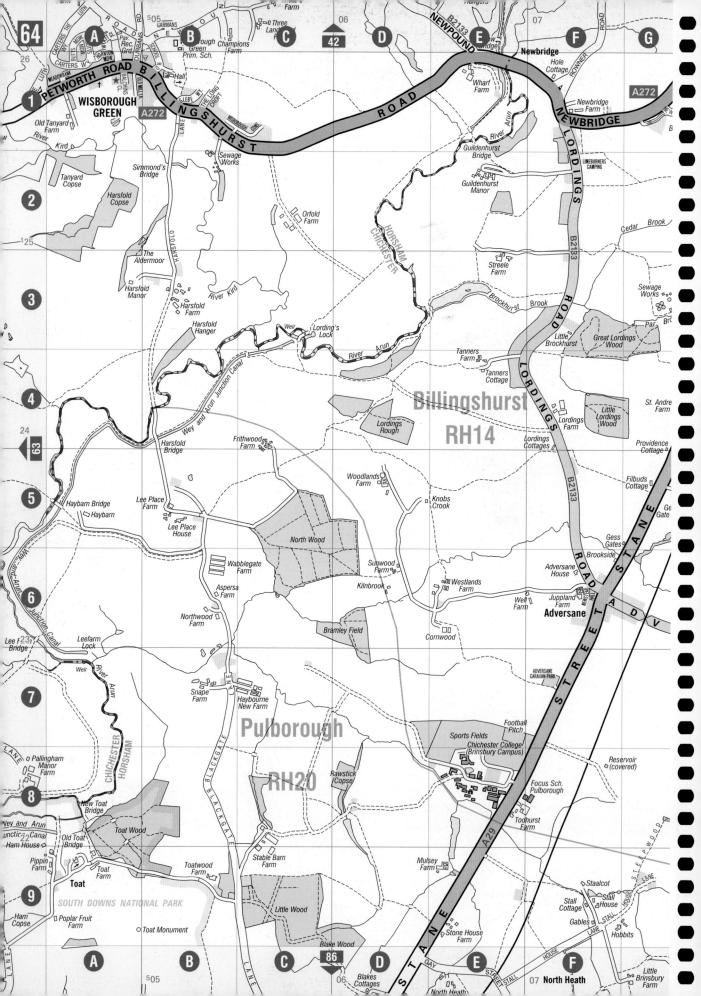

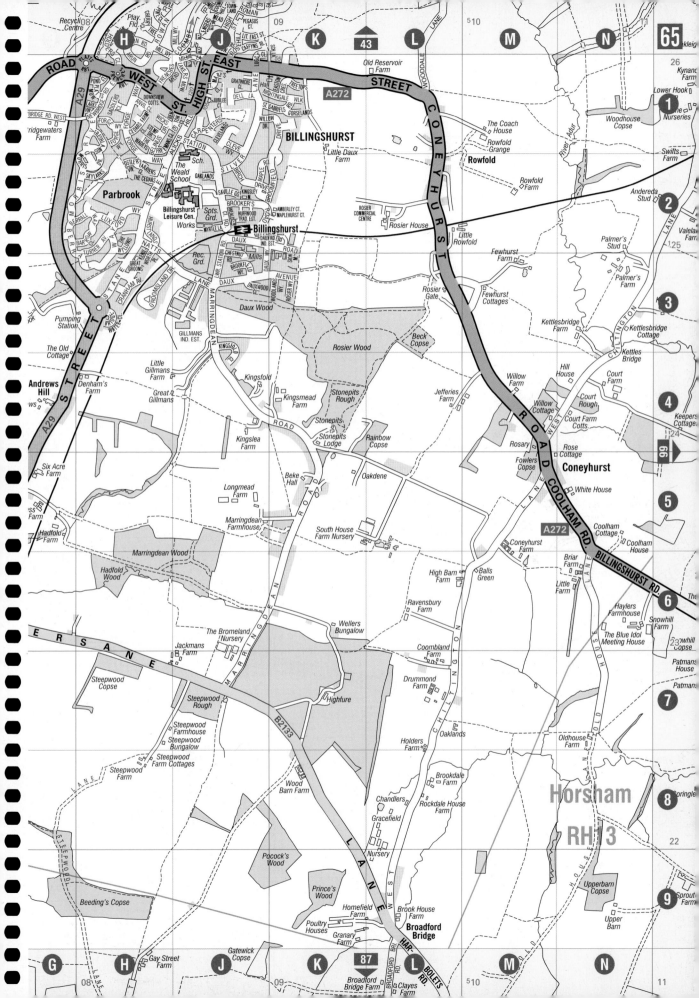

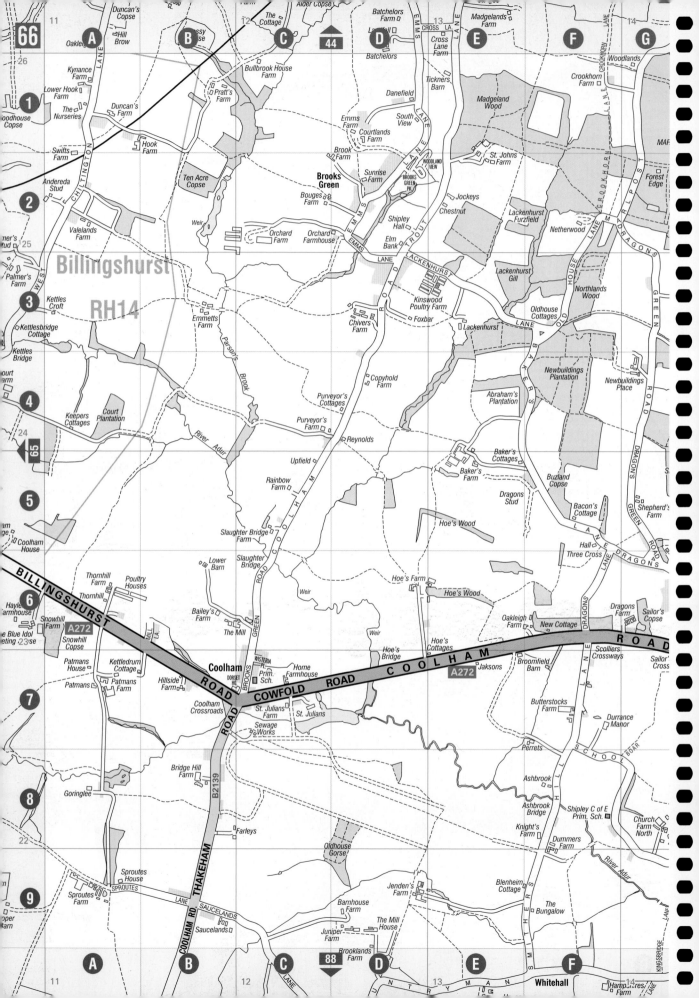

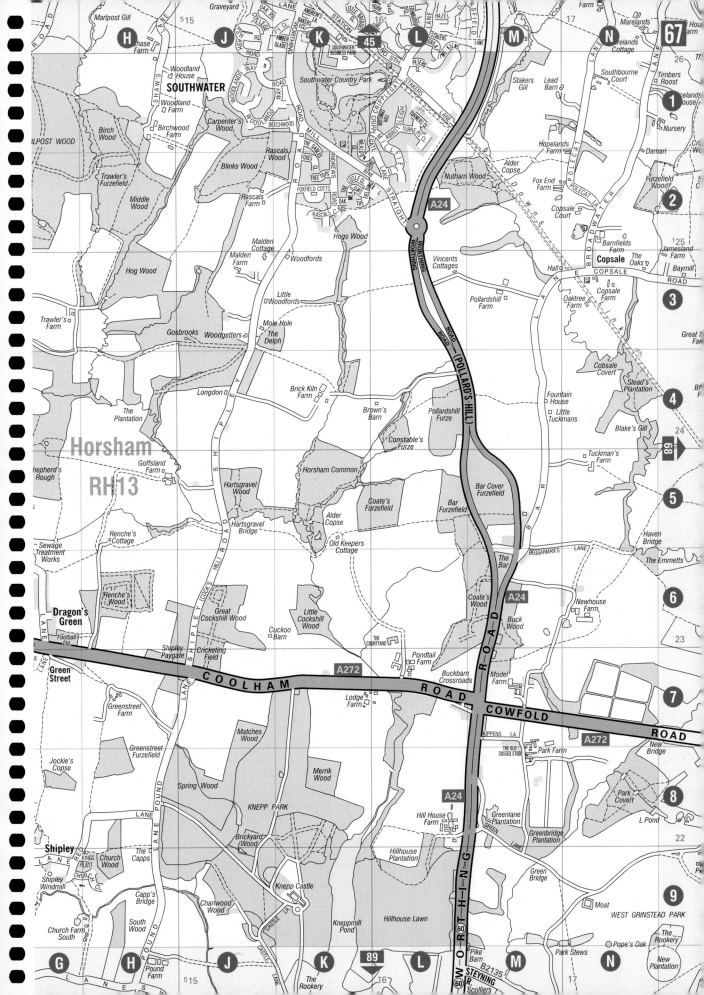

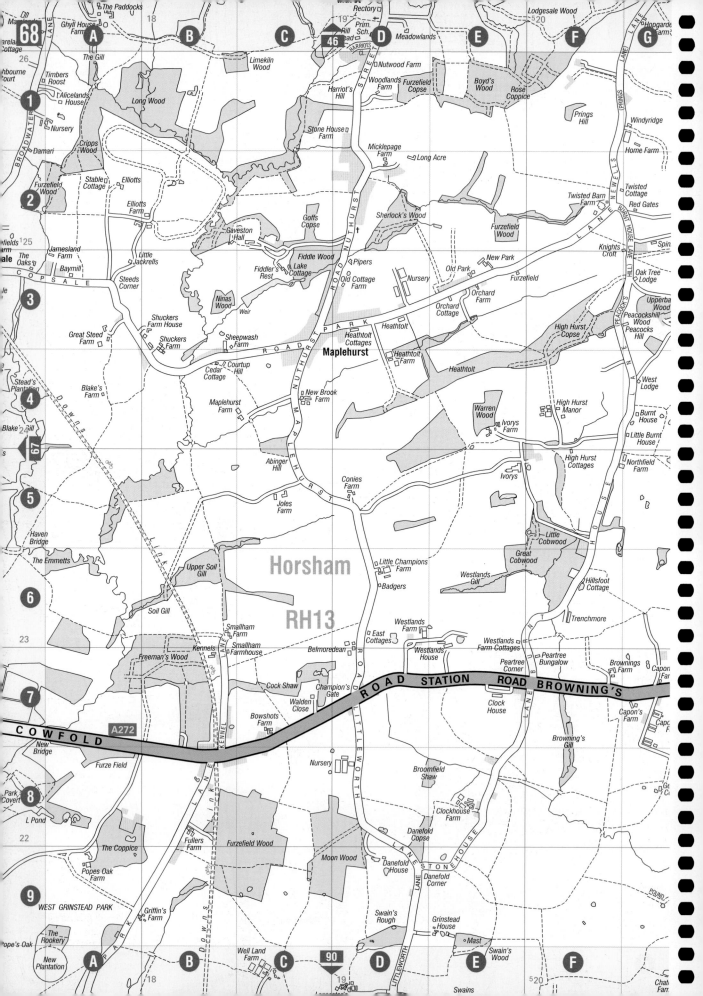

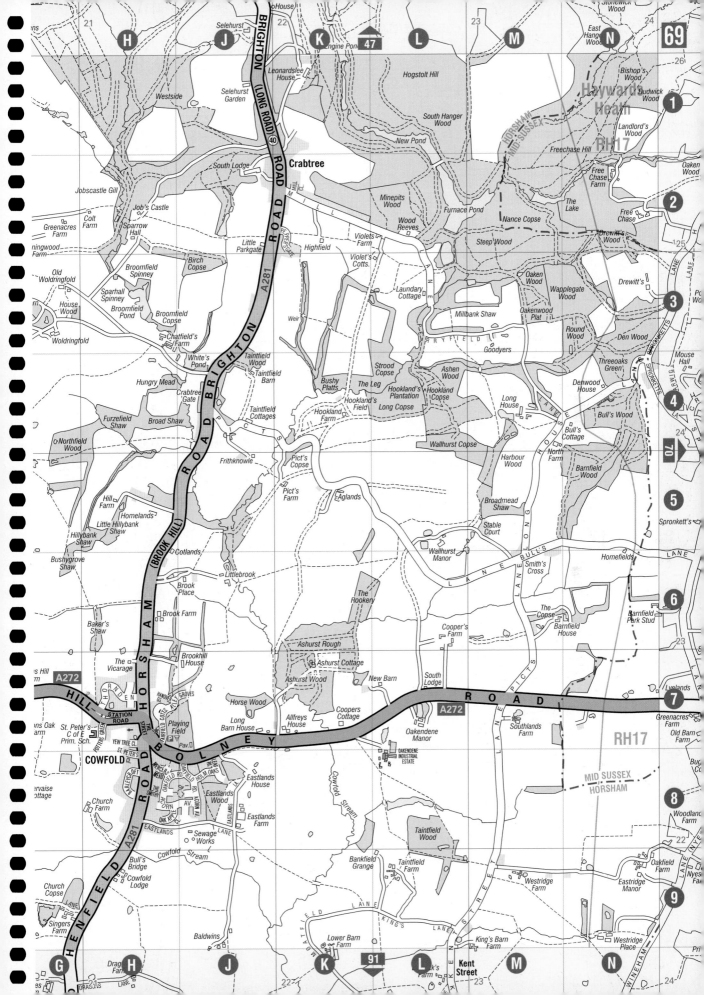

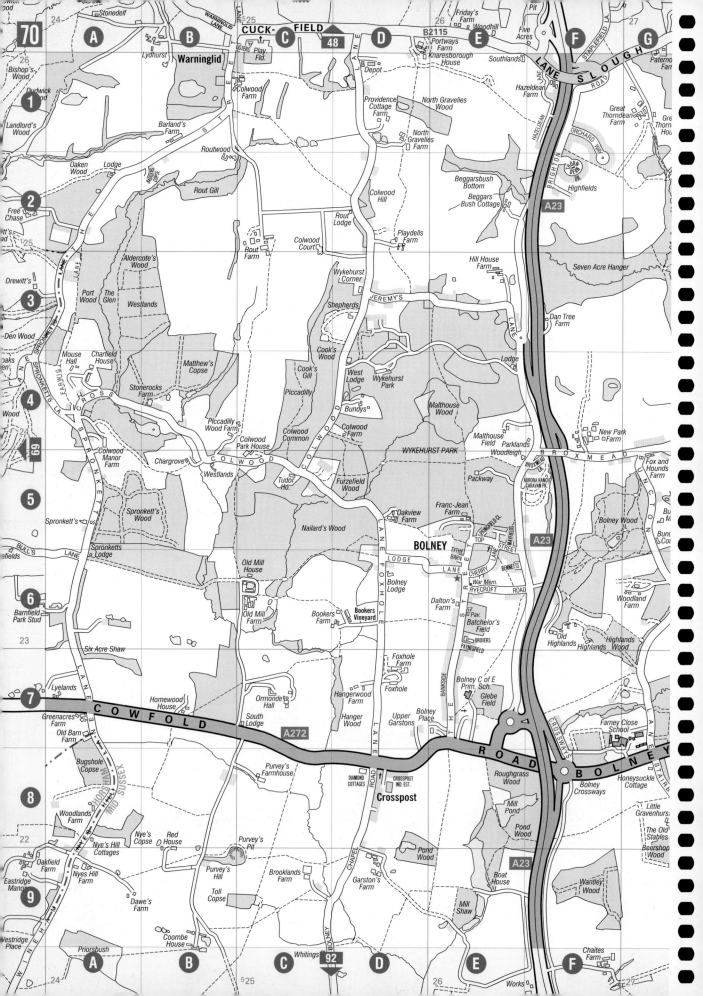

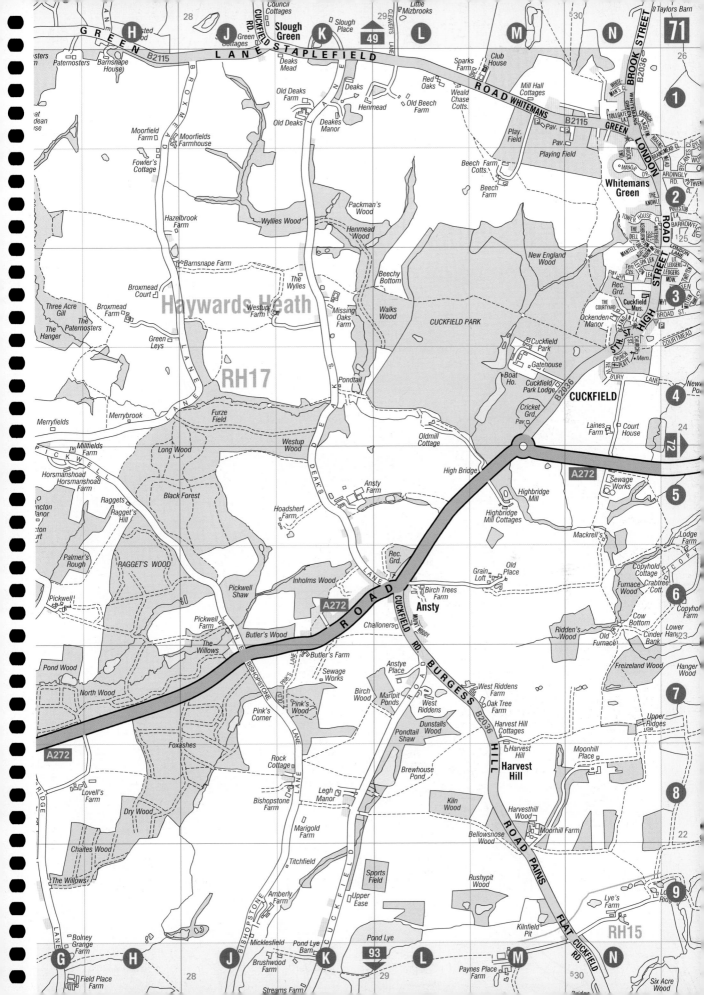

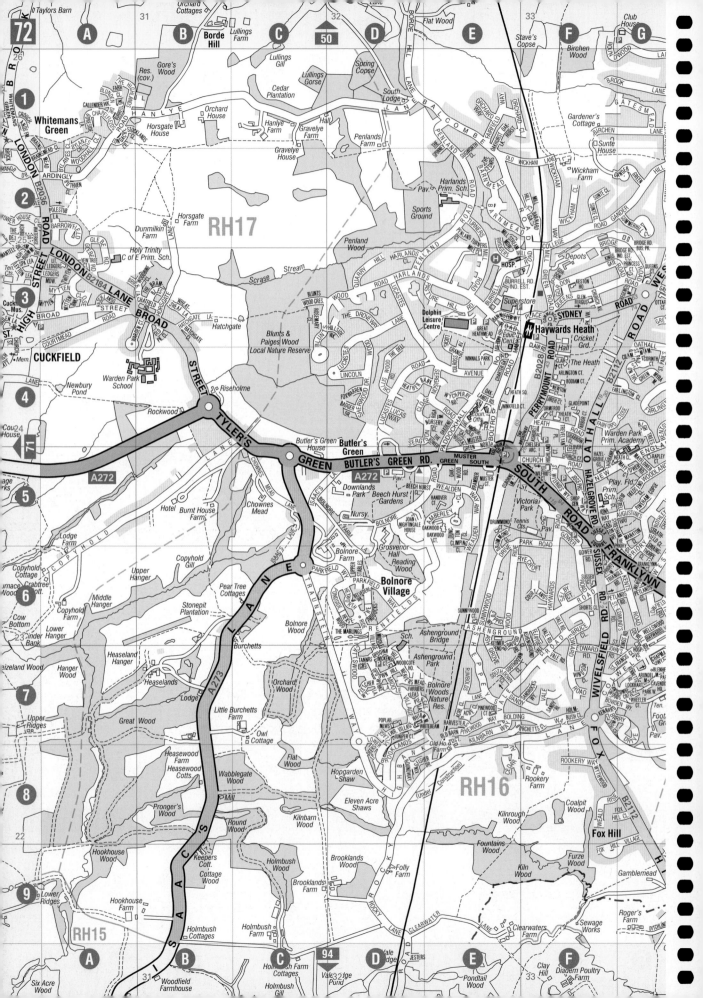

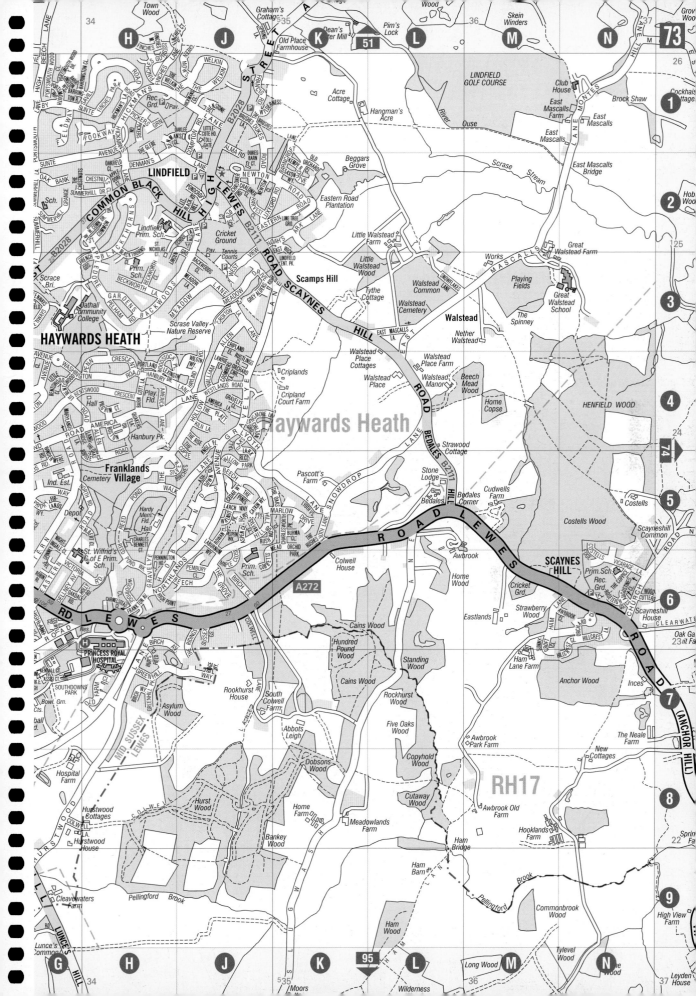

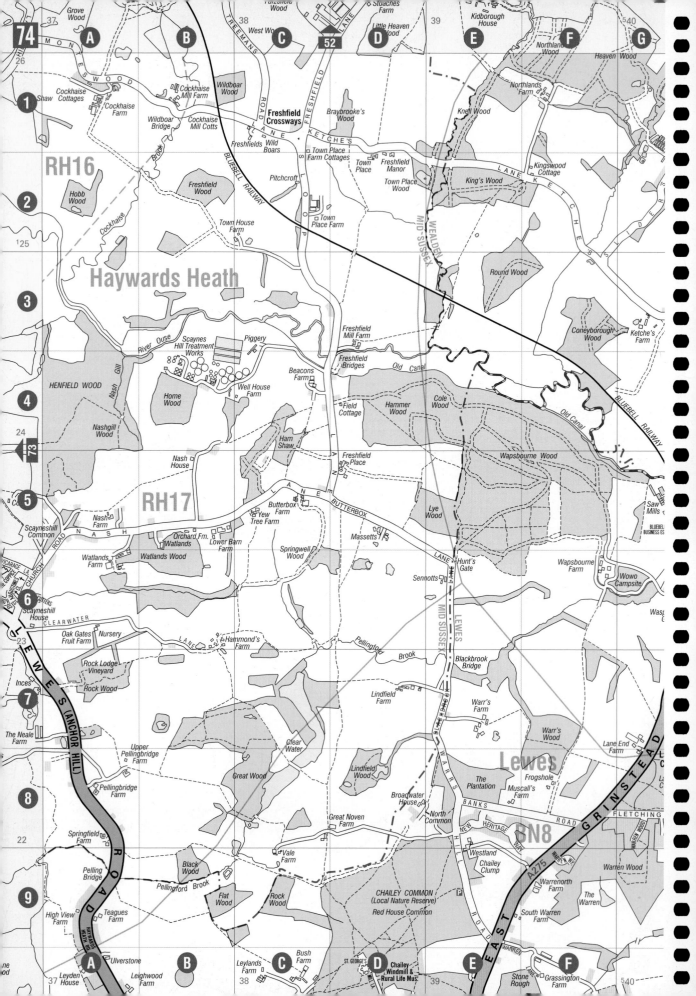

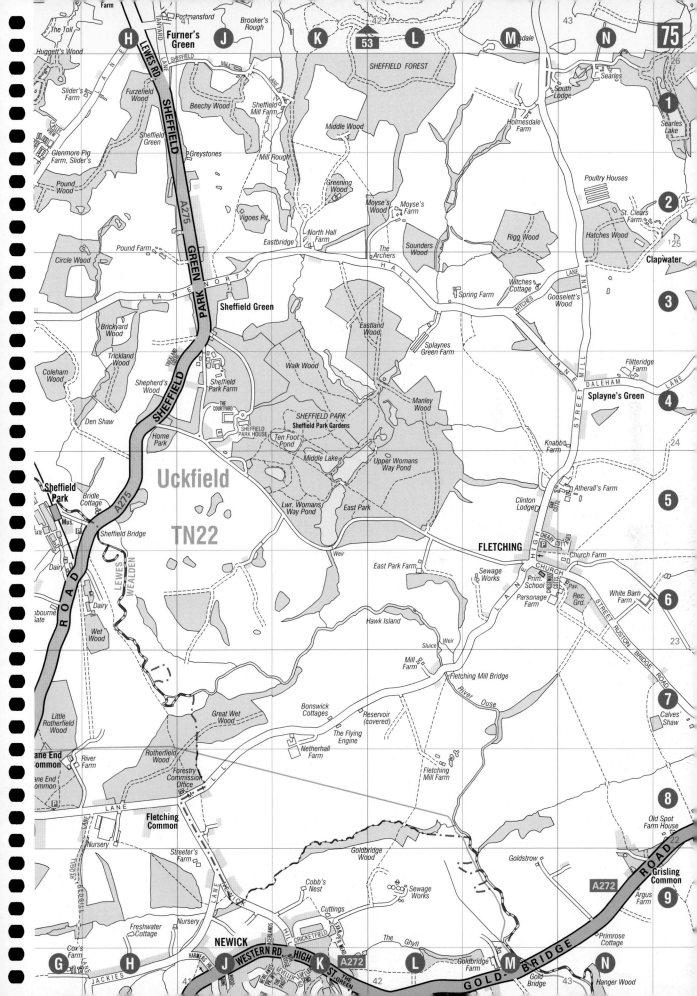

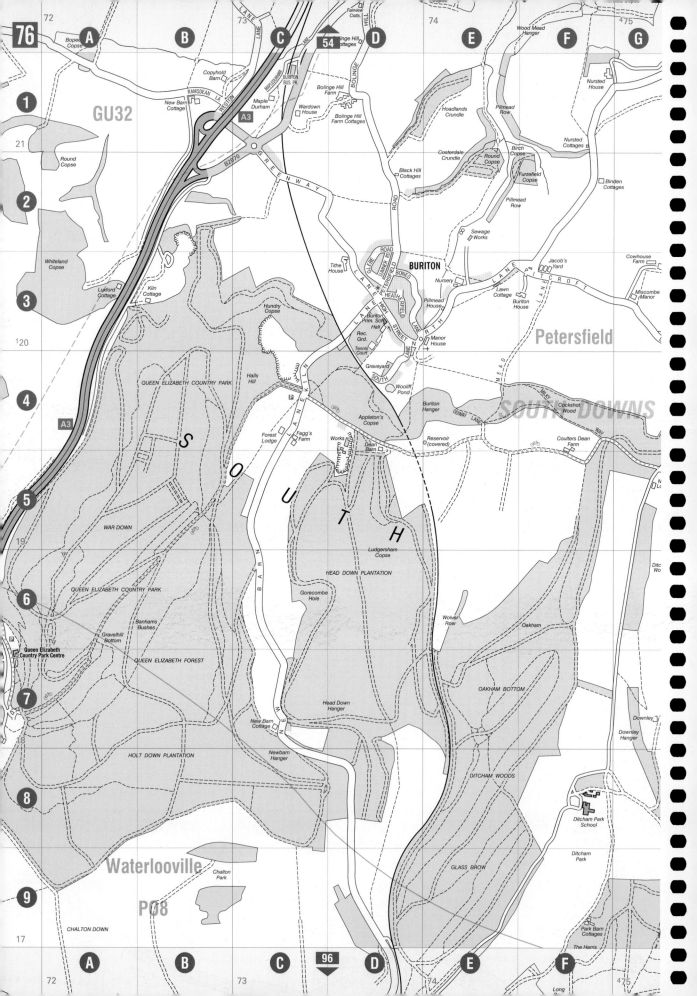

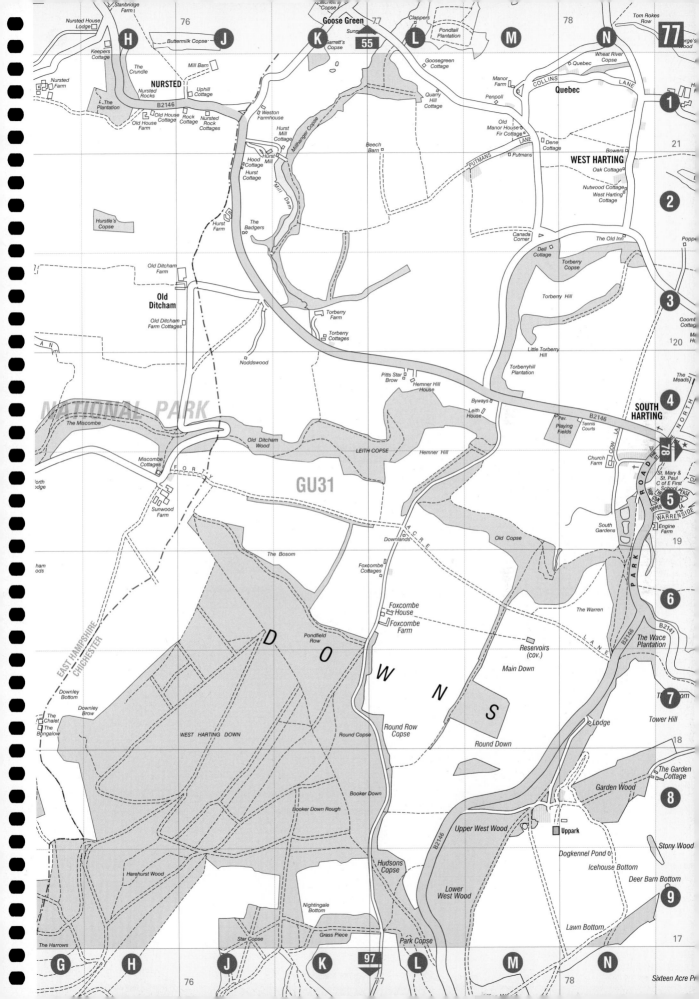

Labels and place names:

Stanbridge Farm, Tom Rokes Row, Gatchell's Copse, Clappers, **77**, Nursted House Lodge, **H**, Buttermilk Copse, **J**, Goose Green, **K**, Barrett's Copse, **55**, **L**, Pondtail Plantation, **M**, **N**, Keepers Cottage, The Crundle, Mill Barn, Wheat River Copse, Quebec, **1**, Nursted Farm, The Plantation, NURSTED, Nursted Rocks, Uphill Cottage, Weston Farmhouse, Manor Farm, COLLINS LANE, Quebec, 21, B2146, Old House Cottage, Rock Cottage, Nursted Rock Cottages, Hurst Mill Cottage, Quarry Hill Cottage, Penpoll, Old Manor House, Fir Cottage, LANE, Dene Cottage, Bowers, WEST HARTING, **2**, Hurstle's Copse, Hurst Farm, Hood Cottage, Hurst Mill, Hurst Cottage, The Badgers, Beech Barn, PUTMANS, Putmans, Oak Cottage, Nutwood Cottage, West Harting Cottage, Mill Dam, Milfranger Copse, Canada Corner, Dell Cottage, The Old Inn, Poppe, Torberry Copse, **3**, Old Ditcham Farm, Old Ditcham, Old Ditcham Farm Cottages, Torberry Farm, Torberry Cottages, Torberry Hill, Torberry Hill, Coomb Cottage, 120, Noddswood, Little Torberry Hill, Torberryhill Plantation, NATIONAL PARK, The Miscombe, Old Ditcham Wood, Pitts Star Brow, Hemner Hill House, Byways, Leith House, LEITH COPSE, Hemner Hill, B2146, Pav., Playing Fields, Tennis Courts, SOUTH HARTING, The Meads, **4**, NORTH, Miscombe Cottages, FORTY, North Lodge, Sunwood Farm, GU31, ACRE, Downlands, The Bosom, Old Copse, Church Farm, COW LA, St. Mary & St. Paul C of E First School, TIPPER LA, WARRENSIDE, **78**, **5**, 19, South Gardens, Engine Farm, Foxcombe Cottages, Foxcombe House, Foxcombe Farm, **6**, The Warren, PARK LANE, The Wace Plantation, B2141, Downley Bottom, Downley Brow, DOWNS, Pondfield Row, Reservoirs (cov.), Main Down, B2146, The Chalet, The Bungalow, WEST HARTING DOWN, Round Copse, Round Row Copse, Round Down, Lodge, **7**, Tower Hill, EAST HAMPSHIRE, CHICHESTER, 18, The Garden Cottage, Garden Wood, **8**, Booker Down, Booker Down Rough, Upper West Wood, Uppark, Stony Wood, Harehurst Wood, Hudsons Copse, Lower West Wood, Dogkennel Pond, Icehouse Bottom, Deer Barn Bottom, **9**, Nightingale Bottom, Grass Piece, Park Copse, Lawn Bottom, 17, The Harrows, Star Copse, **G**, **H**, **J**, **K**, **97**, **L**, **M**, **N**, Sixteen Acre Pi, 76, 77, 78

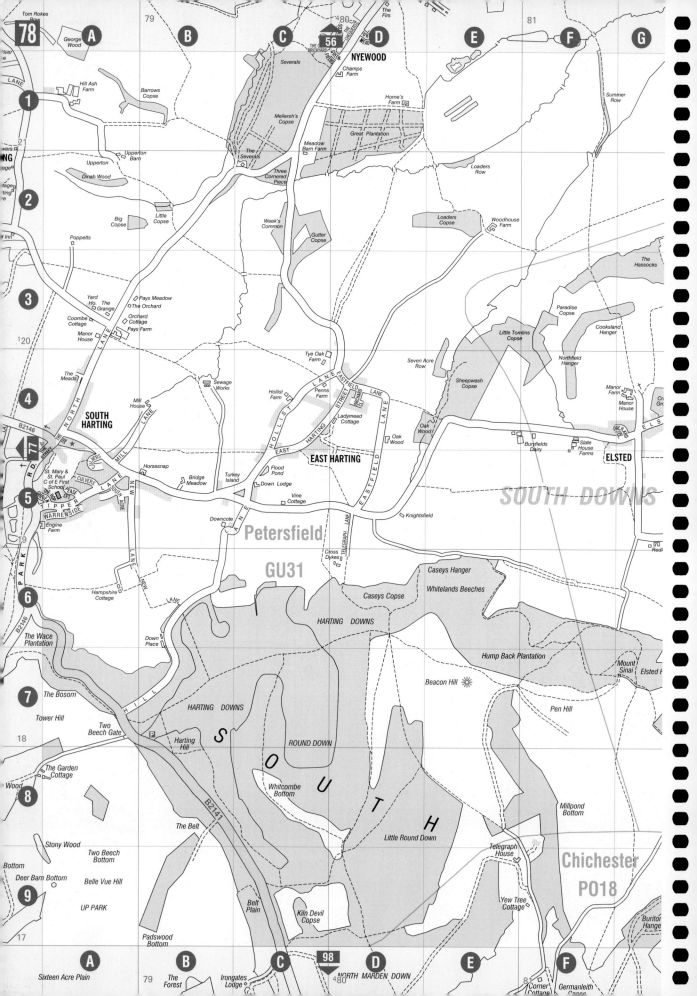

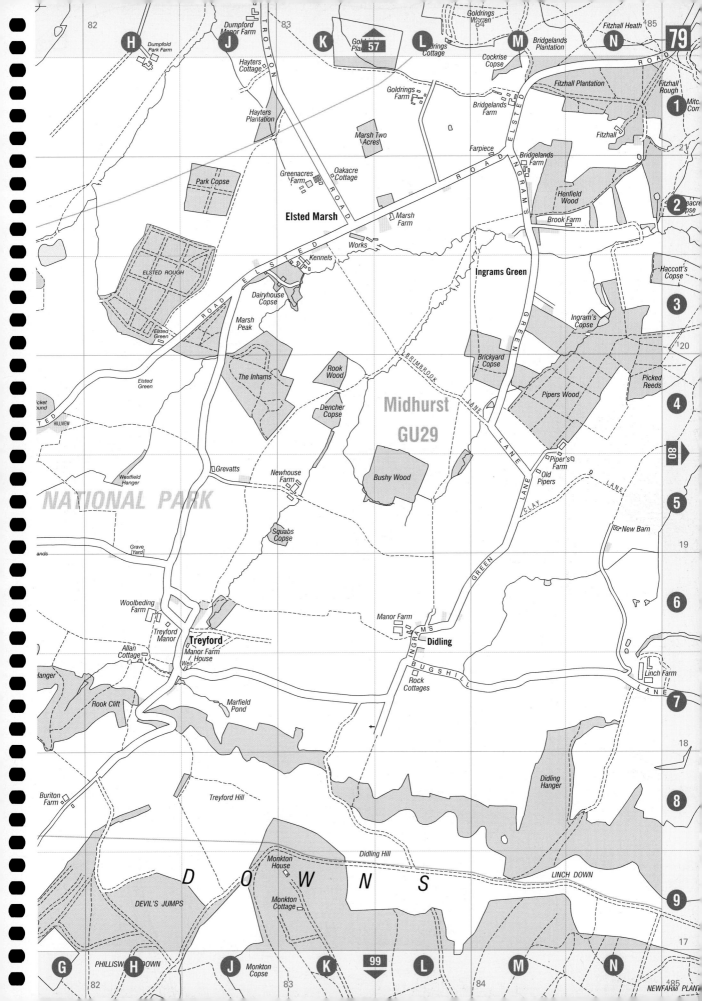

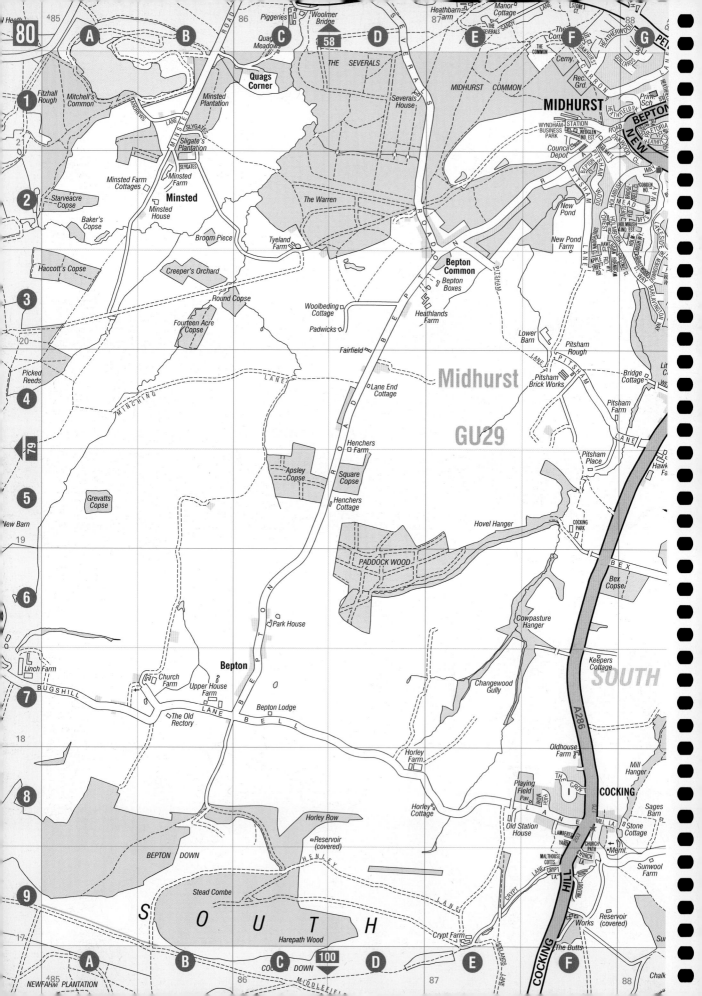

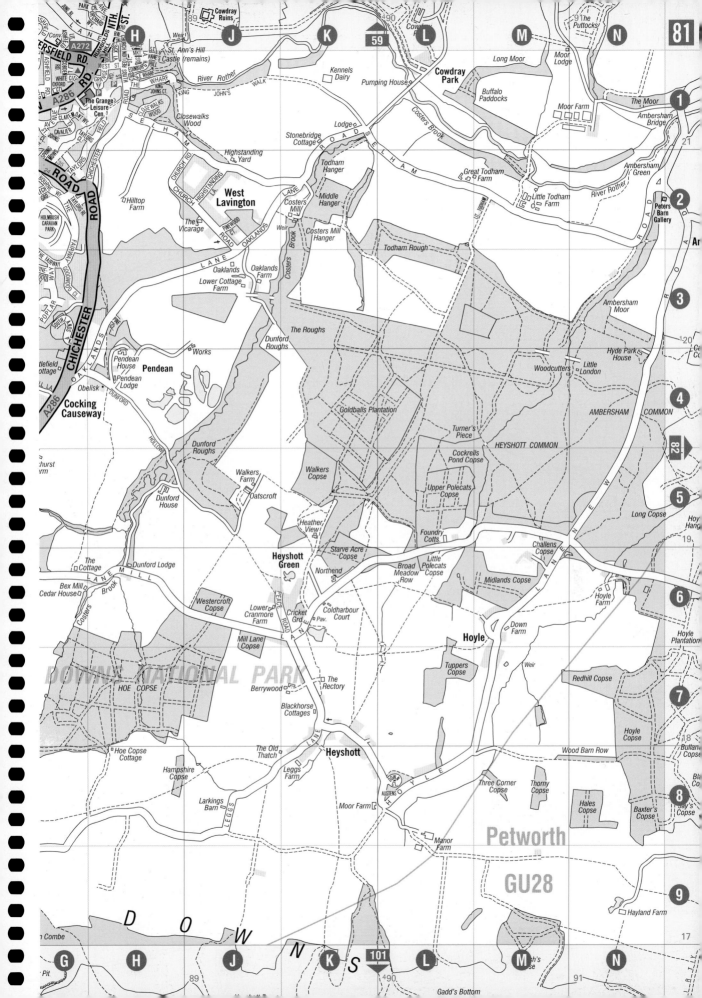

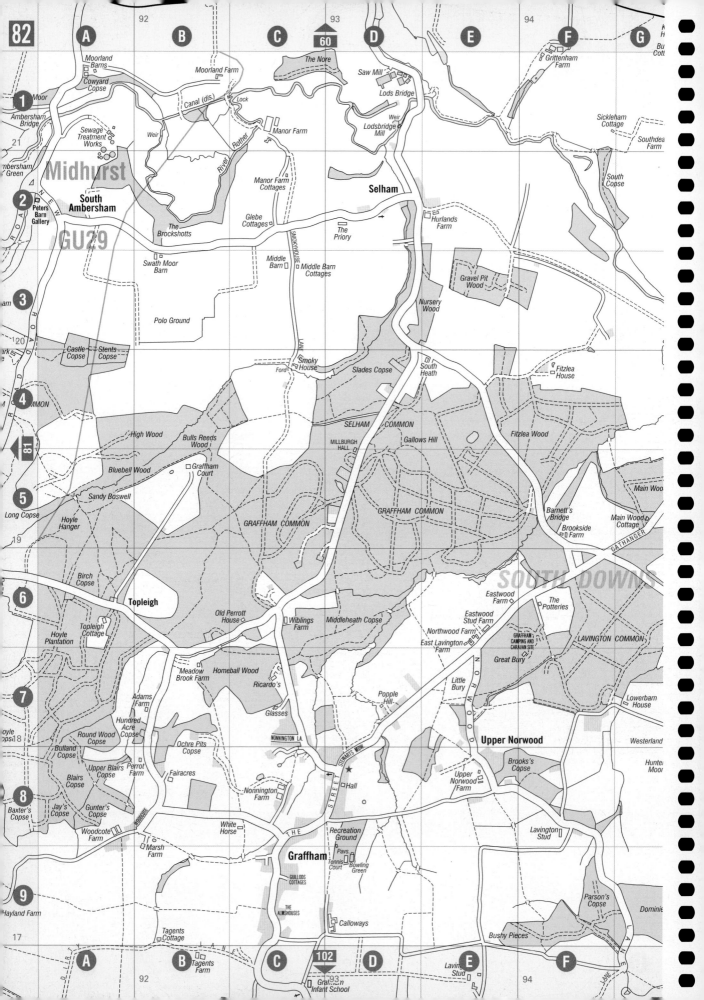

A 92 B C 93 ⬆ 60 D E 94 F G

1
Moor
Moorland Barns
Cowyard Copse
Ambersham Bridge
Moorland Farm
Canal (dis.)
Lock
The Nore
Saw Mill
Lods Bridge
Grittenham Farm

2
Sewage Treatment Works
Ambersham Green
Weir
River Rother
Manor Farm
Weir
Lodsbridge Mill
Sickleham Cottage
Southdean Farm

Midhurst
South Ambersham
Peters Barn Gallery
Manor Farm Cottages
Selham
Hurlands Farm
South Copse

GU29
The Brockshotts
Glebe Cottages
The Priory

3
120
Swath Moor Barn
Middle Barn
Middle Barn Cottages
Gravel Pit Wood
Nursery Wood

Polo Ground
Castle Copse
Stents Copse

4
COMMON
Smoky House
Ford
Slades Copse
South Heath
Fitzlea House

81
High Wood
Bulls Reeds Wood
MILLBURGH HALL
SELHAM COMMON
Gallows Hill
Fitzlea Wood

Bluebell Wood
Graffham Court

5
19
Long Copse
Sandy Boswell
Hoyle Hanger
GRAFFHAM COMMON
GRAFFHAM COMMON
Barnett's Bridge
Brookside Farm
Main Wood
Main Wood Cottage
CATHANGER

6
Birch Copse
Topleigh
Hoyle Plantation
Topleigh Cottage
Old Perrott House
Wiblings Farm
Middleheath Copse
Eastwood Farm
Eastwood Stud Farm
Northwood Farm
SOUTH DOWNS
The Potteries
LAVINGTON COMMON

7
Meadow Brook Farm
Homeball Wood
Ricardo's
Adams Farm
Glasses
Popple Hill
Little Bury
GRAFFHAM CAMPING AND CARAVAN SITE
Great Bury
East Lavington Farm
Lowerbarn House

8
Hoyle Copse
Bulland Copse
Round Wood Copse
Hundred Acre Copse
Upper Blairs Copse
Perrot Farm
Ochre Pits Copse
Fairacres
NONNINGTON LA.
STEWARTS ROW
Hall
Upper Norwood
Brooks's Copse
Upper Norwood Farm
Westerland
Hunter's Moor
Baxter's Copse
Blairs Copse
Jay's Copse
Gunter's Copse
Woodcote Farm
MOORCOTE
Nonnington Farm
White Horse
THE STREET
Recreation Ground
Lavington Stud

9
Hayland Farm
Marsh Farm
Tagents Cottage
Graffham
Pavs.
Tennis Court
Bowling Green
GUILLODS COTTAGES
THE ALMSHOUSES
Calloways
Parson's Copse
Bushy Pieces
Dominie

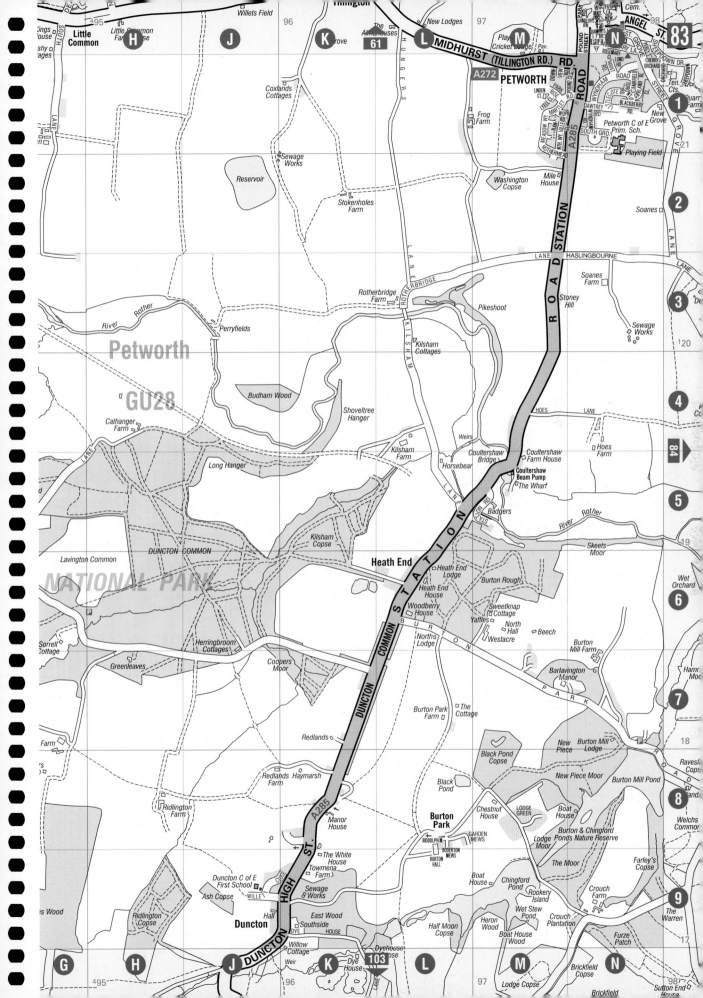

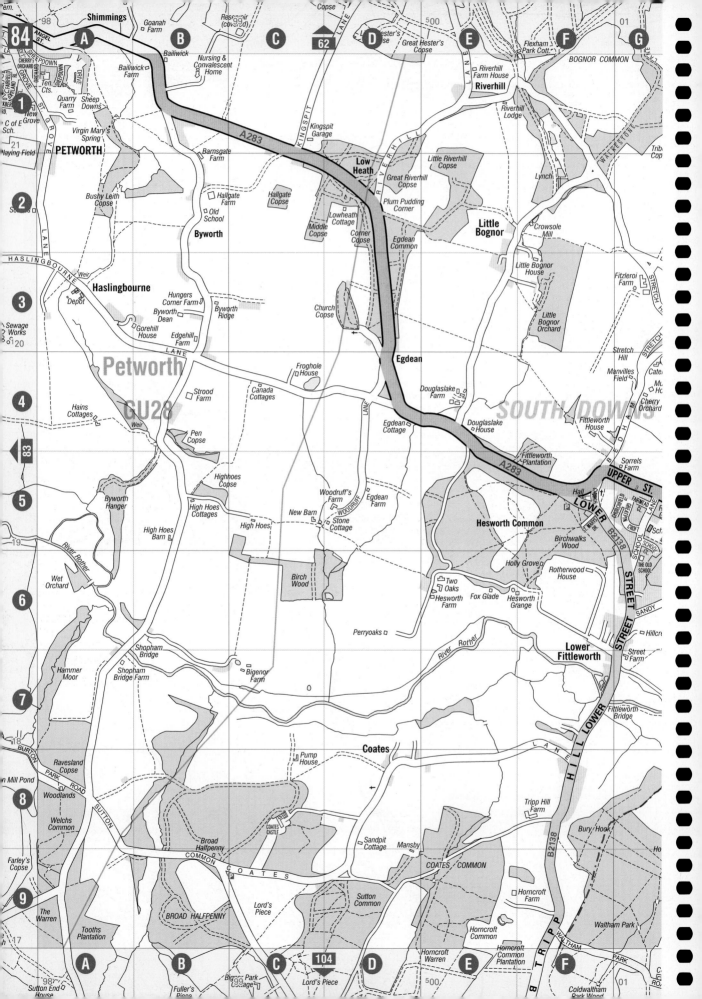

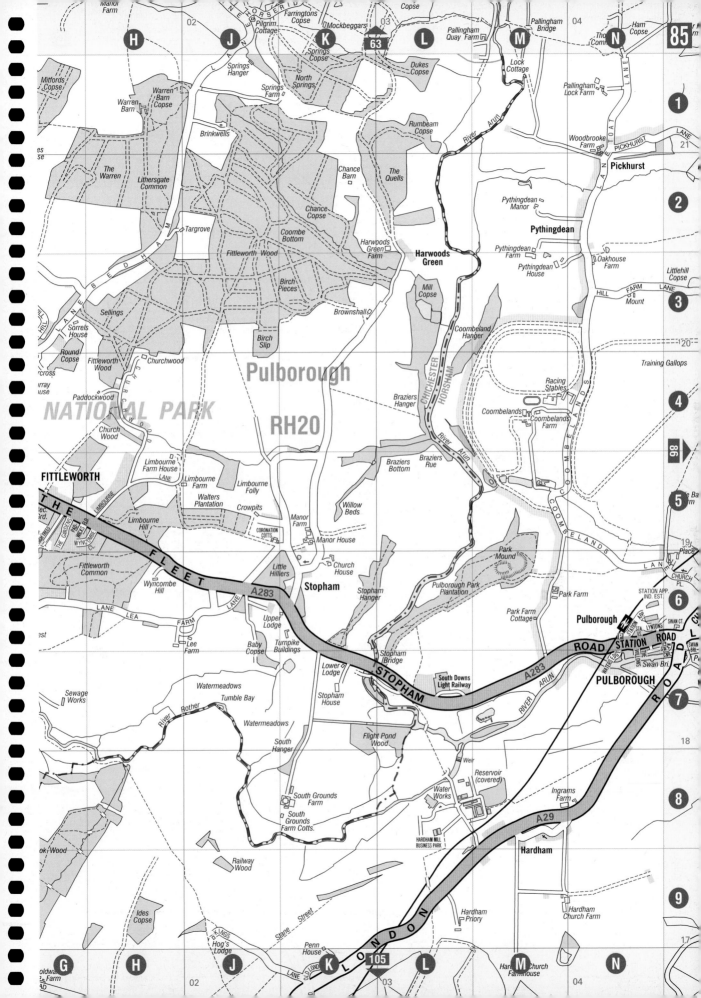

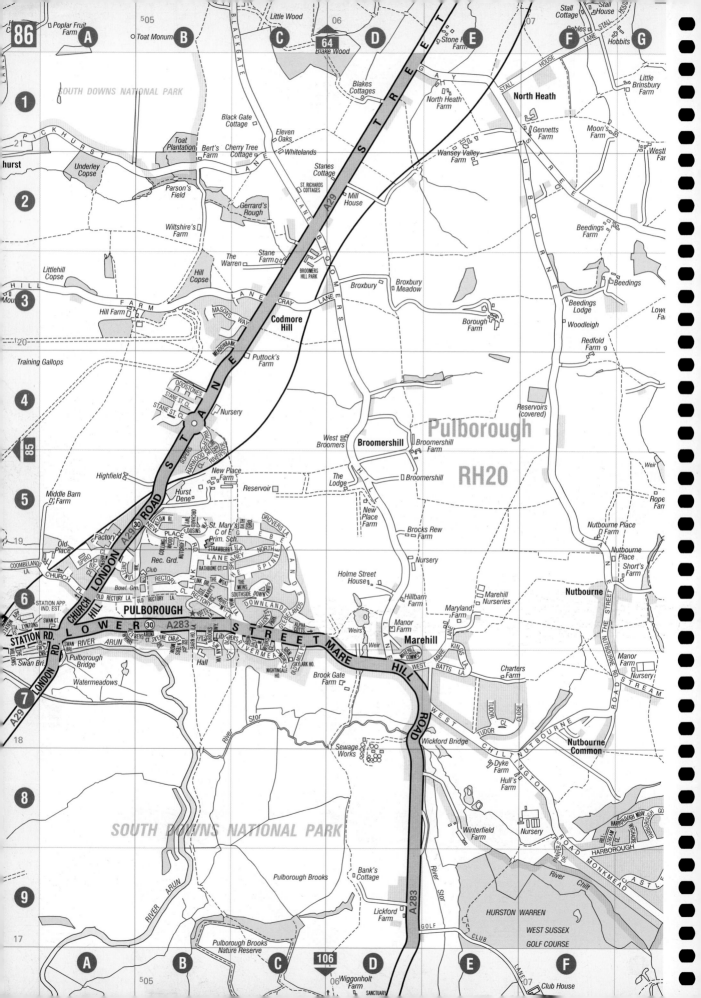

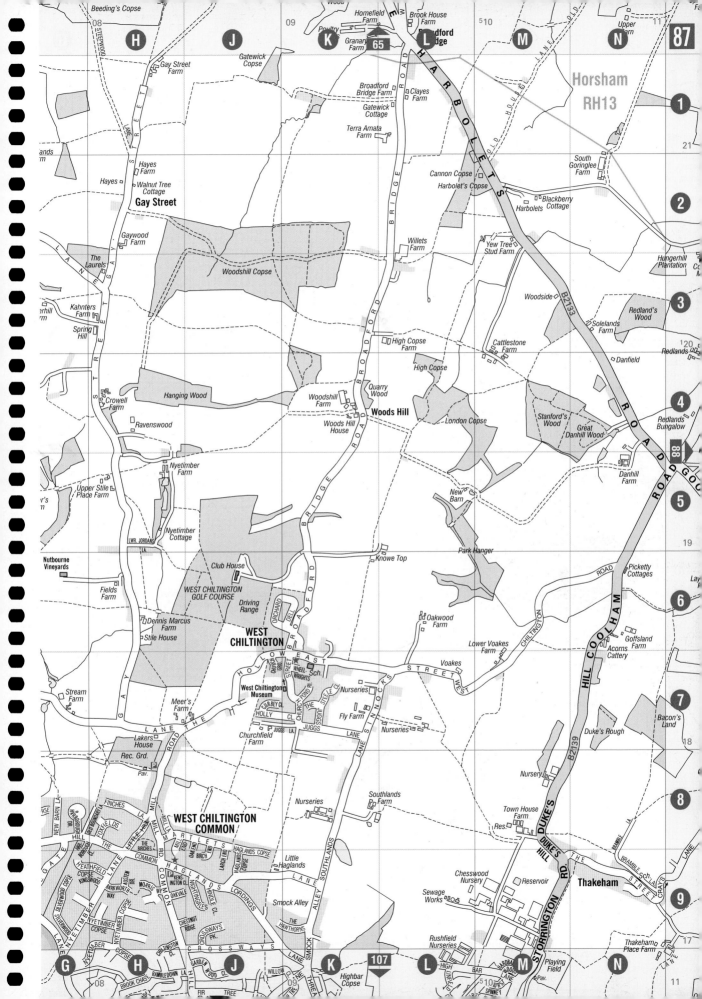

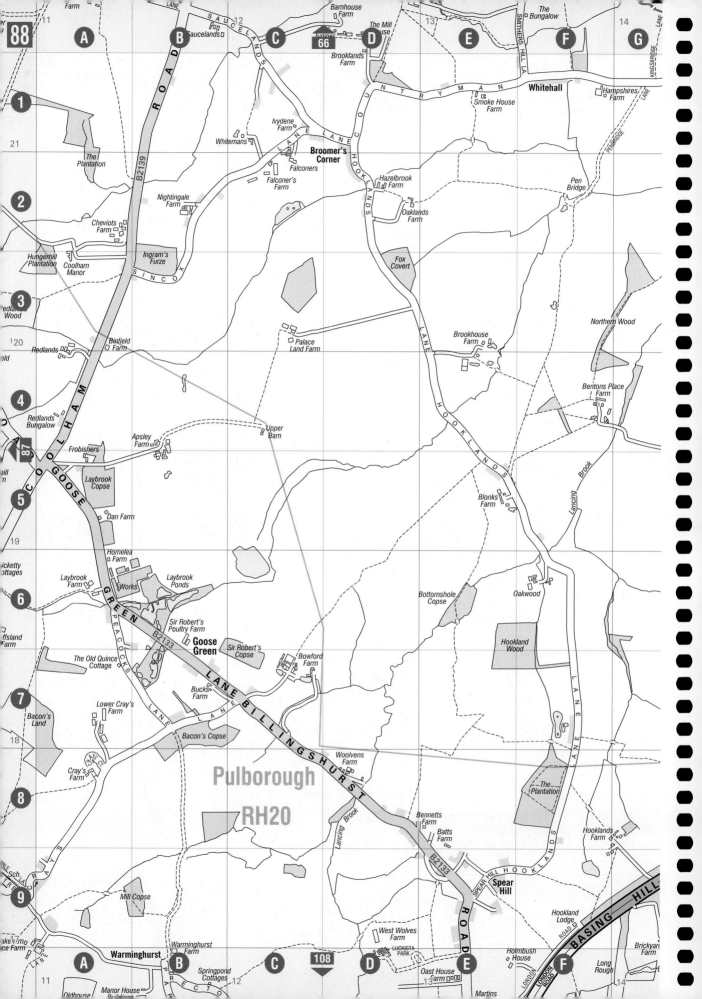

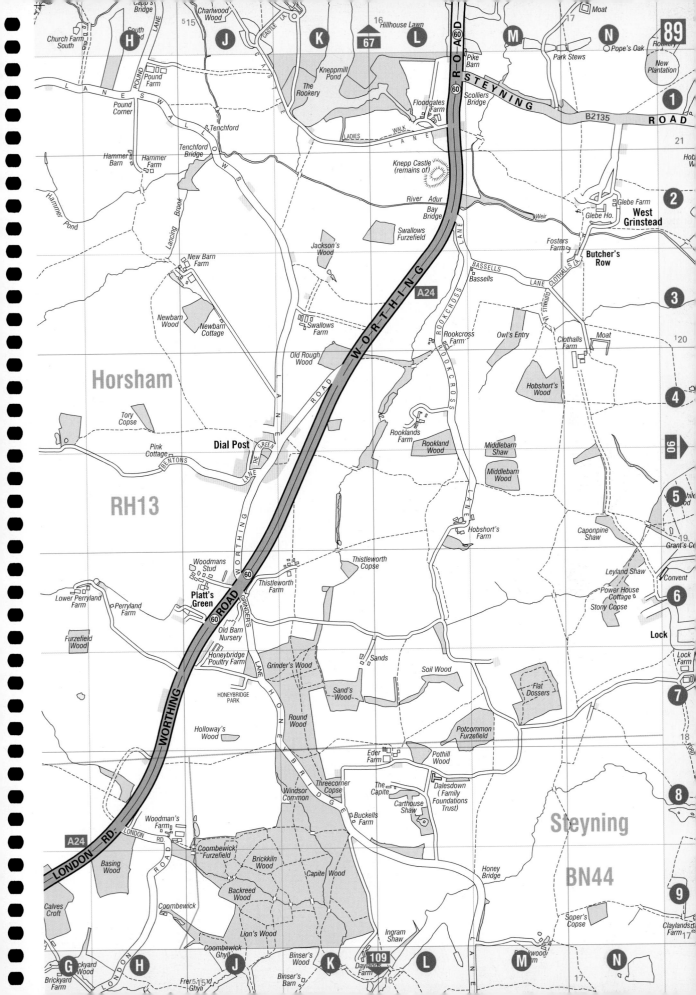

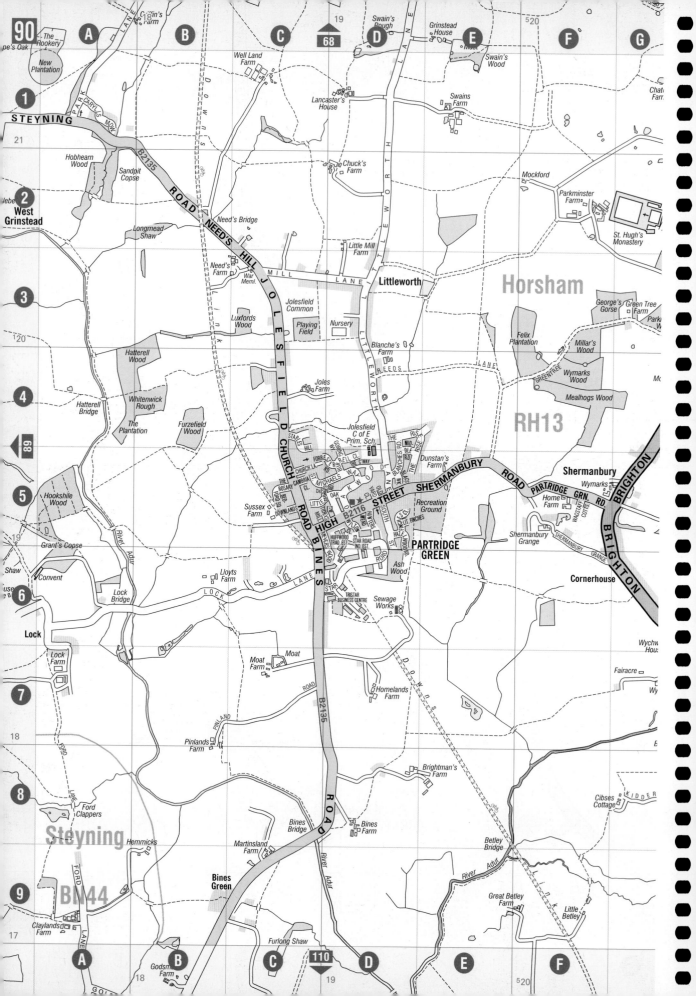

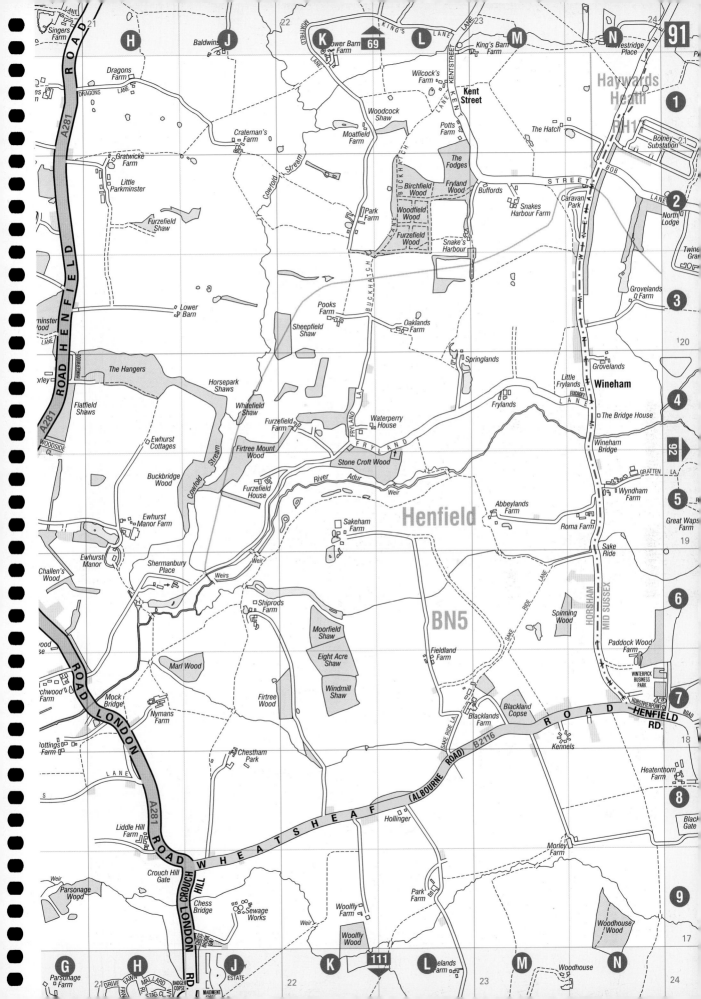

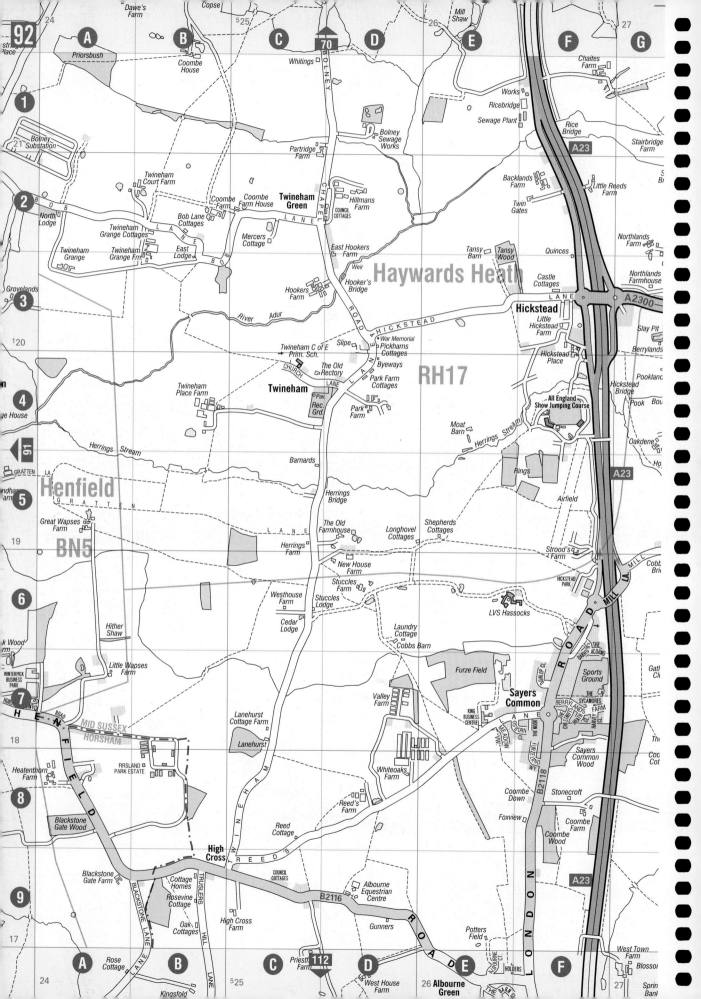

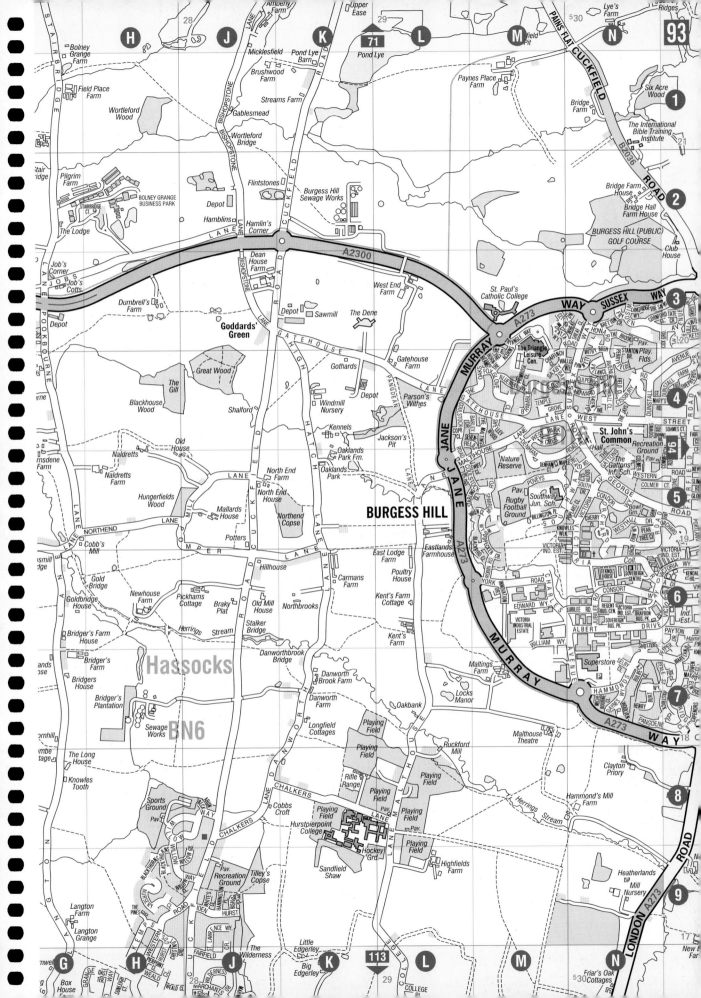

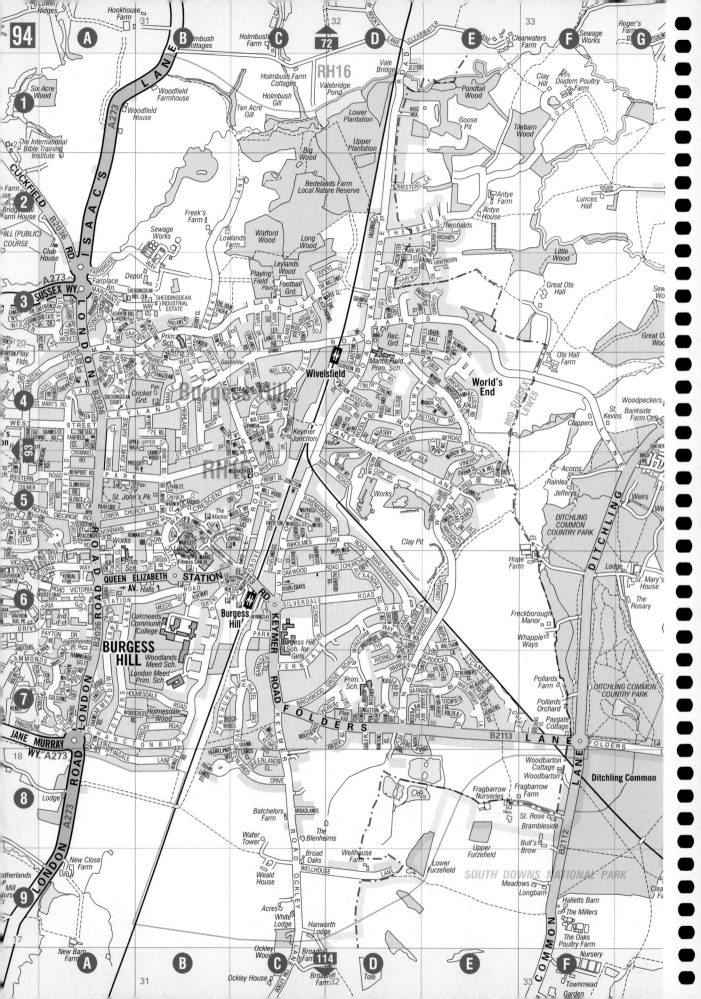

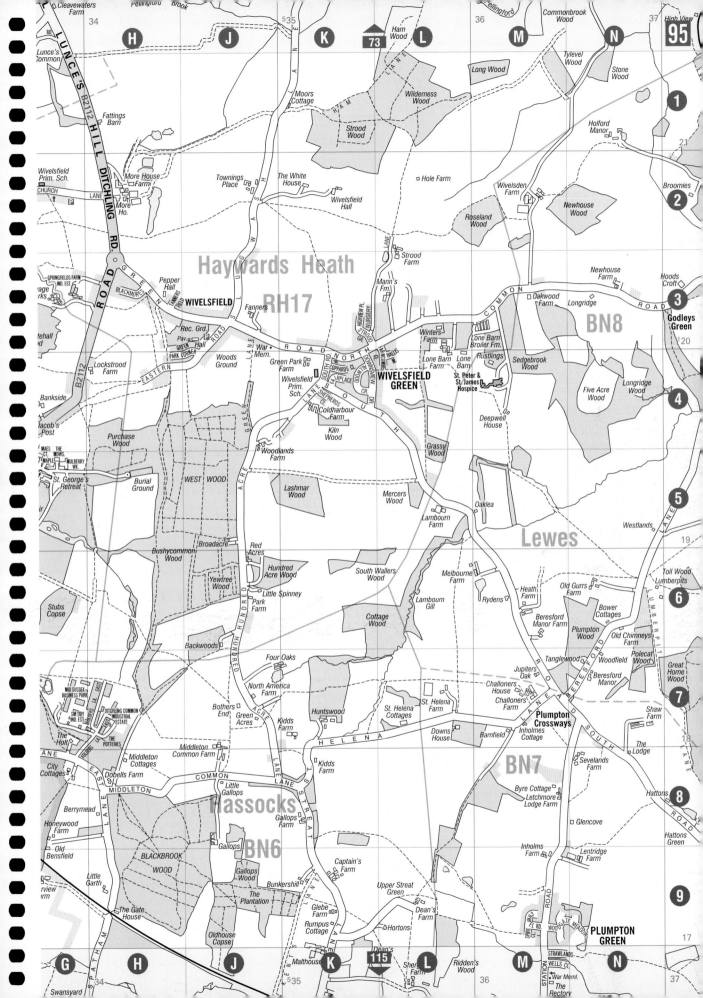

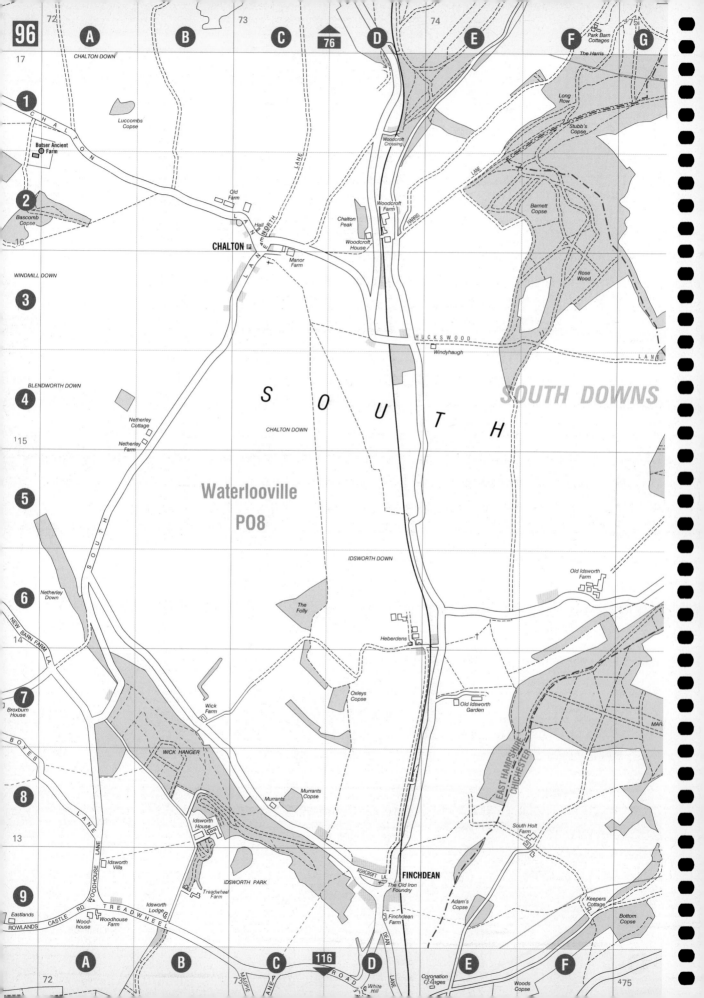

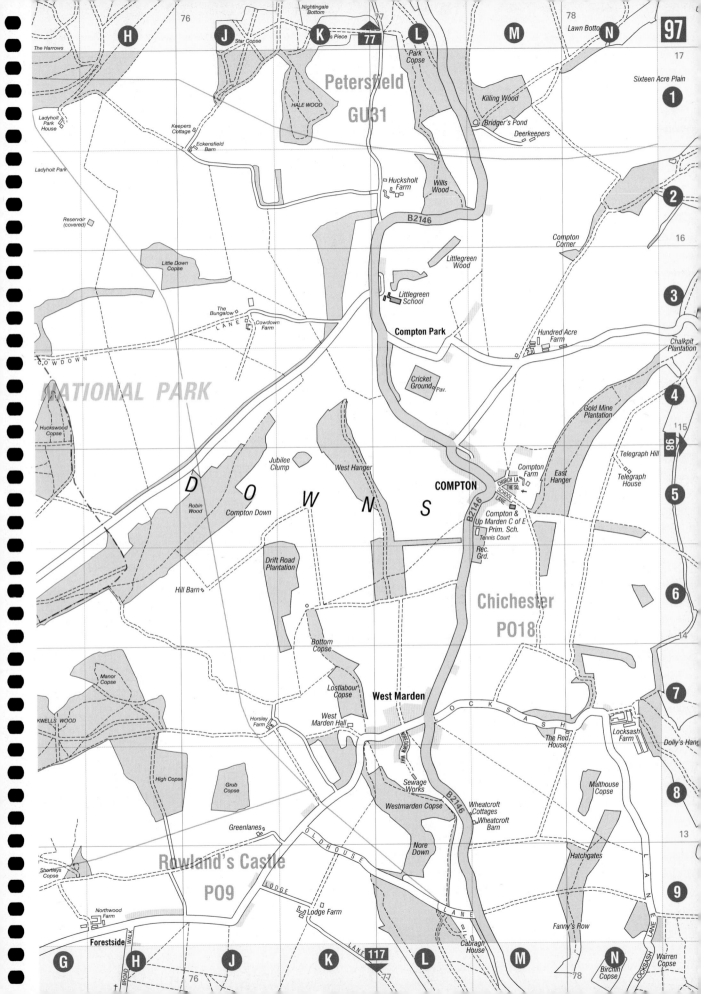

A **B** **C** **D** 78 **E** **F** **G**

UP PARK

Belt Plain

Kiln Devil Copse 480

Yew Tree Cottage 81

Buriton Hanger

Padswood Bottom

79

Petersfield

Sixteen Acre Plain

GU31

The Forest

Irongates Lodge

NORTH MARDEN DOWN

Corner Cottage

Germanleith Copse

Bus

1

17

PADS WOOD

Bushy Piece

Fenced-in-Piece

B2141

Philliswood Cottage

Hooksway

2

16

Fernbeds Down

Edgar Plantation

Church Farm

North Marden

Hill Lands Farm

HOOKSWAY

Handle Down

3

Chalkpit Plantation

Fernbeds Barn

LONG

Batten Hanger

Bevis's Thumb

Fernbeds Farm

LANE

LONG

LANE

4

115

67

Telegraph Hill

Reservoir (covered)

Switchback Barn

Hill Land Corner

Telegraph House

Apple Down

S   **O**   **U**   **T**   **H**

The Glebe House

Battine House

5

6

14

Up Marden Farm

East Marden Farm

East Marden

East Marden Down

Battines Hill Wood

SOUTH DOWNS

Whitelands Copse

Bo F.

Up Marden

Hill Farm

Blinkard Copse

Stripeshill Copse

7

ksash Farm

GREVITTS COPSE

Dolly's Hanger

Coldcroft Copse

WILDHAM WOOD

Lower Farm

8

13

CKSASH

LOWERFARM COPSE

Wildham Barn

9

Lyecommon Cottage

Lye Common

HASLETT COPSE

INHOLMES WOOD

Lambdow

Warren Copse

A **B** 79 **C** 480 **D** 118 78 **E** **F**

Pitlands Farm

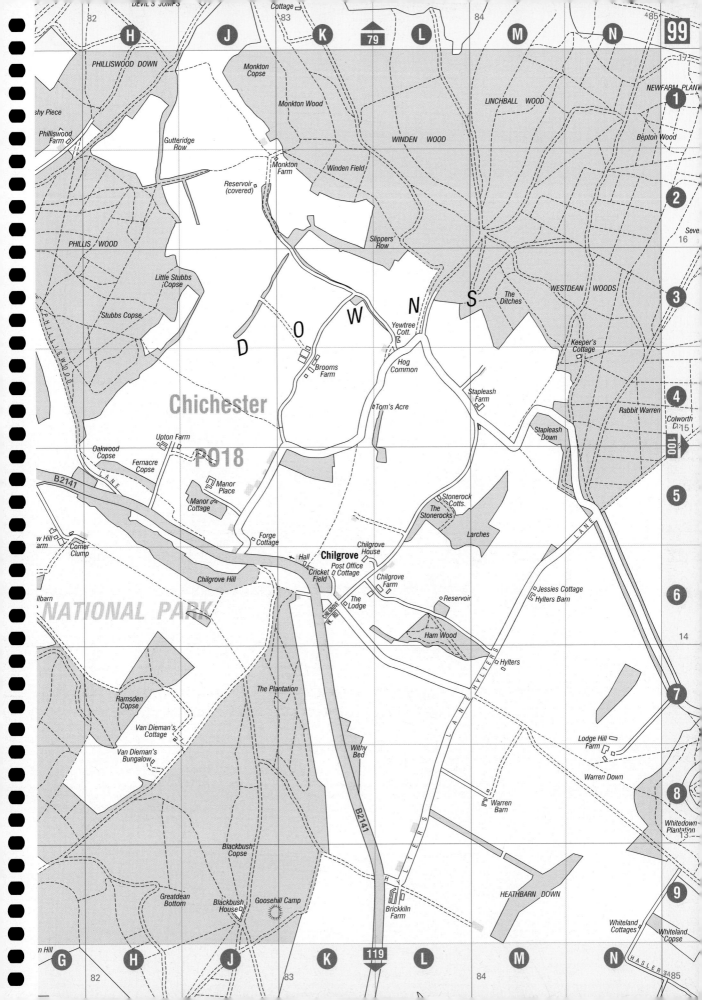

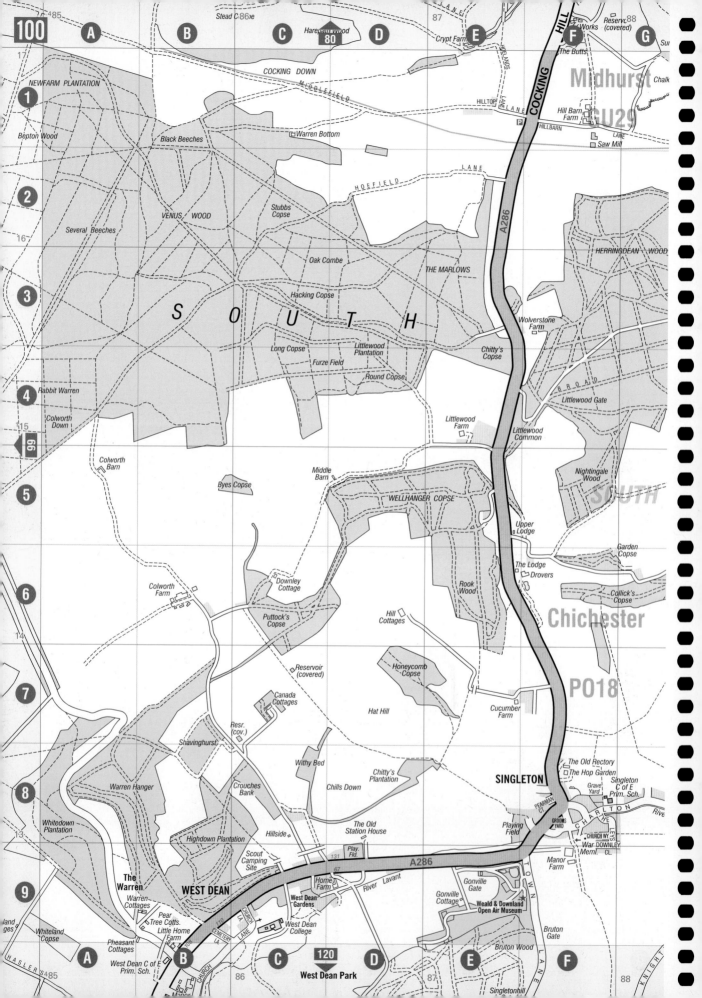

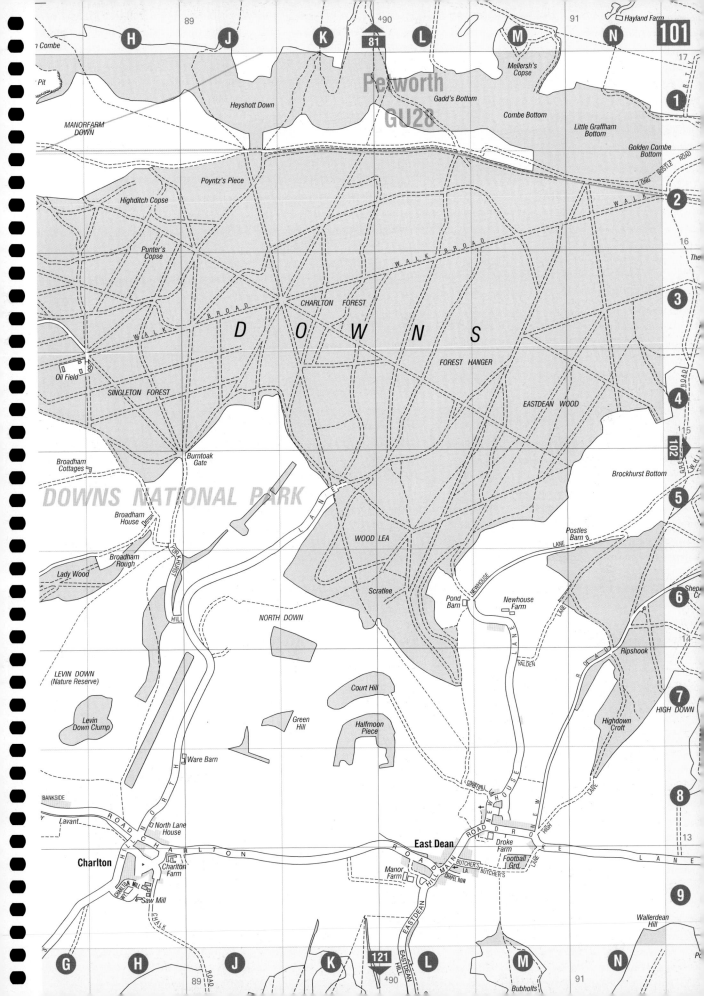

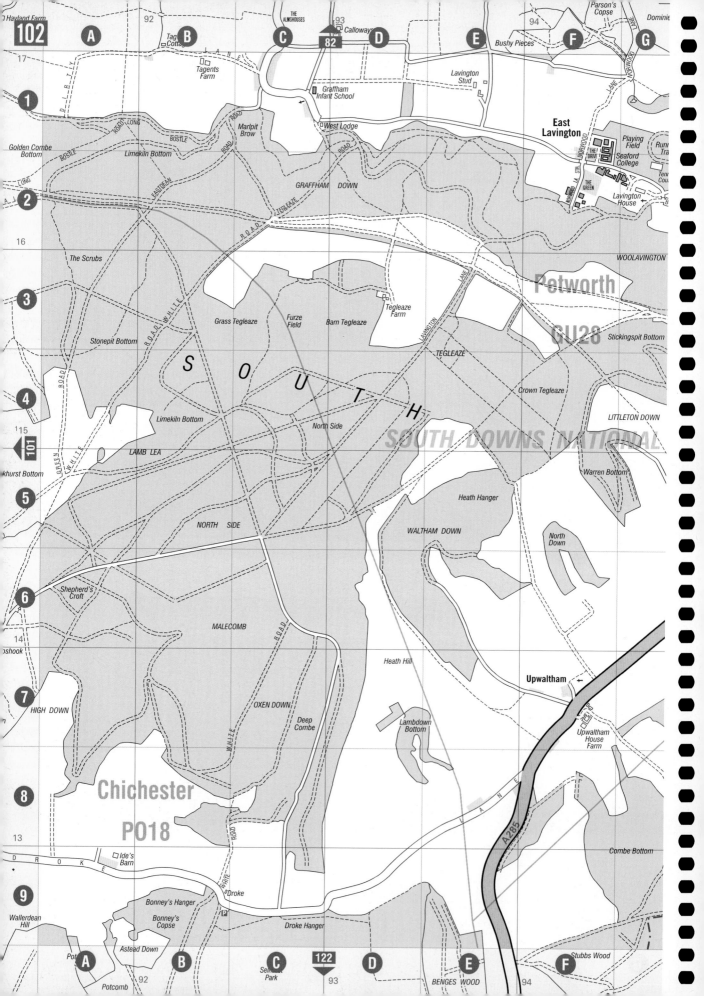

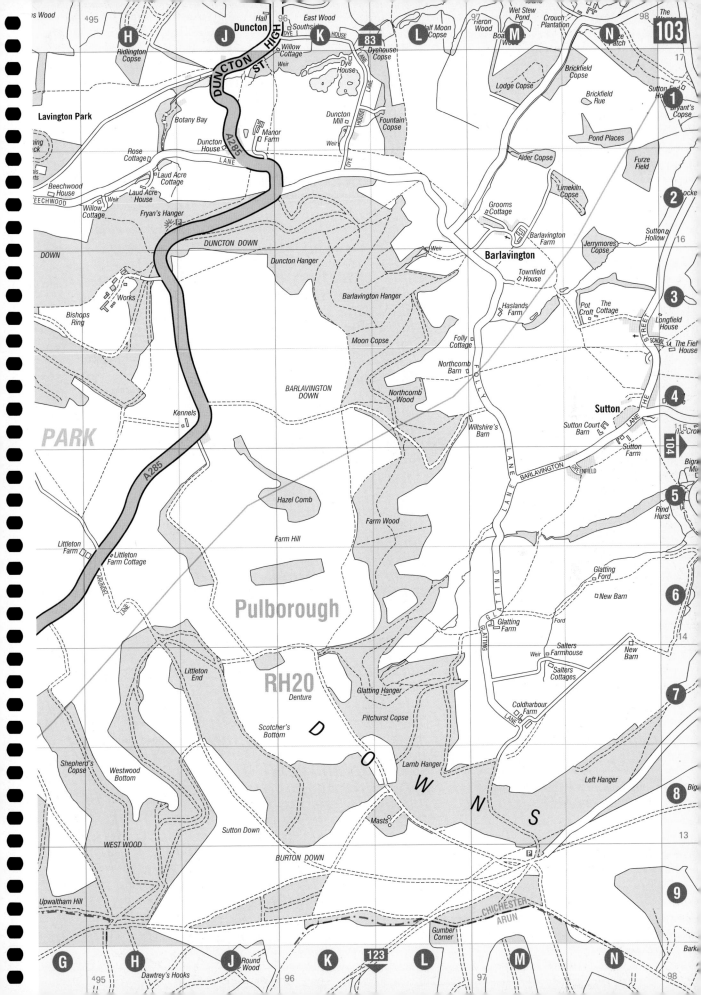

H **J** **K** **83** **L** **M** **N**

Wet Stew
Pond
Crouch
Plantation

es Wood
495
96
Hall
Duncton
East Wood
Southside
97
98
The
Heron
Wood

Ridlington
Copse
Willow
Cottage
DYE
HIGH
ST
DUNCTON
HOUSE
Dyehouse
Copse
Half Moon
Copse
Boa
Wood
Patch
17

Lodge Copse
Brickfield
Copse

Lavington Park
Botany Bay
Duncton
Mill
Fountain
Copse
DYE
HOUSE
LANE
Brickfield
Rue
Sutton End
Bryant's
Copse
1

Manor
Farm
Duncton
House
A285
LANE
Dye
House
Weir
Alder Copse
Pond Places

Rose
Cottage
Weir
Grooms
Cottage
Limekiln
Copse
Furze
Field

Beechwood
House
Laud Acre
Cottage
Laud Acre
House
Barlavington
Farm
Jerrymores
Copse
Sutton
Hollow
2
Locke
16

Willow
Cottage
Weir
BEECHWOOD
Fryan's Hanger
P
DUNCTON DOWN
Weir
Barlavington
Townfield
House
Pot
Croft
The
Cottage
STREET
Longfield
House
3

DOWN
Works
Duncton Hanger
Haslands
Farm
THE
SCHOOL
The Fiel
House

Bishops
Ring
Barlavington Hanger
Folly
Cottage
FOLLY
Sutton Court
Barn
Sutton
4

Moon Copse
Northcomb
Barn
LANE
115
Cron
104

Kennels
BARLAVINGTON
DOWN
Northcomb
Wood
Wiltshire's
Barn
Sutton
Farm
LANE
GREENFIELD
BARLAVINGTON
Bign
Mi

PARK
A285
Hazel Comb
Farm Wood
LANE
5
Rind
Hurst

Littleton
Farm
Littleton
Farm Cottage
Farm Hill
Glatting
Ford
Glatting
Farm
New Barn
6
14

Pulborough
ARUNDEL
LANE
Ford
Salters
Farmhouse
New
Barn

Littleton
End
RH20
Denture
Glatting Hanger
GLATTING
Weir
Salters
Cottages
7

Scotcher's
Bottom
Pitchurst Copse
D
Coldharbour
Farm
LANE

Shepherd's
Copse
Westwood
Bottom
O
Lamb Hanger
Left Hanger
8
Big

West WOOD
Sutton Down
W
Masts
N
S
13

Upwaltham Hill
Burton Down
P
9

CHICHESTER
ARUN
Gumber
Corner
Bark

495
96
97
98

G **H** **J** Round
Wood **K** **123** **L** **M** **N**

Dawtrey's Hooks

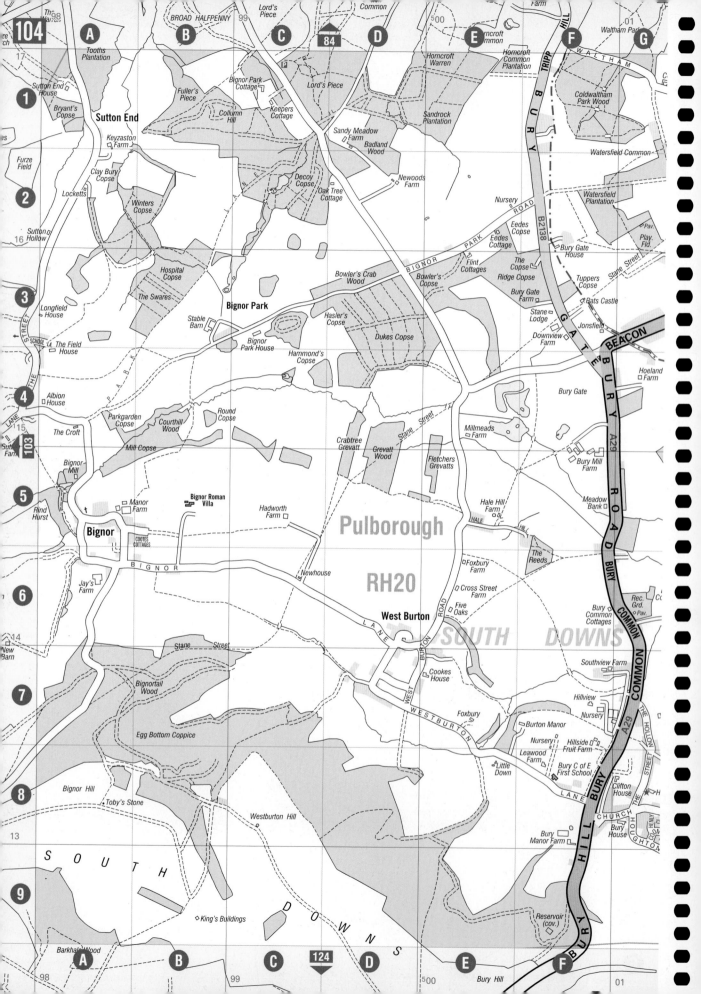

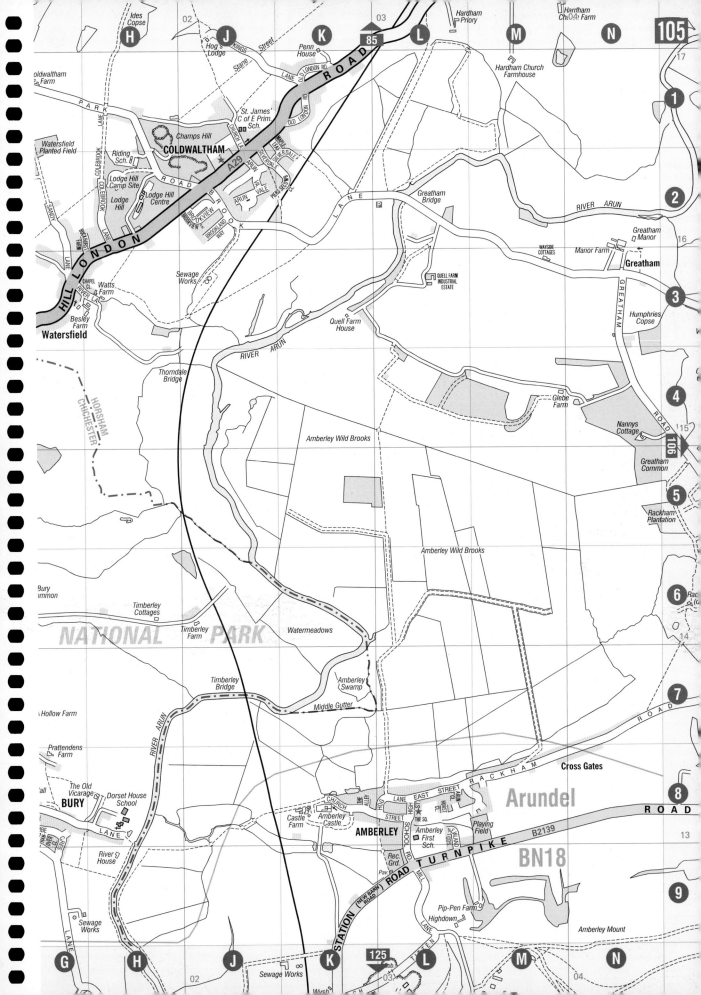

G H J K L M N
H J K L M N

1 2 3 4 5 6 7 8 9

COLDWALTHAM
Watersfield
BURY
AMBERLEY
Greatham
Arundel
BN18
NATIONAL PARK
HORSHAM CHICHESTER

RIVER ARUN
River Arun
London Road
Old London Rd
Kings Street
Stane Lane
Penn House
Hog's Lodge
Ides Copse
Champs Hill
St. James' C of E Prim. Sch.
Riding Sch.
Watersfield Planted Field
Lodge Hill Camp Site
Lodge Hill
Lodge Hill Centre
Brookview
Brookland Way
Chapel
Watts Farm
Besley Farm
Sewage Works
Thorndale Bridge
Quell Farm House
Quell Farm Industrial Estate
Greatham Bridge
Greatham Manor
Manor Farm
Wayside Cottages
Humphries Copse
Glebe Farm
Nannys Cottage
Greatham Common
Rackham Plantation
Amberley Wild Brooks
Amberley Wild Brooks
Bury Common
Timberley Cottages
Timberley Farm
Watermeadows
Timberley Bridge
Amberley Swamp
Middle Gutter
Hollow Farm
Prattendens Farm
The Old Vicarage
Dorset House School
River House
Castle Farm
Amberley Castle
Church
The Alley
Hog Lane
High Street
School Rd
Amberley First Sch.
Rec. Grd.
Playing Field
Cross Gates
Pip-Pen Farm
Highdown
Amberley Mount
Sewage Works
Station Road
New Barn Road
Turnpike Road
Rackham Road
B2139
Hardham Priory
Hardham Church Farm
Hardham Church Farmhouse

A29
85
106
115
125
17
16
14
13
02
03
04

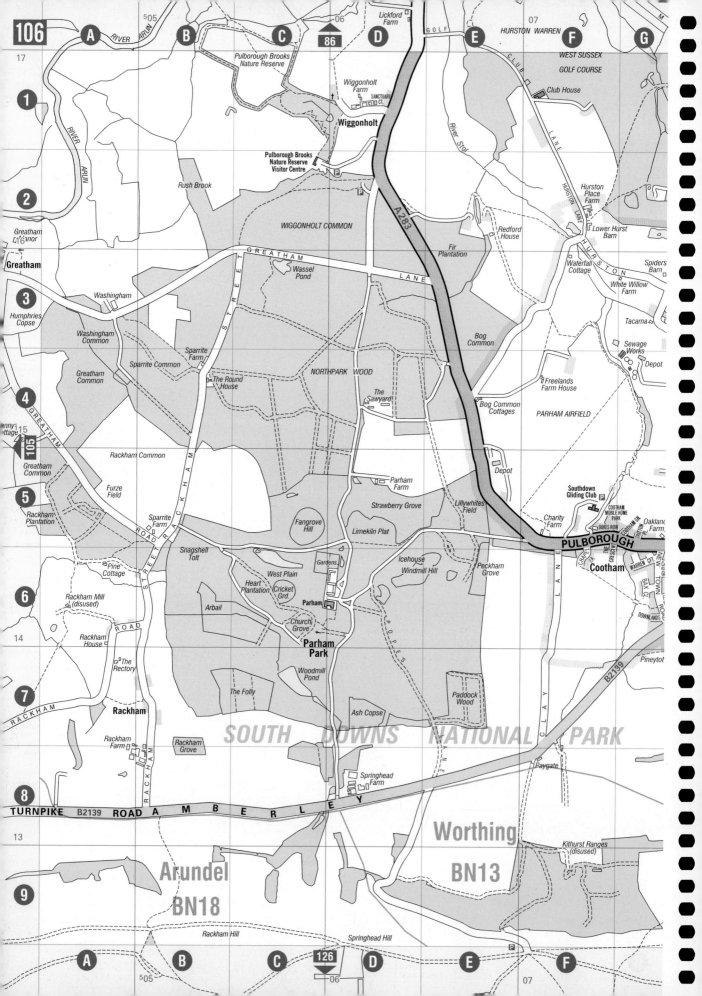

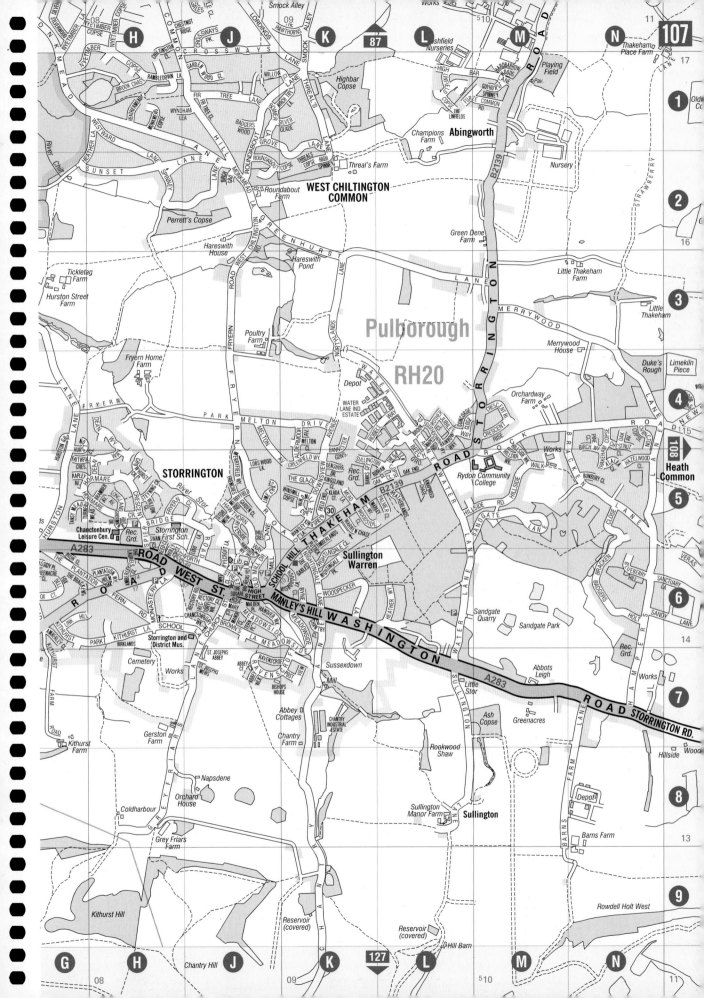

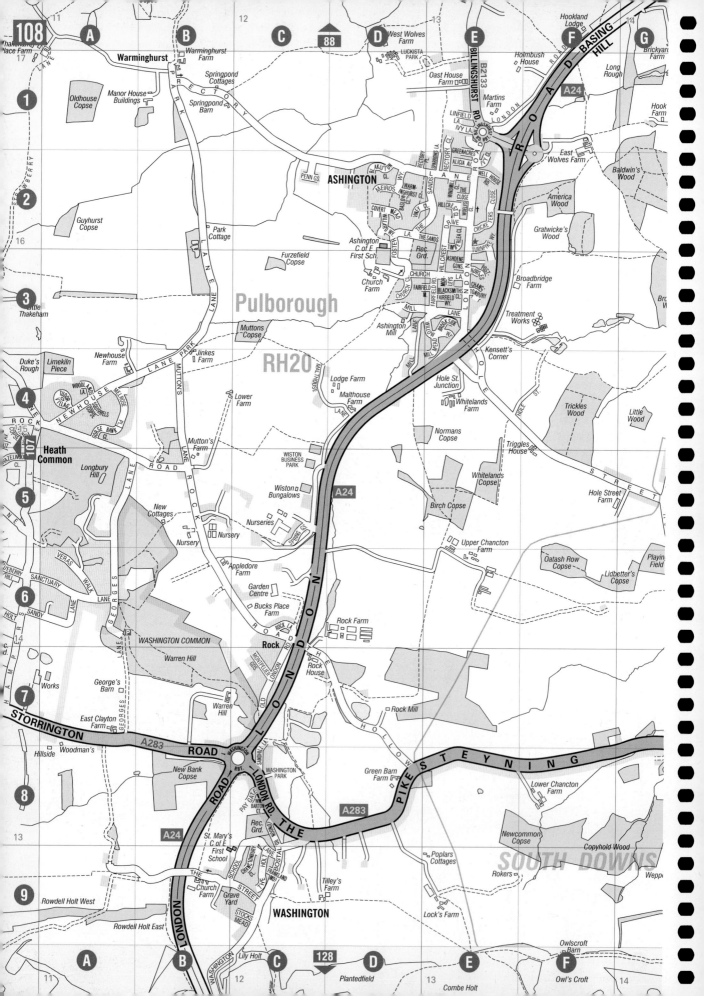

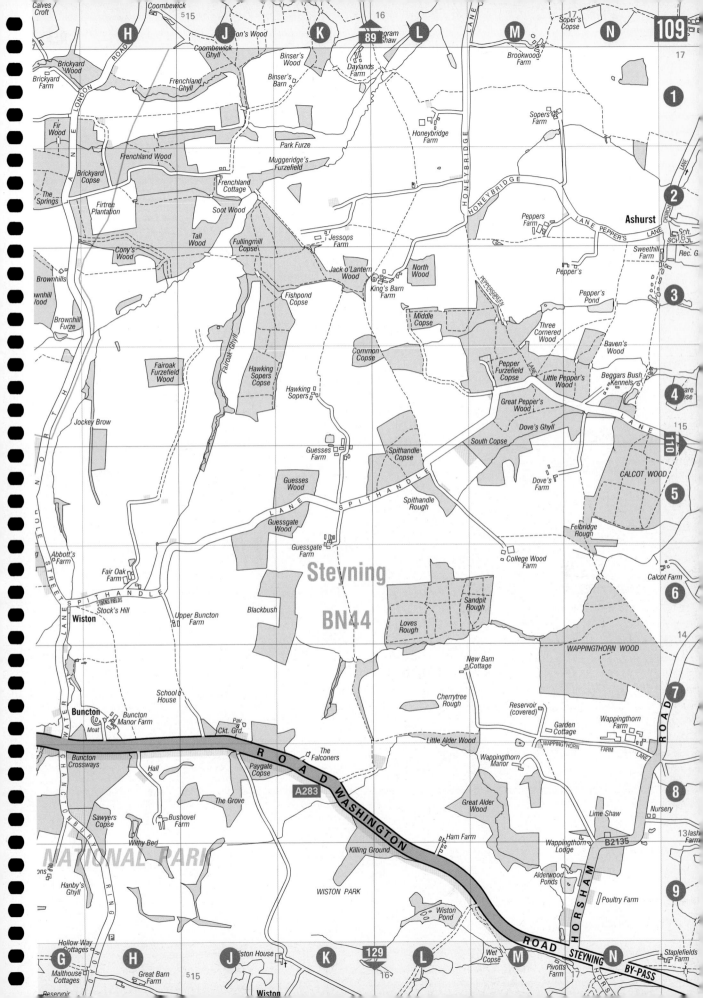

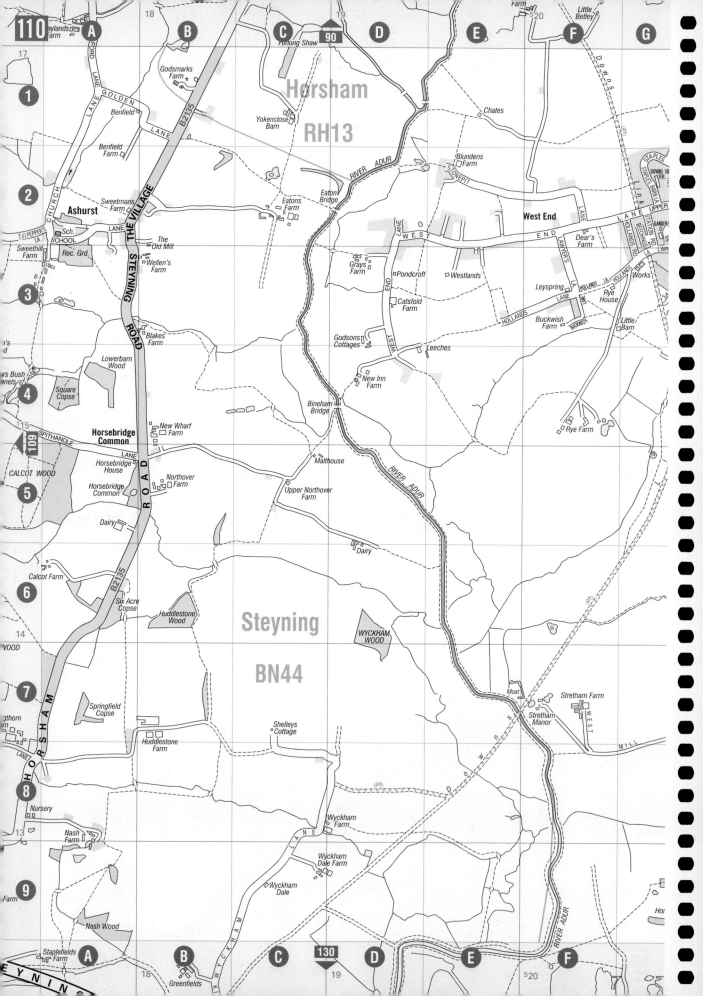

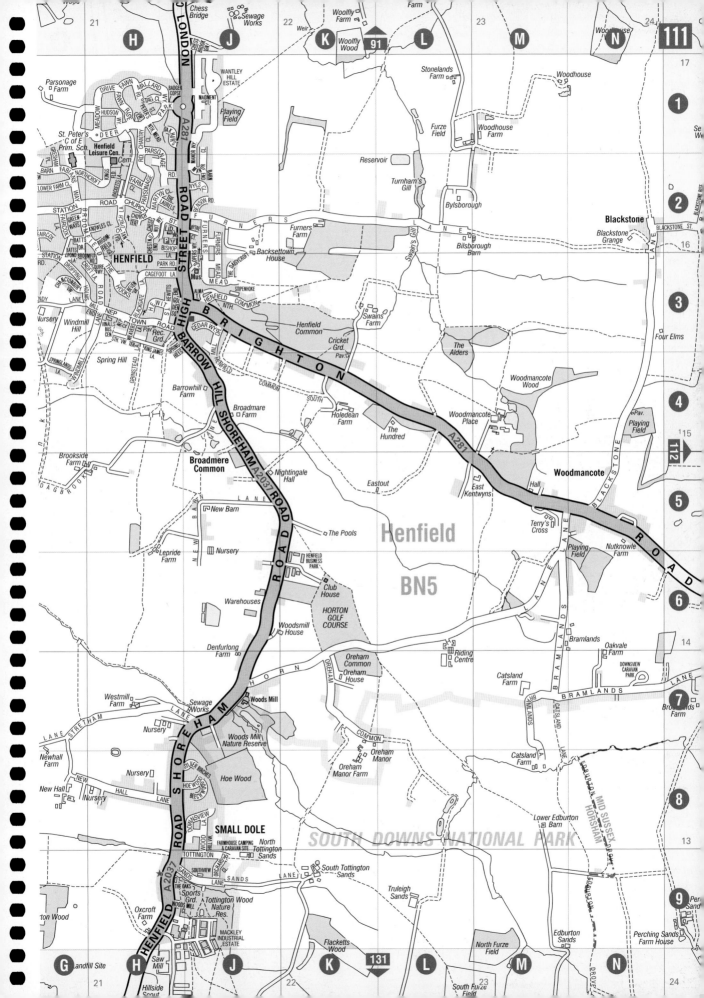

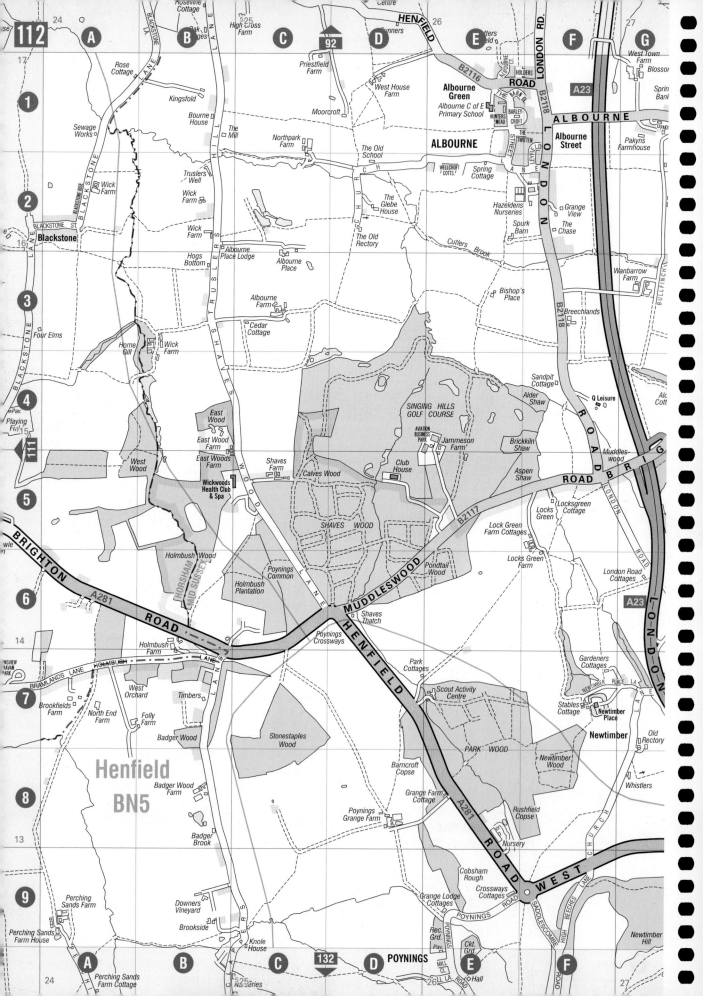

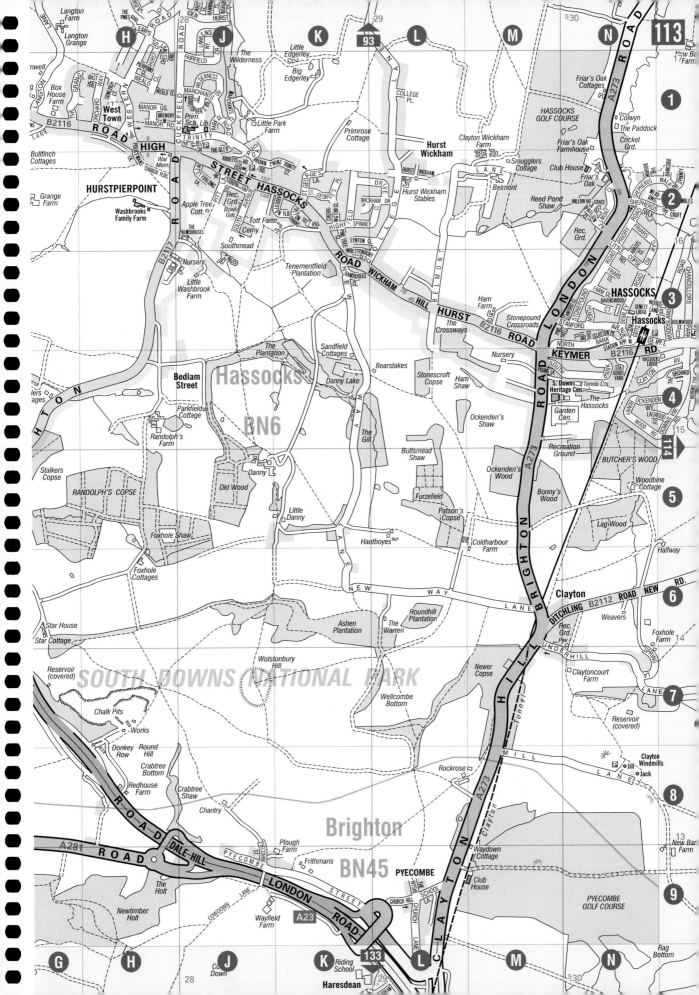

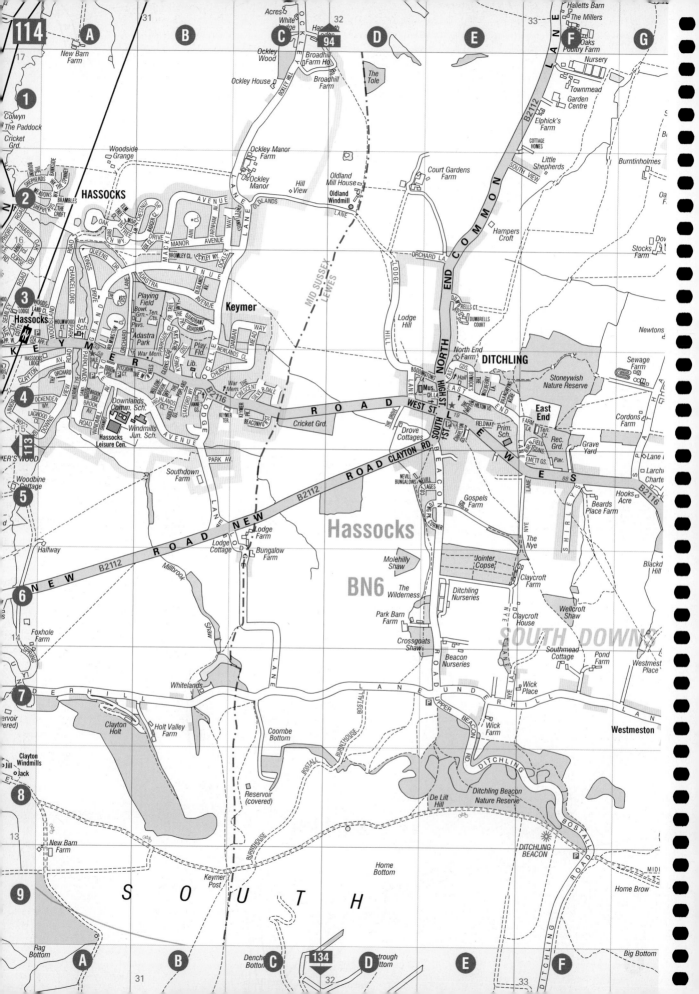

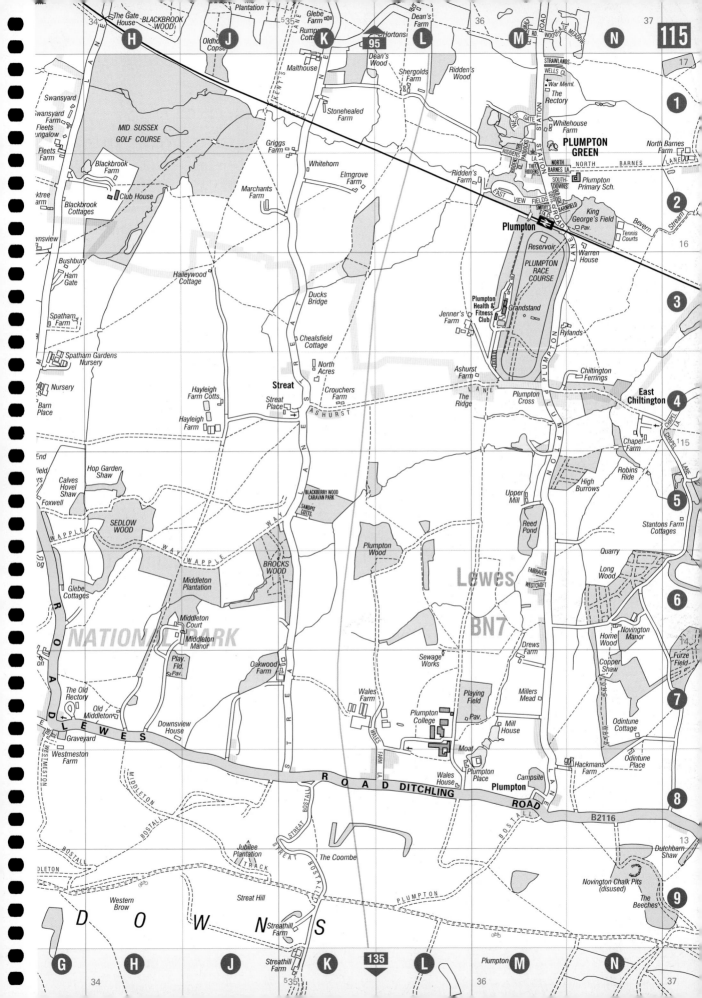

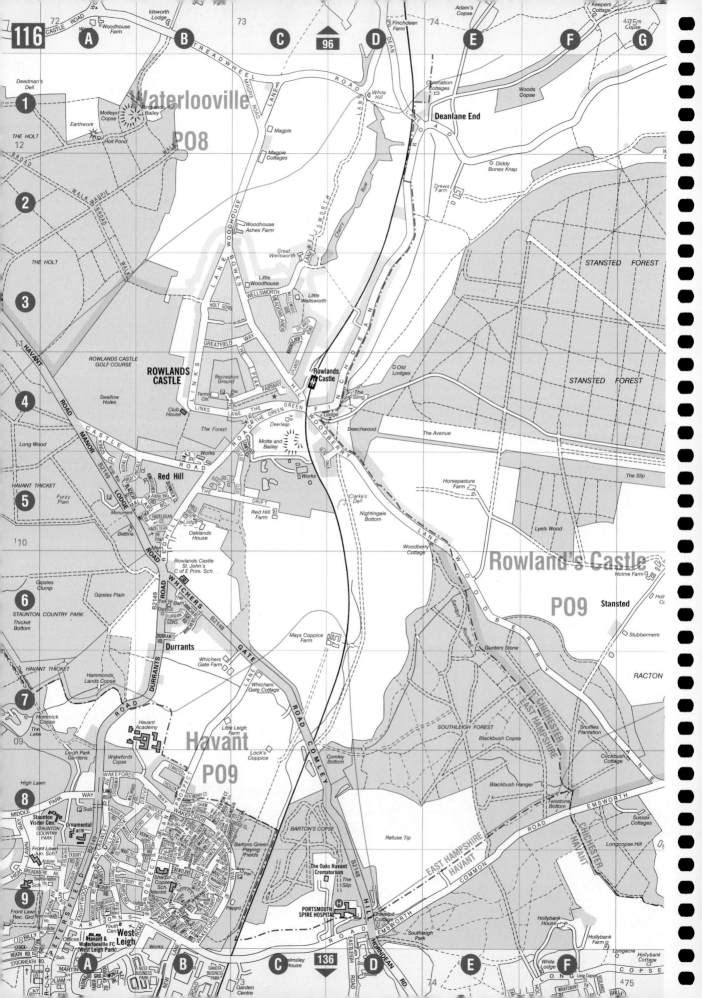

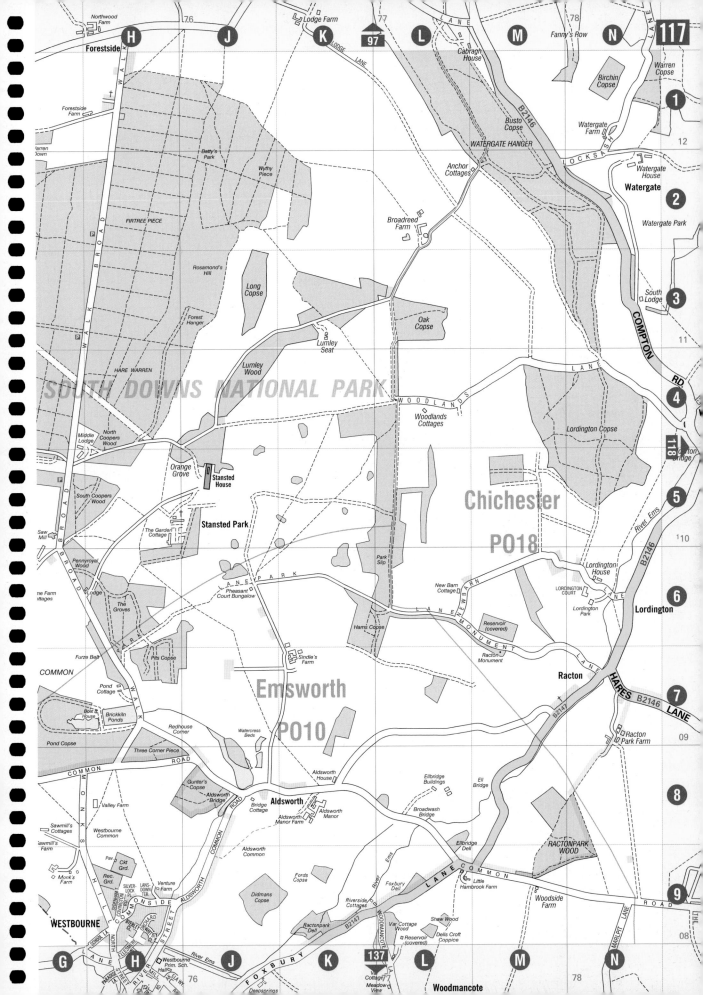

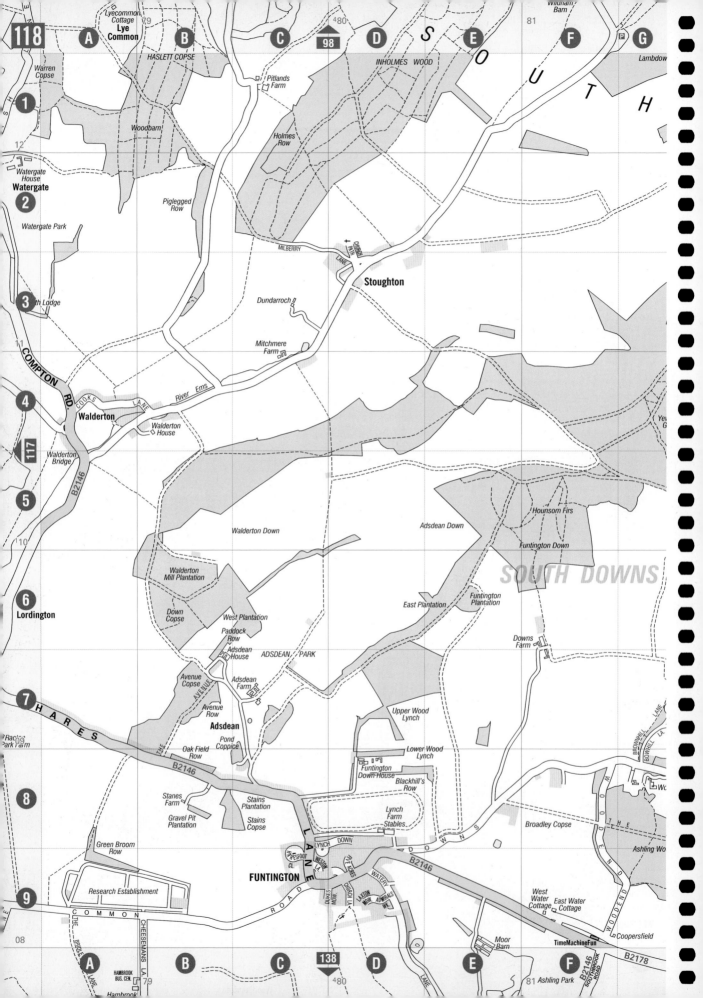

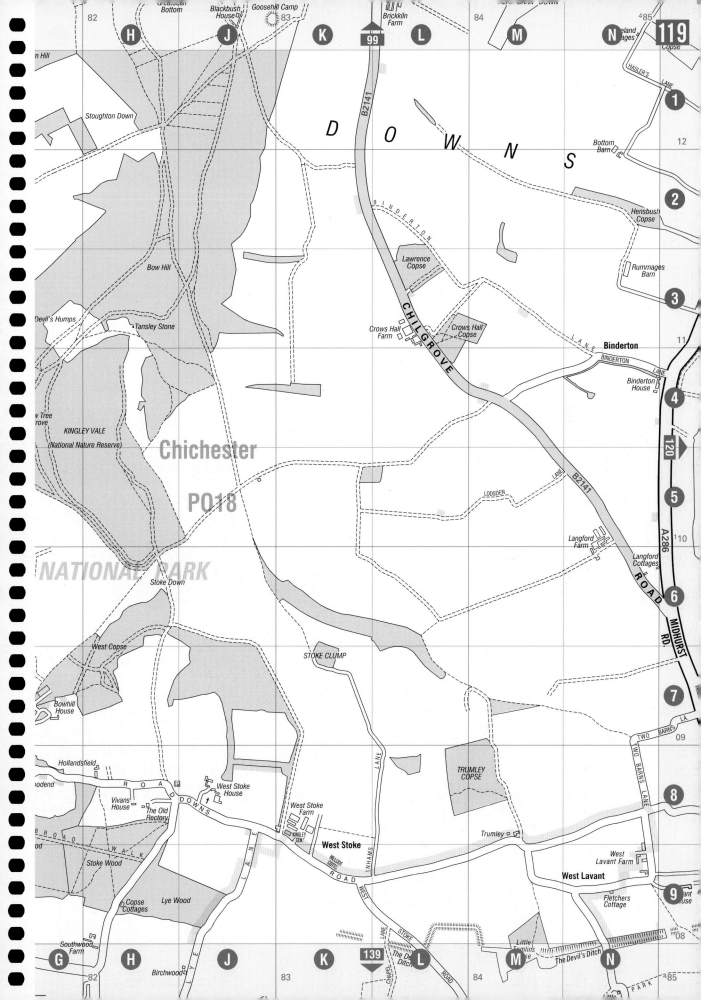

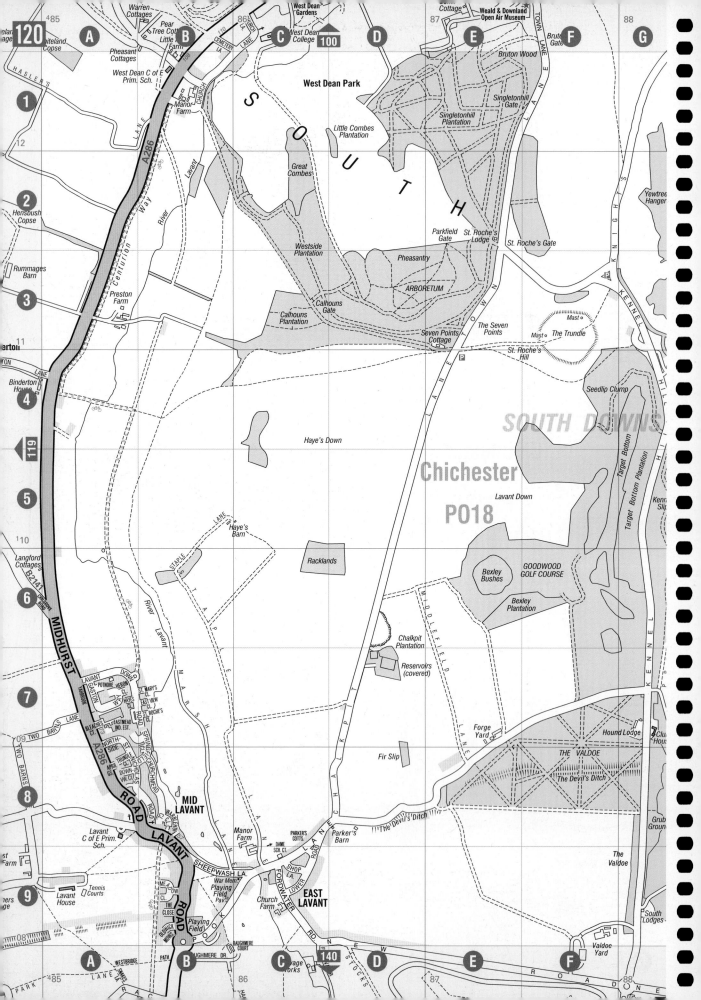

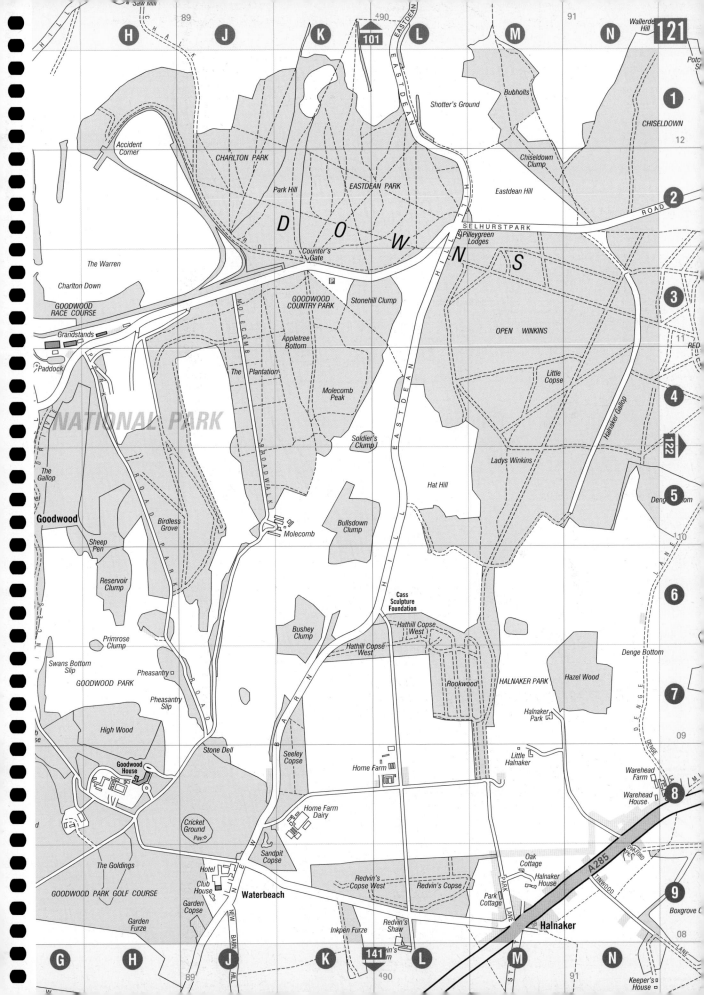

H   J   K   L   M   N

Saw Mill

EASTDEAN

101

Wallerde
Hill

Potc
St

1

Shotter's Ground

Bubholts

CHISELDOWN

12

Accident
Corner

CHARLTON PARK

Chiseldown
Clump

2

Park Hill

EASTDEAN PARK

Eastdean Hill

Eastdean
Hill

SELHURSTPARK

ROAD

D   O   W   N   S

Pilleygreen
Lodges

The Warren

Counter's
Gate

3

Charlton Down

P

GOODWOOD
COUNTRY PARK

Stonehill Clump

GOODWOOD
RACE COURSE

OPEN   WINKINS

11   RED

Grandstands

Appletree
Bottom

Little
Copse

Halnaker Gallop

4

Paddock

The   Plantation

Molecomb
Peak

122

NATIONAL PARK

Soldier's
Clump

Ladys Winkins

The
Gallop

Hat Hill

Deng   om

5

Goodwood

Molecomb

Bullsdown
Clump

110

Sheep
Pen

6

Birdless
Grove

Cass
Sculpture
Foundation

Reservoir
Clump

Bushey
Clump

Hathill Copse
West

Denge Bottom

Primrose
Clump

Hathill Copse
West

Hazel Wood

Swans Bottom
Slip

Pheasantry

Rookwood

HALNAKER PARK

7

GOODWOOD PARK

Halnaker
Park

09

Pheasantry
Slip

Little
Halnaker

High Wood

Stone Dell

Warehead
Farm

8

Goodwood
House

Seeley
Copse

Home Farm

Warehead
House

Cricket
Ground
Pav.

Home Farm
Dairy

Oak
Cottage

A285

The Goldings

Sandpit
Copse

Halnaker
House

Hotel

Redvin's
Copse West

Redvin's Copse

Park
Cottage

9

Club
House

Garden
Copse

Waterbeach

GOODWOOD PARK GOLF COURSE

Halnaker

The
Goldings

Garden
Furze

Inkpen Furze

Redvin's
Shaw

Boxgrove

08

G   H   J   K   L   M   N

NEW   BARN   HILL

141

490

91

Keeper's
House

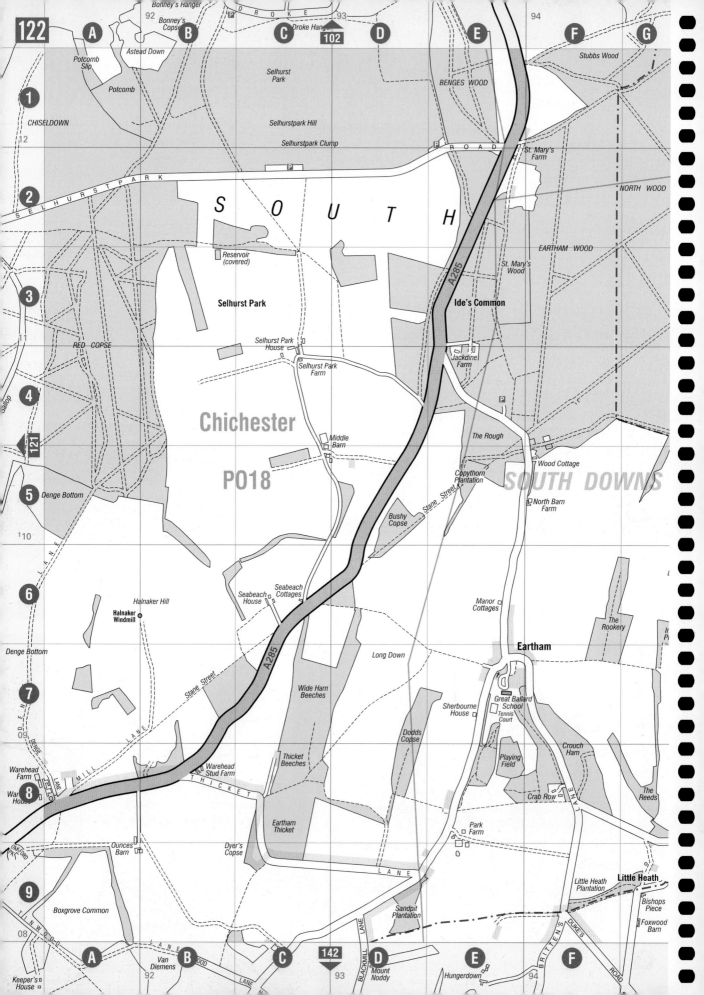

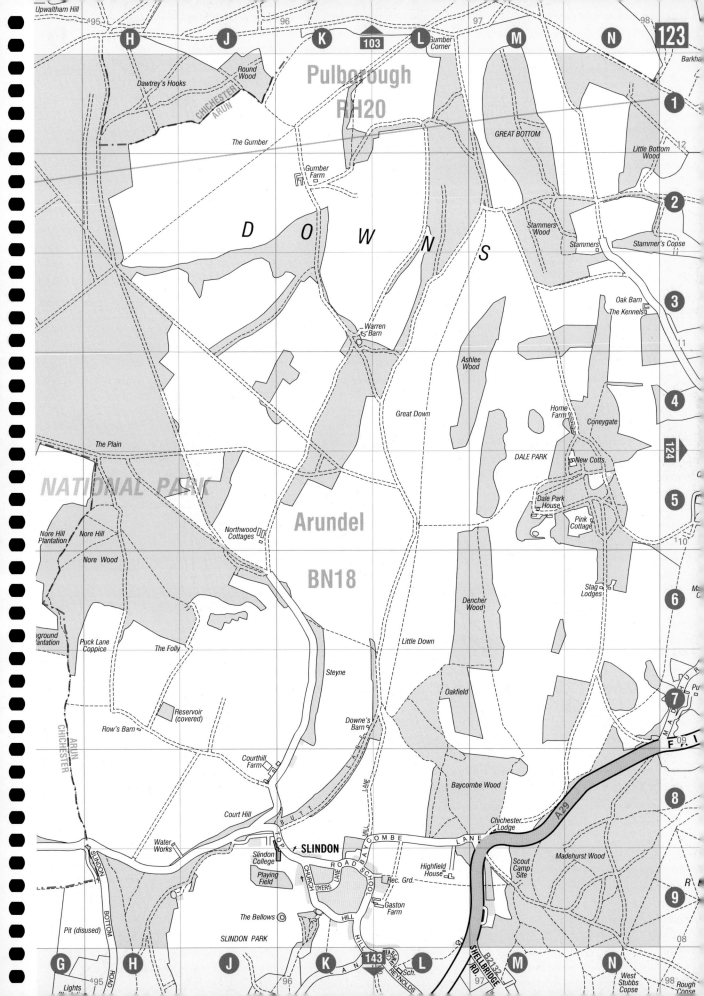

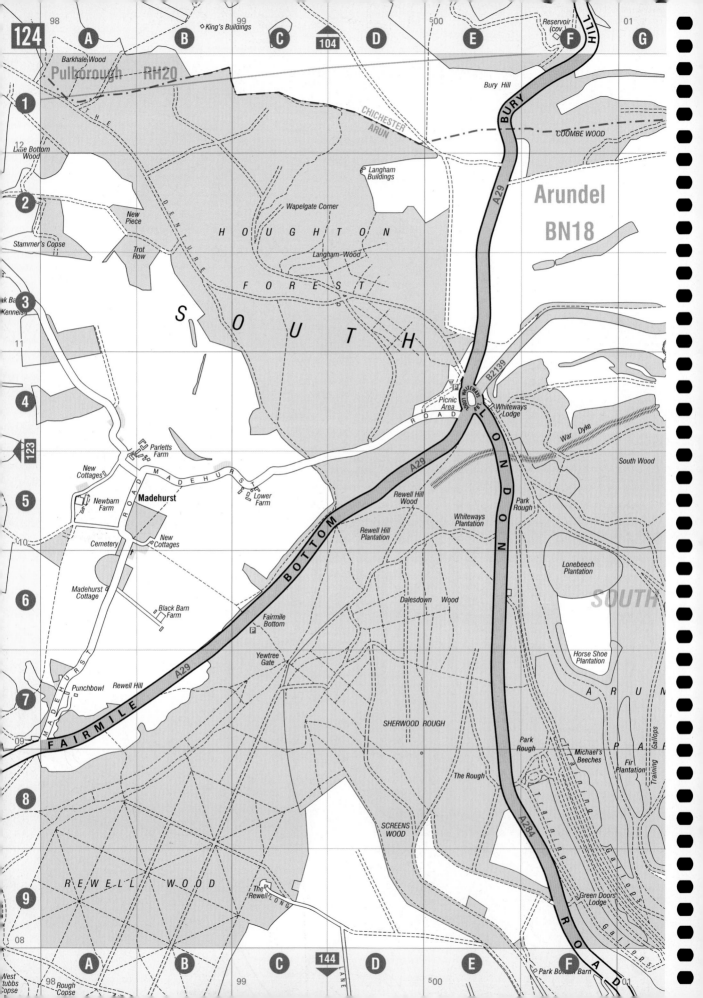

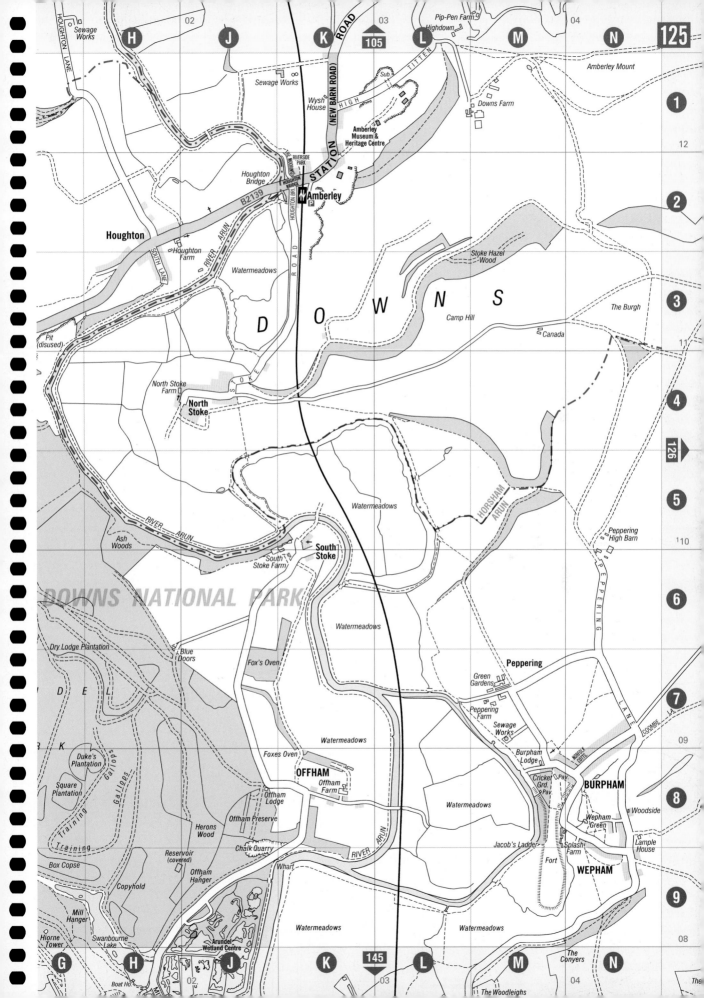

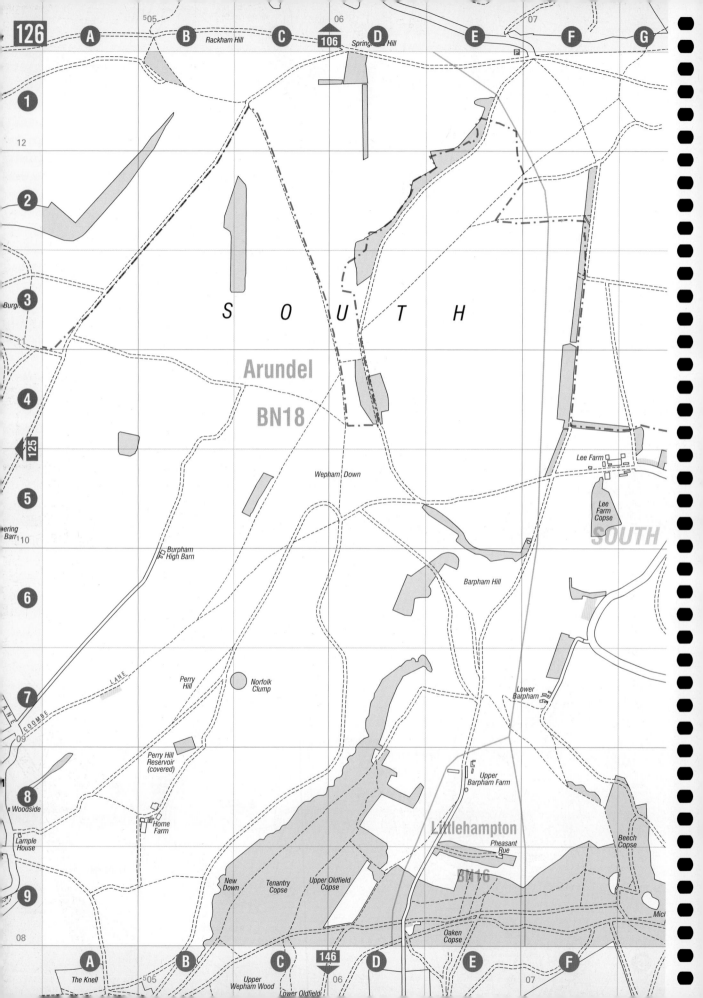

A   B   Rackham Hill   C   106   Springhead Hill   D   E   F   G

1

12

2

3
Burgh

11

4

125

5
ering
Barr
110

6

7
LANE
COOMBE
09

8
Woodside

Lample
House

9

08

A   B   C   146   D   E   F

The Knell   505   Upper Wepham Wood   Lower Oldfield   06   07

S   O   U   T   H

Arundel

BN18

Wepham Down

Burpham
High Barn

Barpham Hill

Lee Farm

Lee
Farm
Copse

SOUTH

Perry
Hill   Norfolk
Clump

Lower
Barpham

Perry Hill
Reservoir
(covered)

Home
Farm

Upper
Barpham Farm

Littlehampton

Pheasant
Rue

Beech
Copse

BN16

New
Down   Tenantry
Copse   Upper Oldfield
Copse

Oaken
Copse

Mich

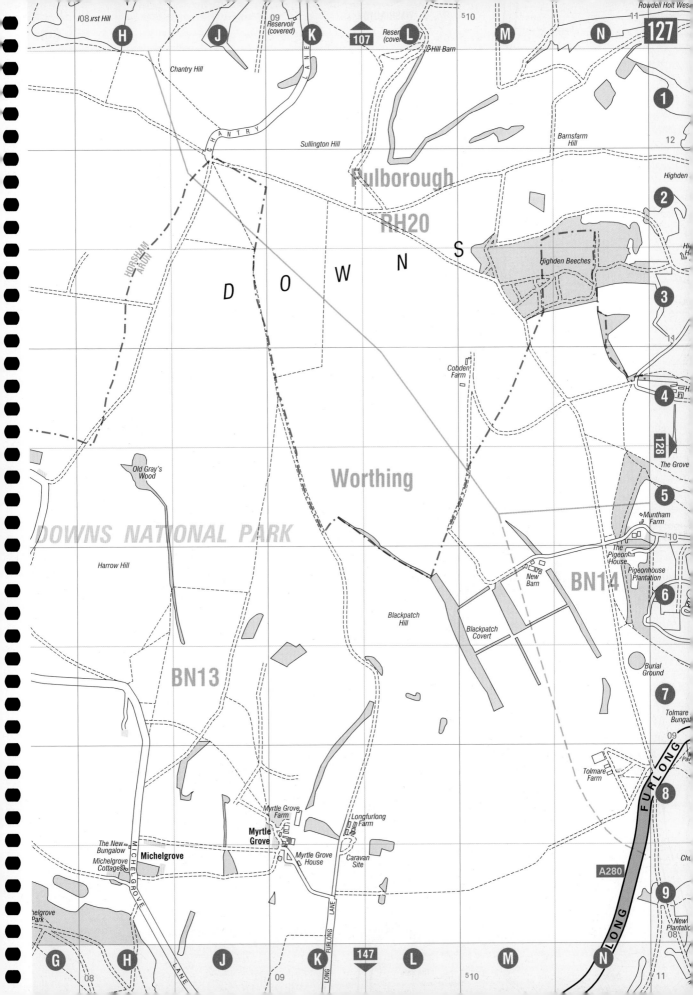

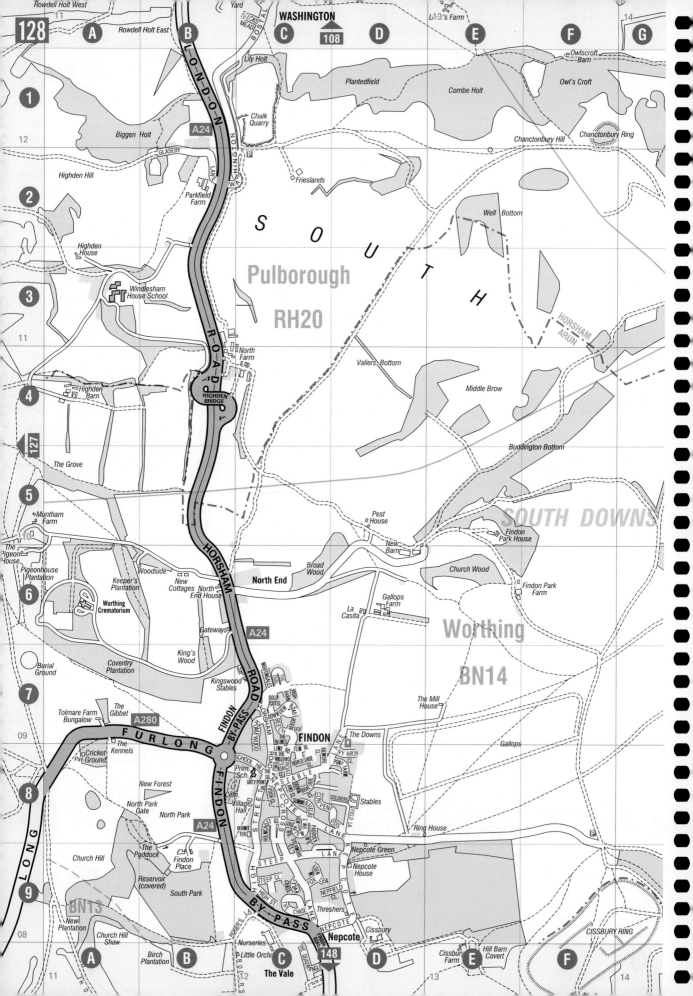

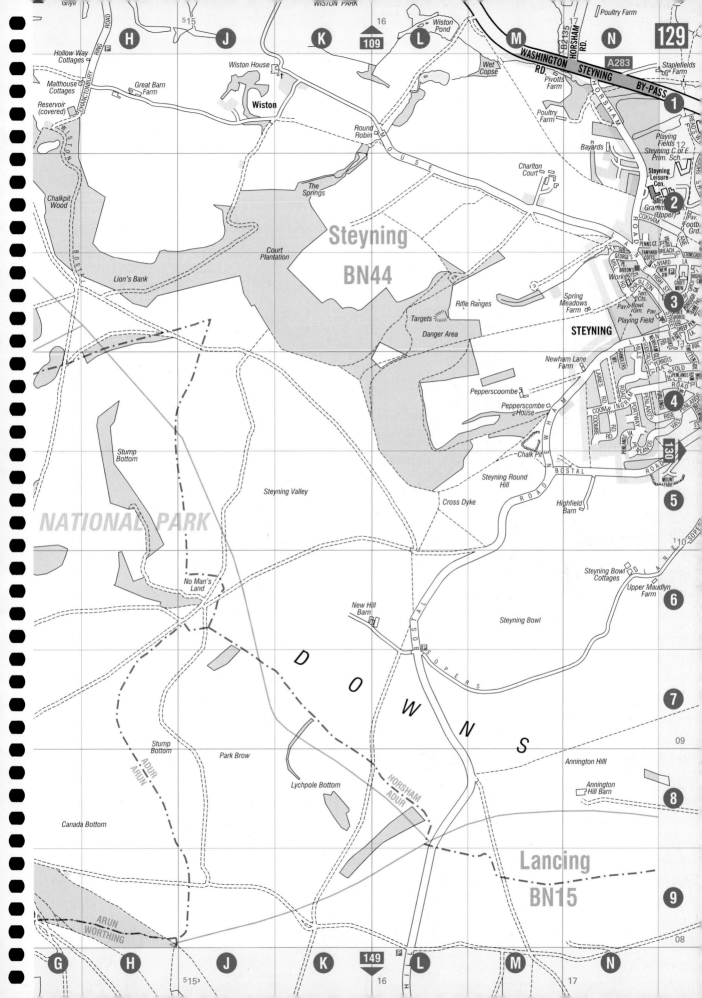

WISTON PARK

Poultry Farm

H J K **109** 16 L M N

Grylis
515
Wiston Pond
Wiston House
Staplefields Farm
Hollow Way Cottages
Wet Copse
WASHINGTON STEYNING BY-PASS
A283
Malthouse Cottages
Great Barn Farm
Pivotts Farm
Reservoir (covered)
Wiston
Poultry Farm
Bayards
Playing Fields 12
Steyning C of E Prim. Sch.
Round Robin
Steyning Leisure Cen.
Chalkpit Wood
The Springs
Charlton Court
Steyning Grammar (Upper)
COXHAM
SIR GEORGE'S
PENNS CT.
Court Plantation
Steyning BN44
Lion's Bank
TANYARD COTTS
NEW RW
Works
CHARLTON
HIGH ST
Rifle Ranges
Spring Meadows Farm
Pav. Bowl. Grn. Pav
WHITE HORSE
Targets
Danger Area
Playing Field
STEYNING
SHEEP PEN LA
Newham Lane Farm
FOLD
PENLANDS
LAINES
Pepperscoombe
Pepperscombe House
NEWHAM
COOM
PORTWAY
PENLANDS RISE
PENLANDS WAY
Chalk Pit
Steyning Round Hill
BOSTAL
130
Stump Bottom
Steyning Valley
Cross Dyke
ROAD
Mount Park
Highfield Barn
NATIONAL PARK
No Man's Land
110 SOPERS
Steyning Bowl Cottages
Upper Maudlyn Farm
LANE
New Hill Barn
Steyning Bowl
BOSTAL
P
SOPERS
09
Stump Bottom
ADUR
ARUN
Park Brow
Annington Hilll
D O W N S
Lychpole Bottom
HORSHAM ADUR
Annington Hill Barn
Canada Bottom
Lancing BN15
ARUN WORTHING
08
G H J K **149** 16 L P M N
515
17

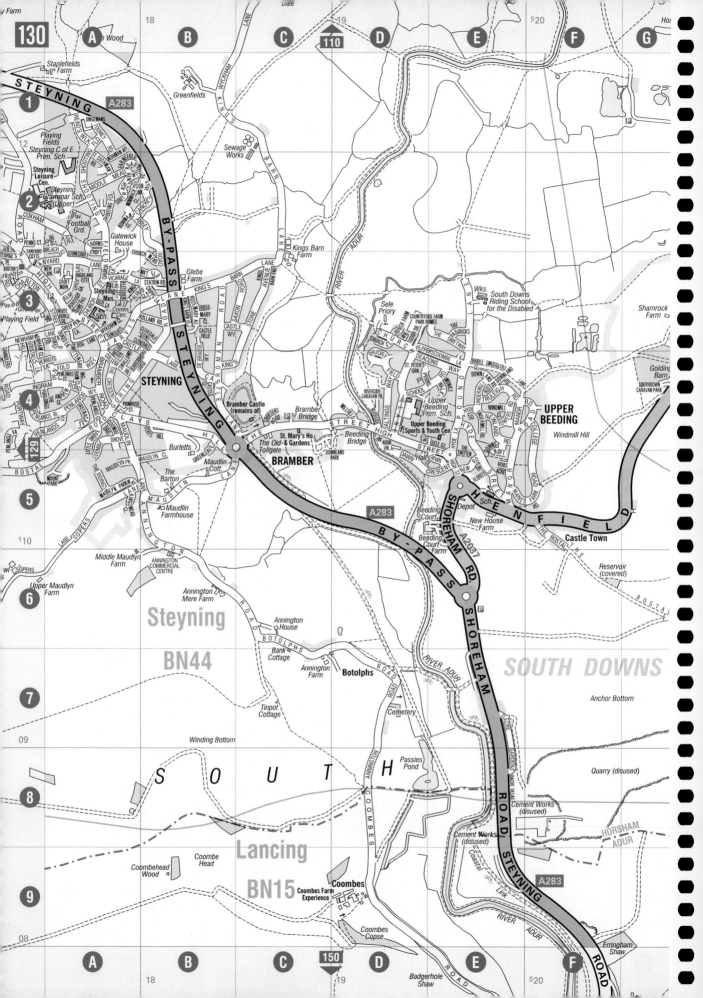

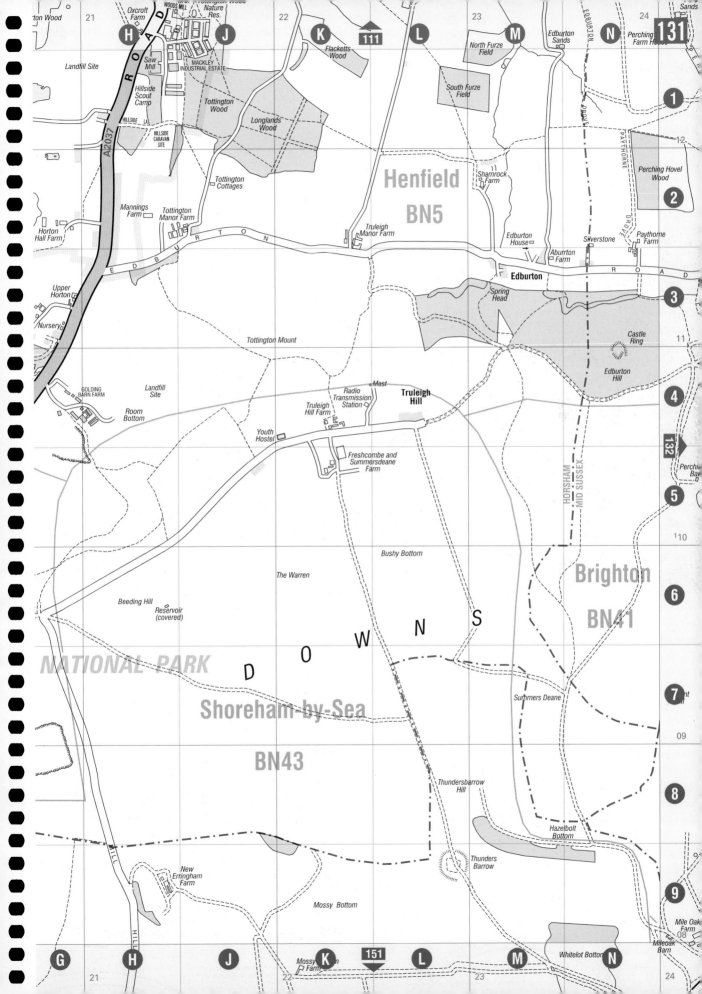

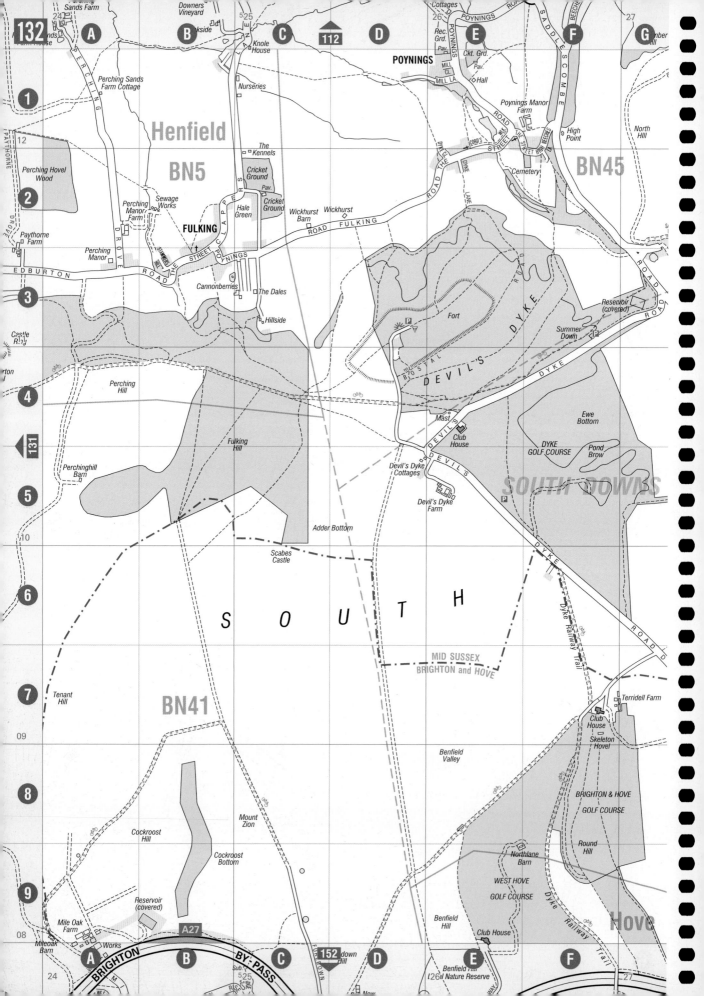

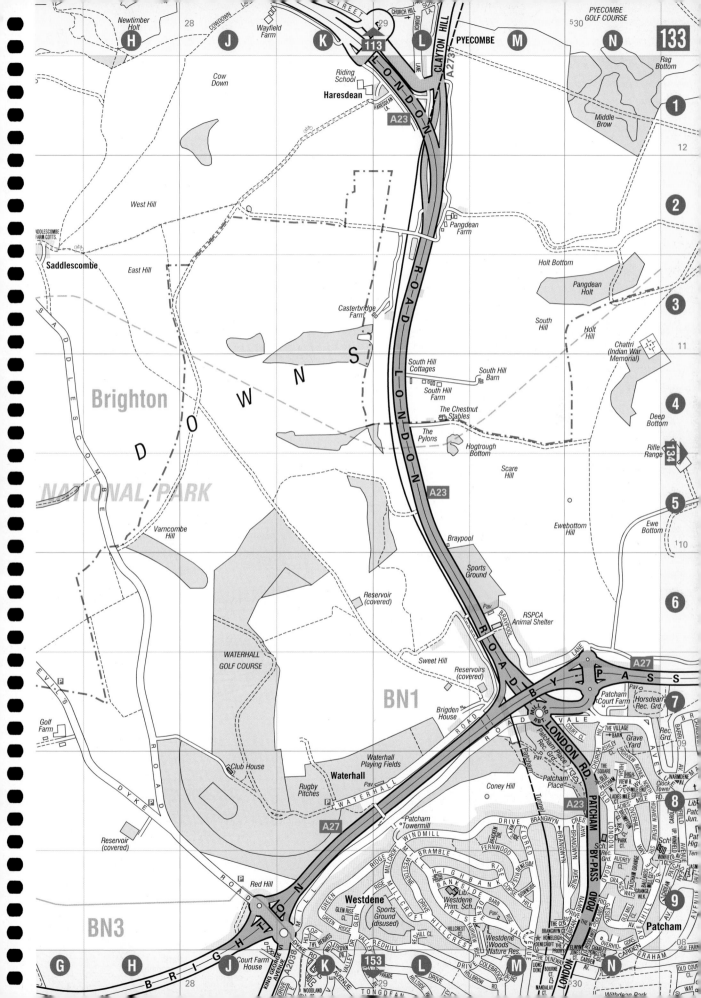

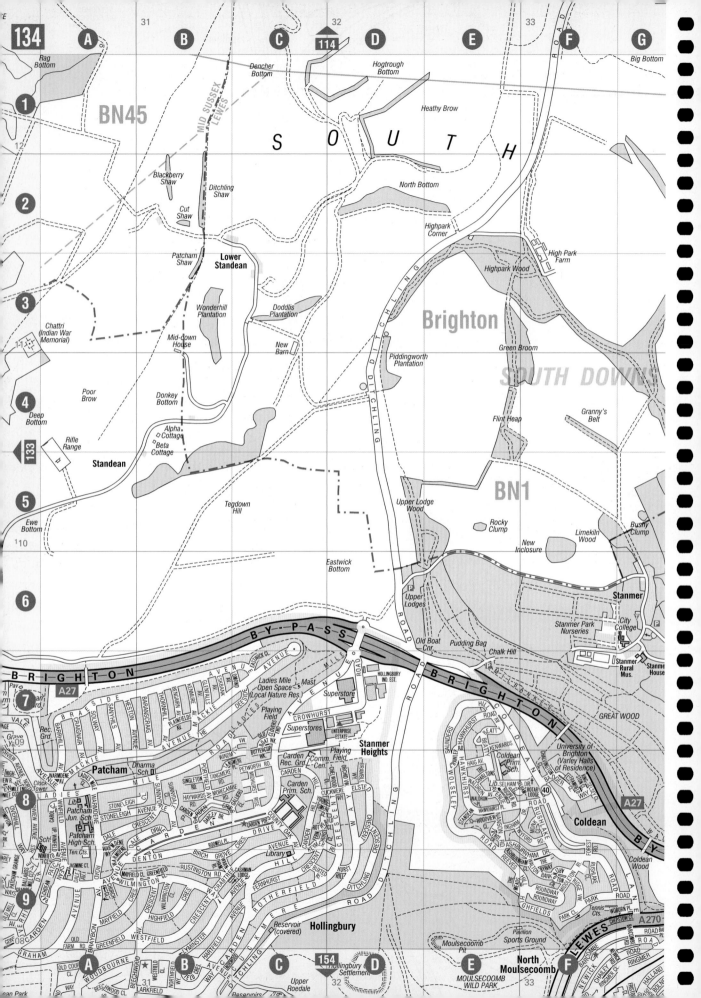

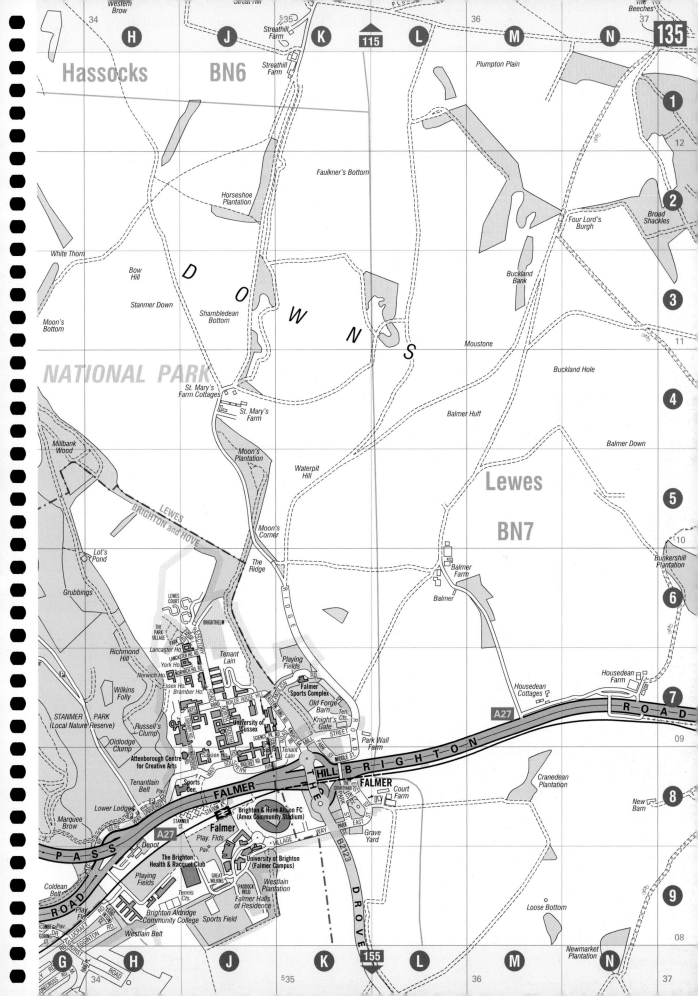

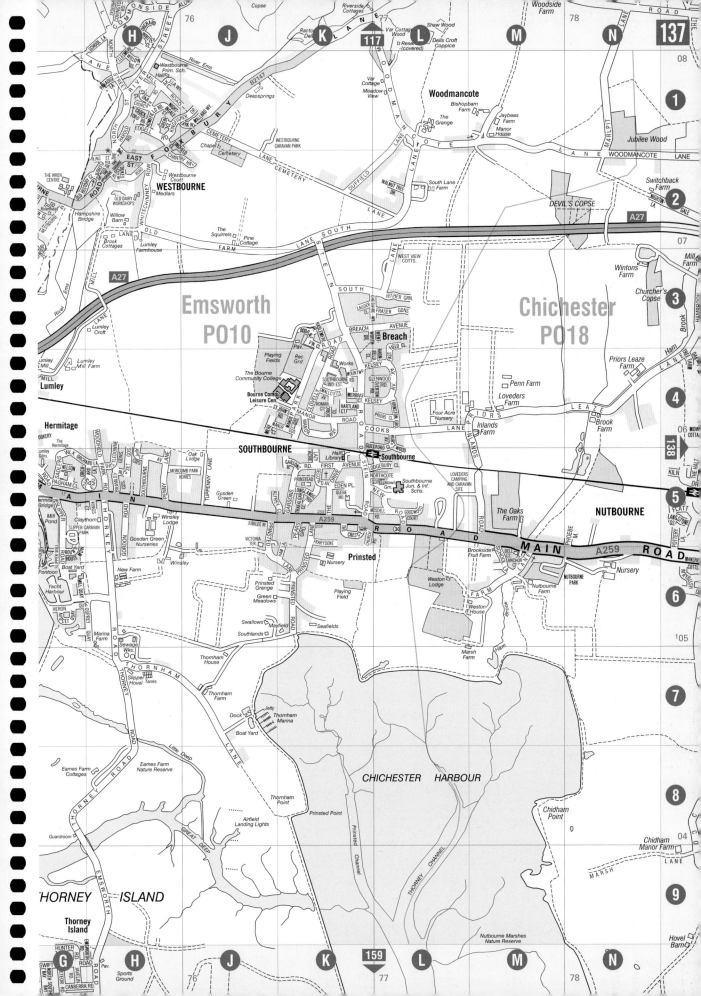

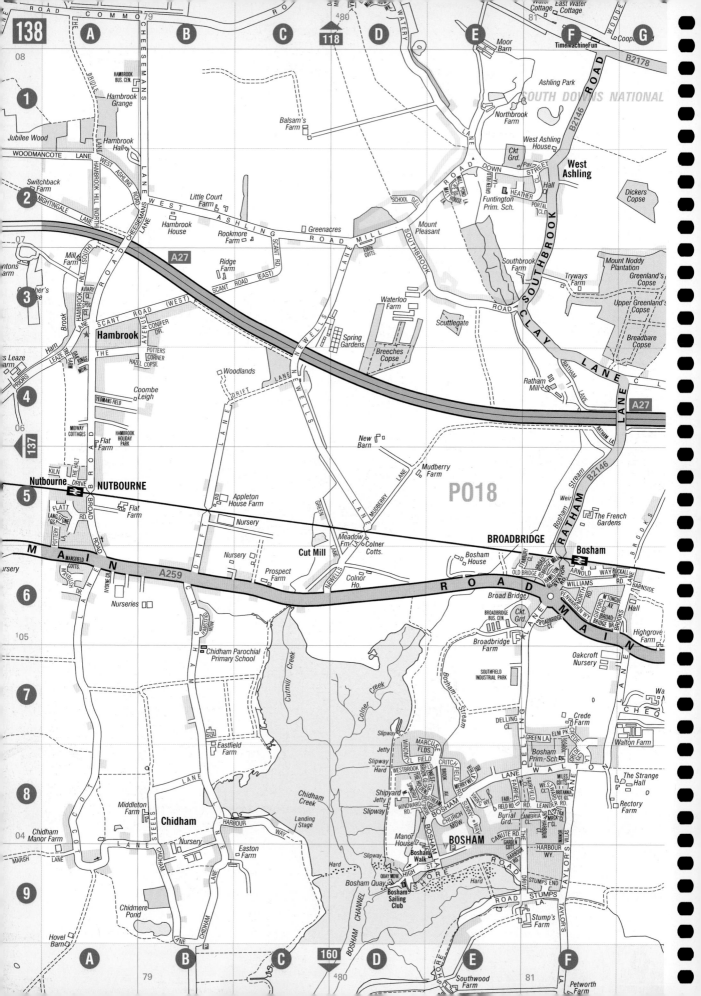

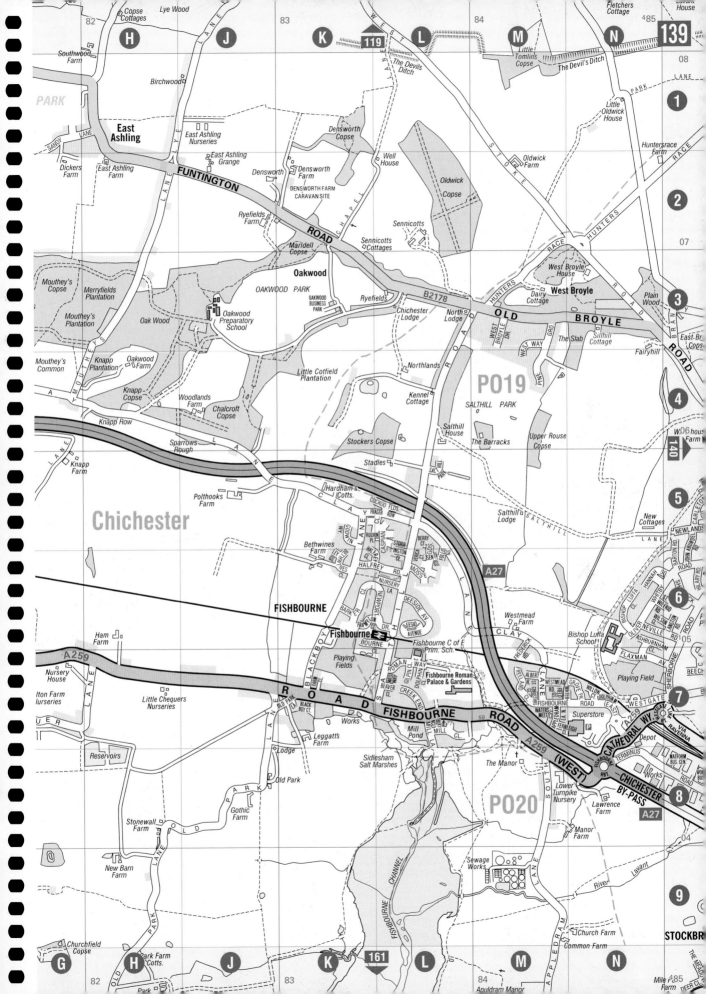

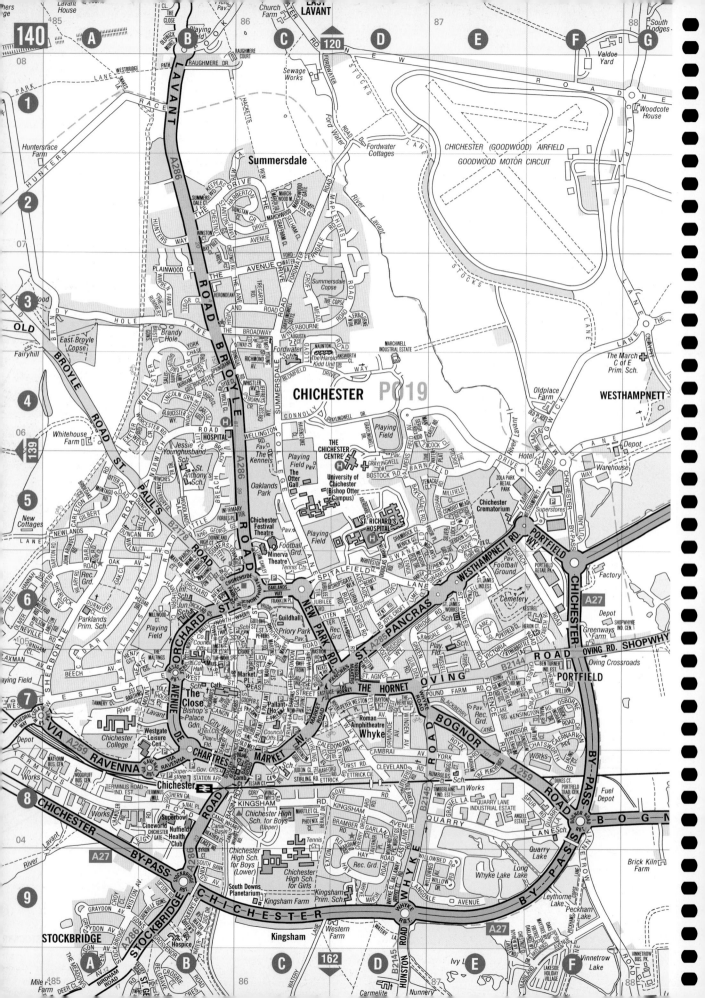

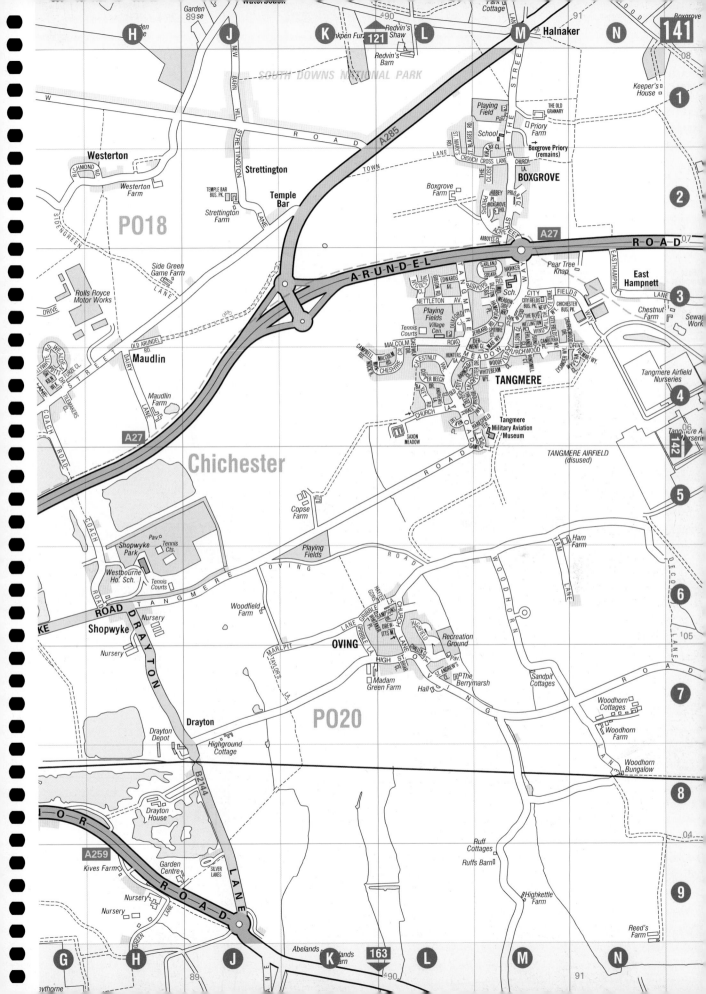

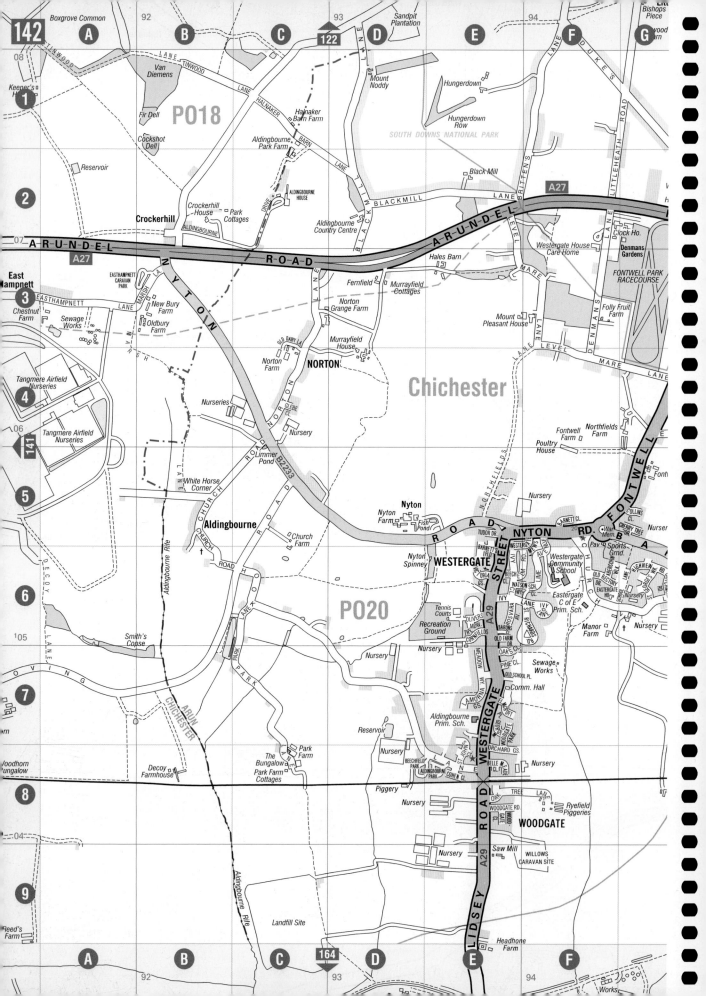

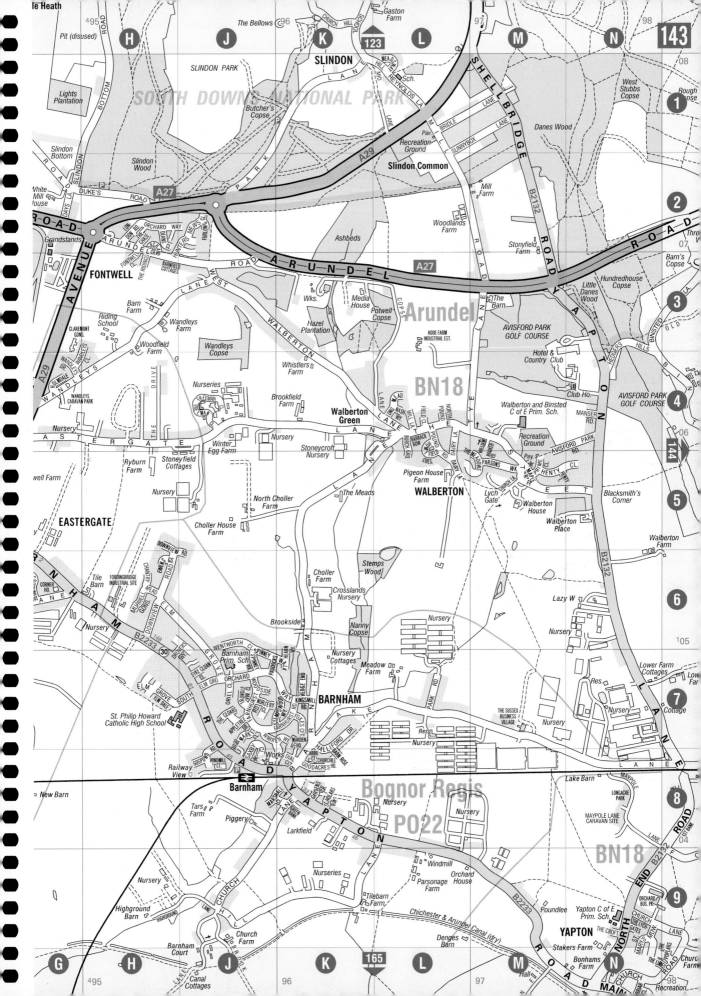

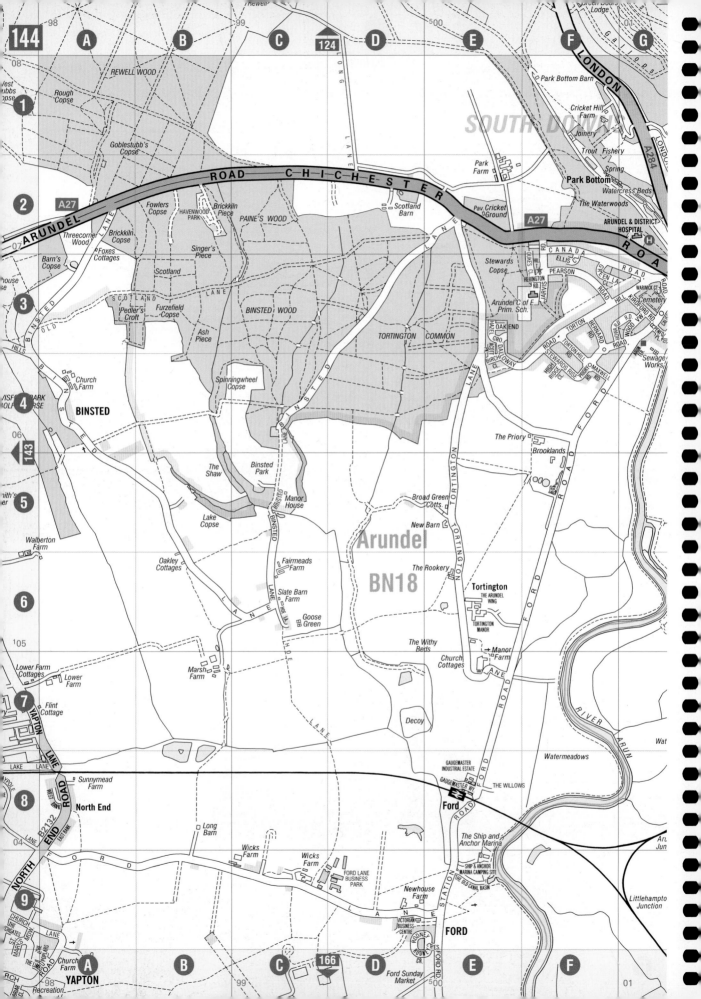

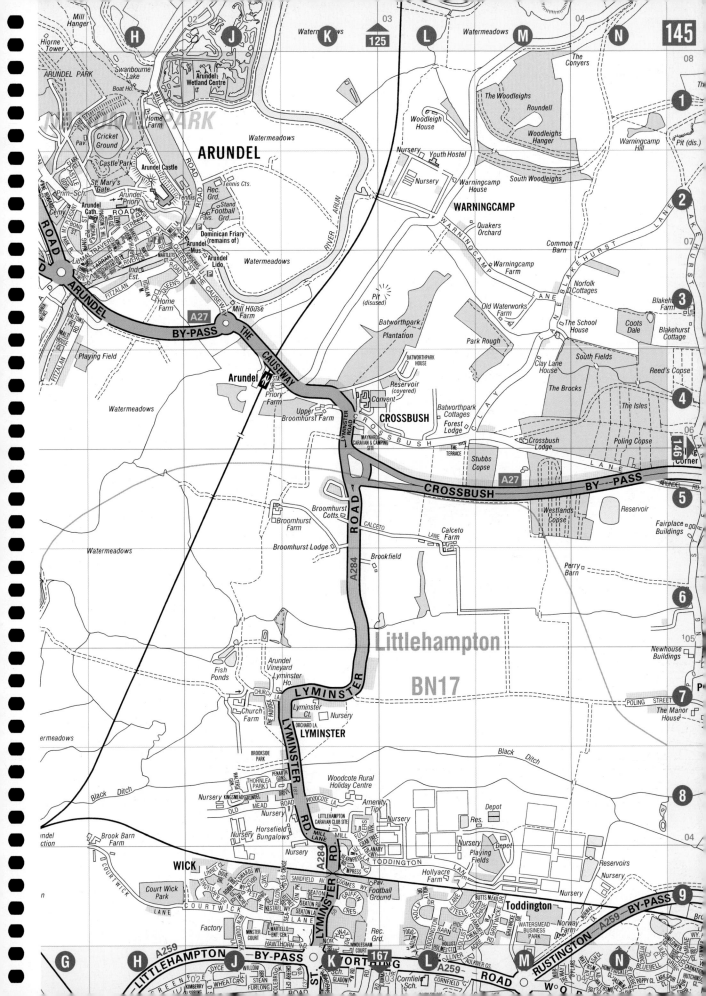

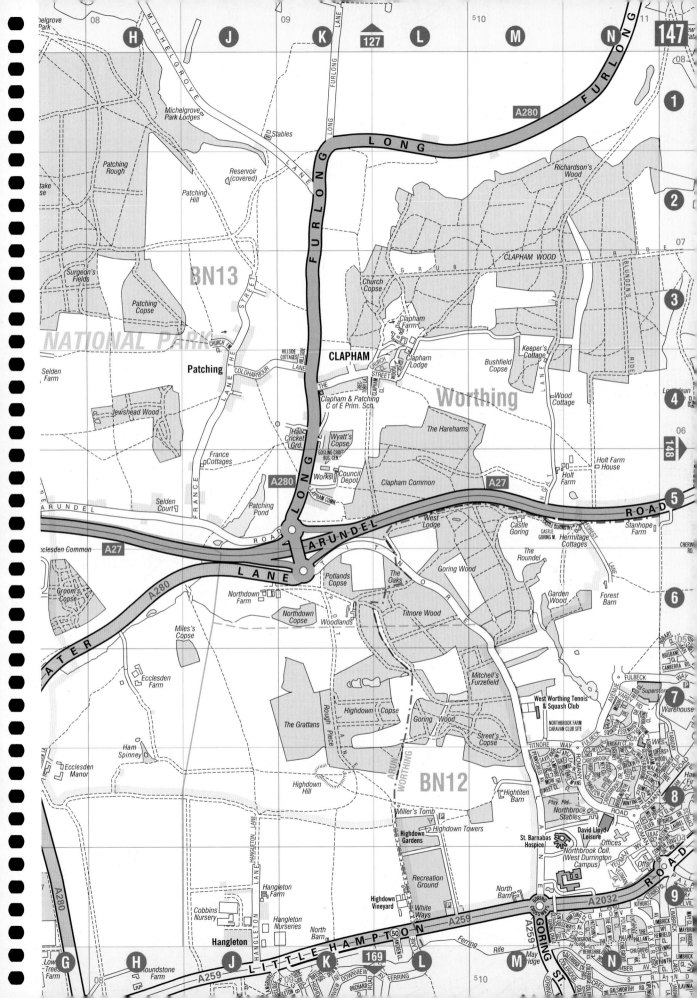

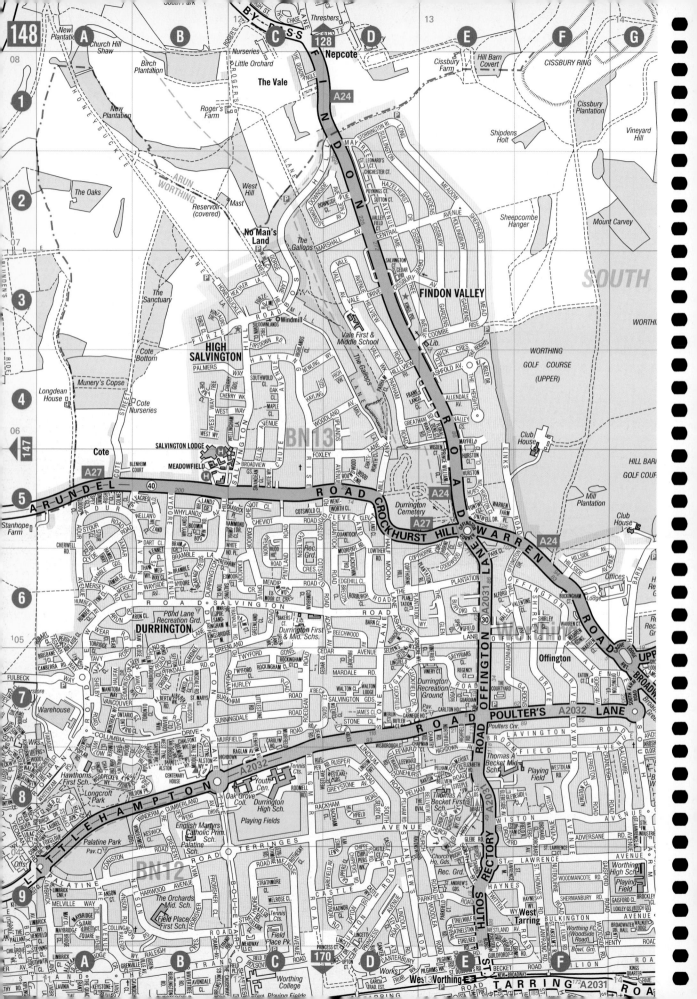

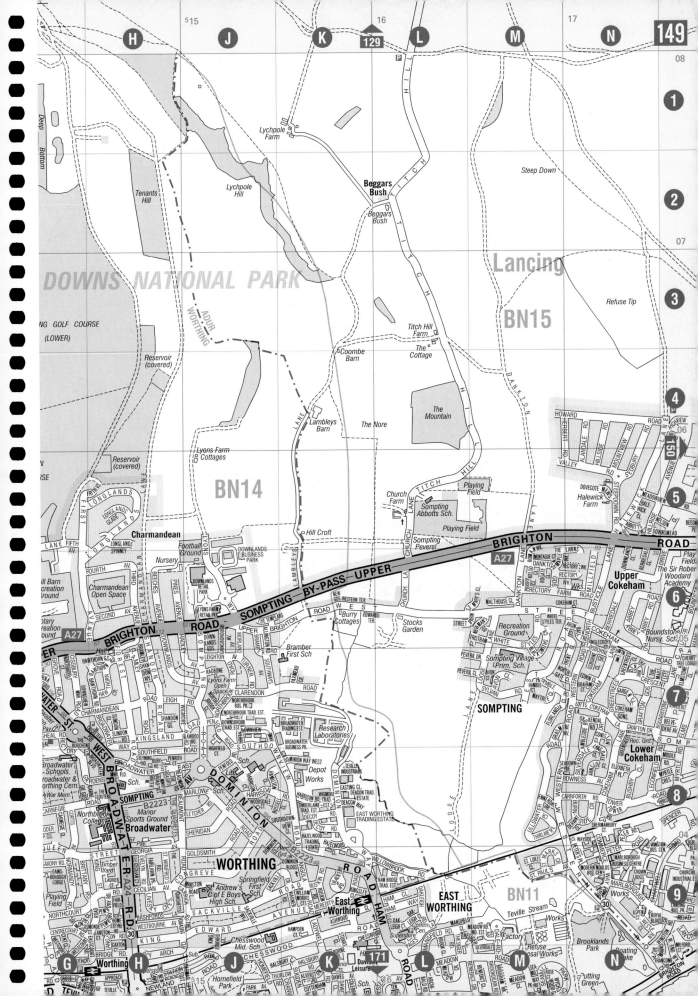

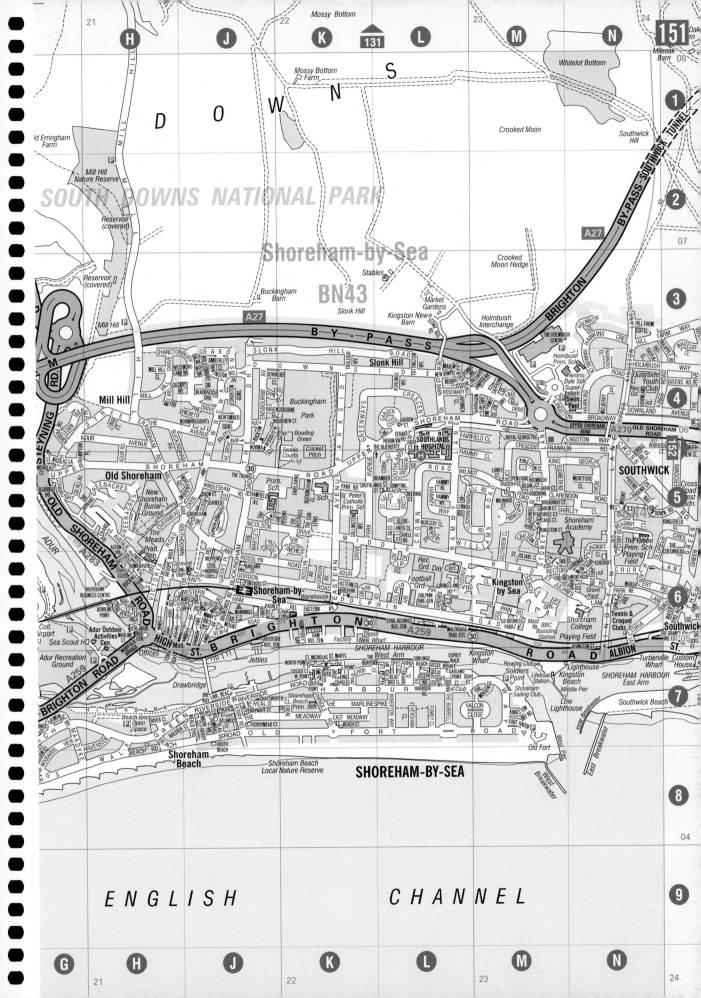

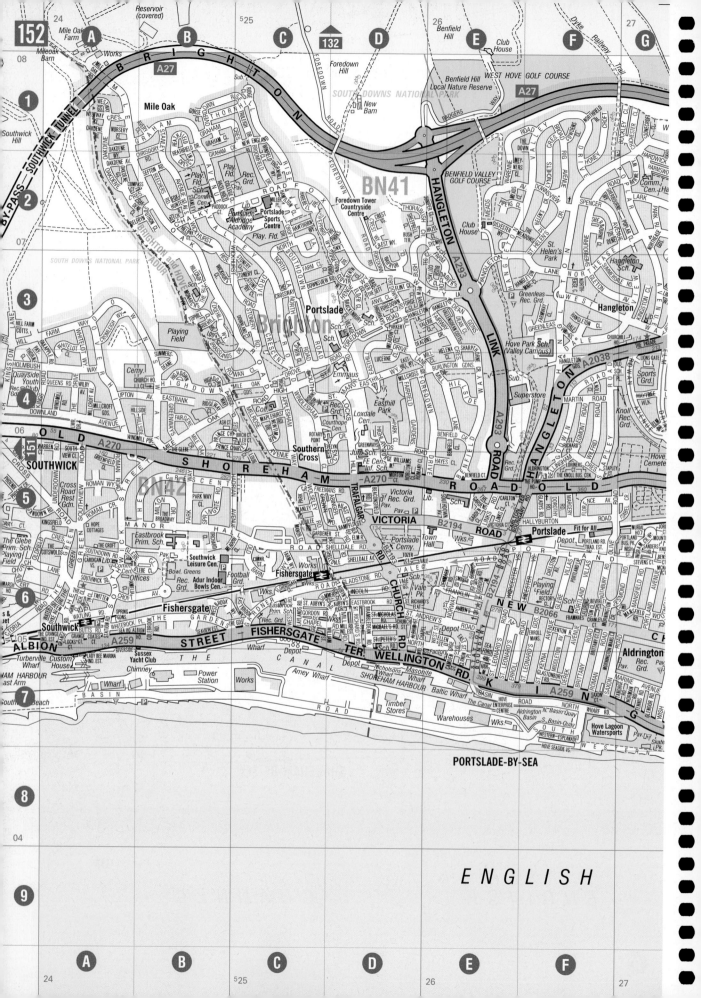

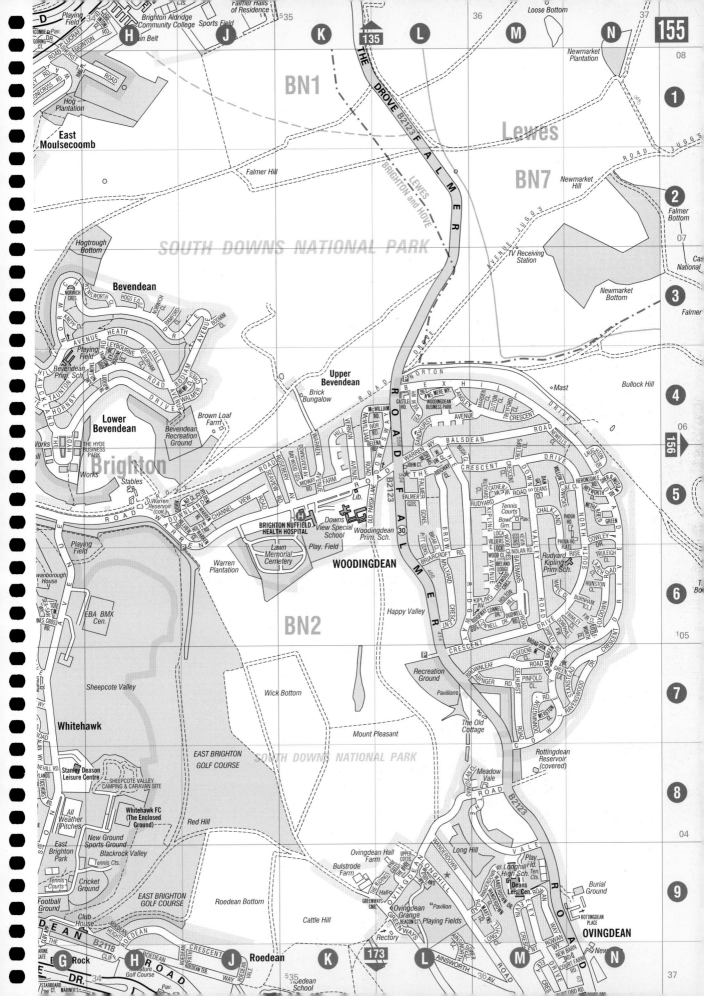

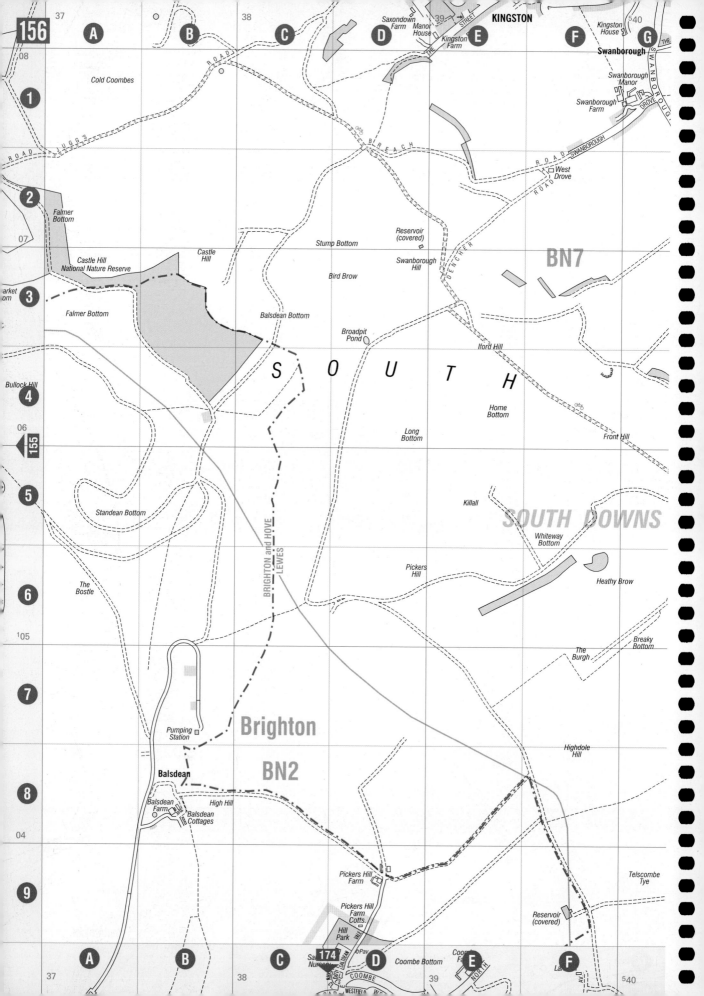

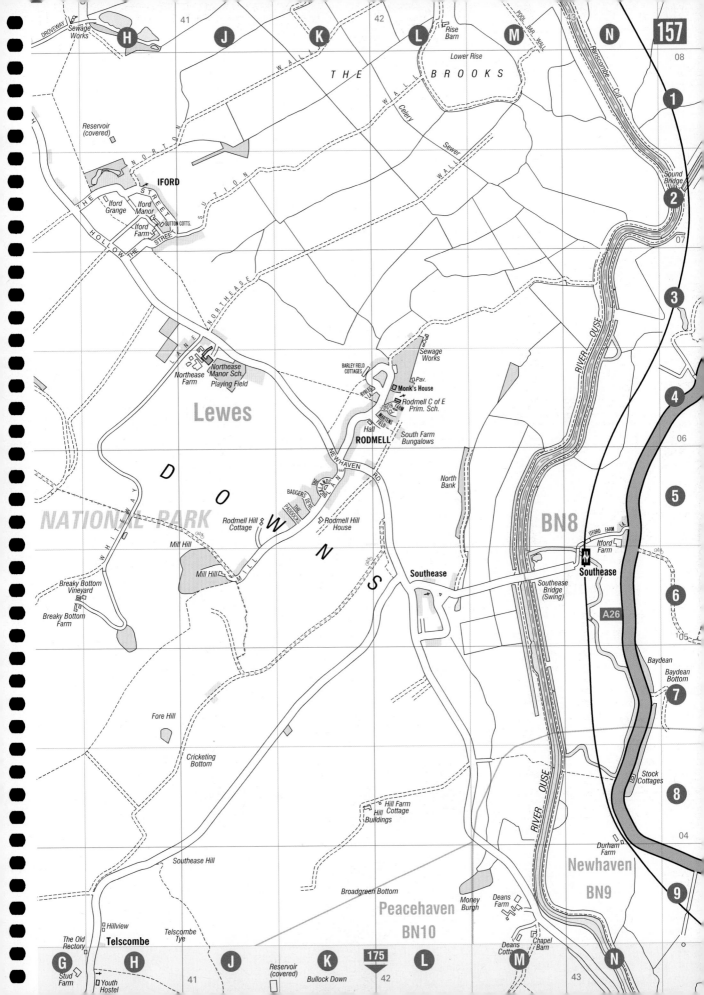

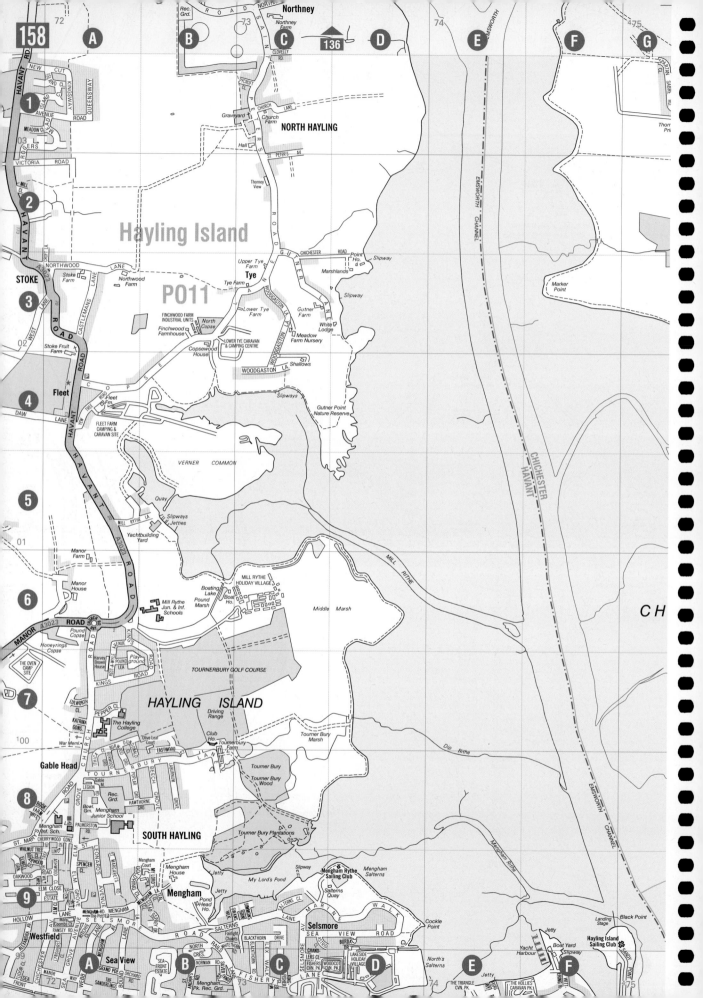

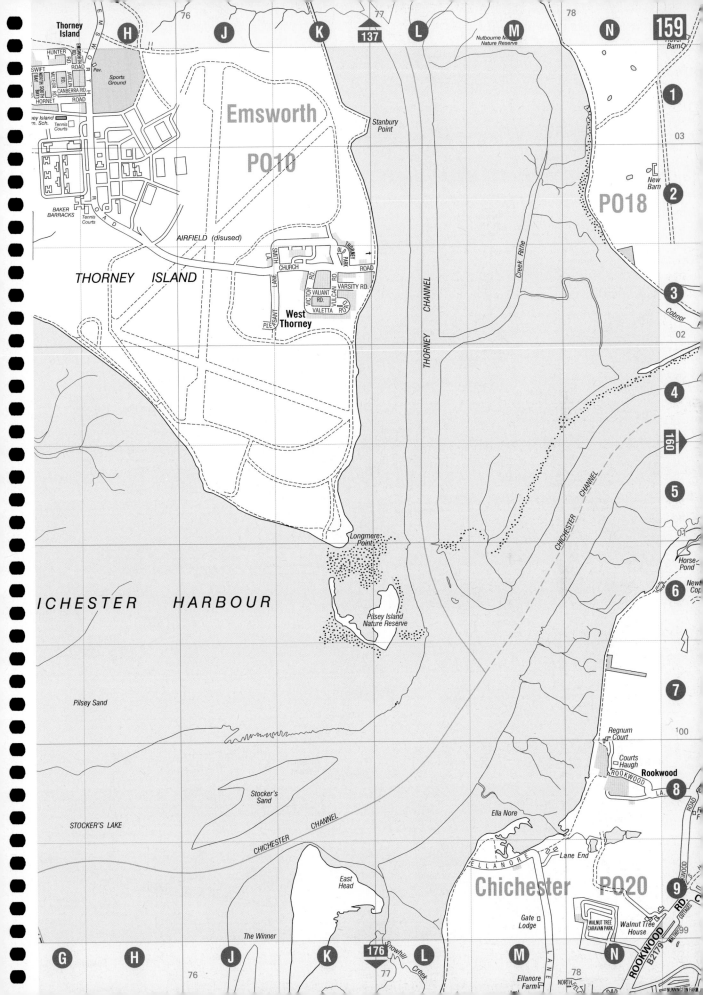

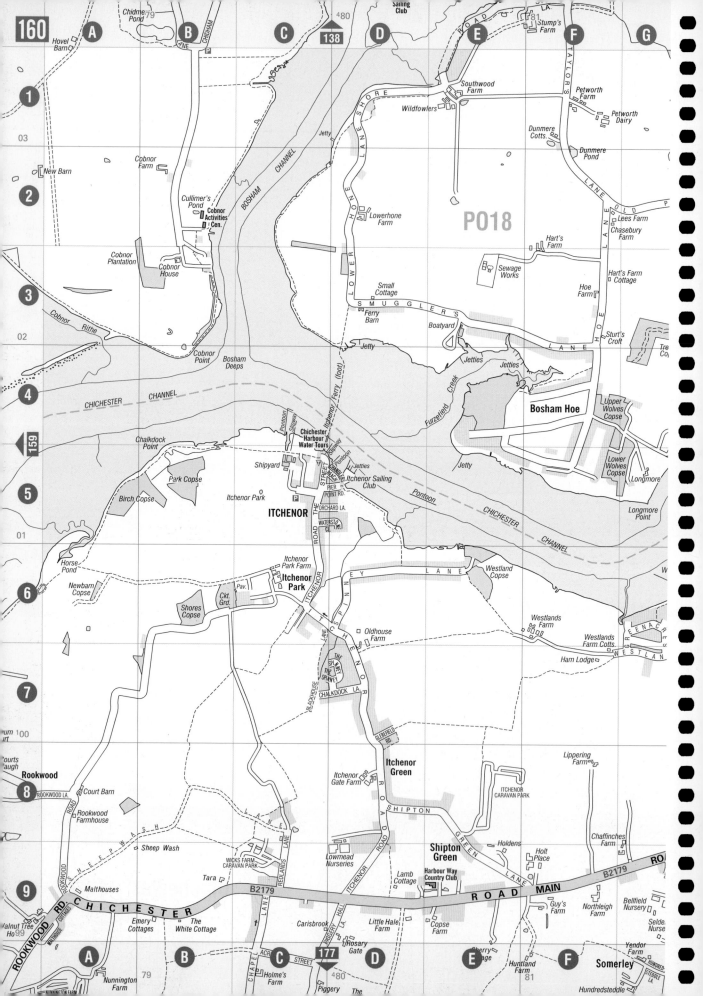

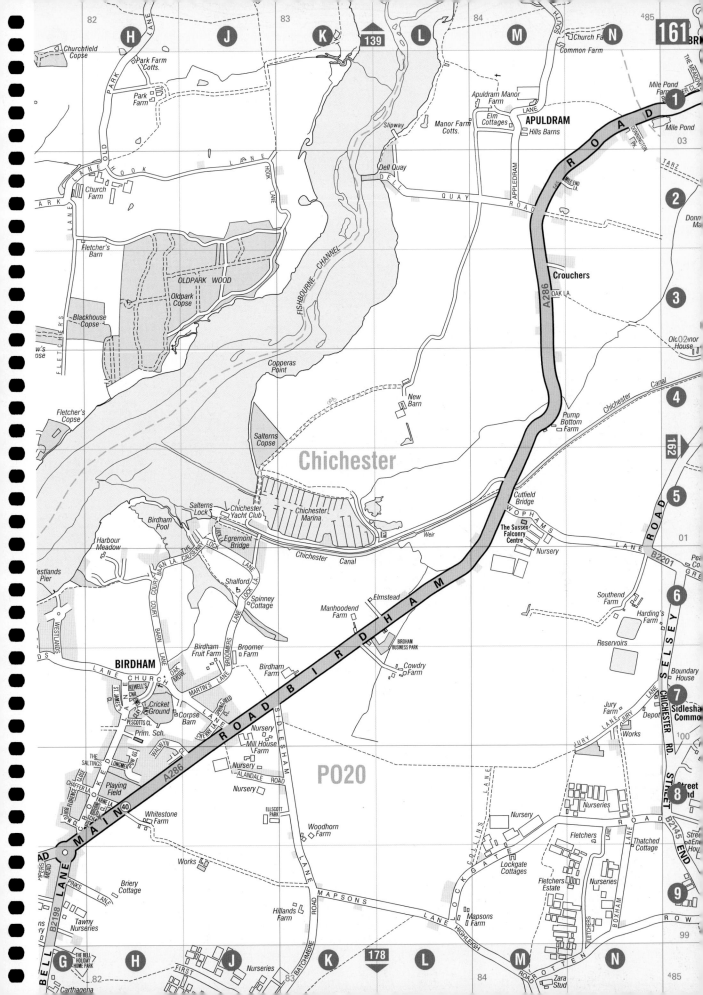

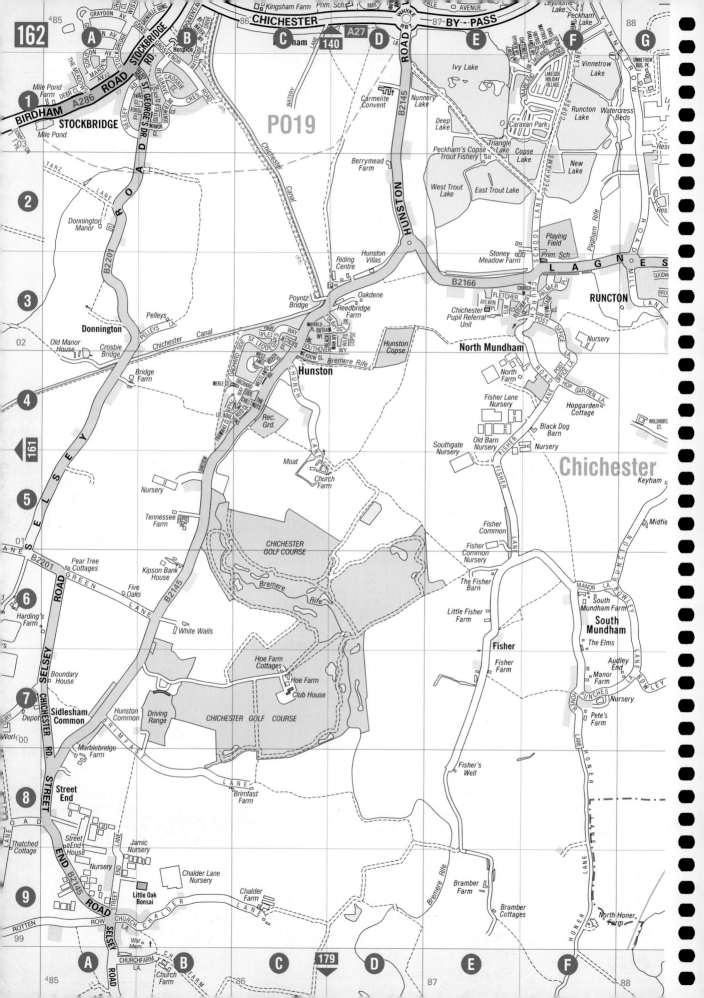

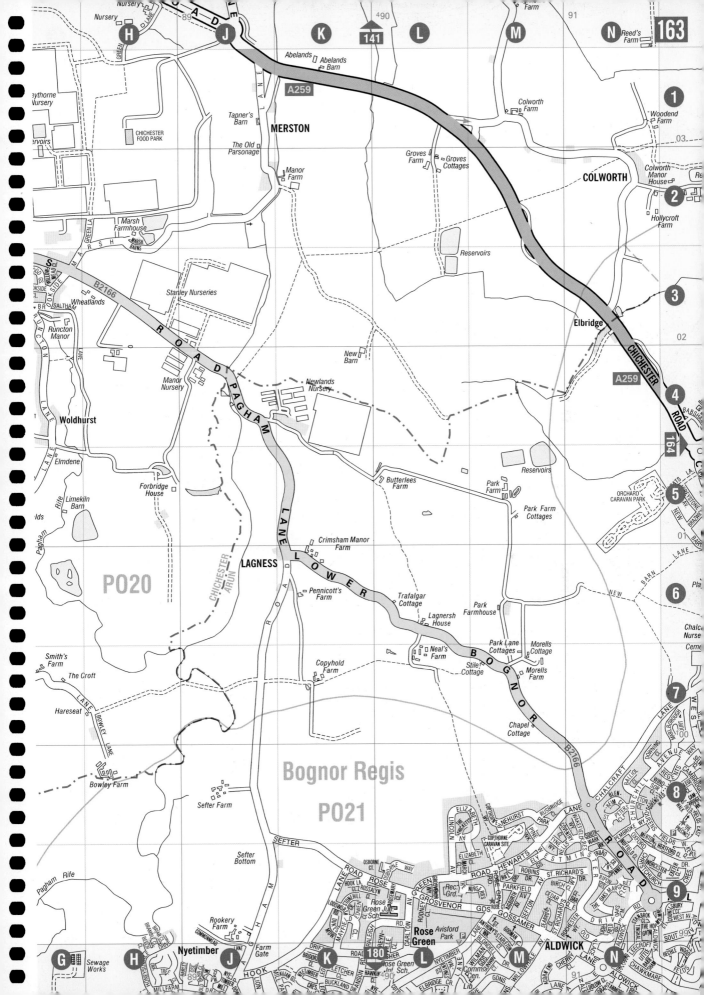

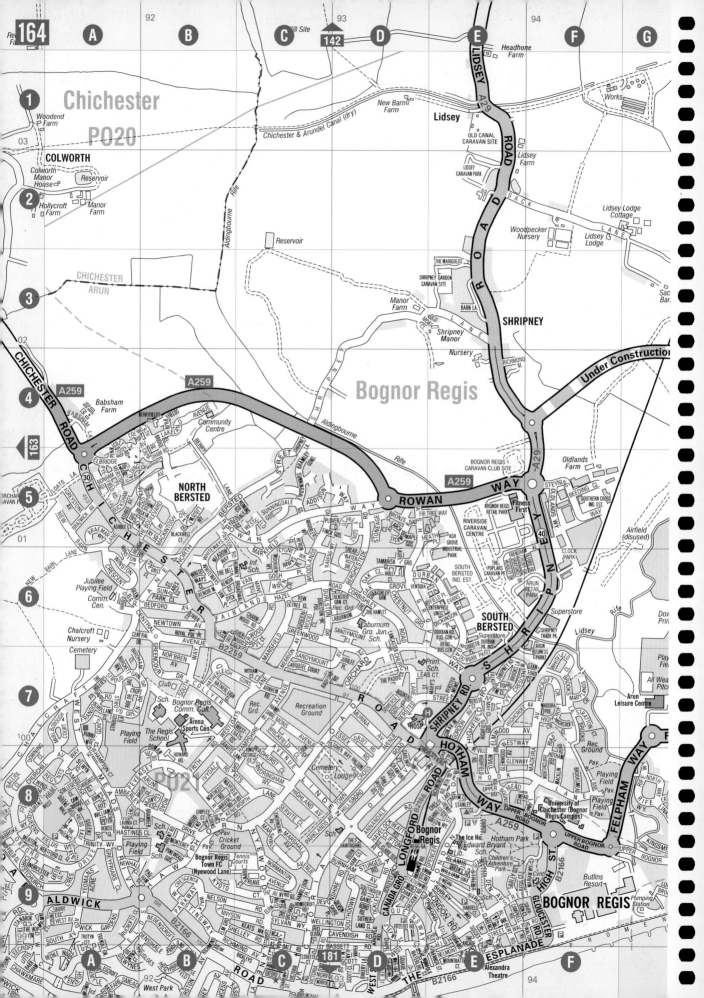

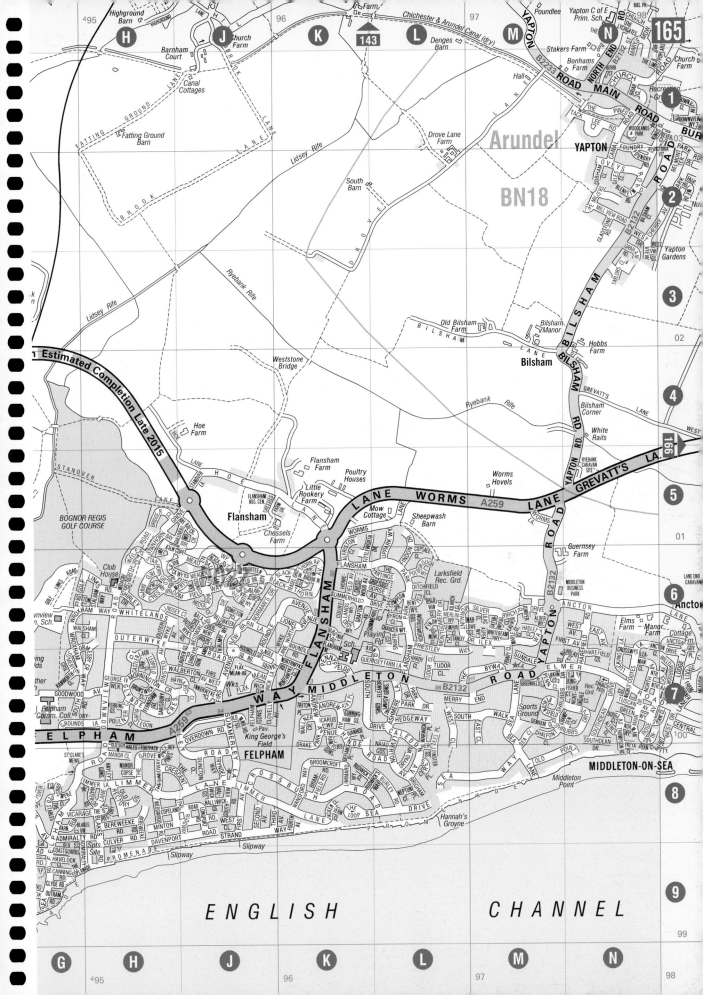

A B C 144 D E F G

Littlehampton Junction

1 YAPTON
Recreation Ground
Church Farm
FORD
Ford Sunday Market
Victorian Business Centre
RODNEY CRES.
Burndell
Ford Airfield Industrial Estate
The Old Canal Basin
FORD AERODROME (disused)
HMP FORD
HMP FORD
Playing Field
Sewage Works

2 BILSHAM
Nursery
Northwood House
B2233 ROAD YAPTON
Rudford Industrial Estate
Church Farm

Yapton Gardens

3 Arundel
Horsemere Green
HORSEMERE GREEN
CLIMPING
Playing Field
Climping Park

BN18
Northwood Farm
B2233 ROAD
JAYBELLE GRANGE LODGE PARK
Hall
A259
Brookpits Barn

4
165 GREVATT'S A259 LANE CROOKTHORN LANE
Waysmeet
Hobb's Farm
St. Mary's C of E Prim. Sch.
BROOKPIT
Kent's Farm
Ryebank Rife

Grevatt's Bridge
Hobb's New Barn
Ryebank House
Sewage Works
Camping Site

5
Ryebank Rife
New Barn

01
Moat

6 Bognor Regis
PO22
Ancton
Lane End Farm Caravan Site
Bailiffscourt Hotel
Tennis Courts
Atherington
Cudlow Barn

7
Elmer
Poole Place

MIDDLETON-ON-SEA

8
ENGLISH

9

A B C D E F

98 99 500 01

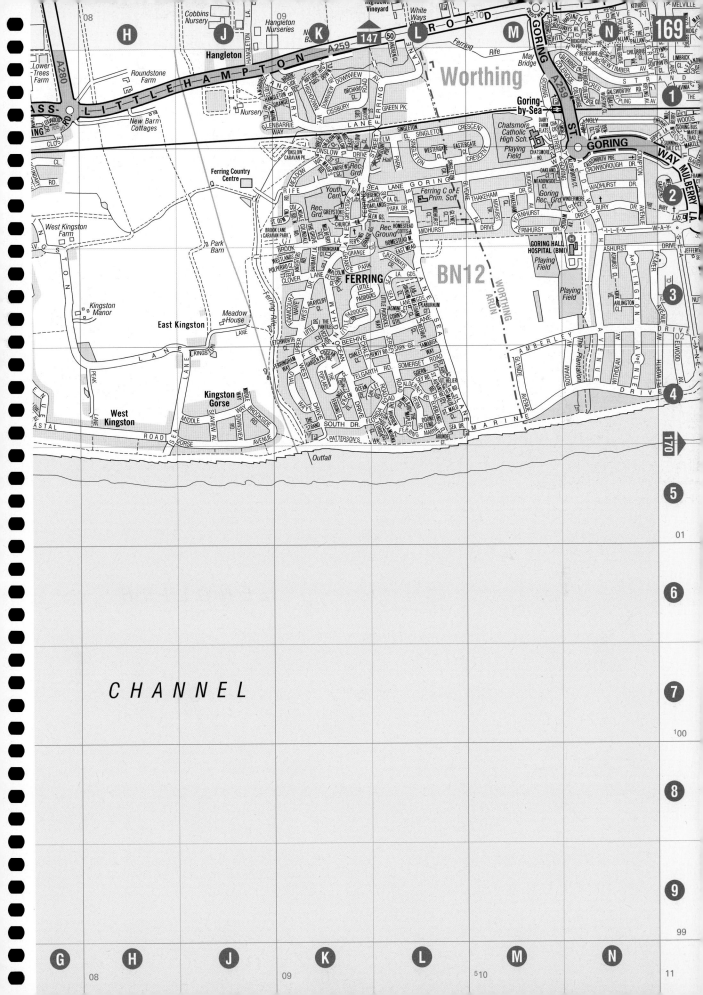

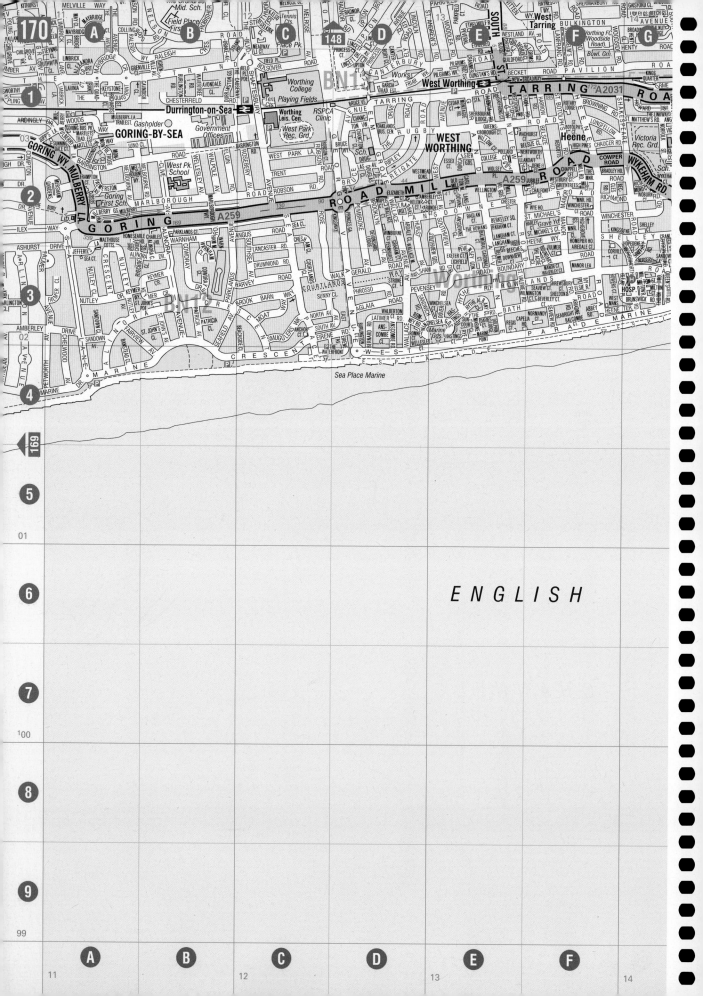

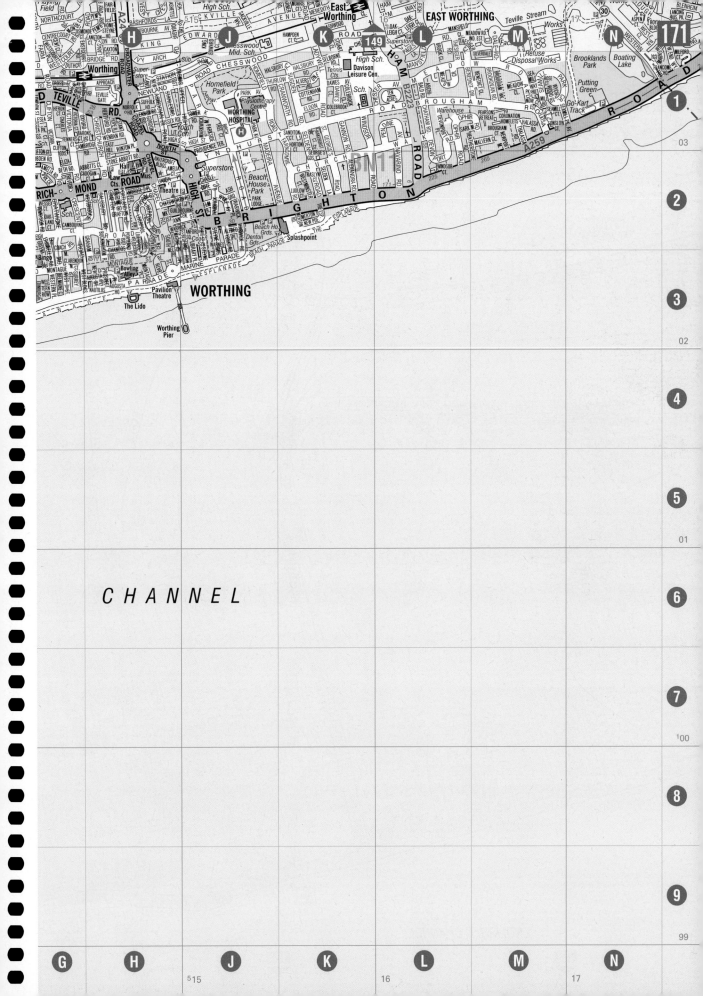

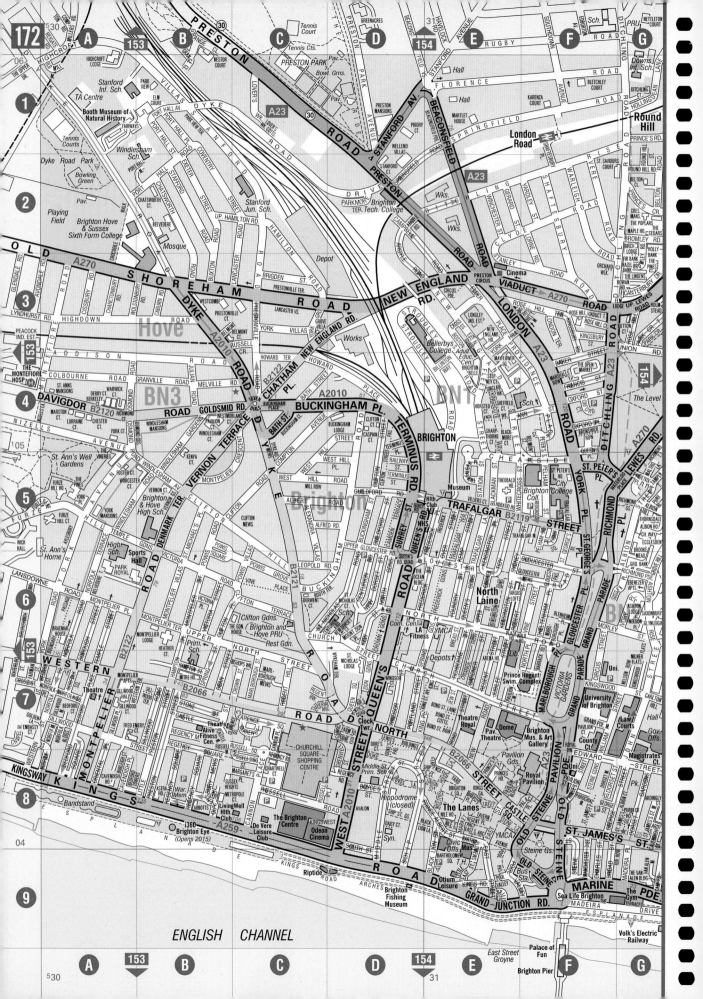

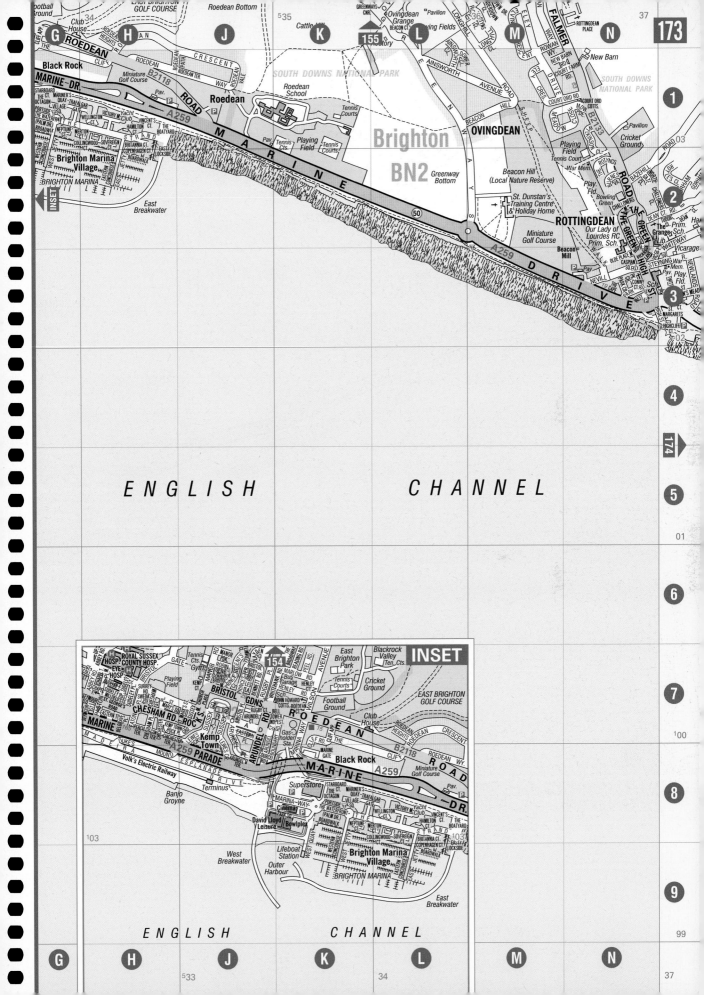

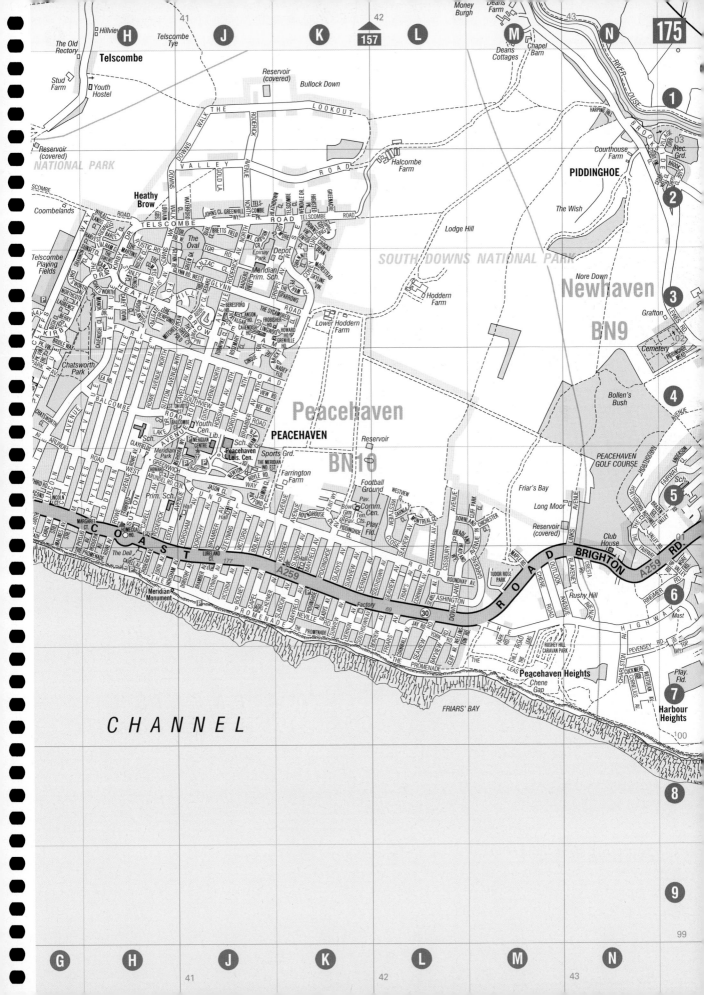

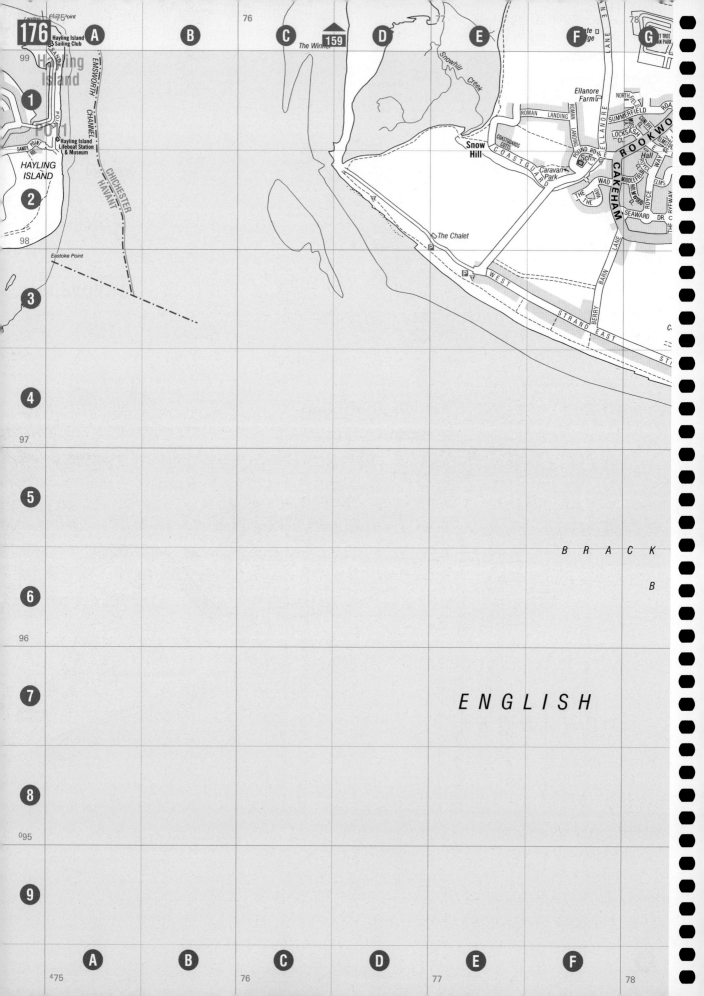

Landing Point

A Hayling Island Sailing Club

B

76

C The Winner 159

D

77

Snowhill Creek

E Ellanore Farm

78

99 Hayling Island

PO11

HAYLING ISLAND

Hayling Island Lifeboat Station & Museum

EMSWORTH CHANNEL

CHICHESTER HARBOUR

98

Eastoke Point

1

2

3

Snowhill Creek

Snow Hill

COASTGUARDS COTTS

COASTGUARD

Caravan Park

The Chalet

P

P

WEST

STRAND EAST

ROMAN LANDING

ROMAN LANDING

ROMAN LANDING

ELLANORE LANE

POUND ROAD

BARN LANE

BERRY LANE

NORTH FIELD

SUMMERFIELD

LOCKSASH CLOSE

ROOKWOOD

CAKEHAM

Hall

SEAWARD

THE WAD

THE

MIDDLETON

ROYCE

ELM'S

DR

THE DRYWAY

SchI

97

4

5

96

6

B R A C K

B

7

E N G L I S H

95

8

9

A

76

B

C

77

D

E

78

F

475

476

477

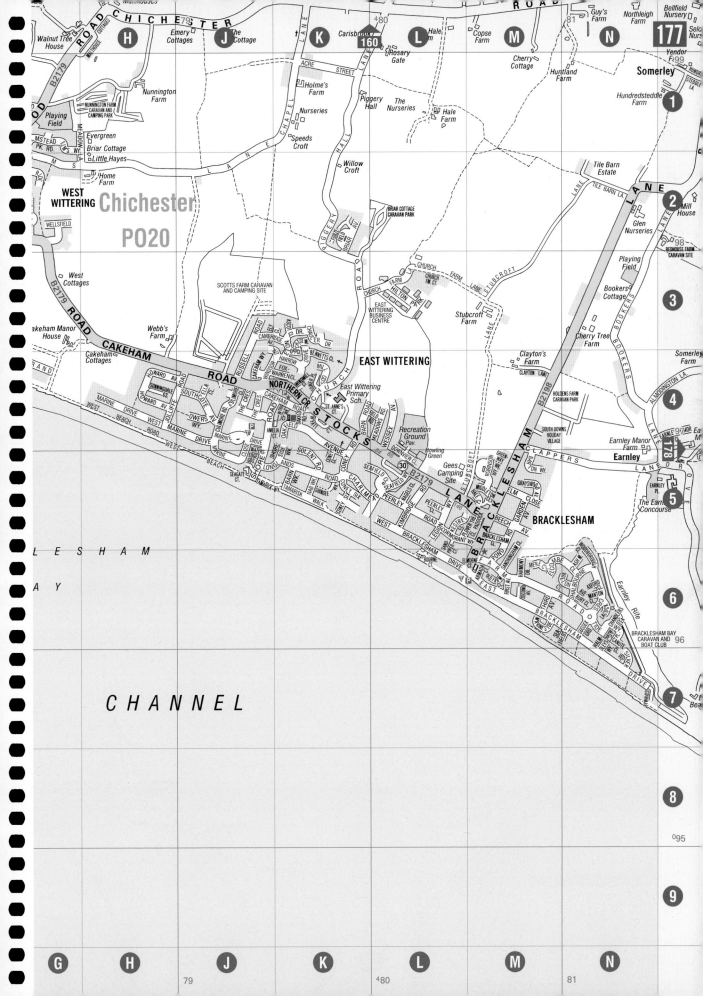

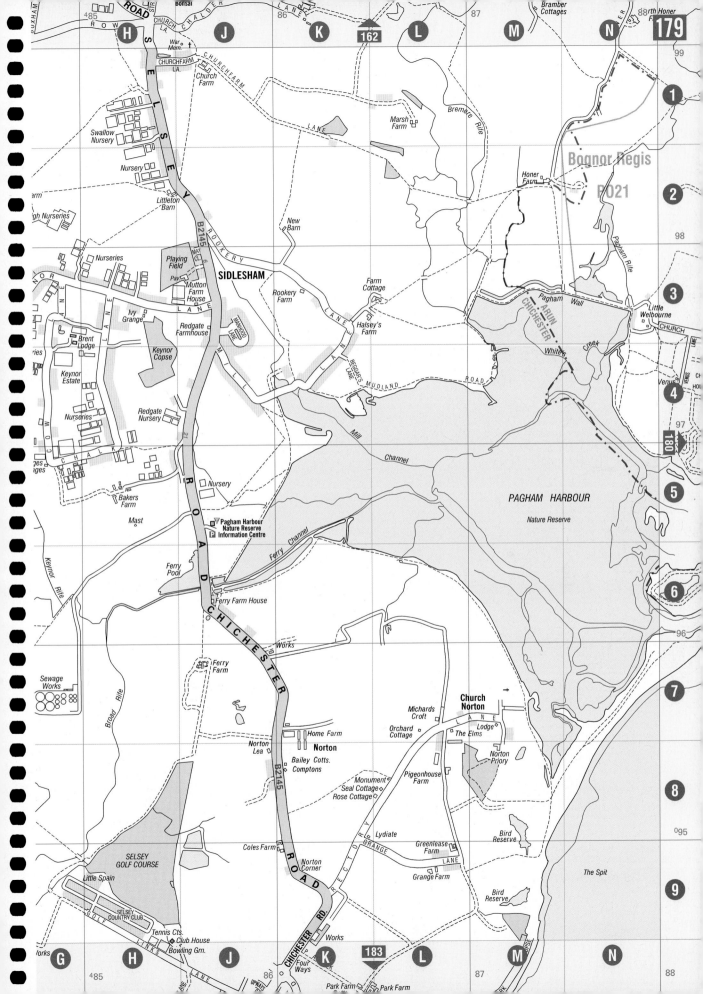

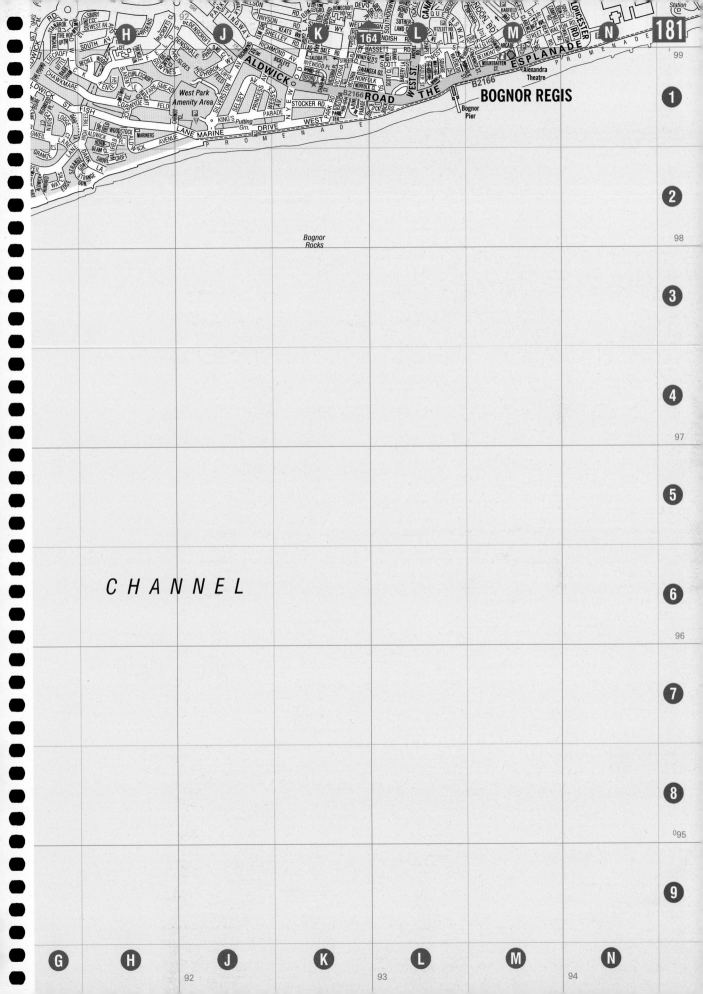

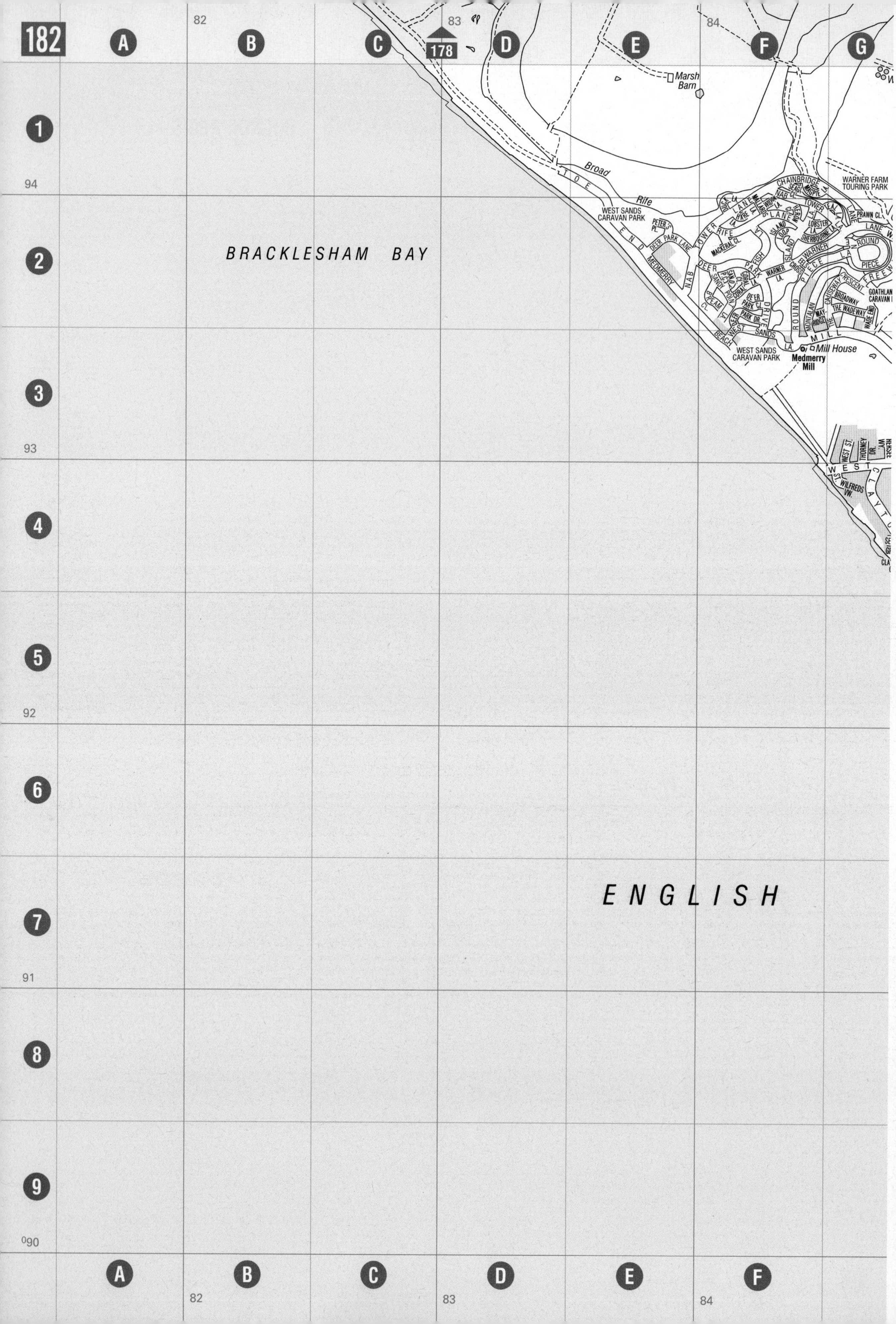

A   82   B   C   178   D   E   84   F   G

1

94

BRACKLESHAM BAY

Broad

Rife

WEST SANDS
CARAVAN PARK

CHAINBRIDGE

WARNER FARM
TOURING PARK

Marsh
Barn

2

DEER PARK LANE

PETER'S
PL

MEDMERRY

NAB

DEER
PARK
DRIVE

WARNER

ROUND

PIECE

GOATHLAND
CARAVAN

3

93

WEST SANDS
CARAVAN PARK

Mill House

Medmerry
Mill

MILL

BROADWAY

THE WADEWAY

WEST ST

THORNEY DR

HORNEY DR

HORSE WY

WEST

CLAYTON

WILFREDS WY

4

5

92

6

7

91

ENGLISH

8

9

⁰90

A   82   B   C   83   D   E   84   F

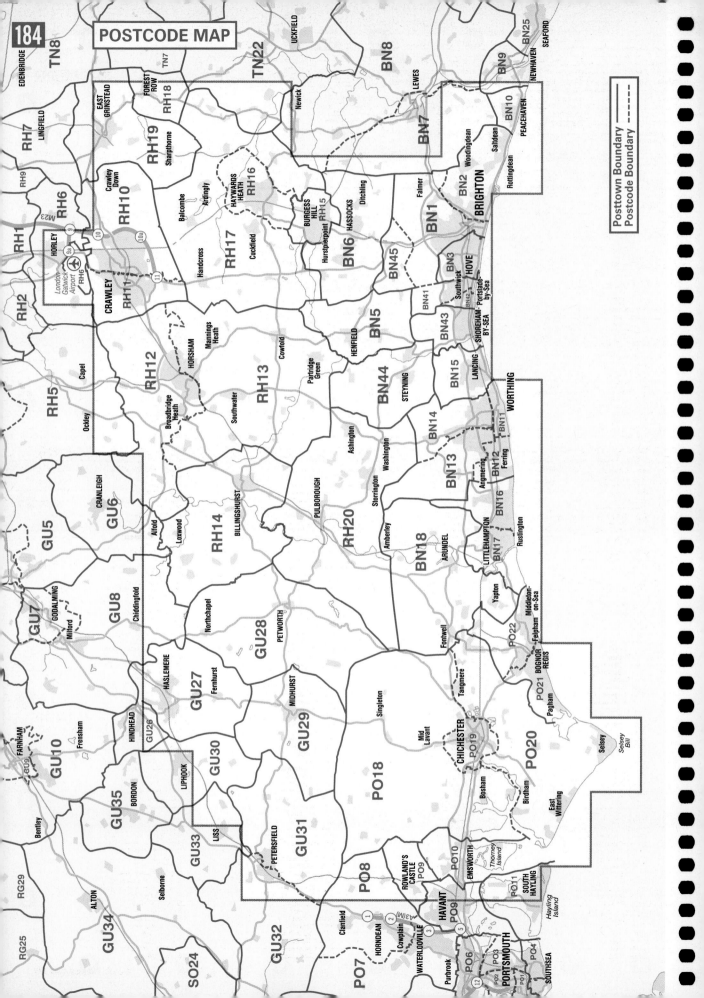

POSTCODE MAP

184

Posttown Boundary ——
Postcode Boundary - - - -

INDEX

Including Streets, Places & Areas, Industrial Estates, Selected Flats & Walkways,
Junction Names & Service Areas, Stations and Selected Places of Interest.

HOW TO USE THIS INDEX

1. Each street name is followed by its Postcode District, then by its Locality abbreviation(s) and then by its map reference;
   e.g. **Abbey Rd.** BN2: Brig . . . .9E **154** is in the BN2 Postcode District and the Brighton Locality and is to be found in square 9E on page **154**.
   The page number is shown in bold type.

2. A strict alphabetical order is followed in which Av., Rd., St., etc. (though abbreviated) are read in full and as part of the street name;
   e.g. **Abbots Cl.** appears after **Abbotsbury Ct.** but before **Abbotsfield Rd.**

3. Streets and a selection of flats and walkways that cannot be shown on the mapping, appear in the index with the thoroughfare to which they are connected shown in brackets;
   e.g. **Abergavenny Ho.** BN3: Hove . . . .7M **153** (off Holland Rd.)

4. Addresses that are in more than one part are referred to as not continuous.

5. Places and areas are shown in the index in BLUE TYPE and the map reference is to the actual map square in which the town centre or area is located and not to the place name shown on the map;
   e.g. ALDRINGTON 6H 153

6. An example of a selected place of interest is Amberley Mus. & Heritage Cen. 1K 125

7. An example of a station is Aldrington Station (Rail) . . . .5J 153, also included is Park & Ride
   e.g. Hop Oast (Horsham) (Park & Ride) 4L 45

8. Junction names and Service Areas are shown in the index in **BOLD CAPITAL TYPE**; e.g. **PEASE POTTAGE SERVICE AREA** 4E 28

9. Map references for entries that appear on large scale page **172** are shown first, with small scale map references shown in brackets;
   e.g. **Abbotts** BN1: Brig 8B **172** (8N **153**)

GENERAL ABBREVIATIONS

All. : Alley	**Cres.** : Crescent	**Intl.** : International	**Quad.** : Quadrant
App. : Approach	**Cft.** : Croft	**Junc.** : Junction	**Ri.** : Rise
Arc. : Arcade	**Dr.** : Drive	**La.** : Lane	**Rd.** : Road
Av. : Avenue	**E.** : East	**Lit.** : Little	**Rdbt.** : Roundabout
Blvd. : Boulevard	**Ent.** : Enterprise	**Lwr.** : Lower	**Shop.** : Shopping
Bri. : Bridge	**Est.** : Estate	**Mnr.** : Manor	**Sth.** : South
B'way. : Broadway	**Fld.** : Field	**Mans.** : Mansions	**Sq.** : Square
Bldgs. : Buildings	**Flds.** : Fields	**Mkt.** : Market	**St.** : Street
Bungs. : Bungalows	**Gdn.** : Garden	**Mdw.** : Meadow	**Ter.** : Terrace
Bus. : Business	**Gdns.** : Gardens	**Mdws.** : Meadows	**Twr.** : Tower
Cen. : Centre	**Gth.** : Garth	**M.** : Mews	**Trad.** : Trading
Cir. : Circus	**Ga.** : Gate	**Mt.** : Mount	**Up.** : Upper
Cl. : Close	**Gt.** : Great	**Mus.** : Museum	**Va.** : Vale
Coll. : College	**Grn.** : Green	**Nth.** : North	**Vw.** : View
Comn. : Common	**Gro.** : Grove	**Pde.** : Parade	**Vs.** : Villas
Cnr. : Corner	**Hgts.** : Heights	**Pk.** : Park	**Vis.** : Visitors
Cott. : Cottage	**Ho.** : House	**Pas.** : Passage	**Wlk.** : Walk
Cotts. : Cottages	**Ind.** : Industrial	**Pl.** : Place	**W.** : West
Ct. : Court	**Info.** : Information	**Pct.** : Precinct	**Yd.** : Yard

LOCALITY ABBREVIATIONS

Adv : **Adversane**	Copt : **Copthorne**	Hay I : **Hayling Island**	N Mun : **North Mundham**
Alb : **Albourne**	Cow : **Cowfold**	Hay H : **Haywards Heath**	Nort : **Norton**
Ald : **Aldingbourne**	Craw : **Crawley**	Henf : **Henfield**	Nor H : **Norwood Hill**
Aldw : **Aldwick**	Craw D : **Crawley Down**	Henl : **Henley**	Nutb : **Nutbourne**
Alf : **Alfold**	Cross : **Crossbush**	Hey : **Heyshott**	N'hrst : **Nuthurst**
Amb : **Amberley**	Cuck : **Cuckfield**	Hick : **Hickstead**	Nut : **Nutley**
Ang : **Angmering**	Dane : **Danehill**	High S : **High Salvington**	N'wd : **Nyewood**
Ans : **Ansty**	Dial P : **Dial Post**	Hill B : **Hill Brow**	Oak : **Oakwoodhill**
Apul : **Apuldram**	Ditch : **Ditchling**	Hind : **Hindhead**	Ock : **Ockley**
Ard : **Ardingly**	Donn : **Donnington**	Hookw : **Hookwood**	Old D : **Old Ditcham**
A'ton : **Ashington**	Dunc : **Duncton**	Horl : **Horley**	Oving : **Oving**
A'hst : **Ashurst**	Duns : **Dunsfold**	Horn : **Horndean**	O'dean : **Ovingdean**
Ash W : **Ashurst Wood**	Durr : **Durrington**	Hors : **Horsham**	Pag : **Pagham**
Bal : **Balcombe**	Earn : **Earnley**	Hors K : **Horsted Keynes**	Part G : **Partridge Green**
Balls C : **Balls Cross**	Eart : **Eartham**	Houg : **Houghton**	Pat : **Patching**
Barn : **Barnham**	E Ash : **East Ashling**	Hove : **Hove**	Peace : **Peacehaven**
B Grn : **Barns Green**	E Chil : **East Chiltington**	Huns : **Hunston**	Pease P : **Pease Pottage**
Bedd : **Beddington**	E Dean : **East Dean**	Hurst : **Hurstpierpoint**	Peters : **Petersfield**
Bep : **Bepton**	E Grin : **East Grinstead**	Ids : **Idsworth**	Petw : **Petworth**
Bers : **Bersted**	E Hart : **East Harting**	Ifield : **Ifield**	Pidd : **Piddinghoe**
Big : **Bignor**	E Lav : **East Lavant**	Ifol : **Ifold**	Pilt : **Piltdown**
Bill : **Billingshurst**	E Pres : **East Preston**	Ifrd : **Iford**	Plais : **Plaistow**
Bils : **Bilsham**	E Witt : **East Wittering**	Ipin : **Iping**	Plum P : **Plummers Plain**
Bins : **Binsted**	Ease : **Easebourne**	Itchen : **Itchenor**	Plump : **Plumpton**
Bir : **Birdham**	E'gate : **Eastergate**	Itch : **Itchingfield**	Plump G : **Plumpton Green**
Blend : **Blendworth**	Eber : **Ebernoe**	Key : **Keymer**	Poling : **Poling**
Bog R : **Bognor Regis**	Els : **Elsted**	King : **Kingsfold**	Ports : **Portslade**
Bol : **Bolney**	Ems : **Emsworth**	K Grn : **Kingsley Green**	Poyn : **Poynings**
Bosh : **Bosham**	Ewh : **Ewhurst**	King G : **Kingston Gorse**	Pulb : **Pulborough**
Box : **Boxgrove**	Falm : **Falmer**	King L : **Kingston near Lewes**	Pye : **Pyecombe**
Brac : **Bracklesham**	Fay : **Faygate**	Kird : **Kirdford**	Rake : **Rake**
Bramb : **Bramber**	Felb : **Felbridge**	Lag : **Lagness**	Rams : **Ramsdean**
Brams : **Bramshott**	Felp : **Felpham**	Lan : **Lancing**	Red : **Redford**
Brig : **Brighton**	Fern : **Fernhurst**	Lstne : **Langstone**	Riv : **River**
Broadb H : **Broadbridge Heath**	Fer : **Ferring**	Lewes : **Lewes**	Rod : **Rodmell**
Broadw : **Broadwater**	Finch : **Finchdean**	Lick : **Lickford**	Rog : **Rogate**
Br Grn : **Brooks Green**	Fin : **Findon**	Linch : **Linchmere**	Rott : **Rottingdean**
Burg H : **Burgess Hill**	Fin V : **Findon Valley**	Lind : **Lindfield**	Rowf : **Rowfant**
Buri : **Buriton**	Fish : **Fishbourne**	Lip : **Liphook**	R'hook : **Rowhook**
Burp : **Burpham**	Fitt : **Fittleworth**	Liss : **Liss**	Row C : **Rowland's Castle**
Bur : **Burstow**	Flan : **Flansham**	L'ton : **Littlehampton**	Rudg : **Rudgwick**
Bury : **Bury**	Flet : **Fletching**	Lods : **Lodsworth**	Runc : **Runcton**
Capel : **Capel**	Font : **Fontwell**	Long C : **Longmoor Camp**	Rusp : **Rusper**
Chalt : **Chalton**	Ford : **Ford**	Lwr Bee : **Lower Beeding**	Rust : **Rustington**
Charlt : **Charlton**	For G : **Forest Green**	Lowf H : **Lowfield Heath**	Salt : **Saltdean**
Charlw : **Charlwood**	F Row : **Forest Row**	Lox : **Loxwood**	Salv : **Salvington**
Char D : **Charman Dean**	Frox : **Froxfield**	Lurg : **Lurgashall**	Say C : **Sayers Common**
Chel C : **Chelwood Common**	Fulk : **Fulking**	Lym : **Lyminster**	Scay H : **Scaynes Hill**
Chel G : **Chelwood Gate**	Funt : **Funtington**	Made : **Madehurst**	Selh : **Selham**
Chich : **Chichester**	Fur G : **Furner's Green**	Mann H : **Mannings Heath**	Sel : **Selsey**
Chidd : **Chiddingfold**	Gatw : **Gatwick**	Map : **Maplehurst**	Sharp : **Sharpthorne**
Chid'm : **Chidham**	God G : **Goddard's Green**	Mard : **Marden**	Shef P : **Sheffield Park**
Chil : **Chilgrove**	Good : **Goodwood**	Midd S : **Middleton-on-Sea**	Sherm : **Shermanbury**
Chit : **Chithurst**	G Grn : **Goose Green**	Midh : **Midhurst**	Ship : **Shipley**
Clap : **Clapham**	Gor S : **Goring-by-Sea**	Mid L : **Mid Lavant**	Ship B : **Shipley Bridge**
Clay : **Clayton**	Graff : **Graffham**	Mill : **Milland**	Shor B : **Shoreham Beach**
Climp : **Climping**	Gray : **Grayshott**	Mins : **Minsted**	Shor S : **Shoreham-by-Sea**
C'ing : **Cocking**	G'wd : **Grayswood**	Monks G : **Monks Gate**	Shrip : **Shripney**
Cold : **Coldwaltham**	Great : **Greatham**	Newd : **Newdigate**	Sidle : **Sidlesham**
Colg : **Colgate**	Hal : **Halnaker**	Newh : **Newhaven**	Sid : **Sidlow**
Comp : **Compton**	Hamb : **Hambrook**	Newick : **Newick**	Sing : **Singleton**
Cool : **Coolham**	Hamm : **Hammerwood**	Newt : **Newtimber**	Slau : **Slaugham**
Coom : **Coomes**	Hand : **Handcross**	N Cha : **North Chailey**	Slind : **Slindon**
Coot : **Cootham**	Has : **Haslemere**	N'chpl : **Northchapel**	Slinf : **Slinfold**
Cops : **Copsale**	Hass : **Hassocks**	N Hth : **North Heath**	Small D : **Small Dole**
	Hav : **Havant**	N Lan : **North Lancing**	Somp : **Sompting**

Anderson Rd.—Ayshe Ct. Dr.

Anderson Rd. RH10: Craw 1G 28
Anderson Way RH6: Horl 2G 4
Andover Ho. PO9: Hav 9A 116
Andrew Av. PO22: Felp 7K 165
Andrew Cl. BN16: Rust 2A 168
BN44: Stey 4A 130
ANDREWS HILL 4G 65
Andrews La. GU29: Mins 1A 80
RH13: Southw 9K 45
Andrews Rd. RH13: Southw 2K 67
Andromeda Cl. RH11: Craw 8A 10
Angela Ct. PO9: Hav 1A 136
Angell Cl. RH10: Craw 7L 11
Angell Est. PO19: Chich 8E 140
Angel St. GU28: Petw 9N 61
Anglesea St. BN11: Wor 1G 170
Anglesey Cl. RH11: Craw 9E 10
ANGMERING 8E 146
Angmering Ct. *BN1: Brig* 9G 134
(off Newick Rd.)
Angmering La. BN16: E Pres 4D 168
Angmering Motor Sports Cen. 6G 146
ANGMERING-ON-SEA 2E 168
Angmering Park 2D 146
Angmering Station (Rail) 2E 168
Angmering Way BN16: Rust 1D 168
Angola Rd. BN14: Broadw 9K 149
Angus Cl. RH12: Hors 7A 26
Angus Rd. BN12: Gor S 2C 170
Annandale Av. PO21: Bog R 8D 164
Ann Cl. BN6: Key 2B 114
Anne Howard Gdns. BN18: Arun 2G 145
Ann Gream Ho. RH19: E Grin 2E 14
Annington Commercial Cen.
BN44: Bramb 6B 130
Annington Gdns. BN43: Shor S 4J 151
Annington Rd. BN44: Bramb 5B 130
(not continuous)
Ann St. BN1: Brig 4F 172 (6B 154)
BN11: Wor 2H 171
Annweir Av. BN15: Lan 7A 150
Anscombe Cl. BN11: Wor 3D 170
Anscombe Rd. BN11: Wor 3D 170
Anscombe Woods Cres.
RH16: Hay H 7F 72
Anscome *RH16: Hay H* 3E 72
(off Great Heathmead)
Ansisters Rd. BN12: Fer 3K 169
Anson Ct. BN12: Gor S 9A 148
Anson Ho. BN10: Peace 3J 175
Anson Rd. BN12: Gor S 9A 148
PO21: Aldw 1D 180
Anstead GU8: Chidd 1K 19
ANSTEADBROOK 6D 18
ANSTY 6L 71
Ansty Cl. BN2: Brig 8F 154
Answorth Cl. PO19: Chich 4D 140
Anthony Pl. GU26: Hind 1H 17
Anthony Way PO10: Ems 2F 136
Antlands La. RH6: Ship B, Bur 7N 5
Antlands La. E. RH6: Ship B 7N 5
Antlands La. W. RH6: Ship B 7N 5
Anvil Cl. BN41: Ports 3D 152
RH13: Southw 9K 45
RH14: Bill 1H 65
Anzac Cl. BN10: Peace 3J 175
Apperlie Dr. RH6: Horl 4L 5
Appledore Ct. RH16: Lind 2H 73
Appledore Gdns. RH16: Lind 3H 73
Appledore Rd. BN2: Brig 1G 154
Appledram La. Nth. PO19: Chich 7M 139
Appledram La. Sth.
PO20: Apul, Fish 2M 161
Applefield RH10: Craw 5G 10
Apple Gro. BN16: Ang 8F 146
PO10: S'brne 5H 137
PO21: Aldw 2D 180
Applesham Av. BN3: Hove 3G 153
Applesham Ct. BN15: Lan 9B 150
Applesham Way BN41: Ports 4C 152
Appletree Dr. PO22: Barn 7J 143
Apple Tree Rd. GU29: Midh 3F 80
Appletrees BN16: E Pres 4G 168
Appletree Wlk. BN17: Climp 3D 166
Applewalk RH15: Burg H 4A 94
Approach, The BN1: Brig 2N 153
April Cl. BN12: Fer 4K 169
RH12: Hors 7N 25
April Gdns. PO18: Mid L 8A 120
Apsley Ct. RH11: Craw 8B 10
Apsley Way BN13: Durr 8N 147
APULDRAM 1M 161
Aqua Ct. BN10: Tels C 5F 174
Aquarius Cl. BN10: Peace 6J 175
Aquarius Ct. RH11: Craw 8A 10
Arbor Ct. RH16: Hay H 4F 72
Arcade, The *BN17: L'ton* 3K 167
(off Arcade Rd.)
PO21: Bog R 9E 164
Arcade Rd. BN17: L'ton 3K 167
Archer Ct. RH15: Burg H 5B 94
Archers Ct. RH10: Craw 4F 10
Archibald Rd. BN11: Wor 1L 171
Archway Theatre 3K 5
Arcturus Rd. RH11: Craw 9A 10
Ardale Cl. BN11: Wor 2D 170
Arden Rd. RH10: Craw 8H 11
ARDINGLY 2J 51
Ardingly Activity Cen. 4F 50
Ardingly Cl. RH11: Craw 4D 10
Ardingly Ct. BN2: Brig 8G 172
Ardingly Dr. BN12: Gor S 1N 169
Ardingly Reservoir (Local Nature Reserve)
3E 50
Ardingly Rd. BN2: Salt 4D 174
RH16: Ard, Lind 5L 51
RH17: Cuck 2A 72
RH19: W Hoa 5J 31
Ardingly St. BN2: Brig 8G 172 (8C 154)
Ardings Cl. RH17: Ard 3J 51
Ardsheal Cl. BN14: Broadw 7G 148
Ardsheal Rd. BN14: Broadw 7G 148
Arena Ho. BN1: Brig 7E 172
Arena Sports Cen. 7B 164
Argus Lofts BN1: Brig 6E 172
Argus Wlk. RH11: Craw 9C 10
Argyle Cir. *PO21: Bog R* 9D 164
(off Argyle Rd.)
Argyle Rd. BN1: Brig 2D 172 (5A 154)
PO21: Bog R 1L 181
Argyle Vs. *BN1: Brig* 2D 172
(off Argyle Rd.)
Argyll Ct. *RH11: Craw* 7F 10
(off Perryfield Rd.)
Ariadne Rd. BN11: Wor 3F 170
Ariel Ct. BN15: Lan 9A 150
Arlington Av. BN12: Gor S 3N 169
Arlington Cl. BN12: Gor S 3N 169
Arlington Ct.
RH16: Hay H 4F 72
Arlington Cres. BN1: Brig 9F 134
BN16: E Pres 1G 168
Arlington Gdns. BN2: Salt 1D 174
Arlington M. *BN2: Brig* 9E 154
(off Eastern Rd.)
Armada Ct. PO20: Brac 6M 177
Armadale Rd. PO19: Chich 6D 140
Armada Way BN17: L'ton 2N 167
Arndale Rd. BN17: Wick 2H 167
Arne Cl. RH11: Craw 9B 10
Arne Gro. RH6: Horl 1G 4
Arnell Av. PO20: Sel 3J 183
Arnfield Cl. RH11: Ifield 7A 10
Arnhem Rd. PO21: Bog R 7C 164
Arnold St. BN2: Brig 6D 154
Arnold Way PO18: Bosh 6F 138
Arnside Cl. BN15: Somp 8N 149
Arran Cl. RH11: Craw 9D 10
Arrancourt RH12: Hors 9L 25
Arran Ga. *PO21: Bog R* 9F 164
(off Marian Way)
Arrivals Rd. RH6: Gatw 5H 5
(not continuous)
Artel Cft. RH10: Craw 6J 11
Artex Av. BN16: Rust 1B 168
Arthur Rd. RH11: Ifield 6A 10
RH13: Hors 1A 46
Arthur St. BN3: Hove 5J 153
Arts Rd. BN1: Falm 7J 135
Arun Beck BN6: Hurst 8J 93
Arun Bus. Pk.
PO22: Bers 6F 164
Arun Cl. BN13: Durr 6B 148
BN15: Somp 6N 149
BN16: Rust 2B 168
BN18: Amb 8L 105
GU31: Peters 7E 54
RH10: Craw 5J 11
Arun Ct. BN16: E Pres 3F 168
BN43: Shor S 5M 151
RH20: Pulb 6B 86
Arun Cres. BN13: Durr 6A 148
RH14: Bill 9H 43
Arundale M. RH20: Pulb 6C 86
ARUNDEL 2H 145
Arundel Arts, Craft & Antique Market 2H 145
(off Tarrant St.)
Arundel By-Pass BN18: Arun 3G 145
Arundel Castle 2H 145
Arundel Cathedral 2H 145
Arundel Cl. BN43: Shor S 5M 151
PO21: Bog R 8B 164
RH10: Craw 6L 11
RH13: Southw 9L 45
Arundel Ct. *BN1: Brig* 9L 133
(off Mill Ri.)
BN2: Brig 9F 154
BN11: Wor 2D 170
BN12: Fer 4L 169
BN43: Shor S 5M 151
RH14: Bill 2K 65
(off Brooker's Rd.)
RH15: Burg H 4A 94
(off West St.)
Arundel Dr. BN17: Wick 8J 145
Arundel Dr. E. BN2: Salt 3C 174
Arundel Dr. W. BN2: Salt 3B 174
Arundel Gdn. BN16: Rust 3B 168
Arundel Ho. *RH13: Hors* 1B 46
(off Kennedy Rd.)
Arundel La. GU28: Upw 6H 103
Arundel Lido 3J 145
Arundel M. *BN2: Brig* 9F 154
(off Arundel Pl.)
RH16: Hay H 7G 72
Arundel Mus. 2J 145
Arundel Pl. BN2: Brig 9F 154
Arundel Rd. BN2: Brig 8J 173
BN10: Peace 5J 175
BN13: Clap, High S, Pat 5G 147
BN16: Ang 5E 146
BN17: L'ton 2K 167
BN18: Bins, Font, Slind, Walb 2H 143
BN18: Poling 5N 145
PO18: Box, Nort, Tang 3K 141
PO20: Box, Tang 3K 141
Arundel Rd. Cen. BN10: Peace 5H 175
Arundel Rd. W. BN10: Peace 4G 175
Arundel Station (Rail) 4J 145
Arundel St. BN2: Brig 8J 173
Arundel Ter. BN2: Brig 8J 173
Arundel Way PO22: Midd S 7B 166
Arundel Wetland Cen. 9J 125
Arundel Wing, The BN18: Tort 6E 144
Arun Ford Cl. BN18: Ford 1E 166
Arun Gdns. RH13: Hors 1B 46
Arun Leisure Cen. 7G 164
Arun Pde. BN17: L'ton 4K 167
Arun Prospect *RH20: Pulb* 7N 85
(off Station Rd.)
Arun Retail Pk. PO22: Bers 6F 164
Arun Rd. PO21: Bog R 8B 164
RH14: Bill 9H 43
Arunside RH12: Hors 1L 45
Arun St. BN18: Arun 3H 145
Arun Ter. BN18: Arun 3G 144
Arun Va. RH20: Cold 2J 105
Arun Way PO21: Aldw 3D 180
(not continuous)
RH13: Hors 1B 46
Arun Wharf *BN17: L'ton* 3J 167
(off River Rd.)
Arun Yacht Club 4J 167
Ascot Cl. PO20: W Witt 3K 177
Ascot Way BN16: Rust 2D 168
Ashacre La. BN13: Salv 6D 148
Ashacre M. BN13: Salv 6D 148
Ashacre Way BN13: Salv 6D 148
Ashbee Ct. PO21: Bers 5A 164
Ashbee Gdns. PO21: Bers 5A 164
Ashburnham Cl. BN1: Brig 9E 134
BN13: Durr 7N 147
PO19: Chich 6N 139
Ashburnham Dr. BN1: Brig 8E 134
RH17: Cuck 2N 71
Ashburnham M. RH17: Cuck 3N 71
Ashburnham Rd.
RH10: Craw 8J 11
Ashby Ct. RH13: Hors 9B 26
Ash Cl. BN3: Hove 2L 153
BN14: Fin 8C 128
BN17: L'ton 1N 167
RH10: Craw D 4K 13
Ash Ct. BN42: S'wck 4B 152
RH19: E Grin 1E 14
Ashcroft BN43: Shor S 6N 151
Ashcroft Cl. BN43: Shor S 6N 151
Ashcroft Ct. GU32: Peters 5F 54
Ashcroft La. PO8: Finch 9D 96
Ashcroft Way PO21: Pag 3C 180
Ashdene Gdns. RH20: A'ton 3E 108
Ashdown BN3: Hove 7L 153
Ashdown Av. BN2: Salt 3B 174
Ashdown Cl. BN16: Ang 9E 146
RH16: Hay H 5J 73
RH18: F Row 1N 33
Ashdown Ct. RH10: Craw 9H 11
RH13: Hors 7C 26
Ashdown Dr. RH10: Craw 9F 10
Ashdown Forest Centre, The 6N 33
Ashdown Forest Llama Pk. 7M 33
Ashdown Ga. RH19: E Grin 2D 14
Ashdown Ho. RH6: Gatw 6J 5
Ashdown Pl. RH18: F Row 3L 33
Ashdown Rd. BN2: Brig 5C 154
BN11: Wor 1H 171
RH18: F Row 1M 33
Ashdown Vw. RH19: E Grin 5E 14
Ashenground Cl. RH16: Hay H 6F 72
Ashenground Rd.
RH16: Hay H 6E 72
Ashe Rd. PO9: Hav 9B 116
Ashfield RH14: Plais 9E 20
Ashfield Cl. GU29: Midh 9G 59
Ashfield Rd. GU29: Midh 1G 81
Ashfold Av. BN14: Fin V 4E 148
ASHFOLD CROSSWAYS 4N 47
Ashford Rd. BN1: Brig 3B 154
Ash Gro. BN11: Wor 2J 171
GU27: Fern 4J 37
PO22: Bers, Bog R 5D 164
RH16: Hay H 6E 72
Ash Gro. Ind. Pk.
PO22: Bers 5E 164
ASHINGTON 2E 108
Ashington Ct. *BN2: Brig* 7G 154
(off Whitehawk Way)
BN14: Broadw 8H 149
(off Broadway St. E.)
RH12: Hors 6A 26
(off Woodstock Cl.)
Ashington Gdns. BN10: Peace 6L 175
Ash Keys RH10: Craw 7G 10
Ash La. BN16: Rust 3B 168
Ashleigh Cl. BN16: Ang 7E 146
RH6: Horl 2H 5
Ashleigh Rd. RH12: Hors 6N 25
Ashley Cl. BN1: Brig 7N 133
Ashley Ho. BN3: Hove 8K 153
Ashlings Way BN3: Hove 3G 152
BN43: Shor S 4L 151
Ashmead Way BN16: Ang 9F 146
Ashmere Gdns. PO22: Felp 7L 165
Ashmere La. PO22: Felp 7L 165
Ashmore Av. BN16: Ang 9F 146
Ashmore Cl. BN10: Peace 2K 175
Ashmore Ho. RH11: Craw 3F 10
Ashmore La. RH12: Rusp 6F 8
Ashmount Ho. *PO21: Bog R* 9D 164
(off Argyle Rd.)
Ash Rd. RH10: Craw 5J 11
RH13: Southw 9J 45
Ashton Gdns. BN16: Rust 4B 168
Ashton Lodge BN2: Brig 6G 172
Ashton Ri. BN2: Brig 6G 172 (7C 154)
Ash Tree Cl. GU27: G'wd 2A 18
ASHURST 2A 110
Ashurst Av. BN2: Salt 4E 174
Ashurst Cl. BN12: Gor S 3N 169
PO21: Bers 6B 164
RH12: Hors 6D 26
Ashurst Dr. BN12: Gor S 3N 169
RH10: Worth 6M 11
Ashurst La. BN6: Streat 4K 115
BN7: Plump, Streat 4K 115
Ashurst Pl. RH16: Hay H 4F 72
Ashurst Rd. BN2: Brig 9G 135
Ashurst Way BN16: Ang 1E 168
ASHURST WOOD 6K 15
Ash Way RH15: Burg H 6B 94
Ashwood RH11: Craw 7F 10
Ashwood Cl. BN11: Wor 9K 149
PO11: Hay I 9A 158
Ashwood Ct. RH18: F Row 2M 33
Ashwood Dr. BN16: Rust 3B 168
Ashwyn Bus. Cen.
RH15: Burg H 3A 94
Aspen Cl. BN17: L'ton 1N 167
RH16: Hay H 5J 73
Aspen Ct. BN15: Lan 9N 149
RH11: Craw 3E 10
(off Rushetts Pl.)
RH19: E Grin 4G 14
Aspen Wlk. RH16: Hay H 5J 73
Aspen Way PO22: Midd S 6M 165
RH12: Hors 7B 26
Assembly Hall
Worthing 2H 171
Assisi Ct. RH16: Hay H 7G 73
Aston Ct. RH11: Craw 2D 28
Aston Ho. BN43: Shor S 5H 151
Aston Ri. RH20: Pulb 5B 86
Astra Cl. PO18: Bosh 8F 138
Astra Ho. BN1: Brig 8B 172
Astral Towers RH10: Craw 2F 10
Astrid Cl. PO11: Hay I 9C 158
Athelstan Cl. RH10: Worth 6N 11
Athelstan Rd. BN14: W Tar 9E 148
Athelstan Way RH13: Hors 2B 46
Athenaeum, The BN3: Hove 7L 153
ATHERINGTON 6F 166
Atkinson Ct. RH6: Horl 3K 5
Atkinson Rd. RH10: Craw 8L 11
Atlantic Ct. BN43: Shor B 7J 151
Atlantic Hgts. *BN2: Salt* 3C 174
(off Suez Way)
Atlantic Ho. *BN16: Rust* 4A 168
(off Harsfold Cl.)
RH6: Gatw 5J 5
Atlingworth Ct. *BN2: Brig* 9C 154
(off Atlingworth St.)
Atlingworth St. BN2: Brig 9C 154
Atrium, The 3E 14
Atrium Ho. *BN1: Brig* 6E 172
(off Regent St.)
Attenborough Centre for Creative Arts
8H 135
Attenborough Rd. BN1: Falm 8J 135
Attlee Ho. RH11: Craw 1D 28
Attree Ct. BN2: Brig 7D 154
Attree Dr. BN2: Brig 7D 154
Auchinleck Ct. RH10: Craw D 5J 13
Auckland Cl. RH11: Craw 3F 10
Auckland Dr. BN2: Brig 4G 155
Audrey Cl. BN1: Brig 9N 133
Augusta Ct. PO19: Chich 3C 140
Augusta Ho. BN11: Wor 3H 171
Augusta Pl. BN11: Wor 3H 171
Augustines Way RH16: Hay H 5G 72
Aurora Ranch Caravan Pk.
RH17: Bol 5F 70
Aurum Cl. RH6: Horl 3K 5
Austen Cl. RH19: E Grin 3B 14
Austens GU29: Hey 8L 81
Autumn Cl. RH11: Craw 7E 10
Avalon BN1: Brig 8D 172 (8A 154)
Avalon Cl. PO10: Ems 3F 136
Avalon Way BN13: Durr 7B 148
Avebury Cl. PO20: Brac 6N 177
RH12: Hors 4D 26
Aveling Cl. RH10: Craw 8L 11
Avenals, The BN16: Ang 8F 146
Avenue BN1: Brig 8E 172
Avenue, The BN2: Brig 3E 154
BN12: Gor S 9A 148
BN43: Shor S 4H 151
GU26: Gray 1F 16
GU27: Has 4H 17
GU29: Wool 7D 58
GU31: Peters 6F 54
PO18: Funt 8B 118
PO18: Hamb 4A 138
PO19: Chich 3B 140
PO21: Bog R 9C 164
RH6: Horl 3H 5
RH10: Craw 2F 28
RH13: Hors 4H 45
RH17: Hand 2B 48
Avenue App. PO19: Chich 6B 140
Avenue Ct. *BN3: Hove* 7L 153
(off Palmeira Av.)
Avenue de Chartres PO19: Chich 7B 140
Avenue de Chartres Rdbt.
PO19: Chich 7B 140
(off Avenue de Chartres)
Avenue Gdns. RH6: Horl 3L 5
Avenue Lawn Tennis & Squash Club 4B 136
Avenue Rd. PO11: Hay I 1A 158
Avery Cl. BN41: Ports 1B 152
Avian Gdns. PO21: Pag 1D 180
Aviary Cl. PO18: Hamb 3A 138
Aviary Way RH10: Craw D 3K 13
Aviation Bus. Pk. BN6: Alb 4D 112
Avila Ho. *BN11: Wor* 2G 171
(off Gratwicke Rd.)
Avington Grn. PO9: Hav 8B 116
Avisford Park Golf Course 4N 143
Avisford Pk. Rd. BN18: Walb 4M 143
Avisford Ter. *PO21: Aldw* 9M 163
(off Rose Grn. Rd.)
Avocet Quay PO10: S'brne 6G 137
Avocet Trad. Est. RH15: Burg H 6A 94
Avon Cl. BN15: Somp 7M 149
GU31: Peters 8E 54
PO22: Felp 7K 165
Avon Ct. *BN2: Brig* 8C 154
(off Mt. Pleasant)
BN15: Somp 7M 149
Avondale Cl. BN12: Gor S 1B 170
Avondale Rd.
BN3: Hove 3A 172 (6M 153)
Avonhurst RH15: Burg H 5C 94
Avon Rd. BN17: L'ton 3K 167
Avon Wlk. RH11: Craw 7B 10
Awbrook Cl. RH17: Scay H 6N 73
Axford Cl. PO20: Brac 6N 177
Aylesbury BN3: Hove 5A 172 (7N 153)
Aylwin Pl. PO20: N Mun 3E 162
Aymer Ho. BN3: Hove 7J 153
Aymer Rd. BN3: Hove 7J 153
Aynsley Ct. BN3: Hove 5L 153
Ayshe Ct. Dr. RH13: Hors 9B 26

Azalea Cl.—Beggars Bush

Azalea Cl. PO9: Hav .1C 136
RH20: Storr .5N 107
Azalea Dr. GU27: Has .3H 17
Azalea Way RH15: Burg H .4E 94

B

Babsham La. PO21: Bers .4A 164
Back La. RH10: Turn H .1D 30
RH14: Plais .9E 20
RH17: Bal, Turn H .1D 30
Backwoods Cl. RH16: Lind .3J 73
Backwoods La. RH16: Lind .3H 73
Baden Dr. RH6: Horl .1G 5
Baden Powell Rd. GU33: Long C .1C 34
Baden Rd. BN2: Brig .4E 154
Bader Ct. RH10: Craw .4F 10
Badger Cl. BN6: Key .2B 114
BN41: Ports .3D 152
Badger Copse BN5: Henf .1H 111
Badger Dr. RH16: Hay H .4D 72
Badgers Cl. RH12: Hors .5C 26
Badgers Copse RH10: Craw D .4H 13
RH17: W'lid .2B 70
Badgers Dene BN7: Rod .5K 157
Badgers Fld. BN10: Peace .3J 175
Badgers Holt RH20: Storr .6N 107
Badgers Wlk. BN16: Ang .9E 146
RH15: Burg H .6D 94
Badgers Way BN3: Hove .1E 152
RH14: Lox .7N 21
RH19: E Grin .2F 14
Badgers Wood RH20: W Chil .1J 107
Badger Wlk. PO19: Chich .5E 140
(off Swanfield Dr.)
Badger Way BN1: Brig .8F 134
Baffins Ct. PO19: Chich .7C 140
(off Baffins La.)
Baffins La. PO19: Chich .7C 140
Bailey Cl. BN17: L'ton .1N 167
(off Lanyards)
RH12: Hors .4C 26
Bailing Hill RH12: Warnh .4J 25
Baird Cl. RH10: Craw .3J 11
Bakehouse Barn Cl. RH12: Hors .4B 26
Bakehouse Rd. RH6: Horl .1J 5
Baker Cl. RH10: Craw .8F 10
Bakers Arms Hill BN18: Arun .2H 145
Bakers Cl. RH13: Southw .9K 45
Bakers Ct. BN13: Durr .6C 148
Baker's La. RH13: Ship .4F 66
Bakers Mdw. RH14: Bill .9J 43
Bakers M. RH13: Lwr Bee .7K 47
Baker St. BN1: Brig .4F 172 (6B 154)
Bakery La. PO21: Bog R .1L 181
Bakery M. BN2: Brig .4D 154
Bala Cres. PO22: Felp .6J 165
Balchin Ct. BN2: Brig .6D 154
Balchins Cl. RH14: Wisb .1A 64
BALCOMBE .9A 30
Balcombe Av. BN14: Wor .8G 148
Balcombe Ct. BN10: Peace .4J 175
BN11: Wor .3F 170
RH10: Craw .5M 11
Balcombe Gdns. RH6: Horl .3L 5
BALCOMBE LANE .6B 30
Balcombe La. RH17: Ard .2F 50
RH17: Bal .4A 30
RH17: Hand .1E 48
RH17: Hors K, Sharp .8D 32
RH19: Hors K, Sharp .8D 32
Balcombe Rd. BN10: Peace .4H 175
RH6: Horl, Gatw .1K 5
RH10: Craw, Worth .8M 5
RH16: Hay H .1E 72
Balcombe Station (Rail) .1A 50
Baldwin Cl. PO22: Midd S .6L 165
RH10: Craw .9L 11
Baldwins Fld. RH19: E Grin .1D 14
BALDWINS HILL .1D 14
Balfour Gdns. RH18: F Row .3L 33
Balfour Rd. BN1: Brig .3A 154
Balfour Vs. BN1: Brig .3B 154
Ballards Mill Cl. BN1: Brig .9N 133
Ballindune GU27: Has .3L 17
Balliol Cl. PO21: Aldw .8N 163
RH10: Craw .3L 11
BALLS CROSS .9B 40
Balls Cross Rd.
GU28: Balls C, Petw .5N 61
Ball Tree Cft. BN15: Somp .6N 149
Balmoral RH19: E Grin .4G 14
Balmoral Cl. BN16: Rust .1A 168
PO19: Chich .7E 140
PO21: Aldw .1G 180
Balmoral Ct. BN3: Hove .2J 153
BN11: Wor .2E 170
RH11: Craw .1D 28
Balmoral Way GU32: Peters .5F 54
BALSDEAN .8B 156
Balsdean Rd. BN2: W'dean .4L 155
Baltic Vw. BN2: Salt .3C 174
(off Suez Way)
Baltimore Ct. BN3: Hove .6L 153
Bamborough Cl. RH13: Southw .9L 45
Bamford Cl. BN2: Brig .3H 155
Bampfield St. BN41: Ports .5D 152
Bancroft Rd. RH10: Craw .7M 11
Banjo Rd. BN17: L'ton .5L 167
Bank, The RH10: Turn H .8H 13
Bank La. RH10: Craw .6F 10
Bank Pas. BN11: Wor .2H 171
(off Liverpool Rd.)
BN44: Stey .3A 130
Bank Pct. RH10: Craw .3J 11
Banks Cft. RH20: Storr .5K 107
Bankside BN1: Brig .9L 133
BN6: Hass .2A 114
PO18: Sing .8G 101
RH17: Bol .7E 70
Bankside Ct. BN1: Brig .9L 133
(off Bankside)
Banks Rd. BN8: N Cha .8E 74
RH10: Craw .6L 11
Bankview Cl. PO22: Bog R .8E 164
Bannerman Rd. GU32: Peters .5F 54
Bannings Va. BN2: Salt .4D 174
Bannister Gdns. RH20: Storr .5K 107
Bannister Way RH16: Hay H .3E 72
Banstead Cl. BN12: Gor S .4A 170
Baranscraig Av. BN1: Brig .7B 134
Barbary La. BN12: Fer .3K 169
Barber Cl. RH10: Craw .1L 29
Barclay Ho. BN2: Brig .6C 154
Barcombe Pl. BN1: Brig .9G 135
Barcombe Rd. BN1: Brig .1F 154
Barentin Way GU31: Peters .4G 54
Barfield Pk. BN15: Lan .7C 150
Barford Rd. PO19: Chich .8C 140
Barham Rd. GU32: Peters .6F 54
Barkdale RH15: Burg H .3E 94
Barker Cl. PO18: Fish .6K 139
Barkworth Way RH20: W Chil .9H 87
Bar La. RH13: Cops, Southw .5M 67
BARLAVINGTON .2M 103
Barlavington La. RH20: Sutt .5M 103
Barlavington Way GU29: Midh .3G 80
Barley Cl. BN10: Tels C .2H 175
PO21: Pag .1C 180
RH10: Craw .7F 10
Barleycroft BN6: Alb .1E 112
RH13: Cow .8H 69
Barley Dr. RH15: Burg H .4M 93
Barley Fld. Cotts. BN7: Rod .4K 157
Barley Ho. RH10: Craw .7F 10
(off Barley Cl.)
Barleymead RH6: Horl .1K 5
Barlow Rd. PO19: Chich .6A 140
RH11: Craw .9A 10
Barnard Gate RH16: Hay H .2F 72
Barn Cl. BN6: Alb .1E 112
BN13: Durr .6D 148
BN17: Wick .9L 145
PO10: Ems .5D 136
RH10: Craw .6M 11
RH11: Pease P .4D 28
Barn Cottage La. RH16: Hay H .4H 73
Barncroft Cl. PO20: Tang .4L 141
Barncroft Dr. RH16: Lind .2K 73
Barnden Ct. RH15: Burg H .7C 94
Barn End BN5: Henf .2J 111
Barnes Cl. PO20: Sel .5J 183
Barnes Ho. RH13: Hors .5H 45
(off The Avenue)
Barnes M. RH12: Hors .9M 25
Barnes Rd. BN41: Ports .5D 152
Barnes Wallis Av. RH13: Hors .4H 45
Barnett Cl. PO20: E'gate .5F 142
Barnett Rd. BN1: Brig .3C 154
Barnett's Fld. PO20: Westg .6E 142
Barnet Way BN3: Hove .2G 152
BN13: Durr .8B 148
Barn Feld PO22: Felp .8G 165
Barnfield BN7: Plump G .2M 115
RH6: Horl .3J 5
Barnfield Cl. PO10: S'brne .4L 137
Barnfield Cotts. BN18: Font .3H 143
Barnfield Dr. PO19: Chich .5D 140
Barnfield Gdns. BN2: Brig .7D 154
BN6: Ditch .4F 114
Barn Field Pl. RH19: E Grin .1G 14
Barnfield Rd. GU31: Peters .6J 55
RH10: Craw .5F 10
BARNHAM .7J 143
Barnham La. BN18: Walb .8K 143
PO22: Barn .8K 143
Barnham Rd.
PO20: Barn, E'gate .5G 142
PO22: Barn, E'gate .5G 142
Barnham Station (Rail) .8J 143
Barnhouse Cl. RH20: Pulb .6B 86
Barn Ho. La. RH20: Pulb .6B 86
Barn La. PO22: Shrip .3E 164
Barnmead RH16: Hay H .2E 72
Barn Mdw. RH17: Bal .1B 50
Barnplat Cotts. GU29: Midh .3F 58
Barn Ri. BN1: Brig .9M 133
PO22: Barn .8K 143
Barn Rd. PO20: E Witt .4K 177
Barns Farm La. RH20: Storr .8M 107
Barnsfold La. RH12: Rudg .5D 22
BARNS GREEN .8D 44
Barnside PO18: Bosh .6G 138
Barnside Av. RH15: Burg H .7D 94
Barnsite Cl. BN16: Rust .2A 168
Barnsite Gdns. BN16: Rust .2A 168
BARNSNAP .8L 27
Barnsnap Cl. RH12: Hors .5A 26
Barn Theatre, The .6A 152
Barn Wlk. PO20: E Witt .5K 177
Barnwood RH10: Craw .5L 11
Barons Cl. PO20: Westg .6E 142
Barons Ct. BN11: Wor .1G 171
RH15: Burg H .6C 94
Barons Mead PO21: Pag .3C 180
Barque Cl. BN17: L'ton .2N 167
Barrackfield Wlk. RH12: Hors .2M 45
Barrack La. PO21: Aldw .2F 180
Barrack Row BN18: Walb .4L 143
Barrack Yd. BN1: Brig .7F 172
Barrhill Av. BN1: Brig .7A 134
Barrington Cl. BN12: Gor S .2A 170
RH16: Lind .1H 73
Barrington Rd. BN12: Gor S .2A 170
(not continuous)
RH10: Craw .8F 10
RH13: Hors .9B 26
RH16: Lind .1G 73
Barrington Wood RH16: Lind .1G 73
Barrow Cl. BN1: Brig .3D 154
RH14: Bill .2H 65
Barrowfield RH17: Cuck .2A 72
Barrowfield Cl. BN3: Hove .2L 153
Barrowfield Dr. BN3: Hove .3L 153
Barrowfield Lodge BN3: Hove .3L 153
Barrow Hill BN1: Brig .3D 154
BN5: Henf .3J 111
Barry Cl. RH10: Craw .9G 10
Barry Dr. RH16: Hay H .7F 72
Barry Wlk. BN2: Brig .7D 154
Bartholomew Cl. GU27: Has .3M 17
Bartholomews BN1: Brig .8E 172 (8B 154)
Bartholomew Sq. BN1: Brig .9E 172
Bartholomew Way RH12: Hors .5D 26
Bartletts Cotts. BN14: Broadw .8H 149
(off Broadwater St. E.)
Barton Cl. BN13: W Tar .8E 148
PO21: Pag .2C 180
Barton Ct. BN16: Rust .3A 168
Barton Cres. RH19: E Grin .4G 15
Barton Rd. PO19: Chich .6A 140
PO22: Bers .5B 164
Bartons La. GU28: Petw .9N 61
Bartons Rd. PO9: Hav .9A 116
Barton Wlk. RH10: Craw .8K 11
Barton Way PO20: Brac .5M 177
Barttelot Rd. RH12: Hors .1A 46
Barwell Gro. PO10: Ems .2E 136
Barwick Cl. BN16: Rust .1A 168
Basement, The .6E 172
(off Robert St.)
Basepoint Bus. Cen. RH11: Craw .2F 10
Bashfords La. BN14: Broadw .9H 149
Bashford Way RH10: Craw .4M 11
Bashurst Copse RH13: Itch .2D 44
Bashurst Hill RH13: Itch .6B 44
Basildon Way RH11: Craw .9A 10
Basing Hill RH20: A'ton .9F 88
Basin Rd. PO19: Chich .8B 140
Basin Rd. Nth. BN41: Ports .7E 152
Basin Rd. Sth. BN41: Ports .7A 152
BN42: Ports, S'wck .7A 152
Baslow Cl. RH20: A'ton .2D 108
Bassells La. RH13: W Grin .3M 89
Bassett Rd. PO21: Bog R .1L 181
RH10: Craw .9M 11
Bastion Ho. PO19: Chich .7C 140
BATCHMERE .2C 178
Batchmere Rd. PO20: Bir, Earn .3C 178
Bateman Ct. RH10: Craw .9J 11
Batemans Cl. BN13: Durr .8N 147
Batemans Rd. BN2: W'dean .6M 155
Bates Rd. BN1: Brig .3A 154
Bath Ct. BN3: Hove .8K 153
(off King's Esplanade)
Bath Pl. BN11: Wor .3H 171
Bath Rd. BN11: Wor .3E 170
PO10: Ems .6F 136
Bath St. BN1: Brig .4C 172 (6A 154)
Battens Way PO9: Hav .1A 136
Batts Dr. BN5: Henf .2G 111
Batts La. RH20: Pulb .7E 86
Batts Pond La. BN5: Henf .2G 111
Batworthpark Ho. BN18: Cross .4L 145
Bavant Rd. BN1: Brig .3N 153
Bax Cl. RH20: Coot .6G 106
Baxendale Rd. PO19: Chich .5D 140
Baxter Cl. RH10: Craw .8K 11
Baxters La. RH17: Chel C .4J 53
Baxter St. BN2: Brig .6D 154
Bay Bri. Cres. PO22: Felp .5J 165
Baybridge Rd. PO9: Hav .9B 116
Baycombe La. BN18: Slind .9K 123
Bayfield Rd. RH6: Horl .1G 5
Bayford Rd. BN17: L'ton .4K 167
Bayhams Fld. RH19: Sharp .5N 31
Bayhorne La. RH6: Horl .4L 5
Bayley Rd. PO20: Tang .4L 141
Baylis Cres. RH15: Burg H .4M 93
Baylis Wlk. RH11: Craw .2D 28
BAYNARDS .1F 22
Baynards Rd. RH12: Rudg .1E 22
Bayton Ct. PO19: Chich .7D 140
Bay Tree Cl. BN43: Shor S .4M 151
Baytree Cl. PO19: Chich .2B 140
Baytree Ct. BN5: Henf .2J 111
Bay Tree Gdn. BN16: E Pres .3E 168
Bay Trees Cl. BN16: E Pres .3E 168
Bayview Rd. BN10: Peace .7L 175
Bay Wlk. PO21: Aldw .3E 180
Baywood Gdns. BN2: W'dean .5K 155
Bazehill Rd. BN2: Rott .2N 173
Beach Cl. PO21: Aldw .2E 180
Beach Ct. BN17: L'ton .4L 167
(off Irvine Rd.)
BN43: Shor B .7K 151
Beach Cres. BN17: L'ton .5L 167
Beachcroft Pl. BN15: S Lan .9B 150
Beaches, The BN17: Climp .3D 166
Beach Gdns. PO20: Sel .5H 183
(not continuous)
Beach Grn. BN43: Shor B .7G 150
Beach House Pk. .2J 171
Beach Pde. BN11: Wor .3J 171
Beach Rd. BN17: L'ton .3K 167
BN43: Shor B .8H 151
PO10: Ems .5E 136
PO20: Sel .2K 183
(not continuous)
PO21: Pag .4C 180
Beachside Cl. BN12: Gor S .3C 170
Beachy Rd. RH11: Craw .2C 28
Beacon, The RH19: W Hoa .4M 31
Beacon Cl. BN1: Brig .3B 154
Beacon Ct. BN2: O'dean .9L 155
RH13: Hors .7D 26
Beacon Dr. PO20: Sel .4J 183
Beacon Hill BN2: O'dean .1M 173
RH20: Bury, Cold .3G 104
Beacon Hill (Local Nature Reserve) .2M 173
Beacon Ho. BN3: Hove .6F 152
(off Erroll Rd.)
Beaconhurst BN6: Key .4C 114
Beacon Mill .3N 173
Beacon Ri. RH19: E Grin .1H 15
Beacon Rd. BN6: Ditch .5E 114
Beaconsfield Cl. PO22: Midd S .7M 165
RH15: Burg H .5A 94
Beaconsfield Pde. BN1: Brig .1E 172
Beaconsfield Rd. BN1: Brig .1E 172 (5B 154)
BN17: Wick .1K 167
BN41: Ports .5D 152
RH17: Chel G .1J 53
Beaconsfield Vs. BN1: Brig .1D 172 (3A 154)
Beacon Sq. PO10: Ems .5E 136
Beaconsville Ct. BN1: Brig .4A 154
Beacon Way BN17: L'ton .2N 167
Beagle Dr. BN18: Ford .2B 166
Beal Cres. BN1: Brig .3C 154
Beale Ct. RH11: Craw .9C 10
Beale St. RH15: Burg H .7N 93
Bear Rd. BN2: Brig .5D 154
Bearsden Way RH12: Broadb H .8H 25
Beatty Av. BN1: Brig .7E 134
Beatty Rd. PO21: Bog R .8D 164
Beaufield Cl. PO20: Sel .4H 183
Beaufield Ga. GU27: Has .4M 17
Beaufort Ter. BN2: Brig .7D 154
Beau Ho. BN1: Brig .4C 172
(off Bath St.)
Beaumont Cl. RH11: Ifield .7A 10
Beaumont Ct. BN16: E Pres .2E 168
Beaumont Pk. BN17: L'ton .4N 167
Beaumont Rd. BN14: Broadw .8H 149
Beaver Cl. PO19: Fish .7L 139
RH12: Hors .5B 26
Beccles Rd. BN11: Wor .2F 170
Beckers, The RH10: Craw D .3J 13
Becket Rd. BN14: Wor .1E 170
Beckett La. RH11: Craw .3F 10
Beckett Way RH19: E Grin .4F 14
Beckford Way RH10: Craw .1K 29
Beckham La. GU32: Peters .5D 54
Beckley Cl. BN2: Brig .8F 154
Beckworth Cl. BN13: Durr .8N 147
RH16: Lind .3H 73
Beckworth La. RH16: Lind .3H 73
Bedale Cl. RH11: Craw .8E 10
Bedales Hill RH16: Hay H .4L 73
Bedelands Cl. RH15: Burg H .3C 94
Bedelands Farm Local Nature Reserve .2C 94
Bedenscroft PO21: Aldw .9B 164
Bedford Av. PO21: Bers .6B 164
Bedford Cl. PO9: Warbl .5B 136
Bedford Ct. BN1: Brig .7A 172
Bedford Pl. BN1: Brig .7A 172 (8N 153)
Bedford Rd. GU32: Peters .5D 54
RH13: Hors .1A 46
Bedford Row BN11: Wor .2J 171
Bedford Sq. BN1: Brig .8A 172 (8N 153)
RH13: Part G .5C 90
Bedford St. BN2: Brig .9D 154
PO21: Bog R .9E 164
Bedford Towers BN1: Brig .8A 172
BEDHAM .8H 63
Bedham La. RH20: Fitt .4G 84
Bedhampton Way PO9: Hav .2A 136
BEDLAM STREET .4J 113
Beech Av. PO19: Chich .7A 140
PO20: Brac .5M 177
Beech Cl. BN14: Fin .7C 128
BN41: Ports .2B 152
PO20: Westg .6E 142
PO21: Pag .9H 163
RH19: E Grin .2D 14
Beech Ct. RH19: E Grin .2D 14
Beechers Rd. BN41: Ports .2G 152
Beeches, The BN1: Brig .2M 153
Beeches Av. BN14: Char D .6H 149
Beeches Cres. RH10: Craw .8G 10
Beeches La. RH19: Ash W .6K 15
Beechey Cl. RH10: Copt .1C 12
Beechey Way RH10: Copt .1C 12
Beechfield Pk. PO20: Ald .8D 142
Beechfields RH19: E Grin .1F 14
Beech Gdns. BN14: Wor .9G 148
RH10: Craw D .5H 13
Beech Gro. BN2: Brig .2F 154
BN15: S Lan .8D 150
GU29: Midh .2G 81
PO11: Hay I .8B 158
RH20: Storr .5L 107
Beech Hill RH16: Hay H .5J 73
Beech Holme RH10: Craw D .4J 13
Beech Ho. RH10: Craw .2F 10
Beech Hurst Cl. RH16: Hay H .5D 72
Beech Hurst Gdns. .5D 72
Beechings BN5: Henf .2G 110
Beeching Way RH19: E Grin .3E 14
Beechlands Cl. BN16: E Pres .3F 168
Beechlands Ct. BN16: E Pres .3F 168
Beech Rd. BN14: Fin .7C 128
GU27: Has .4M 17
RH12: Hors .6E 26
Beechside RH10: Craw .7G 10
Beech Tree Cl. RH10: Craw .5F 10
Beech Vw. BN16: Ang .6F 146
Beech Way BN16: Ang .9F 146
Beechwood BN1: Brig .2N 153
BN5: Small D .8J 111
RH13: Southw .1K 67
Beechwood Av. BN1: Brig .1A 154
BN13: Durr .6D 148
Beechwood Cl. BN1: Brig .1A 154
Beechwood La. GU28: Dunc, Graff .2G 103
Beechwoods RH15: Burg H .7B 94
Beechworth Rd. PO9: Hav .4A 136
Beeding Av. BN3: Hove .2H 153
Beeding Cl. BN15: Somp .5A 150
PO22: Bers .5F 164
RH12: Hors .6D 26
Beeding Ct. BN1: Brig .9L 133
(off Mill Ri.)
BN43: Shor S .5L 151
Beedingwood Dr. RH12: Colg .5H 27
Beehive Cl. BN12: Fer .3L 169
Beehive La. BN12: Fer .3K 169
Beehive Ring Rd. RH6: Craw .8K 5
Bee Rd. BN10: Peace .4J 175
Beggarman's La. RH13: Southw .6M 67
BEGGARS BUSH .2L 149

Beggar's La.—Blytons, The

Beggar's La. PO20: Sidle 4K 179
Behenna Cl. RH11: Craw 7A 10
Belbourne Ct. *BN1: Brig* 6E 172
(off Tichbourne St.)
Belfast St. BN3: Hove 6K 153
Belgrave Cres. PO19: Chich 1B 162
Belgrave Pl. BN2: Brig 9E 154
Belgrave St. BN2: Brig 7C 154
Belgravia Ct. *RH6: Horl* 2K 5
(off St Georges Cl.)
Belinus Dr. RH14: Bill 1H 65
Bellair Ho. PO9: Hav 4A 136
Bellair Rd. PO9: Hav 4A 136
Bellamy Rd. RH10: Craw 1L 29
Bell Centre, The RH10: Craw 2H 11
Bell Cl. PO19: Chich 5B 140
RH20: Pulb 6A 86
Bell Ct. PO18: Nutb 6M 137
PO21: Aldw 1E 180
Bell Davies Rd. BN17: L'ton 2M 167
Belle Meade Cl. PO20: Westg 8E 142
Belle Vue Cotts. BN2: Brig 5G 154
Belle Vue Ct. BN2: Brig 8E 154
Bellevue Ct. BN1: Brig 4A 154
Belle Vue Gdns. BN2: Brig 8D 154
Bellevue La. PO10: Ems 3F 136
Bell Hammer RH19: E Grin 4E 14
BELL HILL 4E 54
Bell Hill GU32: Peters 3E 54
Bell Hill Ridge GU32: Peters 4E 54
Bell Holiday Home Park, The PO20: Bir 1A 178
Bellingham Cres. BN3: Hove 5F 152
Bell La. GU29: Bep, C'ing 7C 80
PO20: Earn, Bir, E Witt 1A 178
TN22: Nut 7N 53
Bell Mead BN3: Hove 6M 153
Belloc Cl. RH10: Craw 5K 11
Belloc Ct. RH13: Hors 8D 26
Belloc Rd. BN17: Wick 1J 167
Bell Rd. GU27: Has 7J 17
RH12: Warnh 3K 25
Bellscroft Cl. BN17: L'ton 2M 167
Bell Twr. Ind. Est. BN2: Brig 9G 154
Bell Va. La. GU27: Has 7K 17
Bellview Ct. BN13: W Tar 8E 148
Bellview Rd. BN13: W Tar 8E 148
Belmaine Ct. BN11: Wor 3G 171
Belmer Ct. BN11: Wor 3E 170
Belmont BN1: Brig 3B 172 (6N 153)
Belmont Cl. BN6: Hass 2N 113
Belmont Ct. BN1: Brig 3C 172
Belmont La. BN6: Hass 3L 113
Belmont St. BN1: Brig 4F 172 (6B 154)
PO21: Bog R 1M 181
Belmont Ter. BN18: Yap 2A 166
Belmont Wlk. BN13: Durr 8B 148
Belsize Cl. BN11: Wor 1E 170
Belsize Rd. BN11: Wor 1F 170
Beltane Cl. BN16: E Pres 4F 168
Belton Cl. BN2: Brig 2G 172
Belton Rd. BN2: Brig 2G 172 (5C 154)
Belvedere BN1: Brig 2B 172 (5N 153)
Belvedere Av. BN15: Lan 7A 150
Belvedere Ct. RH10: Craw 5K 11
Belvedere Pl. GU32: Peters 5F 54
Belvedere Ter. BN1: Brig 6A 172
Belvedere Wlk. RH16: Hay H 6D 72
Belyngham Cres. BN17: Wick 2J 167
Bembridge St. BN2: Brig 5D 154
Benbow Cl. BN43: Shor B 7J 151
Benchfield Cl. RH19: E Grin 4H 15
Benedict Cl. BN11: Wor 1M 171
Benedict Dr. BN11: Wor 1L 171
Benett Av. BN3: Hove 3K 153
Benett Dr. BN3: Hove 3K 153
Benfield Cl. BN41: Ports 4E 152
Benfield Ct. BN41: Ports 5E 152
Benfield Cres. BN41: Ports 4E 152
Benfield Hill Local Nature Reserve 1E 152
Benfield Valley Golf Course 2E 152
Benfield Way BN41: Ports 5E 152
Bengairn Av. BN1: Brig 7B 134
Benham Ct. *BN3: Hove* 8K 153
(off King's Esplanade)
Benhams Dr. RH6: Horl 1J 5
Benizi Ct. *PO21: Bog R* 9E 164
(off Clarence Rd.)
Benjamin Lodge *RH15: Burg H* 5E 94
(off Kings Way)
Benjamin Rd. RH10: Craw 8M 11
Benland Cotts. RH12: Warnh 1H 25
Bennett Cl. RH10: Craw 1K 29
Bennett Rd. BN2: Brig 9F 154
Bennetts RH17: Bol 6E 70
Bennetts Cl. PO20: W Witt 4K 177
Bennetts Ri. RH16: Hay H 7G 72
Bennetts Rd. RH13: Hors 1B 46
Bennetts Ter. *GU29: Midh* 1G 81
(off Bepton Rd.)
Bens Acre RH13: Hors 9D 26
Benson Ct. BN3: Hove 6G 152
Benson Rd. BN5: Henf 2J 111
Bensons La. RH12: Fay 2F 26
Bentham Rd. BN2: Brig 6D 154
Bentley Cl. BN16: Ang 9F 146
Bentley Ct. PO9: Hav 9B 116
Bentons La. RH13: Dial P 5H 89
Bentswood Cres. RH16: Hay H 4G 73
Bentswood Rd. RH16: Hay H 4G 72
Ben Turner Ind. Est. PO19: Chich 7F 140
BEPTON 7C 80
Bepton Cl. GU29: Midh 2F 80
BEPTON COMMON 3E 80
Bepton Down GU31: Peters 6G 54
Bepton Rd. GU29: Bep, Midh 7C 80
Berberis Ct. BN43: Shor S 4L 151
Beresford Ct. BN3: Hove 6M 153
Beresford Ho. BN10: Peace 3J 175
Beresford La. BN8: N Cha, Plump G 7N 95
Beresford Rd. BN2: Brig 8E 154
Bereweeke Rd. PO22: Felp 8H 165
Bergamot Cres. BN43: Shor S 4M 151
Berghestede Rd. PO22: Bers 6D 164
Berkeley Cl. RH11: Craw 1A 28
Berkeley Ct. BN3: Hove 4A 172
BN12: Fer 2K 169
(off Ferringham La.)
PO21: Bog R 1M 181
(off The Esplanade)
Berkeley M. PO19: Chich 6D 140
Berkeley Sq. BN11: Wor 2E 170
PO9: Warbl 4B 136
Berkshire Ct. BN12: Gor S 1N 169
Bermuda Ct. BN17: L'ton 2N 167
Bernard Pl. BN2: Brig 6D 154
Bernard Powell Ho. PO9: Hav 4A 136
Bernard Rd. BN2: Brig 6D 154
BN11: Wor 3D 170
BN18: Arun 3F 144
Bernard Sunley Outdoor Education Centre, The 6K 33
Berrall Way RH14: Bill 2G 65
Berri Ct. BN18: Yap 1N 165
Berriedale Av. BN3: Hove 7G 153
Berriedale Cl. BN15: Somp 6N 149
Berriedale Dr. BN15: Somp 6N 149
Berriedale Ho. BN3: Hove 7G 153
Berry Barn La. PO20: W Witt 3F 176
Berry Cl. BN10: Tels C 3G 175
RH15: Burg H 3B 94
Berry Ct. PO19: Fish 5L 139
Berryfields PO21: Bers 4B 164
Berryfields Ct. PO21: Bers 4B 164
Berrylands GU33: Liss 3A 34
Berrylands Farm BN6: Say C 7F 92
Berry La. BN17: L'ton 4M 167
PO22: Bers 4B 164
RH17: Ard 3K 51
Berrymeade Wlk. RH11: Ifield 7A 10
Berrymill Cl. PO21: Bog R 8E 164
Berstead Wlk. RH11: Craw 9B 10
Bersted Grn. Ct. PO22: Bers 6D 164
Bersted M. PO22: Bog R 7E 164
Bersted St. PO22: Bog R 7D 164
(not continuous)
Berwick Rd. BN2: Salt 1D 174
Bessborough Ter. BN15: Lan 9A 150
Besson Ho. *BN41: Ports* 6E 152
(off Gordon Cl.)
Betchley Cl. RH19: E Grin 1E 14
Betchworth Works RH6: Charlw 7A 4
Bethune Cl. RH10: Worth 7M 11
Bethune Rd. RH13: Hors 1B 46
Bethwines Cl. PO18: Fish 6K 139
Betts Way RH10: Craw 2F 10
Beulah Ct. RH6: Horl 2J 5
Bevan Ct. RH11: Craw 2D 28
BEVENDEAN 4H 155
Bevendean Av. BN2: Salt 3D 174
Bevendean Cres. BN2: Brig 3F 154
Bevendean Down Local Nature Reserve 3F 154
Bevendean Rd. BN2: Brig 5E 154
Beverley Cl. BN18: Yap 1A 166
PO20: Sel 3K 183
Beverley Ct. BN3: Hove 6F 152
BN11: Wor 3F 170
Beverley Gdns. BN16: Rust 2A 168
Beverley Ho. BN15: S Lan 9B 150
Beverley M. RH10: Craw 7J 11
BEWBUSH 9B 10
Bewbush Cen. 9A 10
Bewbush Dr. RH11: Craw 9A 10
Bewbush Mnr. Rdbt. RH11: Craw 1A 28
Bewbush Pl. RH11: Craw 9A 10
Bewbush Water Garden 8N 9
Bewick Gdns. PO19: Chich 5D 140
Bewley Rd. BN16: Ang 7E 146
Bexhill Rd. BN2: W'dean 4L 155
Bex La. GU29: C'ing, Hey 6G 80
BEXLEYHILL 2N 59
Bickley Ct. RH11: Craw 9C 10
Bickleys Ct. PO21: Bog R 1K 181
Biddulph M. GU28: Dunc 8L 83
Biggin Cl. RH11: Craw 8E 10
BIGNOR 5A 104
Bignor Cl. BN16: Rust 2C 168
RH12: Hors 5D 26
Bignor La. RH20: Big, Bury 6B 104
BIGNOR PARK 3C 104
Bignor Pk. Rd. RH20: Bury 3D 104
Bignor Roman Villa 5B 104
Bigwood Av. BN3: Hove 5M 153
Bilberry Cl. RH11: Craw 9D 10
Bilbets *RH12: Hors* 8N 25
(off North Pde.)
Billam Ho. *BN2: Brig* 7C 154
(off Belgrave St.)
Billam Ter. *BN2: Brig* 7C 154
(off Belgrave St.)
BILLINGSHURST 9J 43
Billingshurst Leisure Cen. 2H 65
Billingshurst Rd. RH12: Broadb H 8G 24
RH13: Cool 6N 65
RH14: Cool 6N 65
RH14: Wisb 1B 64
RH20: A'ton 7C 88
Billingshurst Rd. Rdbt. RH20: A'ton 1E 108
Billingshurst Station (Rail) 2J 65
Billington Ct. RH19: E Grin 2E 14
Billington Pl. RH15: Burg H 5M 93
Billinton Dr. RH10: Craw 6K 11
Billinton Way BN1: Brig 4E 172 (6B 154)
Billy Lawn Av. PO9: Hav 9A 116
BILSHAM 4N 165
Bilsham Ct. BN18: Yap 2N 165
Bilsham La. BN18: Bils 3L 165
Bilsham Rd. BN18: Bils, Yap 3N 165
BINDERTON 4N 119
Binderton La. PO18: Chil, W Dean 2L 119
BINES GREEN 9B 90
Bines Rd. RH13: Part G 5C 90
Binney Ct. RH10: Craw 3N 11
Binstead Cl. RH11: Craw 4D 10
BINSTED 4A 144
Binsted Av. PO22: Felp 7H 165
Binsted Cl. BN16: Rust 4A 168
Binsted La. BN18: Arun, Bins, Tort 3N 143
Biology Rd. BN1: Falm 8J 135
Birch Av. RH17: Hay H 6H 73
Birch Cl. BN15: Lan 9A 150
BN16: Ang 9E 146
BN18: Arun 4E 144
GU33: Liss 3C 34
PO21: Aldw 9M 163
RH10: Craw D 4K 13
RH17: Hay H 6J 73
Birch Ct. BN42: S'wck 4C 152
Birch Dr. RH14: Bill 2J 65
Birch End RH20: W Chil 9J 87
Birchen La. RH16: Hay H 1F 72
Birches, The RH10: Craw 4J 11
RH13: Mann H 3F 46
RH20: W Chil 8H 87
Birches Cl. BN13: Durr 8A 148
PO20: Sel 3G 183
Birches Ind. Est. RH19: E Grin 1A 14
Birches Rd. RH12: Hors 6E 26
Birchfield Est. RH6: Charlw 9A 4
BIRCH GROVE 9G 32
Birch Gro. RH20: W Chil 2J 107
Birch Gro. Cres. BN1: Brig 9B 134
Birchgrove La. RH17: Hors K 1E 52
Birch Gro. Rd. RH17: Hors K 5D 52
Birch Ho. RH19: E Grin 2C 14
Birch Lea RH10: Craw 3J 11
Birch Lodge BN2: Brig 2G 172
Birch Tree Cl. PO10: Ems 1F 136
Birch Tree Ct. BN11: Wor 1J 171
GU27: Has 7E 16
Birch Tree Dr. PO10: Ems 1F 136
Birch Tree Gdns. RH19: E Grin 1B 14
Birch Tree La. RH20: W Chil 1K 107
Birch Wlk. RH15: Ditch 5G 94
Birch Way BN6: Key 2A 114
RH17: Hay H 7H 73
RH20: Storr 4N 107
Birchwood Cl. RH6: Horl 1K 5
RH10: Craw 9L 11
RH14: Ifol 8K 21
Birchwood Gro. Rd. RH15: Burg H 7C 94
BIRDHAM 7H 161
Birdham Bus. Pk. PO20: Bir 6L 161
Birdham Cl. PO21: Bers 7A 164
RH11: Craw 4D 10
Birdham Pl. BN2: Brig 2F 154
Birdham Rd. BN2: Brig 2F 154
PO19: Apul, Chich 7K 161
PO20: Bir, Donn, Apul 7K 161
Birkdale Cl. BN13: Durr 7B 148
Birkdale Dr. RH11: Ifield 7N 9
Birkdale Rd. BN13: Durr 7B 148
Birklands RH20: Storr 6H 107
Birling Cl. BN2: Brig 4E 154
Birthday Ho. GU29: Ease 7J 59
Biscay Cl. BN17: L'ton 2A 168
Bisham Cl. RH10: Craw 8M 11
Bishop La. BN5: Henf 2H 111
Bishop Luffa Cl. PO19: Chich 6N 139
Bishopric RH12: Hors 9M 25
Bishopric Ct. RH12: Hors 9M 25
Bishops Cl. BN6: Hurst 9J 93
BN14: W Tar 9E 148
BN15: Lan 7C 150
GU27: Fern 4J 37
PO21: Pag 3C 180
Bishops Ct. RH12: Hors 1N 45
Bishops Courtyard *PO19: Chich* 7D 140
(off The Hornet)
Bishopsfield RH14: Bill 5L 43
Bishopsgate Wlk. PO19: Chich 6D 140
Bishops Ho. RH20: Storr 7J 107
Bishop's Palace Garden 7B 140
Bishops Rd. BN3: Hove 4L 153
PO20: Tang 3L 141
Bishopstone Dr. BN2: Salt 2B 174
Bishopstone La. BN6: God G 3J 93
RH17: Ans, God G 7J 71
Bishopstone Wlk. RH11: Craw 2E 28
Bishops Wlk. BN1: Brig 7C 172 (8A 154)
Bitmead Cl. RH11: Ifield 7A 10
Bittern Cl. RH11: Ifield 7N 9
Blackberry Copse PO22: Felp 6J 165
Blackberry La. PO19: Chich 7E 140
PO20: Sel 3G 183
Blackberry Rd. GU28: Petw 1N 83
Blackberry Wood Caravan Pk. BN6: Streat 5K 115
Blackbird Cl. RH15: Burg H 5M 93
Blackbird Hill RH10: Turn H 7K 13
Blackbird Way PO20: Sel 2J 183
Black Boy Ct. PO18: Fish 7K 139
Blackboy La. PO18: Fish 7K 139
Blackbridge Ct. RH12: Hors 9M 25
Blackbridge La. RH12: Hors 1L 45
Blackbrook La. BN8: N Cha, Shef P 7E 74
RH17: Scay H, Shef P 7E 74
Blackcap Cl. PO9: Row C 5A 116
RH11: Craw 8E 10
BLACK CORNER 8M 5
Black Dog Wlk. RH10: Craw 4G 10
BLACKDOWN 4B 38
Black Down 1A 38
Blackdown BN2: Brig 6G 154
Blackdown Cl. RH11: Craw 8F 10
Blackdown Rd. BN13: Durr 6D 148
Blackett Rd. RH10: Craw 7L 11
Blackfold Rd. RH10: Craw 7J 11
Blackgate La. BN5: Henf 3H 111
RH20: Pulb 8B 64
Blackheath RH10: Craw 4M 11
Black Hill RH16: Lind 2H 73
Black Horse Caravan Pk. *PO20: Sel* 2G 182
(off Mill La.)
Blackhorse Way RH12: Hors 9M 25
Blackhouse Farm Ind. Est. RH13: Colg 6N 27
Blackhouse La. GU28: Petw 7D 62
PO20: Itchen 7C 160
RH15: Burg H 4C 94
Blackhouse Rd. RH13: Colg 5M 27
Blacklands Cres. RH18: F Row 1M 33
Black Lion La. BN1: Brig 8D 172 (8A 154)
Black Lion St.
BN1: Brig 9E 172 (9B 154)
Blackman St. BN1: Brig 5E 172 (7B 154)
Blackman Way PO20: Huns 3C 162
Blackmill La. PO18: Eart, Nort 2D 142
Blackmoor Wlk. PO9: Hav 9B 116
Blackmore Ct. BN1: Brig 4E 172
Blackmores RH17: Wivel 3H 95
Blackpatch Gro. BN43: Shor S 4J 151
BLACK ROCK 8K 173
Blacksmiths Cl. RH20: A'ton 3E 108
Blacksmiths Cres.
BN15: Somp 7M 149
Blacksmiths M. *BN11: Wor* 3G 171
(off Montague St.)
Blacksmith Way PO22: Felp 6J 165
BLACKSTONE 2A 112
Blackstone La. BN5: W'cote 5N 111
(not continuous)
BN6: Alb 9B 92
Blackstone Ri. BN5: W'cote 2A 112
Blackstone St. BN5: W'cote 2N 111
Blackstone Way RH15: Burg H 3B 94
Black Swan Cl. RH11: Pease P 4D 28
Blackthorn Av. PO22: Felp 6K 165
Blackthorn Cl. BN1: Brig 2M 153
BN41: Ports 3D 152
RH11: Craw 4E 10
RH13: Hors 9D 26
Blackthorn Dr. PO11: Hay I 9C 158
Blackthorn Rd. PO11: Hay I 9C 158
Blackthorns BN6: Hurst 9H 93
RH16: Lind 2H 73
Blackthorns, The RH15: Burg H 3C 94
Blackthorns Cl. RH16: Lind 3H 73
Blackwater La. RH10: Craw 7L 11
BLACKWELL 2E 14
Blackwell Ct. PO21: Bers 5B 164
Blackwell Farm Rd. RH19: E Grin 1F 14
Blackwell Hollow RH19: E Grin 2F 14
Blackwell Rd. RH19: E Grin 2F 14
Bladon Cl. PO9: Hav 2C 136
Blake Cl. RH10: Craw 1H 29
Blake Ct. *BN2: Brig* 5G 172
(off Richmond Pl.)
BLAKEHURST 3A 146
Blakehurst La. BN18: Poling, W'camp 3M 145
Blakehurst Way BN17: L'ton 2K 167
Blakemyle PO21: Aldw 1H 181
Blakeney Av. BN10: Peace 6N 175
Blakeney Cl. PO19: Fish 7L 139
Blaker St. BN2: Brig 8C 154
Blakes Farm Rd. RH13: Southw 5L 45
Blakes Rd. PO22: Felp 8H 165
Blakes Vw. PO22: Felp 8G 165
Blakiston Cl. RH20: A'ton 2D 108
Blanches Rd. RH13: Part G 5D 90
Blanches Wlk. RH13: Part G 5D 90
Blatchen, The BN17: L'ton 4M 167
Blatchford Cl. RH13: Hors 8C 26
Blatchford Rd. RH13: Hors 8C 26
Blatchington Rd. BN3: Hove 6J 153
Bleaches Ct. PO18: Mid L 7A 120
Blenheim Av. BN13: Durr 7C 148
Blenheim Cl. BN16: Rust 1A 168
RH10: Craw 3M 11
RH19: E Grin 1G 15
Blenheim Ct. *BN3: Hove* 7J 153
(off New Church Rd.)
BN13: High S 5B 148
PO21: Aldw 8N 163
Blenheim Dr. BN16: Rust 1A 168
Blenheim Flds. RH18: F Row 9L 15
Blenheim Gdns. PO9: Hav 3B 136
PO19: Chich 7E 140
Blenheim M. RH16: Hay H 7G 72
Blenheim Pl. BN1: Brig 6F 172 (7B 154)
Blenheim Rd. BN15: Lan 9A 150
BN18: Yap 2N 165
RH12: Hors 6A 26
Blessing Lodge *BN43: Shor B* 7L 151
(off Britannia Av.)
Bletchley Ct. BN1: Brig 1F 172 (5B 154)
Bligh Cl. RH10: Craw 8H 11
Blind La. GU28: Eber 7L 39
Blindley Rd. RH10: Craw 3M 11
Blissford Cl. PO9: Hav 8B 116
Blomfield Dr. PO19: Chich 4C 140
Blondell Dr. PO21: Aldw 9M 163
Bloomsbury Pl. BN2: Brig 9D 154
Bloomsbury St. BN2: Brig 9D 154
Bloor Cl. RH12: Hors 4A 26
Blount Av. RH19: E Grin 3C 14
Bluebell Bus. Est. TN22: Shef P 5G 74
Bluebell Cl. RH11: Craw 9D 10
RH12: Hors 6B 26
RH16: Hay H 5G 72
RH19: E Grin 3B 14
Bluebell Dr. BN17: L'ton 1N 167
Bluebell Hill RH13: Sharp 5N 31
Bluebell Railway
East Grinstead Station 3D 14
Horsted Keynes Station 3A 52
Kingscote Station 8N 13
Sheffield Park Station 5G 75
Bluebell Railway Mus. 5G 75
Bluebell Way RH15: Burg H 4M 93
Blueberry Hill RH20: Storr 6N 107
Bluebird Cl. BN43: Shor B 7L 151
Bluebird Dr. BN3: Hove 7J 153
Blue Cedars Cl. BN16: Ang 9D 146
Bluecoat Pond RH13: Hors 4H 45
Bluecoat Sports Health & Fitness Club 4H 45
Blundell Av. RH6: Horl 1H 5
Blunden Dr. RH17: Cuck 1A 72
Blunden's Ride BN13: Clap 3N 147
Blunts & Paiges Wood Local Nature Reserve 3C 72
Blunts Way RH12: Hors 8N 25
Blunts Wood Cres. RH16: Hay H 3C 72
Blunts Wood Rd. RH16: Hay H 3C 72
Blytons, The RH19: E Grin 3B 14

Boardwalk—Bristol Ct.

Boardwalk BN2: Brig 8K 173
PO19: Chich 6C 140
(off Northgate)
Boar La. RH13: Ship 8G 66
Boatyard, The BN2: Brig 8L 173
Bob La. RH17: Twine 2N 91
Boddingtons La. BN6: Ditch 4D 114
(not continuous)
Boderton M. GU28: Dunc 9L 83
Bodiam Av. BN2: Brig 4J 155
BN12: Gor S 4N 169
(Amberley Dr.)
BN12: Gor S 2N 169
(Fernhurst Dr.)
Bodiam Cl. BN2: Brig 3J 155
RH10: Craw 6L 11
RH13: Southw 8L 45
Bodiam Ct. RH16: Hay H 4F 72
Bodiham Ho. BN3: Hove 6M 153
(off Davigdor Rd.)
Bodmin Cl. BN13: Durr 5B 148
Bodmin Rd. BN13: Durr 5B 148
Bognor Pier 1M 181
BOGNOR REGIS 9E 164
Bognor Regis Caravan Club Site
PO22: Bers 5E 164
Bognor Regis Golf Course 6H 165
Bognor Regis Mus. 1M 181
(off Little High St.)
Bognor Regis Retail Pk. PO22: Bers 5E 164
Bognor Regis Station (Rail) 9D 164
Bognor Regis Town FC 9B 164
Bognor Regis Wireless Mus. 1M 181
(off Little High St.)
Bognor Rd. PO19: Chich 7E 140
PO20: Oving 8G 140
RH12: Oak, Warnh, Broadb H, R'hook 7G 7
Bognor Rd. Rdbt.
PO19: Chich, Oving, Runc 8F 140
Boiler Ho. Hill BN1: Falm 7J 135
Bolding Way RH16: Hay H 7E 72
Boleyn Cl. RH10: Craw 9M 11
Boleyn Dr. PO21: Pag 2D 180
Bolinge Hill GU31: Buri 1D 76
BOLNEY 6E 70
Bolney Av. BN10: Peace 6J 175
(not continuous)
Bolney Chapel Rd. RH17: Bol, Twine 9C 70
Bolney Ct. RH11: Craw 9B 10
Bolney Grange Bus. Pk. RH17: Bol 2H 93
Bolney Rd. BN2: Brig 1G 154
RH13: Cow 8H 69
RH17: Ans, Bol 8F 70
Bolnore Farm La. RH16: Hay H 5C 72
Bolnore Rd. RH16: Hay H 5D 72
BOLNORE VILLAGE 6D 72
Bolnore Woods Local Nature Reserve 7E 72
Bolsover Rd. BN3: Hove 6G 153
BN13: Wor 1C 170
Bolton Rd. RH10: Craw 2K 29
Boltro Rd. RH16: Hay H 4E 72
Bonaventure BN43: Shor B 7L 151
(off Britannia Av.)
Bonchurch Rd. BN2: Brig 5D 154
Bond St. BN1: Brig 7E 172 (8B 154)
BN18: Arun 2G 145
Bond St. Cotts. BN1: Brig 7E 172
Bond St. Laine BN1: Brig 7E 172
Bond St. Row BN1: Brig 7E 172
Bones La. GU31: Buri 3D 76
Bonfire Hill RH13: Southw 8H 45
Bonfire La. RH17: Hors K 6C 52
Bonham Rd. PO21: Bers 5A 164
Bonnar Cl. PO20: Sel 4G 183
Bonnar Rd. PO20: Sel 4H 183
Bonnetts La. RH11: Ifield 2C 10
Bonny Wood Rd. BN6: Hass 4N 113
Bookers Cl. PO22: Bog R 7D 164
Bookers La. PO20: Earn 3N 177
Bookers Vineyard 6D 70
Booth Museum of Natural History
1A 172 (5N 153)
Booth Rd. RH11: Craw 9A 10
Booth Way RH13: Hors 8B 26
Borage Cl. RH11: Craw 9C 10
BORDE HILL 9B 50
Borde Hill Gdns. 9D 50
Borde Hill La. RH16: Hay H 4D 50
RH17: Bal, Hay H 4D 50
BORDEN 3J 57
Borden La. GU30: Mill 3J 57
Border Chase RH10: Copt 2B 12
Border Cl. GU33: Hill B 9A 34
Border Ct. RH19: E Grin 1F 14
Border End GU27: Has 5F 16
Border Rd. GU27: Has 5F 16
Borers Arms Rd. RH10: Copt 1C 12
Borers Cl. RH10: Copt 1D 12
Borers Yd. Ind. Est. RH10: Copt 1D 12
Borough, The GU32: Peters 6E 54
(off Borough Hill)
Borough Gate BN44: Stey 3A 130
Borough Gro. GU32: Peters 7E 54
Borough Hill GU32: Peters 6E 54
Borough Ho. GU29: Midh 9H 59
Borough Rd. GU32: Peters 7D 54
Borough St. BN1: Brig 7A 172 (7N 153)
Borrowdale Cl. RH11: Craw 8D 10
Borrow King Cl. BN2: Brig 4E 154
BOSHAM 9D 138
BOSHAM HOE 4F 160
Bosham La. PO18: Bosh 8E 138
Bosham Rd. RH10: Craw 9L 11
Bosham Sailing Club 9D 138
Bosham Station (Rail) 6F 138
Bosham Walk 9D 138
Bosmere Gdns. PO10: Ems 4E 136
Bostal, The BN44: Up B 5F 130
Bostal Rd. BN44: Bramb, Stey 6L 129
BN45: Poyn 4D 132
Bost Hill BN13: Fin V, High S 3C 148
Bostock Av. RH12: Hors 7D 26
Bostock Rd. PO19: Chich 5D 140
Boston Ct. RH16: Hay H 4H 73
(off Allen Rd.)
Boston Rd. RH16: Hay H 4H 73
Boston St. BN1: Brig 3E 172 (6B 154)
Boswell Rd. RH10: Craw 9G 10
Botany Cl. BN16: Rust 4C 168
BOTOLPHS 7D 130
Botolphs Rd. BN44: Bramb 6C 130
Bottings Hill RH13: Southw 1L 67
Bough Beeches RH15: Burg H 7D 94
Boulevard, The BN12: Wor 8B 148
BN13: Wor 8B 148
PO20: Tang 3M 141
PO21: Bers 5B 164
RH10: Craw 6F 10
(not continuous)
RH12: Hors 1J 45
Boulevard Ho. BN1: Brig 7E 172
Boundary Cl. BN11: Wor 3F 170
RH10: Craw 5G 11
Boundary Pas. BN1: Brig 6A 172
Boundary Rd. BN2: Brig 8J 173
BN3: Hove 7E 152
BN11: Wor 3E 170
BN15: S Lan 8E 150
GU26: Gray 1F 16
RH10: Craw 5G 11
RH17: Bal 8A 30
Boundary Way BN16: E Pres 2G 169
Bound La. PO11: Hay I 9A 158
Boundstone Cl. BN15: Lan 6A 150
Boundstone La. BN15: Lan, Somp 7N 149
Bourg-de-Peage Av. RH19: E Grin 3G 14
Bourne, The BN6: Hass 2N 113
Bourne Cl. BN13: Durr 7N 147
PO19: Fish 6K 139
Bourne Community Leisure Cen. 4J 137
Bourne Ct. BN1: Brig 1M 153
BN17: Wick 1H 167
(off Phoenix Cl.)
PO20: E Witt 6L 177
RH13: Hors 8B 26
Bournemouth Ho. PO9: Hav 9A 116
Bourne Vw. Cl. PO10: S'brne 3K 137
Bourne Way GU29: Midh 2G 81
Bowater Rd. RH10: Craw 9L 11
Bowcroft La. RH12: Rudg 4K 23
Bowden Way RH16: Hay H 7F 72
Bowen Ct. BN3: Hove 7L 153
Bowen La. GU31: Peters 6F 54
Bower, The RH10: Craw 7L 11
RH16: Hay H 4E 72
Bowerhill Cotts. RH19: F Row 5F 32
Bower La. RH20: W Chil 1J 107
Bowers Pl. RH10: Craw D 4J 13
Bowes Cl. RH13: Hors 8B 26
Bowes Hill PO9: Row C 3C 116
Bowhill La. PO18: W Sto 8G 118
Bowley La. PO20: S Mun 6G 162
Bowline Point BN43: Shor S 6H 151
Bowling Grn. Cl. PO21: Aldw 2D 180
Bowling Grn. La. RH12: Hors 8A 26
Bowlplex
Brighton 8K 173
Bowman Ct. RH10: Craw 5F 10
(off London Rd.)
Bowmans Cl. BN44: Stey 2A 130
Bowness Av. BN15: Somp 8N 149
Bowness Cl. RH11: Ifield 7N 9
Bowring Way BN2: Brig 9E 154
Bowser Ct. BN11: Wor 3F 170
Boxall Wlk. RH13: Hors 1A 46
Box Cl. RH11: Craw 2E 28
Boxes La. RH17: Hors K 5C 52
BOXGROVE 2M 141
Boxgrove BN12: Gor S 9N 147
Boxgrove Cl. BN15: N Lan 5C 150
Boxgrove Gdns. PO21: Aldw 1E 180
Boxgrove Ho. PO18: Box 2M 141
Boxgrove Pde. BN12: Gor S 9N 147
Boxgrove Priory (remains) 2M 141
Boxham La. PO20: Sidle 9N 161
Box La. RH19: Ash W 6L 15
Box's La. RH17: Chel C 4J 53
Box Tree Av. BN16: Rust 3A 168
Boyce's St. BN1: Brig 8D 172 (8A 154)
Boyes La. PO8: Blend, Ids 7A 96
Boyles La. BN2: Brig 9F 154
Brackenbury Cl. BN41: Ports 3D 152
Bracken Cl. RH10: Copt 1C 12
RH10: Craw 4G 11
RH20: Storr 6N 107
Bracken Gro. RH12: Hors 6E 26
Bracken La. RH20: Storr 4N 107
Bracken Rd. GU31: Peters 7J 55
Brackens, The RH20: Storr 6G 107
Brackenside RH6: Horl 1K 5
BRACKLESHAM 6M 177
Bracklesham Bay Caravan & Boat Club
PO20: Brac 6N 177
Bracklesham Cl. PO20: Brac 5M 177
Bracklesham La. PO20: Brac, E Witt 5M 177
Bracknell Wlk. RH11: Craw 1A 28
Bradbury Rd. RH10: Craw 9L 11
Brading Rd. BN2: Brig 6D 154
Bradley Ct. PO9: Hav 8B 116
RH15: Burg H 6C 94
(off Grove Rd.)
Bradley Ho. BN11: Wor 2F 170
Bradlond Cl. PO21: Aldw 1J 181
Bradshaw Rd. PO19: Chich 5E 140
Braeburn Rd. RH11: Ifield 3C 10
Braemar Ho. BN1: Brig 6A 172
Braemar Way PO21: Bers 5A 164
Braemore Ct. BN3: Hove 7H 153
Braemore Rd. BN3: Hove 7G 153
Braeside Av. BN1: Brig 7A 134
Braeside Cl. BN14: Fin 8C 128
GU27: Has 3H 17
Brainsmead RH17: Cuck 1N 71
Brainsmead Cl. RH17: Cuck 2N 71
Braishfield Rd. PO9: Hav 1A 136
BRAMBER 4C 130
Bramber Av. BN3: Hove 2H 153
BN10: Peace 6J 175
(not continuous)
RH20: Storr 5H 107
Bramber Av. Nth. BN10: Peace 4J 175
Bramber Castle (remains of) 4B 130
Bramber Cl. BN10: Peace 4J 175
BN15: Somp 5A 150
PO21: Bog R 8B 164
RH10: Craw 4G 10
RH12: Hors 6E 26
RH16: Hay H 5E 72
Bramber Ct. BN3: Hove 6K 153
BN43: Shor S 5L 151
Bramber Ho. RH13: Hors 1B 46
(off Kennedy Rd.)
Bramber Rd. BN14: Broadw 6J 149
BN44: Stey 4A 130
PO19: Chich 8D 140
Bramber Sq. BN16: Rust 2B 168
Bramber Way RH15: Burg H 4B 94
Bramble Cl. BN13: Durr 6B 148
PO9: Hav 2C 136
PO21: Pag 9H 163
RH10: Copt 1C 12
Bramble Ct. GU31: Peters 6J 55
(off Rival Moor Rd.)
Bramble Cres. BN13: Durr 5B 148
Brambledean Rd. BN41: Ports 6D 152
Bramble Gdns. RH15: Burg H 4M 93
Bramble Hill RH17: Bal 9A 30
Bramble Hill Farm RH13: Slinf 2D 44
Bramble La. BN13: Durr 6B 148
RH20: Thake 9N 87
Bramble Mead RH17: Bal 1A 50
Bramble Ri. BN1: Brig 9L 133
Bramble Rd. GU31: Peters 6J 55
Brambles BN6: Hass 2A 114
Brambles, The RH17: Cuck 3B 72
Bramble Twitten RH19: E Grin 3G 14
Brambletye La. RH18: F Row 8K 15
Brambletye Rd. RH10: Craw 7J 11
Brambletyne Av. BN2: Salt 3D 174
Brambletyne Cl. BN16: Ang 7F 146
Bramble Way BN1: Brig 8D 134
Brambling Cl. RH13: Hors 1D 46
Brambling La. GU29: Wool 6D 58
Brambling Rd. PO9: Row C 5B 116
RH13: Hors 1D 46
Bramblings, The BN16: Rust 3C 168
Bramfield Rd. PO22: Felp 8K 165
Bramlands La. BN5: W'cote 7M 111
Bramley Cl. BN14: Broadw 7H 149
RH10: Craw 6H 11
RH14: Kird 7H 41
Bramley Gdns. PO10: S'brne 5H 137
PO22: Bers 5C 164
Bramley Rd. BN14: Broadw 7H 149
Bramley Wlk. RH6: Horl 2L 5
Bramley Way BN16: Ang 9F 146
Brampton Cl. PO20: Sel 3H 183
Brampton Ct. PO19: Chich 8B 140
(off Stockbridge Rd.)
Bramshaw Ct. PO9: Hav 9B 116
BRAMSHOTT CHASE 3D 16
Bramshott Chase La. GU26: Brams 2D 16
Brandon Cl. RH10: Craw 8M 11
Brandy Hole La. PO19: Chich, W Bro 3A 140
Brangwyn Av. BN1: Brig 8N 133
Brangwyn Ct. BN1: Brig 9M 133
Brangwyn Cres. BN1: Brig 8M 133
Brangwyn Dr. BN1: Brig 8M 133
Brangwyns Acre BN6: Ditch 4E 114
Brangwyn Way BN1: Brig 9N 133
Brantridge La. RH17: Bal, S'fld 9J 29
Brantridge Rd. RH10: Craw 8H 11
Brasslands Dr. BN41: Ports 3C 152
Braybon Av. BN1: Brig 1A 154
Braybon Bus. Pk. RH15: Burg H 6N 93
Bray Cl. RH10: Craw 8M 11
Braypool La. BN1: Brig 6M 133
Brazen Cl. BN9: Newh 5N 175
Brazwick Av. PO21: Bers 5A 164
BREACH 3L 137
Breach Av. PO10: S'brne 4K 137
Breach Cl. BN44: Stey 2A 130
Breach Rd. BN7: King L 1D 156
Bread La. BN17: Climp 4E 166
Bread St. BN1: Brig 6E 172 (7B 154)
Breaky Bottom Vineyard 6G 157
Bream La. PO20: Sel 2F 182
Brecon Cl. BN13: Durr 6D 148
Brecon Ct. BN3: Hove 6L 153
Brede Cl. BN2: Brig 8F 154
Breezehurst Dr. RH11: Craw 9A 10
Breezehurst Rdbt.
RH11: Craw 1C 28
Bremere La. PO20: Sidle 1F 178
Bremner Av. RH6: Horl 1H 5
Brendon Rd. BN13: Durr 5C 148
Brendon Way BN16: Rust 2A 168
Brent Ct. PO10: Ems 5E 136
Brent Rd. PO21: Bog R 8B 164
Brentwood Cl. BN1: Brig 2C 154
Brentwood Cres. BN1: Brig 2C 154
Brentwood Rd. BN1: Brig 2C 154
Brettingham Cl. RH11: Craw 9A 10
Bretton RH15: Burg H 3N 93
Bretts Fld. BN10: Peace 2J 175
Bretts Orchard RH17: Bal 1B 50
Brewells La. GU33: Liss, Rake 4D 34
Brewer Rd. RH10: Craw 8G 10
Brewer St. BN2: Brig 6C 154
Brewers Yd. RH20: Storr 6J 107
Brewery Hill BN18: Arun 2H 145
Brewery M. BN6: Hurst 1H 113
Brewhurst La. RH14: Lox 9N 21
Breydon Wlk. RH10: Craw 8K 11
Briar Av. PO20: W Witt 2K 177
Briar Cl. BN2: W'dean 5L 155
BN16: Ang 9E 146
BN18: Yap 1N 165
PO20: Oving 7L 141
Briar Cl. PO21: Pag 9H 163
RH11: Craw 3E 10
Briar Cott. Caravan Pk. PO20: E Witt 2L 177
Briarcroft Rd. BN2: W'dean 6L 155
Briars Wood RH6: Horl 1L 5
Briarswood Cl. RH10: Craw 4M 11
Briarwood Gdns. PO11: Hay I 9A 158
Brickfield Cl. PO21: Bog R 7C 164
Brickfield La. RH6: Hookw 4F 4
Brick Kiln Cl. RH13: Lwr Bee 7K 47
BRICKKILN COMMON 6L 63
Bricklands RH10: Craw D 5J 13
Brick La. RH17: Cuck 3A 72
Bricky, The BN10: Peace 4J 175
Brickyard Copse RH5: Ock 1G 7
Brickyard La. RH10: Craw D 4J 13
Brideake Cl. RH11: Craw 9C 10
Brideoake Cl. PO19: Chich 5A 140
Bridge Cl. BN12: Gor S 9A 148
BN15: S Lan 8B 150
RH15: Burg H 4A 94
RH20: Pulb 4B 86
Bridgefield Cl. GU29: Midh 2G 80
Bridgefoot Path PO10: Ems 5F 136
Bridge Ind. Est. RH6: Horl 2K 5
Bridgelands RH10: Copt 1B 12
Bridger Cl. PO22: Felp 5H 165
Bridge Rd. BN14: Broadw 1H 171
BN17: L'ton 3H 167
GU27: Has 4L 17
PO10: Ems 4F 136
PO19: Chich 6D 140
RH12: Rudg 4J 23
RH16: Hay H 2F 72
Bridge Rd. Bus. Pk. RH16: Hay H 2G 72
Bridge Rd. Ind. Est. RH16: Hay H 3G 72
Bridgers Mill RH16: Hay H 2E 72
Bridges Cl. RH6: Horl 2M 5
Bridges Ct. RH12: Hors 6C 26
Bridges Pl. RH12: Hors 1N 45
Bridgestone Pl. RH13: Hors 1B 46
Bridgewater Cl. RH14: Bill 3H 65
Bridge Way BN43: Shor B 7J 151
Bridgeway, The PO20: Sel 4H 183
Bridgnorth Cl. BN13: Durr 8N 147
Bridle Cl. BN44: Up B 4E 130
Bridle La. BN18: Slind 1L 143
Bridle Lane, The PO18: Hamb 9A 118
Bridle Way BN10: Tels C 3G 175
RH10: Craw 5M 11
Bridle Way, The PO20: Sel 3H 183
Bridorley Cl. PO21: Pag 1D 180
Brier La. GU31: Chit, Rog 5K 57
Brierley Gdns. BN15: Lan 7C 150
Brigden St. BN1: Brig 3C 172 (6A 154)
Brigham Pl. PO22: Felp 8L 165
Brighthelm BN1: Falm 6J 135
BRIGHTON 8E 172 (8B 154)
Brighton & Hove Albion FC 8J 135
Brighton & Hove Golf Course 7F 132
Brighton & Hove School Sports Hall & Fitness Suite
6A 172 (7N 153)
Brighton & Hove Stadium (Greyhound) 4J 153
Brighton Belle BN1: Brig 4E 172
Brighton By-Pass BN1: Brig 1B 152
BN3: Hove 1B 152
BN41: Ports 1B 152
BN43: Shor S 3M 151
Brighton Centre, The 8C 172 (8A 154)
Brighton Dome 7E 172 (8B 154)
Brighton Eye i360 8B 172 (8N 153)
Brighton Fishing Mus. 9D 172 (9A 154)
Brighton Health & Racquet Club, The 9H 135
Brighton Little Theatre 7B 172
Brighton Marina 9K 173
BRIGHTON MARINA VILLAGE 8K 173
Brighton Museum & Art Gallery 7F 172 (8B 154)
Brighton Pier 9F 172 (9B 154)
Brighton Pl. BN1: Brig 8E 172
Brighton Racecourse 6F 154
Brighton Rd. BN5: Henf, W'cote 3J 111
BN6: Clay, Hass 6M 113
BN6: Hurst, Newt 5G 112
BN7: Falm, Lewes 8L 135
BN9: Newh, Peace 6N 175
BN11: Wor 2J 171
BN15: Lan, S Lan 9B 150
BN43: Shor S 6J 151
(New Rd.)
BN43: Shor S 7G 151
(Ormonde Way)
RH6: Gatw, Craw 4H 5
RH6: Horl 3H 5
RH10: Craw 9F 10
RH11: Craw 3E 28
RH11: Hand, Pease P 7D 28
RH13: Cow, Hors, Lwr Bee, Mann H, Monks G
1A 46
RH13: Sherm 5G 90
RH17: Hand 8E 28
(Coopers Wood)
RH17: Hand 2E 48
(High St.)
RH17: W'lid 2F 70
Brighton Sq. BN1: Brig 8E 172
Brighton Station (Rail) 5E 172 (7B 154)
Brighton Toy & Model Museum, The
5E 172 (7B 154)
Brighton Youth Cen. 8C 154
(off Edward St.)
Brills La. BN1: Brig 9E 172 (9B 154)
Brimbrook La. GU29: Trey 4L 79
Brimfast La. PO20: Sidle 7A 162
BRINKSOLE 8D 62
BRINKSWAY 7F 16
Brisbane Cl. BN13: Durr 7A 148
RH11: Craw 3F 10
Brisbane Ct. GU29: Midh 2G 81
(off The Fairway)
Bristol Av. BN15: S Lan 8E 150
Bristol Cl. RH10: Craw 3M 11
Bristol Ct. BN2: Brig 9E 154
(off Marine Pde.)

Bristol Gdns.—Butts Cl.

Bristol Gdns. BN2: Brig 9F 154
PO19: Chich 3B 140
Bristol Ga. BN2: Brig 9E 154
Bristol M. BN2: Brig 9F 154
Bristol Pl. BN2: Brig 9F 154
Bristol Ri. *BN2: Brig* *9E 154*
(off Bowring Way)
Bristol Rd. BN2: Brig 9D 154
Bristol St. BN2: Brig 9F 154
Britannia Av. BN43: Shor B 7L 151
Britannia Ct. BN2: Brig 8L 173
Britannia Ct. Gdns. PO18: Bosh 8F 138
Britannia St. GU31: Peters 4G 54
British Engineerium, The 3K 153
British Rail New Yd. RH10: Craw 2K 11
Britnell Ho. GU32: Peters 5F 54
Briton's Cft. BN44: Stey 3N 129
Brittany Ct. BN3: Hove 6F 152
Brittany Rd. BN3: Hove 7F 152
BN14: Broadw 9G 149
Britten Cl. RH11: Craw 9B 10
RH13: Hors 7E 26
Britten's La. BN18: Eart, Font 2E 142
Brittleware Cotts. RH6: Charlw 2B 4
BROADBRIDGE 6F 138
Broadbridge Bus. Cen. PO18: Bosh 6E 138
Broadbridge Ct. PO18: Bosh 6F 138
Broadbridge Dr. PO18: Bosh 6F 138
BROADBRIDGE HEATH 8H 25
Broadbridge Heath By-Pass
RH12: Broadb H 8G 25
Broadbridge Heath Leisure Cen. 9H 25
Broadbridge Heath Rd.
RH12: Broadb H, Warnh 7H 25
Broadbridge Mill PO18: Bosh 6F 138
Broadbridge Retail Pk. RH12: Broadb H 8J 25
Broadcroft PO9: Row C 3C 116
BROADFIELD 1D 28
Broadfield RH19: W Hoa 4M 31
Broadfield Barton RH11: Craw 1D 28
Broadfield Dr. RH11: Craw 9D 10
Broadfield Park 2E 28
Broadfield Pk. RH11: Craw 1F 28
Broadfield Pl. RH11: Craw 1D 28
Broadfield Rdbt. RH11: Craw 9D 10
Broadfields BN2: Brig 2F 154
Broadfields Rd. BN2: Brig 2F 154
Broadfield Stadium 1E 28
BROADFORD BRIDGE 9L 65
Broadford Bri. Rd. RH20: Bill, W Chil 6K 87
Broad Grn. BN2: W'dean 7M 155
Broad Grn. Av. RH15: Burg H 6D 94
Broad Grn. M. BN2: W'dean 6M 155
Broadhurst Mnr. Rd. RH17: Hors K, Sharp 1D 52
Broadlands RH6: Horl 1L 5
RH15: Burg H 8C 94
Broadlands Bus. Campus RH12: Hors 8N 7
Broadmark Av. BN16: Rust 4B 168
Broadmark Beach BN16: Rust 5B 168
Broadmark Ho. *BN16: Rust* *3B 168*
(off Ash La.)
Broadmark La. BN16: Rust 5B 168
Broadmark Pde. BN16: Rust 3B 168
Broadmark Way BN16: Rust 4B 168
Broadmead RH6: Horl 1L 5
Broadmere Av. PO9: Hav 9A 116
BROADMERE COMMON 5J 111
Broad Piece BN17: L'ton 2H 167
Broad Reach BN43: Shor S 6H 151
Broad Rig Av. BN3: Hove 1F 152
Broad Rd. PO18: Nutb, Hamb 5A 138
Broadstone RH18: F Row 1N 33
Broad Strand BN16: Rust 5C 168
Broad St. BN2: Brig 9F 172 (9B 154)
RH17: Cuck 3A 72
Broad Vw. PO20: Sel 3K 183
Broadview Gdns. BN13: High S 5C 148
Broad Wlk. PO8: Horn 2A 116
PO9: Row C 5G 117
PO10: Row C, W'brne 6G 117
PO18: Graff, Sing 4F 100
Broad Walk, The PO18: W Sto 8G 118
Broadwalk RH10: Craw 6F 10
BROADWATER 9H 149
Broadwater Blvd. BN14: Broadw 8H 149
Broadwater Blvd. Flats *BN14: Broadw* *8H 149*
(off Broadwater Rd.)
Broadwater Bus. Pk. BN14: Broadw 7K 149
Broadwater Hall BN14: Wor 9G 148
Broadwater La. RH13: Cops, Hors 3N 67
Broadwater M. BN14: Broadw 8H 149
Broadwater Rd. BN11: Wor 8H 149
BN14: Broadw 8H 149
Broadwater St. E. BN14: Broadw 8H 149
Broadwater St. W. BN14: Broadw 7G 148
Broadwater Trad. Est. BN14: Broadw 7K 149
Broadwater Way BN14: Broadw 7H 149
Broad Way GU32: Frox, Steep 1A 54
Broadway PO20: Sel 2G 182
Broadway, The BN2: Brig 9G 154
BN11: Wor *2J 171*
(off Brighton Rd.)
BN15: S Lan 8E 150
BN42: S'wck 5B 152
PO19: Chich 3B 140
RH10: Craw 6F 10
RH16: Hay H 4E 72
RH17: Bal *9A 30*
(off Bramble Hill)
Broadway Ct. BN15: S Lan 8E 150
BN43: Shor S 5M 151
Broadway Pk. BN15: S Lan 7E 150
GU31: Peters 8F 54
Broadwood Cl. RH12: Hors 6D 26
Broadwood Ri. RH11: Craw 2C 28
Brock End RH17: Cuck 2N 71
Brockham Keep *RH6: Horl* *1L 5*
(off Langshott La.)
Brockhurst BN2: Brig 5G 154
Brockhurst Cl. RH12: Hors 1K 45
Brockley Cl. BN14: Wor 9G 148
Brock Rd. RH11: Craw 3D 10
Bromley Cl. BN6: Key 3B 114
Bromley Rd. BN2: Brig 2G 172 (6C 154)
Brompton Cl. BN1: Brig 8N 133
Brontes, The RH19: E Grin 3D 14
Bronze Cl. PO22: Bers 5D 164
Brook, The RH10: Craw 5F 10
RH13: Southw 8L 45
Brook Av. BN6: Key 4A 114
PO18: Bosh 8E 138
Brook Barn Way BN12: Gor S 3C 170
Brook Chase RH20: W Chil 1H 107
Brook Cl. BN11: Wor 9L 149
PO21: Bog R 8B 164
RH19: E Grin 3H 15
RH20: Storr 4L 107
Brookdean Rd. BN11: Wor 1M 171
Brooke Mead BN2: Brig 5G 172
Brookenbee Cl. BN16: Rust 1A 168
Brooker Pl. BN3: Hove 6J 153
Brooker's Rd. RH14: Bill 2J 65
Brooker St. BN3: Hove 6K 153
Brookfield La. GU28: Riv 8E 60
Brookfield Way RH14: Bill 3J 65
Brook Gdns. PO10: Ems 5D 136
Brook Grn. RH17: Cuck 9N 49
Brook Hill GU28: Lurg 7E 38
RH13: Cow 6H 69
Brookhill Cl. RH10: Copt 1B 12
Brookhill Rd. RH10: Copt 2B 12
Brookhouse Bottom TN22: Fur G 5J 53
Brookhurst Fld. RH12: Rudg 3J 23
Brooklands PO21: Pag 2C 180
RH16: Hay H 8D 72
Brooklands New Salt Farm BN43: Shor S 7F 150
Brooklands Pk. 1N 171
Brooklands Rd. RH11: Craw 2E 28
Brooklands Way RH19: E Grin 4D 14
Brookland Way RH20: Cold 2J 105
Brook La. BN12: Fer 3K 169
BN16: Rust 1B 168
PO22: Barn 1J 165
RH12: Fay 3F 26
RH16: Hay H 1F 72
RH20: Cold, Great 2J 105
Brook La. Caravan Pk. BN12: Fer 2J 169
Brooklyn Av. BN11: Wor 2D 170
Brooklyn Chambers *BN11: Wor* *2D 170*
(off Brooklyn Av.)
Brook Mnr. RH19: E Grin 5D 14
Brook Mdw. GU8: Chidd 1K 19
Brook Meadow Nature Reserve 4G 136
Brookpit La. BN17: Climp 4E 166
Brook Rd. RH12: Hors 5B 26
Brooks, The RH15: Burg H 3N 93
Brooks End PO21: Pag 1C 180
BROOKS GREEN 2D 66
Brooks Grn. Pk. RH13: Br Grn 2D 66
Brooks Grn. Rd. RH13: Cool 7C 66
Brookside BN6: Key 4A 114
BN9: Pidd 1N 175
PO20: Runc 3G 163
RH10: Copt 1B 12
RH10: Craw 5H 11
RH10: Craw D 4J 13
RH20: A'ton 3E 108
Brookside Av. BN16: Rust 1B 168
Brookside Bus. Pk. BN16: Rust 1B 168
Brookside Cl. BN12: Fer 1K 169
PO20: Runc 3G 162
Brookside Ind. Est. BN16: Rust 1B 168
Brookside Pk. BN17: Lym 8J 145
Brookside Rd. BN16: King G 4J 169
Brookside Rural Pk. RH12: Rudg 1L 23
Brooks La. PO18: Bosh 6G 138
(not continuous)
PO22: Bog R 7F 164
Brooks La. W. PO22: Bog R 7E 164
Brooksmead PO22: Bog R 8F 164
BROOK STREET 8N 49
Brook St. RH17: Cuck 1N 71
Brooks Way RH20: Pulb 6B 86
Brookview RH10: Copt 1B 12
RH20: Cold 2J 105
Brookview Sth. RH20: Cold 2J 105
Brook Way BN15: S Lan 8C 150
RH15: Burg H 5D 94
Brookway RH16: Lind 1H 73
Brookwood RH6: Horl 1K 5
Brookwood Pk. RH6: Horl 3K 5
Broomcroft Rd. PO22: Felp 8K 165
Broomdashers Rd. RH10: Craw 5H 11
Broome Cl. RH12: Hors 6A 26
BROOMER'S CORNER 1D 88
BROOMERSHILL 4D 86
Broomers Hill La. RH20: Pulb 2C 86
Broomers Hill Pk. RH20: Pulb 3C 86
Broomers La. PO20: Bir 7J 161
Broomfield Av. BN10: Tels C 5F 174
BN14: Wor 7E 148
Broomfield Dr. BN41: Ports 1C 152
RH14: Bill 2K 65
Broomfield Gdns. BN5: Henf 2H 111
Broomfield Rd. BN5: Henf 2G 111
PO20: Sel 2K 183
Broom Fld. Way PO22: Felp 6H 165
Broom Rd. GU31: Peters 7J 55
Broom Squires Ct. GU27: Has 5J 17
Broomwicks Pl. *RH12: Broadb H* *8J 25*
(off Sullington Mead)
Brou Cl. BN16: E Pres 3G 168
Brougham Ct. BN11: Wor 1M 171
Brougham Rd. BN11: Wor 1L 171
Brougham Wlk. BN11: Wor 1M 171
Brow, The BN2: W'dean 5L 155
RH15: Burg H 6B 94
Brow Cl. RH20: Storr 6G 107
Brownfield Ho. GU32: Peters 5F 54
Brownhill La. PO18: W Sto 7G 118
Browning Cl. RH10: Craw 5L 11
Browning Rd. BN11: Wor 1F 170
BN15: N Lan 5B 150
Brownings, The RH19: E Grin 3C 14
Browning's Hill RH13: Cow 7F 68
Brownjohn Ct. RH10: Craw 5J 11
Brownleaf Rd. BN2: W'dean 7M 155
Brown's La. RH20: Storr 6J 107
Browns Wood RH19: E Grin 1E 14
Brown Twins Rd. BN6: Hurst 2J 113
Broxhead Rd. PO9: Hav 8A 116
Broxmead La. RH17: Bol, Cuck 1J 71
(not continuous)
Broyle Cl. PO19: Chich 4B 140
Broyle Rd. PO19: Chich 4B 140
Bruce Av. BN11: Wor 2D 170
Bruce Cl. RH16: Hay H 6F 72
Bruce Vs. BN11: Wor 1D 170
Bruce Way BN11: Wor 1D 170
Brunel Centre, The RH10: Craw 2H 11
Brunel Pl. RH10: Craw 7G 10
Brunswick Cl. PO22: Felp 7H 165
RH10: Craw 8J 11
Brunswick Ct. *RH10: Craw* *8J 11*
(off Brunswick Cl.)
Brunswick M. BN3: Hove 8M 153
Brunswick Pl. BN3: Hove 7M 153
Brunswick Rd. BN3: Hove 6A 172 (7M 153)
BN11: Wor 3G 170
BN43: Shor S 6J 151
Brunswick Row BN1: Brig 4F 172
Brunswick Sq. BN3: Hove 8M 153
Brunswick St. E. BN3: Hove 8M 153
Brunswick St. W. BN3: Hove 8M 153
Brunswick Ter. BN3: Hove 8M 153
Brushes La. RH16: Lind 1J 73
(not continuous)
Brushwood Gro. PO10: Ems 1G 136
Brushwood Rd. RH12: Hors 5E 26
Bryce Cl. RH12: Hors 6D 26
Buchan Country Pk. 1A 28
Buchan Country Pk. Countryside Cen. 1B 28
BUCHAN HILL 3C 28
Buchan Pk. RH11: Craw 1B 28
Buchans Lawn RH11: Craw 1D 28
Buci Cres. BN43: Shor S 5M 151
Buckhatch La. BN5: Sherm 3K 91
RH13: Cow 2L 91
Buckhurst Cl. RH19: E Grin 1C 14
Buckhurst Farm RH20: Cold 2G 105
Buckhurst Mead RH19: E Grin 1C 14
Buckhurst Rd. BN10: Tels C 4F 174
Buckhurst Way RH19: E Grin 1C 14
Buckingham Av. BN43: Shor S 4H 151
Buckingham Cl. BN1: Brig 4C 172
BN43: Shor S 5K 151
Buckingham Ct. BN14: Salv 6F 148
PO22: Midd S 7M 165
RH11: Craw 1D 28
Buckingham Dr. PO19: Chich 7F 140
RH19: E Grin 4G 14
Buckingham Ga. RH6: Gatw 6L 5
Buckingham Lodge BN1: Brig 4D 172
Buckingham M. BN43: Shor S 4J 151
Buckingham Pl.
BN1: Brig 4C 172 (6A 154)
BN16: Rust 1A 168
Buckingham Rd. BN1: Brig 6C 172 (7A 154)
BN11: Wor 2H 171
BN43: Shor S 6J 151
GU32: Peters 6D 54
Buckingham St. BN1: Brig 5D 172 (7A 154)
BN43: Shor S 6H 151
Buckland Dr. PO21: Aldw, Pag 1D 180
Buckler St. BN41: Ports 5D 152
Buckley Cl. BN3: Hove 1G 152
Buckley La. RH13: Hors, Mann H 4C 46
Buckley Pl. RH10: Craw D 4H 13
Buckmans Rd. RH11: Craw 5F 10
Buckmore Av. GU32: Peters 4D 54
Bucknor Cl. PO21: Aldw 1E 180
BUCKS GREEN 4J 23
Bucksham Av. PO21: Bers 5A 164
Buckshead Hill RH13: Plum P 3J 47
Buckswood Dr. RH11: Craw 8C 10
Buckwish La. BN5: Henf 3F 110
Buddington La. GU29: Ease 7G 59
Budgen Cl. RH10: Craw 3M 11
BUDGENOR 6J 59
Budgenor Lodge GU29: Ease 6H 59
Buffbeards La. GU27: Has 4G 17
Bugshill La. GU29: Bep, Trey 7L 79
Bulbeck Cl. RH15: Burg H 7N 93
Bulbeck Way PO22: Felp 6H 165
Bulkington Av. BN14: Wor 9F 148
Bulldogs Bank RH19: Sharp 6N 31
Buller Rd. BN2: Brig 4E 154
Bullfinch Cl. RH6: Horl 1G 4
RH12: Hors 4N 25
Bullfinch La. BN6: Hurst 3G 112
Bull Hill GU33: Rake 6D 34
Bullocks La. GU27: Has 2D 38
GU28: Has 2D 38
Bull's La. RH13: Cow 6M 69
RH17: Cow 6M 69
Bulrushes Farm RH19: E Grin 5L 15
Bunbury Cl. RH20: Storr 5N 107
Bunch La. GU27: Has 4J 17
Bunch Way GU27: Has 5J 17
BUNCTON 7G 109
Buncton La. RH17: Bol 5G 70
Bunting Cl. RH13: Hors 8C 26
Bunyan Cl. RH11: Craw 9A 10
Burbeach Cl. RH11: Craw 1B 28
Burchell Ct. BN15: Lan 6C 150
Burchens, The BN14: Broadw 7G 149
Burchetts Cl. RH16: Hay H 7F 72
Burchett Wlk. PO21: Bers 7A 164
Burch Gro. BN18: Walb 4L 143
Burdale Dr. PO11: Hay I 9D 158
Burdett Cl. RH10: Worth 7M 11
Burdock Cl. RH11: Craw 1C 28
Burdocks Dr. RH15: Burg H 7E 94
Burford Cl. BN14: Salv 6E 148
Burford Rd. RH13: Hors 9B 26
Burgesmede Ho. GU31: Peters 6F 54
BURGESS HILL 5B 94
Burgess Hill (Public) Golf Course 2A 94
Burgess Hill Rd. RH17: Ans 7L 71
Burgess Hill Station (Rail) 6C 94
Burghclere Rd. PO9: Hav 8B 116
Burgh Cl. RH10: Craw 3M 11
BURITON 3D 76
Buriton Bus. Pk. GU32: West 1C 76
Burlands RH11: Craw 3C 10
Burleigh Cl. RH10: Craw D 4J 13
Burleigh Ct. BN1: Brig 8A 172
Burleigh La. RH10: Craw D 5J 13
Burleigh Way RH10: Craw D 5J 13
Burley Cl. BN15: Lan 7B 150
PO9: Hav 8B 116
RH14: Lox 7N 21
Burley Rd. PO22: Felp 8L 165
Burleys Rd. RH10: Craw 6L 11
Burlington Ct. BN11: Wor 3D 170
Burlington Gdns. BN41: Ports 4E 152
PO20: Sel 4K 183
Burlington Pde. *BN41: Ports* *4E 152*
(off Burlington Gdns.)
Burlington Rd. BN12: Gor S 1B 170
Burlington St. BN2: Brig 9D 154
Burlow Cl. BN2: Brig 8F 154
PO20: Bir 8G 161
Burma Cl. RH16: Hay H 5K 73
Burmill Ct. BN16: Rust 1D 168
BURNDELL 2B 166
Burndell Rd. BN18: Ford, Yap 1A 166
Burners Cl. RH15: Burg H 7E 94
Burnes Va. BN2: Rott 2N 173
Burney Ct. RH11: Craw 9C 10
Burngreave Ct. PO21: Bog R 9C 164
Burnham Av. PO21: Bog R 9D 164
Burnham Cl. BN2: W'dean 6N 155
Burnham Gdns. PO21: Bog R 9D 164
Burnham Pl. RH13: Hors 1A 46
Burnham Rd. BN13: Durr 7B 148
Burns Cl. RH12: Hors 4B 26
Burns Gdns. PO22: Felp 6L 165
Burnside Cres. BN15: Somp 8N 149
Burns Rd. RH10: Craw 4L 11
Burns Way RH12: Fay 2M 27
RH19: E Grin 3C 14
Burnthouse Bostall BN6: Ditch 9C 114
Burnt Ho. La. RH12: Rusp 5J 9
RH13: Cow, Lwr Bee 2G 68
(not continuous)
BURPHAM 8N 125
Burrell Av. BN15: Lan 8A 150
Burrell Bldgs. BN15: Lan 8A 150
Burrell Cl. RH13: Part G 5D 90
Burrell Ct. RH11: Craw 8B 10
Burrell Grn. RH17: Cuck 1A 72
Burrell Rd. RH16: Hay H 3E 72
Burrell Rd. Ind. Est. RH16: Hay H 3E 72
Burrells, The BN43: Shor B 7L 151
Burrows Cl. PO9: Hav 2A 136
Bursledon Cl. PO22: Felp 7H 165
Burstead Cl. BN1: Brig 2C 154
Burston Gdns. RH19: E Grin 1D 14
BURSTOW HILL 4L 51
Burstow Hill La. RH17: Ard 4L 51
Burton & Chingford Ponds Nature Reserve
8M 83
Burton Cl. RH6: Horl 3J 5
Burton Hall GU28: Dunc 9L 83
BURTON PARK 8L 83
Burton Pk. Rd. GU28: Petw 6L 83
Burtons Ct. RH12: Hors 9N 25
Burton Vs. BN3: Hove 5M 153
Burton Wlk. *BN3: Hove* *6M 153*
(off Wilbury Cres.)
Burwash Cl. BN16: E Pres 1G 168
Burwash Lodge *BN1: Brig* *4D 154*
(off Liphook Cl.)
Burwash Rd. BN3: Hove 2G 153
RH10: Craw 7J 11
Burwood Gro. PO11: Hay I 7A 158
BURY 8G 104
Bury, The BN12: Gor S 2N 169
Bury Comn. RH20: Bury 6F 104
Bury Dr. BN12: Gor S 2N 169
Bury Ga. RH20: Bury, Fitt 1F 104
Bury Hill BN18: Bury 1E 124
RH20: Bury 1E 124
Bury Ho. BN14: Broadw 8H 149
Bury Rd. RH20: Bury 4F 104
Bushby Av. BN16: Rust 3B 168
Bushby Cl. BN15: Somp 8N 149
Bush Cl. BN2: W'dean 5L 155
BN10: Tels C 3G 175
Bush Cott. Cl. BN41: Ports 3E 152
Bush Farm Dr. BN41: Ports 3D 152
Bushfield RH14: Plais 9F 20
Bush La. RH12: Hors 3D 26
Bush Ter. BN41: Ports 2D 152
Busticle La. BN15: Somp 6N 149
Butcher Cl. BN16: Ang 8F 146
Butcher's La. PO18: E Dean 9L 101
BUTCHER'S ROW 3N 89
Bute St. BN2: Brig 8E 154
Butler Ct. BN13: Salv 7D 148
BUTLER'S GREEN 5D 72
Butler's Grn. Rd. RH16: Hay H 5D 72
Butlers Rd. RH13: Hors 7D 26
Butlins Resort
Bognor Regis 9F 164
Butser Ancient Farm 1A 96
Butser Wlk. GU31: Peters 5H 55
Butterbox La. RH17: Scay H 5D 74
Buttercup Gro. PO22: Felp 6J 165
Buttercup Wlk. BN1: Brig 8C 134
Buttercup Way RH13: Southw 8L 45
Butterfield RH19: E Grin 1B 14
Buttermere Cl. RH12: Hors 5E 26
Buttermere Ct. *RH10: Craw* *8M 11*
(off Grayrigg Rd.)
Buttermere Way BN17: L'ton 1N 167
Butt La. BN18: Slind 8K 123
Button Ct. BN2: Brig 3G 172
Butts, The *BN17: Wick* *9M 145*
(off Butts Mead)
Butts Cl. RH11: Craw 5D 10

Butts Mead—Chaloner Cl.

Butts Mead BN17: Wick 9M 145
Butts Mdw. RH14: Wisb 1A 64
Butts Rd. BN42: S'wck 6A 152
Buxted Ri. BN1: Brig 9C 134
Buxton Rd. BN1: Brig 3B 172 (6N 153)
Bybles La. BN7: Rod 4K 157
Bycroft Way RH10: Craw 4K 11
Byerley Cl. PO10: W'brne 9H 117
Byerley Way RH10: Craw 5M 11
Bye Way, The PO21: Aldw 3E 180
Byeway, The PO20: W Witt 2G 176
Byfield Pl. PO22: Bers 6E 164
Byfleets La. RH12: Broadb H, Warnh 5H 25
Bylands BN2: Brig 8G 155
Bylanes Cl. RH17: Cuck 2A 72
Bylanes Cres. RH17: Cuck 1A 72
Byne Cl. RH20: Storr 6K 107
Byrd Rd. RH11: Craw 9B 10
Byre, The BN2: O'dean 9L 155
Byre Cotts. BN2: O'dean 9L 155
Byron Cl. PO22: Felp 6L 165
RH10: Craw 5K 11
RH12: Hors 5B 26
Byron Ct. PO19: Chich 9B 140
RH16: Hay H 4E 72
(off Winnals Pk.)
Byron Gro. RH19: E Grin 4C 14
Byron Rd. BN11: Wor 2G 170
BN16: Rust 3N 167
Byron St. BN3: Hove 6J 153
Byron Ter. *BN3: Hove 6J 153*
(off Byron St.)
By Sunte RH16: Lind 1G 73
Bywater Way PO19: Chich 9B 140
Bywaves PO20: Brac 7N 177
Byway, The BN1: Brig 9F 134
PO22: Midd S 7L 165
Byways PO20: Sel 5J 183
BYWORTH 2B 84
Byworth Cl. BN2: Brig 7G 154

C

Caburn Ct. RH11: Craw 8E 10
Caburn Hgts. RH11: Craw 8E 10
Caburn Rd. BN3: Hove 3B 172 (6N 153)
Cackstones, The RH10: Craw 4M 11
Cadogan Ct. BN11: Wor 2H 171
Caedwalla Dr. PO20: Tang 3L 141
Caen Stone Ct. *BN18: Arun 3H 145*
(off Queen St.)
Caernarvon Rd. PO19: Chich 7F 140
Caffins Cl. RH10: Craw 4G 11
Caffyns Ri. RH14: Bill 9J 43
Cagefoot La. BN5: Henf 3H 111
Cairo Av. BN10: Peace 5G 175
Cairo Av. Sth. BN10: Peace 5G 175
Caisters Cl. BN3: Hove 5L 153
Caius Ct. BN43: Shor S 5M 151
Cakeham Rd. PO20: W Witt 2F 176
Cakeham Way PO20: W Witt 4J 177
Calbourne RH16: Hay H 4E 72
Calceto La. BN17: Lym 5K 145
Caldbeck Ho. *RH11: Craw 9B 10*
(off Salvington Rd.)
Calderdale Cl. RH11: Craw 8D 10
Caledon Av. PO22: Felp 7L 165
Caledonian Ct. *BN2: Brig 5C 154*
(off Caledonian Rd.)
Caledonian Ho. *RH10: Craw 4F 10*
(off Barnfield Rd.)
Caledonian Pl. *BN11: Wor 3H 171*
(off West Bldgs.)
Caledonian Rd. BN2: Brig 5C 154
PO19: Chich 7C 140
Caledonian Way RH6: Gatw 6K 5
California M. BN18: Arun 3G 144
Callender Wlk. RH17: Cuck 1A 72
Callisto Cl. RH11: Craw 9A 10
Callon Cl. BN13: Durr 7N 147
Calluna Dr. RH10: Copt 2B 12
Calvin Wlk. RH11: Craw 9A 10
Camargue Ct. *BN11: Wor 1E 170*
(off Downview Rd.)
Camber Cl. BN2: Brig 8G 154
RH10: Craw 6L 11
Cambourne Ct. BN11: Wor 2G 171
Cambrai Av. PO19: Chich 8D 140
Cambria Cl. PO18: Bosh 8F 138
RH13: Part G 5C 90
Cambridge Av. PO20: W Witt 3J 177
Cambridge Dr. PO21: Aldw 8A 164
Cambridge Gro. BN3: Hove 6L 153
Cambridge M. BN3: Hove 6L 153
Cambridge Pl. *BN2: Brig 8C 154*
(off Park Rd. Ter.)
Cambridge Rd. BN3: Hove 7M 153
BN11: Wor 1G 171
RH13: Hors 9A 26
Cambridge Wlk. PO21: Aldw 8A 164
Camden St. BN41: Ports 7E 152
Camden Ter. BN1: Brig 5D 172
Camelford St. BN2: Brig 9G 172 (9C 154)
Camelia Cl. BN17: L'ton 1N 167
PO9: Hav 2C 136
Camelot Cl. RH13: Southw 8L 45
Camelot Ct. RH11: Ifield 6A 10
CAMELSDALE 6H 17
Camelsdale Rd. GU27: Has 6G 17
Campbell Ct. *BN12: Gor S 1M 169*
(off Goring St.)
Campbell Cres. RH19: E Grin 3B 14
Campbell Dr. BN16: Rust 2A 168
Campbell Rd. BN1: Brig 2D 172 (5A 154)
PO20: Tang 4K 141
PO21: Bog R 9E 164
RH10: Craw 8L 11
Campion Cl. BN16: Rust 9A 146
Campion Rd. RH12: Hors 6B 26
Canada Cl. BN10: Tels C 3H 175
Canada Cotts. *GU29: Ease 6J 59*
(off Canada Gro.)
Canada Gro. GU29: Ease 6J 59
PO21: Bog R 9D 164
Canada Rd. BN18: Arun 2F 144
Canadian Cres. PO20: Sel 5J 183
Canal Pl. PO19: Chich 8B 140
Canal Rd. BN18: Yap 2N 165
Canal Wharf PO19: Chich 8B 140
Canal Wharf Rd. PO19: Chich 8B 140
Canberra Cl. RH11: Craw 3F 10
Canberra Pl. PO20: Tang 3M 141
RH12: Hors 7C 26
Canberra Rd. BN13: Durr 7A 148
PO10: Tho I 1G 159
Canfield Cl. BN2: Brig 4E 154
Canfield Rd. BN2: Brig 4E 154
Canhouse La. GU31: Rake, Rog 6D 34
GU33: Rake 6D 34
Canning Rd. PO22: Felp 9G 165
Canning St. BN2: Brig 8D 154
Cannon Pl. BN1: Brig 8C 172 (8A 154)
(not continuous)
Canns La. RH15: Burg H 5E 94
Canonbury Cotts. RH12: Rusp 6J 9
Canon La. PO19: Chich 7B 140
Canon's Cl. PO21: Aldw 2F 180
Canons Way BN44: Stey 2B 130
Cansiron La. RH19: Ash W 6M 15
Cantelupe Ho. *RH19: E Grin 3F 14*
(off Cantelupe Rd.)
Cantelupe M. *RH19: E Grin 3F 14*
(off Cantelupe Rd.)
Cantelupe Rd. RH19: E Grin 3F 14
Canter, The RH10: Craw 5N 11
Canterbury Cl. PO19: Chich 5B 140
PO21: Pag 2C 180
Canterbury Ct. BN13: Wor 1D 170
RH13: Southw 8L 45
(off Porchester Cl.)
Canterbury Dr. BN2: Brig 3G 172 (6C 154)
Canterbury Rd. BN13: Wor 1D 170
BN16: Rust 2D 168
RH10: Craw 1G 28
Canton *RH16: Hay H 3E 72*
(off Great Heathmead)
Cants Cl. RH15: Burg H 5D 94
Cants La. RH15: Burg H 4D 94
Canute Cl. PO20: Brac 6N 177
Canute Rd. PO18: Bosh 8E 138
Canvas Ct. GU27: Has 5K 17
Canvey Cl. RH11: Craw 9E 10
Cape, The BN2: Rott 3N 173
BN17: L'ton 3N 167
Cape Copse RH12: Rudg 4J 23
Capel Av. BN10: Peace 6J 175
(not continuous)
Capelia Ho. BN11: Wor 3E 170
Capel La. RH11: Craw 7B 10
Capel Rd. RH12: Capel, Rusp 5C 8
Capenors RH15: Burg H 7A 94
Capitol, The 9A 26
Capricorn Cl. RH11: Craw 8A 10
Capsey Rd. RH11: Ifield 6A 10
Capstan Dr. BN17: L'ton 1N 167
Captains Wlk. RH11: Craw 8E 10
Capua Ct. RH10: Craw 2L 11
Caraway Cl. RH11: Craw 1D 28
Carden Av. BN1: Brig 1N 153
Carden Cl. BN1: Brig 8B 134
Carden Cres. BN1: Brig 8B 134
Carden Hill BN1: Brig 8C 134
Carden Pde. BN1: Brig 8C 134
Cardew Rd. GU33: Liss 7A 34
Card Hill RH18: F Row 2M 33
Cardigan Vs. BN42: S'wck 6A 152
Cardinal Ct. BN11: Wor 3E 170
Cardinal's Dr. PO21: Pag 2C 180
Carey Down BN10: Tels C 3H 175
Carey Ho. RH11: Craw 6E 10
Carfax RH12: Hors 9N 25
Cargo Forecourt Rd. RH6: Gatw 6F 4
Cargo Rd. RH6: Gatw 5F 4
Carina Dr. BN16: Ang 9E 146
Carisbrooke Cl. BN15: N Lan 5B 150
PO9: Hav 3B 136
Carisbrooke Dr. BN13: Durr 8N 147
Carisbrooke Lodge BN44: Stey 4A 130
Carisbrooke Rd. BN2: Brig 6E 154
Carleton Rd. PO19: Chich 5A 140
Carlingford Ct. PO21: Bog R 8D 164
Carlisle Gdns. PO19: Chich 4B 140
Carlisle Rd. BN3: Hove 7H 153
Carlton Av. PO21: Aldw 9L 163
Carlton Cl. RH10: Craw 7G 10
Carlton Ct. BN41: Ports 5E 152
Carlton Hill BN2: Brig 7G 172 (8C 154)
Carlton Ho. BN1: Brig 3N 153
BN13: Salv 7E 148
Carlton M. BN11: Wor 2E 170
Carlton Mt. *BN2: Brig 8C 154*
(off Carlton Pl.)
Carlton Pl. BN2: Brig 8C 154
Carlton Ter. BN41: Ports 5E 152
Carlton Tye RH6: Horl 2L 5
Carlyle Av. BN2: Brig 4E 154
Carlyle Ho. *BN14: Broadw 1H 171*
(off Bridge Rd.)
Carlyle St. BN2: Brig 6D 154
Carman Wlk. RH11: Craw 2D 28
Carmel Ho. BN3: Hove 6J 153
Carmelstead Cl. RH16: Hay H 6H 73
Carnation Cl. BN17: L'ton 1A 168
Carn Ct. *BN2: Brig 7D 154*
(off North Dr.)
Carnegie Cl. BN14: Broadw 8G 149
Carnegie Gdns. BN14: Broadw 8H 149
Carnegie Ho. BN13: Salv 7D 148
Carnegie Rd. BN14: Broadw 8G 149
Carnforth Rd. BN15: Somp 8N 149
Carnot Cl. PO21: Aldw 1J 181
Carnoustie Ct. *RH16: Hay H 5F 72*
(off Caxton Way)
Carol Cl. BN1: Brig 8A 134
Caroline Ct. RH11: Craw 7F 10
Carolyn Ho. BN13: Durr 7C 148
Caron Cl. BN15: S Lan 8B 150
Carousel Ct. PO22: Bog R 7C 164
Carpenters RH14: Bill 1J 65
Carpenters Lodge *BN11: Wor 1J 171*
(off Markwick M.)
Carpenters Mdw. RH20: Pulb 6B 86
Carrick Wlk. *BN43: Shor S 6H 151*
(off Broad Reach)
Carrier Bus. Pk. RH10: Craw 5K 11
Carron La. GU29: Midh 1F 80
Carse Rd. PO19: Chich 4E 140
Carter Rd. RH10: Craw 9M 11
Cartersland Cnr. GU30: Mill 7L 35
Carterslodge La. RH17: Hand 3N 47
Cartersmead Cl. RH6: Horl 1K 5
Carters Way RH14: Wisb 9A 42
Carvel Way BN17: L'ton 2N 167
Carylls Cotts. RH12: Fay 2J 27
Carylls Mdw. RH13: W Grin 1A 90
Casher Rd. RH10: Craw 9L 11
Cashman Lodge BN1: Brig 9C 134
Caspian Cl. PO18: Fish 5L 139
Caspian Ct. BN1: Brig 4D 172
Caspian Hgts. *BN2: Salt 3C 174*
(off Suez Way)
Caspian Sq. BN2: Rott 3N 173
Cassells Rd. PO19: Chich 3C 140
Cassidy Pl. RH20: Storr 6G 107
Cass Sculpture Foundation 6L 121
Castle, The RH12: Hors 4B 26
Castle Av. PO9: Warbl 4B 136
Castle Cl. BN13: Wor 8D 148
BN44: Bramb 4B 130
Castle Ct. BN13: Wor 9D 148
Castle Dr. RH6: Horl 4L 5
Castle Fld. BN44: Stey 3B 130
Castle Gdn. GU32: Peters 6E 54
Castle Gdns. BN18: Arun 2G 145
GU29: Midh 1H 81
(off Duck La.)
Castlegate RH20: W Chil 9G 86
Castle Goring M. BN13: Clap 5M 147
Castle Goring Way BN13: Clap 5M 147
Castle Hill National Nature Reserve 3A 156
Castle Ho. BN2: W'dean 4L 155
Castle La. BN44: Bramb, Stey 3A 130
(not continuous)
RH13: W Grin 9J 67
Castlemans La. PO11: Hay I 3A 158
Castle M. BN1: Brig 7B 172
Castle of Mey Ho. GU27: Has 5H 17
Castlereagh Grn. PO22: Felp 7H 165
Castlerigg Way RH10: Craw 8M 11
Castle Rd. BN13: Wor 9D 148
PO9: Row C 4A 116
RH12: Broadb H 8H 25
Castle Sq. BN1: Brig 8E 172 (8B 154)
Castle St. BN1: Brig 7B 172 (8N 153)
CASTLE TOWN 5F 130
Castle Way BN13: Wor 9D 148
BN44: Stey 3B 130
Castleway PO9: Warbl 4B 136
Castlewood Rd. RH13: Southw 8L 45
Caterways RH12: Hors 8L 25
Cathanger La. GU28: Graff 5G 82
Cathedral Ct. *PO19: Chich 7B 140*
(off South St.)
Cathedral St. *PO19: Chich 7C 140*
(off South St.)
Cathedral Way PO19: Chich 7N 139
Catherine Va. BN2: W'dean 5M 155
Cat Hill RH5: Ock 1F 6
Cathill La. RH5: Ock 1F 6
Catkin Way RH16: Hay H 5J 73
Catsland La. BN5: W'cote 7M 111
Cattswood La. RH16: Hay H 7D 72
Caudle St. *BN5: Henf 3J 111*
(off Coopers Way)
CAUSEWAY 7F 54
Causeway RH12: Hors 1N 45
Causeway, The BN2: Brig 7E 154
BN12: Gor S 1B 170
BN18: Arun 3J 145
GU31: Peters 9D 54
PO20: Bir 6J 161
PO20: Sel 2G 182
PO21: Pag 3C 180
RH13: Part G 5D 90
Causeway Ct. BN18: Arun 3J 145
Causewayside *GU27: Has 4M 17*
(off High St.)
Cavalier Cl. GU29: Midh 1G 81
Cavalier Way RH19: E Grin 5F 14
Cavell Av. BN10: Peace 5H 175
(Homecoast Ho.)
BN10: Peace 6H 175
(Roderick Av.)
Cavell Av. Nth. BN10: Peace 4J 175
Cavell Ct. *BN10: Peace 5H 175*
(off Cavell Av.)
Cavell Ho. BN43: Shor S 5L 151
Cavell Way RH10: Craw 7L 11
Cavendish Cl. BN10: Tels C 3H 175
BN12: Gor S 1B 170
RH12: Hors 4A 26
Cavendish Ho. BN1: Brig 8A 172
BN10: Peace 3J 175
PO21: Bog R 1M 181
(off Lennox St.)
RH16: Hay H 7G 72
Cavendish M. *BN3: Hove 8M 153*
(off Ivy Pl.)
BN11: Wor 3G 170
(off Heene Pl.)
Cavendish Pl. BN1: Brig 8A 172 (8N 153)
Cavendish Rd. PO21: Bog R 9D 164
Cavendish St. BN2: Brig 8G 172 (8C 154)
PO19: Chich 6B 140
Caversham Ct. *BN11: Wor 3F 170*
(off West Pde.)
Cawley Rd. PO19: Chich 8C 140
Caxton Cl. RH10: Craw 9F 10
Caxton Ct. BN14: Broadw 9H 149
GU27: Has 4L 17
Caxton Way RH16: Hay H 5F 72
Cecil Ct. BN15: S Lan 9B 150
Cecilian Av. BN14: Broadw 9H 149
Cecilian Ct. BN14: Broadw 9H 149
Cecil Norris Ho. BN43: Shor S 6J 151
Cecil Pashley Way BN43: Shor S 5F 150
Cecil Rd. BN15: S Lan 9B 150
Cedar Av. BN13: Durr 7D 148
RH16: Hay H 8E 72
Cedar Chase BN14: Fin 9C 128
Cedar Cl. BN12: Fer 3K 169
BN13: Durr 7D 148
BN15: Lan 9A 150
BN16: Ang 9F 146
PO10: W'brne 1H 137
PO21: Aldw 9M 163
RH11: Craw 3E 10
RH12: Hors 8M 25
RH15: Burg H 3C 94
Cedar Cl. E. PO21: Aldw 9N 163
Cedar Ct. BN11: Wor 1E 170
GU27: Has 5K 17
GU28: Petw 1M 83
(off Ranville Cl.)
Cedar Dr. PO19: Chich 7A 140
RH13: Southw 8K 45
Cedar Gdns. PO9: Hav 3A 136
Cedar Ho. BN14: Fin V 3D 148
BN43: Shor S 4L 151
Cedar Lodge *BN16: Rust 4B 168*
(off Cudlow Gdn.)
GU27: Has 6N 17
RH10: Craw 8F 10
Cedars, The BN1: Brig 2M 153
BN2: Brig 2G 172
BN10: Peace 3J 175
BN16: Rust 2D 168
PO22: Barn 7J 143
RH14: Bill 2H 65
RH16: Hay H 2E 72
Cedars Farm Cl. RH14: Bill 1H 65
Cedars Gdns. BN1: Brig 2M 153
Cedar Way BN5: Henf 3J 111
RH16: Hay H 5J 73
Cedarwell Cl. BN9: Pidd 2N 175
Cedarwood *BN1: Brig 2N 153*
(off Curwen Pl.)
Celandine Cl. RH11: Craw 9D 10
Celicia M. RH16: Hay H 4G 72
Cello Ct. *BN2: Brig 8D 154*
(off Somerset St.)
Cemetery La. GU28: Till 9J 61
PO10: W'brne, W'cote 1J 137
PO18: W Dean 9B 100
Cemetery Wlk. RH17: Hand 1A 48
Centenary Gdns. PO9: Hav 3A 136
Centenary Ho. *BN1: Brig 3N 153*
(off Cumberland Rd.)
BN13: Durr 8B 148
Centenary Ind. Est. BN2: Brig 5C 154
Central Av. BN10: Tels C 5G 174
BN14: Fin V 2D 148
BN16: Rust 4B 168
PO21: Bers 6B 164
Central Ct. BN10: Tels C 5G 174
Central Dr. PO21: Bers 6A 164
PO22: Midd S 7A 166
Central Pde. RH6: Horl 3J 5
Centrecourt Cl. BN14: Broadw 9G 149
Centrecourt Rd. BN14: Broadw 9G 149
Centurion Rd. BN1: Brig 6D 172 (7A 154)
(not continuous)
Centurion Way 3A 120
Ceres Pl. PO22: Felp 8L 165
Chadborn Cl. BN2: Brig 9E 154
Chadwick Cl. RH11: Craw 2D 28
Chaffer La. PO20: Bir 8G 161
Chaffinch Cl. BN13: Durr 8A 148
RH11: Craw 4F 10
RH12: Hors 4A 26
RH15: Burg H 4M 93
Chaffinch Way RH6: Horl 1G 4
Chailey Av. BN2: Rott 2A 174
Chailey Cl. RH11: Craw 9C 10
Chailey Common (Local Nature Reserve) 9D 74
Chailey Ct. *BN1: Brig 9L 133*
(off Mill Ri.)
RH16: Hay H 6G 72
(off Whitelands)
Chailey Cres. BN2: Salt 3E 174
Chailey Rd. BN1: Brig 1F 154
Chailey Windmill & Rural Life Mus. 9D 74
Chainbridge La. PO20: Sel 1F 182
Chain Pier Ho. *BN2: Brig 9C 154*
(off Marine Pde.)
Chalcraft La. PO21: Aldw, Bers, Lag 8N 163
Chalder La. PO20: Sidle 9B 162
Chaldon Rd. RH11: Craw 2E 28
Chalet Cl. BN12: Fer 4K 169
Chalet Gdns. BN12: Fer 4L 169
Chalet Rd. BN12: Fer 4K 169
Chalfont Cl. PO22: Midd S 7M 165
Chalfont Ct. BN11: Wor 2F 170
Chalfont Dr. BN3: Hove 2L 153
Chalfont Way BN13: Durr 7B 148
Chalkdock La. PO20: Itchen 7C 160
Chalkers La. BN6: Hurst 8J 93
Chalkland Ri. BN2: W'dean 5M 155
Chalk La. PO20: Sidle 5G 179
Chalkpit La. PO18: E Lav 8D 120
Chalk Rd. PO18: Charlt, E Dean, Good 9H 101
RH14: Ifol 9J 21
Chalky Rd. BN41: Ports 2B 152
Challen Cl. PO20: Oving 7L 141
Challen Ct. RH12: Hors 8M 25
Challoners RH17: Hors K 6C 52
Challoners Cl. BN2: Rott 2N 173
Challoners M. BN2: Rott 2N 173
Challow Cl. BN6: Hass 3N 113
Chalmers Cl. RH6: Charlw 7A 4
Chaloner Cl. RH16: Lind 2J 73

Chaloner Rd.—Church Hill

Chaloner Rd. RH16: Lind . . . 2J 73
CHALTON . . . 3C 96
Chalton La. PO8: Chalt . . . 1A 96
Chalvington Cl. BN1: Brig . . . 8F 134
Champions Row BN3: Hove . . . 5L 153
Chancellors Pk. BN6: Hass . . . 3A 114
Chanctonbury RH20: A'ton . . . 3E 108
Chanctonbury Cl. BN16: Rust . . . 4A 168
RH20: Wash . . . 9C 108
Chanctonbury Dr. BN43: Shor S . . . 4H 151
Chanctonbury Leisure Cen. . . . 5G 107
Chanctonbury Ring . . . 1F 128
Chanctonbury Ring Rd.
BN44: Wis . . . 8G 109
Chanctonbury Rd.
BN3: Hove . . . 3A 172 (6N 153)
BN16: Rust . . . 4A 168
(not continuous)
RH15: Burg H . . . 7A 94
Chanctonbury Vw. BN5: Henf . . . 3G 111
Chanctonbury Wlk. RH20: Storr . . . 6J 107
Chanctonbury Way RH11: Craw . . . 8E 10
Chancton Cl. BN11: Wor . . . 1D 170
Chancton Copse RH20: Storr . . . 4N 107
Chancton Vw. Rd. BN11: Wor . . . 1D 170
Chandler Cl. RH10: Craw . . . 8F 10
Chandler Ct. RH6: Horl . . . 2K 5
Chandler Rd. PO19: Chich . . . 8A 140
Chandlers Cl. PO11: Hay I . . . 9C 158
Chandlers Lea PO20: Brac . . . 6N 177
Chandlers Reach PO20: Itchen . . . 5D 160
Chandlers Way BN44: Stey . . . 4N 129
Chandos Rd. BN11: Wor . . . 2H 171
Channel Ct. BN15: S Lan . . . 9B 150
Channel Grange BN10: Tels C . . . 5G 174
Channel Keep BN17: L'ton . . . 4L 167
Channel Vw. BN42: S'wck . . . 6A 152
(off Whiterock Pl.)
PO21: Pag . . . 3C 180
Channel Vw. Rd. BN2: W'dean . . . 5J 155
Channings BN3: Hove . . . 7H 153
Chantlers Cl. RH19: E Grin . . . 2C 14
Chantrelles, The BN16: Ang . . . 8F 146
Chantrey Rd. RH10: Craw . . . 9G 10
Chantry Cl. BN5: Henf . . . 1H 111
RH6: Horl . . . 1H 5
RH20: Storr . . . 6K 107
Chantryfield Rd. BN16: Ang . . . 7E 146
Chantry Hall PO10: W'brne . . . 2H 137
Chantry Ind. Est. RH20: Storr . . . 7K 107
Chantry La. RH20: Storr . . . 1J 127
Chantry Mead PO22: Barn . . . 6H 143
Chantry Orchard BN44: Stey . . . 3A 130
(off Tanyard La.)
Chantry Rd. BN13: W Tar . . . 7E 148
Chapel Cl. BN17: Wick . . . 2J 167
RH15: Burg H . . . 4A 94
RH20: Cold . . . 3H 105
Chapelfields RH17: Cuck . . . 1A 72
Chapel Ho. BN2: Brig . . . 8C 154
(off Chapel St.)
Chapel La. BN7: E Chil . . . 4N 115
PO18: E Ash, W Sto . . . 2K 139
PO20: W Witt . . . 1K 177
RH10: Craw D . . . 1G 12
RH17: Hors K . . . 5C 52
RH18: F Row . . . 2M 33
RH19: Ash W . . . 6K 15
RH20: Coot . . . 6F 106
Chapel M.
BN3: Hove . . . 7A 172 (8M 153)
Chapel Pl. BN41: Ports . . . 6D 152
Chapel Rd. BN7: Plump G . . . 9M 95
BN11: Wor . . . 1H 171
BN41: Ports . . . 6C 152
RH6: Charlw . . . 6A 4
RH13: B Grn . . . 8D 44
Chapel Row PO18: E Dean . . . 9L 101
RH19: W Hoa . . . 4M 31
Chapel St. BN2: Brig . . . 8C 154
GU32: Peters . . . 5F 54
PO19: Chich . . . 6B 140
PO21: Bog R . . . 9D 164
Chapel Ter. BN2: Brig . . . 9E 154
Chapel Ter. M. BN2: Brig . . . 9E 154
Chapel Wlk. BN16: Ang . . . 8E 146
Chapman Ct. BN13: W Tar . . . 7E 148
Chapman Rd. RH10: Craw . . . 1L 29
Chapman's La. RH19: E Grin . . . 3B 14
(not continuous)
Chapman Way RH16: Hay H . . . 7G 72
Chappell Cft. BN11: Wor . . . 2F 170
Charis Ct. BN3: Hove . . . 6L 153
(off Eaton Rd.)
Charlecote Rd. BN11: Wor . . . 2J 171
Charles Av. PO19: Chich . . . 7F 140
RH15: Burg H . . . 6M 93
Charles Bennet Ct. RH16: Hay H . . . 5H 73
Charles Busby Ho. BN1: Brig . . . 6F 172
(off Marlborough Pl.)
Charles Cl. BN3: Hove . . . 2J 153
Charles Ct. BN11: Wor . . . 1G 171
Charlesfield Rd. RH6: Horl . . . 1H 5
Charles Ho. BN12: Gor S . . . 2B 170
Charles Kingston Gdns. BN1: Brig . . . 9N 133
Charles St. BN2: Brig . . . 9F 172 (9B 154)
GU32: Peters . . . 6E 54
Charleston Ct. RH10: Craw . . . 9K 11
Charlesworth Pk. RH16: Hay H . . . 5K 73
Charlmead PO20: E Witt . . . 5K 177
Charlock Cl. RH11: Craw . . . 1C 28
Charlock Way RH13: Southw . . . 8L 45
Charlotte Ct. RH11: Craw . . . 6E 10
(off Leopold Rd.)
Charlotte St. BN2: Brig . . . 9C 154
Charlston Av. BN9: Newh . . . 7N 175
CHARLTON . . . 9H 101
Charlton Dr. GU31: Peters . . . 4G 54
Charlton Gdns. BN6: Ditch . . . 4E 114
Charlton Mill Way PO18: Charlt . . . 9H 101
Charlton Rd. PO18: Charlt, Sing . . . 8F 100
Charltons, The BN1: Brig . . . 8K 134
Charlton St. BN44: Stey . . . 3N 129
CHARLWOOD
RH6 . . . 6A 4
RH19 . . . 2D 32
Charlwood Cl. RH10: Copt . . . 1B 12
Charlwood Gdns. RH15: Burg H . . . 3D 94
Charlwood M. RH6: Charlw . . . 6A 4
Charlwood Rd. RH6: Gatw . . . 5E 4
RH11: Gatw, Lowf H . . . 9D 4
RH11: Ifield . . . 9A 4
RH15: Burg H . . . 2D 94
Charlwoods Bus. Cen.
RH19: E Grin . . . 1D 14
Charlwoods Pl. RH19: E Grin . . . 1E 14
Charlwoods Rd. RH19: E Grin . . . 1E 14
Charlwood St. PO21: Bog R . . . 1K 181
Charlwood Wlk. RH11: Craw . . . 3D 10
CHARMANDEAN . . . 5H 149
Charmandean La. BN14: Char D . . . 6H 149
Charmandean Rd. BN14: Broadw . . . 7G 149
Charmans Cl. RH12: Hors . . . 6E 26
Charm Cl. RH6: Horl . . . 1G 4
Charnwood Rd. PO22: Bers . . . 6C 164
Charrington Way RH12: Broadb H . . . 8G 25
Charter Ga. RH16: Hay H . . . 4E 72
Charterhouse M. PO20: W Witt . . . 3K 177
Charter Wlk. GU27: Has . . . 5L 17
(off West St.)
Chartfield BN3: Hove . . . 3J 153
Chartfield Way BN3: Hove . . . 3J 153
(off Woodland Dr.)
Chartness BN1: Brig . . . 8A 134
(off Warmdene Rd.)
Chart Way RH12: Hors . . . 9N 25
Chartwell Ct. BN1: Brig . . . 8C 172
Chartwell Dr. PO9: Hav . . . 2C 136
Chartwell Rd. BN15: Lan . . . 9N 149
Chase, The BN14: Fin . . . 9C 128
BN18: Font . . . 2H 143
RH10: Craw . . . 7J 11
Chase Cl. GU33: Liss . . . 6A 34
Chase La. GU27: Has . . . 7M 17
Chase Plain GU26: Hind . . . 2E 16
Chatelet Cl. RH6: Horl . . . 1K 5
Chates Farm Ct. BN2: Brig . . . 7C 154
Chatfield Rd. RH17: Cuck . . . 3B 72
Chatfields RH11: Craw . . . 8D 10
Chatham Pl. BN1: Brig . . . 4C 172 (6A 154)
Chatham Rd. BN11: Wor . . . 1L 171
Chatsmore Cres. BN12: Gor S . . . 1M 169
Chatsmore Ho. BN12: Gor S . . . 2M 169
Chatsworth Av. BN10: Tels C . . . 3G 175
GU27: Has . . . 3L 17
Chatsworth Cl. BN10: Tels C . . . 4G 175
BN13: High S . . . 5D 148
BN16: Rust . . . 1A 168
Chatsworth Ct. BN1: Brig . . . 2B 172
BN43: Shor B . . . 7J 151
Chatsworth Dr. BN16: Rust . . . 1A 168
Chatsworth Lodge BN11: Wor . . . 1F 170
(off St Botolph's Rd.)
Chatsworth Pk. BN10: Tels C . . . 3H 175
Chatsworth Rd. BN1: Brig . . . 2B 172 (5N 153)
BN11: Wor . . . 2H 171
PO19: Chich . . . 7F 140
Chatsworth Sq. BN3: Hove . . . 6M 153
Chaucer Av. BN16: Rust . . . 3A 168
RH19: E Grin . . . 4C 14
Chaucer Ct. RH16: Hay H . . . 4E 72
(off Winnals Pk.)
Chaucer Dr. PO20: W Witt . . . 3K 177
Chaucer Rd. BN11: Wor . . . 1F 170
RH10: Craw . . . 4K 11
Chaucer Way PO22: Felp . . . 6L 165
Chawkmare Coppice PO21: Aldw . . . 1G 181
Chayle Gdns. PO20: Sel . . . 4J 183
Cheal Cl. BN43: Shor B . . . 7J 151
Cheal Ct. BN17: Wick . . . 9M 145
(off Cheal Way)
Cheals Rdbt. RH11: Craw . . . 8D 10
Cheal Way BN17: Wick . . . 9L 145
Cheam Rd. BN16: Rust . . . 4C 168
Cheapside BN1: Brig . . . 5E 172 (7B 154)
Cheeleys RH17: Hors K . . . 5C 52
Cheesemans La. PO18: Hamb . . . 9B 118
Cheetahs Gym . . . 8J 153
Chelsea Arc. RH16: Hay H . . . 4F 72
Chelston Av. BN3: Hove . . . 6F 152
Cheltenham Pl. BN1: Brig . . . 6F 172 (7B 154)
Chelwood Av. BN12: Gor S . . . 3A 170
Chelwood Cl. BN1: Brig . . . 8D 134
RH10: Craw . . . 8H 11
CHELWOOD COMMON . . . 4K 53
CHELWOOD GATE . . . 2K 53
Chelwood Ga. Rd. RH17: Chel G . . . 3L 53
TN22: Nut . . . 3L 53
Chene Rd. BN10: Peace . . . 6M 175
Chenies Cotts. RH5: Oak . . . 5E 6
Chennells Brook Cotts. RH12: Hors . . . 4C 26
(off Giblets La.)
Chennells Way RH12: Hors . . . 6A 26
Chepstow Cl. RH10: Craw . . . 6N 11
Chepstow Ct. BN1: Brig . . . 9F 134
Chequer Grange RH18: F Row . . . 2L 33
Chequer La. PO18: Bosh . . . 7G 138
Chequer Mead Theatre & Arts Cen. . . . 3F 14
Chequer Rd. RH19: E Grin . . . 3F 14
Chequers, The GU31: N'wd . . . 9D 56
Chequers Cl. RH6: Horl . . . 1J 5
Chequers Ct. RH13: Hors . . . 8B 26
Chequers Dr. RH6: Horl . . . 1J 5
Chequers Quay PO10: Ems . . . 5G 136
(off Queen St.)
Chermont Ct. BN16: E Pres . . . 2E 168
Cherrimans Orchard GU27: Has . . . 5H 17
Cherrington Cl. BN6: Hurst . . . 2K 113
Cherry Av. BN18: Yap . . . 2N 165
Cherry Cl. PO21: Aldw . . . 1F 180
RH15: Burg H . . . 5N 93
Cherry Cotts. TN22: Flet . . . 5M 75
Cherry Ct. RH13: Hors . . . 1A 46
Cherry Cft. BN17: Wick . . . 1K 167
Cherrycroft BN1: Brig . . . 9A 134
(off Warmdene Rd.)
Cherry Gdns. BN13: High S . . . 4C 148
PO20: Sel . . . 5H 183
Cherrylands Cl. GU27: Fern . . . 4K 37
Cherry La. PO20: Bir . . . 7J 161
RH11: Craw . . . 3E 10
RH17: Bal, Cuck . . . 5N 49
RH17: Bol . . . 6E 70
Cherry Orchard GU28: Petw . . . 1N 83
Cherry Orchard Rd.
PO19: Chich . . . 8D 140
Cherry Pl. RH16: Hay H . . . 7D 72
(off Lower Village)
Cherry Tree Av. GU27: Has . . . 4H 17
Cherry Tree Cl. BN13: High S . . . 4B 148
RH10: Craw . . . 4M 11
RH14: Bill . . . 9H 43
Cherry Tree Dr. PO20: E'gate . . . 5G 142
Cherry Tree Lodge BN15: Lan . . . 7A 150
Cherry Tree Wlk. GU28: Petw . . . 1M 83
(off Meadow Way)
RH12: Hors . . . 5E 26
Cherry Wlk. BN13: High S . . . 4B 148
Cherrywood BN1: Brig . . . 2N 153
(off Curwen Pl.)
Cherrywood Gdns.
PO11: Hay I . . . 8A 158
Cherwell Rd. BN13: Durr . . . 5A 148
Cherwell Wlk. RH11: Craw . . . 7B 10
Chesham Cl. BN12: Gor S . . . 2C 170
Chesham Mans. BN2: Brig . . . 9E 154
(off Eaton Pl.)
Chesham Pl. BN2: Brig . . . 9E 154
Chesham Rd. BN2: Brig . . . 9E 154
Chesham St. BN2: Brig . . . 9E 154
Cheshire Cl. PO21: Bog R . . . 8E 164
Cheshire Cres. PO20: Tang . . . 4L 141
Cheshire Way PO10: S'brne . . . 3L 137
Chesholt Cl. GU27: Fern . . . 4K 37
Chesley Cl. BN13: Durr . . . 7A 148
Chess Brook Grn. BN5: Henf . . . 9J 91
Chessels Farm Dr. PO22: Flan . . . 5J 165
Chesswood Av. PO22: Felp . . . 6K 165
Chesswood Cl. BN11: Wor . . . 9K 149
Chesswood Rd. BN11: Wor . . . 1J 171
Chester Av. BN11: Wor . . . 1L 171
BN15: Lan . . . 9A 150
Chester Bldgs. BN14: Wor . . . 9E 148
Chester Cl. PO10: Ems . . . 4D 136
Chester Ct. BN3: Hove . . . 4A 172
BN11: Wor . . . 2E 170
Chesterfield Cl. RH19: Felb . . . 1K 13
Chesterfield Ct. BN2: Brig . . . 8C 154
(off Marine Vw.)
Chesterfield Rd. BN12: Gor S . . . 1B 170
Chesters RH6: Horl . . . 1G 4
Chester Ter. BN1: Brig . . . 3B 154
Chesterton Cl. RH19: E Grin . . . 5F 14
Chesterton Ct. RH13: Hors . . . 7D 26
Chestnut Av. GU27: Has . . . 4L 17
PO19: Chich . . . 2B 140
Chestnut Cl. BN16: Ang . . . 9F 146
(Foxwood Av.)
BN16: Ang . . . 9E 146
(Sycamore Cl.)
GU29: Midh . . . 3G 80
PO20: N Mun . . . 9E 140
RH15: Burg H . . . 3C 94
RH19: E Grin . . . 3G 15
RH20: Storr . . . 4N 107
Chestnut Cotts. TN22: Flet . . . 6M 75
Chestnut Ct. BN11: Wor . . . 1G 171
(off Victoria Rd.)
BN16: E Pres . . . 3F 168
PO9: Row C . . . 6B 116
RH13: Hors . . . 9B 26
Chestnut Dr. BN6: Key . . . 2B 114
GU31: Peters . . . 8F 54
Chestnut End BN5: Henf . . . 2H 111
Chestnut Gdns. RH12: Hors . . . 6N 25
Chestnut Gro. BN6: Hurst . . . 1H 113
PO22: Bog R . . . 6D 164
Chestnut Ridge RH20: W Chil . . . 9H 87
Chestnut Rd. RH6: Horl . . . 1K 5
RH14: Bill . . . 2J 65
Chestnuts, The BN2: Brig . . . 5C 154
(off Prince's Cres.)
BN6: Say C . . . 7F 92
PO20: Huns . . . 4C 162
RH6: Horl . . . 1K 5
RH16: Lind . . . 2G 73
Chestnuts Cl. RH16: Lind . . . 2H 73
Chestnut Wlk. BN13: Durr . . . 8A 148
PO20: Tang . . . 4L 141
RH11: Craw . . . 3E 10
RH20: Pulb . . . 6A 86
Chestnut Way BN5: Henf . . . 2H 111
Chesworth Cl. RH13: Hors . . . 2N 45
Chesworth Cres. RH13: Hors . . . 1N 45
Chesworth Gdns. RH13: Hors . . . 1N 45
Chesworth La. RH13: Hors . . . 1N 45
Chetnole RH19: E Grin . . . 2D 14
Chetwood Rd. RH11: Craw . . . 1N 27
Cheveley Gdns. PO21: Aldw . . . 1F 180
Chevening Cl. RH11: Craw . . . 2E 28
Cheviot Cl. BN13: Durr . . . 5C 148
BN16: E Pres . . . 2F 168
Cheviot Rd. BN13: Durr . . . 5C 148
Cheviot Wlk. RH11: Craw . . . 6D 10
Cheyne Ct. BN43: Shor S . . . 6M 151
Cheynell Wlk. RH11: Craw . . . 8B 10
Cheyne Wlk. RH6: Horl . . . 4H 5
CHICHESTER . . . 7C 140
Chichester Av. PO11: Hay I . . . 9A 158
Chichester Bus. Pk. PO20: Tang . . . 3M 141
Chichester By-Pass
PO19: Chich, Westh, Oving . . . 8N 139
Chichester Cathedral . . . 7B 140
Chichester Cl. BN2: Brig . . . 9E 154
(off Chichester Pl.)
BN2: Salt . . . 3C 174
BN3: Hove . . . 1G 152
BN10: Peace . . . 5M 175
RH10: Craw . . . 1G 28
Chichester Ct. BN11: Wor . . . 3E 170
(off Pevensey Gdn.)
BN14: Fin V . . . 2D 148
BN16: Rust . . . 2B 168
Chichester Crematorium PO19: Chich . . . 5E 140
Chichester Dr. PO20: Tang . . . 4L 141
Chichester Dr. E. BN2: Salt . . . 3C 174
Chichester Dr. W. BN2: Salt . . . 3B 174
Chichester Festival Theatre . . . 5C 140
Chichester Food Pk. PO20: Runc . . . 1H 163
Chichester Ga. PO19: Chich . . . 8B 140
Chichester Golf Course . . . 7C 162
Chichester Harbour Water Tours . . . 4C 160
Chichester Ho. PO9: Hav . . . 2A 136
Chichester Marina . . . 5K 161
Chichester Minerva Theatre . . . 6C 140
Chichester Pl. BN2: Brig . . . 9E 154
Chichester Rd. BN18: Arun . . . 2C 144
GU29: Midh . . . 4G 81
PO11: Hay I . . . 3C 158
PO20: Sel . . . 6J 179
PO20: Sidle . . . 7A 162
PO20: W Witt . . . 9A 160
PO21: Bers, Bog R . . . 4N 163
Chichester Station (Rail) . . . 8B 140
Chichester Ter. BN2: Brig . . . 9E 154
RH12: Hors . . . 9A 26
Chichester Way PO20: Sel . . . 2L 183
RH15: Burg H . . . 3D 94
Chicken's La. RH14: Kird, Wisb . . . 3H 63
Chiddingfold Golf Course . . . 2J 19
Chiddingly Cl. BN2: Brig . . . 8G 154
RH10: Craw . . . 7J 11
Chiddingly Ho. BN3: Hove . . . 6M 153
(off Chatsworth Sq.)
CHIDHAM . . . 8B 138
Chidham La. PO18: Chid'm . . . 6B 138
Chilbolton Ct. PO9: Hav . . . 8B 116
Chilcomb RH15: Burg H . . . 7D 94
Chilcroft La. GU27: K Grn . . . 1K 37
Chilcroft Rd. GU27: Has . . . 4H 17
Chilcrofts Rd. GU27: K Grn . . . 1J 37
CHILGROVE . . . 6K 99
Chilgrove BN1: Brig . . . 8A 134
(off Warmdene Rd.)
Chilgrove Cl. BN12: Gor S . . . 1N 169
Chilgrove Pk. Rd. PO18: Chil . . . 6K 99
Chilgrove Pl. BN18: Yap . . . 2A 166
Chilgrove Rd. PO18: Mid L . . . 3L 119
Chilling St. RH19: Sharp . . . 6C 32
Chillis Wood Rd. RH16: Hay H . . . 4D 72
Chiltern Cl. BN16: E Pres . . . 2F 168
BN43: Shor S . . . 5M 151
GU27: Has . . . 6K 17
RH11: Craw . . . 6D 10
Chiltern Cres. BN13: Durr . . . 5C 148
Chiltington Cl. BN2: Salt . . . 2C 174
RH15: Burg H . . . 3A 94
RH20: W Chil . . . 1H 107
Chiltington Ct. RH12: Hors . . . 7A 26
(off Blenheim Rd.)
Chiltington Way BN2: Salt . . . 2C 174
Chiltley La. GU30: Lip . . . 8A 16
Chilton Cl. GU6: Alf . . . 1M 21
Chilton Gro. RH16: Hay H . . . 4J 73
Chine, The BN17: L'ton . . . 4N 167
Chipley Ct. PO21: Bog R . . . 8B 164
Chippendale Rd. RH11: Craw . . . 2D 28
Chippers Cl. BN13: Wor . . . 9D 148
Chippers Rd. BN13: Wor . . . 9D 148
Chippers Wlk. BN13: Wor . . . 9D 148
CHITHURST . . . 7M 57
Chithurst La. GU30: Mill . . . 3L 57
GU31: Chit, Trot . . . 5M 57
(not continuous)
Choda Ho. RH10: Craw . . . 7H 11
Chorley Av. BN2: Salt . . . 2B 174
Chownes Mead La. RH16: Hay H . . . 5C 72
Chrisdory Rd. BN41: Ports . . . 2B 152
Christchurch Cres. PO21: Aldw . . . 9N 163
Christchurch Ho. BN1: Brig . . . 7A 172
(off Montpelier Rd.)
Christchurch Rd. BN11: Wor . . . 1H 171
Christie Pl. PO22: Bers . . . 6E 164
Christies RH19: E Grin . . . 4D 14
Christopher Rd. RH19: E Grin . . . 3E 14
Christopher Way PO10: Ems . . . 3F 136
Christ's Hospital Rd. RH13: Hors . . . 4H 45
RH13: Itch . . . 4F 44
Christs Hospital Station (Rail) . . . 3H 45
Church App. BN17: L'ton . . . 3L 167
Church Av. RH16: Hay H . . . 3F 72
Church Bungs. RH14: Plais . . . 8E 20
Church Cl. BN1: Brig . . . 9A 134
BN13: Clap . . . 4L 147
BN15: N Lan . . . 5B 150
BN44: Up B . . . 3D 130
GU27: G'wd . . . 1A 18
PO21: Pag . . . 4A 180
RH13: Lwr Bee . . . 7K 47
RH13: Ship . . . 9G 67
RH15: Burg H . . . 5B 94
RH20: A'ton . . . 3D 108
CHURCH COMMON . . . 1E 54
Church Ct. BN3: Hove . . . 4H 153
RH16: Hay H . . . 5F 72
Churcher Rd. PO10: W'brne . . . 1H 137
Church Farm Cl. BN13: Pat . . . 3J 147
Church Farm Ct. PO20: E Witt . . . 3L 177
Church Farm Holiday Village PO21: Pag . . . 4A 180
Church Farm La. PO20: E Witt . . . 3L 177
Churchfarm La. PO20: Sidle . . . 1H 179
Church Farm Wlk. BN44: Up B . . . 3D 130
Churchfield RH20: Fitt . . . 5G 84
Churchfield Rd. GU31: Peters . . . 5H 55
Church Flds. BN6: Hurst . . . 2H 113
Churchfields BN16: E Pres . . . 2E 168
Church Grn. BN43: Shor S . . . 6M 151
GU27: Has . . . 4L 17
Church Gro. RH20: W Chil . . . 7J 87
Church Hill BN1: Brig . . . 8N 133
BN16: Ang . . . 8E 146
BN18: Slind . . . 9K 123

Church Hill—Colgate

Church Hill BN45: Pye 9L 113
GU27: Has 4L 17
GU29: Midh 9H 59
RH19: W Hoa 5M 31
RH20: Pulb 6A 86
Church Ho. Cl. BN42: S'wck 4B 152
Church Ho. M. PO22: Felp 8H 165
(off Felpham Rd.)
Churchill Av. PO21: Aldw 8N 163
RH12: Hors 8M 25
Churchill Ct. RH10: Craw 3J 11
Churchill Dr. PO10: Ems 1F 136
Churchill Ho. BN3: Hove 3F 152
PO22: Barn 8K 143
Churchill Ind. Est. BN15: Lan 9A 150
Churchill Pde. BN16: Rust 3B 168
Churchill Sq. Shop. Cen.
BN1: Brig 7C 172 (8A 154)
Churchill Wlk. PO21: Pag 3C 180
(off Ashcroft Way)
Churchill Way RH15: Burg H 6D 94
Church La. BN5: Henf 2H 111
BN6: Alb 2D 112
BN6: Ditch 4E 114
BN6: Newt 8F 112
BN12: Fer 2K 169
BN15: Somp 6L 149
BN17: Climp 3E 166
BN17: Lym 7J 145
BN18: Walb 5M 143
BN18: Yap 9N 143
BN42: S'wck 6N 151
BN44: A'hst 2A 110
BN44: Stey 3A 130
BN44: Up B 3D 130
BN45: Newt 8F 112
BN45: Pye 9L 113
GU27: Has 4L 17
GU28: Lods 7C 60
GU29: C'ing 9F 80
PO9: Warbl 5B 136
PO11: Hay I 1C 158
PO18: Box 2M 141
PO18: Comp 5M 97
PO18: Funt 9D 118
PO18: W Dean 9C 100
PO20: Bir 7H 161
PO20: E'gate 6F 142
PO20: Huns 4C 162
PO20: N Mun 3F 162
PO20: Oving 6L 141
PO20: Sidle 9A 162
PO20: Tang 4L 141
PO21: Pag 3A 180
PO22: Barn 9J 143
PO22: Bog R 7D 164
RH5: Oak 3D 6
RH6: Bur, Horl 7N 5
RH10: Copt 2B 12
RH10: Craw 5H 11
RH12: Broadb H 8H 25
RH13: Part G 5C 90
RH13: Plum P, Lwr Bee 4K 47
RH13: Southw 9J 45
RH17: Ard 3G 51
RH17: Dane 7G 53
RH17: Hors K 5C 52
RH17: Twine 4C 92
RH17: Wivel 2G 95
RH19: E Grin 3F 14
RH20: A'ton 3D 108
RH20: Bury 8F 104
RH20: Cold 1J 105
RH20: Fitt 5F 84
Church Mead BN6: Key 4B 114
BN44: Stey 3A 130
Churchmead Cl. PO18: Mid L 8B 120
Church Mdw. PO18: Bosh 8E 138
Church M. PO20: N Mun 3E 162
CHURCH NORTON 7M 179
Church Pk. RH11: Lowf H 8G 5
Church Path GU29: C'ing 8F 80
PO9: Warbl 6B 136
PO10: Ems 6D 136
(Maisemore Gdns.)
PO10: Ems 5F 136
(St James' Rd.)
PO18: Stou 2D 118
PO21: Bog R 8E 164
PO22: Midd S 7N 165
RH12: Rusp 7F 8
Church Pl. BN2: Brig 9F 154
RH20: Pulb 6A 86
Church Platt RH17: Cuck 4N 71
Church Rd. BN3: Hove 7J 153
BN13: W Tar 8E 148
BN16: Ang 8E 146
BN16: Rust 3B 168
BN18: Yap 1N 165
BN41: Ports 6D 152
GU27: Fern 5K 37
GU27: Has 4L 17
(Rosemary Ct.)
GU27: Has 5H 17
(St Stephens Cl.)
GU29: W Lav 2H 81
GU32: Steep 2D 54
PO10: S'brne 5K 137
PO10: Tho I 3K 159
PO10: W'brne 2H 137
PO11: Hay I 8A 158
PO19: Chich 5E 140
PO20: Ald 5B 142
PO20: E Witt 4K 177
PO20: Sel 2J 183
RH6: Horl 3H 5
RH10: Copt 1C 12
RH10: Turn H 9G 13
RH10: Worth 6N 11
RH11: Lowf H 8G 5
RH12: Broadb H 8H 25
RH12: Hors 6E 26
RH13: Mann H 5F 46
Church Rd. RH13: Part G 4C 90
RH15: Burg H 6B 94
RH16: Hay H 5F 72
RH17: Scay H 6N 73
Church Rd. Ind. Est. RH11: Lowf H 8H 5
Church Rd. Rdbt. PO11: Hay I 6A 158
Churchside PO19: Chich 6B 140
Church Sq. PO19: Chich 7C 140
Church St. BN1: Brig 6C 172 (7A 154)
BN5: Henf 2H 111
BN17: L'ton 3L 167
BN18: Amb 8K 105
BN41: Ports 6D 152
BN43: Shor S 6J 151
BN44: Stey 3A 130
GU28: Petw 9N 61
RH11: Craw 6E 10
RH12: Rudg 4H 23
RH12: Warnh 4K 25
RH17: Cuck 3N 71
RH20: Storr 6J 107
RH20: W Chil 7K 87
TN22: Flet 6M 75
Church Ter. BN5: Henf 2H 111
Church Vw. GU28: Till 8K 61
(off Cemetery La.)
PO10: W'brne 2H 137
Church Vw. Cl. RH6: Horl 3H 5
Church Wlk. BN11: Wor 2K 171
RH6: Horl 3H 5
RH10: Craw 6F 10
RH12: Colg 3L 27
RH15: Burg H 5B 94
Church Wlk. M. RH15: Burg H 5B 94
(off Church Rd.)
Church Way BN2: Brig 5G 172
BN13: W Tar 8E 148
PO18: Sing 8F 100
PO21: Pag 2C 180
Church Way Cl. BN13: W Tar 8E 148
Churchwood RH20: Fitt 4H 85
Churchwood Dr. PO20: Tang 4M 141
Churt Dr. PO22: Bers 6E 164
Chute Av. BN13: High S 5C 148
Chute Way BN13: High S 5C 148
CINDER HILL 2B 52
Cinder Hill RH19: Sharp 1B 52
Cinder Hill La. RH17: Hors K 4A 52
Cinders La. BN18: Yap 2A 166
Cineworld Cinema
Brighton 8K 173
Chichester 8B 140
Crawley 5F 10
Cinque Foil BN10: Peace 4J 175
Circle, The BN16: E Pres 4F 168
Circus Pde. BN1: Brig 3E 172
Circus St. BN2: Brig 7F 172 (8B 154)
Cissbury Av. BN10: Peace 6L 175
BN14: Fin V 3D 148
Cissbury Cl. RH12: Hors 5D 26
Cissbury Cres. BN2: Salt 3E 174
Cissbury Dr. BN14: Fin V 2D 148
Cissbury Gdns. BN14: Fin V 2E 148
Cissbury Hill RH11: Craw 8E 10
Cissbury Ring 9F 128
Cissbury Rd. BN3: Hove 3A 172 (6N 153)
BN12: Fer 1K 169
BN14: Broadw 7G 149
RH15: Burg H 4N 93
Cissbury Way BN43: Shor S 4H 151
City Bus. Cen. PO19: Chich 8B 140
(off Basin Rd.)
RH13: Hors 1A 46
City Bus. Centre, The RH11: Craw 2F 10
City Flds. Bus. Pk. PO20: Tang 3M 141
City Flds. Way PO20: Tang 3M 141
City Pk. BN3: Hove 4K 153
City Pl. RH6: Craw 8K 5
Civic Way RH15: Burg H 6B 94
Claigmar Rd. BN16: Rust 3B 168
Clair Ct. RH16: Hay H 4F 72
Clair Rd. RH16: Hay H 3F 72
Clammer Hill GU27: G'wd 2A 18
Clammer Hill Rd. GU27: G'wd 3A 18
Clapgate La. RH13: Slinf 6A 24
CLAPHAM 4K 147
Clapham Cl. BN13: Clap 4L 147
Clapham Comn. BN13: Clap 5K 147
Clappers Ga. RH10: Craw 5F 10
Clappers La. BN5: Fulk 2B 132
PO20: Brac, Earn 5M 177
Clappers Mdw. GU6: Alf 1N 21
Clappers Orchard GU6: Alf 1M 21
CLAPWATER 3N 75
Clare Cl. RH10: Craw 3L 11
Clare Gdns. GU31: Peters 6J 55
Clare Lodge BN16: Rust 3A 168
(off Sea La.)
Claremont Cl. BN16: Ang 7E 146
Claremont Ct. PO21: Bog R 9E 164
(off Campbell Rd.)
Claremont Gdns. PO20: E'gate 3G 143
Claremont Way GU29: Midh 1G 81
Clarence Av. BN17: Wick 1J 167
Clarence Ct. BN11: Wor 2K 171
(off Brighton Rd.)
RH6: Horl 1M 5
Clarence Dr. BN16: E Pres 2E 168
RH19: E Grin 5F 14
Clarence Gdns. BN1: Brig 7B 172
Clarence Ga. PO21: Bog R 9E 164
(off High St.)
Clarence Rd. PO21: Bog R 9E 164
RH13: Hors 1A 46
Clarence Sq. BN1: Brig 7C 172 (8A 154)
Clarence Ter. BN5: Henf 3H 111
(off Nep Town Rd.)
Clarence Way RH6: Horl 1M 5
Clarence Yd. BN1: Brig 8E 172 (8B 154)
Clarendon Ho. BN3: Hove 6K 153
Clarendon M. BN11: Wor 3G 171
Clarendon Pl. BN2: Brig 9D 154
BN41: Ports 7E 152
Clarendon Rd. BN3: Hove 6K 153
BN14: Broadw 7J 149
BN43: Shor S 5M 151
Clarendon Ter. BN2: Brig 9E 154
Clarendon Vs. BN3: Hove 6K 153
Clare Wlk. BN2: Brig 8E 154
Claridge Ho. BN17: L'ton 3L 167
Clarke Av. BN3: Hove 3G 153
Clarke Ct. BN3: Hove 7H 153
Clarke Ho. RH10: Craw 4J 11
Clark Rd. RH11: Craw 2C 28
CLARK'S GREEN 1N 7
Clarks Grn. Rd. RH5: Capel, Newd, Rusp 2D 8
Clarks Ind. Est. BN3: Hove 5K 153
Clayfields BN10: Peace 4H 175
Clay La. BN18: Cross, W'camp 4M 145
GU29: Bep, Trey 5M 79
PO18: W Ash, E Ash, Fish 3F 138
PO19: Chich, Fish 5K 139
RH20: Coot 7F 106
Claypit La. PO18: Good, Westh 1G 140
Clays Cl. RH19: E Grin 4E 14
Clays Hill BN44: Bramb 4A 130
CLAYTON 6M 113
Clayton Av. BN6: Hass 4N 113
Clayton Ct. PO20: Sel 4G 183
Clayton Dr. RH15: Burg H 7A 94
Clayton Hill BN6: Clay, Pye 1L 133
BN45: Pye 1L 133
RH11: Craw 8E 10
Clayton La. PO20: Brac 4M 177
Clayton Pk. BN6: Hass 3N 113
Clayton Rd. BN2: Brig 6E 154
BN6: Ditch 5D 114
PO20: Sel 4G 182
Claytons Cnr. PO20: Bir 7H 161
Clayton Wlk. BN13: Durr 8B 148
(off Chalfont Way)
Clayton Way BN3: Hove 2H 153
Clayton Windmills (Jack & Jill) 8N 113
Clearwater La. RH16: Hay H 9D 72
RH17: Scay H 6A 74
Cleaver's La. RH17: Cuck 7K 49
Cleeves Ct. BN16: Rust 2C 168
Cleeves Way BN16: Rust 2D 168
Clements Ct. BN43: Shor S 6J 151
(off Raven's Rd.)
Clerks Acre BN6: Key 3B 114
(not continuous)
Clermont Ct. BN1: Brig 3N 153
Clermont Rd. BN1: Brig 3N 153
Clermont Ter. BN1: Brig 3N 153
Cleveland Cl. BN13: Durr 5D 148
Cleveland Copse BN13: Durr 5D 148
(off Cleveland Cl.)
Cleveland Gdns. RH15: Burg H 6C 94
Cleveland Rd. BN1: Brig 3B 154
BN13: Durr 5D 148
PO19: Chich 8D 140
Clevelands RH14: Bill 1J 65
RH16: Hay H 3F 72
(off Perrymount Rd.)
Clevets, The PO21: Aldw 2E 180
Cleve Way RH14: Bill 1J 65
Cliff, The BN2: Brig 9G 155
Cliff App. BN2: Brig 9G 155
Cliff Av. BN10: Peace 7L 175
Cliff Ct. BN2: Rott 3N 173
(off Park Rd.)
Cliff Gdns. BN10: Tels C 4F 174
Cliff Pk. Cl. BN10: Peace 5M 175
Cliff Rd. BN2: Brig 9G 154
Clifton Cl. RH6: Horl 2M 5
Clifton Ct. BN1: Brig 4D 172
BN11: Wor 1G 170
PO21: Bog R 9D 164
(off Clifton Rd.)
Clifton Gdns. BN11: Wor 1G 171
Clifton Hill BN1: Brig 5B 172 (7N 153)
Clifton M. BN1: Brig 5C 172
Clifton Pl. BN1: Brig 6B 172 (7N 153)
Clifton Rd. BN1: Brig 5B 172 (7A 154)
BN11: Wor 1G 171
BN17: L'ton 4K 167
PO21: Bog R 8D 164
RH10: Craw 7L 11
RH15: Burg H 3M 93
Clifton St. BN1: Brig 5D 172 (7A 154)
Clifton St. Pas. BN1: Brig 5D 172
Clifton Ter. BN1: Brig 6C 172 (7A 154)
Cliftonville Ct. BN3: Hove 6K 153
Clifton Way BN10: Tels C 4G 174
CLIMPING 3F 166
Climping Cl. RH16: Hay H 5E 72
Climping Pk. BN17: L'ton 3F 166
Climping Rd. RH11: Craw 4D 10
Climping St. BN17: Climp 4D 166
Clitherow Gdns. RH10: Craw 7G 10
Clive Av. BN12: Gor S 2B 170
Clivedale BN44: Stey 3A 130
Clivedale Gdns. BN44: Stey 3B 130
Cliveden Cl. BN1: Brig 2N 153
Cliveden Ct. BN1: Brig 3N 153
Clive Way RH10: Craw 6L 11
Clock Ho. Cotts. RH5: Capel 2N 7
Clockhouse Ct. GU27: Has 5L 17
Clock Pk. PO22: Bers 6F 164
Clock Tower
Brighton 7D 172 (8A 154)
Cloisters, The BN14: Broadw 8H 149
BN17: L'ton 4M 167
CLOSE, THE 7B 140
Close, The BN1: Brig 9M 133
BN6: Key 3A 114
BN15: S Lan 9C 150
BN16: Rust 4C 168
BN43: Shor S 5J 151
PO18: Box 2M 141
PO18: Mid L 9B 120
PO19: Chich 7B 140
PO20: Sel 2L 183
PO21: Aldw 2E 180
PO22: Midd S 7A 166
Close, The RH6: Horl 4L 5
RH14: Ifol 8J 21
RH15: Burg H 4D 94
RH17: Ard 3J 51
RH19: E Grin 4D 14
RH20: A'ton 2E 108
Closewalks Wood GU29: Midh 1H 81
Clothalls La. RH13: W Grin 3M 89
Clovelly Av. PO22: Felp 7J 165
Clovelly Rd. PO10: Ems 5E 136
PO10: S'brne 4K 137
PO11: Hay I 9C 136
Clover Ct. RH16: Hay H 5F 72
Cloverfield RH13: Slinf 8B 24
Cloverfields RH6: Horl 1K 5
Cloverlands RH10: Craw 4H 11
Clover La. BN12: Fer 3K 169
Clover Mead PO22: Felp 6K 165
Clovers Cotts. RH12: Fay 2J 27
Clovers End BN1: Brig 7C 134
RH12: Hors 6D 26
Clovers Way RH12: Fay 4G 26
Clover Way BN41: Ports 3D 152
Club Wlk. BN16: E Pres 4F 168
Clun Rd. BN17: L'ton, Wick 1H 167
Clyde Cl. BN13: Durr 5A 148
Clyde Rd. BN1: Brig 2E 172 (5B 154)
BN13: Durr 6A 148
PO22: Felp 9G 165
Clydesdale Av. PO19: Chich 8C 140
Clydesdale Gdns. PO22: Bers 5B 164
Clyde Ter. BN44: Stey 3B 130
(off Station Rd.)
Coach & Horses La. RH17: Chel C 4J 53
Coach Ho. Cl. BN16: Rust 2D 168
PO20: Sel 3J 183
Coach Ho. M. BN11: Wor 2G 171
Coach La. RH17: Chel C 4J 53
Coachman's Dr. RH11: Craw 1D 28
Coach Rd. PO18: Westh 4G 141
PO20: Oving 5H 141
RH6: Gatw 5H 5
Coastal Counties Ho. BN2: Brig 7C 154
(off Sussex St.)
Coastal Link 9E 130
Coastal Pl. BN3: Hove 7H 153
Coastal Rd. BN16: E Pres, King G 4G 168
Coastguard Cotts. PO9: Lstne 7A 136
Coastguard La. PO20: W Witt 2E 176
Coastguard Pde. PO21: Aldw 2F 180
(off Barrack La.)
Coastguard Rd. BN17: L'ton 5K 167
(off Arun Pde.)
Coastguards Cotts. PO20: W Witt 1E 176
COATES 8D 84
Coates Castle RH20: Fitt 8C 84
Coates Ct. BN42: S'wck 6A 152
Coates La. RH20: Fitt 9C 84
Cobbett Cl. RH10: Craw 4L 11
Cobbetts Mead RH16: Hay H 6J 73
Cobbetts M. RH20: Pulb 6N 85
(off Lyntons)
Cobblers RH13: Slinf 8B 24
Cobbles Cres. RH10: Craw 5G 10
Cobblewood PO10: Ems 2F 136
Cob Cl. RH10: Craw D 4K 13
Cobden Ho. GU29: Midh 2G 80
Cobden La. GU27: Has 4M 17
Cobden Rd. BN2: Brig 6D 154
BN11: Wor 2G 171
GU29: Midh 1G 81
Cobham Cl. BN18: Yap 2N 165
Cobham Way RH10: Craw 9K 5
Cob La. RH17: Ard 2J 51
Cobnor Activities Cen. 2B 160
Cobnor Cl. RH11: Craw 8B 10
Cobton Dr. BN3: Hove 2J 153
Coburn Ho. RH10: Craw 5K 11
(off Trafalgar Gdns.)
Cob Wlk. RH11: Craw 6C 10
COCKING 8F 80
COCKING CAUSEWAY 4G 81
Cocking Hill GU29: C'ing 1F 100
Cocking Pk. GU29: C'ing 5F 80
Cock's Hill RH13: Ship, Southw 6J 67
CODMORE HILL 3C 86
Cohen Cl. PO20: Ald 8E 142
Cokeham Ct. BN15: Somp 6M 149
Cokeham Gdns. BN15: Somp 7N 149
Cokeham La. BN15: Somp 7N 149
Cokeham Rd. BN15: Somp 6N 149
Colbourne Av. BN2: Brig 3E 154
Colbourne Rd. BN3: Hove 4A 172 (6N 153)
Colchester Va. RH18: F Row 1L 33
Colchins RH15: Burg H 7A 94
COLD ASH HILL 5A 16
COLDEAN 8E 134
Coldean La. BN1: Brig 7E 134
Coldharbour Farm Rd. PO10: Ems 4F 136
Coldharbour La. BN13: Pat 4J 147
Coldicott M. PO22: Midd S 7A 166
COLDWALTHAM 2J 105
Cold Waltham La. RH15: Burg H 6E 94
Colebrook Cl. BN11: Wor 1K 171
Colebrook Ct. BN11: Wor 1K 171
Colebrook La. RH20: Cold 2H 105
Colebrook Rd. BN1: Brig 1M 153
BN17: Wick 1J 167
BN42: S'wck 6B 152
Cole Cl. RH11: Craw 2D 28
Coleman Av. BN3: Hove 6G 153
Colemans Hatch Rd. RH18: Wych C 6L 33
Coleman St. BN2: Brig 7C 154
Coleridge Cl. BN12: Gor S 1N 169
RH12: Hors 5B 26
Coleridge Cres. BN12: Gor S 1N 169
Coleridge Ho. RH13: Hors 5H 45
(off The Avenue)
Coleridge M. BN12: Gor S 1N 169
Coleridge Rd. BN12: Gor S 1N 169
Coleridge St. BN3: Hove 5J 153
Colet Rd. RH10: Craw 9F 10
COLGATE 5M 27

Coxes Mdw.—Dean La.

Coxes Mdw. GU32: Peters 4E 54
Coxes Rd. PO20: Sel 4G 183
COX GREEN 1K 23
Cox Grn. Rd. RH12: Rudg 1K 23
Cox Gro. RH15: Burg H 3A 94
Coxham La. BN44: Stey 2N 129
Cox Ho. RH12: Hors 9M 25
Cox's La. GU29: Ipin 3N 57
Coxswain Way PO20: Sel 5J 183
CRABBET PARK 5N 11
Crabbet Pk. RH10: Worth 5A 12
Crabbet Rd. RH10: Craw 5K 11
Crablands PO20: Sel 3G 183
Crablands Cl. PO20: Sel 3G 183
CRABTREE 2K 69
Crabtree Arc. BN15: Lan 7B 150
(off Grand Av.)
Crabtree Av. BN1: Brig 9B 134
Crab Tree Cl. BN17: Wick 8K 145
Crabtree Ct. RH11: Craw 5E 10
Crabtree La. BN15: Lan 7A 150
Crabtree Lodge BN15: Lan 6A 150
Crabtree Rd. RH11: Craw 5E 10
Cradock Pl. BN13: Durr 5C 148
Crafts La. GU31: Peters 4G 54
Craggits La. BN5: Henf 2H 111
(off Church St.)
Craigans RH11: Craw 6C 10
Craignair Av. BN1: Brig 7A 134
Craigweil La. PO21: Aldw 1G 180
Craigweil Mnr. PO21: Aldw 2F 180
Cranborne Wlk. RH10: Craw 8H 11
Cranbourne Cl. RH6: Horl 1K 5
Cranbourne St. BN1: Brig 7D 172 (8A 154)
Cranbrook BN2: Brig 7C 154
(off John St.)
Crane St. PO19: Chich 7C 140
Cranford Gdns. PO21: Bog R 8D 164
Cranford Rd. GU32: Peters 7D 54
Cranham Av. RH14: Bill 3B 65
Cranleigh Av. BN2: Rott 3B 174
Cranleigh Ct. BN11: Wor 2G 170
Cranleigh Rd. BN14: Wor 8F 148
Cranley Ct. BN3: Hove 6F 152
Cranmer Av. BN3: Hove 4H 153
Cranmer Rd. BN13: Wor 1E 170
Cranmer Wlk. RH10: Craw 7L 11
Cranston Gdns. RH19: E Grin 2E 14
Cranston Rd. RH19: E Grin 2E 14
Cranston Way RH10: Craw D 4K 13
Cranworth Rd. BN11: Wor 1K 171
Craven Ct. BN15: Lan 6B 150
RH19: E Grin 2F 14
(off Badger's Way)
Craven Path BN2: Brig 7E 154
Craven Pl. BN2: Brig 8E 154
Craven Rd. BN2: Brig 7E 154
RH10: Craw 7K 11
Crawford Gdns. RH13: Hors 7B 26
Crawfurd Way RH19: E Grin 1G 15
CRAWLEY 6F 10
Crawley Av. PO9: Hav 8A 116
RH10: Craw 4G 10
RH11: Craw 5D 10
Crawley Bus. Quarter RH10: Craw 2G 11
CRAWLEY DOWN 5J 13
Crawley Down Rd. RH19: Felb 1M 13
Crawley Foyer RH11: Craw 6E 10
Crawley Goods Yd. RH10: Craw 1K 11
Crawley Karting 2K 11
Crawley La. RH10: Craw 5L 11
RH17: Bal 6M 29
Crawley Lawn Tennis Club 4K 11
Crawley Leisure Pk.
RH10: Craw 5F 10
Crawley Museum Cen. 7E 10
Crawley Rd. BN1: Brig 8E 134
RH11: Fay 4F 26
RH12: Hors, Fay 7C 26
Crawley Sth. West By-Pass
RH11: Pease P, Craw 1A 28
Crawley Station (Rail) 7G 10
Crawley Town FC 1E 28
Crawters Cl. RH10: Craw 5H 11
Crawters La. GU31: Peters 6F 54
(off College St.)
Crayford Rd. BN2: Brig 4E 154
Cray La. RH20: Pulb 3C 86
Crays Ct. RH20: G Grn 8A 88
Cray's La. RH20: G Grn, Thake 9N 87
Creasys Dr. RH11: Craw 2C 28
Crede Cl. PO18: Bosh 8F 138
Crede La. PO18: Bosh 7F 138
Creek End PO10: Ems 6F 136
PO19: Fish 7L 139
Cremorne Pl. GU32: Peters 5F 54
Crescent, The BN2: Brig 3F 154
BN6: Key 4C 114
BN15: Lan 9A 150
BN16: E Pres 4F 168
BN16: Rust 4N 167
BN42: S'wck 5B 152
BN44: Stey 4A 130
PO10: S'brne 5K 137
PO20: W Witt 4J 177
PO21: Pag 3C 180
PO22: Felp 8H 165
RH6: Horl 4J 5
RH12: Hors 1L 45
RH20: Coot 6F 106
Crescenta Wlk. PO21: Bog R 9B 164
Crescent Cl. BN2: W'dean 5M 155
RH15: Burg H 5C 94
Crescent Ct. BN2: Brig 6C 154
(off Park Cres. Ter.)
BN11: Wor 1M 171
(off Seamill Pk. Cres.)
RH6: Horl 4J 5
Crescent Dr. Nth. BN2: W'dean 5L 155
Crescent Dr. Sth. BN2: W'dean 7L 155
Crescent Mans. BN2: Brig 2G 172
Crescent Pl. BN2: Brig 9D 154
Crescent Ri. RH20: Storr 4M 107
Crescent Rd. BN2: Brig 5C 154
BN11: Wor 2G 171
PO21: Bog R 9D 164
RH15: Burg H 5B 94
RH19: E Grin 3D 14
Crescent Way RH6: Horl 4J 5
RH15: Burg H 5B 94
Crespin Way BN1: Brig 3D 154
Cressey Way PO19: Chich 4C 140
Cresta Ct. BN10: Peace 5J 175
(off Sth. Coast Rd.)
Cresta Rd. BN9: Newh 6N 175
Crest Way BN41: Ports 2D 152
Crestway, The BN1: Brig 3D 154
Crestway Pde. BN1: Brig 3D 154
(off The Crestway)
Crewdson Rd. RH6: Horl 2K 5
Cricket Ct. RH19: E Grin 1E 14
Cricketers Cl. RH20: A'ton 2E 108
Cricketers Pde. BN14: Broadw 7H 149
Cricketfield BN8: Newick 9K 75
Cricketfield Rd. RH12: Hors 1M 45
Crimbourne La. RH14: Wisb 5J 63
Crimsham Rd. PO21: Bers 5B 164
Cripland Cl. RH16: Hay H 3J 73
Cripplecrutch Hill GU27: Chidd 6G 18
Cripplegate La. RH13: Southw 1L 67
Cripps Av. BN10: Peace 3K 175
Cripps Ho. RH11: Craw 1D 28
Cripps La. BN44: Stey 3B 130
Critchel's La. PO20: Sidle 2E 178
Critchfield Rd. PO18: Bosh 8E 138
CRITCHMERE 4G 16
Critchmere Hill GU27: Has 4G 16
Critchmere La. GU27: Has 5G 16
Critchmere Rd. PO20: E'gate 6G 142
Critchmere Va. GU27: Has 5G 16
CROCKERHILL 2B 142
Crockford Rd. PO10: W'brne 1H 137
Crockham Cl. RH11: Craw 8E 10
Crockhurst RH13: Southw 8L 45
Crockhurst Hill BN13: Salv 5D 148
Crocks Dean BN10: Peace 2K 175
Crocodile Wlk. BN3: Hove 3A 172 (5N 153)
Croft, The BN6: Hass 2A 114
BN16: E Pres 3F 168
BN18: Yap 9N 143
BN42: S'wck 5A 152
GU28: Lods 6C 60
GU29: C'ing 8F 80
PO21: Bers 7A 164
RH11: Craw 6C 10
Croft Av. BN42: S'wck 6A 152
Croftcost La. PO22: Felp 6L 165
Croft Dr. BN41: Ports 2C 152
Crofters Wood BN44: Bramb 4C 130
Croft La. BN5: Henf 3H 111
PO11: Hay I 3A 158
Croft Mead PO19: Chich 3C 140
Croft Mdw. BN44: Stey 3A 130
Croft Rd. BN1: Brig 1M 153
PO20: Sel 4H 183
Croft Vs. BN5: Henf 2H 111
(off Church St.)
Croft Way PO20: Sel 3H 183
PO22: Felp 6K 165
RH12: Hors 8L 25
Cromleigh Way BN42: S'wck 3A 152
Crompton Flds. RH10: Craw 3G 10
Crompton Way RH10: Craw 4G 10
Cromwell Ct. BN3: Hove 6L 153
Cromwell M. RH15: Burg H 4A 94
Cromwell Pl. RH19: E Grin 5F 14
Cromwell Rd. BN3: Hove 6L 153
RH15: Burg H 5A 94
Cromwell St. BN2: Brig 6D 154
Crooked La. PO20: Bir 8G 161
Crookhorn La. RH13: Br Grn, Southw 2F 66
Crookthorn La. BN17: Climp 4D 166
Cropthorne Dr. BN17: Climp 3E 166
Crosbie Cl. PO19: Chich 1B 162
Crosby Cl. BN13: Durr 7B 148
Croshaw Cl. BN15: Lan 8A 150
CROSSBUSH 4K 145
Crossbush By-Pass BN18: Cross, Poling 5L 145
Crossbush La. BN18: Cross, Poling 4K 145
Crossbush Rd. BN2: Brig 7F 154
PO22: Felp 8J 165
Cross Colwood La. RH17: Bol 4A 70
Crossfield GU27: Fern 5K 37
CROSS GATES 8M 105
Crosshaven BN17: L'ton 2N 167
Cross Keys RH10: Craw 6F 10
Crossland Dr. PO9: Hav 2A 136
Cross La. BN14: Fin 8C 128
RH13: B Grn 9E 44
Crossman Ct. RH11: Craw 2C 28
Crosspath RH10: Craw 5G 11
CROSSPOST 8D 70
Crosspost Ind. Est. RH17: Bol 8D 70
Cross Rd. BN16: Rust 3D 168
BN42: S'wck 5N 151
Cross Rd. Cl. BN42: S'wck 5N 151
Cross St. BN1: Brig 3E 172 (6B 154)
BN3: Hove 7A 172 (8M 153)
BN11: Wor 1G 171
Crossway RH6: Gatw 5H 5
Crossway, The BN1: Brig 3C 154
BN41: Ports 3C 152
Crossways BN16: E Pres 1G 168
GU29: Ease 7J 59
PO22: Midd S 7N 165
RH10: Craw 5H 11
RH17: Bol 7F 70
RH20: W Chil 9J 87
Crossways, The BN17: Wick 1J 167
Crossways Av. BN12: Gor S 9M 147
RH19: E Grin 3C 14
Crossways Cl. RH10: Craw 5H 11
Crossways Ct. GU27: Fern 4K 37
(off Vann Rd.)
Crossways Pk. RH20: W Chil 9J 87
Crossways Rd. GU26: Gray, Hind 1F 16
Crouch Cross La. PO18: Box 2L 141
CROUCHERS 3M 161
Crouch Hill BN5: Henf 9J 91
Crouchlands Farm RH17: Cuck 1N 71
Crowberry Cl. RH11: Craw 1C 28
Crowborough Dr. BN12: Gor S 2N 169
Crowborough Rd. BN2: Salt 3D 174
Crowhurst Cl. RH10: Worth 6N 11
Crowhurst Cres. RH20: Storr 5H 107
Crowhurst Keep RH10: Worth 6N 11
Crowhurst Rd. BN1: Brig 7C 134
Crown All. RH12: Hors 9N 25
(off Carfax)
Crown Bldgs. BN15: Lan 9N 149
Crown Cl. BN3: Hove 7M 153
(off Palmeira Av.)
Crown Gdns. BN1: Brig 6D 172
Crown Hill BN2: Brig 7D 154
(off Finsbury Rd.)
Crown Rd. BN41: Ports 5C 152
BN43: Shor S 5L 151
Crown St. BN1: Brig 7C 172 (8A 154)
Crown Yd. M. BN18: Arun 2H 145
(off River Rd.)
Crowsbury Cl. PO10: Ems 2E 136
Croxton La. RH16: Hay H 3J 73
Croy Cl. PO19: Chich 9A 140
Crundens Cnr. BN16: Rust 2D 168
Crundles GU31: Peters 6G 55
Crutchfield La. RH6: Hookw, Sid 1E 4
Crypt La. GU29: C'ing 9E 80
Cubitt Ter. BN2: Brig 9E 154
(off Chichester Pl.)
CUCKFIELD 3N 71
Cuckfield Cl. RH11: Craw 9B 10
Cuckfield Cres. BN13: Salv 7D 148
Cuckfield Golf Course 1M 71
Cuckfield La. RH17: W'lid 9C 48
Cuckfield Mus. 3N 71
Cuckfield Rd. BN6: God G, Hurst 1J 113
RH15: Burg H 1N 93
RH17: Ans 6L 71
RH17: Cuck, S'fld 5H 49
(not continuous)
Cuckmere Cres. RH11: Craw 7B 10
Cuckmere Rd. BN9: Newh 7N 175
Cuckmere Way BN1: Brig 8D 134
Cuckoo Cl. PO10: Ems 2G 136
Cuckoo Flds. PO18: Fish 5L 139
Cudlow Av. BN16: Rust 3B 168
Cudlow Gdn. BN16: Rust 3B 168
(not continuous)
Culimore Cl. PO20: W Witt 4J 177
Culimore Rd. PO20: W Witt 4J 177
Cullum Cl. PO19: Chich 5E 140
Culpepper RH15: Burg H 4N 93
Culpepper Cl. BN2: Brig 3E 154
Culross Av. RH16: Hay H 4E 72
Culver Ct. BN15: Lan 7B 150
Culver Rd. BN15: Lan 7B 150
PO22: Felp 8H 165
Culvers GU31: S Hart 5A 78
(not continuous)
Cumberland Av. BN12: Gor S 8B 148
PO10: Ems 1E 136
Cumberland Cl. BN16: Ang 8F 146
Cumberland Cres. BN16: Ang 8E 146
Cumberland Dr. BN1: Brig 3N 153
Cumberland Lodge BN1: Brig 3N 153
(off Cumberland Rd.)
Cumberland Rd. BN1: Brig 3N 153
BN16: Ang 8F 146
Cumbernauld Wlk. RH11: Craw 1A 28
Cumber's La. GU31: Rog 5J 57
Cumbrian Cl. BN13: Durr 6C 148
Cunliffe Cl. PO20: W Witt 1G 176
Cunningham Gdns.
PO22: Felp 7K 165
Curbey Cl. RH20: W Chil 7J 87
Curdridge Cl. PO9: Hav 9A 116
Curf Way RH15: Burg H 5D 94
Curlescroft PO21: Aldw 1H 181
Curlew Cl. PO10: Ems 5E 136
Curlews, The BN43: Shor S 5K 151
Curteys Wlk. RH11: Craw 9B 10
Curtis's Cotts. RH12: Hors 8C 8
Curve, The BN2: Brig 7G 172
Curvins Way BN15: Lan 6C 150
Curwen Pl. BN1: Brig 2N 153
Curzon Av. RH12: Hors 8M 25
Curzon Cl. BN13: Durr 7D 148
Curzon Ct. BN2: Salt 4C 174
Cutfield Cl. PO19: Chich 1B 162
Cuthbert Rd. BN2: Brig 8D 154
Cuthbert Row GU27: Has 4L 17
CUT MILL 5D 138
Cutten Way PO19: Chich 7D 140
Cuttinglye La. RH10: Craw D 3H 13
Cuttinglye Rd. RH10: Craw D 2J 13
CUTTINGLYE WOOD 2K 13
Cygnets, The BN43: Shor S 5J 151
Cygnet Wlk. PO22: Bers 6C 164
Cylinders, The GU27: Fern 5J 37
Cypress Av. BN13: Durr 8A 148
Cypress Cl. BN43: Shor S 4J 151
Cypress Way GU26: Hind 1F 16
PO21: Aldw 1F 180
Cyprus M. RH15: Burg H 5C 94
Cyprus Rd. RH15: Burg H 5B 94
Cyril Richings Bus. Cen. BN43: Shor S 6L 151

D

Dacre Gdns. BN44: Up B 7E 130
Dacre Vs. BN44: Up B 8E 130
Dagbrook La. BN5: Henf 5G 111
Dagmar St. BN11: Wor 1H 171
Dairy Farm Flats BN12: Gor S 1M 169
Dairyfields RH11: Craw 7C 10
Dairy La. BN18: Walb 4K 143
PO18: Westh 4H 141
Daisy Ct. BN1: Brig 8D 172
Daisycroft, The BN5: Henf 3J 111
Daisy Flds. Touring Pk. BN17: Wick 1L 167
Dakin Cl. RH10: Craw 1L 29
Dakins, The RH19: E Grin 4E 14
Dakota Bus. Pk. PO9: Hav 1B 136
Dale Av. BN1: Brig 9A 134
BN6: Key 4A 114
Dale Cl. RH12: Hors 6C 26
Dale Copse GU27: Fern 4K 37
(off Old Glebe)
Dale Cres. BN1: Brig 8A 134
Daledene RH19: E Grin 4F 14
(off Lewes Rd.)
Dale Dr. BN1: Brig 8A 134
Daleham La. TN22: Flet, Pilt 4N 75
Dale Hill BN45: Pye 9J 113
Dale Rd. BN11: Wor 9M 149
RH18: F Row 2M 33
Dale Ter. BN6: Key 4A 114
Dale Vw. BN3: Hove 3F 152
GU27: Has 6J 17
Dale Vw. Gdns. BN3: Hove 3F 152
Dale Way PO22: Felp 6J 165
Dalewood Gdns. RH10: Craw 4H 11
RH15: Burg H 6D 94
Dallaway Gdns. RH19: E Grin 3E 14
Dallaway Rd. PO19: Chich 9D 140
Dallington Rd. BN3: Hove 5H 153
Dalloway Rd. BN18: Arun 3E 144
Dalton Cl. RH11: Craw 2C 28
Daltons Pl. BN18: Arun 3G 145
Damascus Ct. RH16: Hay H 4G 72
(off St Paul's on the Green)
Damer's Bri. GU28: Petw 9N 61
Dame School Ct. PO18: E Lav 8C 120
Damian Way BN6: Key 3C 114
Damon Cl. BN10: Peace 5J 175
Dampier Wlk. RH11: Craw 2D 28
Dana Lodge BN10: Tels C 5G 174
Danbury Ct. PO10: Ems 3G 136
Danby Ct. RH6: Horl 1J 5
Danefield Rd. PO20: Sel 4G 183
DANEHILL 6G 53
Danehill La. RH17: Hors K 5D 52
Danehill Rd. BN2: Brig 8G 155
Danehurst Cres. RH13: Hors 9C 26
Daneswood Ho. BN11: Wor 2E 170
(off Southview Dr.)
Daniel Cl. BN15: Lan 6C 150
Daniels Ho. RH10: Craw 5K 11
(off Trafalgar Gdns.)
Dankton Gdns. BN15: Somp 6M 149
Dankton La. BN15: Somp 4M 149
Danley La. GU27: Linch 8C 16
Danny Sheldon Ho. BN2: Brig 9D 154
(off Eastern Rd.)
Danworth La. BN6: Hurst 8J 93
Dapper's La. BN16: Ang 7F 146
Darcey Dr. BN1: Brig 8B 134
Dark Hollow GU32: Peters 5E 54
Dark La. PO21: Aldw 1G 181
Darleydale RH11: Craw 9E 10
Darlington Cl. BN16: Ang 8F 146
Darlingtons, The BN16: Rust 1D 168
Darlington Wlk. BN16: Rust 1D 168
(off The Leas)
Dart Cl. BN13: Durr 5B 148
Dart Ct. RH19: E Grin 1G 14
Dartmouth Cl. BN2: Brig 4G 154
Dartmouth Cres. BN2: Brig 4F 154
Darwin Cl. RH12: Hors 7C 26
D'Aubigny Rd. BN2: Brig 5C 154
Daux Av. RH14: Bill 3J 65
Daux Hill RH12: Warnh 4M 25
Daux Rd. RH14: Bill 2J 65
Daux Rd. Ind. Est. RH14: Bill 2J 65
Daux Way RH14: Bill 3J 65
Dauxwood Cl. RH14: Bill 3J 65
Davenport Ct. BN11: Wor 2D 170
Davenport Rd. PO22: Felp 8H 165
Davey Dr. BN1: Brig 4C 154
David Lloyd Leisure
Brighton 8J 173
Worthing 8N 147
Davids Cl. PO21: Bers 7A 164
Davies Ct. BN11: Wor 3E 170
Davigdor Rd. BN3: Hove 4A 172 (6M 153)
Davis Cl. RH11: Craw 2C 28
Davison Leisure Cen. 1K 171
Davits Dr. BN17: L'ton 2N 167
Dawes Av. BN11: Wor 1K 171
Dawes Cl. BN11: Wor 1K 171
Daw La. PO11: Hay I 4A 158
Dawlish Cl. BN2: Brig 4F 154
Dawn Cl. BN44: Up B 5E 130
Dawn Cres. BN44: Up B 5D 130
Dawn Ri. RH10: Copt 1B 12
Dawson Ct. BN11: Wor 1G 171
(off Victoria Rd.)
Dawson Ter. BN2: Brig 7D 154
Dawtrey Cl. BN16: Rust 2D 168
Dawtrey Rd. GU28: Petw 1N 83
Daynes Way RH15: Burg H 7N 93
Days La. BN18: Font 2G 143
Deacons Dr. BN41: Ports 3D 152
Deacons Way BN44: Up B 4D 130
Deacon Trad. Est. BN14: Broadw 8K 149
Deacon Way BN14: Broadw 8K 149
Deak's La. RH17: Ans, Cuck 4K 71
Dean Cl. BN2: Rott 2A 174
BN17: Wick 1J 167
BN41: Ports 3E 152
Dean Ct. Rd. BN2: Rott 2N 173
Deane Ct. PO9: Hav 9B 116
Deanery Cl. PO19: Chich 7B 140
Deanery Farm La. PO19: Chich 7B 140
(off Southgate)
Deanery Sq. PO21: Bers 5A 164
Dean Gdns. BN41: Ports 3E 152
Deanland Rd. RH17: Bal 1B 50
Dean La. GU28: Till 9G 61
PO8: Finch, Row C 9D 96
PO9: Row C 9D 96

Deanlane End—Dryad Way

DEANLANE END . . . 1E 116
Deans Cl. BN2: W'dean . . . 5M 155
BN18: Font . . . 2H 143
Deans Leisure Cen. . . . 9M 155
Dean St. BN1: Brig . . . 7B 172 (8N 153)
Dean Way RH20: Storr . . . 5H 107
Deanway BN3: Hove . . . 2K 153
Deborah Ter. BN10: Tels C . . . 5G 174
De Braose Way BN44: Bramb . . . 4B 130
Deco Building, The *BN2: Brig* . . . *4D 154*
(off Coombe Rd.)
De Courcel Rd. BN2: Brig . . . 8J 173
Decoy Dr. BN16: Ang . . . 6E 146
Decoy La. BN18: Poling . . . 6C 146
PO20: Tang . . . 6A 142
Decoy Rd. BN14: Broadw . . . 8K 149
Dedisham Cl. RH10: Craw . . . 7J 11
Deepdene GU27: Has . . . 5G 16
Deepdene Cl. PO22: Midd S . . . 7A 166
Deer Cl. PO19: Apul . . . 1A 162
Deerhurst Pk. RH18: F Row . . . 1N 33
Deer Pk. BN5: Henf . . . 1H 111
Deer Pk. Cl. PO20: Sel . . . 2F 182
Deer Pk. Dr. PO20: Sel . . . 2F 182
Deer Pk. La. PO20: Sel . . . 2E 182
Deers Leap RH16: Hay H . . . 8D 72
Deers Leap Pk. . . . 8C 14
Deerswood Cl. BN13: Durr . . . 8N 147
RH11: Craw . . . 5D 10
Deerswood Ct. RH11: Craw . . . 5C 10
Deerswood Rd. RH11: Craw . . . 6D 10
Deer Way RH12: Hors . . . 1L 45
Deeside, The BN1: Brig . . . 7B 134
Deeside Av. PO19: Fish . . . 6L 139
Defiance Pl. PO22: Felp . . . 8K 165
Delancey Ct. *RH12: Hors* . . . *7N 25*
(off Wimblehurst Rd.)
De La Warr Rd. RH19: E Grin . . . 3F 14
Delfont Cl. RH10: Craw . . . 8M 11
Delfryn BN41: Ports . . . 2A 152
Delius Gdns. RH13: Hors . . . 7E 26
Dell, The PO22: Bers . . . 6B 164
RH6: Horl . . . 1K 5
RH16: Hay H . . . 4D 72
RH17: Cuck . . . 2N 71
RH19: E Grin . . . 3H 15
Dell Cl. GU27: Has . . . 4J 17
Dell Dr. BN16: Ang . . . 9E 146
Delling Cl. PO18: Bosh . . . 7E 138
Delling La. PO18: Bosh . . . 8F 138
Dell La. RH14: Bill . . . 1J 65
Dellney Av. RH16: Hay H . . . 6G 73
Dell Quay Rd. PO20: Apul . . . 2L 161
Delrogue Rd. RH11: Ifield . . . 3C 10
Delta Bungs. *RH6: Horl* . . . *4J 5*
(off Delta Dr.)
Delta Dr. RH6: Horl . . . 4J 5
Delta Ho. *RH6: Horl* . . . *4J 5*
(off Delta Dr.)
De Montfort Rd. BN2: Brig . . . 6D 154
Dempsey Rd. PO19: Chich . . . 3C 140
Dempsey Wlk. RH11: Craw . . . 4C 10
Den Av. PO21: Bog R . . . 9E 164
Denbigh Rd. GU27: Has . . . 6M 17
Dencher Rd. BN7: King L . . . 3E 156
Denchers Plat RH11: Craw . . . 3F 10
Dene, The BN3: Hove . . . 2F 152
RH13: Southw . . . 8L 45
Dene Cl. GU27: Has . . . 6L 17
RH6: Horl . . . 1G 5
Dene Ct. BN11: Wor . . . 2F 170
Denecroft BN1: Brig . . . 9M 133
Deneside BN1: Brig . . . 9M 133
Dene Tye RH10: Craw . . . 5M 11
Dene Vale BN1: Brig . . . 9M 133
Deneway, The BN1: Brig . . . 1M 153
BN15: Somp . . . 7N 149
Denge La. PO18: Hal . . . 7N 121
Denham Cl. PO22: Midd S . . . 7M 165
Denham Ct. RH15: Burg H . . . 5M 93
Denham Rd. RH15: Burg H . . . 4M 93
Denmans RH10: Craw . . . 5M 11
Denman's Cl. RH16: Lind . . . 1H 73
Denmans Gdns. . . . 2G 142
Denmans La. BN18: Font . . . 3F 142
PO20: Font . . . 3F 142
RH16: Lind . . . 2H 73
Denmark M. BN3: Hove . . . 6K 153
Denmark Rd. BN41: Ports . . . 6E 152
Denmark Ter.
BN1: Brig . . . 5B 172 (7N 153)
Denmark Vs. BN3: Hove . . . 6K 153
Denne Pde. RH12: Hors . . . 1N 45
DENNE PARK . . . 1N 45
Denne Rd. RH11: Craw . . . 7F 10
RH12: Hors . . . 1N 45
Dennis Hobden Cl. BN2: Brig . . . 4F 154
Dennis Way GU33: Liss . . . 7A 34
Denny's Cl. PO20: Sel . . . 3J 183
Denshare Rd. PO20: Sel . . . 2J 183
Denshire Dr. RH20: Storr . . . 5K 107
Densihale PO21: Aldw . . . 9B 164
Densworth Farm Caravan Site
PO18: E Ash . . . 2K 139
Denton Cl. BN12: Gor S . . . 1N 169
Denton Dr. BN1: Brig . . . 9B 134
Denton Gdns. . . . 2J 171
Denture, The BN18: Houg . . . 1A 124
Den Vale Trade Pk. RH10: Craw . . . 7G 11
DENVILLES . . . 3B 136
Denvilles Cl. PO9: Hav . . . 3B 136
Departures Rd. RH6: Gatw . . . 5H 5
Depot Rd. RH11: Craw . . . 3F 10
RH13: Hors . . . 9B 26
Derby Ct. BN3: Hove . . . 4A 172
Derby Pl. *BN2: Brig* . . . *8C 154*
(off Up. Park Pl.)
Derby Rd. GU27: Has . . . 4K 17
Derek Av. BN3: Hove . . . 7F 152
Derek Ho. BN3: Hove . . . 6H 153
Derek Rd. BN15: N Lan . . . 5A 150
Dervia Ho. *BN3: Hove* . . . *6M 153*
(off Palmeira Av.)
Derwent Cl. BN15: Somp . . . 8N 149
BN17: L'ton . . . 2N 167
PO20: Tang . . . 3M 141
RH11: Craw . . . 7B 10
RH12: Hors . . . 5E 26
Derwent Ct. BN1: Brig . . . 6C 172
Derwent Dr. BN12: Gor S . . . 8B 148
Derwent Gro. PO22: Felp . . . 6J 165
Desmond Way BN2: Brig . . . 7G 154
Detling Rd. RH11: Craw . . . 2E 28
De Vere Leisure Club . . . 8C 172
Devil's Dyke . . . 4E 132
Devil's Dyke Rd. BN1: Brig . . . 4E 132
BN3: Brig . . . 7G 133
Devils La. GU30: Lip . . . 7A 16
Devonian Cl. BN2: Brig . . . 6C 154
Devonian Ct. *BN2: Brig* . . . *6C 154*
(off Park Cres. Pl.)
Devon Lodge *BN2: Brig* . . . *8C 154*
(off Carlton Hill)
Devonport Pl. BN11: Wor . . . 1L 171
Devonport Rd. BN11: Wor . . . 1L 171
Devonshire Ct. BN3: Hove . . . 6L 153
Devonshire Lodge BN11: Wor . . . 2D 170
Devonshire Mans. *BN2: Brig* . . . *8C 154*
(off Devonshire Pl.)
Devonshire Pl. BN2: Brig . . . 8C 154
PO21: Bog R . . . 9D 164
Devonshire Rd. PO21: Bog R . . . 9C 164
RH13: Hors . . . 9A 26
Dewar Cl. RH11: Ifield . . . 7A 10
Dewe Rd. BN2: Brig . . . 4D 154
Dewpond, The BN10: Peace . . . 3H 175
Dew Pond Cl. RH13: Hors . . . 8C 26
Dexter Dr. RH19: E Grin . . . 4E 14
Dial Cl. PO22: Barn . . . 8K 143
DIAL GREEN . . . 7C 38
DIAL POST . . . 5J 89
Diamond Cotts. RH17: Bol . . . 8D 70
Diana Cl. PO10: Ems . . . 1E 136
Diana Wlk. *RH6: Horl* . . . *2K 5*
(off High St.)
Dickens Cl. RH19: E Grin . . . 3C 14
Dickens Rd. RH10: Craw . . . 9F 10
Dickins La. GU31: Peters . . . 4G 55
Dickinson Pl. PO22: Bers . . . 6E 164
Dickins Way RH13: Hors . . . 2C 46
Dicklands, The BN7: Rod . . . 5K 157
DIDLING . . . 6L 79
Diggers, The BN1: Brig . . . 2C 154
Dinapore Ho. *BN2: Brig* . . . *7C 154*
(off John St.)
Dingemans BN44: Stey . . . 1A 130
Dingle, The RH11: Craw . . . 6D 10
Dingle Cl. RH11: Craw . . . 5D 10
Dingley Rd. BN16: Rust . . . 3A 168
Dinsdale Fld. BN16: Rust . . . 1D 168
Dinsdale Gdns. BN16: Rust . . . 2B 168
Dione Wlk. RH11: Craw . . . 9A 10
Dirty La. GU28: Graff . . . 1A 102
RH17: Ash W . . . 6L 15
Discovery Pk. RH10: Craw . . . 1J 11
Ditches Grn. Cotts. RH5: Ock . . . 2C 6
Ditchfield Cl. PO22: Felp . . . 6L 165
DITCHLING . . . 4E 114
Ditchling Beacon . . . 8F 114
Ditchling Beacon Nature Reserve . . . 8E 114
Ditchling Bostall BN6: Ditch, W'ton . . . 8E 114
Ditchling Cl. BN12: Gor S . . . 9N 147
DITCHLING COMMON . . . 7G 95
Ditchling Common Country Pk. . . . 5F 94
Ditchling Comn. Ind. Est. BN6: Ditch . . . 7H 95
Ditchling Ct. BN1: Brig . . . 1G 172
Ditchling Cres. BN1: Brig . . . 9D 134
Ditchling Gdns. BN1: Brig . . . 4B 154
Ditchling Hill RH11: Craw . . . 9E 10
Ditchling Mus. . . . 4E 114
Ditchling Pl. BN1: Brig . . . 4B 154
Ditchling Ri. BN1: Brig . . . 2E 172 (5B 154)
Ditchling Rd.
BN1: Brig, Ditch, Stan . . . 1G 172 (3D 134)
BN6: Clay . . . 6M 113
BN6: W'ton . . . 3D 134
BN7: Plump . . . 8L 115
RH15: Ditch, Wivel . . . 6F 94
RH16: Hay H . . . 9G 72
RH17: Burg H, Wivel . . . 2H 95
Dobbins Pl. RH11: Ifield . . . 7N 9
Dobson Rd. RH11: Craw . . . 3F 10
Doctors La. RH17: Chel G . . . 3K 53
Dodsley Gro. GU29: Ease . . . 7H 59
Dodsley La. GU29: Ease . . . 8H 59
Dog La. BN44: Stey . . . 3A 130
Dolby Ter. RH6: Charlw . . . 7A 4
Dollis Cl. RH10: Craw . . . 7L 11
Dolphin Cl. GU27: Has . . . 5G 16
PO19: Fish . . . 7L 139
Dolphin Ct. *BN3: Hove* . . . *7J 153*
(off Hove St.)
BN16: Rust . . . 4C 168
PO21: Bog R . . . *1L 181*
(off The Steyne)
Dolphin Ent. Cen. BN43: Shor S . . . 6L 151
Dolphin Leisure Cen. . . . 3E 72
Dolphin Lodge BN11: Wor . . . 3E 170
Dolphin M. *BN2: Brig* . . . *9F 172*
(off Steine St.)
BN43: Shor S . . . 6K 151
PO19: Chich . . . 7N 139
Dolphin Quay PO10: Ems . . . 5G 136
Dolphin Rd. BN43: Shor S . . . 6K 151
RH16: Hay H . . . 5E 72
Dolphin Way BN16: Rust . . . 4C 168
BN43: Shor S . . . 6L 151
Dome Cinema . . . *3J 171*
(off Marine Pde.)
Domehouse Cl. PO20: Sel . . . 5J 183
Dominican Friary (remains of) . . . 2J 145
Dominion Bldgs. BN14: Broadw . . . 9K 149
Dominion Cl. BN14: Broadw . . . 9J 149
Dominion Rd. BN14: Broadw . . . 8J 149
Dominion Way BN14: Broadw . . . 8K 149
BN16: Rust . . . 1B 168
Dominion Way W. BN14: Broadw . . . 8K 149
Donald Hall Rd. BN2: Brig . . . 8E 154
Donaldson Cl. PO20: Sel . . . 2G 183
Doncaster Wlk. RH10: Craw . . . 8J 11
Donegal Rd. PO19: Chich . . . 4C 140
Donkey La. RH6: Horl . . . 6M 5
Donkey M. BN3: Hove . . . 8M 153
Donne Cl. RH10: Craw . . . 4K 11
DONNINGTON . . . 3A 162
Donnington Ct. RH11: Craw . . . 9B 10
Donnington Pk. PO20: Apul . . . 1N 161
Donnington Pl. *BN16: Rust* . . . *2B 168*
(off Woodlands Av.)
Donnington Rd. BN2: W'dean . . . 7M 155
Doomsday Gdn. RH13: Hors . . . 1D 46
DOOMSDAY GREEN . . . 2D 46
Doomsday La. RH13: Hors . . . 2D 46
Doone End BN12: Fer . . . 4L 169
Dorchester Ct. *BN1: Brig* . . . *7A 172*
(off Norfolk Sq.)
Dorchester Gdns. BN11: Wor . . . 2E 170
Doric Cl. PO10: S'brne . . . 4K 137
Dorita Ct. *BN10: Peace* . . . *5J 175*
(off Sth. Coast Rd.)
Dorking Rd. RH12: King, Warnh . . . 2L 25
Dormans RH11: Craw . . . 7C 10
Dormans Pk. Rd. RH19: E Grin . . . 1D 14
Dorothy Av. BN10: Peace . . . 6J 175
(not continuous)
Dorothy Av. Nth. BN10: Peace . . . 4J 175
Dorothy Rd. BN3: Hove . . . 5F 152
Dorothy Stringer Sports Cen. . . . 2A 154
Dorset Av. RH19: E Grin . . . 1C 14
Dorset Cl. BN17: L'ton . . . 2L 167
Dorset Ct. BN3: Hove . . . 7H 153
Dorset Gdns. BN2: Brig . . . 8G 172 (8C 154)
RH19: E Grin . . . 1C 14
Dorset Ho. RH13: Cool . . . 7B 66
Dorset M. BN2: Brig . . . 8F 172
RH19: E Grin . . . 1C 14
Dorset Pl. BN2: Brig . . . 8C 154
BN14: W Tar . . . 8E 148
Dorset Rd. PO21: Bog R . . . 7D 164
Dorset St. BN2: Brig . . . 8F 172 (8B 154)
Dorsten Pl. RH11: Craw . . . 9A 10
Dorsten Sq. RH11: Craw . . . 9B 10
Doubledays RH15: Burg H . . . 6C 94
Douglas Av. BN11: Wor . . . 2D 170
Douglas Cl. BN11: Wor . . . 2D 170
BN18: Ford . . . 2B 166
PO22: Midd S . . . 7N 165
Douglas Gdns. PO9: Hav . . . 1A 136
Douglas Martin Rd. PO19: Chich . . . 6D 140
Dove Cl. RH11: Craw . . . 4F 10
Dovecote M. BN15: Somp . . . 5N 149
Dove Ct. PO22: Bers . . . 6C 164
Dovedale Cres. RH11: Craw . . . 8D 10
Dover Cl. RH13: Southw . . . 8K 45
Dover La. BN18: Poling, W'camp, Ang . . . 5D 146
Dover Rd. BN1: Brig . . . 3B 154
BN11: Wor . . . 3E 170
Dower Cl. BN2: O'dean . . . 1L 173
Dower Wlk. RH11: Craw . . . 7C 10
Down, The BN3: Hove . . . 1E 152
Downash Cl. BN2: Brig . . . 7F 154
Down Cl. GU29: Hey . . . 8L 81
Downe Cl. RH6: Horl . . . 1G 5
Downes Ct. *BN43: Shor S* . . . *5M 151*
(off Wilmot Rd.)
Downe Wlk. *BN13: Durr* . . . *8B 148*
(off East Tyne)
Downford *BN2: Brig* . . . *8G 154*
(off Whitehawk Rd.)
Downhill Vw. BN2: W'dean . . . 6M 155
Downing Cl. PO21: Aldw . . . 8N 163
Downland Av. BN10: Peace . . . 5L 175
BN42: S'wck . . . 4N 151
Downland Cl. BN2: W'dean . . . 5H 155
BN14: Fin . . . 8C 128
BN42: S'wck . . . 4N 151
BN44: Up B . . . 4E 130
Downland Ct. BN41: Ports . . . 3C 152
PO19: Chich . . . 5B 140
RH11: Craw . . . 8E 10
Downland Cres. BN3: Hove . . . 2H 153
Downland Dr. BN3: Hove . . . 2H 153
RH11: Craw . . . 8E 10
Downland Pk. BN44: Bramb . . . 5D 130
Downland Pl. RH11: Craw . . . 8E 10
Downland Rd. BN2: W'dean . . . 5H 155
BN44: Up B . . . 4E 130
Downlands BN13: High S . . . 3C 148
RH13: Part G . . . 5C 90
RH20: Coot . . . 6G 106
RH20: Pulb . . . 6C 86
Downlands Av. BN14: Broadw . . . 6H 149
Downlands Bus. Pk. BN14: Char D . . . 5J 149
Downlands Cl. BN15: Somp . . . 6N 149
PO21: Pag . . . 1C 180
Downlands Gdns. BN14: Broadw . . . 6J 149
Downlands Pde. *BN14: Broadw* . . . *6J 149*
(off Up. Brighton Rd.)
Downlands Retail Pk. BN14: Char D . . . 6J 149
Downley Cl. PO18: Sing . . . 8F 100
Downley Point PO9: Hav . . . 1B 136
Downley Rd. PO9: Hav . . . 2B 136
DOWN PARK . . . 3H 13
Downsbrook Trad. Est. BN14: Broadw . . . 7J 149
Downs Cl. BN15: S Lan . . . 7E 150
Downs Crematorium BN2: Brig . . . 5F 154
Downscroft BN44: Up B . . . 4E 130
RH15: Burg H . . . 2E 94
Downshire Ter. *RH17: Ard* . . . *2H 51*
(off Street La.)
Downside BN1: Brig . . . 9M 133
BN3: Hove . . . 2K 153
BN43: Shor S . . . 4K 151
Downside Av. BN14: Fin V . . . 2C 148
Downside Cl. BN14: Fin V . . . 2D 148
BN43: Shor S . . . 4J 151
Downs Link . . . 6G 45
Downsman Ct. RH10: Craw . . . 9F 10
Downsmead BN15: Somp . . . 5N 149
Downs Rd. PO18: Funt, W Sto . . . 8E 118
RH15: Burg H . . . 4N 93
Down St. PO18: W Ash . . . 2E 138
Downs Valley Rd. BN2: W'dean . . . 5M 155
Downs Vw. BN10: Peace . . . 2K 175
Downsview BN3: Hove . . . 2F 152
BN5: Small D . . . 8J 111
Downsview Av. BN2: W'dean . . . 5K 155
RH20: Storr . . . 5K 107
Downsview Caravan Pk. BN5: W'cote . . . 7N 111
Downsview Cotts. RH14: Bill . . . 1H 65
Downsview Dr. GU29: Midh . . . 3G 80
RH17: Wivel G . . . 4K 95
Downsview Mnr. BN14: Broadw . . . 7G 149
Downs Vw. Rd. BN6: Hass . . . 4A 114
Downsview Rd. BN16: King G . . . 4J 169
BN41: Ports . . . 3C 152
RH12: Hors . . . 5E 26
Downs Vw. Ter. BN5: Henf . . . 2G 110
Downs Wlk. BN10: Peace . . . 2J 175
Downs Way BN16: Ang . . . 1E 168
Downsway BN2: W'dean . . . 5L 155
BN42: S'wck . . . 3A 152
BN43: Shor S . . . 4J 151
Down Ter. BN2: Brig . . . 7D 154
Downview Av. BN12: Fer . . . 1K 169
Downview Cl. BN18: Yap . . . 1A 166
PO18: Mid L . . . 8A 120
PO20: E Witt . . . 5L 177
Downview Ct. BN11: Wor . . . 3E 170
Downview Rd. BN11: Wor . . . 1E 170
BN12: Fer . . . 1K 169
BN14: Fin . . . 7C 128
BN18: Yap . . . 1A 166
GU28: Petw . . . 1M 83
PO22: Barn . . . 6H 143
PO22: Felp . . . 7H 165
Downview Way BN18: Yap . . . 1A 166
Doyle Ct. GU27: Has . . . 5J 17
DRAGON'S GREEN . . . 6G 67
Dragons Grn. Rd. RH13: Br Grn, Ship . . . 2G 66
Dragons La. RH13: Cow . . . 1H 91
RH13: Ship . . . 6F 66
Dragon St. GU31: Peters . . . 6F 54
Drake Av. BN12: Gor S . . . 9B 148
Drake Cl. RH12: Hors . . . 5B 26
Drake Gro. BN18: Ford . . . 2B 166
Drakeleys Fld. GU30: Mill . . . 8L 35
Drake Pk. PO22: Felp . . . 7K 165
Drake Rd. RH6: Horl . . . 2G 5
RH10: Craw . . . 8G 11
Drakes Cl. BN15: S Lan . . . 7E 150
Draxmont Way BN1: Brig . . . 2A 154
Draycliff Cl. BN12: Fer . . . 3K 169
DRAYTON . . . 7J 141
Drayton La. PO20: Oving . . . 6H 141
Drewetts Cl. BN16: Rust . . . 1A 168
Drewitts M. PO20: Oving . . . 6L 141
Drift, The PO9: Row C . . . 5B 116
Drift La. PO18: Bosh . . . 6B 138
PO20: Sel . . . 2G 183
Drift Rd. PO20: Sel . . . 1K 183
PO21: Aldw, Pag . . . 1D 180
Driftway, The BN16: Rust . . . 2A 168
BN44: Up B . . . 3E 130
RH11: Craw . . . 5F 10
Drills, The *BN16: Ang* . . . *8E 146*
(off High St.)
Drive, The BN3: Hove . . . 7L 153
BN11: Wor . . . 1D 170
BN15: Lan . . . 9A 150
BN16: E Pres . . . 4G 168
BN42: S'wck . . . 4A 152
BN43: Shor S . . . 5J 151
GU28: Graff . . . 1F 102
PO10: S'brne . . . 5K 137
PO18: Bosh . . . 8F 138
PO18: Westh . . . 3G 140
PO19: Chich . . . 2B 140
PO20: E'gate . . . 4H 143
PO21: Aldw . . . 2F 180
RH6: Horl . . . 3K 5
RH10: Copt . . . 1D 12
RH10: Craw . . . 2J 11
RH12: Rusp . . . 5H 9
RH14: Ifol . . . 8K 21
RH15: Burg H . . . 4C 94
Drive Lodge BN3: Hove . . . 6L 153
Driveway, The BN43: Shor S . . . 5J 151
Droke La. GU28: Upw . . . 8M 101
PO18: E Dean . . . 8M 101
Dropping Holms BN5: Henf . . . 3G 111
Drove, The BN1: Brig . . . 4M 153
BN1: Falm . . . 8K 135
BN6: Ditch . . . 4D 114
Drove Av. BN2: King L . . . 3L 155
BN7: King L . . . 3L 155
Drove Cres. BN41: Ports . . . 3C 152
Drove La. BN18: Yap . . . 3K 165
PO20: Earn . . . 5A 178
Drove Rd. BN2: W'dean . . . 5H 155
BN41: Ports . . . 4C 152
Drovers RH17: Bol . . . 6E 70
Drovers Cl. BN41: Ports . . . 3E 152
Drovers La. RH20: Pulb . . . 5C 86
Drovers Way PO22: Barn . . . 7H 143
RH15: Burg H . . . 6D 94
Droveway, The BN3: Hove . . . 3J 153
(not continuous)
BN7: King L . . . 1G 156
RH16: Hay H . . . 3D 72
Drum La. GU32: Peters . . . 5F 54
Drum Mead GU32: Peters . . . 6E 54
Drummond Cl. RH16: Hay H . . . 5E 72
Drummond Ct. *BN12: Gor S* . . . *3B 170*
(off Marine Cres.)
RH16: Hay H . . . 5E 72
Drummond Rd. BN12: Gor S . . . 3C 170
RH11: Ifield . . . 7A 10
Drungewick La.
RH14: Lox, Wisb . . . 4B 42
Drury Cl. RH10: Craw . . . 8M 11
Dryad Way PO22: Felp . . . 8L 165

Drygrounds La.—Elmers Rd.

Drygrounds La. PO22: Felp 7G 165
Duck La. GU29: Midh 9H 59
PO20: Sel 2F 182
Duckmead La. GU33: Liss 4A 34
Dudeney Lodge BN1: Brig 4C 154
Dudley M. BN3: Hove 8M 153
(off Brunswick St. W.)
Dudley Rd. BN1: Brig 4C 154
Dudwell Rd. BN2: W'dean 6M 155
Duffield La. PO10: W'cote 2K 137
Duke Cl. RH10: Craw 1L 29
Duke of York's Picture House 3E 172 (6B 154)
Dukes Barn Ct. RH16: Lind 2J 73
Dukes Cl. BN18: Arun 3F 144
GU32: Peters 5D 54
PO10: W'brne 2H 137
Dukes Ct. BN1: Brig 7D 172
BN17: L'ton 3K 167
PO19: Chich 8F 140
Dukes Head RH10: Craw D 1F 12
Duke's Hill RH20: Thake, W Chil 8M 87
Dukes La.
BN1: Brig 8D 172 (8A 154)
BN44: Stey 3A 130
Dukes Mdw. PO18: Funt 9C 118
PO21: Pag 9K 163
Duke's Mound BN2: Brig 9E 154
Duke's Pas. BN1: Brig 8D 172
Dukes Rd. BN18: Font 9F 122
RH16: Lind 1J 73
Dukes Row RH20: Coot 5F 106
Dukes Sq. RH12: Hors 1N 45
Duke St. BN1: Brig 8D 172 (8A 154)
BN17: L'ton 3K 167
Dukes Yd. BN44: Stey 3A 130
Dulcima Ho. RH12: Hors 9N 25
Dumbrells Ct. BN6: Ditch 3E 114
Dumbrells Ct. Rd.
BN6: Ditch 3E 114
Dumbrills Cl. RH15: Burg H 3B 94
DUMPFORD 9J 57
Dumpford La. GU31: N'wd, Trot 9E 56
Duncan Ct. BN2: Salt 3C 174
Duncan Ho. BN10: Peace 3J 175
(off Collingwood Cl.)
Duncan Rd. PO19: Chich 5B 140
DUNCTON 9J 83
Duncton Cl. PO22: Felp 8J 165
RH11: Craw 4D 10
RH16: Hay H 5E 72
Duncton Comn. GU28: Dunc 7K 83
Duncton High St. GU28: Dunc 1J 103
Duncton Rd. BN16: Rust 2D 168
Dundonald Cl. PO11: Hay I 7A 158
Dunes, The PO21: Aldw 3E 180
Dunford Hollow GU29: W Lav 4H 81
Dunhurst Cl. PO9: Hav 2A 136
Dunlop Cl. BN6: Say C 7F 92
Dunning's Rd. RH19: E Grin 6E 14
Dunnock Cl. PO9: Row C 5B 116
Dunsfold Cl. RH11: Craw 7C 10
Dunsfold Rd. RH14: Plais 5D 20
Dunstall Av. RH15: Burg H 4N 93
Dunstall Farm Rd.
RH15: Burg H 4A 94
Dunstan Cl. PO19: Chich 2C 140
Dunster Cl. BN1: Brig 4C 154
Dunwich BN43: Shor B 7L 151
(off Sea Spray Av.)
Durban Pk. PO22: Bers 7E 164
Durban Pk. Ind. Est.
PO22: Bers 6E 164
Durban Rd. PO22: Bers 6D 164
Durban Rd. Bus. Cen.
PO22: Bers 6E 164
Durbans Rd. RH14: Wisb 8A 42
Durfold Hill RH12: Warnh 9M 7
Durfold Rd. RH12: Hors 4A 26
Durfold Wood RH14: Plais 5C 20
Durford Rd. GU31: Peters 6H 55
DURFORD WOOD 2M 55
Durham Cl. BN2: Brig 4H 155
PO21: Pag 3C 180
RH10: Craw 1G 29
(not continuous)
Durham Ct. BN3: Hove 7K 153
Durham Gdns. PO19: Chich 4B 140
Durkins Rd. RH19: E Grin 1D 14
DURLEIGHMARSH 5N 55
Durlston Dr.
PO22: Bers, Bog R 6C 164
Durlston Pde. PO22: Bers 6C 164
Durnford Cl. PO19: Chich 6A 140
DURRANTS 6B 116
Durrants Gdns. PO9: Row C 6B 116
Durrants Rd. PO9: Row C 7B 116
DURRINGTON 6B 148
Durrington Ct. BN1: Brig 9M 133
(off Mill Ri.)
Durrington Gdns. BN12: Gor S 1B 170
Durrington Hill BN13: Durr 6B 148
Durrington La. BN13: Durr 6B 148
Durrington-on-Sea Station (Rail) 1C 170
Dutchells Copse RH12: Hors 5B 26
Duxford Cl. PO20: Tang 3L 141
Dyall Cl. RH15: Burg H 4N 93
Dye Ho. La. GU28: Dunc 9K 83
Dyers Almshouses RH10: Craw 5F 10
Dyers La. BN18: Slind 9K 123
Dyke Cl. BN3: Hove 1K 153
BN45: Poyn 1E 132
Dyke Golf Course 4E 132
Dyke La. BN45: Poyn 2E 132
Dyke Railway Trail 6F 132
Dyke Rd. BN1: Brig 1A 172 (3M 153)
BN3: Hove 1A 172 (3M 153)
Dyke Rd. Av. BN1: Brig 9K 133
BN3: Hove 9K 133
Dyke Rd. Dr.
BN1: Brig 1B 172 (5N 153)
Dyke Rd. M. BN1: Brig 4C 172
Dyke Rd. Pl. BN1: Brig 2L 153
Dymock's, The BN6: Ditch 4E 114
Dymoke St. PO10: Ems 1E 136
Dyson Wlk. RH11: Craw 2D 28

E

Eady Cl. RH13: Hors 9C 26
Eagle Ct. BN2: Brig 5D 154
(off Lewes Rd.)
Eagles Chase BN17: Wick 9K 145
Eagle Trad. Est. RH14: Bill 2J 65
(off Brooker's Rd.)
Eames Farm Nature Reserve 8H 137
Eardley, The BN11: Wor 2J 171
(off Marine Pde.)
Earle Ho. RH19: E Grin 2F 14
(off Badger's Way)
Earles Mdw. RH12: Hors 5D 26
Earlswood Cl. RH13: Hors 7C 26
Early Commons RH10: Craw 5H 11
(not continuous)
EARNLEY 5A 178
Earnley Butterflies, Birds & Beasts 3B 178
Earnley Mnr. Cl. PO20: Earn 4A 178
Earnley Pl. PO20: Earn 5N 177
EARTHAM 7E 122
Earwig La. RH17: Bol, W'lid 4A 70
EASEBOURNE 7J 59
Easebourne La. GU29: Ease 8J 59
Easebourne St. GU29: Ease 7K 59
EAST ASHLING 1H 139
East Av. BN12: Gor S 3D 170
PO22: Midd S 6N 165
East Bank BN18: Yap 8A 144
PO20: Sel 3K 183
Eastbank BN42: S'wck 4B 152
E. Bank Wlk. BN17: L'ton 4N 167
(off Ketch Rd.)
EAST BEACH 2K 183
E. Beach Rd. PO20: Sel 2L 183
Eastbourne Rd. BN2: Brig 4E 154
E. Bracklesham Dr. PO20: Brac 6M 177
East Brighton Golf Course 9G 155
Eastbrook Rd. BN41: Ports 6D 152
Eastbrook Way BN41: Ports 6C 152
EAST CHILTINGTON 4N 115
East Cl. PO22: Midd S 7M 165
East Court 2F 14
Eastcourt Rd. BN14: Broadw 9G 149
East Ct. Way BN16: Rust 2D 168
Eastcroft M. RH12: Hors 1K 45
Eastdale Rd. RH15: Burg H 4E 94
EAST DEAN 8M 101
Eastdean Hill PO18: E Dean, Hal 9L 101
Eastdean Rd. GU28: Graff 2B 102
East Dr. BN2: Brig 8D 154
BN16: Ang 9D 146
PO22: Midd S 7A 166
Easteds La. RH13: Southw 8L 45
EAST END 4F 114
East End La. BN6: Ditch 4E 114
EASTERGATE 6F 142
Eastergate Cl. BN12: Gor S 1L 169
Eastergate Grn. BN16: Rust 3B 168
Eastergate Ho. PO20: E'gate 6F 142
Eastergate La. BN18: Walb 4G 143
PO20: E'gate 4G 143
Eastergate Rd. BN2: Brig 1G 154
Eastern Av. BN43: Shor S 6K 151
Eastern Cl. BN16: E Pres 2G 168
BN43: Shor S 6K 151
Eastern Concourse BN2: Brig 9L 173
Eastern Pl. BN2: Brig 9F 154
Eastern Ring Rd. BN1: Falm 7J 135
Eastern Rd. BN2: Brig 8C 154
PO9: Hav 3A 136
RH16: Hay H 6G 73
RH16: Lind 2J 73
RH17: Wivel 4H 95
Eastern St. BN2: Brig 9E 154
(off Eastern Ter.)
Eastern Ter. BN2: Brig 9E 154
Eastern Ter. M. BN2: Brig 9E 154
(off Eastern Ter.)
East Fld. Cl. PO10: S'brne 4L 137
Eastfield Cres. BN1: Brig 1B 154
Eastfield La. GU31: E Hart 4D 78
E. Front Rd. PO21: Pag 4C 180
East Gdns. BN6: Ditch 4E 114
Eastgate Ct. PO19: Chich 7D 140
(off The Hornet)
Eastgate M. RH13: Hors 1A 46
Eastgate Sq. PO19: Chich 7C 140
EAST GRINSTEAD 3E 14
East Grinstead Mus. 3F 14
E. Grinstead Rd. BN8: N Cha 9E 74
TN22: N Cha, Shef P 9E 74
East Grinstead Sports Club 7B 14
East Grinstead Station
Bluebell Railway 3D 14
East Grinstead Station (Rail) 3D 14
East Gun Copse RH13: Hors 5J 45
EAST HAMPNETT 3N 141
Easthampnett Caravan Pk.
PO18: Tang 3A 142
Easthampnett La. PO18: Tang 3N 141
East Ham Rd. BN17: L'ton 3J 167
EAST HARTING 4C 78
E. Harting St. GU31: E Hart 5C 78
East Hill Ct. BN11: Wor 1H 171
Easthill Dr. BN41: Ports 4D 152
Easthill Pk. 4D 152
Easthill Way BN41: Ports 4D 152
Easting Cl. BN14: Broadw 8K 149
East Jetty BN2: Brig 9L 173
EAST KINGSTON 3J 169
East Lake PO21: Bog R 8E 164
Eastlake Cl. GU31: Peters 6J 55
Eastland Rd. PO19: Chich 9D 140
Eastlands La. RH13: Cow 8H 69
EAST LAVANT 9C 120
EAST LAVINGTON 2F 102
Eastleigh Rd. PO9: Hav 2C 136
EAST LISS 6A 34
East Lockside BN2: Brig 9L 173
East Lodge BN15: S Lan 9B 150
(off The Terrace)
GU31: Rog 5E 56
EAST MARDEN 5E 98
E. Mascalls La.
RH16: Hay H, Wals 3L 73
East Mead BN12: Fer 3L 169
PO21: Pag 3C 180
Eastmead Ind. Est. PO18: Mid L 7A 120
East Meadway BN43: Shor B 7K 151
East M. RH12: Hors 9N 25
EAST MOULSECOOMB 1G 154
Easton Cres. RH14: Bill 1K 65
Easton La. PO20: Sidle 3C 178
E. Onslow Cl. BN12: Fer 1K 169
Eastover Way PO22: Felp 8G 164
East Pallant PO9: Hav 4A 136
PO19: Chich 7C 140
East Pk. RH10: Craw 7F 10
East Point BN43: Shor B 7K 151
Eastpoint PO20: Sel 2J 183
EAST PRESTON 3F 168
East Row PO19: Chich 7C 140
Eastshaw La. GU29: Wool 6E 58
East Strand PO20: W Witt 3F 176
East St. BN1: Brig 8E 172 (8B 154)
BN1: Falm 8K 135
BN15: S Lan 9B 150
BN17: L'ton 3K 167
BN18: Amb 8L 105
BN41: Ports 6E 152
BN43: Shor S 6J 151
GU28: Petw 9N 61
GU31: Rog 5E 56
PO10: W'brne 2H 137
PO19: Chich 7C 140
PO20: Sel 3H 183
RH10: Turn H 8H 13
RH12: Hors 1N 45
RH12: Rusp 5G 8
RH14: Bill 1J 65
RH20: W Chil 7K 87
East St. Arc. BN1: Brig 8E 172
East Tyne BN13: Durr 7B 148
East Vw. Cl. PO18: Mid L 7B 120
East Vw. Flds. BN7: Plump G 2M 115
East Wlk. BN16: E Pres 4E 168
East Walls PO19: Chich 7C 140
E. Walls Cl. PO19: Chich 7C 140
(off East Walls)
East Way PO20: Sel 3K 183
Eastway RH6: Gatw 6K 5
East Wick RH16: Lind 2K 73
Eastwick Cl. BN1: Brig 7C 134
EAST WITTERING 4K 177
E. Wittering Bus. Cen. PO20: E Witt 3L 177
Eastwood RH10: Craw 6H 11
Eastwood Cl. PO11: Hay I 8B 158
Eastwoods BN1: Brig 4B 154
EAST WORTHING 9K 149
East Worthing Station (Rail) 9K 149
E. Worthing Trad. Est. BN14: Broadw 8K 149
Eaton Ct. BN2: Brig 9E 154
(off Eaton Pl.)
BN3: Hove 6K 153
(off Eaton Gdns.)
BN14: Salv 7F 148
Eaton Gdns. BN3: Hove 6L 153
Eaton Gdns. Mans. BN3: Hove 6L 153
(off Eaton Gdns.)
Eaton Gate BN3: Hove 6L 153
Eaton Gro. BN3: Hove 6L 153
Eaton Hall BN3: Hove 6K 153
Eaton Mnr. BN3: Hove 6L 153
Eaton Pl. BN2: Brig 9E 154
Eaton Rd. BN3: Hove 6K 153
Eaton Vs. BN3: Hove 6K 153
Ebenezer Apartments BN2: Brig 6G 172
EBERNOE 6M 39
Ecclesden BN2: Brig 5G 172
Ecclesden La. BN16: Ang 8G 146
EDBURTON 3M 131
Edburton Av. BN1: Brig 1F 172 (3B 154)
Edburton Drove BN5: Fulk 8N 111
Edburton Gdns. BN43: Shor S 4J 151
Edburton Rd.
BN5: Small D, Henf, Fulk 3H 131
Eddington Hill RH11: Craw 2C 28
Eden Ct. BN17: Wick 9M 145
(off Gratwicke Dr.)
Eden Pl. PO10: S'brne 5K 137
Eden Rd. RH11: Craw 8B 10
Eden Va. RH19: E Grin 1D 14
Edgar Cl. RH10: Worth 7N 11
Edgehill Cl. BN13: Durr 6D 148
Edgehill Way BN41: Ports 3B 152
Edge Leisure Centre, The 3F 16
Edgell Rd. PO10: W'brne 1H 137
Edinburgh Cl. PO21: Aldw 1G 180
RH13: Southw 9L 45
Edinburgh Cotts. BN11: Wor 3G 171
Edinburgh Ho. RH11: Craw 1D 28
Edinburgh Rd. BN2: Brig 5C 154
Edinburgh Sq. GU29: Midh 1H 81
Edinburgh Way RH19: E Grin 5F 14
Edith Av. BN10: Peace 6H 175
(not continuous)
Edith Av. Nth. BN10: Peace 4J 175
Edith Cotts. PO18: W Ash 3D 138
Edmonds Ho. GU28: Petw 1N 83
(off Wyndham Rd.)
Edmonton Rd. BN13: Durr 7A 148
Edrich Rd. RH11: Craw 2C 28
Edser Ct. BN41: Ports 2B 152
(off Mile Oak Rd.)
Edward Av. BN2: Salt 1D 174
BN3: Hove 2J 153
Edward Cl. BN3: Hove 2J 153
Edward Ct. BN3: Hove 7H 153
Edward Rd. RH16: Hay H 6F 72
Edwards Av. PO20: Tang 3L 141
Edwards Ter. BN15: Somp 6K 149
Edward St. BN2: Brig 8F 172 (8B 154)
Edwards Way BN17: Wick 9J 145
Edward Way RH15: Burg H 6M 93
Edwen Cl. PO21: Pag 9K 163
Edwin Cl. BN15: Somp 7N 149
PO21: Bers 5B 164
Eels Cross PO20: Sel 2F 182
Effingham Cl. BN2: Salt 2C 174
Effingham La. RH10: Copt 1F 12
Effingham Park Golf Course 1G 12
Egan Way BN17: Wick 2H 167
EGDEAN 4D 84
Egginton Cl. BN2: Brig 9H 135
Egginton Rd. BN2: Brig 9G 135
Egmont Ho. GU29: Ease 8J 59
Egmont M. GU29: Midh 1H 81
(off Rumbolds Hill)
Egmont Rd. BN3: Hove 4F 152
GU29: Ease 8J 59
Egremont Almshouses GU28: Petw 8N 61
Egremont Pl. BN2: Brig 8C 154
Egremont Row GU28: Petw 9N 61
(off Angel St.)
Eighth Av. BN15: Lan 6B 150
Eileen Av. BN2: Salt 3B 174
Eileen Beard Ho. PO9: Hav 9A 116
Eirene Av. BN12: Gor S 3D 170
Eirene Rd. BN12: Gor S 3C 170
Elbourne Ho. RH6: Horl 2K 5
(off Lumley Rd.)
ELBRIDGE 3N 163
Elbridge Av. PO21: Bers 5A 164
Elbridge Cres. PO21: Aldw 1E 180
Elbridge Sq. PO21: Bers 4B 164
Elcombe Cl. PO20: Brac 6M 177
Elder Cl. BN41: Ports 3D 152
RH11: Craw 3E 10
Elderfield Cl. PO10: Ems 2G 136
Elder Pl. BN1: Brig 3E 172 (6B 154)
Elder Rd. PO9: Hav 2B 136
Eldon Rd. BN11: Wor 1K 171
Eldon Way BN17: Wick 1H 167
Eldred Av. BN1: Brig 8M 133
Eleanor Ct. BN11: Wor 2D 170
(off Bruce Av.)
Eleanor Gdns. PO22: Felp 7L 165
Eley Cres. BN2: Rott 1M 173
Eley Dr. BN2: Rott 9M 155
Elfin Gro. PO21: Bog R 9C 164
Elfin M. PO21: Bog R 9C 164
Elgar Way RH13: Hors 7E 26
Elger Way RH10: Copt 1B 12
Elgin Cl. RH13: Hors 8C 26
Elgin Ct. PO19: Chich 8C 140
(off Stirling Rd.)
Elgin Rd. BN12: Gor S 2B 170
Elim Ct. BN2: Brig 6C 154
Eliot Dr. GU27: Has 5G 17
Elizabethan Way RH10: Craw 7L 11
Elizabeth Av. BN3: Hove 2J 153
PO21: Aldw 8L 163
Elizabeth Cl. BN3: Hove 2J 153
PO21: Aldw 9L 163
Elizabeth Ct. BN3: Hove 6L 153
(off Wilbury Rd.)
BN11: Wor 2D 170
PO21: Bog R 1K 181
(off Park Ter.)
RH6: Horl 2J 5
Elizabeth Cres. RH19: E Grin 1F 14
Elizabeth Ho. BN13: W Tar 8E 148
Elizabeth Pl. BN15: Somp 8N 149
Elizabeth Rd. BN11: Wor 2G 171
BN43: Shor S 5M 151
PO19: Chich 6F 140
Ella Cl. PO20: W Witt 4J 177
Ellanore La. PO20: W Witt 1F 176
Ellasdale Rd. PO21: Bog R 9C 164
Ella Ter. BN18: Poling 5B 146
Ellen Ho. BN3: Hove 6K 153
Ellen St. BN3: Hove 6K 153
BN41: Ports 6E 152
Ellesmere Orchard PO10: W'brne 1H 137
Elliot Cl. RH10: Craw 7L 11
Ellis Av. BN13: High S 5C 148
Ellis Cl. BN18: Arun 3F 144
Ellis Sq. PO20: Sel 1K 183
Ellis Way PO21: Pag 3C 180
Ellman Rd. RH11: Craw 8B 10
Ellscott Pk. PO20: Bir 8J 161
Ellson Cl. RH10: Craw 8L 11
Ellwood Pl. RH11: Craw 6B 10
Elm Av. BN16: E Pres 3G 168
Elm Cl. BN3: Hove 3L 153
BN43: Shor S 4L 151
PO11: Hay I 9A 158
PO20: Brac 5M 177
PO20: N Mun 3E 162
PO21: Pag 2C 180
Elm Cl. Est. PO11: Hay I 9A 158
Elm Ct. BN1: Brig 1B 172 (5N 153)
BN41: Ports 5D 152
(off Elm Rd.)
RH19: E Grin 2D 14
(Newlands Cres.)
RH19: E Grin 4E 14
(The Jordans)
Elmcroft Ct. RH10: Craw 6G 11
Elmcroft Pl. PO20: Westg 7E 142
Elm Dale PO22: Barn 7H 143
Elmdale GU31: Peters 5G 54
Elmdene Ct. PO20: Brac 6M 177
Elm Dr. BN3: Hove 4G 152
GU31: Peters 8E 54
PO22: Midd S 7B 166
RH19: E Grin 3G 14
ELMER 7B 166
Elmer Cl. PO22: Midd S 7B 166
Elmer Ct. PO22: Midd S 7C 166
Elmer Rd. PO22: Midd S 7N 165
ELMERS MARSH 5C 36
Elmers Rd. RH5: Ock 1G 7

Elm Gro.—Fidler Cl.

Elm Gro. BN2: Brig .6C 154
BN11: Wor .1D 170
BN15: Lan .8A 150
PO11: Hay I .9A 158
PO20: Sel .3H 183
PO21: Bog R .9B 164
PO22: Barn .6H 143
RH13: Hors .1B 46
Elm Gro. La. BN44: Stey .3A 130
Elm Gro. Rd. BN17: L'ton .2L 167
Elm Gro. Sth. PO22: Barn .7H 143
Elmhurst Cl. BN16: Ang .7F 146
Elmhurst La. RH13: Slinf .4N 43
Elmleigh GU29: Midh .9F 58
Elmleigh Ct. GU29: Midh .9G 58
Elm Lodge BN2: Brig .3G 172
Elm M. BN13: Durr .7B 148
Elmore Ct. BN2: Brig .7C 154
(off Elmore Rd.)
Elmore Rd. BN2: Brig .7C 154
Elm Pk. BN12: Fer .1L 169
PO18: Bosh .7F 138
Elm Pl. BN16: Rust .2C 168
Elm Ri. BN14: Fin .8C 128
Elm Rd. BN11: Wor .2J 171
BN41: Ports .5D 152
PO9: Hav .5A 136
PO20: Westg .6F 142
Elms Dr. BN15: Lan .7A 150
Elmsfield PO20: Sel .3J 183
Elms La. PO20: W Witt .2G 177
Elms Lea Av. BN1: Brig .3N 153
Elms Ride PO20: W Witt .2G 176
Elmstead Gdns. PO20: W Witt .1G 176
Elmstead Pk. Rd. PO20: W Witt .1G 177
Elmstone Cl. BN15: Lan .7A 150
Elms Way PO20: W Witt .1G 177
Elm Ter. BN44: Stey .3A 130
(off Elm Gro. La.)
Elm Tree Cl. BN6: Key .2A 114
PO20: Sel .2J 183
PO21: Bers .6B 164
RH6: Horl .1J 5
Elmwood Av. PO22: Bog R .7E 164
Elrington Rd. BN3: Hove .4L 153
Elsaw Ct. PO19: Chich .8C 140
Elsie Rd. BN11: Wor .3F 170
Elspring Mead BN17: Wick .1J 167
ELSTED .4G 78
Elsted Cl. RH11: Craw .4D 10
Elsted Cres. BN1: Brig .8D 134
ELSTED MARSH .2K 79
Elsted Rd. GU29: Els, Ipin .4G 78
Elverlands Cl. BN12: Fer .4L 169
Elvin Cres. BN2: Rott .9M 155
Elwell Grn. PO11: Hay I .9A 158
Elwood Cl. RH15: Burg H .7A 94
Elwyn Jones Ct. BN1: Brig .9N 133
Ely Cl. BN13: Wor .9D 148
PO20: W Witt .3J 177
RH10: Craw .1G 29
Ely Gdns. PO21: Aldw .9M 163
Ely Rd. BN13: Wor .1D 170
Embassy Ct. BN1: Brig .7A 172
RH16: Hay H .3F 72
(off Sydney Rd.)
Emberwood RH11: Craw .4E 10
Emerald Quay BN43: Shor B .7K 151
Emett Gdns. BN6: Ditch .5F 114
Emlyn Rd. RH6: Horl .1G 5
Emmabrook Ct. BN16: Rust .5N 167
(off Sea Rd.)
Emmanuel Ct. BN11: Wor .1L 171
(off Chatham Rd.)
Emms La. RH13: B Grn, Br Grn .8D 44
Empire Ct. PO9: Hav .4A 136
Empress Cl. BN17: Wick .9K 145
Emsbrook Dr. PO10: Ems .3F 136
EMSWORTH .5F 136
Emsworth By-Pass PO10: Ems .4C 136
Emsworth Centre, The PO10: Ems .5F 136
Emsworth Cl. RH10: Craw .9L 11
Emsworth Comn. Rd. PO9: Ems .9D 116
PO10: Ems, W'brne .8F 116
Emsworth Ho. PO10: Ems .4D 136
Emsworth Ho. Cl. PO10: Ems .4E 136
Emsworth Mus. .5F 136
Emsworth Rd. PO9: Hav, Warbl .4A 136
PO10: Tho I .9H 137
Emsworth Station (Rail) .4F 136
Enclosed Ground, The .8H 155
Ends Pl. RH12: Warnh .3G 25
Enfield Rd. RH11: Craw .1D 28
Engalee RH19: E Grin .2C 14
Englefield RH12: Hors .9K 25
English Bus. Pk. BN3: Hove .5G 153
English Cl. BN3: Hove .5G 153
English Martyrs Catholic Church .2N 169
Enholms La. RH17: Dane .6G 52
Ennerdale Cl. RH11: Craw .8D 10
Ennerdale Dr. BN15: Somp .8M 149
Ensign Way BN17: L'ton .2N 167
Enterprise Centre, The RH10: Craw .2H 11
Enterprise Ct. BN12: Gor S .1A 170
(off Woodsway)
RH11: Craw .2F 10
Enterprise Est. BN1: Brig .7D 134
Enterprise Ho. RH12: Hors .1M 45
Enterprise Units PO22: Bers .6E 164
Epping Wlk. RH10: Craw .8H 11
Epsom Gdns. BN16: Rust .2D 168
Epsom Rd. RH10: Craw .8J 11
Erica Way RH10: Copt .1B 12
RH12: Hors .6A 26
Eridge Cl. RH10: Craw .6L 11
Eridge Rd. BN3: Hove .3J 153
Erin Way RH15: Burg H .5N 93
Eriskay Ct. BN13: Durr .7N 147
Eriswell Rd. BN11: Wor .2G 171
Ermenild Ho. RH19: E Grin .2E 14
Ernest Cl. PO10: Ems .4F 136
Erringham Rd. BN43: Shor S .4H 151
Erroll Mans. BN3: Hove .6F 152
Erroll Rd. BN3: Hove .7E 152
Erskine Cl. RH11: Craw .1A 28
Esher Cl. PO21: Pag .1D 180
Esher Dr. BN17: L'ton .3M 167
Eskbank Av. BN1: Brig .7B 134
Eskdale Way RH10: Craw .8M 11
Esmond Cl. PO10: Ems .5F 136
Esmonde Cl. BN17: L'ton .2M 167
Esplanade BN1: Brig .8A 172 (8N 153)
BN2: Brig .8J 173
(Lewes Cres.)
BN2: Brig .9F 172 (9B 154)
(Madeira Dr.)
BN11: Wor .4D 170
Esplanade, The BN10: Tels C .5F 174
BN11: Wor .2K 171
PO21: Bog R .1L 181
PO22: Felp .9G 165
Esplanade Ct. BN11: Wor .2K 171
(off The Esplanade)
Essenhigh Dr. BN13: Durr .7N 147
Essex Cotts. BN2: Brig .9D 154
(off Essex St.)
Essex Ct. BN11: Wor .2E 170
Essex Pl. BN2: Brig .9D 154
(off Montague St.)
Essex Rd. PO21: Bog R .7D 164
Essex St. BN2: Brig .9D 154
Estcots Dr. RH19: E Grin .3F 14
Estuary, The BN17: L'ton .3M 167
Ethelred Rd. BN14: W Tar .9E 148
Ethel St. BN3: Hove .6K 153
Ethelwulf Rd. BN14: W Tar .9E 148
Eton Cl. PO21: Aldw .8N 163
Eton Dr. PO20: W Witt .3K 177
Eton Rd. BN11: Wor .1E 170
Ettrick Cl. PO19: Chich .8D 140
Ettrick Rd. PO19: Chich .8C 140
Evans Cl. RH10: Craw .7M 11
Evans Pl. PO22: Bers .6E 164
Evelyn Av. BN16: Rust .4C 168
Evelyn Cl. RH19: Felb .1M 13
Evelyn Ct. BN41: Ports .4D 152
Evelyn Glennie Ct. BN2: Brig .8D 154
(off Somerset St.)
Evelyn Lancaster Ho. RH12: Hors .5B 26
Evelyn Rd. BN14: Broadw .9H 149
Evelyn Ter. BN2: Brig .8D 154
Evelyn Wlk. RH10: Craw .9G 10
Everest Ho. BN3: Hove .6H 153
Eversfield RH13: Southw .9L 45
Eversfield Rd. RH13: Hors .1B 46
Evershed Ct. BN10: Tels C .5F 174
Evershed Way BN43: Shor S .6L 151
Eversleigh Ct. GU29: Ease .7J 59
(off High Path)
Ewart St. BN2: Brig .7C 154
Ewelands RH6: Horl .1L 5
Ewens Gdns. PO22: Barn .6H 143
Ewhurst Cl. RH11: Craw .6E 10
Ewhurst Rd. BN2: Brig .5D 154
RH11: Craw .6D 10
Exbury Rd. PO9: Hav .9A 116
Excalibur Cl. RH11: Ifield .7A 10
Exceat Cl. BN2: Brig .7F 154
Excelsior, The BN1: Brig .1M 153
Exchange Rd. RH10: Craw .6G 10
Exeter Cl. PO10: Ems .2F 136
PO21: Aldw .9A 164
RH10: Craw .1G 28
Exeter Ct. BN11: Wor .3E 170
Exeter Rd. PO19: Chich .4A 140
Exeter St. BN1: Brig .2B 172 (5N 153)
Exford Wlk. BN13: Durr .8B 148
Exmoor Cl. BN13: Durr .6C 148
Exmoor Ct. BN13: Durr .6C 148
Exmoor Cres. BN13: Durr .6C 148
Exmoor Dr. BN13: Durr .5C 148
Exton Rd. PO9: Hav .9B 116
PO19: Chich .9C 140
Eyles Cl. RH12: Hors .7M 25

F

Faber Cl. PO9: Hav .1A 136
Fabians Way BN5: Henf .2G 111
Fairbank Rd. RH13: Southw .9K 45
Fairbanks RH16: Hay H .5F 72
Fairbridge Way RH15: Burg H .3A 94
Faircox La. BN5: Henf .2G 111
Fairdene BN42: S'wck .4B 152
Fairfield BN10: Peace .5H 175
Fairfield Av. RH6: Horl .3J 5
Fairfield Cl. BN43: Shor S .4L 151
PO10: Ems .3F 136
PO18: Bosh .8F 138
RH15: Burg H .4A 94
RH17: Ard .2H 51
Fairfield Cotts. RH13: Cow .7H 69
Fairfield Ct. RH13: Cow .7H 69
(off Fairfield Cotts.)
Fairfield Cres. BN6: Hurst .1J 113
Fairfield Gdns. BN41: Ports .4D 152
RH15: Burg H .4A 94
(off Fairfield Rd.)
Fairfield M. RH20: A'ton .3D 108
Fairfield Ri. GU28: Petw .1N 83
Fairfield Rd. PO9: Hav .4A 136
PO18: Bosh .8E 138
RH15: Burg H .5A 94
RH19: E Grin .4F 14
RH20: A'ton .3E 108
Fairfields BN14: Broadw .9H 149
BN14: W Tar .8E 148
Fairfield Ter. PO9: Hav .4A 136
(off Fairfield Rd.)
Fairfield Way RH16: Hay H .1E 72
RH20: A'ton .3E 108
Fairford Cl. RH16: Hay H .4F 72
Fairhaven BN7: Plump .6M 115
Fairholme Dr. BN18: Yap .2A 166
Fairhurst BN10: Tels C .5F 174
Fairlands BN16: E Pres .3E 168
PO22: Bers .6B 164
Fairlawn BN16: Rust .2B 168
RH16: Hay H .5F 72
(off Oathall Rd.)
Fairlawn Cres. RH19: E Grin .2B 14
Fairlawn Dr. BN14: Broadw .9H 149
RH19: E Grin .2B 14
Fairlawns BN3: Hove .7H 153
BN43: Shor S .5K 151
RH6: Horl .3K 5
Fairlea Cl. RH15: Burg H .4A 94
Fairlead BN17: L'ton .4M 167
Fairlea Rd. PO10: Ems .2F 136
Fairlie Gdns. BN1: Brig .2N 153
Fairlight Av. BN10: Tels C .5F 174
Fairlight Chalets PO11: Hay I .9B 158
Fairlight Ct. BN10: Tels C .4F 174
BN17: L'ton .4K 167
Fairlight Pl. BN2: Brig .5D 154
(off Pevensey Rd.)
Fairmead Cl. RH20: Fitt .5G 84
Fairmile Bottom .8C 124
Fairmile Bottom BN18: Made .7A 124
Fair Oak Dr. PO9: Hav .2A 136
Fairplace RH17: Wivel G .4K 95
Fairstone Ct. RH6: Horl .1K 5
Fair Vw. RH12: Hors .8L 25
Fairview Av. BN12: Gor S .3A 170
Fairview Cotts. RH13: Southw .7M 45
Fairview Ct. RH19: E Grin .4F 14
(off Fairfield Rd.)
Fairview Gdns. BN15: N Lan .5B 150
Fairview Ri. BN1: Brig .9M 133
Fairview Rd. BN15: N Lan .5B 150
Fairway BN17: L'ton .4M 167
RH10: Copt .2C 12
RH11: Ifield .7N 9
Fairway, The BN9: Newh .5N 175
BN15: S Lan .8D 150
GU29: Midh .2G 81
PO9: Row C .4B 116
PO21: Aldw .3D 180
Fairway Bus. Cen. BN2: Brig .1F 154
Fairway Cl. RH10: Copt .2B 12
Fairway Cres. BN41: Ports .3E 152
Fairways BN1: Brig .1A 172 (5N 153)
Fairway Trad. Est. BN2: Brig .1F 154
Faithfull Cres. RH20: Storr .5G 107
Falcon Cl. BN43: Shor B .7L 151
RH11: Craw .4F 10
Falcon Ct. BN2: Brig .6G 154
(off Swanborough Pl.)
Falcon Gdns. BN17: Wick .9J 145
Falkland Av. BN17: L'ton .2M 167
Falklands Cl. PO22: Bog R .7E 164
Falklands Dr. RH13: Hors .7E 26
Fallow Deer Cl. RH13: Hors .8E 26
Fallowfield Cl. BN3: Hove .3H 153
Fallowfield Cres. BN3: Hove .3G 153
Fallowfield Way RH6: Horl .1K 5
FALMER .8K 135
Falmer Av. BN2: Salt .1B 174
BN12: Gor S .3N 169
Falmer Cl. BN12: Gor S .3A 170
RH11: Craw .8F 10
Falmer Gdns. BN2: W'dean .5L 155
Falmer Hill BN1: Falm .8J 135
Falmer Rd. BN2: Brig, Falm, W'dean, Rott .2L 155
Falmer Sports Complex .7K 135
Falmer Station (Rail) .8J 135
Falmouth M. RH13: Southw .9L 45
Famet Ct. RH19: E Grin .1C 14
Family Court
Brighton .7G 172 (8C 154)
Faraday Av. RH19: E Grin .6F 14
Faraday Centre, The RH10: Craw .3H 11
Faraday Cl. BN13: Durr .7A 148
Faraday Ct. RH10: Craw .2G 11
Faraday Rd. RH10: Craw .2H 11
Farebrothers RH12: Warnh .3K 25
Faresmead PO21: Aldw .1H 181
Farhalls Cres. RH12: Hors .6C 26
Farlington Av. RH16: Hay H .4G 72
Farlington Cl. RH16: Hay H .4G 72
Farm Acre BN16: E Pres .2E 168
Farman St. BN3: Hove .7A 172 (8M 153)
Farm Av. RH12: Hors .8M 25
Farm Cl. BN5: Henf .2H 111
BN6: Hass .3N 113
BN41: Ports .3C 152
PO18: Fish .7K 139
PO22: Midd S .7B 166
RH10: Craw .5J 11
RH12: Warnh .4K 25
RH13: B Grn .8D 44
RH14: Lox .8N 21
RH19: E Grin .4H 15
Farm Cnr. PO22: Midd S .7A 166
Farm Cotts. RH16: Hay H .6D 72
(off Parkfield Way)
Far Mdw. Way PO10: Ems .5D 136
Farmfield Cotts. RH6: Charlw .6D 4
Farmfield Dr. RH6: Charlw .5D 4
Farm Hill BN2: W'dean .5K 155
Farmhouse Camping & Caravan Site
BN5: Small D .8J 111
Farm La. BN6: Ditch .4F 114
PO18: Nutb .6M 137
Farmleigh Cl. RH10: Craw .4L 11
Farm M. BN3: Hove .7M 153
Farm Rd. BN3: Hove .7M 153
PO20: Brac .6M 177
RH17: Ard .4G 51
Farm Vw. PO10: Ems .2F 136
Farm Wlk. RH6: Horl .2H 5
Farm Way BN16: Rust .3A 168
BN42: S'wck .6C 152
RH15: Burg H .7E 94
Farmway Cl. BN3: Hove .3F 152
Farm Yd. BN1: Brig .7D 172
Farncombe Cl. RH17: Wivel G .4L 95
Farncombe Rd. BN11: Wor .1K 171
Farndell Cl. PO19: Chich .6E 140
Farne Cl. PO20: Bir .8H 161
Farnefold Rd. BN44: Stey .2A 130
Farne La. PO20: Bir .8H 161
Farnham Av. BN6: Key .2B 114
Farnham Cl. RH11: Craw .3E 28
Farnham La. GU27: Has .3H 17
Farnham Rd. GU32: Peters, Steep .2H 55
Farnhurst Rd. PO22: Barn .7J 143
Farnlea RH15: Burg H .3E 94
Faroes, The BN17: L'ton .2N 167
Farr Cl. RH17: Cuck .1A 72
Farren Ct. RH13: Cow .7H 69
(off The Street)
Farriers Cl. RH14: Bill .2H 65
Farriers Ct. RH12: Hors .9N 25
Farriers Lea RH16: Hay H .7D 72
Farriers Wlk. RH12: Hors .9J 25
Farringdon Rd. PO9: Hav .1A 136
Farthings Hill RH12: Hors .8K 25
(off Guildford Rd.)
Farthings Hill Interchange
RH12: Broadb H, Hors .8J 25
Farthings Wlk. RH12: Hors .8K 25
Fastnet Way BN17: L'ton .2N 167
Fatting Ground La. PO22: Barn .1H 165
Faulkner Cl. RH11: Craw .3D 28
Faulkner Gdns. BN17: Wick .1L 167
Faulkners Way RH15: Burg H .3B 94
Fawley Ct. PO9: Hav .9B 116
Fawn Ri. BN5: Henf .1H 111
Fay Cotts. RH12: Fay .8H 9
FAYGATE .2J 27
Faygate Bus. Cen. RH12: Fay .2J 27
Faygate Ct. BN2: Brig .7F 154
Faygate La. RH12: Rusp, Fay .5H 9
Faygate Station (Rail) .2J 27
Fay Rd. RH12: Hors .6N 25
FELBRIDGE .1A 14
Felbridge Av. RH10: Craw .5M 11
Felbridge Centre, The RH19: E Grin .1A 14
Felbridge Cl. RH19: E Grin .1C 14
Felbridge Rd. RH19: Felb .1L 13
Felcot Rd. RH19: Felb .1K 13
Feld, The RH19: E Grin .1A 14
Fellcott Way RH12: Hors .1K 45
Fellows Gdns. BN18: Yap .2A 166
FELPHAM .8J 165
Felpham Gdns. PO22: Felp .7J 165
Felpham Rd. PO22: Felp .9G 165
Felpham Way PO22: Bog R, Felp .8F 164
Felride RH16: Hay H .6F 72
Felwater Ct. RH19: E Grin .1A 14
Fenby Cl. RH13: Hors .7E 26
Fenchurch Mans. BN11: Wor .1G 171
(off Cross St.)
Fenchurch Rd. RH10: Craw .8K 11
Fenchurch Wlk. BN1: Brig .4E 172
Fender Ho. RH12: Hors .9M 25
Fenhurst Cl. RH12: Hors .1K 45
Fennel Cres. RH11: Craw .1D 28
Fennel Wlk. BN43: Shor S .4L 151
Fenners Ct. BN11: Wor .1G 171
Fereday Cl. BN15: Lan .7B 150
Fermandy La. RH10: Craw D .3H 13
Fern Cl. GU31: Peters .6J 55
Ferndale Rd. BN3: Hove .6M 153
PO19: Chich .3C 140
RH15: Burg H .7C 94
Ferndale Wlk. BN16: Ang .7F 146
Fernden Hgts. GU27: Has .9K 17
Fernden La. GU27: Has, Fern, K Grn .8K 17
Ferndown RH6: Horl .1J 5
RH10: Craw .2M 11
Ferndown Gdns. PO22: Felp .7H 165
Fern Dr. PO9: Hav .3A 136
FERNHILL .6N 5
Fernhill Cl. RH10: Craw D .3J 13
Fernhill Rd. RH6: Horl .6M 5
FERNHURST .4K 37
Fernhurst Cl. BN1: Brig .8C 134
RH11: Craw .4D 10
Fernhurst Ct. BN11: Wor .2D 170
Fernhurst Cres. BN1: Brig .9C 134
Fernhurst Dr. BN12: Gor S .2M 169
Fernhurst Gdns. PO21: Aldw .1F 180
Fernhurst Grn. GU27: Fern .4K 37
Fernhurst Rd. GU30: Mill .7L 35
Fernleigh Cl. PO19: Chich .7M 139
Fern Rd. RH20: Storr .6H 107
Fern Way RH12: Hors .6A 26
Fernwood Ri. BN1: Brig .8M 133
Feroners Cl. RH10: Craw .8J 11
Feroners Ct. RH10: Craw .8J 11
(off Feroners Cl.)
FERRING .2K 169
Ferring Cl. BN12: Fer .4K 169
RH11: Craw .5D 10
Ferring Country Cen. .2J 169
Ferring Ct. BN1: Brig .9G 134
(off Newick Rd.)
Ferring Gdns. PO22: Felp .7H 165
Ferring Grange Flats BN12: Fer .2K 169
(off Ferringham La.)
Ferring Grange Gdns. BN12: Fer .2K 169
Ferringham Ct. BN12: Fer .3K 169
Ferringham La. BN12: Fer .4K 169
Ferringham Way BN12: Fer .4K 169
Ferring La. BN12: Fer .1L 169
Ferring Marine BN12: Fer .4L 169
Ferring St. BN12: Fer .2K 169
Ferrymead Ct. BN43: Shor B .7J 151
Ferry Rd. BN17: L'ton .4G 166
BN43: Shor B .7J 151
Ferrywaye Ct. BN43: Shor B .7J 151
Festival Ct. PO19: Chich .6C 140
(off Somerstown)
RH10: Craw .8L 11
Fetherston Rd. BN15: Lan .6A 150
Feversham Cl. BN43: Shor B .7L 151
Fiddlers Copse GU27: Fern .4J 37
(off Nappers Wood)
Fidler Cl. PO20: Sel .1K 183

Field Cl.—Freeman Rd.

Field Cl. BN15: Lan 7A 150
BN18: Walb 4L 143
RH6: Horl 1L 5
RH15: Burg H 4N 93
Field Dr. RH10: Craw D 5H 13
Field End RH20: Storr 5K 107
Fieldend RH12: Hors 6D 26
Fieldgate Cl. RH13: Monks G 6F 46
Field Ho. BN16: E Pres 2E 168
Fieldings, The RH6: Horl 1K 5
RH13: Southw 2K 67
Fieldings Cotts. RH14: Bill 5L 43
FIELD PLACE 6H 25
Field Pl. BN13: Wor 1C 170
BN17: L'ton 3K 167
Field Pl. Cotts. RH12: Broadb H 6H 25
Field Pl. Pde. BN12: Gor S 1C 170
Field Place Pk. 9C 148
Field Rd. PO20: E Witt 4L 177
Field Row BN11: Wor 2H 171
Fields, The *PO20: Westg* 6E 142
(off Meadow Way)
Fields End Cl. RH16: Hay H 5G 72
Fieldview RH6: Horl 1K 5
Field Wlk. *RH6: Horl* 2H 5
(off Court Lodge Rd.)
Fieldway BN6: Ditch 4E 114
GU27: Has 4L 17
RH16: Lind 1G 73
Fifth Av. BN14: Char D 5G 149
BN15: Lan 6B 150
PO9: Hav 3B 136
Filbert Cres. RH11: Craw 6C 10
Filey Cl. RH11: Craw 8B 10
Filton Wlk. *BN13: Durr* 8B 148
(off West Tyne)
Fincham Cl. BN16: E Pres 3E 168
Finch Ct. BN10: Tels C 5G 174
Finch Cres. RH10: Turn H 7K 13
FINCHDEAN 9D 96
Finchdean Rd. PO9: Row C 4C 116
Finches, The BN43: Shor S 5K 151
Finches Cl. BN15: Lan 8A 150
BN17: Wick 9J 145
RH13: Part G 5D 90
Finches Ct. RH16: Lind 9H 51
Finches Gdns. RH16: Lind 1H 73
Finches La. RH16: Lind 1H 73
RH20: W Chil 8H 87
Finches Pk. Rd. RH16: Lind 1H 73
Finch Gdns. PO22: Bers 5C 164
Finchmead La. GU32: Stro 5B 54
Finchwood Farm Ind. Units PO11: Hay I 3B 158
FINDON 8C 128
Findon Av. BN2: Salt 3E 174
Findon By-Pass BN14: Fin 7B 128
Findon Cl. BN3: Hove 2H 153
Findon Dr. PO22: Felp 6L 165
Findon Rd. BN2: Brig 8G 154
BN14: Fin, Fin V 9C 128
RH11: Craw 4D 10
FINDON VALLEY 3D 148
Findon Way RH12: Broadb H 8H 25
Finians Fld. RH13: B Grn 8D 44
Finisterre Way BN17: L'ton 4N 167
Finlat Ct. RH10: Craw 6H 11
Finsbury Cl. RH11: Craw 1E 28
Finsbury Lodge *BN2: Brig* 7D 154
(off Finsbury Rd.)
Finsbury Rd. BN2: Brig 7C 154
Fir Bank BN2: Brig 3G 172
Firbank Way RH19: E Grin 3D 14
Fir Cl. BN2: W'dean 6N 155
Fircroft Av. BN15: N Lan 5A 150
Fircroft Cl. BN1: Brig 2N 153
BN13: Durr 7D 148
Fircroft Cres. BN16: Rust 2C 168
Firlands RH6: Horl 1K 5
RH16: Hay H 5G 73
Firle Cl. RH10: Craw 4G 10
Firle Rd. BN2: Brig 7E 154
BN10: Peace, Tels C 3H 175
BN15: N Lan 5A 150
Firs Av. PO22: Felp 7J 165
Firs Av. W. PO22: Felp 7J 165
Firsdown Cl. BN13: High S 3C 148
Firsdown Rd. BN13: High S 3C 148
Firsland Pk. Est. BN6: Alb 8A 92
Firs Pk. GU31: Peters 6J 55
First Av. BN3: Hove 8L 153
BN14: Char D 5G 149
BN15: Lan, N Lan 7B 150
PO9: Hav 3B 136
PO10: S'brne 5K 137
PO20: Bir 1B 178
PO20: Brac 6M 177
PO22: Felp 8J 165
PO22: Midd S 6M 165
Firtoft Cl. RH15: Burg H 5C 94
Fir Tree Av. GU27: Has 5F 16
Fir Tree Cl. RH11: Craw 3D 10
RH13: Lwr Bee 7K 47
RH20: W Chil 1J 107
Firtree Cl. PO20: N Mun 9F 140
Fir Tree La. RH20: W Chil 1J 107
Fir Tree Rd. PO11: Hay I 9A 158
Fir Tree Way BN6: Key 3B 114
PO22: Bers 5C 164
FISHBOURNE 6L 139
Fishbourne Rd. (East)
PO19: Chich 7M 139
Fishbourne Rd. (West)
PO19: Fish 7L 139
Fishbourne Roman Palace & Gardens 7L 139
Fishbourne Rdbt. PO19: Chich 8N 139
Fishbourne Station (Rail) 6K 139
FISHER 6E 162
Fisher Cl. RH10: Craw 8G 10
Fisher La. GU8: Chidd, Duns 4L 19
PO20: N Mun, S Mun 4E 162
Fishermans, The PO10: Ems 5G 136
Fishermans Quay *BN17: L'ton* 4K 167
(off Surrey St.)
Fishermans Wlk. BN43: Shor B 8G 150
PO11: Hay I 9E 158
PO20: Sel 4K 183
PO21: Aldw 2F 180
Fishers RH6: Horl 1L 5
Fishers Caravan Pk. PO11: Hay I 9C 158
Fishers Cl. BN17: L'ton 4N 167
Fishers Ct. RH12: Hors 7N 25
Fishers Farm Pk. 8C 42
FISHERSGATE 6C 152
Fishersgate Cl. BN41: Ports 6C 152
Fishersgate Station (Rail) 6C 152
Fishersgate Ter. BN41: Ports 6C 152
FISHERSTREET 8H 19
Fisher St. GU8: Chidd 7G 19
GU28: Chidd, N'chpl 2H 39
Fishery La. PO11: Hay I 9C 158
Fish La. PO20: Sel 2F 182
PO21: Aldw 1H 181
Fitch Dr. BN2: Brig 4F 154
Fitchet Cl. RH11: Craw 4D 10
Fit for All 5F 152
Fitness First
Bognor Regis 5E 164
Brighton 5E 172 (7B 154)
FITTLEWORTH 5G 84
Fittleworth Cl. BN12: Gor S 9M 147
Fittleworth Dr. PO22: Felp 6K 165
Fittleworth Gdn. BN16: Rust 3B 168
Fittleworth Rd. RH14: Wisb 6L 63
Fitzalan Ct. *BN10: Peace* 5H 175
(off Cavell Av.)
BN16: Rust 5A 168
(off Rackham Rd.)
Fitzalan M. BN18: Arun 3H 145
Fitzalan Pl. RH10: Worth 6M 11
Fitzalan Rd. BN17: L'ton 4L 167
BN18: Arun 3H 145
(Arundel By-Pass)
BN18: Arun 4G 145
(Malthouse Cl.)
RH13: Hors 7D 26
Fitzhamon Ho. *GU31: Peters* 6G 54
(off Herne Rd.)
Fitzherbert Ct. *BN2: Brig* 5E 154
(off Fitzherbert Dr.)
Fitzherbert Dr. BN2: Brig 5E 154
Fitzjohn Ct. BN6: Key 4A 114
Fitzleet Ho. PO21: Bog R 9D 164
Fitzroy Ct. BN17: L'ton 3L 167
Fitzwilliam Cl. PO21: Aldw 8A 164
Five Acres PO18: Funt 9D 118
RH10: Craw 4G 10
FIVE OAKS 5L 43
Five Oaks Rd. RH13: Slinf, Itch, Broadb H 4N 43
Five Ways BN1: Brig 3B 154
Fixcroft BN5: Wine 4N 91
Flag Ct. BN3: Hove 8K 153
Flag Sq. BN43: Shor B 7J 151
Flamsteed Hgts. RH11: Craw 2C 28
FLANSHAM 5J 165
Flansham Bus. Cen. PO22: Flan 5J 165
Flansham La. PO22: Felp 7K 165
Flansham M. PO22: Felp 6K 165
Flansham Pk. PO22: Felp 6K 165
FLATHURST 8A 62
Flatt Rd. PO18: Nutb 5A 138
Flaxman Av. PO19: Chich 7N 139
Flax Mean PO22: Felp 7J 165
Flax Mean Ho. PO22: Felp 7J 165
FLEET 4A 158
Fleet, The RH20: Fitt 5G 85
Fleet Cl. BN17: L'ton 2N 167
Fleet Farm Camping & Caravan Site
PO11: Hay I 4A 158
Fleet St. BN1: Brig 4E 172 (6B 154)
Fleming Centre, The RH10: Craw 2G 11
Fleming Ct. PO21: Pag 2C 180
Fleming Wlk. RH19: E Grin 6F 14
Fleming Way RH10: Craw 2G 10
Fleming Way Ind. Cen. RH10: Craw 1H 11
Fleming Way Rdbt. RH10: Craw 2F 10
Fletcher Cl. PO20: N Mun 3E 162
PO21: Pag 1D 180
RH10: Craw 8G 10
Fletcher Pl. PO20: N Mun 3E 162
Fletcher Rd. BN14: Broadw 8J 149
RH13: Southw 9K 45
(off College Rd.)
Fletchers RH13: Southw 7K 45
Fletchers Cl. RH13: Hors 1B 46
Fletchers Cft. BN44: Stey 3A 130
RH20: Storr 5J 107
(off Spierbridge Rd.)
Fletchers La. PO18: Bosh 4G 161
PO20: Sidle 9N 161
Fletcher Way BN16: Ang 7E 146
PO21: Bog R 7C 164
RH16: Hay H 7D 72
FLETCHING 6M 75
Fletching Cl. BN2: Brig 7G 154
FLETCHING COMMON 8H 75
Fletching La. BN8: N Cha 8G 74
Flexford Gdns. PO9: Hav 2A 136
(not continuous)
Flimwell Cl. BN2: Brig 8F 154
(not continuous)
Flint Cl. BN16: E Pres 2E 168
BN41: Ports 3D 152
RH6: Horl 1L 5
RH10: Craw 9K 11
Flint Way BN10: Peace 5K 175
Flora Ct. *BN17: Wick* 1H 167
(off Phoenix Cl.)
Floral Clock
Brighton 7L 153
(off Western Rd.)
Floraldene Ct. BN14: Fin V 4E 148
Flora Twort Gallery 6F 54
Florence Av. BN3: Hove 5F 152
Florence Cl. PO20: Bir 8G 161
Florence Ct. *BN1: Brig* 3A 154
(off Gordon Rd.)
Florence Pl. BN1: Brig 1G 172 (4C 154)
Florence Rd. BN1: Brig 1E 172 (5B 154)
PO19: Chich 7E 140
Florets, The BN44: Up B 5E 130
Florida Cl. BN12: Fer 4L 169
Florida Gdns. BN12: Fer 4L 169
Florida Rd. BN12: Fer 4L 169
Florlandia Cl. BN15: Somp 7M 149
Flower Farm Cl. BN5: Henf 2G 111
Foamcourt Waye BN12: Fer 3K 169
Folders Cl. RH15: Burg H 7E 94
Folders Gdns. RH15: Burg H 7D 94
Folders Grange RH15: Burg H 7D 94
Folders La. RH15: Burg H, Ditch 7C 94
Folders La. E. BN6: Ditch 7F 94
Folders Vs. RH15: Burg H 7F 94
Follett Cl. PO21: Aldw 2G 180
Follis Gdns. PO19: Fish 6L 139
Folly La. GU31: Peters 6F 54
RH20: Sutt 4M 103
Fontana Cl. RH10: Worth 7M 11
Fonthill Rd. BN3: Hove 5K 153
FONTWELL 2H 143
Fontwell Av.
BN18: Font, Slind, Walb 5G 142
PO20: E'gate, Font 5G 142
Fontwell Cl. BN14: Fin V 5E 148
BN16: Rust 4A 168
BN18: Font 3H 143
Fontwell Dr. BN14: Fin V 5E 148
Fontwell Park Racecourse 3G 142
Fontwell Rd. PO20: Sel 2L 183
RH10: Craw 9J 11
Forbes Cl. RH10: Craw 1K 29
Forbes Pl. PO19: Chich 5B 140
FORD 9E 144
Ford Airfield Ind. Est. BN18: Ford 1B 166
Fordingbridge Cl. RH12: Hors 1N 45
Fordingbridge Ind. Site PO22: Barn 6H 143
Ford La. BN18: Ford, Yap 9A 144
BN44: Part G, A'hst 8A 90
(not continuous)
Ford La. Bus. Pk. BN18: Ford 9D 144
Ford Rd. BN18: Arun, Ford, Tort 8E 144
BN18: Climp, Ford 1E 166
Ford Station (Rail) 8E 144
Fordwater Gdns. BN18: Ford 2B 166
Fordwater La. PO19: Chich 3C 140
Fordwater Rd. PO18: E Lav 9C 120
PO19: Chich 3C 140
Foredown Cl. BN41: Ports 3D 152
Foredown Dr. BN41: Ports 4D 152
Foredown Rd. BN41: Ports 1C 152
(not continuous)
Foredown Tower Countryside Cen. 2D 152
Forest Cl. RH10: Craw D 4J 13
RH12: Hors 7E 26
RH13: Mann H 4F 46
Forester Rd. RH10: Craw 8G 10
Foresters, The RH13: Hors 1C 46
Forestfield RH10: Craw 9K 11
RH13: Hors 8D 26
Forest Ga. RH11: Craw 2F 28
Forest Grange RH13: Hors, Colg 6G 27
Forest Grange Mnr. RH13: Colg 7H 27
Forest La. BN13: Clap 5N 147
Forest Lodge RH19: E Grin 4F 14
FOREST MERE 1G 34
Forest M. RH12: Hors 6E 26
Forest Oaks RH13: Hors 7E 26
Forest Pk. RH13: Mann H 4H 47
Forest Recreation Cen. 1C 46
Forest Ridge RH19: Sharp 5A 32
Forest Rd. BN1: Brig 9F 134
BN14: Broadw 7H 149
GU29: Midh 2F 80
RH11: Pease P 5A 28
RH12: Hors, Colg, Pease P 7E 26
FOREST ROW 9M 15
Forest Row Bus. Pk. RH18: F Row 9M 15
Forestry Road, The RH14: Plais 8H 21
(not continuous)
FORESTSIDE 9H 97
Forestside Av. PO9: Hav 9A 116
Forest Vw. RH10: Craw 9J 11
Forest Vw. Rd. RH19: E Grin 6E 14
Forest Way RH18: F Row 8J 15
RH19: E Grin 5G 15
Forge, The PO20: Sel 3H 183
RH6: Charlw 6A 4
RH12: Warnh 3J 25
RH13: Southw 9K 45
RH17: Hand 2E 48
Forge Cl. BN16: E Pres 2E 168
BN41: Ports 3D 152
PO19: Chich 1A 162
RH12: Broadb H 7H 25
Forge Cotts. *RH12: Broadb H* 7H 25
(off Forge Cl.)
Forge La. RH10: Craw 5J 11
RH12: Broadb H 7H 25
Forge Pl. RH6: Hookw 4G 4
Forge Rd. RH10: Craw 5J 11
Forge Way RH14: Bill 1H 65
RH15: Burg H 4A 94
Forge Wood RH10: Craw 1M 11
Forge Wood Ind. Est. RH10: Craw 2K 11
Forrester Rd. RH13: Part G 5C 90
Forsters Yd. BN17: L'ton 3H 167
Forsythia Cl. PO9: Hav 1B 136
Fort Haven BN43: Shor B 7M 151
Fort Rd. BN17: L'ton, Wick 2H 167
Fort Rd. E. BN17: Wick 2J 167
Fort Rd. Ind. Est. BN17: L'ton 2H 167
Forty Acre La.
GU31: Old D, S Hart 5J 77
Forum, The RH12: Hors 9N 25
Foster Ct. BN3: Hove 5A 172
Foster La. RH20: A'ton 3D 108
Fosters BN16: E Pres 4D 168
Fosters Cl. BN16: E Pres 4D 168
Fosters Pl. RH19: E Grin 2D 14
Foundry Cl. RH13: Hors 7B 26
Foundry Ct. RH13: Hors 8B 26
RH15: Burg H 5C 94
(off Mill Rd.)
Foundry La. GU27: Has 5J 17
RH13: Hors 8B 26
Foundry Rd. BN18: Yap 1N 165
Foundry St. BN1: Brig 6E 172 (7B 154)
Fountains Cl. BN1: Brig 3C 154
RH11: Craw 8C 10
Founthill Av. BN2: Salt 3B 174
Founthill Rd. BN2: Salt 3B 174
Four Marks Grn. PO9: Hav 8B 116
Four Oaks RH18: F Row 1M 33
Fourteen Acre Av. PO22: Felp 6J 165
Fourth Av. BN3: Hove 8K 153
BN14: Char D 6H 149
BN15: Lan 6B 150
PO9: Hav 3B 136
PO22: Felp 8K 165
Fowey Cl. BN43: Shor B 7L 151
Fowler Cl. RH10: Craw 8L 11
Foxbridge Dr. PO20: Huns 3D 162
Foxbridge Golf Course 1J 41
Foxbridge La. RH14: Kird, Lox 2H 41
Foxbury La. PO10: W'brne, W'cote 2H 137
Fox Cl. BN6: Key 2B 114
PO19: Chich 5E 140
RH11: Craw 3D 10
RH15: Burg H 7A 94
Fox Ct. RH20: Storr 6G 107
Foxdale Dr. BN16: Ang 9E 146
Fox Dell RH20: Storr 6G 107
Foxdown Rd. BN2: W'dean 6N 155
Foxes Cl. BN16: Rust 9A 146
RH13: Southw 2K 67
Foxes Cft. PO22: Barn 7K 143
Foxfield Cotts. RH13: Southw 2K 67
Foxfields RH20: W Chil 8H 87
Foxglove Av. RH12: Hors 5B 26
Foxglove Cl. RH15: Burg H 4M 93
Foxglove Ct. BN1: Brig 2C 154
Foxglove Wlk. BN13: Durr 8A 148
RH11: Craw 9D 10
Foxglove Way BN17: L'ton 1N 167
FOX HILL 8F 72
FOXHILL 7E 62
Fox Hill RH16: Hay H 7F 72
Foxhill BN10: Peace 3H 175
Fox Hill Cl. RH16: Hay H 8G 72
Foxhill Ct. *RH16: Hay H* 6F 72
(off Sussex Rd.)
Fox Hill Village RH16: Hay H 9F 72
Foxhole La. RH17: Bol 6D 70
Foxholes RH12: Rudg 3J 23
Foxhunters Rd. BN41: Ports 2B 152
Fox Lea BN14: Fin 9C 128
Foxleigh Chase RH12: Hors 7C 26
Foxley La. BN13: High S 5C 148
Fox Rd. GU27: Has 5G 17
GU29: Ease 7J 59
Foxwarren RH16: Hay H 4D 72
Foxwarren Cl. PO20: W Witt 4K 177
Fox Way BN41: Ports 2C 152
Foxwells RH17: Bal 1B 50
Foxwood RH12: King 6M 7
Foxwood Av. BN16: Ang 9F 146
Framfield *BN2: Brig* 8G 154
(off Whitehawk Rd.)
Framfield Cl. BN1: Brig 8F 134
RH11: Craw 4C 10
Framnaes BN3: Hove 6F 152
Frampton Cl. PO19: Fish 6K 139
Frampton Ct. BN12: Gor S 2A 170
Frampton Pl. BN43: Shor S 5G 151
Framptons, The BN16: E Pres 3G 168
Framroze Ct. BN1: Brig 2C 154
France La. BN13: Pat 5J 147
Franciscan Way BN17: L'ton 3K 167
Francis Ct. BN17: L'ton 3L 167
Francis Edwards Way RH11: Craw 1A 28
Francis Rd. RH16: Lind 1J 73
Francis St. BN1: Brig 4F 172 (6B 154)
Francome Ho. BN15: Lan 1N 171
Frandor Rd. PO21: Bers 7A 164
Frankalan M. PO21: Bog R 1L 181
Frankland Mead RH20: Wash 9C 108
Franklands Cl. BN14: Fin V 4D 148
RH15: Burg H 7C 94
Franklands Gdns. RH15: Burg H 8B 94
FRANKLANDS VILLAGE 6H 73
Franklands Way RH15: Burg H 8B 94
Frankland Ter. PO10: Ems 5G 136
Franklin Pl. PO19: Chich 6C 140
Franklin Rd. BN2: Brig 5D 154
BN13: Durr 6C 148
BN41: Ports 6E 152
BN43: Shor S 4M 151
RH10: Craw 7L 11
Franklin St. BN2: Brig 5D 154
Franklynn Ct. RH16: Hay H 6G 72
Franklynn Rd. RH16: Hay H 6G 72
Frankton Av. RH16: Hay H 6H 73
Frant Rd. BN3: Hove 3J 153
Fraryden PO10: S'brne 5K 137
Fraser Cl. PO20: Sel 4K 183
Fraser Ct. BN43: Shor S 5M 151
Fraser Gdns. PO10: S'brne 3L 137
Fraser Row PO18: Fish 5L 139
Fraser Wlk. RH17: Hand 3D 48
Fred Emery Ct. BN1: Brig 7A 172
Frederick Gdns. BN1: Brig 6E 172
Frederick Pl. BN1: Brig 5E 172 (7B 154)
Frederick Rd. PO19: Chich 7M 139
Frederick St. BN1: Brig 6D 172 (7B 154)
Frederick Ter. BN1: Brig 5E 172
Freefolk Grn. PO9: Hav 8B 116
Freehold St. BN43: Shor S 6H 151
Freehold Ter. BN2: Brig 5C 154
Freek's La. RH15: Burg H 3B 94
(not continuous)
Freeland Cl. PO19: Chich 7M 139
Freeman Cl. BN18: Walb 4J 143
Freeman Rd. RH12: Warnh 3K 25

Freemans Cl.—Godstalls La.

Freemans Cl. RH14: Bill 1H 65
Freemans Rd. BN41: Ports 5C 152
Freeways PO20: Sel 2G 182
Freeways Caravan Site PO20: Sel 2G 183
Frenches RH20: Storr 5J 107
Frenches Mead RH14: Bill 1H 65
Frenches Rdbt. RH14: Bill 1H 65
French Gdns. RH16: Lind 3H 73
Frenchman's Rd. GU32: Peters 5E 54
Frensham Av. PO22: Bers 6E 164
Freshbrook Cl. BN15: S Lan 8B 150
Freshbrook Ct. *BN15: Lan* *8B 150*
(off Freshbrook Rd.)
Freshbrook Rd. BN15: Lan, S Lan 8B 150
Freshfield Bank RH18: F Row 1L 33
Freshfield Cl. RH10: Craw 7J 11
FRESHFIELD CROSSWAYS 1C 74
Freshfield Ind. Est. BN2: Brig 8D 154
Freshfield La. RH17: Dane, Hors K 1C 74
Freshfield Pl. BN2: Brig 8D 154
Freshfield Rd. BN2: Brig 8D 154
Freshfields Cl. BN15: Lan 7A 150
Freshfields Dr. BN15: Lan 7A 150
Freshfield St. BN2: Brig 7D 154
Freshfield Way BN2: Brig 8D 154
Freshlands RH14: Bill 1H 65
Freshwater Pde. *RH12: Hors* *9M 25*
(off Bishopric)
Freshwoods RH12: Rudg 3J 23
Freya Cl. PO22: Midd S 8N 165
Friar Cl. BN1: Brig 1B 154
Friar Cres. BN1: Brig 1B 154
Friar Rd. BN1: Brig 1A 154
Friars Av. BN10: Peace 7L 175
(not continuous)
Friars Cl. BN6: Hass 3N 113
Friars Oak Rd. BN6: Hass 2N 113
Friars Rookery RH10: Craw 6H 11
Friar Wlk. BN1: Brig 1A 154
BN13: Wor 1D 170
Friary Cl. PO22: Midd S 7M 165
Friary La. PO19: Chich 7C 140
Friary Way RH10: Craw 7F 10
FRIDAYS HILL 3K 37
Friday St. RH5: Ock 1J 7
RH12: Rusp 7B 8
RH12: Warnh 4J 25
Friends Cl. RH11: Craw 3F 10
Frimley Cl. BN2: W'dean 6N 155
Friston Cl. BN2: Brig 1G 154
Friston Wlk. RH11: Craw 4C 10
Frith Pk. RH19: E Grin 1E 14
Frith Rd. BN3: Hove 5J 153
PO21: Bog R 8B 164
Frobisher Cl. BN12: Gor S 9B 148
Frobisher Gdns. PO10: Ems 5F 136
Frobisher Ho. BN10: Peace 3J 175
Frobisher Rd. PO21: Aldw 1E 180
Frobisher Way BN12: Gor S 9B 148
BN16: Rust 4D 168
Froggetts La. RH5: Wall 3A 6
Froxfield Rd. PO9: Hav 9B 116
Froyle Ct. PO9: Hav 9B 116
Fryan's Hanger Viewpoint 2H 103
Fry Cl. RH11: Craw 2D 28
Fry Cres. RH15: Burg H 3N 93
Fryern Cl. RH20: Storr 5H 107
Fryern Pk. RH20: Storr 4H 107
Fryern Rd. RH20: Storr 4J 107
Fryland La. BN5: Sherm, Wine 4K 91
Fuel Farm Rd. RH6: Gatw 4G 4
Fulbeck Av. BN13: Durr 7N 147
Fulbeck Way BN13: Durr 7N 147
Fulfords Hill RH13: Itch 4E 44
Fulfords Rd. RH13: Itch 4F 44
Fulham Cl. RH11: Craw 1D 28
FULKING 3B 132
Fulking Rd. BN45: Poyn 2D 132
Fullers Wlk. BN17: Wick 8K 145
Fullerton Cl. PO9: Hav 9B 116
Fulmar Cl. BN3: Hove 4M 153
RH11: Ifield 7N 9
Fulmar Dr. RH19: E Grin 1G 15
Fulmar Way PO20: Tang 4N 141
Fulmer Ct. BN11: Wor 2F 170
FUNTINGTON 9D 118
Funtington Rd. PO18: E Ash 2J 139
Furlong Cl. BN18: Walb 2J 143
Furlonge Ho. PO10: Ems 4E 136
Furlongs, The BN44: Stey 4A 130
Furlong Way RH6: Gatw 5H 5
Furnace Dr. RH10: Craw 8H 11
Furnace Farm Rd. RH10: Craw 8J 11
RH19: Felb 1J 13
FURNACE GREEN 8J 11
Furnace Pde. RH10: Craw 8J 11
Furnace Pl. RH10: Craw 8J 11
FURNACE WOOD 1K 13
FURNER'S GREEN 9H 53
Furners La. BN5: Henf, W'cote 2J 111
Furners Mead BN5: Henf 2J 111
Furnston Gro. PO10: S'brne 4L 137
Furse Feld PO21: Aldw 1J 181
Furze Cl. BN13: High S 3B 148
PO18: Westh 4G 141
RH6: Horl 2M 5
Furze Comn. Rd. RH20: Thake 1L 107
Furze Cft. BN3: Hove 7M 153
Furzedene BN3: Hove 5A 172 (7M 153)
Furzedown BN17: L'ton 4L 167
Furzedown Cres. PO9: Hav 9A 116
Furzefield PO20: W Witt 2K 177
RH11: Craw 5D 10
Furzefield Cl. BN16: Ang 6E 146
Furzefield Rd. RH12: Hors 6E 26
RH19: E Grin 1D 14
Furze Hill BN3: Hove 5A 172 (7M 153)
Furze Hill Ct. BN3: Hove 5A 172 (7M 153)
Furze Hill Ho. BN3: Hove 5A 172 (7N 153)
Furzeholme BN13: High S 3C 148
Furzeland Way BN6: Say C 7F 92
Furze La. RH19: E Grin 1B 14
Furze Mdw. GU31: N'wd 9D 56
Furzen La. RH5: Wall 8A 6
RH12: Wall 8A 6
Furze Rd. BN13: High S 3B 148
RH12: Rudg 3J 23
Furze Vw. RH13: Slinf 4N 43
Fushia Cl. PO9: Hav 1C 136
FYNING 5F 56
Fyning La. GU31: Rog 5F 56

G

G3 Bus. Pk. BN43: Shor S 6M 151
GABLE HEAD 8A 158
Gable M. PO11: Hay I 8A 158
Gables, The RH6: Horl 3J 5
RH10: Copt 1C 12
RH12: Hors 7A 26
RH13: Southw 1K 67
RH20: Storr 6K 107
Gableson Av. BN1: Brig 1K 153
Gabriel Rd. RH10: Craw 1L 29
Gage Cl. RH10: Craw D 3K 13
Gage Ridge RH18: F Row 1L 33
Gaggle Wood RH13: Mann H 4F 46
Gainsboro Rd. PO21: Bog R 9D 164
Gainsborough Av. BN14: Broadw 6J 149
Gainsborough Dr. PO20: Sel 3J 183
Gainsborough Ho. *BN3: Hove* *6L 153*
(off Eaton Gdns.)
Gainsborough Lodge BN14: Broadw 9G 149
Gainsborough Rd. RH10: Craw 1H 29
Gaisford Cl. BN14: Wor 9G 148
Gaisford Rd. BN14: Wor 9F 148
Gala Bingo
Brighton 8D 154
Worthing 3G 171
Galahad Rd. RH11: Ifield 6A 10
Gales Cl. GU27: Has 6G 17
Gales Dr. RH10: Craw 6H 11
Gales Pl. RH10: Craw 6H 11
Galleries, The *BN3: Hove* *6M 153*
(off Palmeira Av.)
Galliers Cl. BN1: Brig 8C 134
Galsworthy Cl. BN12: Gor S 1N 169
Galsworthy Rd. BN12: Gor S 1N 169
Gamecock Ter. PO20: Tang 5M 141
Gammon Cl. GU31: Peters 5G 54
Gander Cl. RH15: Burg H 3B 94
Gander Grn. RH16: Hay H 2G 72
Gander Hill RH16: Hay H 2G 72
Ganders Cl. BN5: Henf 2G 110
Gandersgate La. RH14: Kird 2F 62
Gannet Ho. BN3: Hove 4K 153
Gannon Rd. BN11: Wor 1K 171
Ganymede Ct. RH11: Craw 9A 10
Garbitts La. GU31: Rog 6E 56
Garcia Trad. Est. BN13: Wor 1D 170
Garden Av. PO20: Brac 5M 177
Garden Cl. BN15: Somp 7N 149
BN16: Ang 6F 146
BN41: Ports 5E 152
BN43: Shor S 4L 151
RH19: E Grin 5F 14
RH20: Storr 5J 107
Garden Cott. PO18: Bosh 8E 138
Garden Ct. *BN3: Hove* *6M 153*
(off Somerhill Av.)
BN43: Shor S 4L 151
PO21: Aldw 1G 181
Garden Cres. PO22: Barn 8K 143
Gardener Ho. *RH13: Southw* *9J 45*
(off College Rd.)
Gardeners Cl. RH12: Warnh 3J 25
Gardeners Ct. RH13: Hors 1A 46
Gardeners Grn. RH12: Rusp 6F 8
Gardener St. BN41: Ports 5C 152
Garden House, The BN1: Brig 6C 172
Garden Ho. La. RH19: E Grin 5F 14
Garden Lodge *PO21: Pag* *1C 180*
(off Pagham Rd.)
Garden Mead RH19: W Hoa 5M 31
Garden M. GU28: Dunc 8M 83
GU31: Peters 6F 54
Garden Pk. BN12: Fer 4K 169
Garden Pl. RH12: Hors 7N 25
Gardens, The BN41: Ports 5E 152
BN42: S'wck 6B 152
PO9: Warbl 4B 136
PO18: W Ash 2E 138
RH20: Fitt 5G 85
Garden Wlk. RH11: Craw 6E 10
RH12: Hors 7N 25
Garden Wood Cl. RH20: W Chil 1J 107
Garden Wood Rd. RH19: E Grin 3B 14
Gardner La. RH10: Craw D 4H 13
Gardner Rd. BN41: Ports 6C 152
Gardner St. BN1: Brig 7E 172 (8B 154)
Garland Av. PO10: Ems 2F 136
Garland Cl. GU28: Petw 1N 83
PO19: Chich 8D 140
Garland Ct. *RH19: E Grin* *3D 14*
(off Garland Rd.)
Garland Point BN43: Shor B 7L 151
Garland Rd. RH19: E Grin 2D 14
Garland Sq. PO20: Tang 3M 141
Garmans RH14: Wisb 9B 42
Garnet Ho. *BN2: Brig* *9D 154*
(off St George's Rd.)
Garrett Cl. RH10: Craw 8L 11
Garrick Rd. BN14: Broadw 9H 149
Garrick Wlk. RH10: Craw 9G 11
Garrones, The RH10: Craw 5M 11
Garsons Rd. PO10: S'brne 5K 137
Garton Cl. RH11: Ifield 7A 10
Gaskyns Cl. RH12: Rudg 4J 23
Gasson Wood Rd.
RH11: Craw 8A 10
Gaston Way PO18: Mid L 7A 120
Gatcombe Cl. BN13: Durr 8M 147
Gateford Dr. RH12: Hors 5C 26
Gate Ho. *GU29: Midh* *1H 81*
(off Edinburgh Sq.)
Gatehouse La. BN6: God G 3K 93
GU31: Rog, Trot 3J 57
RH15: Burg H 4M 93
Gates Cl. RH10: Craw 1L 29
Gatesmead RH16: Hay H 1G 72
Gateway Lodge *PO22: Felp* *8G 165*
(off Felpham Rd.)
Gatewycke Ter. *BN44: Stey* *3A 130*
(off Tanyard La.)
Gatton Manor Golf Course 2D 6
Gattons, The RH15: Burg H 5N 93
GATWICK AIRPORT
North Terminal 5G 5
South Terminal 6J 5
Gatwick Airport Beehive Area RH6: Craw 8J 5
Gatwick Airport Station (Rail) 6K 5
Gatwick Aviation Mus. 7B 4
Gatwick Bus. Pk. RH6: Craw 9K 5
RH6: Hookw 3E 4
Gatwick Ga. RH11: Lowf H 8G 4
Gatwick Ga. Ind. Est. RH11: Lowf H 8G 4
(not continuous)
Gatwick Intl. Distribution Cen. RH10: Craw 9K 5
Gatwick Metro Cen. RH6: Horl 2K 5
Gatwick Rd. RH6: Craw 8J 5
RH10: Craw 3J 11
Gatwick Rd. Rdbt. RH6: Craw 8J 5
Gatwick Way RH6: Gatw 5H 5
Gaugemaster Ind. Est. BN18: Ford 8E 144
Gaugemaster Way BN18: Ford 8E 144
Gaulter Cl. PO9: Hav 2A 136
GAY STREET 2H 87
Gay St. RH20: Bill, Pulb 7H 87
Gay St. La. RH20: N Hth, Bill 1E 86
Gaywood Wlk. BN13: Durr 8B 148
Geddes Way GU31: Peters 5J 55
Gemini Cl. RH11: Craw 8A 10
Genesis Bus. Cen. RH13: Hors 8C 26
Genistas, The *BN6: Hass* *3N 113*
(off Semley Rd.)
Genoa Cl. BN17: L'ton 2N 167
George IV Wlk. PO22: Felp 7H 165
George V Av. BN11: Wor 1D 170
BN15: S Lan 8E 150
George Denyer Cl. GU27: Has 4L 17
George Pinion Ct. RH12: Hors 8M 25
Georges La. RH20: Wash 7A 108
George St. BN2: Brig 8F 172 (8B 154)
BN3: Hove 7K 153
BN41: Ports 6C 152
(Chapel Rd.)
BN41: Ports 6E 152
(Ellen St.)
PO19: Chich 6C 140
George Williams M. BN41: Ports 5D 152
Georgia Av. BN14: Broadw 9H 149
Georgian Cl. RH10: Craw 7M 11
Georgian Gdns. BN16: Rust 2D 168
Gerald Cl. RH15: Burg H 5E 94
Gerald Ct. RH13: Hors 9B 26
Gerald Rd. BN11: Wor 3D 170
Gerardes Lodge GU27: Has 3M 17
Gerard St. BN1: Brig 2E 172 (5B 154)
Gerrard Ho. Bus. Cen. *BN16: E Pres* *2E 168*
(off Worthing Rd.)
Ghyll Ct. *RH13: Southw* *9K 45*
(off Station Rd.)
Ghyll Cres. RH13: Hors 2C 46
Ghyllside BN2: Brig 4F 154
Gibbons Cl. RH10: Craw 9L 11
Giblets La. RH12: Hors 4C 26
Giblets Way RH12: Hors 4B 26
Gibson Pl. RH10: Craw 4G 10
Gibson Rd. PO20: Tang 3L 141
Gibson Way PO21: Bog R 8E 164
Giffards Cl. RH19: E Grin 3F 14
Gifford Rd. PO18: Bosh 6F 138
Gilbert Rd. PO19: Chich 5A 140
Gilberts, The BN16: Rust 5N 167
Giles Cl. BN18: Yap 2N 165
Gilham La. RH18: F Row 1L 33
Gillett Ct. RH13: Hors 7E 26
Gillham's La. GU27: Has 7B 16
Gilligan Cl. RH12: Hors 9M 25
Gilligans, The RH15: Burg H 3A 94
Gillmans Ind. Est. RH14: Bill 3J 65
Gill Way PO20: Sel 2L 183
Gilmore Rd. PO19: Chich 7E 140
Gilmour Ho. BN3: Hove 7K 153
Gilpin Cl. PO19: Fish 7L 139
Gilwynes PO21: Aldw 1H 181
Gilwynes Ct. PO21: Aldw 1H 181
Ginhams Rd. RH11: Craw 6D 10
Girton Ho. BN3: Hove 7H 153
Glade, The PO21: Pag 3C 180
RH10: Craw 8J 11
RH13: Hors 8D 26
RH20: Storr 5K 107
Gladepoint RH16: Hay H 4F 72
Glades, The RH19: E Grin 3H 15
Gladonian Rd. BN17: Wick 1K 167
Gladstone Ct. *BN2: Brig* *5D 154*
(off Hartington Rd.)
Gladstone Pl. BN2: Brig 5D 154
Gladstone Rd. BN18: Yap 2N 165
BN41: Ports 6D 152
RH12: Hors 8A 26
RH15: Burg H 4D 94
Gladstone Ter. BN2: Brig 6C 154
BN17: Wick 1K 167
Gladys Av. BN10: Peace 6K 175
(not continuous)
Gladys Rd. BN3: Hove 5F 152
Glamis Ct. PO21: Bog R 9E 164
Glamis St. PO21: Bog R 9E 164
Glanville Wlk. RH11: Craw 9C 10
Glaseby La. RH20: Wash 2B 128
Glasshouse La. GU28: Kird, Petw 7E 62
RH14: Kird 4G 63
Glass Pavilion BN2: Brig 8F 172
Glastonbury Rd. BN3: Hove 7F 152
Glatting La. RH20: Sutt 6M 103
Glawood Ho. BN14: Broadw 7J 149
Glaziers La. GU29: Ease 7J 59
Gleave Cl. RH19: E Grin 2G 14
Glebe, The BN6: Hurst 1J 113
BN42: S'wck 4B 152
PO20: Tang 4L 141
RH6: Horl 2H 5
RH10: Copt 1C 12
RH16: Lind 1H 73
Glebe Cl. BN15: Lan 6B 150
BN42: S'wck 6A 152
PO20: Nort 4C 142
RH10: Craw 5G 10
Glebefield Rd. PO20: Itchen 7D 160
Glebe Gdns. PO9: Warbl 4B 136
Glebe Ho. PO10: S'brne 5K 137
Glebelands RH10: Craw D 5H 13
RH14: Lox 7M 21
RH20: Pulb 5C 86
Glebelands Cl. BN43: Shor S 5L 151
Glebelands Mdw. GU6: Alf 2M 21
Glebe Rd. BN14: W Tar 8E 148
GU27: Fern 5K 37
GU31: Buri 3D 76
RH17: Cuck 2A 72
Glebeside Av. BN14: Wor 8E 148
Glebeside Cl. BN14: Wor 8E 148
Glebe Twitten *RH17: Cuck* *3A 72*
(off London La.)
Glebe Vw. RH17: Bal 1B 50
Glebe Vs. BN3: Hove 6F 152
Glebe Way BN15: Lan 6B 150
RH14: Wisb 1B 64
Glen, The BN13: Salv 6E 148
RH13: Southw 8L 45
Glenavon M. *BN17: Wick* *2J 167*
(off Lineside Way)
Glenbarrie Way BN12: Fer 1J 169
Glencathara Rd. PO21: Bog R 9C 164
Glen Cres. PO20: Sel 3J 183
Glen Dale PO9: Row C 4C 116
Glendale Cl. RH12: Hors 5D 26
Glendale Rd. BN3: Hove 3A 172 (6M 153)
RH15: Burg H 6C 94
Glendon Ho. RH10: Craw 7F 10
Glendor Rd. BN3: Hove 7G 152
Glendyne Cl. RH19: E Grin 4G 15
Glendyne Way RH19: E Grin 4G 14
Gleneagles Ct. RH10: Craw 7F 10
RH16: Hay H *5F 72*
(off Iona Way)
Glenelg Cl. PO21: Bers 6A 164
Glenfalls Av. BN1: Brig 7B 134
Glenfergus RH16: Hay H 3F 72
Glen Gdns. BN12: Fer 2L 169
Glen Lea GU26: Hind 2G 16
Glenlea Hollow GU26: Hind 3G 16
Glenleigh Pk. PO9: Warbl 3B 136
Glen Pl. PO10: Ems 1G 136
Glen Ri. BN1: Brig 9K 133
Glen Ri. Cl. BN1: Brig 9K 133
Glenview Cl. RH10: Craw 4H 11
Glenville Rd. BN16: Rust 3B 168
Glen Vue RH19: E Grin 3E 14
Glenway PO22: Bog R 8E 164
Glenwood Av. PO22: Bog R 8E 164
Glenwood Rd. PO10: S'brne 4K 137
Gleton Av. BN3: Hove 3F 152
Globe Pl. BN17: Wick 1K 167
Gloster Dr. PO21: Pag 2D 180
Gloucester Cl. GU32: Peters 6D 54
RH19: E Grin 4G 14
Gloucester Ct. *BN11: Wor* *3D 170*
(off George V Av.)
GU32: Peters 5F 54
Gloucester La. BN17: L'ton 3K 167
Gloucester M. BN1: Brig 6F 172
Gloucester Pas. BN1: Brig 6F 172
Gloucester Pl. BN1: Brig 6F 172 (7B 154)
BN17: L'ton 3K 167
Gloucester Rd. BN1: Brig 6E 172 (7B 154)
(not continuous)
BN17: L'ton 3J 167
PO21: Bog R 9F 164
RH10: Craw 1G 28
RH15: Burg H 5A 94
Gloucester St. BN1: Brig 6F 172 (7B 154)
Gloucester Way PO19: Chich 5B 140
Gloucester Yd. *BN1: Brig* *6F 172*
(off Gloucester Rd.)
Glovers Fld. GU27: Has 5H 17
Glover's Yd. BN1: Brig 4A 154
Glynde Av. BN2: Salt 2D 174
BN12: Gor S 4M 169
(Amberley Dr.)
BN12: Gor S 2M 169
(Thakeham Dr.)
Glyndebourne Av. BN2: Salt 2C 174
Glyndebourne Ct. *BN43: Shor S* *6J 151*
(off Ham Rd.)
Glynde Cl. BN12: Fer 2L 169
Glynde Cres. PO22: Felp 7H 165
Glynde Ho. BN3: Hove 7M 153
RH10: Craw 4G 11
Glynde Pl. *RH12: Hors* *9N 25*
(off South St.)
Glynde Rd. BN2: Brig 7E 154
Glynleigh BN2: Brig 6G 172
Glynn Ho. Cl. *PO20: Sel* *3J 183*
(off Malthouse Rd.)
Glynn Ri. BN10: Peace 3H 175
Glynn Rd. BN10: Peace 3J 175
Glynn Rd. W. BN10: Peace 3J 175
GOAT CROSSROAD 5G 32
Goatlands Caravan Pk. PO20: Sel 2G 182
Gochers Ct. *BN2: Brig* *6D 154*
(off Islingword Rd.)
Goda Rd. BN17: L'ton 3L 167
Goddard Cl. RH10: Craw 9K 11
GODDARDS' GREEN 3J 93
GODLEYS GREEN 3N 95
Godman Cl. PO21: Aldw 9M 163
Godolphin Ct. RH10: Craw 8F 10
Godstalls La. BN44: Stey 3N 129

Godwin Cl.—Greystone Av.

Godwin Cl. PO10: Ems .2E 136
Godwin Rd. BN3: Hove .4F 152
Godwin Way PO18: Fish .5K 139
RH13: Hors .7C 26
Goepel Ct. RH10: Craw .5J 11
Goffs Cl. RH11: Craw .7E 10
Goffs La. RH11: Craw .6D 10
(not continuous)
GOFFS PARK .7D 10
Goffs Pk. Rd. RH11: Craw .7E 10
Golby Ct. BN10: Tels C .5G 174
Goldbridge Rd. BN8: Newick .9M 75
TN22: Pilt .9M 75
Goldcrest Av. BN17: Wick .9J 145
Goldcrest Cl. RH6: Horl .1G 4
Golden Acre BN16: E Pres .4G 168
PO21: Pag .3C 180
Golden Av. BN16: E Pres .2G 168
Golden Av. Cl. BN16: E Pres .4G 168
Golden Hill RH15: Burg H .5E 94
Golden La. BN1: Brig .7A 172 (8M 153)
BN44: A'hst .1A 110
Golden Sands Caravan Pk. BN15: S Lan .9D 150
Golden Sq. BN5: Henf .3H 111
GU28: Petw .9N 61
Goldfinch Cl. RH11: Craw .4F 10
RH12: Hors .4N 25
Goldfinch Way PO20: Sel .1H 183
Golding Barn Farm BN5: Small D .4H 131
Golding Cl. RH10: Craw .7L 11
Golding La. RH13: Mann H .4F 46
Golding's Hill RH13: Mann H .3G 46
Gold La. BN10: Peace .2J 175
Goldring Cl. PO11: Hay I .9A 158
Goldsmid M. BN3: Hove .7M 153
(off Farm M.)
Goldsmid Rd. BN3: Hove .4B 172 (6N 153)
Goldsmith Rd. BN14: Broadw .9J 149
Goldstone Cl. BN3: Hove .3J 153
Goldstone Ct. BN3: Hove .2J 153
Goldstone Cres. BN3: Hove .2J 153
Goldstone Ho. BN3: Hove .6K 153
(off Clarendon Rd.)
Goldstone La. BN3: Hove .5K 153
Goldstone Retail Pk. BN3: Hove .5K 153
Goldstone Rd. BN3: Hove .6K 153
Goldstone St. BN3: Hove .6K 153
Goldstone Vs. BN3: Hove .6K 153
Goldstone Way BN3: Hove .3J 153
Golf Club La. RH20: Pulb .9E 86
Golf Dr. BN1: Brig .2C 154
Golfers La. BN16: Ang .9C 146
Golf Links La. PO20: Sel .9H 179
Golf Links Rd. PO22: Felp .6G 165
(not continuous)
Goodacres PO22: Barn .8K 143
Goodhew Cl. BN18: Yap .1A 166
Goodwin Cl. RH11: Craw .9B 10
Goodwins Cl. RH19: E Grin .1D 14
GOODWOOD .5G 120
Goodwood Av. PO22: Felp .7G 165
Goodwood Cl. BN16: Rust .2D 168
GU29: Midh .3G 81
RH10: Craw .9J 11
Goodwood Country Pk. .3K 121
Goodwood Ct. BN3: Hove .6M 153
PO10: S'brne .5L 137
PO20: Sel .2J 183
Goodwood Gdns. PO20: Runc .3G 162
Goodwood Golf Course .7G 120
Goodwood House .8H 121
Goodwood Motor Circuit .2E 140
Goodwood Park Golf Course .9J 121
Goodwood Pl. PO21: Bog R .1L 181
(off West St.)
Goodwood Race Course .3G 121
Goodwood Rd. BN13: Salv .6E 148
Goodwood Way BN2: Brig .2F 154
Goodyer Cl. GU32: Peters .7E 54
GOOSE GREEN
GU31 .9L 55
RH12 .5J 25
RH20 .6B 88
Goosegreen Cl. RH12: Hors .6A 26
Goose Grn. La. RH20: G Grn .5A 88
Gordon Av. BN43: Shor S .6K 151
PO19: Chich .1A 162
PO22: Bog R .8E 164
(not continuous)
Gordon Av. W. PO22: Bog R .7E 164
Gordon Cl. BN41: Ports .6E 152
RH16: Hay H .3F 72
Gordon Ho. PO19: Chich .7C 140
(off Church Sq.)
Gordon M. BN41: Ports .6E 152
Gordon Rd. BN1: Brig .3A 154
BN11: Wor .1H 171
BN15: Lan .7A 150
BN41: Ports .6C 152
(Chapel Rd.)
BN41: Ports .6E 152
(Gordon Cl.)
BN43: Shor S .6J 151
PO10: S'brne .6H 137
RH12: Hors .7A 26
RH15: Burg H .4D 94
RH16: Hay H .3F 72
Gordon Ter. BN18: Poling .5B 146
Goreside La. RH17: Cuck .1A 72
Gorham Av. BN2: Rott .2A 174
Gorham Cl. BN2: Rott .2A 174
Gorham Ct. BN10: Tels C .4E 174
Gorham Way BN10: Tels C .4E 174
Goring Bus. Pk. BN12: Gor S .1A 170
GORING-BY-SEA .2A 170
Goring-by-Sea Station (Rail) .1M 169
Goring Chase BN12: Gor S .9M 147
Goring Ct. BN1: Brig .9G 135
BN44: Stey .4A 130
(off Bramber Rd.)
Goring Crossways BN12: Gor S .9M 147
Goring Rd. BN12: Gor S, Wor .2A 170
BN44: Stey .4A 130
Goring's Mead RH13: Hors .1A 46
Goring St. BN12: Gor S .9M 147
Goring Way BN12: Fer, Gor S .2L 169
RH13: Part G .4D 90
Gorling Cl. RH11: Ifield .7A 10
Gorringe Cl. BN43: Shor S .6N 151
Gorringes Brook
RH12: Hors .5A 26
Gorse Av. BN14: Salv .7F 148
BN16: King G .4J 169
PO22: Felp .6L 165
Gorse Bank Cl. RH20: Storr .4A 108
Gorse Cl. BN41: Ports .1B 152
RH10: Copt .2C 12
RH11: Craw .3D 28
Gorse End RH12: Hors .6A 26
Gorselands RH14: Bill .1K 65
Gorse La. BN13: High S .3C 148
Gorse Rd. GU31: Peters .6J 55
Gosden Cl. RH10: Craw .7J 11
Gosden Rd. BN17: L'ton .2M 167
Gosling Croft Bus. Cen. BN13: Clap .5K 147
GOSPEL GREEN .8F 18
Gospond Rd. PO22: Barn .8J 143
Gosport Ct. BN43: Shor B .7L 151
(off Harbour Way)
Gosport Ho. PO9: Hav .9B 116
Gossamer La. PO21: Aldw .9M 163
Gossops Dr. RH11: Craw .7B 10
GOSSOPS GREEN .7B 10
Gossops Grn. La. RH11: Craw .7C 10
Gossops Pde. RH11: Craw .7B 10
(off Gossops Dr.)
Gostrode La. GU8: Chidd .5H 19
Goudhurst Cl. RH10: Worth .6N 11
Goudhurst Keep RH10: Worth .6N 11
Gower Rd. RH6: Horl .2G 5
RH16: Hay H .5F 72
Gowers Cl. RH17: Ard .2J 51
Grace Ct. BN6: Hass .2N 113
RH12: Hors .7D 26
Grace Rd. RH11: Craw .2C 28
GRAFFHAM .8D 82
Graffham Camping & Caravan Site
GU28: Graff .6F 82
Graffham Cl. BN2: Brig .7F 154
PO19: Chich .2C 140
RH11: Craw .4D 10
Grafton Av. PO22: Felp .6K 165
Grafton Cl. BN16: Rust .2B 168
Grafton Ct. PO20: Sel .4J 183
Grafton Dr. BN15: Somp .7N 149
Grafton Gdns. BN15: Somp .7N 149
Grafton Pl. BN11: Wor .2H 171
Grafton Rd. BN11: Wor .2H 171
PO20: Sel .5J 183
Grafton St. BN2: Brig .9C 154
Graham Av. BN1: Brig .1N 153
BN41: Ports .1B 152
Graham Cl. BN41: Ports .1B 152
Graham Ct. BN11: Wor .2D 170
BN15: Somp .7N 149
Graham Cres. BN41: Ports .1B 152
Graham Rd. BN11: Wor .2H 171
BN18: Yap .3N 165
Grailands Cl. GU27: Fern .4L 37
Granary Cl. RH12: Hors .1K 45
Granary La. PO20: Sel .2H 183
Granary Way BN17: Wick .9K 145
RH12: Hors .1K 45
Grand Av. BN3: Hove .8L 153
BN6: Key .3A 114
BN11: Wor .1E 170
BN15: Lan .7B 150
BN17: Wick .1J 167
Grand Av. Mans. BN3: Hove .7L 153
(off Grand Av.)
Grand Cres. BN2: Rott .3A 174
Grand Junc. Rd. BN1: Brig .9E 172 (9B 154)
Grand Ocean BN2: Salt .3D 174
Grand Pde. BN2: Brig .7F 172 (8B 154)
PO11: Hay I .9A 158
RH10: Craw .6F 10
Grand Pde. M. BN2: Brig .7F 172 (8B 154)
Grange, The BN2: Salt .4D 174
BN6: Hurst .1G 113
PO10: Ems .3F 136
(off New Brighton Rd.)
Grange Cl. BN1: Brig .1B 172 (4N 153)
BN12: Fer .3K 169
PO9: Hav .3B 136
RH10: Craw .4J 11
RH15: Burg H .3D 94
Grange Ct. BN3: Hove .5H 153
(off Payne Av.)
BN12: Fer .2K 169
(off Ferring Grange Gdns.)
BN42: S'wck .6A 152
PO21: Aldw .2G 181
Grange Cres. RH10: Craw D .5J 13
Grange Farm Cotts. BN2: O'dean .9L 155
(off Greenways)
Grange Fld. Way PO21: Aldw .1F 180
Grange Ind. Estate, The BN42: S'wck .6A 152
Grange La. PO20: Sel .9K 179
Grange Leisure Centre, The .1H 81
Grange Museum & Art Gallery, The .2A 174
Grange Pk. BN12: Fer .3K 169
Grange Rd. BN3: Hove .6G 153
BN42: S'wck .6A 152
GU29: Midh .1H 81
GU32: Peters .7E 54
RH10: Craw D .5H 13
Grange Wlk. BN1: Brig .9N 133
Grange Way RH13: Southw .8K 45
Grangeway, The BN16: Rust .3B 168
Grangeways BN1: Brig .9N 133
Grangewood Dr. PO21: Aldw .1F 180
Grant Cl. PO20: Sel .3H 183
Grantham Rd. BN1: Brig .4B 154
Grantsmead BN15: N Lan .5B 150
Grant St. BN2: Brig .6C 154
Granville Cl. PO9: Warbl .4A 136
Granville Ct. BN3: Hove .6K 153
(off Denmark Vs.)
Granville Rd. BN3: Hove .4B 172 (6N 153)
BN17: L'ton .4L 167
Graperies, The BN2: Brig .8D 154
Grasmere Av. BN15: Somp .7M 149
Grasmere Ct. RH10: Craw .8M 11
(off Grayrigg Rd.)
Grasmere Gdns. RH12: Hors .5E 26
Grassmere RH6: Horl .1L 5
Grassmere Av. BN10: Tels C .4F 174
Grassmere Cl. BN17: L'ton .1N 167
PO22: Felp .8G 165
Grassmere Ct. BN10: Tels C .4G 174
Gratten La. BN5: Wine .5N 91
RH17: Twine, Wine .5A 92
Grattons, The RH13: Slinf .8C 24
Grattons Dr. RH10: Craw .3L 11
Gratwicke Cl. RH14: Bill .1J 65
Gratwicke Ct. BN17: Wick .9M 145
(off Gratwicke Dr.)
Gratwicke Dr. BN17: Wick .9M 145
Gratwicke Rd. BN11: Wor .2G 171
Gravel La. PO19: Chich .8E 140
Gravelly Cres. BN15: Lan .7C 150
Gravelye Cl. RH16: Hay H .4J 73
Gravelye La. RH16: Hay H .6H 73
(not continuous)
Graveney Rd. RH10: Craw .7L 11
Gravett Ct. RH15: Burg H .6A 94
GRAVETYE .1N 31
Gravetye Cl. RH10: Craw .8J 11
Gravits La. PO21: Bog R .7B 164
Graydon Av. PO19: Chich .9A 140
Graylingwell Cotts. PO19: Chich .3C 140
Graylingwell Dr. PO19: Chich .4D 140
(not continuous)
Grayrigg Rd. RH10: Craw .8M 11
Grays Cl. GU27: Has .3N 17
GRAYSHOTT .1E 16
Grayshott Dr. PO22: Bers .6E 164
GRAYSWOOD .1A 18
Grays Wood RH6: Horl .2L 5
Grayswood Av. PO20: Brac .5M 177
Grayswood Comn. GU27: G'wd .2A 18
Grayswood M. GU27: G'wd .1A 18
Grayswood Pl. GU27: Has .3N 17
Grayswood Rd. GU27: Has, G'wd .4M 17
Gt. College St. BN2: Brig .9D 154
GREAT COMMON .6H 41
Gt. Daux Rdbt. RH12: Warnh .4M 25
Great Fld. Pl. RH19: E Grin .1H 15
Greatfield Way PO9: Row C .3B 116
Great Grooms RH14: Bill .3H 65
GREATHAM .3N 105
Greatham Ct. BN1: Brig .8N 133
(off Old London Rd.)
Greatham La. RH20: Pulb .3C 106
Greatham Rd. BN14: Fin V .4D 148
RH10: Craw .9L 11
RH20: Great, Pulb .3N 105
Great Hanger GU31: Peters .6H 55
Great Heathmead RH16: Hay H .3E 72
Great Ho. Ct. RH19: E Grin .4F 14
Greatlake Ct. RH6: Horl .1K 5
(off Tanyard Way)
Gt. Lime Kilns RH13: Southw .9L 45
Greatpin Cft. RH20: Fitt .5G 84
Great Wilkins BN1: Falm .9J 135
Grebe Cl. PO10: W'brne .1H 137
Grebe Cres. RH13: Hors .1D 46
Grecians E. RH13: Hors .5J 45
(off East Gun Copse)
Grecians W. RH13: Hors .5H 45
(off West Gun Copse)
Green, The BN2: Rott .2N 173
BN3: Hove .3L 153
BN5: Henf .3H 111
(off Golden Sq.)
BN8: Newick .9K 75
BN42: S'wck .6A 152
GU28: Graff .2F 102
PO9: Row C .4C 116
PO19: Chich .5E 140
PO21: Pag .3C 180
RH10: Copt .1C 12
RH11: Craw .5E 10
RH13: Dial P .5J 89
RH17: Hors K .5D 52
RH20: Pulb .4B 86
(off Stane St. Cl.)
RH20: Storr .5L 107
Greena Ct. BN11: Wor .2G 171
Greenacre BN10: Peace .2K 175
Greenacre Cl. RH20: Storr .6G 107
Greenacre Ct. RH15: Burg H .6B 94
(off Station Rd.)
Greenacres BN1: Brig .1D 172 (4A 154)
BN10: Tels C .5G 174
BN43: Shor S .5H 151
BN44: Stey .4A 130
PO20: Bir .6G 160
RH10: Craw .7J 11
RH12: Hors .7N 25
RH20: A'ton .2E 108
Greenacres Ring BN16: Ang .7F 146
Green Bank PO22: Barn .8K 143
Greenbank Av. BN2: Salt .3C 174
Greenbushes Cl. BN16: Rust .4A 168
Green Cl. BN42: S'wck .6A 152
RH13: Southw .7K 45
Green Ct. BN17: L'ton .4K 167
BN42: S'wck .6A 152
(off The Green)
PO20: E Witt .4K 177
(off Cakeham Rd.)
Greencourt Dr. PO21: Bers .7B 164
Greenfield RH20: Sutt .5N 103
Greenfield Cl. BN1: Brig .9B 134
BN42: S'wck .5A 152
Greenfield Cres. BN1: Brig .9A 134
Greenfield La. PO18: W Ash .2E 138
Greenfield Rd. RH13: Slinf .8B 24
Greenfields BN17: Wick .1H 167
GU31: N'wd .1D 78
PO22: Midd S .7M 165
Greenfields Cl. GU31: N'wd .9D 56
RH12: Hors .5D 26
Greenfields Rd. RH6: Horl .1H 5
RH12: Hors .6D 26
Greenfields Way RH12: Hors .5D 26
Greenfield Way RH20: Storr .5K 107
Greenfinch Way RH12: Hors .4N 25
Green Gate BN10: Peace .3J 175
Greengates GU28: Lurg .8E 38
Green Hedges Av. RH19: E Grin .2D 14
Green Hedges Cl. RH19: E Grin .2D 14
Greenhill Pk. RH17: Hay H .7H 73
Greenhill Way BN10: Peace .2J 175
RH17: Hay H .7H 73
Greenhurst La. RH20: Storr .2J 107
Greenland Cl. BN13: Durr .6C 148
Greenland Rd. BN13: Durr .7B 148
Greenlands Cl. RH15: Burg H .8C 94
Greenlands Dr. RH15: Burg H .8C 94
Greenland Wlk. BN13: Durr .6C 148
Green La. BN2: W'dean .7M 155
GU27: Has .7K 17
GU31: Mill .3J 57
PO18: Bosh .7F 138
(Delling La.)
PO18: Bosh .5C 138
(Newells La.)
PO19: Chich .6D 140
PO20: Donn, Huns .6A 162
PO20: Oving .1H 163
PO20: Runc .2H 163
PO20: Sel .4H 183
PO20: Sidle .2F 178
RH5: Ock .1C 6
RH10: Craw .4G 11
RH10: Craw D .1G 13
RH10: Worth .6M 11
(not continuous)
RH12: Hors .8B 8
RH13: Southw .5L 45
RH13: W Grin .8M 67
RH17: Wivel .4J 95
Green La. Cl. BN18: Arun .3F 144
Green Lawns Caravan Pk. PO20: Sel .1J 183
Greenlea Av. PO21: Aldw, Pag .1D 180
Greenleas BN3: Hove .3F 152
Greenleaves BN44: Bramb .5B 130
Green Mdws. RH16: Lind .9J 51
RH20: Pulb .7C 86
Greenoaks BN15: N Lan .5A 150
Green Pk. BN12: Fer .1L 169
Green Pk. Cnr. RH17: Wivel .3H 95
Green Pond Cnr. PO9: Warbl .4B 136
Green Ridge BN1: Brig .9K 133
Green Rd. PO18: E Dean .5A 102
RH17: Wivel, Wivel G .3H 95
Greens La. RH13: Mann H .3G 46
Greenstede Av. RH19: E Grin .1F 14
GREEN STREET .7G 67
Greentree La. RH13: Sherm .4F 90
Greentrees BN11: Wor .2F 170
BN15: Somp .8N 149
Greentrees Cl. BN15: Somp .7N 149
Greentrees Cres. BN15: Somp .7N 149
Green Vw. RH15: Burg H .5N 93
Green View, The RH11: Pease P .4E 28
Green Wlk. RH10: Craw .4G 10
Green Way PO22: Midd S .7N 165
Green Way, The BN12: Gor S .9N 147
Greenway RH12: Hors .8M 25
Greenway, The PO10: Ems .2F 136
Greenway Ct. BN2: Rott .3A 174
Greenway La. GU31: Buri .2C 76
Greenways BN2: O'dean .9L 155
BN5: Henf .2G 111
BN41: Ports .4D 152
BN42: S'wck .4B 152
PO21: Pag .2D 180
RH16: Hay H .3G 72
Greenways Cnr. BN2: O'dean .9K 155
Greenways Cres. BN12: Fer .3L 169
BN43: Shor S .4K 151
Greenways Wlk. RH11: Craw .2E 28
Greenway Wlk. PO20: E Witt .5M 177
Greenwich Cl. RH11: Craw .1E 28
Greenwich Way BN10: Peace .5H 175
Greenwood Av. PO22: Bers, Bog R .6C 164
Greenwood Cl. PO22: Bers .6C 164
Greenwood Ct. RH11: Craw .2D 28
Greenwood Dr. BN16: Ang .9E 146
Greet Rd. BN15: Lan .6A 150
Gregory Cl. RH10: Craw .1L 29
Gregsons RH12: Warnh .3J 25
Grendon Cl. RH6: Horl .1H 5
Grenehurst Way GU31: Peters .6F 54
Grenfield Ct. PO10: Ems .2F 136
Grenville Av. BN12: Gor S .1B 170
Grenville Cl. BN12: Gor S .1A 170
Grenville Gdns. PO19: Chich .9B 140
Grenville Ho. BN10: Peace .3K 175
Grenville St. BN1: Brig .8D 172 (8A 154)
Gresham Pl. BN5: Henf .1G 111
Gresham Wlk. RH10: Craw .9G 10
(not continuous)
Grevatt's La. BN17: Climp .5N 165
BN18: Bils .5N 165
Grevatt's La. W. BN18: Bils .4N 165
Greville Grn. PO10: Ems .1E 136
Grey Alders RH16: Hay H .3J 73
Greyfriars BN3: Hove .5M 153
Greyfriars Cl. BN13: Salv .7E 148
PO21: Aldw .9A 164
Greyfriars La. RH20: Storr .8H 107
Greyhound Slip RH10: Craw .5M 11
Greynville Cl. PO21: Aldw .1E 180
Grey Point Ho. BN14: Fin .8C 128
Greystoke M. BN12: Fer .2K 169
Greystoke Rd. BN12: Fer .2K 169
Greystone Av. BN13: Wor .8D 148
PO21: Bers .5A 164

Gribble La.—Hascombe Ct.

Gribble La. PO20: Oving .6K 141
Grier Cl. RH11: Ifield .7A 10
Griffin Cres. BN17: Wick .9K 145
Griffiths Av. BN15: N Lan .5A 150
Griffits Path RH18: F Row .1L 33
Grinder's La. RH13: Dial P .6J 89
Grinstead Av. BN15: Lan .7B 150
Grinstead La. BN5: Henf .4H 111
BN15: Lan .8B 150
RH19: F Row .2B 32
Grinstead Mt. BN2: Brig .8G 154
Grisedale Cl. RH11: Craw .8E 10
GRISLING COMMON .9N 75
Groombridge Way RH12: Hors .1K 45
Grooms, The RH10: Craw .4M 11
Grooms Cl. BN16: Ang .8F 146
Groomsland Dr. RH14: Bill .3H 65
Grooms Yd. PO18: Sing .8F 100
Grosvenor Cl. RH6: Horl .4J 5
Grosvenor Ct. BN1: Brig .2N 153
PO9: Hav .4A 136
(off East St.)
RH19: E Grin .3D 14
(off Grosvenor Rd.)
Grosvenor Gdns. PO21: Aldw .9L 163
Grosvenor Mans. BN3: Hove .7K 153
Grosvenor Rd. BN11: Wor .2H 171
PO19: Chich .9B 140
RH19: E Grin .3D 14
Grosvenor St. BN2: Brig .8C 154
Grosvenor Way PO21: Aldw .9L 163
Grouse Rd. RH11: Colg, Pease P .7A 28
RH13: Plum P, Colg .3J 47
Grove, The BN12: Fer .2K 169
PO10: W'brne .2H 137
PO22: Felp .8H 165
RH6: Horl .3K 5
RH11: Craw .6E 10
RH16: Hay H .6J 73
Grove Bank BN2: Brig .6G 172
Grove Ct. BN3: Hove .7L 153
RH10: Craw .6J 11
Grove Cres. BN17: L'ton .2L 167
Grove Hill BN2: Brig .6G 172 (7C 154)
Grovelands RH6: Horl .3K 5
Grovelands, The BN15: S Lan .9B 150
Grovelands Cl. RH15: Burg H .7A 94
Grove La. GU28: Petw .1A 84
RH20: W Chil .1J 107
Grove Lodge BN14: Broadw .7G 148
Grove Lodge Rdbt. BN14: Broadw .6G 148
Grove Pk. PO19: Chich .7N 139
Grover Av. BN15: Lan .6A 150
Grove Rd. BN14: Broadw .7G 149
PO9: Hav .4A 136
PO19: Chich .8D 140
PO20: Sel .4J 183
RH6: Horl .1G 5
RH15: Burg H .6C 94
Grove St. BN2: Brig .7C 154
GU28: Petw .9N 61
Grove Villa BN1: Brig .3C 172
Grub Ride BN13: Clap .3L 147
G's Health Club .8C 14
Guardian Ct. BN13: Salv .7E 148
Guernsey Cl. RH11: Craw .1C 28
Guernsey Farm La. PO22: Felp .7K 165
Guernsey Rd. BN12: Fer .4L 169
Guildbourne Centre, The BN11: Wor .2H 171
Guilden Rd. PO19: Chich .7D 140
Guildford Cl. BN14: Wor .9E 148
PO10: S'brne .4K 137
Guildford Pl. PO19: Chich .4B 140
Guildford Rd. BN1: Brig .5D 172 (7A 154)
BN14: Wor .1E 170
BN16: Rust .2D 168
GU6: Alf, Rudg .1A 22
RH12: Hors .8K 25
RH12: Rudg .3E 22
RH12: Slinf, Broadb H .4B 24
RH13: Rudg, Slinf .3E 22
RH14: Lox .6M 21
Guildford St. BN1: Brig .5D 172 (7A 154)
Guildhall
Chichester .6C 140
Guildhall St. PO19: Chich .6C 140
Guild Pl. RH15: Burg H .7D 94
Guillards Oak GU29: Midh .1G 80
Guillemot Path RH11: Ifield .7N 9
Guillods Cotts. GU28: Graff .9C 82
Guinevere Rd. RH11: Ifield .6A 10
Guinness Ct. RH11: Craw .1E 28
Gullivers Mead PO22: Felp .5J 165
Gunning Cl. RH11: Craw .9C 10
Gunwin Ct. PO21: Aldw .1F 180
Gutner La. PO11: Hay I .3C 158
Gutner Point Nature Reserve .4C 158
Guyhurst Spinney RH20: Thake .1M 107
Gwydyr Mans. BN3: Hove .7M 153
Gwynne Gdns. RH19: E Grin .2C 14
Gym, The
Brighton .9G 172 (9C 154)

H

HABIN .7E 56
Habin Hill GU31: Rog .5E 56
Hackenden Cl. RH19: E Grin .1E 14
Hackenden Cotts. RH19: E Grin .1E 14
Hackenden La. RH19: E Grin .1E 14
Hacketts La. BN5: Henf .2H 111
Hacketts Rew PO19: Chich .1C 140
Haddington Cl. BN3: Hove .7K 153
Haddington St. BN3: Hove .6K 153
Hadlands PO21: Pag .2C 180
Hadley Av. BN14: Broadw .6H 149
Hadley Cl. PO22: Midd S .6M 165
Hadlow Cl. BN2: Brig .7E 154
Hadlow Way BN15: Lan .7C 150
Hadmans Cl. RH12: Hors .1N 45
Hadrian Av. BN42: S'wck .5C 152
Haglands Copse RH20: W Chil .9J 87
Haglands La. RH20: W Chil .9H 87
Haig Av. BN1: Brig .8E 134
Haigh Cl. BN15: S Lan .7E 150
Hailsham Av. BN2: Salt .1D 174
Hailsham Cl. BN16: E Pres .1G 168
Hailsham Rd. BN11: Wor .3D 170
Hairpin Cft. BN10: Peace .3J 175
Hale Cl. PO20: E Witt .5M 177
HALECOMMON .4D 56
Hale Hill RH20: Bury .5E 104
Hales Fld. GU27: Has .5L 17
Hales Footpath PO22: Felp .7H 165
Halewick Cl. BN15: Somp .5N 149
Halewick La. BN15: Somp .5N 149
Haleybridge Wlk. PO20: Tang .4L 141
Halfacres RH10: Craw .5G 10
Half Moon Cotts. GU29: Midh .9F 58
(off Petersfield Rd.)
Half Moon Ct. BN13: Salv .6D 148
(off Half Moon La.)
Half Moon Hill GU27: Has .5L 17
Half Moon La. BN13: Salv .5D 148
Half Moon Pde. BN13: Salv .6D 148
(off Half Moon La.)
Halfrey Cl. PO18: Fish .6K 139
Halfrey Rd. PO18: Fish .6K 139
HALFWAY BRIDGE .9D 60
Halifax Cl. RH10: Craw .3N 11
Halifax Dr. BN13: Durr .7A 148
Halland Cl. RH10: Craw .5J 11
Halland Rd. BN2: Brig .1G 154
Hallands, The RH15: Burg H .4D 94
(off St Andrews Rd.)
Hall Av. BN14: Salv .6E 148
Hall Cl. BN14: Salv .6E 148
Hallett Rd. BN2: Brig .6E 154
PO9: Hav .3B 136
Halley Cl. RH11: Craw .2D 28
Hall Hurst Cl. RH14: Lox .7M 21
Halliford Dr. PO22: Barn .7K 143
Halliwick Gdns. PO22: Felp .8J 165
Halls Dr. RH12: Fay .2J 27
Hallsland RH10: Craw D .4K 13
Hallyburton Rd. BN3: Hove .5F 152
HALNAKER .9M 121
Halnaker Barn La. PO18: Box .1C 142
Halnaker Gdns. PO21: Aldw .1E 180
Halnaker Wlk. RH11: Craw .9B 10
Halnaker Windmill .6A 122
Halsbury Cl. BN11: Wor .1J 171
Halsbury Rd. BN11: Wor .1K 171
Halsford Cft. RH19: E Grin .1B 14
Halsford Grn. RH19: E Grin .1B 14
Halsford La. RH19: E Grin .2B 14
Halsford Pk. Rd. RH19: E Grin .2C 14
Halson Cl. PO21: Bog R .8D 164
Halt, The PO18: Nutb .5A 138
Halton Shaws BN6: Hurst .2K 113
HAM .8F 178
Hamble Ct. BN15: Somp .7M 149
Hambledon Pl. PO21: Bog R .9C 164
Hamble Gdns. BN13: Durr .6A 148
Hamble Rd. BN15: Somp .7M 149
Hamble Ter. BN17: Wick .2J 167
Hambleton Ct. RH11: Craw .8E 10
Hambleton Hill RH11: Craw .8E 10
Hamble Way BN13: Durr .6A 148
Ham Bri. Trad. Est. BN14: Broadw .9L 149
HAMBROOK .3A 138
Hambrook RH15: Burg H .7D 94
Hambrook Bus. Cen. PO18: Hamb .1A 138
Hambrook Hill Nth. PO18: Hamb .2A 138
Hambrook Hill Sth. PO18: Hamb .3A 138
Hambrook Holiday Pk. PO18: Hamb .4A 138
Ham Bus. Cen. BN43: Shor S .6K 151
Ham Cl. BN11: Wor .9L 149
Hamfield Av. BN43: Shor S .5J 151
Hamilton Cl. BN14: Broadw .8J 149
BN16: Rust .9A 146
BN41: Ports .2C 152
GU29: S'ham .8B 58
PO9: Lstne .5A 136
RH6: Horl .3J 5
Hamilton Ct. BN2: Brig .8L 173
BN12: Gor S .9B 148
(off Drake Av.)
Hamilton Dr. BN16: Rust .9A 146
Hamilton Gdns. PO18: Bosh .6F 138
PO21: Aldw .1F 180
Hamilton Mans. BN3: Hove .8K 153
Hamilton M. BN15: Somp .7N 149
Hamilton Rd. BN1: Brig .2C 172 (5A 154)
BN15: Lan .6A 150
RH12: Hors .8M 25
Ham La. PO10: S'brne .6K 137
PO20: Tang, Oving .5M 141
RH17: Scay H .6M 73
RH17: Wivel .1K 95
Hamlet, The BN17: Climp .3D 166
PO22: Bog R .6D 164
Ham Mnr. Cl. BN16: Ang .9D 146
Ham Manor Golf Course .9C 146
Ham Mnr. Way BN16: Ang .9D 146
HAMMER .6F 16
HAMMER BOTTOM .5E 16
Hammer Hill GU27: Has .7E 16
RH17: Cuck .7J 49
Hammer La. GU27: Lip .6C 16
GU31: Chit, Ipin .6M 57
Hammerpond Rd.
RH13: Hors, Colg, Mann H, Plum P .1C 46
HAMMERPOT .5E 146
Hammer Va. GU27: Lip .5E 16
Hammerwood Copse GU27: Has .6F 16
Hammerwood Rd. RH19: Ash W .6K 15
Hammer Yd. RH10: Craw .7F 10
Hammingden La.
RH17: Ard, Sharp .3L 51
Hammond Cl. BN13: Durr .5C 148
BN16: Ang .9F 146
Hammond Dr. BN13: Durr .5C 148
Hammond Pl. RH20: Storr .6J 107
(off Hanover Wlk.)
Hammond Rd. RH11: Craw .3D 28
Hammonds Gdns. RH15: Burg H .7A 94
Hammonds Ridge RH15: Burg H .7N 93
Hammy Cl. BN43: Shor S .5L 151
Hammy La. BN43: Shor S .5L 151
Hammy Way BN43: Shor S .5L 151
Hampden Cl. PO22: Midd S .7N 165
RH10: Craw .3N 11
Hampden Ct. BN11: Wor .9K 149
Hampden Pl. PO20: Tang .3M 141
Hampden Rd. BN2: Brig .6D 154
Hampers Comn. Ind. Est. GU28: Petw .7N 61
Hampers Ct. RH13: Hors .9A 26
HAMPERS GREEN .7N 61
Hampers Grn. GU28: Petw .7M 61
Hampers La. RH13: Hors .9D 26
RH20: Storr .7C 107
Hampshire Av. PO21: Bog R .7C 164
Hampshire Ct. BN2: Brig .9C 154
Hampshire Hill RH13: Plum P .5A 48
RH17: Plum P, Slau .5A 48
Hampstead Rd. BN1: Brig .4M 153
Hampstead Wlk. RH11: Craw .1E 28
Hampton Ct. PO21: Bog R .8A 164
Hampton Flds. BN17: Wick .2K 167
Hampton Lodge RH6: Horl .3J 5
Hampton Pl. BN1: Brig .7B 172 (8N 153)
BN17: Wick .1J 167
Hampton St. BN1: Brig .7B 172 (8N 153)
Hampton Ter. BN1: Brig .6B 172
(off Upper Nth. St.)
Hampton Way RH19: E Grin .5F 14
Ham Rd. BN11: Wor .9L 149
BN43: Shor S .6J 151
PO20: Sidle .4F 178
Hamsey Cl. BN2: Brig .8G 154
Hamsey Rd. BN2: Salt .3D 174
Hamsland RH19: Sharp .5A 32
Hamstead RH17: Hors K .6C 52
Hamstead Mdw. PO18: Chid'm .6B 138
Ham Way BN11: Wor .9L 149
Hanbury La. RH16: Hay H .4H 73
Hanbury Rd. RH11: Ifield .7A 10
Hanbury Sq. GU31: Peters .4G 54
Hancock Way BN43: Shor B .7L 151
HANDCROSS .2E 48
HANDCROSS PARK .9E 28
Handcross Rd. RH13: Plum P .5M 47
RH17: Bal .8K 29
RH17: Hand, S'fld .3F 48
Handford Way RH13: Plum P .4N 47
Hangdown Mead Bus. Pk. RH19: Sharp .6B 32
Hanger Way GU31: Peters .6H 55
Hangerwood RH13: Sherm .4G 91
HANGLETON
BN3 .3G 152
BN12 .9J 147
Hangleton Cl. BN3: Hove .3F 152
Hangleton Gdns. BN3: Hove .4F 152
Hangleton Grange BN12: Fer .1J 169
Hangleton La. BN3: Hove .3E 152
BN12: Fer .1J 169
BN41: Ports .3D 152
(not continuous)
Hangleton Link Rd. BN41: Ports .2E 152
Hangleton Mnr. Cl. BN3: Hove .3E 152
Hangleton Rd. BN3: Hove .5F 152
Hangleton Valley Dr. BN3: Hove .3E 152
Hangleton Way BN3: Hove .4F 152
Hanlye La. RH16: Hay H .1B 72
RH17: Cuck .1B 72
Hannah Peschar Sculpture Garden .2E 6
Hannah Sq. PO19: Chich .6N 139
Hannington Pl. BN6: Hurst .9J 93
Hanover Cl. PO20: Sel .3K 183
RH10: Craw .8H 11
(not continuous)
RH20: Bury .8G 105
Hanover Ct. BN2: Brig .6C 154
BN14: Broadw .7G 149
(off Rectory Gdns.)
GU29: Ease .7J 59
RH13: Hors .8C 26
RH16: Hay H .5E 72
Hanover Cres. BN2: Brig .6C 154
Hanover Gdns. RH13: Cow .7H 69
Hanover Lofts BN2: Brig .7C 154
(off Finsbury Rd.)
Hanover M. BN2: Brig .6C 154
Hanover Pl. BN2: Brig .6C 154
(off Lewes Rd.)
Hanover St. BN2: Brig .6C 154
Hanover Ter. BN2: Brig .6C 154
Hanover Wlk. RH20: Storr .6J 107
Hansworth Ho. RH10: Craw .7F 10
(off Brighton Rd.)
Happy Days Caravan Pk. BN15: S Lan .8D 150
Hapstead Ho. RH17: Ard .2J 51
Hapstead M. RH17: Ard .2J 51
Harberton Cres. PO19: Chich .2B 140
Harbolets Rd. RH14: Bill .9L 65
RH20: Bill, W Chil .9L 65
Harborough Cl. RH20: W Chil .8G 87
Harborough Dr. RH20: W Chil .8G 87
Harborough Gorse RH20: W Chil .8G 86
Harborough Hill RH20: W Chil .9F 86
Harborough Mdw. RH20: W Chil .8G 86
Harbour Ct. BN42: S'wck .6B 152
(off Whiterock Pl.)
PO18: Bosh .8F 138
HARBOUR HEIGHTS .7N 175
Harbour Ho. BN43: Shor B .7L 151
Harbour M. BN3: Hove .7E 152
Harbour Park .5K 167
Harbour Rd. PO18: Bosh .9E 138
PO21: Pag .5B 180
Harbour Vw. Pk. BN17: L'ton .4J 167
Harbour Vw. Rd. PO21: Pag .2C 180
Harbour Way BN43: Shor B .7K 151
PO10: Ems .5G 136
PO18: Bosh .9F 138
PO18: Chid'm .8B 138
Harbour Way Country Club .9E 160
Harcourt Way PO20: Sel .2K 183
Hard, The PO22: Midd S .7C 166
Hardbarrow Woods RH20: Thake .1M 107
HARDHAM .8M 85
Hardham Cl. BN16: Rust .4A 168
RH11: Craw .4C 10
RH16: Hay H .7F 72
Hardham Mill Bus. Pk. RH20: Pulb .8L 85
Hardham Rd. PO19: Chich .8D 140
Harding Cl. PO20: Sel .1K 183
Hard's Hill RH13: Hors .5A 46
Hardwick Rd. BN3: Hove .2G 152
Hardwick Way BN3: Hove .2G 152
(not continuous)
Hardy Av. GU31: Peters .4G 54
Hardy Cl. BN43: Shor B .7J 151
PO22: Felp .7L 165
RH6: Horl .2G 5
RH10: Craw .5L 11
RH12: Hors .7M 25
Hardys Gdn. PO20: Sidle .3G 178
Harebell Cl. BN17: L'ton .1A 168
Harebell Dr. BN41: Ports .2C 152
Harefield Av. BN13: Wor .9D 148
Harefield Gdns. PO22: Midd S .7N 165
Harefield Rd. PO22: Midd S .7N 165
Hare La. PO20: Sel .2F 182
RH11: Craw .3D 10
HARESDEAN .1K 133
Haresdean La. BN45: Pye .1L 133
Haresfield Ter. PO20: Tang .4M 141
Haresfoot Cl. PO18: Funt .9C 118
Hares La. PO18: Wald, Funt .7N 117
Harewood Cl. RH10: Craw .3J 11
Harewood Ct. BN3: Hove .7L 153
Harfield Ct. PO21: Bog R .9E 164
Harlands Cl. RH16: Hay H .3D 72
Harlands Rd. RH16: Hay H .3D 72
Harlech Cl. BN13: Durr .8N 147
Harley Ct. BN11: Wor .2F 170
Harmans Dr. RH19: E Grin .3H 15
Harmans Mead RH19: E Grin .3H 15
Harmers Hill BN8: Newick .9J 75
Harmony Cl. RH11: Craw .8A 10
Harmony Dr. PO20: Brac .6M 177
Harmsworth Cres. BN3: Hove .2G 152
Harold Cl. PO21: Bers .6A 164
Harold Rd. PO10: W'brne .1H 137
RH10: Worth .7N 11
Haroldslea RH6: Horl .4M 5
Haroldslea Cl. RH6: Horl .4L 5
Haroldslea Dr. RH6: Horl .4L 5
Harold Ter. PO10: Ems .4F 136
Harper Dr. RH10: Craw .1L 29
Harping Hill BN9: Pidd .1N 175
Harrier Ct. RH10: Craw .3M 11
(off Bristol Cl.)
Harrier Way GU31: Peters .7J 55
Harriet Pl. BN43: Shor B .7L 151
Harrington Ct. BN1: Brig .3N 153
Harrington Mans. BN1: Brig .3N 153
Harrington Pl. BN1: Brig .3C 154
Harrington Rd. BN1: Brig .3N 153
Harrington Vs. BN1: Brig .3A 154
Harriots Cl. RH13: N'hrst .9D 46
Harris Cl. RH11: Craw .9D 10
Harris La. PO8: Chalt .2D 96
Harrison Ct. BN14: Broadw .8J 149
Harrison Rd. BN14: Broadw .8J 149
Harris Path RH11: Craw .9D 10
Harrow Dr. PO20: W Witt .4K 177
Harrow La. GU32: Peters .3F 54
Harrow Rd. BN11: Wor .1F 170
Harrows, The GU28: Till .9J 61
Harrowsley Ct. RH6: Horl .1K 5
Harrowsley Grn. La. RH6: Horl .3L 5
Harsfold Cl. BN16: Rust .4A 168
Harsfold La. RH14: Wisb .3B 64
Harsfold Rd. BN16: Rust .5A 168
Hartfield Av. BN1: Brig .1B 154
Hartfield Ct. BN3: Hove .7L 153
Hartfield Rd. BN2: Salt .3D 174
RH18: F Row .9M 15
Harting Cl. BN12: Gor S .9N 147
Harting Ct. RH11: Craw .9B 10
Harting Down GU31: Peters .6H 55
Harting Rd. BN17: Wick .1K 167
Hartings, The PO22: Felp .6L 165
Hartington Pl. BN2: Brig .5D 154
Hartington Rd. BN2: Brig .5D 154
Hartington Ter. BN2: Brig .5D 154
Hartington Vs. BN3: Hove .5K 153
Hartland Ct. PO10: S'brne .4K 137
Hartland Ho. BN11: Wor .2E 170
(off Southview Dr.)
Hartley Ct. BN1: Brig .4D 172
(off Howard Pl.)
Hartnetts Cotts. BN16: Rust .3A 168
(off Sea La.)
Harvest Cl. BN10: Tels C .2H 175
RH16: Lind .2J 73
Harvester Cl. PO19: Chich .6D 140
Harvesters RH12: Hors .7A 26
RH16: Hay H .7E 72
HARVEST HILL .8M 71
Harvest Hill RH19: E Grin .4E 14
Harvest Rd. RH10: Craw .8L 11
Harvestside RH6: Horl .1L 5
Harvey Brown Ho. PO11: Hay I .7A 158
Harvey Cl. BN6: Say C .7F 92
RH11: Craw .2C 28
Harvey Rd. BN12: Gor S .3C 170
Harwood Av. BN12: Gor S .9B 148
Harwood Cl. RH20: Pulb .5B 86
Harwood Ind. Est. BN17: L'ton .2J 167
Harwood Rd. BN17: L'ton .2J 167
RH13: Hors .8B 26
Harwood Rd. Ent. Units BN17: Wick .2J 167
(off Harwood Rd.)
Harwoods Cl. RH19: E Grin .5F 14
HARWOODS GREEN .3L 85
Harwoods La. RH19: E Grin .5F 14
Hascombe Ct. RH11: Craw .7C 10

Hasle Dr.—Highcroft Lodge

Hasle Dr. GU27: Has .5K 17
HASLEMERE .5L 17
Haslemere Educational Mus. .4M 17
Haslemere Hall .4L 17
Haslemere Ind. Est. GU27: Has .4K 17
Haslemere Rd. GU27: K Grn, Fern .1K 37
GU30: Lip .7A 16
PO10: S'brne .3K 137
Haslemere Station (Rail) .5K 17
Hasler's La. PO18: W Dean .1N 119
Haslett Av. E. RH10: Craw .6G 11
Haslett Av. W. RH10: Craw .7F 10
HASLINGBOURNE .3A 84
Haslingbourne La. GU28: Petw .3N 83
HASSOCKS .3A 114
Hassocks Ct. RH11: Craw .9B 10
Hassocks Golf Course .2N 113
Hassocks Leisure Cen. .4A 114
Hassocks Lodge BN6: Hass .4N 113
Hassocks Rd. BN6: Hurst .2J 113
Hassocks Station (Rail) .3N 113
Haste Hill GU27: Has .6M 17
Hastings Cl. PO21: Bog R .8A 164
Hastings Ct. BN11: Wor .3E 170
Hastings Rd. BN2: Brig .5D 154
BN11: Wor .3E 170
RH10: Craw .6L 11
Hatch Cl. GU6: Alf .1N 21
Hatch End RH18: F Row .1M 33
Hatchetts Dr. GU27: Has .5E 16
Hatchgate RH6: Horl .3H 5
Hatchgate Cl. RH17: Cuck .3B 72
Hatchgate La. RH17: Cuck .3B 72
Hatch Hill GU27: K Grn .1K 37
Hatchlands RH12: Hors .4D 26
RH17: Cuck .3A 72
Hatch La. GU27: K Grn .9K 17
GU33: Liss .6A 34
Hatfield Wlk. BN13: Durr .8B 148
RH11: Craw .9A 10
Hatherleigh Cl. PO21: Bog R .7B 164
Hatherleigh Gdns. PO21: Bog R .7B 164
Haughton Ho. GU27: Has .5K 17
HAVANT .2A 136
Havant & Waterlooville FC .9A 116
Havant By-Pass PO9: Hav, Warbl .5A 136
Havant Farm Cl. PO9: Hav .2A 136
Havant Rd. PO8: Horn .4A 116
PO9: Row C .4A 116
PO10: Ems .5C 136
PO11: Hay I .1A 158
Havelock Cl. PO22: Felp .9G 165
Havelock Rd. BN1: Brig .1E 172 (3A 154)
PO21: Bog R .8D 164
HAVEN, THE .9J 23
Haven, The BN15: S Lan .9C 150
BN17: L'ton .3N 167
Haven Gdns. RH10: Craw D .3J 13
Havengate RH12: Hors .6C 26
Haven Rd. RH12: Rudg .5H 23
RH14: Bill, Slinf, T Haven .9J 23
Havenside BN43: Shor B .7H 151
Havenstoke Cl. PO19: Chich .4C 140
Havenwood Pk. BN18: Bins .2B 144
Havercroft Bldgs. BN11: Wor .2H 171
Haversham Cl. RH10: Craw .6H 11
Hawarden Cl. RH10: Craw D .4K 13
Haweswater Pl. RH10: Craw .8M 11
(off Castlerigg Way)
Hawke Cl. BN16: Rust .3D 168
Hawker Cl. PO20: Tang .3M 141
Hawkesbourne Rd. RH12: Hors .6C 26
Hawkesmoor Rd. RH11: Craw .8A 10
Hawkhurst Ct. RH14: Kird, Wisb .6J 63
Hawkhurst Pl. BN1: Brig .8E 134
Hawkhurst Rd. BN1: Brig .7E 134
Hawkhurst Wlk. RH10: Craw .8K 11
Hawkins Cl. BN43: Shor S .4N 151
PO21: Aldw .1D 180
Hawkins Cres. BN43: Shor S .3N 151
Hawkins Rd. BN43: Shor S .4N 151
RH10: Craw .9G 11
Hawkridge RH12: Rudg .2K 23
Hawksfold La. E. GU27: Fern .5H 37
Hawksfold La. W. GU27: Fern .4J 37
Hawks Pl. PO22: Bers .6C 164
Hawley Rd. BN16: Rust .4A 168
Hawmead RH10: Craw D .4K 13
Haworth Rd. RH10: Craw .7K 11
Hawth Av. RH10: Craw .8G 11
Hawth Cl. RH10: Craw .8G 10
Hawthorn Bank BN2: Brig .1G 154
Hawthorn Cl. BN2: Salt .2C 174
BN16: Rust .4B 168
GU29: Midh .2F 80
PO19: Chich .6B 140
RH11: Craw .3E 10
RH12: Hors .7N 25
RH15: Burg H .3E 94
Hawthorn Ct. GU31: Peters .6J 55
Hawthorn Cres. BN14: Broadw .7H 149
Hawthorne Gro. PO11: Hay I .8A 158
Hawthorn Gdns. BN14: Broadw .7H 149
Hawthorn Pl. RH16: Hay H .7D 72
(off Lower Village)
Hawthorn Rd. BN14: Broadw .7H 149
BN17: Wick .9J 145
PO21: Bog R .9B 164
Hawthorns, The PO21: Bog R .8D 164
RH15: Burg H .3B 94
RH20: W Chil .9K 87
Hawthorn Way BN41: Ports .2C 152
RH20: Storr .5J 107
Hawth Theatre .7H 11
Haybarn Dr. RH12: Hors .4B 26
Haybourne Cl. BN2: Brig .6F 154
Haybourne Rd. BN2: Brig .6F 154
Haydon Cl. PO21: Aldw .2E 180
Hayes Cl. BN41: Ports .5E 152
PO18: Mid L .7A 120
Hayes La. RH13: Slinf .2M 43
Hayes Wood Rd. RH14: Bill .5L 43
Hayfields RH6: Horl .1K 5
Hayley Rd. BN15: Lan .6C 150
Hayley's Gdns. PO22: Felp .8H 165
Haylind Rd. RH16: Hay H .4J 73
Hayling Ct. RH11: Craw .9E 10
Hayling Gdns. BN13: High S .4C 148
HAYLING ISLAND .7A 158
Hayling Island Lifeboat Station & Mus. .1A 176
Hayling Island Sailing Club .9F 158
Hayling Ri. BN13: High S .4C 148
Haynes Rd. BN14: Wor .9E 148
Haynes Way BN14: Wor .9F 148
Hay Rd. PO19: Chich .9D 140
Hays Cotts. GU32: Steep .2D 54
Hayter Gdns. PO20: Oving .6L 141
Hayton Ct. BN13: Durr .8N 147
(off Chestnut Wlk.)
Hayward Bus. Cen. PO9: Hav .2B 136
Haywards RH10: Craw .3M 11
Haywards Cl. PO22: Felp .7H 165
HAYWARDS HEATH .5F 72
Haywards Heath Golf Course .9G 50
Haywards Heath Rd. BN8: N Cha .9A 74
RH17: Bal .9A 30
RH17: N Cha .9A 74
Haywards Heath Station (Rail) .3F 72
Haywards Pl. PO20: Brac .6N 177
Haywards Rd. BN1: Brig .8B 134
RH16: Hay H .6F 72
Haywards Vs. RH16: Hay H .6G 72
Hazel Bank BN2: Brig .3G 172
Hazelbank Cl. GU30: Lip .7A 16
GU31: Peters .5H 55
Hazel Cl. BN41: Ports .2E 152
RH10: Craw D .4K 13
RH11: Craw .3E 10
RH13: Southw .9L 45
Hazel Copse PO18: Hamb .4A 138
Hazeldean Ct. PO9: Row C .5B 116
Hazeldean Dr. PO9: Row C .5B 116
Hazeldean La. RH17: W'lid .1F 70
Hazeldene Meads BN1: Brig .2M 153
Hazelden Pl. RH19: E Grin .6A 14
Hazeley Grn. PO9: Hav .9B 116
(off Sharps Rd.)
Hazel Gro. BN18: Arun .3E 144
GU26: Hind .2G 16
PO21: Aldw .9M 163
RH15: Burg H .7C 94
Hazelgrove Gdns. RH16: Hay H .5F 72
Hazelgrove Rd. RH16: Hay H .5F 72
Hazel Holt BN41: Ports .2B 152
Hazelhurst RH6: Horl .1L 5
Hazelhurst Cres. BN14: Fin V .2D 148
RH12: Hors .1K 45
Hazelhurst Dr. RH10: Worth .6N 11
Hazel Lodge BN16: Rust .4B 168
(off Cudlow Gdn.)
Hazelmead Dr. BN16: E Pres .3F 168
Hazel Rd. BN16: Ang .9F 146
PO22: Bers .6C 164
Hazel Wlk. GU31: Peters .8F 54
Hazel Way RH10: Craw D .4K 13
Hazelwick Av. RH10: Craw .4J 11
Hazelwick Ct. RH10: Craw .4J 11
(off Hazelwick Av.)
Hazelwick M. RH10: Craw .4J 11
Hazelwick Mill La. RH10: Craw .4J 11
(not continuous)
Hazelwick Rd. RH10: Craw .5J 11
Hazelwick Rdbt. RH10: Craw .4J 11
Hazelwood BN1: Brig .2M 153
(off Curwen Pl.)
RH11: Craw .6C 10
Hazelwood Cl. BN14: Broadw .8K 149
GU29: Ease .6J 59
RH10: Craw D .4G 13
RH20: Storr .5N 107
Hazelwood Lodge BN15: S Lan .8C 150
Hazelwood Rd. RH13: Part G .5D 90
Hazelwood Trad. Est. BN14: Broadw .8K 149
Headborough BN15: S Lan .9B 150
(off Alma St.)
Headborough Ct. BN15: S Lan .9B 150
Head Down GU31: Peters .6H 55
Headland Cl. BN10: Peace .5L 175
Headland Way BN10: Peace .6L 175
Headley Cl. RH10: Craw .3M 11
Headley Dr. PO22: Bers .6E 164
Hearn Cl. PO20: Tang .4L 141
Hearnfield Rd. BN17: Wick .9K 145
Heasewood RH16: Hay H .6D 72
Heath Cl. BN6: Say C .7F 92
PO20: Huns .4C 162
RH12: Broadb H .8J 25
RH13: Mann H .4G 46
RH16: Hay H .5G 72
HEATH COMMON .4N 107
Heathcote Dr. RH19: E Grin .2B 14
Heathcotes RH10: Craw .8M 11
Heath Ct. GU31: Peters .7F 54
RH12: Broadb H .8J 25
RH16: Hay H .4F 72
Heathcourt BN17: L'ton .3L 167
Heathdown Cl. BN10: Peace .2K 175
HEATH END .6L 83
Heather Bank RH16: Hay H .4D 72
Heather Cl. PO18: W Ash .2E 138
RH10: Copt .2C 12
RH12: Hors .6A 26
Heather Ct. BN1: Brig .6B 172 (7N 153)
PO19: Chich .8B 140
Heatherfield GU31: Buri .3D 76
Heather Ho. BN15: Lan .6C 150
Heatherlands RH6: Horl .1K 5
(not continuous)
RH20: Storr .5L 107
Heather La. BN13: High S .3C 148
RH20: W Chil .2H 107
Heatherleigh Ct. RH12: Hors .7N 25
(off North Pde.)
Heathermead RH20: W Chil .1H 107
Heather Rd. GU31: Peters .6J 55
Heathers, The BN16: Ang .7E 146
Heatherstone Rd. BN11: Wor .1L 171
Heatherton M. PO10: Ems .2F 136
Heather Wlk. RH11: Craw .9D 10
Heather Way RH20: Storr .6L 107
Heatherwood GU29: Midh .9F 58
Heathfeild Ga. GU29: Midh .1G 80
(off Bepton Rd.)
Heathfield RH10: Craw .3M 11
(not continuous)
Heathfield Av. BN2: Salt .2D 174
BN16: Ang .1E 168
Heathfield Cl. BN13: Wor .8D 148
GU29: Midh .1G 80
Heathfield Copse RH20: W Chil .9G 87
Heathfield Cres. BN41: Ports .1B 152
Heathfield Dr. BN41: Ports .2B 152
Heathfield Gdns. GU29: Midh .1G 80
Heathfield Grn. GU29: Midh .1G 80
Heathfield Pk. GU29: Midh .1F 80
Heathfield Rd. GU31: Peters .6J 55
Heath Hill Av. BN2: Brig .3G 154
Heath Pl. PO22: Bers .5E 164
Heath Rd. GU27: Has .6F 16
GU31: Peters .6F 54
RH16: Hay H .4F 72
Heath Rd. E. GU31: Peters .7H 55
Heath Rd. W. GU31: Peters .7G 54
Heath Sq. RH16: Hay H .4E 72
Heath Way RH12: Hors .6A 26
HEATHY BROW .3H 175
Heathy Brow BN10: Peace, Tels C .3H 175
Heaven Farm .9H 53
Hebe Rd. BN43: Shor S .6K 151
Hechle Wood PO21: Aldw .1H 181
Heckfield Cl. PO9: Hav .9B 116
Hectors La. RH19: E Grin .5J 15
Hedge End PO22: Barn .7K 143
Hedge End Wlk. PO9: Hav .8C 116
Hedgehog La. GU27: Has .5K 17
Hedgerow Cl. PO22: Felp .6J 165
Hedgerow Gdns. PO10: Ems .2F 136
Hedgers Hill BN18: Bins, Walb .4N 143
Hedgeside RH11: Craw .2E 28
Hedgeway PO22: Felp .7L 165
Hedingham Cl. RH6: Horl .1L 5
HEENE .1F 170
Heene Pl. BN11: Wor .3F 170
Heene Rd. BN11: Wor .1F 170
Heene Ter. BN11: Wor .3F 170
Heene Way BN11: Wor .2F 170
Heghbrok Way PO21: Aldw .1J 181
Heights, The BN1: Brig .9K 133
BN14: Fin V .4E 148
RH16: Hay H .5F 72
(off Church Rd.)
Heights Health & Fitness Cen. .6B 94
Helena Cl. BN41: Ports .3E 152
Helena Rd. BN2: W'dean .4K 155
Helen Ct. BN11: Wor .2D 170
Helicon Ho. RH11: Craw .7E 10
Hellingly Cl. BN2: Brig .8G 154
Helston Dr. PO10: Ems .2E 136
Helyer's Grn. BN17: Wick .2J 167
Hempstead Rd. BN2: Salt .2D 174
Hemsby Wlk. RH10: Craw .8K 11
Hemsleys, The RH11: Pease P .5D 28
Henbane Ct. RH11: Craw .1C 28
Henderson Rd. RH11: Craw .2D 28
Henderson Wlk. BN44: Stey .2A 130
Henderson Way RH12: Hors .2K 45
Hendon Av. BN16: Rust .5N 167
Hendon St. BN2: Brig .8E 154
HENFIELD .2H 111
Henfield Bus. Pk. BN5: Henf .6K 111
Henfield Cl. BN2: Brig .8G 154
BN12: Gor S .9A 148
Henfield Comn. Nth. BN5: Henf .3J 111
Henfield Comn. Sth.
BN5: Henf .4J 111
Henfield Leisure Cen. .1H 111
Henfield Mus. .3J 111
Henfield Rd. BN5: Small D .5E 130
BN5: Wine .7N 91
BN6: Alb, Wine .7N 91
BN44: Up B .5E 130
BN45: Poyn .6D 112
RH13: Cow, Part G, Sherm .3G 91
Henfield Way BN3: Hove .2H 153
PO22: Felp .6L 165
Henge Way BN41: Ports .3D 152
Hengist Cl. RH12: Hors .1L 45
HENLEY .1K 59
Henley Cl. RH10: Craw .9M 11
HENLEY COMMON .9H 37
Henley Ct. BN2: Brig .9G 154
Henley Hill GU27: Henl .9H 37
Henley La. GU29: C'ing .9C 80
Henley Rd. BN2: Brig .9G 154
Henly Cl. RH20: Bury .8G 104
Henry Av. BN16: Rust .3N 167
Henry Burt Way RH15: Burg H .7N 93
Henry Cl. PO19: Chich .7F 140
Henry Fletcher Cl. BN16: Ang .8F 146
Henry St. PO21: Bog R .8E 164
Henshaw Cl. RH11: Craw .8B 10
Henson Rd. RH10: Craw .5K 11
Henty Cl. BN14: Wor .9G 148
BN18: Walb .5M 143
RH11: Craw .9A 10
Henty Gdns. PO19: Chich .7A 140
Henty Rd. BN12: Fer .4L 169
BN14: Wor .9G 148
Henwood Down GU31: Peters .6G 55
Heo Grn. BN17: Wick .1H 167
Hepplewhite Cl. RH11: Craw .2D 28
Herald Dr. PO19: Chich .8C 140
Herbert Rd. BN1: Brig .3A 154
BN15: Somp .4M 149
Hercules Pl. PO22: Felp .8L 165
Hereford Cl. PO19: Chich .4B 140
RH10: Craw .1G 29
Hereford Ct. BN2: Brig .8D 154
BN3: Hove .6L 153
Hereford Ho. BN2: Brig .8D 154
(off Hereford St.)
BN12: Gor S .1M 169
(off Goring St.)
Hereford St. BN2: Brig .8C 154
Herington Rd. BN18: Arun .3F 144
Heritage, The PO19: Chich .7D 140
Heritage Lawn RH6: Horl .1L 5
Heritage Pl. BN16: Rust .4B 168
(off Broadmark La.)
Herm Cl. RH11: Craw .1C 28
Hermione Cl. BN12: Fer .1J 169
HERMITAGE .4G 137
Hermitage, The PO10: S'brne .4G 137
PO20: N Mun .3F 162
(off Hermitage Cl.)
Hermitage Cl. PO20: N Mun .3F 162
Hermitage La. RH19: E Grin .4F 14
Hermitage Rd. RH19: E Grin .1D 14
Hermits Rd. RH10: Craw .5H 11
Hermit Ter. BN14: Fin .8C 128
HERMONGERS .2M 23
Hermonger's La. RH12: Rudg .1L 23
Herm Rd. BN12: Fer .4L 169
Hernbrook Dr. RH13: Hors .2B 46
Herne Ct. BN16: Rust .2C 168
(off Station Rd.)
Herne Farm Leisure Centre, The .6G 55
Herne Gdns. BN16: Rust .2C 168
Herne La. BN16: Rust .2C 168
Herne Rd. GU31: Peters .6G 54
Heron Cl. PO18: Mid L .7A 120
PO20: Sel .2F 182
PO22: Bers .5C 164
RH11: Craw .4E 10
Heron Ct. BN2: Brig .6G 154
(off Swanborough Pl.)
BN11: Wor .1G 171
PO19: Chich .6F 140
Herondale GU27: Has .5G 17
Herondean PO19: Chich .3B 140
Heron Mead PO21: Pag .4B 180
Heron Pl. RH19: E Grin .4F 14
Heron Quay PO10: S'brne .6G 137
Herons, The BN15: S Lan .9C 150
BN43: Shor S .5K 151
PO20: Sel .3H 183
Herons Cl. RH14: Kird .8H 41
Heron's Ct. Cl. BN16: Rust .4B 168
Heronsdale Rd. BN2: W'dean .5N 155
Herons Farm La. RH14: Kird .7H 41
Herons Leisure Club, The .5H 17
Herons Rye RH20: Pulb .6B 86
(off Lower St.)
Herons Tye BN6: Key .4A 114
Heronswood Ct. RH6: Horl .1K 5
Herontye Dr. RH19: E Grin .4F 14
Herontye Ho. RH19: E Grin .5F 14
Heron Vw. BN43: Shor S .4L 151
Heron Way RH13: Hors .9D 26
Herrick Cl. RH10: Craw .4L 11
Herschel Wlk. RH11: Craw .2D 28
Hersee Way PO20: Sel .3G 182
Hertford Cl. PO21: Aldw .9A 164
Hertford Ho. RH13: Hors .4J 45
(off The Avenue)
Hertford Rd. BN1: Brig .3C 154
BN11: Wor .1H 171
Heston Av. BN1: Brig .7A 134
Heston Gro. PO21: Aldw .2E 180
HESWORTH COMMON .5E 84
Hett Cl. RH17: Ard .2J 51
Hevers Av. RH6: Horl .1H 5
Hevers Cnr. RH6: Horl .1H 5
Hewarts La. PO21: Aldw .9M 163
Hewells Ct. RH12: Hors .1N 45
Hewitts BN5: Henf .3H 111
Hewitts End BN5: Henf .3H 111
Hewshott Gro. GU30: Lip .6A 16
Hewshott La. GU30: Lip .6A 16
Hexham Cl. RH10: Craw .6N 11
HEYSHOTT .7K 81
Heyshott Cl. BN15: N Lan .5B 150
HEYSHOTT GREEN .6K 81
Heyshott Lodge BN2: Brig .7F 154
(off Crossbush Rd.)
Heyworth Cl. BN2: W'dean .5N 155
Heyworth Ride RH16: Hay H .6D 72
Hickling Wlk. RH10: Craw .8K 11
Hickmans Cl. RH16: Lind .1J 73
Hickman's La. RH16: Lind .1H 73
(not continuous)
HICKSTEAD .3F 92
Hickstead La. RH17: Hick, Twine .3D 92
Hickstead Pk. BN6: Say C .6F 92
Hide Cl. BN17: Wick .9L 145
Hide Gdns. BN16: Rust .2A 168
Higgins Way RH13: Hors .1B 46
Highams Hill RH11: Craw .7B 10
Highbank BN1: Brig .9L 133
RH16: Hay H .8D 72
High Bar La. RH20: Thake .1L 107
Highbarn BN14: Fin .7C 128
High Beeches BN11: Wor .2E 170
High Beeches Cotts. RH17: Hand .9G 29
High Beeches Gdns. .9H 29
High Beeches La. BN45: Newt .9F 112
BN45: Poyn .1F 132
RH17: Bal, Hand .9G 28
High Beech La. RH16: Hay H .1G 73
Highbirch Cl. RH12: Hors .6E 26
HIGHBROOK .1M 51
Highbrook Cl. BN2: Brig .3E 154
Highbrook La. RH19: W Hoa .9M 31
Highbury Gro. GU27: Has .3L 17
Highclere Way BN13: Durr .8N 147
Highcliff Ct. BN2: Rott .3A 174
High Cl. BN41: Ports .4C 152
Highcroft Av. PO22: Bog R .7E 164
Highcroft Cl. PO22: Bog R .7F 164
Highcroft Cres. PO22: Bog R .7F 164
Highcroft Dr. RH12: Rudg .2K 23
Highcroft Lodge BN1: Brig .1A 172 (5N 153)

Highcroft M.—Homing Gdns.

Highcroft M. BN1: Brig 1A 172 (4M 153)
Highcroft Rd. RH19: Sharp 6A 32
Highcroft Vs. BN1: Brig 1A 172 (5N 153)
HIGH CROSS 9B 92
Highden BN2: Brig 7D 154
Highden Bri. RH20: Wash 4B 128
Highdown BN42: S'wck 4B 152
Highdown Av. BN13: W Tar 8E 148
Highdown Cl. BN12: Fer 1K 169
BN16: Ang 8F 146
BN42: S'wck 4B 152
Highdown Ct. BN1: Brig 2N 153
BN13: Durr 8B 148
RH10: Craw 9K 11
Highdown Dr. BN17: L'ton, Wick 1K 167
Highdown Gdns. 8L 147
Highdown Hill 8K 147
Highdown Rd. BN3: Hove 3A 172 (6N 153)
Highdown Vineyard 9L 147
Highdown Way BN12: Fer 1K 169
RH12: Hors 5C 26
Highercombe Rd. GU27: Has 3N 17
Highfield BN17: Wick 1H 167
Highfield Cl. BN16: Ang 8F 146
GU29: Ease 7J 59
Highfield Ct. BN14: Broadw 7J 149
RH16: Hay H 5F 72
(off Church Rd.)
Highfield Cres. BN1: Brig 9B 134
Highfield Dr. BN6: Hurst 2K 113
Highfield Gdns. BN16: Rust 3A 168
GU33: Liss 6A 34
PO22: Bog R 7E 164
Highfield Ho. *RH11: Craw 5F 10*
(off Town Mead)
Highfield La. GU30: Lip 9A 16
PO20: Oving 6L 141
Highfield Rd. BN13: W Tar 7E 148
GU32: Peters 5F 54
PO22: Bog R 7E 164
(not continuous)
RH19: E Grin 1D 14
Highfields BN1: Brig 9F 134
RH18: F Row 1M 33
Highgate Ct. RH11: Craw 1E 28
Highgate Dr. PO21: Bers 5A 164
Highgate Rd. RH18: F Row 2L 33
Highgate Works RH18: F Row 2L 33
HIGHGREEN 2M 33
Highground La. PO22: Barn 9H 143
HIGH GROVE 5B 14
Highgrove Gdns. BN11: Wor 2F 170
High Hatch La. BN6: God G, Hurst 4K 93
Highland Av. PO21: Bog R 8C 164
Highland Cl. PO10: Ems 5E 136
Highland Ct. RH16: Hay H 5F 72
Highland Cft. BN44: Stey 3A 130
Highland Rd. PO10: Ems 4E 136
PO19: Chich 3B 140
RH16: Hay H 6G 73
Highlands, The RH17: Cuck 1A 72
Highlands Av. RH13: Hors 9B 26
Highlands Cl. BN6: Key 4B 114
BN13: High S 4C 148
Highlands Cres. RH13: Hors 9B 26
Highlands Dr. RH15: Burg H 4B 94
Highlands Rd. BN41: Ports 4D 152
RH13: Hors 9B 26
High La. GU27: Has 3L 17
GU28: Lurg 6D 38
PO18: E Dean 8M 101
High Lawn Way PO9: Hav 9A 116
HIGHLEIGH 1F 178
Highleigh BN2: Brig 7C 154
Highleigh Rd. PO20: Sidle 9L 161
High Mdw. GU29: C'ing 8F 80
High Oaks RH11: Craw 8D 10
High Pk. Av. BN3: Hove 2G 153
High Path GU29: Ease 7J 59
High Pines BN11: Wor 1F 170
High Pitfold GU26: Hind 2F 16
High Point RH16: Hay H 6H 73
High Ridge Cl. BN18: Arun 4F 144
HIGH SALVINGTON 3C 148
High Salvington Windmill 3C 148
High Seat Copse RH14: Bill 9J 43
High Seat Gdns. RH14: Bill 9J 43
High Spinney RH20: W Chil 2K 107
Highstanding La. GU29: W Lav 2J 81
Highstead La. GU28: Lick 1B 60
Highsted Pk. BN10: Peace 2K 175
High St. BN2: Brig 8C 154
BN2: Rott 3N 173
BN5: Henf 3J 111
BN6: Ditch 4E 114
BN6: Hurst 1H 113
BN8: Newick 9K 75
BN11: Wor 1J 171
(not continuous)
BN14: Fin 9C 128
BN14: W Tar 8E 148
BN16: Ang 8E 146
BN17: L'ton 3K 167
BN18: Amb 8L 105
BN18: Arun 2H 145
BN41: Ports 4C 152
BN43: Shor S 6H 151
BN44: Stey 3N 129
BN44: Up B 4D 130
GU27: Has 5M 17
GU28: Petw 9N 61
GU31: Buri 3D 76
GU31: Peters 6F 54
GU32: Peters 6F 54
PO10: Ems 5F 136
PO18: Bosh 9D 138
PO19: Chich 5B 140
PO20: Oving 7L 141
PO20: Sel 3H 183
PO21: Bog R 9E 164
RH6: Horl 2K 5
RH10: Craw 7F 10
RH12: Rusp 5F 8
High St. RH13: Part G 5C 90
RH14: Bill 1J 65
RH14: Lox 8M 21
RH16: Lind 2J 73
RH17: Ard 2J 51
RH17: Bal 8K 29
RH17: Cuck 3N 71
RH17: Hand 2E 48
RH19: E Grin 4F 14
RH20: Storr 6J 107
TN22: Flet 5M 75
HIGHSTREET GREEN 1A 20
High St. Grn. GU8: Chidd 2M 19
High Titten BN18: Amb 1K 125
High Trees PO20: Huns 3C 162
PO21: Aldw 1H 181
RH16: Hay H 4G 72
RH20: Fitt 5G 85
High Trees Ct. RH6: Sid 1C 4
High Vw. BN13: High S 4D 148
GU32: Peters 5F 54
Highview BN15: Somp 4A 150
Highview Av. Nth. BN1: Brig 8N 133
Highview Av. Sth. BN1: Brig 8N 133
Highview Pl. RH17: Wivel G 3K 95
High Vw. Rd. BN10: Tels C 4E 174
Highview Rd. BN1: Brig 8N 133
PO20: E'gate 6G 142
Highview Way BN1: Brig 8N 133
Highway, The BN2: Brig 3E 154
(not continuous)
BN9: Newh, Peace 6M 175
BN10: Peace 6M 175
Highway Cl. BN2: Brig 3E 154
Highways BN41: Ports 3D 152
Highwood Cres. RH12: Hors 9J 25
Highwood Pk. RH11: Craw 1E 28
Highworth RH13: Hors 1C 46
Hilary Lodge BN2: Brig 8D 154
Hilary Rd. PO19: Chich 6A 140
Hilda Duke's Way RH19: E Grin 1E 14
Hildon Cl. BN13: Durr 8B 148
Hildon Pk. BN13: Durr 8B 148
Hilgrove Rd. BN2: Salt 1D 174
Hilland Rdbt. RH14: Bill 8J 43
Hillary Cl. RH19: E Grin 1G 15
Hillbank Cl. BN41: Ports 2B 152
Hillbarn Av. BN15: Somp 4A 150
Hill Barn Golf Course 5G 148
Hill Barn La. BN14: Char D 6G 148
Hillbarn La. GU29: C'ing 1F 100
Hillbarn Pde. *BN15: Somp 5N 149*
(off Up. Brighton Rd.)
HILL BROW 8A 34
Hill Brow BN3: Hove 1K 153
Hill Brow Cl. PO9: Row C 5B 116
Hill Brow Rd. GU33: Hill B, Liss 8A 34
Hillbrow Rd. BN1: Brig 1L 153
Hill Ct. GU27: Has 5K 17
Hillcrest BN1: Brig 9L 133
GU27: Fern 5K 37
RH17: Hors K 5C 52
RH20: Storr 5J 107
Hillcrest Cl. RH10: Craw 6M 11
RH17: Scay H 7N 73
RH20: A'ton 2E 108
Hillcrest Ct. BN1: Brig 9L 133
Hillcrest Dr. RH20: A'ton 3E 108
Hillcrest La. RH17: Scay H 6N 73
Hillcrest Pk. RH20: Pulb 6C 86
Hillcroft BN41: Ports 3B 152
Hill Dr. BN3: Hove 2K 153
Hill Farm Cl. GU27: Has 6H 17
Hill Farm Cotts. BN42: S'wck 3N 151
Hill Farm La. RH20: Pulb 3N 85
Hill Farm Way BN42: S'wck 3N 151
Hillfield Cotts. RH13: Itch 2F 44
Hillfield Rd. PO20: Sel 5H 183
Hillfoot GU29: C'ing 9F 80
HILLGROVE 4F 38
Hill Ho. Cl. RH10: Turn H 8H 13
Hillhouse La. RH12: Rudg 2D 22
Hillingdale RH11: Craw 2E 28
Hill La. GU31: E Hart, S Hart 7A 78
PO22: Barn 9J 143
Hill Mead RH12: Hors 8L 25
Hillmead RH11: Craw 7B 10
Hill Pl. RH11: Craw 7E 10
Hillrise Av. BN15: Somp 5N 149
Hill Rd. BN2: Salt 3B 174
BN10: Peace 7M 175
BN17: L'ton 2L 167
GU27: Has 5L 17
Hillsboro Rd. PO21: Bog R 8D 164
Hills Ct. *PO21: Bog R 9E 164*
(off London Rd.)
Hills Farm La. RH12: Hors 1K 45
HILL SIDE 8A 34
Hillside BN2: Brig 2F 154
BN13: Pat 4K 147
BN41: Ports 4E 152
BN42: S'wck 4A 152
RH10: Craw D 4J 13
RH12: Hors 1K 45
RH18: F Row 9M 15
Hillside Av. BN14: Char D 6F 148
Hillside Caravan Site BN5: Small D 1H 131
Hillside Cl. RH11: Craw 8D 10
RH19: E Grin 1E 14
Hillside Cotts. BN13: Pat 4K 147
PO18: W Sto 9K 119
Hillside Cres. BN16: Ang 8F 146
Hill Side La. GU33: Hill B 8A 34
Hillside La. BN5: Small D 1H 131
Hillside Rd. BN15: Somp 5N 149
GU27: Has 6H 17
RH20: Storr 5L 107
Hillside Ter. BN44: Stey 4A 130
Hillside Wlk. RH16: Hay H 3D 72
RH20: Storr 4M 107
Hillside Way BN1: Brig 1L 153
BN2: Brig 3F 154
Hills Pl. RH12: Hors 9L 25
Hills Rd. BN44: Stey 3N 129
Hillstream Cl. RH20: W Chil 8F 86
Hill Ter. BN18: Arun 3F 144
Hilltop BN1: Brig 9K 133
GU28: Till 8K 61
GU29: C'ing 1E 100
Hilltop Rd. RH19: W Hoa 5M 31
Hill Top Way BN9: Newh 6N 175
Hill Vw. BN5: Small D 8J 111
RH18: F Row 2M 33
Hillview GU29: Els 4G 79
Hillview Cres. BN16: E Pres 2F 168
Hillview Gdns. RH11: Craw 3E 28
Hillview Ri. BN14: Fin V 4D 148
Hillview Rd. BN2: W'dean 5J 155
BN14: Fin V 3D 148
Hillybarn Rd. RH11: Ifield 3M 9
Hiltingbury Rd. PO9: Hav 9A 116
Hilton Ct. RH6: Horl 1L 5
Hilton Pk. PO20: E Witt 3L 177
Hinde Rd. PO22: Felp 7K 165
Hindhead Cl. RH11: Craw 8E 10
Hindhead Rd. GU26: Hind 4G 17
GU27: Has, Hind 4G 17
Hindleap La. RH18: F Row, Wych C 5G 32
Hindleap Warren 6K 33
Hindle Cl. RH20: W Chil 9J 87
Hinton Cl. BN1: Brig 3D 154
Hipley Rd. PO9: Hav 2A 136
Hislop Wlk. PO21: Bog R 9E 164
Hither Grn. PO10: S'brne 3L 137
HMP Ford BN18: Ford 2D 166
Hoadlands GU31: Peters 5G 55
Hoadlands Cotts. RH17: Hand 9E 28
Hoad La. RH16: Lind 6K 51
Hoathdown Av. BN9: Newh 5N 175
Hoathly Hill RH19: W Hoa 5N 31
Hobart Cl. BN13: Durr 6A 148
Hobbs Rd. RH11: Craw 2C 28
Hobbs Sq. GU31: Peters 4G 54
Hobbs Way BN16: Rust 3B 168
Hobdens La. RH17: Ard 3H 51
Hoblands RH16: Hay H 6H 73
Hobs Acre BN44: Up B 5E 130
Hocken Mead RH10: Craw 4M 11
Hoddern Av. BN10: Peace 5H 175
(not continuous)
Hodges Cl. PO9: Hav 2A 136
Hodgkin Cl. RH10: Craw 7L 11
Hodshrove La. BN2: Brig 2F 154
Hodshrove Pl. BN2: Brig 2F 154
Hodshrove Rd. BN2: Brig 2F 154
Hoe Ct. BN15: N Lan 4C 150
Hoefield La. PO18: C'ing 2D 100
Hoelands La. GU29: C'ing 1E 100
Hoe La. BN18: Bins 6C 144
PO18: Bosh 3F 160
PO22: Flan 4H 165
Hoes La. GU28: Petw 4M 83
Hoewood BN5: Small D 8J 111
Hogarth Rd. BN3: Hove 6H 153
RH10: Craw 9H 11
Hoggarth Cl. GU31: Peters 5G 54
Hog La. BN18: Amb 8L 105
Hogs Edge BN2: Brig 3H 155
Hogs Hill GU27: Fern 4K 37
RH10: Craw 9F 10
Hogshill Gdns. RH10: Craw 8F 10
Hogwood Rd. RH14: Ifol 8J 21
Holbein Rd. RH10: Craw 9H 11
HOLBROOK 3B 26
Holbrook *BN2: Brig 8G 154*
(off Findon Rd.)
Holbrook Club, The 5B 26
Holbrook School La. RH12: Hors 4A 26
Holbury Ct. PO9: Hav 9B 116
Holcroft Ct. RH19: E Grin 1F 14
Holden Brook La. RH5: Ock 1C 6
Holdens, The PO18: Bosh 8D 138
Holdens Farm Caravan Pk. PO20: Brac 4M 177
Holder Rd. RH10: Craw 9K 11
Holders BN6: Alb 1E 112
Holders Cl. RH14: Bill 9H 43
Holdfast La. GU27: Has 3A 18
Hole St. BN44: Wis 5G 109
RH20: A'ton, Wis 4E 108
Holford Grn. PO20: Sel 2K 183
Holland Cl. PO21: Bers 7A 164
Holland M. BN3: Hove 8M 153
Holland Rd. BN3: Hove 8M 153
BN44: Stey 3B 130
Hollands Ct. RH19: E Grin 1G 14
Hollands Fld. RH12: Broadb H 7J 25
Hollands La. BN5: Henf 3E 110
Hollands Rd. BN5: Henf 2G 110
Holland St. BN2: Brig 7C 154
Hollands Way RH12: Warnh 3K 25
RH19: E Grin 1G 14
Hollies, The PO21: Bers 7A 164
Hollies Caravan Park, The PO11: Hay I 9E 158
Hollihurst Rd. GU28: Lods 6C 60
Hollin Ct. RH10: Craw 3G 10
Hollingbourne Ct. *BN2: Brig 9F 154*
(off Bristol Pl.)
Hollingbourne Cres. RH11: Craw 3E 28
HOLLINGBURY 1B 154
Hollingbury Copse BN1: Brig 1B 154
Hollingbury Cres. BN1: Brig 3C 154
Hollingbury Gdns. BN14: Fin V 2E 148
Hollingbury Ind. Est. BN1: Brig 7D 134
Hollingbury Pk. Av. BN1: Brig 3B 154
Hollingbury Pk. Golf Course 1C 154
Hollingbury Pl. BN1: Brig 3C 154
Hollingbury Ri. BN1: Brig 2C 154
Hollingbury Ri. W. BN1: Brig 3B 154
Hollingbury Rd. BN1: Brig 3B 154
Hollingbury Ter. BN1: Brig 3B 154
HOLLINGDEAN 3C 154
Hollingdean La. BN1: Brig 1G 172 (5C 154)
Hollingdean Rd. BN2: Brig 5C 154
Hollingdean St. BN1: Brig 4C 154
Hollingdean Ter. BN1: Brig 4C 154
Hollist Chase BN17: Wick 9L 145
Hollist Ct. BN17: Wick 9L 145
Hollist La. GU29: Ease, Midh, Wool 7E 58
GU31: E Hart 4C 78
Hollow, The RH11: Craw 7B 10
RH16: Hay H 5H 73
RH19: W Hoa 5N 31
RH20: Bury 7G 104
RH20: W Chil 7J 87
RH20: Wash 7C 108
Hollow La. PO11: Hay I 9A 158
Hollyacres BN13: Durr 5B 148
Holly Bank BN2: Brig 2G 172
Hollybank La. PO10: Ems 1F 136
Hollybush Bus. Cen. RH10: Ship B 1A 12
Hollybush Cl. RH10: Craw 5G 11
Hollybush Rd. RH10: Craw 5G 11
Holly Cl. BN1: Brig 2N 153
BN13: Durr 8A 148
RH10: Craw 4J 11
RH12: Hors 6E 26
RH20: W Chil 7J 87
HOLLYCOMBE 2N 35
Hollycombe Cl. GU30: Lip 1M 35
Hollycombe Gdns. 3A 36
Hollycombe Steam Collection 3A 36
Holly Ct. PO22: Bers 6D 164
RH20: Storr 6H 107
Holly Dr. BN17: Wick 9L 145
Hollyhock Way BN17: L'ton 1N 167
Holly M. BN6: Hurst 2J 113
Hollyridge GU27: Has 5K 17
Holly Rd. RH16: Hay H 6H 73
Hollywood Bowl
Crawley 5F 10
Hollywood Ct. *RH16: Hay H 4F 72*
(off Oathall Rd.)
Holman Cl. RH11: Craw 3D 28
Holmans RH17: Ard 2H 51
Holmbury Cl. RH11: Craw 8E 10
Holmbury Keep *RH6: Horl 1L 5*
(off Maize Cft.)
Holmbush Caravan Pk. GU29: Midh 2G 81
Holmbush Centre, The BN43: Shor S 3M 151
Holmbush Cl. BN43: Shor S 3N 151
RH12: Hors 5A 26
RH16: Hay H 7F 72
Holmbush Ct. BN43: Shor S 5M 151
RH12: Fay 2L 27
Holmbush Farm World 2L 27
Holmbush Ind. Est. GU29: Midh 2G 80
Holmbush La. BN5: Fulk 7A 112
Holmbush Potteries Ind. Est. RH12: Fay 2M 27
Holmbush Way BN42: S'wck 4N 151
GU29: Midh 2F 80
Holmcroft RH10: Craw 7G 10
Holmcroft Gdns. BN14: Fin 8C 128
Holmdale PO20: E'gate 4G 143
Holmes Av. BN3: Hove 4H 153
Holmesdale Rd. RH15: Burg H 7A 94
Holmes Foundation *BN18: Arun 3H 145*
(off Fitzalan Rd.)
Holmes La. BN16: Rust 4A 168
Holmes Way BN17: Wick 1L 167
Holming End RH12: Hors 6E 26
Holm Oak RH20: Storr 6H 107
Holm Oaks RH13: Cow 8J 69
Holmstead BN2: Brig 3G 172 (6C 154)
Holmsted Hill RH17: Cuck 8J 49
Holmwood Cl. PO20: W Witt 2G 176
Holmwood Ct. BN6: Hass 3A 114
Holt, The RH15: Burg H 6D 94
RH20: Wash 9C 108
Holt Down GU31: Peters 6H 55
Holt Gdns. PO9: Row C 3B 116
Holt La. BN13: Clap 5M 147
Holt Lodge *BN2: Brig 5C 154*
(off Canterbury Dr.)
Holton Hill BN2: W'dean 6M 155
Holtview Rd. BN2: W'dean 5J 155
Holtye Av. RH19: E Grin 1F 14
Holtye Pl. RH19: E Grin 1G 15
Holtye Rd. RH19: E Grin, Hamm 2F 14
Holtye Wlk. RH10: Craw 8J 11
Holyrood RH19: E Grin 5G 14
Holyrood Pl. RH11: Craw 1D 28
Homebush Av. BN2: Salt 3D 174
BN7: Tels C 1F 174
Home Cl. RH10: Craw 4L 11
Homecoast Ho. BN10: Peace 5H 175
Homecroft Ho. PO21: Bog R 9C 164
Homedrive Ho. BN3: Hove 5L 153
Home Farm Bus. Cen. BN1: Brig 2E 154
Home Farm Ct. RH17: Hors K 5C 52
Home Farm Ho. *RH12: Hors 9N 25*
(off Springfield Rd.)
Home Farm Rd. BN1: Brig 2E 154
Homefield Av. PO22: Felp 6K 165
Homefield Cl. BN16: Rust 2B 168
RH6: Horl 1K 5
Homefield Cres. BN18: Walb 4L 143
Homefield Rd. BN11: Wor 1J 171
PO10: W'brne 1H 137
Homegreen Ho. GU27: Has 5J 17
Homehaven Ct. BN43: Shor S 6H 151
Homelands Av. BN16: E Pres 4F 168
Homelands Copse GU27: Fern 6M 37
Homeleigh BN1: Brig 9M 133
Homepier Ho. BN11: Wor 2F 170
Home Platt RH19: Sharp 5A 32
Homeridge Ho. BN2: Salt 3D 174
Home Rd. BN1: Brig 3N 153
Homesearle Ho. BN12: Gor S 2A 170
Homestall Rd. RH19: Ash W 3L 15
Homestead, The BN16: E Pres 3F 168
Homestead Cotts. BN12: Fer 2L 169
Homestead La. RH15: Burg H 2D 94
Homestead M. BN12: Fer 2L 169
Homesteyne Ho. BN14: Broadw 9H 149
Homestream Ho. RH12: Hors 1M 45
Homethorne Ho. RH11: Craw 7E 10
Home Way GU31: Peters 6J 55
Homewood BN14: Fin 7C 128
Homing Gdns. PO22: Bers 5C 164

Honer La.—Jaybelle Grange Lodge Pk.

Honer La. PO20: S Mun 7F 162
Honeybridge La.
BN44: A'hst, Dial P 2L 109
RH13: A'hst, Dial P 7J 89
Honeybridge Pk. RH13: Dial P 7J 89
Honey Cft. BN3: Hove 2F 152
Honeydown Cotts. GU28: N'chpl 2J 39
Honey La. BN16: Ang 8F 146
RH5: Oak 9C 6
RH12: Oak, R'hook 9C 6
Honeysuckle Cl. BN15: N Lan 4A 150
BN17: L'ton 1N 167
RH6: Horl 1L 5
Honeysuckle Dr. PO21: Pag 1B 180
Honeysuckle La. BN13: High S 1A 148
PO20: Sel 2G 183
RH11: Craw 3E 10
Honeysuckle Wlk. RH12: Hors 6D 26
Honeywood La. RH5: Oak 7C 6
Honeywood Rd. RH13: Hors 7D 26
Hooe, The BN17: L'ton 3N 167
Hooe Farm Ind. Est. BN18: Walb 3L 143
Hooklands La. RH13: Ship 2D 88
RH20: A'ton, Ship 9E 88
Hook La. PO18: Bosh 2H 161
PO20: Ald 6C 142
PO21: Pag 1C 180
PO22: Bog R 8E 164
RH19: W Hoa 9K 31
Hook La. Cl. PO21: Aldw 9K 163
Hooks, The BN5: Henf 3H 111
Hook St. GU6: Alf 2A 22
HOOKSWAY 2G 98
Hooksway La. PO18: Mard 2G 98
HOOKWOOD 3F 4
Hope Cotts. BN42: S'wck 5A 152
Hope Ct. RH11: Craw 2D 28
Hopedene Ct. BN11: Wor 2G 170
Hopewell Cl. BN43: Shor B 7L 151
Hop Garden, The GU31: S Hart 5A 78
Hop Garden La. PO20: N Mun 4F 162
Hopgarton, The PO21: Aldw 9N 163
Hophurst Cl. RH10: Craw D 4J 13
Hophurst Dr. RH10: Craw D 4J 13
Hophurst Hill RH10: Craw D 2L 13
Hophurst La. RH10: Craw D 4J 13
Hopkins Ct. RH11: Craw 2D 28
Hop Oast (Horsham) (Park & Ride) 4L 45
Hop Oast Rdbt. RH13: Hors 5L 45
Horatio Ho. BN1: Brig 5E 172
Hordens, The RH13: B Grn 8D 44
Hordern Ho. RH12: Hors 1L 45
Horizon Cl. BN41: Ports 5D 152
Horizon Ct. *BN3: Hove 7H 153*
(off Kingsway)
HORLEY 2K 5
Horley Leisure Cen. 2G 4
Horley Pl. BN2: Brig 7F 154
Horley Rd. RH6: Charlw 7B 4
Horley Row RH6: Horl 1H 5
Horley Station (Rail) 3K 5
Hormare Cres. RH20: Storr 5G 107
Hornbeam Cl. PO21: Aldw 1H 181
RH13: Hors 1C 46
Hornbeam Rd. PO9: Hav 2B 136
Hornbeams, The RH15: Burg H 4M 93
Hornbeam Way GU29: Midh 3F 80
Hornbrook Copse RH13: Hors 2C 46
Hornbrook Hill RH13: Hors 2C 46
Hornby Pl. *BN2: Brig 4H 155*
(off Hornby Rd.)
Hornby Rd. BN2: Brig 4G 155
Horndean Cl. RH10: Craw 2M 11
Horndean Rd. PO10: Ems 1D 136
Hornet, The PO19: Chich 7D 140
Hornet Rd. PO10: Tho I 1G 159
Hornets, The RH13: Hors 1A 46
Horn La. BN5: Henf, W'cote 7J 111
Hornshill La. RH12: Rudg 5E 22
Horns La. PO21: Pag 2B 180
HORSEBRIDGE COMMON 5A 110
Horsebridge Rd. PO9: Hav 1A 136
Horsefield Rd. PO20: Sel 3H 183
Horse Hill RH6: Sid 1C 4
HORSEMERE GREEN 3D 166
Horsemere Grn. La. BN17: Climp 3C 166
Horseridge Hill RH14: Wisb 9J 63
RH20: Fitt, Wisb 9J 63
Horse Shoe, The PO20: Sel 3H 183
Horseshoe Cl. BN14: Fin 8C 128
RH10: Craw 5M 11
Horsgate La. RH17: Cuck 3B 72
HORSHAM 9N 25
Horsham Av. BN10: Peace 6H 175
(not continuous)
Horsham Av. Nth. BN10: Peace 4J 175
Horsham Cl. BN2: Brig 7G 154
Horsham Gates RH13: Hors 8B 26
Horsham Golf Course 4M 45
Horsham Indoor Bowls Cen. 9H 25
Horsham Mus. *1N 45*
(off Morth Gdns.)
Horsham Northern By-Pass
RH12: Warnh, Hors 5M 25
Horsham Rd. BN14: Fin 6B 128
BN17: L'ton 3M 167
BN44: Stey 9N 109
(not continuous)
GU6: Alf 1N 21
GU28: Petw 8N 61
RH5: Capel 4N 7
RH5: For G, Ock, Wall 4B 6
RH5: Wall 3A 6
RH11: Craw 1N 27
RH11: Pease P 5C 28
RH12: Rusp 8D 8
RH13: Cow 7H 69
RH14: Bill, Slinf 5L 43
RH17: Plum P, Hand 4A 48
Horsham Rd. W. BN17: L'ton 2M 167
Horsham Station (Rail) 8A 26
Horsham Trad. Est. RH13: Hors 7B 26
Horsted Ct. BN1: Brig 4E 172
Horsted Ho. *RH16: Hay H 6G 72*
(off Whitelands)
HORSTED KEYNES 5C 52
Horsted Keynes Ind. Pk. RH17: Hors K 2B 52
Horsted Keynes Rd. RH17: Chel G, Hors K . . . 1H 53
Horsted Keynes Station
Bluebell Railway 3A 52
Horsted La. RH17: Dane 6F 52
RH19: Sharp 6B 32
Horton Ct. BN11: Wor 1K 171
Horton Golf Course 6K 111
Horton Pl. BN16: Ang 9F 146
Horton Rd. BN1: Brig 4C 154
Hoskins Pl. RH19: E Grin 1G 14
Hospital Vs. RH16: Hay H 7G 72
Hotham Gdns. PO22: Bog R 8F 164
Hotham Park 8E 164
Hotham Way PO21: Bog R 8E 164
PO22: Bog R 8E 164
HOUGHTON 2H 125
Houghton Bri. BN18: Amb 2K 125
Houghton Cl. PO9: Hav 8B 116
Houghton La. BN18: Bury 8G 104
RH20: Bury 8G 104
Houghton Rd. RH10: Craw 9L 11
Hova Vs. BN3: Hove 7K 153
HOVE 7K 153
Hove Bus. Cen. BN3: Hove 5K 153
Hovedene BN3: Hove 6L 153
Hove Ent. Cen. BN41: Ports 7E 152
Hove Lagoon Watersports 7F 152
Hove Mnr. BN3: Hove 7J 153
Hove Museum & Art Gallery 7J 153
Hove Pk. Gdns. BN3: Hove 4K 153
Hove Pk. Rd. BN3: Hove 4K 153
Hove Pk. Vs. BN3: Hove 5K 153
Hove Pk. Way BN3: Hove 4L 153
Hove Pl. BN3: Hove 8K 153
Hove Seaside Vs. BN41: Ports 7F 152
Hove Sea Wall BN3: Hove 8L 153
Hove Station (Rail) 5K 153
Hove St. BN3: Hove 7J 153
Hove St. Sth. BN3: Hove 8J 153
Howard Av. PO20: W Witt 4H 177
RH15: Burg H 3N 93
Howard Ct. BN3: Hove 3H 153
BN10: Peace 5H 175
Howard Ho. BN10: Peace 3K 175
PO21: Bog R 8B 164
Howard Pl. BN1: Brig 4C 172 (6A 154)
BN17: L'ton 3K 167
Howard Rd. BN2: Brig 6D 154
BN15: Somp 4M 149
BN17: L'ton 3J 167
BN18: Arun 3F 144
RH11: Craw 1A 28
RH13: Hors 7D 26
Howard St. BN11: Wor 1G 170
Howards Way BN16: Rust 5A 168
Howard Ter. BN1: Brig 4C 172 (6A 154)
Howberry Chase GU27: Has 5K 17
Howlands Ct. RH10: Craw 6H 11
Hoylake Cl. RH11: Ifield 7N 9
Hoyland Ho. RH11: Craw 6B 10
HOYLE 6M 81
Hoyle La. GU29: Hey 8L 81
Hoyle Rd. BN10: Peace 5J 175
Huckswood La. PO8: Chalt, Ids 3E 96
Huddlestones BN16: Ang 7E 146
Hudson Cl. BN13: Durr 7B 148
Hudson Dr. BN16: Rust 4C 168
Hudson Rd. RH10: Craw 8G 11
Hudson Way BN5: Henf 1H 111
Huffwood Trad. Est. RH13: Part G 5D 90
RH14: Bill 2J 65
Hughes Cl. PO21: Aldw 8A 164
Hughes Rd. BN2: Brig 5C 154
Hugo Platt GU31: Rog 5D 56
Humber Av. BN13: Durr 6A 148
Humber Cl. BN13: Durr 6A 148
BN17: L'ton 4M 167
Humphrey Lodge *RH15: Burg H 5E 94*
(off Kings Way)
Humphrey's Gap BN43: Shor S 6K 151
Humphry's Almshouses *BN11: Wor 2H 171*
(off Humphrys Rd.)
Humphrys Rd. BN11: Wor 2H 171
Hundred Acre La. BN6: Streat, Wivel 6J 95
RH17: Wivel, Wivel G 6J 95
Hundredsteddle La. PO20: Bir 1A 178
Hungers La. GU28: Petw, Till 9L 61
Hunnisett Cl. PO20: Sel 1K 183
Hunns Mere Way BN2: W'dean 4L 155
Hunstanton Cl. RH11: Ifield 7N 9
HUNSTON 3C 162
Hunston Cl. BN2: W'dean 6N 155
Hunston Rd. PO20: Huns, N Mun 2D 162
Hunter Ho. RH10: Craw 9F 10
Hunter Rd. PO10: Tho I 1G 159
RH10: Craw 9F 10
Hunters Cl. PO21: Aldw 2E 180
Hunters Ga. PO20: Tang 4L 141
Hunters Mead BN6: Alb 1E 112
RH13: Part G 5D 90
Hunters M. BN18: Font, Walb 3H 143
Hunters Race PO19: Mid L, W Bro 3M 139
Hunters Way PO19: Chich 2B 140
Huntingdon Way RH15: Burg H 3E 94
Huntsbottom La.
GU33: Hill B, Liss 6A 34
Hurlands La. GU8: Duns 1F 20
Hurley Rd. BN13: Durr 7C 148
Hurn Ct. PO9: Hav 8B 116
Hurst-An-Clays RH19: E Grin 4E 14
Hurst Av. BN11: Wor 2D 170
RH12: Hors 8A 26
Hurst Cl. BN18: Amb 8L 105
RH11: Craw 8B 10
Hurst Ct. *BN1: Brig 4M 153*
(off Reigate Rd.)
RH12: Hors 8A 26
Hurst Cres. BN41: Ports 5D 152
Hurst Farm Rd. RH19: E Grin 4D 14
Hurstfield BN15: Lan 8A 150
Hurstfield Cl. RH17: Hay H 7H 73
Hurstfold Ind. Est. GU27: Fern 8M 37
Hurst Gdns. BN6: Hurst 1H 113
Hurst Hill BN1: Brig 9D 134
RH12: Hors 1D 26
Hurstlands RH14: Bill 2H 65
Hurston Cl. BN14: Fin V 5E 148
RH20: Storr 4G 107
Hurston Gro. RH20: Storr 5G 107
Hurston La. RH20: Pulb, Storr 2F 106
Hurst Pk. GU29: Midh 2F 58
RH12: Hors 8A 26
HURSTPIERPOINT 2J 113
Hurstpierpoint Rd. BN5: Wine 7N 91
BN6: Wine 7N 91
Hurst Rd. BN6: Hass 3L 113
BN16: E Pres 2D 168
RH6: Horl 1G 5
RH12: Hors 7N 25
HURST WICKHAM 1L 113
Hurst Wickham Cl. BN6: Hurst 2L 113
Hurstwood BN2: Brig 8G 154
Hurstwood Av. PO10: S'brne 4L 137
Hurstwood Ct. GU29: Midh 3G 80
Hurstwood La. RH17: Hay H 9G 73
RH17: Hors K, Sharp 1C 52
RH19: Sharp 1C 52
Hutchinson Cl. BN16: Rust 1A 168
Hutchins Way RH6: Horl 1H 5
Hutton Rd. BN1: Brig 2C 154
Huxley's (Bird of Prey & Garden) 2C 46
Hyde, The BN2: Brig 4G 155
Hyde Bus. Park, The BN2: Brig 4H 155
Hyde Dr. RH11: Ifield 7A 10
Hyde Heath Ct. RH10: Craw 4M 11
Hydehurst La. RH10: Craw 1G 10
Hyde La. BN44: Up B 4E 130
Hyde Sq. BN44: Up B 4E 130
Hyde St. BN44: Up B 4E 130
Hylands Cl. RH10: Craw 7J 11
Hylden Cl. BN2: W'dean 5J 155
Hylters La. PO18: Chil 9L 99
Hylton Rd. GU32: Peters 6F 54
Hyndman Cl. RH11: Craw 3D 28
Hyperion Ct. RH11: Craw 8A 10
Hyperion Wlk. RH6: Horl 4K 5
Hythe Cl. BN11: Wor 3E 170
Hythe Rd. BN1: Brig 3B 154
BN11: Wor 3E 170

I

i360 Brighton Eye 8B 172 (8N 153)
Icarus Way PO22: Felp 7K 165
Ice House, The 8E 164
Icklesham Ho. *RH11: Craw 9B 10*
(off Salvington Rd.)
Iden Cl. BN2: Brig 8F 154
Iden Hurst BN6: Hurst 9J 93
IDE'S COMMON 3E 122
Idsworth Down GU31: Peters 6G 54
IFIELD 5C 10
Ifield Av. RH11: Craw 3C 10
Ifield Barn Theatre 4B 10
Ifield Cl. BN2: Salt 2E 174
Ifield Dr. RH11: Craw, Ifield 5B 10
Ifield Golf Course 6A 10
IFIELD GREEN 4C 10
Ifield Grn. RH11: Craw, Ifield 3C 10
Ifield Pk. RH11: Craw 6B 10
Ifield Pond 7A 10
Ifield Rd. RH6: Charlw 9A 4
RH10: Craw 6F 10
RH11: Craw 5D 10
Ifield Rd. Rdbt. RH11: Craw 6F 10
Ifield Rdbt. RH11: Craw 5E 10
Ifield Station (Rail) 6C 10
Ifield St. RH11: Ifield 4B 10
Ifield Watermill 7A 10
IFIELDWOOD 3N 9
Ifield Wood RH11: Ifield 5M 9
IFOLD 8K 21
Ifold Bri. La. RH14: Ifol 7J 21
Ifoldhurst RH14: Ifol 9J 21
IFORD 2H 157
Iford Ct. PO9: Hav 8B 116
Ilex Cl. BN16: Rust 4B 168
Ilex Ct. *BN12: Gor S 2N 169*
(off Goring St.)
BN42: S'wck 4C 152
Ilex Wlk. PO11: Hay I 9C 158
Ilex Way BN12: Gor S 2N 169
PO22: Midd S 6M 165
Imberhorne Bus. Cen. RH19: E Grin 2B 14
Imberhorne La. RH19: E Grin 1B 14
Imberhorne Way RH19: E Grin 1B 14
Imperial Arc. BN1: Brig 7C 172 (8A 154)
Independent Bus. Park, The RH19: E Grin 1A 14
Infirmary Dr. RH13: Hors 4J 45
Infirmary Ter. PO19: Chich 5B 140
INGFIELD MANOR 4K 43
Ingfield Mnr. Dr. RH14: Bill 4K 43
Ingham Dr. BN1: Brig 8E 134
Inglecroft Ct. BN15: Somp 6N 149
Inglegreen Cl. BN12: Fer 4K 169
Ingleside Cres. BN15: S Lan 8B 150
Ingleside Rd. BN15: S Lan 8B 150
Inglewood Cl. PO21: Aldw 2E 180
Inglewood Dr. PO21: Aldw 2D 180
Ingram Cl. BN16: Rust 3A 168
BN44: Stey 4A 130
RH12: Hors 9L 25
Ingram Ct. BN3: Hove 6G 153
Ingram Cres. E. BN3: Hove 6G 153
Ingram Cres. W. BN3: Hove 6G 152
Ingram Rd. BN44: Stey 4N 129
INGRAMS GREEN 3M 79
Ingram's Grn. La. GU29: Ipin, Trey 2M 79
Inhams La. PO18: W Sto 9K 119
Inholmes RH10: Craw 6J 11
Inholmes Cl. RH15: Burg H 6D 94
Inholmes Pk. Rd. RH15: Burg H 5C 94
Inkpen La. RH18: F Row 2M 33
Inlands Rd. PO18: Nutb 4M 137
Inmans La. GU32: Peters 4H 55
Innerwyke Cl. PO22: Felp 7J 165
Innes Rd. RH12: Hors 7C 26
Innovation Dr. RH15: Burg H 6M 93
Institute Wlk. RH19: E Grin 3E 14
International Dr. RH10: Craw 7G 10
INVAL 2L 17
Inval Hill GU27: Has 3L 17
Inverness Rd. BN2: Brig 5D 154
Inwood Cres. BN1: Brig 4M 153
Iona Cl. RH11: Craw 9D 10
Iona Way RH16: Hay H 5F 72
Ionian Hgts. *BN2: Salt 3C 174*
(off Suez Way)
IPING 7A 58
Iping La. GU29: Ipin 2N 57
Iping Rd. GU29: Ipin 8L 35
GU30: Ipin, Mill 8L 35
Ireland Lodge BN2: W'dean 6M 155
Irene Av. BN15: Lan 6A 150
Iris Cl. BN17: L'ton 1A 168
Irvine Rd. BN17: L'ton 4K 167
Irving Wlk. RH10: Craw 9G 11
Irwin Dr. RH12: Hors 8L 25
Isaac's La. RH15: Burg H, Hay H 2A 94
RH16: Hay H 6C 72
(not continuous)
Isabel Cres. BN3: Hove 5G 152
Isetta Sq. BN1: Brig 3E 172
Isfield Rd. BN1: Brig 3D 154
ISLAND 1D 54
Island Cl. PO11: Hay I 1A 158
Island Farm La. GU32: Steep 1D 54
Island La. PO20: Sel 2F 182
Island Loop PO20: Sel 2F 182
ISLE OF THORNS 1K 53
Islingword Pl. BN2: Brig 7D 154
Islingword Rd. BN2: Brig 6C 154
Islingword St. BN2: Brig 7C 154
Itchen Cl. GU31: Peters 7E 54
ITCHENOR 5C 160
Itchenor Caravan Pk. PO20: Itchen 8E 160
ITCHENOR GREEN 8D 160
ITCHENOR PARK 6C 160
Itchenor Rd. PO20: Itchen, W Witt 6C 160
Itchen Rd. PO9: Hav 8B 116
ITCHINGFIELD 4E 44
Itchingfield Rd. RH13: Itch 4E 44
Itford Farm La. BN8: Bedd 5N 157
Ithica Cl. PO11: Hay I 8A 158
Ivanhoe Cl. RH11: Craw 3F 10
Ivanhoe Pl. PO22: Felp 7K 165
Iveagh Cl. RH11: Craw 2E 28
Ivor Rd. BN2: W'dean 4K 155
Ivory Pl. BN2: Brig 6G 172 (7C 154)
Ivory Wlk. RH11: Craw 8A 10
Ivy Arch Cl. BN14: Fin 8D 128
Ivy Arch Rd. BN14: Broadw 1H 171
Ivy Cl. PO20: Westg 6E 142
RH13: Southw 9K 45
RH20: A'ton 2E 108
Ivy Cres. PO22: Bog R 7E 164
Ivydale Rd. PO21: Bog R 8B 164
Ivydene Cres. PO18: Chid'm 6A 138
Ivydene Ind. Est. RH19: Ash W 5K 15
Ivy Dene La. RH19: Ash W 6K 15
Ivydore Av. BN13: Durr 5B 148
Ivydore Cl. BN13: Durr 6B 148
Ivyhouse Cotts. RH5: Newd 1K 9
Ivy La. PO20: Westg 6E 142
PO22: Bog R 7E 164
RH20: A'ton 1E 108
Ivy M. *BN3: Hove 8M 153*
(off Ivy Pl.)
Ivy Pl. BN3: Hove 8M 153
BN11: Wor 3F 170
Ivyview Way PO20: N Mun 9E 140

J

Jackdaw Cl. RH11: Craw 4E 10
Jackdaw La. RH12: Hors 6B 26
Jacken Cl. PO22: Felp 8K 165
Jackies La. BN8: Newick 9H 75
Jackrells La. RH13: Southw 7M 45
Jackson Rd. RH11: Craw 3D 28
Jackson St. BN2: Brig 6C 154
Jacobean Cl. RH10: Craw 7L 11
Jacobs Ct. RH10: Craw 5L 11
Jacobs Ladder GU28: Riv 6E 60
Jacqueline Du Pre Ct. *BN2: Brig 8D 154*
(off Somerset St.)
James Bradford Almshouses *RH16: Hay H . . . 5D 72*
(off Butler's Grn. Rd.)
James Cl. BN13: Durr 7D 148
James Pl. RH10: Craw 7F 10
James Searle Ind. Est. RH12: Hors 7B 26
James St. PO20: Sel 4J 183
James Watt Way RH10: Craw 1J 11
Jane Murray Way RH15: Burg H, Hass 4L 93
Janes Cl. RH15: Burg H 3D 94
Janes La. GU28: Riv 6F 60
RH15: Burg H 3D 94
Janeston Ct. BN3: Hove 6L 153
Jan Smuts Cl. GU33: Long C 1C 34
Japonica Cl. BN43: Shor S 4L 151
Japonica Way PO9: Hav 2C 136
Jarvis Cl. RH11: Craw 3D 28
Jarvis La. BN44: Stey 3A 130
Jarvis Rd. BN18: Arun 3F 144
Jasmine Cl. BN17: L'ton 1N 167
Jasmine Ct. BN1: Brig 9A 134
BN3: Hove 6M 153
BN12: Fer 3L 169
RH12: Hors 9N 25
Jason Cl. BN10: Peace 5J 175
Javelin Ct. RH10: Craw 3M 11
Javelin Rd. PO10: Tho I 1G 159
Jaybelle Grange Lodge Pk. BN17: Climp 4C 166

Jay Cl.—Kingston by Sea

Jay Cl. RH13: Southw 8L 45
Jay Rd. BN10: Peace 6L 175
Jays, The BN17: L'ton 2K 167
RH15: Burg H 4N 93
Jays Cl. BN17: L'ton 2K 167
Jay's La. GU27: Has 9C 18
Jay Wlk. *PO19: Chich* *7C 140*
(off St Martins St.)
RH10: Turn H 7K 13
Jeans Ct. RH11: Craw 2D 28
Jefferies RH17: Hors K 6C 52
Jefferies La. BN12: Gor S 3A 170
Jeffreys Av. PO19: Chich 4C 140
Jengers La. *RH14: Bill* *9J 43*
(off Jengers Mead)
Jengers Mead RH14: Bill 9J 43
Jengers Pas. *RH14: Bill* *9J 43*
(off Jengers Mead)
Jenner Rd. RH10: Craw 1H 11
Jennings Way RH6: Horl 2M 5
Jeremy's La. RH17: Bol 3D 70
Jerrard Rd. PO20: Tang 3M 141
Jersey Rd. BN12: Fer 3L 169
RH11: Craw 1C 28
Jersey St. BN2: Brig 7C 154
Jervis Av. BN16: Rust 4C 168
Jesmond Cl. BN3: Hove 6G 152
Jesmond Rd. BN3: Hove 6G 152
Jessamine Ter. RH13: B Grn 7D 44
Jesters RH16: Burg H 1D 94
Jestico's Cl. PO20: Huns 3C 162
Jetty, The PO22: Midd S 7A 166
Jevington Cl. BN13: Durr 8N 147
Jevington Ct. *BN13: Durr* *8N 147*
(off Jevington Cl.)
BN43: Shor S 6N 151
Jevington Dr. BN2: Brig 4E 154
Jewel Wlk. RH11: Craw 9C 10
Jew St. BN1: Brig 7E 172 (8B 154)
Jib Cl. BN17: L'ton 1N 167
Jireh Ct. RH16: Hay H 4F 72
Joan Nightingale Ho. RH16: Hay H 5D 72
Jobes RH17: Bal 1A 50
Jobs La. RH17: God G, Hick 3G 93
Jobson's La. GU8: Has 4C 38
GU27: Has 4C 38
Jockey Mead RH12: Hors 1L 45
John Arundel Rd. PO19: Chich 6A 140
John Ct. BN2: W'dean 5L 155
John Howard Cotts. BN2: Brig 9G 154
John Pound's Ho. RH11: Craw 8E 10
Johns Cl. BN10: Peace 2J 175
Johnson Bank *BN2: Brig* *6D 154*
(off Wellington Rd.)
Johnson Dr. RH15: Burg H 5E 94
JOHNSON'S COMMON 4A 4
Johnson Wlk. RH10: Craw 9G 10
Johnson Way BN18: Ford 2B 166
John St. BN2: Brig 7G 172 (8C 154)
BN43: Shor S 6H 151
PO21: Bog R 9E 164
John Whittle Lodge BN2: Brig 4D 154
Jolesfield RH13: Part G 3C 90
Jolesfield Ct. RH11: Craw 9B 10
Jolliffe Ct. *GU32: Peters* *6F 54*
(off Hylton Rd.)
Jolliffe Rd. PO20: W Witt 4H 177
Jones Sq. PO20: Sel 4J 183
Jordan Ct. BN3: Hove 5G 152
JORDANS, THE 1G 9
Jordans, The RH19: E Grin 4E 14
Jordans Cl. RH11: Craw 4F 10
Jordans Cres. RH11: Craw 3F 10
Joseph Wlk. BN43: Shor B 7L 151
Joyce Cl. BN17: Wick 1J 167
Joys Cft. PO19: Chich 6D 140
Joys Cft. Ct. *PO19: Chich* *6D 140*
(off Joys Cft.)
Jubilee Av. BN16: Rust 2B 168
Jubilee Cl. RH16: Hay H 5H 73
Jubilee Ct. BN2: Brig 3F 154
BN10: Peace *5H 175*
(off Cavell Av.)
BN11: Wor 2F 170
RH14: Bill 1J 65
Jubilee Est. RH13: Hors 7B 26
Jubilee Gdns. PO21: Pag 2D 180
Jubilee Ho. PO10: Ems 4E 136
Jubilee La. GU26: Gray 1E 16
Jubilee M. PO10: S'brne 5J 137
Jubilee Pde. PO22: Midd S 7A 166
Jubilee Pl. PO22: Bog R 7D 164
Jubilee Rd. BN41: Ports 5C 152
PO19: Chich 6C 140
RH12: Rudg 3J 23
RH15: Burg H 6N 93
Jubilee St. BN1: Brig 7E 172 (8B 154)
Jubilee Ter. PO19: Chich 6C 140
Jubilee Wlk. RH10: Craw 6J 11
RH12: Hors *9N 25*
(off Albion Way)
Jubilee Way RH20: Storr 4L 107
Judge's Ter. RH19: E Grin 4E 14
Juggs, The RH20: W Chil 7K 87
Juggs La. RH20: W Chil 7J 87
Jugg's Rd. BN7: King L 2M 155
Jugshill La. RH5: Oak 5F 6
Julian Ct. BN43: Shor S 5M 151
Julian Rd. BN3: Hove 4B 172 (6N 153)
Junction Cl. BN18: Ford 2B 166
RH15: Burg H 4D 94
Junction M. RH15: Burg H 5C 94
Junction Pl. GU27: Has 5H 17
Junction Rd. BN1: Brig 5D 172 (7A 154)
RH15: Burg H 6C 94
June Cl. PO21: Pag 3B 180
June La. GU29: Midh 9F 58
June Mdws. GU29: Midh 9F 58
June Ri. GU29: Midh 9G 59
Juniper Cl. BN13: Durr 8A 148
BN41: Ports 2E 152
PO22: Midd S 6M 165
Juniper Ct. RH16: Hay H 7D 72
Juniper Rd. RH11: Craw 3E 10
Juniper Sq. PO9: Hav 5A 136
Juniper Wlk. BN43: Shor S 4M 151
Juno Cl. BN12: Gor S 1A 170
Jupp's La. BN12: Gor S 1N 169
Jura Cl. RH11: Craw 9D 10
Jury La. PO20: Sidle 7N 161
Juventu Cl. PO9: Hav 1A 136
Juxon Cl. PO19: Chich 8C 140
RH11: Craw 8B 10

K

K2 Leisure Cen. 1F 28
Kandy Pk. BN17: L'ton 3J 167
Karenza Ct. BN1: Brig 1F 172 (5B 154)
RH13: Hors 8B 26
Katherine's Lodge BN15: S Lan 8B 150
Kathleen Gdns. PO19: Chich 7E 140
Katrina Gdns. PO11: Hay I 7A 158
Kearsley Dr. BN14: Fin V 4E 148
Keats Cl. RH12: Hors 4C 26
Keats Pl. RH19: E Grin 3D 14
Keats Wlk. PO21: Bog R 9C 164
Keats Way PO19: Chich 7C 140
Kebbell Lodge *BN2: Brig* *8C 154*
(off High St.)
Keble Cl. PO21: Aldw 9A 164
RH10: Craw 3M 11
Keelson Way BN17: L'ton 2N 167
Keepers Wood PO19: Chich 2B 140
Keir Hardie Ho. RH11: Craw 2D 28
Kelly Rd. BN3: Hove 4M 153
Kelmscott Ri. RH11: Craw 3D 28
Kelmscott Way PO21: Bers 5B 164
Kelsey Av. PO10: S'brne 4K 137
Kelsey Cl. RH6: Horl 2H 5
Kelsey Ct. *RH15: Burg H* *5E 94*
(off Kings Way)
Kelso Cl. BN13: Wor 9C 148
BN15: Somp 6M 149
RH10: Craw 5N 11
Kelvin Bus. Cen. RH10: Craw 3H 11
Kelvin La. RH10: Craw 2H 11
Kelvin Way RH10: Craw 2H 11
Kemnal Pk. GU27: Has 4M 17
Kemp Ct. BN2: Brig 9F 154
Kempe Rd. RH16: Lind 2K 73
Kemps BN6: Hurst 9H 93
Kempshott M. RH12: Hors 7M 25
Kempshott Rd. RH12: Hors 7M 25
Kemp St. BN1: Brig 6E 172 (7B 154)
KEMP TOWN 9F 154
Kemptown M. *BN2: Brig* *9F 154*
(off Arundel Pl.)
Kemp Town Pl. BN2: Brig 9E 154
Ken Berry Ct. PO9: Hav 8B 116
Kendal Cl. BN17: L'ton 1N 167
Kendale Cl. RH10: Craw 1L 29
Kendal Ho. RH15: Burg H 6A 94
Kendall Ct. RH16: Hay H 7G 73
Kendal Rd. BN3: Hove 5H 153
BN15: Somp 7N 149
Kenhurst BN16: E Pres 3F 168
Kenilworth Cl. BN2: Brig 3H 155
RH11: Craw 1D 28
Kenilworth Pl. RH14: Bill 3H 65
Kenilworth Rd. PO21: Bog R 8B 164
Kenlegh PO21: Aldw 1H 181
Kenmara Cl. RH10: Craw 3J 11
Kenmara Ct. RH10: Craw 2J 11
Kenmure Av. BN1: Brig 7B 134
Kennard Ct. RH18: F Row 9L 15
Kennard La. RH16: Hay H 7F 72
Kennedy Av. RH19: E Grin 1D 14
Kennedy Rd. RH13: Hors 1A 46
Kennel Hill PO18: Charlt, E Lav, Good 3G 120
Kennel La. RH6: Hookw 3F 4
RH13: W Grin 7B 68
Kennet Cl. BN13: Durr 6B 148
RH11: Craw 7B 10
Kennet Rd. GU31: Peters 7E 54
Kensington Cl. RH20: W Chil 9H 87
Kensington Gdns. BN1: Brig 6E 172 (7B 154)
Kensington Pl. BN1: Brig 6E 172 (7B 154)
Kensington Rd. PO19: Chich 7E 140
RH11: Craw 1D 28
Kensington St. BN1: Brig 6E 172 (7B 154)
Kent Cl. BN43: Shor S 6M 151
Kenton Rd. BN3: Hove 6F 152
Kent Rd. BN17: L'ton 2K 167
PO19: Chich 6D 140
Kent's La. BN6: Streat 1K 115
Kents Rd. RH16: Hay H 6G 72
KENT STREET 1L 91
Kent St. RH13: Cow 1L 91
Kentstreet La. RH13: Cow 1L 91
Kentwyns Dr. RH13: Hors 2B 46
Kentwyns Pl. RH13: Hors 2B 46
Kenwards BN1: Brig 7E 134
Kenwood Bus. Pk. PO9: Hav 3A 136
Kenwood Quay BN15: S Lan 8C 150
Kenya Ct. BN1: Brig 5B 172
RH6: Horl 1H 5
Kerrison M. *BN3: Hove* *8M 153*
(off Lwr. Market St.)
Kerry Gdns. BN16: E Pres 2F 168
Kerves La. RH13: Hors 4A 46
(not continuous)
Kerwin Ct. RH13: Slinf 9F 24
Keston Ho. RH16: Hay H 3F 72
Kestrel Cl. BN3: Hove 5M 153
PO20: E Witt 5L 177
RH11: Craw 4E 10
RH12: Hors 6B 26
Kestrel Ct. *BN2: Brig* *6G 154*
(off Swanborough Pl.)
PO19: Chich 6F 140
PO21: Pag 4B 180
Kestrels, The BN43: Shor S 5K 151
Kestrel Wlk. RH10: Turn H 7K 13
Kestrel Way BN17: Wick 9J 145
Keswick Cl. BN12: Gor S 8B 148
RH11: Ifield 8N 9
Ketches La. RH17: Scay H 1C 74
TN22: Shef P 2F 74
Ketch Rd. BN17: L'ton 4N 167
Kevin Gdns. BN2: W'dean 5M 155
Kewell's Cnr. PO20: Bir 7H 161
Kew Gdns. PO21: Bog R 8A 164
Kew St. BN1: Brig 6D 172 (7A 154)
KEYMER 4B 114
Keymer Av. BN10: Peace 6J 175
(not continuous)
Keymer Ct. *RH15: Burg H* *6C 94*
(off Station Rd.)
Keymer Cres. BN12: Gor S 3B 170
Keymer End RH16: Hay H 6E 72
Keymer Gdns. RH15: Burg H 7C 94
Keymer Pde. *RH15: Burg H* *6C 94*
(off Station Rd.)
Keymer Pk. BN6: Key 4C 114
Keymer Rd. BN1: Brig 8C 134
BN6: Hass, Key, Ditch 4N 113
RH11: Craw 7E 10
RH15: Burg H, Key 6C 94
Keymer Ter. BN6: Key 4B 114
Keymer Way BN12: Gor S 3A 170
Keynor La. PO20: Sidle 3G 178
Keysford La. RH16: Lind 7M 51
RH17: Hors K, Lind 7M 51
Keystone Cl. BN12: Gor S 1A 170
Kidborough Rd. RH11: Craw 7B 10
Kidbrook RH16: Hay H 3J 73
KIDBROOKE PARK 2K 33
Kidbrooke Ri. RH18: F Row 1L 33
Kidders La. BN5: Henf 8G 90
Kidd Rd. PO19: Chich 4D 140
Kidmans Cl. RH12: Hors 6C 26
Kidworth Cl. RH6: Horl 1H 5
Killinghurst La. GU8: Chidd 5D 18
GU27: Chidd, Has 5D 18
KILLINGHURST PARK 3E 18
Kilmore Cl. BN14: Fin 8C 128
Kiln, The RH15: Burg H 5D 94
Kiln Av. GU27: Has 3L 17
Kilnbarn Ct. *RH16: Hay H* *7E 72*
(off Kilnbarn Way)
Kilnbarn Way RH16: Hay H 7E 72
Kiln Cl. RH10: Craw D 5J 13
Kiln Dr. PO18: Nutb 5A 138
Kilnfield Rd. RH12: Rudg 3J 23
Kiln Ho. *RH19: E Grin* *2D 14*
(off Fosters Pl.)
Kiln La. GU31: Buri 4C 76
RH6: Horl 1J 5
RH16: Hay H 4J 73
Kilnmead RH10: Craw 5F 10
Kilnmead Cl. RH10: Craw 5G 10
Kiln Rd. RH10: Craw D 5J 13
Kiln Wlk. PO18: Westh 4G 141
Kilnwood Cl. PO20: Sel 3K 183
Kilnwood La. RH11: Fay 9J 9
RH12: Fay 9J 9
Kilsham La. GU28: Petw 3L 83
Kilwich Cl. PO22: Midd S 6L 165
Kimber Cl. BN15: Lan 8A 150
Kimberley Cl. RH6: Horl 2G 5
Kimberley Rd. BN2: Brig 4E 154
GU33: Long C 1B 34
RH10: Craw 5K 11
Kimberry BN17: Wick 1J 167
Kimbers GU32: Peters 5E 54
Kimbridge Cres. PO9: Hav 8A 116
Kimbridge Pk. *PO20: E Witt* *5L 177*
(off Nagels Cl.)
Kimbridge Rd. PO20: E Witt 5L 177
Kimpton Ct. PO9: Hav 8B 116
Kindersley Cl. RH19: E Grin 1H 15
Kinfauns Dr. BN13: High S 3B 148
King Alfred Cl. BN44: Stey 3A 130
King Alfred Leisure Cen. 8J 153
King Bus. Cen. BN6: Say C 7E 92
King Charles Pl. BN43: Shor B 7K 151
King Edward Av. BN14: Broadw 9H 149
King Edward Cl. BN14: Broadw 9J 149
RH13: Hors 4H 45
King Edward Rd. RH13: Hors 4H 45
Kingfisher Cl. BN13: Durr 8A 148
PO9: Row C 5B 116
PO11: Hay I 9C 158
RH10: Craw 2J 11
Kingfisher Ct. *BN2: Brig* *6G 154*
(off Albourne Cl.)
PO9: Hav 2B 136
PO22: Midd S 7N 165
Kingfisher Dr. BN17: Wick 9J 145
PO10: W'brne 1H 137
RH16: Hay H 8D 72
Kingfisher La. RH10: Turn H 7K 13
Kingfisher Pde. *PO20: E Witt* *4K 177*
(off Cakeham Rd.)
Kingfisher Ri. RH19: E Grin 4F 14
Kingfisher Way RH12: Hors 6N 25
King George VI Av. BN3: Hove 2H 153
King George VI Dr. BN3: Hove 2J 153
King George VI Mans. BN3: Hove 3H 153
King George Av. GU32: Peters 5F 54
RH19: E Grin 1C 14
King George Ct. PO21: Bog R 8C 164
King George Gdns. PO19: Chich 5B 140
King George M. *GU32: Peters* *5F 54*
(off King George Av.)
King George Rd. BN43: Shor S 5M 151
King James La. BN5: Henf 3H 111
King John Ct. *BN43: Shor B* *7K 151*
(off Emerald Quay)
King Johns Ct. GU29: Midh 1H 81
King John's Wlk. GU29: W Lav 1J 81
King La. GU32: Frox 1A 54
Kingley Cen. PO18: W Sto 8K 119
Kingley Va. PO20: Sel 1J 183
Kingley Vale (National Nature Reserve) 4G 119
Kingmere *BN17: L'ton* *4L 167*
(off South Ter.)
King Pl. BN1: Brig 7D 172 (8B 154)
Kings Arms Hill BN18: Arun 2H 145
Kings Av. PO19: Chich 9B 140
Kings Barn End BN44: Stey 3C 130
King's Barn La. BN44: Stey 1B 130
King's Barn Vs. BN44: Stey 3B 130
Kingsbridge La. RH13: Ship 1G 88
Kingsbridge M. BN13: Durr 6B 148
Kingsbury Rd. BN1: Brig 3F 172 (6B 154)
Kingsbury St. BN1: Brig 3F 172 (6B 154)
Kings Cl. BN10: Peace 3H 175
BN15: S Lan 8C 150
BN18: Yap 1N 165
PO9: Row C 4A 116
Kings Copse RH19: E Grin 4F 14
KINGSCOTE 8M 13
Kingscote Hill RH11: Craw 8D 10
Kingscote Lodge *BN1: Brig* *9G 134*
(off Ringmer Dr.)
Kingscote Station
Bluebell Railway 8N 13
Kingscote Way BN1: Brig 4E 172 (6B 154)
Kings Ct. *BN1: Brig* *7E 172*
(off Church St.)
BN11: Wor *3D 170*
(off Aglaia Rd.)
BN15: S Lan 9C 150
BN43: Shor B 8G 150
PO10: S'brne 5H 137
PO20: Sel 2J 183
PO21: Bog R *9F 164*
(off The Esplanade)
RH13: Hors 8B 26
Kings Cres. BN43: Shor B 8G 150
Kingsdene BN11: Wor 2F 170
Kings Dr. BN6: Key 3A 114
BN43: Shor B 7G 150
GU29: Midh 2F 58
PO21: Pag 3D 180
King's Esplanade BN3: Hove 8J 153
(not continuous)
Kingsey Av. PO10: Ems 5E 136
Kingsfernsden La. GU32: Peters 4G 55
Kings Fld. BN5: Henf 2H 111
Kingsfield RH20: Storr 5K 107
Kingsfield Cl. BN42: S'wck 5A 152
KINGSFOLD 6M 7
Kingsfold BN2: Brig 8G 154
Kingsfold Cl. RH14: Bill 3J 65
Kingsfold Ct. RH12: King 7M 7
Kings Gap BN43: Shor B 8G 150
King's Gdns. BN3: Hove 8K 153
Kings Ga. BN1: Brig 8E 172
BN3: Hove 5L 153
RH12: Hors 9M 25
RH16: Hay H 3F 72
Kingsgate RH10: Craw 6G 10
KINGSHAM 8D 140
Kingsham Av. PO19: Chich 8D 140
Kingsham Rd. PO19: Chich 8C 140
Kingsland Cl. BN43: Shor S 6L 151
RH20: Storr 5K 107
Kingsland Ct. RH10: Craw 6J 11
Kingsland Ho. BN43: Shor S 6L 151
Kingsland Rd. BN14: Broadw 7H 149
Kings La. RH13: Cow 9L 69
RH13: Southw 6L 45
RH20: Cold 9J 85
RH20: Pulb 6E 86
Kingslea RH13: Hors 8B 26
Kings Leisure Cen. 3E 14
Kingsley Cl. BN14: Broadw 9K 149
Kingsley Ct. *BN1: Brig* *8A 172*
(off Kings Rd.)
KINGSLEY GREEN 1K 37
Kingsley Ho. PO10: Ems 5E 136
Kingsley M. RH14: Bill 2J 65
Kingsley Rd. BN1: Brig 4M 153
RH11: Craw 9C 10
Kingsmead BN17: Wick 8J 145
PO22: Felp 8G 164
Kingsmead Cl. BN44: Bramb 5A 130
RH12: Hors 5E 26
Kingsmead Gdns. PO22: Midd S 6A 166
Kings Mdw. PO18: Hamb 4A 138
Kingsmead Pl. RH12: Broadb H 8G 25
Kingsmead Rd. PO22: Midd S 7A 166
RH12: Broadb H 8H 25
Kingsmere BN1: Brig 3N 153
Kings M. BN3: Hove 7L 153
RH12: Hors 9M 25
Kingsmill Rd. PO22: Barn 7K 143
Kings Pde. BN1: Brig 3B 154
BN14: Fin V 3D 148
PO21: Aldw 1J 181
Kingspit La. GU28: Petw 1C 84
Kings Pl. RH13: Hors 8B 26
Kings Platt RH13: Ship 9H 67
Kings Quarter BN11: Wor 1G 170
Kings Ride RH15: Burg H 7E 94
Kings Rd.
BN1: Brig 8A 172 (8N 153)
BN15: S Lan 8B 150
BN42: S'wck 4N 151
GU27: Has 5H 17
GU32: Peters 5D 54
PO10: Ems 5E 136
PO11: Hay I 6A 158
RH6: Horl 2J 5
RH12: Rudg 3J 23
RH13: Hors 8B 26
RH16: Hay H 6G 72
Kings Rd. Arches
BN1: Brig 9C 172 (9A 154)
King's Rd. Ind. Est. GU27: Has 5H 17
King's Stone 5B 116
King's Stone Av. BN44: Stey 4B 130
King's Ter. PO10: Ems 5F 136
Kingsthorpe Rd. BN3: Hove 5G 153
KINGSTON 1E 156
Kingston Bay Rd. BN43: Shor B 7M 151
Kingston B'way. BN43: Shor S 4M 151
KINGSTON BY SEA 6M 151

Leigh Pk. Gdns.—Longcroft

Leigh Pk. Gdns. . . . 8A 116
Leigh Rd. BN14: Broadw . . . 7H 149
PO9: Hav . . . 3A 136
PO19: Chich . . . 8B 140
Leighton Av. BN14: Broadw . . . 7J 149
Leighton Rd. BN3: Hove . . . 5J 153
RH17: Hors K . . . 5C 52
Leighton Vs. RH17: Hors K . . . 5C 52
(off Leighton Rd.)
Leinster Gdns. PO22: Felp . . . 8L 165
Leisure Pursuits . . . 6L 15
Leith Va. Cotts. RH5: Ock . . . 1E 6
Leith Vw. Cotts. RH12: King . . . 6M 7
Leith Vw. Rd. RH12: Hors . . . 6D 26
Le May Cl. RH6: Horl . . . 1J 5
Lemmington Way RH12: Hors . . . 4C 26
Lenham Av. BN2: Salt . . . 3B 174
Lenham Rd. E. BN2: Rott, Salt . . . 3B 174
Lenham Rd. W. BN2: Rott . . . 3A 174
Lenhurst Way BN13: Wor . . . 9D 148
Lennox M. BN11: Wor . . . 1H 171
(off Chapel Rd.)
Lennox Rd. BN3: Hove . . . 5H 153
BN11: Wor . . . 1H 171
BN43: Shor S . . . 5L 151
PO19: Chich . . . 6D 140
Lennox St. BN2: Brig . . . 8C 154
PO21: Bog R . . . 1M 181
Leonardslee Ct. RH10: Craw . . . 8K 11
Leonard Way RH13: Hors . . . 9C 26
Leonora Dr. PO21: Aldw, Pag . . . 1D 180
Leopold Cl. PO22: Felp . . . 7H 165
Leopold Rd. BN1: Brig . . . 6C 172 (7A 154)
RH11: Craw . . . 6E 10
Lesser Foxholes BN43: Shor S . . . 4G 151
Letchworth Cl. BN12: Fer . . . 3K 169
Letchworth Ct. RH11: Craw . . . 9A 10
Level, The . . . 4G 172 (6C 154)
Leveller End BN8: Newick . . . 9K 75
Leveller Rd. BN8: Newick . . . 9K 75
Level Mare La. PO20: E'gate, Font . . . 2E 142
Leveret La. RH11: Craw . . . 4D 10
Leverton Av. PO22: Felp . . . 7L 165
Levin Down (Nature Reserve) . . . 7G 101
Lewes Cl. BN2: Salt . . . 3E 174
PO21: Bog R . . . 8A 164
RH10: Craw . . . 6L 11
Lewes Ct. BN1: Falm . . . 6H 135
Lewes Cres. BN2: Brig . . . 9F 154
(not continuous)
Lewes M. BN2: Brig . . . 8J 173
(off Arundel Pl.)
Lewes Rd. BN1: Brig . . . 4D 154
BN2: Brig . . . 5G 172 (6C 154)
BN6: Ditch, Streat, W'ton . . . 4E 114
BN7: Plump . . . 7H 115
BN9: Newh . . . 3N 175
RH16: Hay H . . . 6H 73
RH16: Hay H, Lind . . . 2J 73
RH17: Chel G . . . 2J 53
RH17: Dane . . . 6G 53
RH17: Hay H, Scay H . . . 5M 73
RH17: Hors K . . . 6C 52
RH18: Chel G, F Row, Wych C . . . 3K 33
RH19: Ash W, E Grin, F Row . . . 4F 14
TN22: Fur G . . . 6G 53
Lewes St. BN2: Brig . . . 7C 154
Lewin Cl. BN15: Lan . . . 6C 150
Lewis Ct. BN13: Durr . . . 8N 147
Lewisham Cl. RH11: Craw . . . 1E 28
Lewis La. BN18: Ford . . . 2B 166
Lewis Rd. BN15: N Lan . . . 5A 150
PO10: Ems . . . 2G 136
PO19: Chich . . . 6D 140
PO20: Sel . . . 3H 183
(not continuous)
Lewis's Bldgs. BN1: Brig . . . 7D 172
Lexington Dr. RH16: Hay H . . . 4H 73
Leybourne Cl. BN2: Brig . . . 4H 155
RH11: Craw . . . 2E 28
Leybourne Pde. BN2: Brig . . . 4H 155
(off Leybourne Rd.)
Leybourne Pl. RH19: Felb . . . 1N 13
Leybourne Rd. BN2: Brig . . . 3H 155
Leyfield BN6: Alb . . . 2F 112
Leylands Pk. RH15: Burg H . . . 3C 94
Leylands Rd. RH15: Burg H . . . 4A 94
Ley Rd. PO22: Felp . . . 7J 165
Leys, The GU27: Fern . . . 5J 37
PO18: Sing . . . 8F 100
Leyton Lea RH17: Cuck . . . 3N 71
Liam Cl. PO9: Hav . . . 1A 136
Library Pl. BN11: Wor . . . 2J 171
Library Rd. BN1: Falm . . . 7J 135
Lichfield Ct. BN2: Brig . . . 8G 154
BN11: Wor . . . 3E 170
Lichfield Gdns. PO21: Aldw . . . 9N 163
LICKFOLD . . . 1B 60
Lickfold Rd. GU27: Fern . . . 7M 37
GU28: Fern . . . 7M 37
Lido, The
Worthing . . . 3H 171
LIDSEY . . . 1E 164
Lidsey Caravan Pk. PO22: Shrip . . . 2E 164
Lidsey Cl. RH10: Craw . . . 8L 11
Lidsey La. PO21: Bers . . . 5A 164
Lidsey Rd. PO20: W'gate . . . 8E 142
PO22: Shrip, W'gate . . . 9E 142
Lifeboat Museum, The
Selsey . . . 4K 183
Lifeboat Station
Hayling Island . . . 1A 176
Littlehampton . . . 4K 167
Lifeboat Way PO20: Sel . . . 5J 183
Lilac Cl. BN13: Durr . . . 8N 147
BN17: L'ton . . . 1N 167
PO9: Hav . . . 2C 136
PO22: Midd S . . . 6M 165
Lilac Ct. BN1: Brig . . . 1M 153
Lillian Ter. BN18: Poling . . . 5B 146
Lillywhite Cl. RH15: Burg H . . . 3A 94
Lillywhite Rd. PO18: Westh . . . 4G 141
Limbourne La. RH20: Fitt . . . 5H 85
Limbrick Cl. BN12: Gor S . . . 1A 170
Limbrick Cnr. BN12: Gor S . . . 9A 148
Limbrick La. BN12: Gor S . . . 9A 148
(not continuous)
Limbrick Way BN12: Gor S . . . 9N 147
Lime Av. PO20: Westg . . . 6F 142
RH12: Hors . . . 7D 26
Limeburners Camping RH14: Bill . . . 2F 64
Lime Chase RH20: Storr . . . 5J 107
Lime Cl. PO19: Chich . . . 6D 140
RH10: Copt . . . 1C 12
RH11: Craw . . . 3E 10
Lime Gro. BN16: Ang . . . 9E 146
Lime Kiln Coppice PO22: Felp . . . 6H 165
Lime Kiln Rd. RH13: Mann H . . . 4F 46
Lime Rd. BN14: Fin . . . 8C 128
Limes, The BN2: Brig . . . 5C 154
(off Bromley Rd.)
BN14: Fin . . . 7C 128
BN16: Rust . . . 2B 168
BN18: Yap . . . 1N 165
RH12: Hors . . . 7N 25
(off Trafalgar Rd.)
Limes Av. RH6: Horl . . . 3K 5
Lime Tree Av. BN14: Fin V . . . 2D 148
Limetree Cl. BN16: E Pres . . . 2E 168
Lime Tree Gro. RH16: Lind . . . 2K 73
Limmard Way PO22: Felp . . . 8K 165
Limmer La. PO22: Felp . . . 8H 165
Limney Rd. BN2: Brig . . . 6F 154
Linacre Dr. RH12: Rudg . . . 1H 23
Lincett Av. BN13: Wor . . . 9D 148
Lincett Ct. BN13: Wor . . . 9D 148
Lincett Dr. BN13: Wor . . . 1D 170
LINCH . . . 6C 36
LINCHMERE . . . 9D 16
Linchmere BN2: Brig . . . 6G 154
Linchmere Av. BN2: Salt . . . 3C 174
Linchmere Pl. RH11: Craw . . . 5C 10
Linchmere Ridge GU27: Has . . . 8F 16
Linchmere Rd. GU27: Linch, Has . . . 8D 16
Linch Rd. GU29: Red, Wool . . . 6C 36
GU30: Mill, Red . . . 6C 36
Lincoln Av. BN10: Peace . . . 5G 175
PO21: Aldw . . . 8L 163
Lincoln Av. Sth. BN10: Peace . . . 5G 174
Lincoln Cl. RH6: Horl . . . 3J 5
RH10: Craw . . . 9G 11
Lincoln Cotts. BN2: Brig . . . 7C 154
Lincoln Ct. BN3: Hove . . . 5L 153
BN10: Peace . . . 5G 175
BN15: Lan . . . 9B 150
Lincoln Grn. PO19: Chich . . . 4B 140
Lincoln Rd. BN13: Wor . . . 9D 148
BN41: Ports . . . 6D 152
Lincoln St. BN2: Brig . . . 7C 154
Lincoln Wood RH16: Hay H . . . 4D 72
Lindale Pl. RH20: Storr . . . 6J 107
(off Hanover Wlk.)
Linden Av. RH19: E Grin . . . 2C 14
Linden Cl. RH10: Craw . . . 9J 11
RH12: Hors . . . 7B 26
Linden Ct. GU28: Petw . . . 1M 83
Linden Gro. PO11: Hay I . . . 9A 158
RH16: Lind . . . 3H 73
Linden Lodge BN11: Wor . . . 2G 171
(off Tennyson Rd.)
Linden Pk. BN17: L'ton . . . 3J 167
Linden Rd. BN17: L'ton . . . 3J 167
PO21: Bog R . . . 8C 164
Lindens, The BN2: Brig . . . 3G 172
RH10: Copt . . . 1C 12
Lindens Cl. PO10: Ems . . . 3F 136
Linden Way PO9: Hav . . . 2A 136
LINDFIELD . . . 2J 73
Lindfield BN41: Ports . . . 4D 152
(off Windlesham Cl.)
Lindfield Cl. BN2: Salt . . . 2B 174
Lindfield Ct. BN1: Brig . . . 4D 154
(off The Crestway)
Lindfield Ent. Pk. RH16: Lind . . . 3K 73
Lindfield Golf Course . . . 1N 73
Lindfield Rd. RH16: Ard . . . 3J 51
RH17: Ard . . . 3J 51
Lindgren Wlk. RH11: Craw . . . 2D 28
Lindisfarne Ho. RH11: Craw . . . 8D 10
(off St Aidan Cl.)
Lindsey Ct. PO22: Felp . . . 6H 165
Lindum Rd. BN13: W Tar . . . 8D 148
Lindum Way BN13: Wor . . . 8D 148
Linemans Vw. BN43: Shor S . . . 6H 151
(off Broad Reach)
Lineside Ind. Est. BN17: Wick . . . 2H 167
Lineside Way BN17: Wick . . . 2H 167
Linfield Cl. BN16: Ang . . . 9F 146
Linfield Copse RH20: Thake . . . 1L 107
Linfield La. RH20: A'ton . . . 1E 108
Linfields, The RH20: Thake . . . 1L 107
Lingfield Cl. BN13: Salv . . . 7D 148
PO10: W'brne . . . 1H 137
Lingfield Dr. RH10: Craw . . . 5N 11
Lingfield Rd. RH19: E Grin . . . 1D 14
Lingfield Way PO20: Sel . . . 3J 183
Link, The RH11: Craw . . . 6F 10
(not continuous)
Link 10 RH10: Craw . . . 3H 11
Link Dr. RH20: Pulb . . . 6B 86
Link Hill RH20: Storr . . . 6G 107
Link La. RH20: Pulb . . . 6B 86
Link Pl. BN1: Brig . . . 4C 154
Links, The PO20: Sel . . . 1J 183
Links Av. BN10: Peace . . . 5N 175
PO22: Felp . . . 8G 164
Links Cl. BN41: Ports . . . 5E 152
PO9: Row C . . . 5B 116
Links La. PO9: Row C . . . 4B 116
Links Rd. BN14: Fin V . . . 5E 148
BN15: Lan . . . 7C 150
BN41: Ports . . . 5E 152
Link Way PO21: Pag . . . 2C 180
Linkway, The BN1: Brig . . . 4C 154
BN11: Wor . . . 1G 170
Linnell Cl. RH11: Craw . . . 3D 28
Linnet Cl. BN17: Wick . . . 9J 145
GU31: Peters . . . 7J 55
Linnett Cl. RH10: Turn H . . . 7K 13
Linthouse Cl. BN10: Peace . . . 2K 175
Linton Ho. GU28: Till . . . 8K 61
Linton Rd. BN3: Hove . . . 5H 153
Lintot Sq. RH13: Southw . . . 9K 45
(off Fairbank Rd.)
Lintott Gdns. RH13: Hors . . . 8B 26
Lion Cl. GU27: Has . . . 4H 17
Lion Ct. PO21: Pag . . . 1D 180
(off Mill Pk. Rd.)
Lionel Av. PO22: Felp . . . 6K 165
Lion Grn. GU27: Has . . . 5H 17
Lion La. GU27: Has . . . 3H 17
RH10: Turn H . . . 8H 13
Lion Mead GU27: Has . . . 5H 17
Lion M. BN3: Hove . . . 6H 153
Lion Rd. PO21: Pag . . . 1C 180
Lions Ct. BN2: Brig . . . 8F 154
Lions Dene BN1: Brig . . . 1M 153
Lions Gdns. BN1: Brig . . . 3M 153
Lions Ga. BN3: Hove . . . 4G 152
Lion St. PO19: Chich . . . 7C 140
LIPHOOK . . . 8A 16
Liphook Cl. BN1: Brig . . . 4D 154
Liphook Golf Course . . . 2K 35
Liphook Ho. PO9: Hav . . . 9B 116
Liphook Rd. GU27: Has . . . 5G 17
GU27: Has, Linch, Lip . . . 8B 16
GU30: Lip . . . 8B 16
LIPSCOMB'S CORNER . . . 5C 8
Lisher Rd. BN15: Lan . . . 6C 150
Lisle Way PO10: Ems . . . 2E 136
Lismore Cres. RH11: Craw . . . 9D 10
LISS FOREST . . . 4A 34
Lister Av. RH19: E Grin . . . 6E 14
Listers RH17: W'lid . . . 9C 48
Litten Ter. PO19: Chich . . . 6C 140
Little Ashfield GU29: Midh . . . 9G 59
Little Babbsham PO21: Aldw . . . 1G 181
Lit. Barn Pl. GU33: Liss . . . 6A 34
Little Bentswood RH16: Hay H . . . 4G 73
Lit. Bentswood Cl. RH16: Hay H . . . 4G 73
Lit. Black Hill RH16: Lind . . . 2J 73
LITTLE BOGNOR . . . 2E 84
Little Boultons PO20: Huns . . . 4B 162
Little Breach PO19: Chich . . . 4B 140
Lit. Bridges Cl. RH13: Southw . . . 9K 45
Little Cl. RH13: Southw . . . 2K 67
LITTLE COMMON . . . 9G 61
Little Comptons RH13: Hors . . . 9C 26
Lit. Copse Rd. BN6: Hass . . . 2N 113
Littlecote GU28: Petw . . . 1N 83
Lit. Cote Ho. RH16: Lind . . . 1J 73
Lit. Court Cl. GU29: Midh . . . 9F 58
Little Crabtree RH11: Craw . . . 5E 10
Little Cres. BN2: Rott . . . 3A 174
Littlecroft Caravan Pk. PO20: Earn . . . 1A 178
Lit. Dipper's RH20: Pulb . . . 7B 86
Little Dr. BN12: Fer . . . 3K 169
Little Drove BN44: Bramb . . . 4A 130
Lit. East St. BN1: Brig . . . 9E 172 (9B 154)
RH14: Bill . . . 9J 43
Littlefield Cl. PO20: Sel . . . 3J 183
Littlefield Rd. PO19: Chich . . . 8D 140
Lit. Finches RH13: Part G . . . 5D 90
Little Gables BN13: Durr . . . 7D 148
Lit. George St. BN2: Brig . . . 8F 172 (8B 154)
Little Grebe RH12: Hors . . . 6N 25
Littlegreen Av. PO9: Hav . . . 1A 136
Lit. Hammer La. GU26: Has . . . 3E 16
LITTLEHAMPTON . . . 3K 167
Littlehampton By-Pass BN17: L'ton, Wick . . . 1H 167
Littlehampton Caravan Club Site
BN17: Wick . . . 8K 145
Littlehampton Golf Club . . . 4J 167
Littlehampton Marina BN17: L'ton . . . 3H 167
Littlehampton Mus. . . . 3L 167
Littlehampton Rd. BN12: Fer, Gor S . . . 1H 169
BN13: Gor S, Salv, Wor . . . 1H 169
BN16: Fer . . . 1H 169
Littlehampton Station (Rail) . . . 3K 167
Littlehampton Swimming & Sports Cen. . . . 5M 167
Little Hatch RH12: Hors . . . 6C 26
LITTLE HAVEN . . . 6B 26
Littlehaven La. RH12: Hors . . . 6C 26
Littlehaven Station (Rail) . . . 6C 26
LITTLE HEATH . . . 9G 122
Littleheath Rd. BN18: Font . . . 2F 142
Little High St. BN11: Wor . . . 1H 171
BN43: Shor S . . . 6H 151
PO21: Bog R . . . 1L 181
Little Hill RH20: W Chil . . . 8H 87
Lit. King St. RH19: E Grin . . . 3E 14
Little Ledgers RH17: Cuck . . . 3A 72
LITTLE LONDON . . . 9H 31
Little London PO19: Chich . . . 7C 140
Lit. London Hill RH12: Warnh . . . 2L 25
Little Mead BN12: Gor S . . . 2A 170
(off Marlborough Rd.)
Little Oak RH13: Part G . . . 5C 90
Little Oak Bonsai . . . 9B 162
Little Oaks RH19: E Grin . . . 1D 14
(off Springfield)
Lit. Paddock Cl. RH11: Craw . . . 4C 10
Little Paddocks BN12: Fer . . . 3K 169
Lit. Paddocks Way BN12: Fer . . . 3L 169
Lit. Park Enterprises RH11: Ifield . . . 1A 10
Lit. Park La. BN6: Hurst . . . 1J 113
Little Pembrokes BN11: Wor . . . 1E 170
Lit. Preston St. BN1: Brig . . . 8B 172 (8N 153)
Littlestone Rd. BN13: Durr . . . 7C 148
Little Todham GU29: S Amb . . . 2M 81
Littleton Gro. PO9: Hav . . . 1A 136
Lit. Western St. BN1: Brig . . . 7A 172 (8M 153)
LITTLEWORTH . . . 3D 90
Littleworth Cl. BN2: W'dean . . . 6N 155
Littleworth La. RH13: Cow, W Grin, Part G . . . 7D 68
Liverpool Bldgs. BN11: Wor . . . 2H 171
(off Liverpool Rd.)
Liverpool Gdns. BN11: Wor . . . 2H 171
Liverpool Rd. BN11: Wor . . . 2H 171
Liverpool Row BN11: Wor . . . 2H 171
Liverpool Ter. BN11: Wor . . . 2H 171
Livesay Cres. BN14: Broadw . . . 9H 149
Livingstone Ho. BN3: Hove . . . 6K 153
Livingstone Rd. BN3: Hove . . . 6K 153
RH10: Craw . . . 8G 11
RH13: Hors . . . 1A 46
RH15: Burg H . . . 5A 94
Livingstone St. BN2: Brig . . . 8E 154
LivingWell Health Club
Brighton . . . 8B 172
Lizard Head BN17: L'ton . . . 2N 167
Llandaff Ct. BN11: Wor . . . 2E 170
Lloyd Cl. BN3: Hove . . . 4L 153
Lloyd Goring Cl. BN16: Ang . . . 7E 146
Lloyd Rd. BN3: Hove . . . 5L 153
PO19: Chich . . . 4C 140
Lloyds Ct. RH10: Craw . . . 3G 11
Loats La. PO21: Bers . . . 5A 164
Lobster La. PO20: Sel . . . 2F 182
Lobs Wood La. RH20: Storr . . . 5J 107
LOCK . . . 6N 89
Lockerley Rd. PO9: Hav . . . 2A 136
Lockgate Rd. PO20: Sidle . . . 9L 161
Lockhart Ct. RH16: Hay H . . . 7G 72
Lock La. PO20: Bir . . . 5J 161
RH13: Part G . . . 6B 90
Locksash Cl. PO20: W Witt . . . 1F 176
Locksash La. PO18: Mard . . . 7L 97
Locks Ct. BN42: S'wck . . . 6A 152
Locks Cres. BN41: Ports . . . 5D 152
Locks Hill BN41: Ports . . . 4D 152
Lockwood Cl. BN2: W'dean . . . 6M 155
RH12: Hors . . . 6D 26
Lockwood Ct. RH10: Craw . . . 4H 11
Lockwood Cres. BN2: W'dean . . . 5M 155
Loddon Cl. BN13: Durr . . . 5A 148
Loder Gdns. BN14: Broadw . . . 8G 149
Loder Pl. BN1: Brig . . . 3A 154
Loder Rd. BN1: Brig . . . 3A 154
Loders RH17: Ard . . . 2J 51
Lodge, The BN2: Brig . . . 5C 154
Lodgebury Cl. PO10: S'brne . . . 5K 137
Lodge Cl. BN41: Ports . . . 3B 152
PO22: Midd S . . . 7A 166
RH11: Craw . . . 6E 10
RH19: E Grin . . . 3C 14
Lodge Ct. BN43: Shor S . . . 4H 151
PO21: Aldw . . . 1G 181
Lodge Grn. GU28: Dunc . . . 8M 83
Lodge Hill La. BN6: Ditch . . . 3D 114
Lodgelands RH17: Ard . . . 4J 51
Lodge La. BN6: Key . . . 4B 114
PO9: Row C . . . 9J 97
RH17: Bol . . . 6D 70
Lodge Wlk. RH6: Horl . . . 2H 5
(off Thornton Pl.)
Lodsden La. PO18: Mid L . . . 5M 119
LODSWORTH . . . 6C 60
Lodsworth BN2: Brig . . . 5G 154
Lodsworth Cl. BN2: Brig . . . 6F 154
Lodsworth Rd. PO21: Pag . . . 9K 163
Lombard St. GU28: Petw . . . 9N 61
Lomond Av. BN1: Brig . . . 7C 134
London Flds. Ho. RH11: Craw . . . 2E 28
LONDON GATWICK AIRPORT
North Terminal . . . 5G 5
South Terminal . . . 6J 5
London La. RH17: Cuck . . . 3A 72
London Rd. BN1: Brig . . . 1M 153
(Coolwater Pk.)
BN1: Brig . . . 7M 133
(Mill Rd. Rdbt.)
BN1: Brig . . . 3E 172 (6B 154)
(Viaduct Rd.)
BN5: Henf . . . 7H 91
(not continuous)
BN6: Alb, Newt, Say C . . . 1F 112
BN6: Hass . . . 3M 113
BN18: Arun, Houg . . . 5E 124
BN18: Font . . . 2H 143
BN45: Newt, Pye . . . 9K 113
GU28: N'chpl, Petw . . . 5H 39
GU31: Hill B, Peters . . . 4H 55
GU33: Hill B, Liss, Rake . . . 9A 34
PO21: Bog R . . . 9E 164
RH10: Craw, Lowf H . . . 5F 10
RH11: Craw . . . 4F 10
RH12: Hors . . . 9N 25
RH15: Burg H . . . 3A 94
RH17: Bal, Cuck . . . 4A 30
RH17: Cuck . . . 1N 71
RH17: Dane . . . 6G 53
RH18: F Row . . . 8L 15
RH19: E Grin . . . 1A 14
RH20: Cold, Pulb . . . 2H 105
(not continuous)
RH20: Wash, A'ton . . . 9B 108
(not continuous)
London Road Station (Rail) . . . 1F 172 (5B 154)
London St. BN11: Wor . . . 1G 171
London Ter. BN1: Brig . . . 3F 172 (6B 154)
Loney Ct. BN43: Shor S . . . 5M 151
Long Acre PO20: Sel . . . 4H 183
RH10: Craw D . . . 4H 13
Longacre Cl. GU33: Liss . . . 6A 34
Longacre Cres. RH17: Cuck . . . 1A 72
Longacre La. PO20: Sel . . . 4H 183
Longacre Pk. BN18: Yap . . . 8N 143
Long Bostle Rd. GU28: Graff . . . 2N 101
Longbridge Ga. RH6: Gatw . . . 5G 5
(off Arrivals Rd.)
Longbridge Rd. RH6: Horl . . . 4H 5
Longbridge Rdbt. RH6: Horl . . . 3G 5
Longbridge Wlk. RH6: Horl . . . 4H 5
Longbridge Way RH6: Gatw . . . 4H 5
Longbrook PO22: Felp . . . 9G 164
Longchamps Cl. RH6: Horl . . . 2L 5
Long Cl. RH10: Craw . . . 6M 11
Long Copse Ct. PO10: Ems . . . 1F 136
Long Copse La. PO10: Ems, W'brne . . . 1F 136
Long Croft, The RH14: Wisb . . . 1B 64
Longcroft BN43: Shor S . . . 6H 151

Longdene Rd.—Manor Paddock

Longdene Rd. GU27: Has . . . 5K 17
Long Down GU31: Peters . . . 5H 55
Longfellow Cl. RH12: Hors . . . 4B 26
Longfellow Rd. BN11: Wor . . . 1F 170
Longfield Rd. PO10: Ems . . . 2E 136
RH12: Hors . . . 2L 45
Longford Rd. PO21: Bog R . . . 9D 164
Long Furlong BN13: Clap, Fin, Pat . . . 5K 147
BN14: Fin . . . 1L 147
Long Furlong La. BN13: Pat . . . 1K 147
Longhill Cl. BN2: O'dean . . . 9M 155
Longhill Rd. BN2: O'dean . . . 9L 155
Long Ho. La. RH13: Cow . . . 5M 69
RH17: Bol, Cow . . . 5M 69
Longhurst RH15: Burg H . . . 6E 94
Longhurst Av. RH12: Hors . . . 9J 25
Longhurst Rd. RH11: Craw . . . 2C 28
Longland Av. RH20: Storr . . . 5H 107
Longlands BN14: Char D . . . 5H 149
Longlands Glade BN14: Char D . . . 5H 149
Longlands Rd. PO10: S'brne . . . 5K 137
PO20: E Witt . . . 5J 177
Longlands Spinney BN14: Char D . . . 5H 149
Long La. BN18: Arun . . . 9C 124
PO18: Mard . . . 4C 98
Longley Ind. Est. BN1: Brig . . . 3E 172 (6B 154)
Long Mead BN18: Walb . . . 4L 143
Long Meadow BN14: Fin V . . . 1D 148
Longmeadow Gdns. PO20: Bir . . . 8H 161
Long Meadow Vs. RH6: Charlw . . . 8A 4
Longmere Rd. RH10: Craw . . . 4F 10
LONGMOOR CAMP . . . 1B 34
Long Pk. Cnr. BN6: Ditch . . . 5E 114
Longport Rd. PO22: Felp . . . 8J 165
Longridge Av. BN2: Salt . . . 4C 174
Long Rd. GU32: Peters . . . 4G 54
RH13: Lwr Bee . . . 9J 47
Longships BN17: L'ton . . . 2N 167
Longstock Rd. PO9: Hav . . . 8B 116
Long Wlk. BN7: Plump . . . 7N 115
RH16: Hay H . . . *5J 73*
(off Walnut Pk.)
Longwall RH19: E Grin . . . 1A 14
Longwood Vw. RH10: Craw . . . 9J 11
Looes Barn Cl. BN2: Salt . . . 1D 174
Look & Sea! . . . 4K 167
Lookout, The BN10: Peace . . . 1J 175
Loop, The PO22: Felp . . . 8K 165
Loose La. BN15: Somp . . . 8L 149
Loppets Rd. RH10: Craw . . . 8H 11
Lordings La. RH20: W Chil . . . 9J 87
Lordings Rd. RH14: Bill, Adv . . . 1F 64
LORDINGTON . . . 6N 117
Lordington Ct. PO18: Wald . . . 6M 117
Loriners RH10: Craw . . . 9F 10
Loriners Ct. BN3: Hove . . . 5F 152
Lorna Rd. BN3: Hove . . . 6L 153
Lorne Rd. BN1: Brig . . . 2F 172 (5B 154)
Lorne Vs. BN1: Brig . . . 3N 153
Lorraine Ct. BN3: Hove . . . 4A 172
(Davigdor Rd.)
BN3: Hove . . . 7K 153
(Osborne Vs.)
Lotts La. BN15: Somp . . . 7N 149
Loudoun Rd. BN17: L'ton . . . 2J 167
Louvain Gdns. BN10: Tels C . . . 2H 175
Loveders Camping & Caravan Site
PO18: Nutb . . . 5L 137
Lovegrove Ct. BN3: Hove . . . 5G 153
Love La. GU31: Peters . . . 5G 54
RH20: Storr . . . 6J 107
Loveletts RH11: Craw . . . 7C 10
Lovell Path RH11: Ifield . . . 7A 10
Lovells Cl. PO21: Aldw . . . 1D 180
Lovers La. RH13: Hors . . . 4N 45
Lover's Wlk. BN1: Brig . . . 1C 172 (5A 154)
Lover's Wlk. Cotts. BN1: Brig . . . 1C 172 (5A 154)
Lovett Ct. BN12: Gor S . . . 9A 148
Loveys Rd. BN18: Yap . . . 2N 165
Lowdell's Cl. RH19: E Grin . . . 1C 14
Lowdells Dr. RH19: E Grin . . . 1C 14
Lowdells La. RH19: E Grin . . . 1B 14
Lowe Cl. RH11: Craw . . . 3D 28
Lwr. Barn Cl. RH12: Hors . . . 6C 26
Lwr. Beach Rd. BN43: Shor B . . . 7J 151
LOWER BEEDING . . . 7K 47
LOWER BEVENDEAN . . . 4G 155
Lwr. Bevendean Av. BN2: Brig . . . 4F 154
Lwr. Bognor Rd. PO20: Lag . . . 6K 163
PO21: Aldw, Lag . . . 8N 163
Lwr. Breache Rd. GU6: Ewh . . . 1A 6
Lwr. Chalvington Pl. BN2: Brig . . . 8F 154
Lwr. Church Rd. RH15: Burg H . . . 5A 94
LOWER COKEHAM . . . 8N 149
Lower Dene RH19: E Grin . . . 3G 14
Lower Dr. BN42: S'wck . . . 4A 152
Lwr. Faircox BN5: Henf . . . 2G 110
LOWER FITTLEWORTH . . . 6F 84
Lower Gro. Rd. PO9: Hav . . . 4A 136
Lower Hanger GU27: Has . . . 5E 16
Lower Heyshott GU31: Peters . . . 6G 54
Lwr. Hone La. PO18: Bosh . . . 3D 160
Lowerhouse La. RH5: For G, Wall . . . 1A 6
Lwr. Jordans La. RH20: Pulb . . . 5H 87
Lower Lodge Shooting Grounds . . . 9L 23
Lwr. Market St. BN3: Hove . . . 8M 153
Lower Mead GU31: Peters . . . 6H 55
Lower Mere RH19: E Grin . . . 4F 14
Lower Rd. GU27: G'wd . . . 1A 18
PO18: E Lav . . . 9C 120
RH18: F Row . . . 9M 15
Lwr. Rock Gdns. BN2: Brig . . . 9C 154
Lower Sq. RH18: F Row . . . 9M 15
LOWER STANDEAN . . . 3B 134
Lwr. Station Rd. BN5: Henf . . . 3G 110
RH14: Bill . . . 3J 65
Lower St. GU27: Has . . . 5K 17
RH20: Fitt . . . 5F 84
RH20: Pulb . . . 6A 86
Lwr. Tanbridge Way RH12: Hors . . . 9M 25
Lwr. Tye Caravan & Camping Cen.
PO11: Hay I . . . 3B 158
Lower Village RH16: Hay H . . . 7D 72

Lwr. Walls Wlk. *PO19: Chich* . . . *7C 140*
(off Keats Way)
Lower Wardown GU31: Peters . . . 5H 55
(not continuous)
Lowestoft Wlk. RH10: Craw . . . 8K 11
LOWFIELD HEATH . . . 8G 5
Lowfield Heath Rd. RH6: Charlw, Gatw . . . 7B 4
Lowfield Heath Rdbt. *RH10: Lowf H* . . . *9G 4*
(off London Rd.)
Lowfield Rd. RH13: Slinf . . . 8B 24
RH16: Hay H . . . 6G 72
Lowfield Way RH11: Lowf H . . . 8G 5
LOW HEATH . . . 2D 84
Lowlands Rd. RH15: Burg H . . . 3C 94
Lowther Rd. BN1: Brig . . . 3B 154
BN13: Durr . . . 6D 148
Loxley Gdns. BN14: Wor . . . 9G 148
Loxmeadow Cl. RH14: Ifol . . . 8K 21
LOXWOOD . . . 7M 21
Loxwood BN16: E Pres . . . 1G 169
Loxwood Av. BN14: Wor . . . 7F 148
Loxwood Farm Pl. RH14: Lox . . . 8M 21
Loxwood Rd. GU6: Alf . . . 3M 21
RH12: Rudg . . . 7D 22
RH14: Lox . . . 8N 21
RH14: Plais . . . 9F 20
Loxwood Wlk. RH11: Craw . . . 4B 10
(not continuous)
Loyal Pde. BN1: Brig . . . 9L 133
Luard Ct. PO9: Warbl . . . 4B 136
Lucas RH17: Hors K . . . 5D 52
Lucas Cl. RH10: Craw . . . 9K 11
RH19: E Grin . . . 3G 14
Lucas Fld. GU27: Has . . . 5G 17
Lucas Grange RH16: Hay H . . . 3E 72
Lucas Rd. RH12: Warnh . . . 3J 25
Lucastes Av. RH16: Hay H . . . 3D 72
Lucastes La. RH16: Hay H . . . 4D 72
Lucastes Rd. RH16: Hay H . . . 4D 72
Lucas Way RH16: Hay H . . . 4D 72
Lucerne Cl. BN41: Ports . . . 4D 152
Lucerne Ct. PO21: Aldw . . . 1G 180
Lucerne Dr. RH10: Craw . . . 9M 11
Lucerne Rd. BN1: Brig . . . 4A 154
Lucking La. PO22: Midd S . . . 7N 165
Luckista Pk. RH20: A'ton . . . 9D 88
Lucksfield Way BN16: Ang . . . 8F 146
Lucraft Rd. BN2: Brig . . . 9G 135
Ludlow Cl. PO21: Aldw . . . 1G 180
Ludlow Ct. BN11: Wor . . . 2K 171
Ludlow Ri. BN2: Brig . . . 4H 155
Luffs Mdw. GU28: N'chpl . . . 3H 39
Luggs Cl. RH14: Bill . . . 1J 65
Luker Dr. GU31: Peters . . . 4G 54
Lulham Cl. BN10: Tels C . . . 2H 175
Lullington Av. BN3: Hove . . . 5H 153
Lulworth Cl. PO11: Hay I . . . 7A 158
RH11: Craw . . . 9C 10
Lumberpit La. BN7: Plump G . . . 6N 95
BN8: N Cha, Plump G, S Chai . . . 6N 95
LUMLEY . . . 4G 137
Lumley Ct. RH6: Horl . . . 1J 5
Lumley Gdns. PO10: S'brne . . . 5G 137
Lumley Path PO10: Ems . . . 4G 136
Lumley Rd. PO10: S'brne . . . 4G 136
RH6: Horl . . . 1J 5
Lumley Ter. PO10: Ems . . . 4G 136
Lunce's Hill RH16: Hay H, Wivel . . . 9G 73
RH17: Wivel . . . 9G 73
Lund Ho. GU28: Petw . . . 1N 83
Lundy Cl. BN17: L'ton . . . 4N 167
RH11: Craw . . . 9E 10
Lupin Cl. BN17: L'ton . . . 1N 167
Lureland Ct. BN10: Peace . . . 6J 175
LURGASHALL . . . 7E 38
Lurgashall RH15: Burg H . . . 6D 94
Lurgashall Winery . . . 6C 38
Lustrells Cl. BN2: Salt . . . 2B 174
Lustrells Cres. BN2: Salt . . . 2B 174
Lustrells Rd. BN2: Rott . . . 2A 174
Lustrells Va. BN2: Salt . . . 2B 174
Lutener Rd. GU29: Ease . . . 8H 59
Luth, The RH14: Wisb . . . 9A 42
(Carters Way)
RH14: Wisb . . . 1N 63
(Petworth Rd.)
Luther M. BN2: Brig . . . 6D 154
Luther St. BN2: Brig . . . 6D 154
Lutman St. PO10: Ems . . . 1E 136
Lutyens Cl. RH11: Craw . . . 8A 10
Luxford Cl. RH12: Hors . . . 6C 26
Luxford Rd. RH16: Lind . . . 2J 73
Luxford's La. RH19: E Grin . . . 7H 15
Luxford Way RH14: Bill . . . 2H 65
Lychgates, The BN18: Yap . . . 9N 143
Lychpole Wlk. BN12: Gor S . . . 9N 147
Lydon Ho. RH11: Craw . . . 3F 10
LYE COMMON . . . 9A 98
Lyefield La. RH5: For G . . . 1A 6
Lye La. PO18: E Ash, W Sto . . . 1H 139
Lymbourn Rd. PO9: Hav . . . 4A 136
LYMINSTER . . . 7K 145
Lyminster Av. BN1: Brig . . . 1B 154
Lyminster Rd. BN17: Lym, Wick . . . 7K 145
BN18: Cross . . . 4K 145
Lynch Down PO18: Funt . . . 8C 118
Lynchet Cl. BN1: Brig . . . 3D 154
Lynchet Down BN1: Brig . . . 3D 154
Lynchets Cres. BN3: Hove . . . 2F 152
Lynchette, The BN43: Shor S . . . 4J 151
Lynchet Wlk. BN1: Brig . . . 3D 154
Lynchmere Av. BN15: N Lan . . . 5A 150
Lynden Ct. BN1: Brig . . . 3N 153
Lyndhurst Cl. PO11: Hay I . . . 9A 158
RH11: Craw . . . 7F 10
Lyndhurst Cnr. *BN3: Hove* . . . *6M 153*
(off Lyndhurst Rd.)
Lyndhurst Ct. BN3: Hove . . . 6M 153
Lyndhurst Rd. BN3: Hove . . . 3A 172 (6M 153)
BN11: Wor . . . 2J 171
PO19: Chich . . . 8D 140
Lyndum Cl. GU32: Peters . . . 5F 54
Lyn Rd. BN13: Durr . . . 7A 148

Lynton Cl. BN6: Hurst . . . 2K 113
RH19: E Grin . . . 2F 14
Lynton Pk. Av. RH19: E Grin . . . 2F 14
Lynton Rd. GU32: Peters . . . 5E 54
Lyntons RH20: Pulb . . . 6N 85
Lynton St. BN2: Brig . . . 6D 154
LYNWICK . . . 3F 22
Lynwick St. RH12: Rudg . . . 4G 23
Lynwood Ct. RH12: Hors . . . 8N 25
Lynwood Rd. BN2: Salt . . . 4C 174
Lyon Cl. BN3: Hove . . . 6M 153
RH10: Craw . . . 1L 29
Lyon Ct. RH13: Hors . . . 9B 26
Lyons Cl. RH13: Slinf . . . 8B 24
Lyons Farm Est. RH13: Slinf . . . 9E 24
Lyons Farm Retail Pk. BN14: Char D . . . 6J 149
Lyons Rd. RH13: Slinf . . . 8B 24
Lyon St. PO21: Bog R . . . 9E 164
Lyon St. W. PO21: Bog R . . . 9E 164
Lyons Way BN14: Char D . . . 5J 149
Lyoth La. RH16: Hay H . . . 4J 73
Lyoth Vs. RH16: Hay H . . . 5K 73
Lyric Cl. RH10: Craw . . . 8M 11
Lysander Way PO20: Tang . . . 4M 141
LYTHE HILL . . . 5B 18
Lythe Hill Pk. GU27: Has . . . 6N 17
Lythe La. GU32: Stro . . . 3A 54
Lytton Dr. RH10: Craw . . . 5M 11

M

McIndoe Rd. RH19: E Grin . . . 1D 14
McIver Cl. RH19: Felb . . . 1N 13
Mackeral Cl. PO20: Sel . . . 2F 182
McKerchar Cl. BN15: Lan . . . 6C 150
MACKEREL'S COMMON . . . 5H 41
Mackie Av. BN1: Brig . . . 8A 134
BN6: Key . . . 2B 114
Mackintosh Dr. PO21: Bers . . . 5B 164
Mackley Ind. Est. BN5: Small D . . . 9J 111
Macklin Rd. PO22: Bog R . . . 8F 164
Macleod Rd. RH13: Hors . . . 1B 46
(not continuous)
McNair Cl. PO20: Sel . . . 2H 183
McNair Ct. BN3: Hove . . . 6G 152
McRae Ct. PO20: Sel . . . 3H 183
McWilliam Rd. BN2: W'dean . . . 4K 155
Maddox Dr. RH10: Worth . . . 7M 11
MADEHURST . . . 5B 124
Madehurst Cl. BN2: Brig . . . 8E 154
BN16: E Pres . . . 4D 168
Madehurst Ct. *BN17: L'ton* . . . *3K 167*
(off Gloucester Rd.)
RH11: Craw . . . 9B 10
Madehurst Rd. BN18: Houg, Made . . . 7A 124
Madehurst Way BN17: L'ton . . . 2K 167
Madeira Av. BN11: Wor . . . 1J 171
PO22: Bog R . . . 8F 164
RH12: Hors . . . 9N 25
Madeira Colonnade *BN2: Brig* . . . *9C 154*
(off Madeira Dr.)
Madeira Dr. BN2: Brig . . . 9F 172 (9C 154)
Madeira Pde. PO22: Bog R . . . 7F 164
Madeira Pl. BN2: Brig . . . 9G 172 (9C 154)
Madeline Rd. GU31: Peters . . . 5F 54
Madgwick La. PO18: Westh . . . 4F 140
PO19: Westh . . . 4F 140
Maes Ct. RH15: Ditch . . . 4G 95
Mafeking Rd. BN2: Brig . . . 4D 154
Magdalene Cl. RH10: Craw . . . 3L 11
Magdalen Row GU32: Peters . . . 6E 54
Magellan Ter. RH10: Craw . . . 2J 11
Magistrates' Court
Brighton . . . 8G 172 (8C 154)
Chichester . . . 8C 140
Crawley . . . 6G 11
Horsham . . . 8A 26
Worthing . . . 2H 171
Magnolia Cl. BN13: Durr . . . 8N 147
Magnolia Ct. RH6: Horl . . . 2J 5
Magnus Pl. *BN43: Shor S* . . . *6H 151*
(off Broad Reach)
Magpie La. PO20: Sel . . . 1F 182
Magpie Rd. PO8: Ids . . . 1C 116
Magpie Wlk. PO8: Horn . . . 2A 116
RH10: Craw . . . 4H 11
MAIDENBOWER . . . 8L 11
Maidenbower Bus. Pk. RH10: Worth . . . 8N 11
Maidenbower Community Sports Cen. . . . 8K 11
Maidenbower Dr. RH10: Craw . . . 8L 11
Maidenbower La. RH10: Craw . . . 7L 11
(Blackett Rd.)
RH10: Craw . . . 8K 11
(Marion Rd.)
Maidenbower Pl. RH10: Craw . . . 8L 11
Maidenbower Sq. RH10: Craw . . . 8L 11
Maiden La. RH11: Craw . . . 4E 10
Maidment Ct. BN5: Henf . . . 1J 111
Main Dr. PO22: Midd S . . . 7N 165
Maine Ho. *RH13: Hors* . . . *5J 45*
(off The Avenue)
Maines Farm Rd. BN44: Up B . . . 5E 130
Mainland Av. PO20: N Mun . . . 1E 162
Main Rd. BN18: Yap . . . 1N 165
PO10: Nutb, S'brne . . . 5G 137
PO18: Bosh, Chid'm, Fish, Nutb . . . 6M 137
PO18: E Dean . . . 9L 101
PO20: Bir . . . 9F 160
Mainstone Rd. BN3: Hove . . . 6H 153
Maisemore Gdns. PO10: Ems . . . 6D 136
Maize Cft. RH6: Horl . . . 1L 5
Major Cl. BN1: Brig . . . 4C 154
Major's Hill RH10: Worth . . . 7D 12
Malcolm Cl. BN12: Fer . . . 3K 169
Malcolm Gdns. RH6: Hookw . . . 4F 4
Malcolm Rd. PO20: Tang . . . 3L 141
(not continuous)
Malden Pl. RH20: Storr . . . 6J 107
Malden Way PO20: Sel . . . 3H 183
Maldon Rd. BN1: Brig . . . 3M 153
Malham Cl. RH10: Craw . . . 9L 11
Malines Av. BN10: Peace . . . 5G 175

Malines Av. Sth. BN10: Peace . . . 5G 175
Malin Rd. BN17: L'ton . . . 3N 167
Mallard Cl. GU27: Has . . . 5G 16
RH12: Hors . . . 6N 25
Mallard Cres. PO21: Pag . . . 4B 180
Mallard Pl. RH19: E Grin . . . 4F 14
Mallard Rd. PO9: Row C . . . 5B 116
Mallards La. PO20: Sel . . . 2F 182
Mallard Way BN5: Henf . . . 1H 111
PO10: W'brne . . . 1J 137
Mallion's La. RH17: S'fld . . . 7G 48
Mallon Dene BN16: Rust . . . 4B 168
Mallory Rd. BN3: Hove . . . 3L 153
Mallow Cl. RH12: Hors . . . 5B 26
Malmayne Ct. PO21: Aldw . . . 9N 163
Malthouse Cl. BN15: Somp . . . 6M 149
BN18: Arun . . . 3G 145
Malthouse Cotts. BN12: Gor S . . . 2A 170
GU29: C'ing . . . 9F 80
PO20: W Witt . . . 9A 160
Malthouse Ct. BN2: Brig . . . 8C 154
Malthouse La. BN2: Brig . . . 5G 172
BN6: Hurst . . . 8L 93
PO18: W Ash . . . 2E 138
RH15: Burg H . . . 5L 93
RH20: A'ton . . . 4C 108
Malthouse Pas. BN17: Wick . . . 2K 167
Malthouse Rd. PO20: Sel . . . 3J 183
RH10: Craw . . . 8F 10
Malthouse Trad. Est.
BN43: Shor S . . . 6L 151
Maltings, The GU30: Lip . . . 7A 16
GU31: Peters . . . 6F 54
PO19: Chich . . . 7B 140
RH14: Bill . . . *9J 43*
(off High St.)
RH15: Burg H . . . 4M 93
Maltings Grn. *BN44: Stey* . . . *4A 130*
(off Castle La.)
Maltravers Dr. BN17: L'ton . . . 4L 167
Maltravers Rd. BN17: L'ton . . . 4L 167
Maltravers St. BN18: Arun . . . 3G 145
Malvern Cl. BN11: Wor . . . 1M 171
Malvern M. PO10: Ems . . . 4F 136
Malvern Rd. GU33: Hill B . . . 8A 34
RH11: Craw . . . 7E 10
Malvern St. BN3: Hove . . . 6K 153
Malvern Way PO21: Pag . . . 2D 180
Malwood Cl. PO9: Hav . . . 8A 116
Manaton Cl. RH16: Hay H . . . 5G 72
Manchester St. BN2: Brig . . . 9F 172 (9B 154)
Mandalay Ct. BN1: Brig . . . 1M 153
Manet Sq. PO22: Bers . . . 6C 164
Manhattan Ct. *BN1: Brig* . . . *1M 153*
(off Tongdean La.)
Manhood Cotts. PO20: Sidle . . . 4C 178
Manhood La. PO20: Sidle . . . 3J 179
Manitoba Way BN13: Durr . . . 7A 148
Manley's Hill RH20: Storr . . . 6J 107
Mann Cl. RH11: Craw . . . 3D 28
Manning Cl. RH19: E Grin . . . 2D 14
Manning Rd. BN17: Wick . . . 1J 167
Mannings BN43: Shor S . . . 6J 151
Mannings Cl. RH10: Craw . . . 3M 11
MANNINGS HEATH . . . 4F 46
Mannings Heath Golf Course . . . 3H 47
Mannock Rd. PO20: Tang . . . 4K 141
Manor, The BN11: Wor . . . 2F 170
Manor Av. BN6: Key . . . 2B 114
Manor Cl. BN2: Brig . . . 8F 154
BN5: Henf . . . 2J 111
BN11: Wor . . . 2F 170
BN15: Lan . . . 6C 150
BN16: E Pres . . . 3E 168
BN42: S'wck . . . 5C 152
GU27: Has . . . 5G 16
PO9: Hav . . . 4A 136
PO19: Chich . . . 1B 162
PO22: Felp . . . 8H 165
RH6: Horl . . . 2H 5
RH14: Bill . . . 9J 43
RH15: Burg H . . . 4E 94
RH20: Storr . . . 6J 107
Manor Copse PO22: Felp . . . 8H 165
Manor Ct. BN11: Wor . . . 3F 170
BN15: N Lan . . . 5A 150
BN42: S'wck . . . 6C 152
PO22: Midd S . . . *7B 166*
(off Manor Way)
RH10: Craw . . . 3H 11
RH12: Hors . . . 6D 26
RH15: Burg H . . . 3D 94
RH20: Storr . . . *6J 107*
(off Church St.)
Manor Cres. BN2: Brig . . . 8F 154
GU27: Has . . . 5G 16
Manor Dr. BN10: Tels C . . . 3H 175
RH6: Horl . . . 2H 5
RH17: Cuck . . . 2N 71
Mnr. Farm Cl. PO20: Sel . . . 2J 183
Mnr. Farm Ct. PO20: Sel . . . 2J 183
PO22: Midd S . . . 7B 166
Manor Fld. Ct. BN14: Broadw . . . 8H 149
Manor Flds. RH13: Hors . . . 7D 26
Manorfields RH11: Craw . . . 1N 27
Manor Gdns. BN2: Brig . . . 8F 154
BN6: Hurst . . . 1H 113
BN16: Rust . . . 3A 168
PO10: S'brne . . . 4K 137
Manor Ga. RH10: Craw . . . 3H 11
Manor Grn. BN2: Brig . . . 8F 154
Manor Hall Rd. BN42: S'wck . . . 5B 152
Manor Hill BN2: Brig . . . 7E 154
Manor Ho. BN11: Wor . . . 2F 170
Manor Ho. Pl. BN15: N Lan . . . 5C 150
Manor La. PO20: S Mun . . . 6F 162
PO20: Sel . . . 2K 183
RH13: Hors . . . 2E 46
Manor Lea BN11: Wor . . . 3F 170
GU27: Has . . . 5G 17
Mnr. Lodge Rd. PO9: Row C . . . 4A 116
Manor Oaks RH15: Burg H . . . 4E 94
Manor Paddock BN2: Brig . . . 9F 154

Mnr. Paddock Ho.—Meath Green

Mnr. Paddock Ho. *BN2: Brig* . . . 9F 154
(off Manor Paddock)
Manor Pde. BN13: Durr . . . 6B 148
Manor Pk. BN15: Lan . . . 6C 150
PO21: Pag . . . 2C 180
Manor Pl. BN2: Brig . . . 9F 154
PO21: Bog R . . . 1L 181
Manor Rd. BN2: Brig . . . 9F 154
BN6: Hurst . . . 1H 113
BN11: Wor . . . 2F 170
BN15: N Lan . . . 5A 150
BN16: E Pres . . . 4F 168
BN16: Rust . . . 2A 168
BN41: Ports . . . 4D 152
BN44: Up B . . . 5E 130
PO10: S'brne . . . 4K 137
PO11: Hay I . . . 6A 158
PO20: Sel . . . 3J 183
RH12: Hors . . . 6D 26
RH15: Burg H . . . 3D 94
RH19: E Grin . . . 2C 14
Manor Royal RH10: Craw . . . 3G 10
Mnr. Royal Ind. Est. RH10: Craw . . . 3G 10
Manor Vw. Ct. BN14: Broadw . . . 8H 149
Manor Vs. PO18: Bosh . . . 8F 138
Manor Wlk. *RH6: Horl* . . . 2H 5
(off Manor Dr.)
Manor Way BN2: Brig . . . 8F 154
BN5: Henf . . . 2J 111
BN15: Lan . . . 6C 150
PO10: S'brne . . . 4K 137
PO11: Hay I . . . 9A 158
PO21: Aldw . . . 2D 180
PO22: Midd S . . . 7B 166
Mansell Ct. RH15: Burg H . . . 5C 94
Mansell Rd. BN43: Shor S . . . 5L 151
Mansergh Rd. PO19: Chich . . . 4D 140
Manser Rd. BN18: Walb . . . 4N 143
Mansfield Cl. BN11: Wor . . . 9L 149
Mansfield Cotts. PO18: Chid'm . . . 6A 138
Mansfield Rd. BN3: Hove . . . 6G 152
BN11: Wor . . . 1L 171
PO22: Bers, Bog R . . . 7C 164
Mansion Cl. RH15: Burg H . . . 5E 94
Mant Cl. BN17: Climp . . . 3D 166
RH20: Storr . . . 6J 107
Mantell Dr. RH17: Cuck . . . 3N 71
Mantell Ho. *BN2: Brig* . . . 8C 154
(off Lennox St.)
Mantling Rd. BN17: L'ton . . . 2K 167
Manton Cl. PO20: Brac . . . 6N 177
Manton Rd. BN2: Brig . . . 4F 154
Mant Rd. GU28: Petw . . . 1N 83
Maple Cl. BN2: W'dean . . . 6M 155
BN13: High S . . . 4C 148
PO10: Ems . . . 3F 136
PO22: Midd S . . . 6M 165
RH11: Craw . . . 3E 10
RH12: Hors . . . 6D 26
RH14: Bill . . . 9H 43
RH15: Burg H . . . 3D 94
RH16: Hay H . . . 6J 73
Maple Ct. BN11: Wor . . . 2D 170
RH15: Burg H . . . 5M 93
RH15: Ditch . . . 5G 95
Mapledown Cl. RH13: Southw . . . 8K 45
Maple Dr. RH15: Burg H . . . 3A 94
RH19: E Grin . . . 3G 15
Mapledurham La. GU32: West . . . 1C 76
Maple Gdns. BN3: Hove . . . 4G 153
PO22: Bers . . . 5D 164
Maple Grn. RH11: Craw . . . 7E 10
Maple Ho. BN2: Brig . . . 2G 172
BN12: Gor S . . . 9M 147
(off Goring Chase)
PO9: Hav . . . 3A 136
MAPLEHURST . . . 3C 68
Maplehurst Ct. RH14: Bill . . . 2K 65
Maplehurst Rd. BN41: Ports . . . 4C 152
PO19: Chich . . . 2D 140
RH13: Cow, Map, W Grin . . . 4C 68
Mapleleaf RH20: Cold . . . 1K 105
Maple Lodge GU27: Has . . . 7N 17
Maple Pde. *BN18: Walb* . . . 5M 143
(off Maple Rd.)
Maple Rd. BN10: Peace . . . 6M 175
BN18: Walb . . . 5M 143
RH14: Bill . . . 2J 65
Maples, The *BN6: Hurst* . . . 9J 93
(off Western Rd.)
BN12: Fer . . . 4L 169
PO21: Bog R . . . 9C 164
(off Hambledon Pl.)
Maple Wlk. BN15: Somp . . . 6M 149
BN16: Rust . . . 2B 168
GU31: Peters . . . 8F 54
Maplewood *BN1: Brig* . . . 2N 153
(off Curwen Pl.)
Mapsons La. PO20: Sidle . . . 9K 161
Marama Gdns. BN16: Rust . . . 5A 168
Marchants Cl. BN6: Hurst . . . 1J 113
Marchants Rd. BN6: Hurst . . . 1J 113
Marchants Way RH15: Burg H . . . 3A 94
March Cl. PO21: Aldw . . . 9L 163
Marches, The GU27: Fern . . . 5K 37
RH12: King . . . 7M 7
Marches Rd. RH12: Warnh, King . . . 8H 7
March Ho. BN3: Hove . . . 4K 153
March Sq. PO19: Chich . . . 2C 140
Marchwell Ind. Est. PO19: Chich . . . 3D 140
Marchwood PO19: Chich . . . 2C 140
Marchwood Ga. PO19: Chich . . . 2C 140
Marchwood M. PO19: Chich . . . 2C 140
Marcuse Flds. PO18: Bosh . . . 7D 138
Mardale Rd. BN13: Durr . . . 7D 148
Marden Av. PO19: Chich . . . 1A 162
Marden Cl. BN2: W'dean . . . 4M 155
Marden Ho. BN17: Wick . . . 1H 167
PO22: Barn . . . 7K 143
Mardens, The RH11: Craw . . . 5D 10
Marden Way GU31: Peters . . . 6G 54
Mardyke BN43: Shor B . . . 7G 151
MAREHILL . . . 7D 86
Marehill Comn. RH20: Pulb . . . 7D 86
Mare Hill Rd. RH20: Pulb . . . 7D 86
Maresfield Rd. BN2: Brig . . . 8F 154
Margaret Cl. PO21: Aldw . . . 9N 163
Margaret Ct. BN10: Peace . . . 5H 175
Margaret St. BN2: Brig . . . 9C 154
Margery Rd. BN3: Hove . . . 5F 152
Marian Way PO21: Bog R . . . 9F 164
Marigolds, The PO22: Shrip . . . 3E 164
Marigolds Lodge *BN16: Rust* . . . 4A 168
(off Holmes La.)
Marina Cl. PO10: Ems . . . 6G 137
Marina Ct. BN15: S Lan . . . 8F 150
Marina Water Tours . . . 8K 173
(off Village Sq.)
Marina Way BN2: Brig . . . 8K 173
(not continuous)
Marine Av. BN3: Hove . . . 7G 152
Marine Cl. BN2: Salt . . . 3B 174
BN11: Wor . . . 3E 170
PO20: W Witt . . . 5J 177
Marine Ct. *BN2: Rott* . . . 3A 174
(off Marine Dr.)
BN2: Salt . . . 4C 174
BN10: Tels C . . . 5F 174
BN17: L'ton . . . 4L 167
BN43: Shor B . . . 7G 150
PO21: Aldw . . . 1K 181
(off Nyewood La.)
Marine Cres. BN12: Gor S . . . 4A 170
Marine Dr. BN2: Brig, O'dean, Rott, Salt . . . 8K 173
BN12: Gor S . . . 4M 169
PO20: Sel . . . 3K 183
PO20: W Witt . . . 4H 177
(not continuous)
Marine Dr. W. PO20: W Witt . . . 4H 177
PO21: Aldw, Bog R . . . 1J 181
Marine Gdns. . . . 3E 170
Marine Gdns. BN2: Brig . . . 9C 154
PO20: Sel . . . 5H 183
Marine Ga. BN2: Brig . . . 8K 173
Marine Pde. BN2: Brig . . . 9F 172 (9C 154)
BN11: Wor . . . 3G 170
PO21: Bog R . . . 1K 181
Marine Path *BN2: Salt* . . . 3C 174
(off Saltdean Pk. Rd.)
Marine Pl. BN11: Wor . . . 2H 171
Marine Point BN11: Wor . . . 3E 170
Mariners PO21: Aldw . . . 1H 181
Mariners, The BN15: Lan . . . 1N 171
Mariners Cl. BN43: Shor B . . . 8G 150
Mariners Quay BN2: Brig . . . 8K 173
BN17: L'ton . . . 3J 167
Mariners Wlk. BN16: Rust . . . 4C 168
Marineside PO20: Brac . . . 6M 177
Marine Sq. BN2: Brig . . . 9D 154
Marine Ter. M. *BN2: Brig* . . . 9D 154
(off Bristol Rd.)
Marine Vw. BN2: Brig . . . 8C 154
Marine Wlk. PO11: Hay I . . . 9C 158
Marion Rd. RH10: Craw . . . 8K 11
Marisfield Pl. PO20: Sel . . . 2K 183
Marjoram Ct. *RH6: Horl* . . . 1L 5
(off Newman Rd.)
Marjoram Pl. BN43: Shor S . . . 4L 151
Market Av. PO19: Chich . . . 8C 140
Market Cl. PO22: Barn . . . 7J 143
Market Fld. BN44: Stey . . . 3B 130
Market House, The *RH19: E Grin* . . . 3F 14
(off Cantelupe Rd.)
Market Place . . . 7C 140
Market Pl. BN14: W Tar . . . 8E 148
GU29: Midh . . . 9H 59
(off Sheep La.)
RH15: Burg H . . . 6B 94
RH16: Hay H . . . 3E 72
Market Rd. PO19: Chich . . . 7C 140
Market Sq. GU28: Petw . . . 9N 61
GU29: Midh . . . 1H 81
RH12: Hors . . . 1N 45
Market St. BN1: Brig . . . 8E 172 (8B 154)
BN11: Wor . . . 2H 171
PO21: Bog R . . . 1L 181
Markfield PO22: Bers . . . 6C 164
Markway Cl. PO10: Ems . . . 4D 136
Markwick M. BN11: Wor . . . 1J 171
Marlborough Bus. Cen.
BN15: Lan . . . 9N 149
Marlborough Cl. PO19: Chich . . . 7F 140
RH11: Craw . . . 1E 28
RH12: Hors . . . 6A 26
Marlborough Ct. BN3: Hove . . . 6L 153
PO21: Aldw . . . 7A 164
RH15: Burg H . . . 5N 93
(off Condor Way)
Marlborough Dr. RH15: Burg H . . . 6D 94
Marlborough M. BN1: Brig . . . 7C 172 (8A 154)
Marlborough Pk. PO9: Hav . . . 2B 136
Marlborough Pl. BN1: Brig . . . 7F 172 (8B 154)
(not continuous)
RH12: Hors . . . 8M 25
(off Rushams Rd.)
Marlborough Rd. BN12: Gor S . . . 2A 170
BN15: Lan . . . 9N 149
Marlborough St. BN1: Brig . . . 7C 172 (8A 154)
Marlborough Way BN12: Gor S . . . 2B 170
Marldell Cl. PO9: Hav . . . 9A 116
Marle Av. RH15: Burg H . . . 4B 94
Marles La. RH14: T Haven . . . 1H 43
Marley Av. GU27: Has . . . 8G 17
Marley Combe Rd. GU27: Has . . . 6H 17
MARLEY COMMON . . . 8H 17
Marley Hanger GU27: Has . . . 8J 17
Marley Hgts. GU27: K Grn . . . 2H 37
Marley La. GU27: Has, K Grn . . . 6G 17
Marley Way RH20: Storr . . . 5K 107
Marlin Ct. BN15: S Lan . . . 9B 150
Marline Ct. BN43: Shor S . . . 6H 151
Marlinespike, The BN43: Shor B . . . 7K 151
Marlings, The RH16: Hay H . . . 6D 72
Marlipins Mus. . . . 6H 151
Marlow Ct. BN2: Brig . . . 6C 154
RH10: Craw . . . 5F 10
Marlow Dr. RH16: Hay H . . . 5K 73
Marlowe Cl. PO22: Midd S . . . 6M 165
Marlowe Rd. BN14: Broadw . . . 8J 149
Marlow Rd. BN2: Brig . . . 9G 154
Marlpit Cl. RH19: E Grin . . . 1E 14
Marlpit La. PO10: W'cote . . . 1N 137
PO20: Oving . . . 7J 141
Marlpit Rd. RH19: Sharp . . . 5A 32
Marlpost Rd. RH13: Br Grn, Southw . . . 2G 66
Marmion Rd. BN3: Hove . . . 6H 153
Marquis Way PO21: Aldw . . . 2G 181
Marringdean Rd. RH14: Bill . . . 3J 65
Marsden Ct. BN10: Tels C . . . 5G 174
Marshall Av. BN14: Fin V . . . 2D 148
PO21: Bog R . . . 8C 164
Marshall Cl. PO22: Barn . . . 8J 143
Marshall Rd. PO11: Hay I . . . 9C 158
RH10: Craw . . . 8L 11
Marshalls Row BN1: Brig . . . 4F 172 (6B 154)
Marshall Way BN3: Hove . . . 4H 153
Marsh Barns PO20: Runc . . . 2H 163
Marsh Ct. RH11: Craw . . . 2D 28
Marsh Ho. BN42: S'wck . . . 6N 151
Marshlands Cotts. RH5: Newd . . . 1F 8
Marsh La. PO18: Chid'm . . . 9N 137
PO18: E Lav . . . 7B 120
PO18: Tang . . . 3B 142
PO20: Oving, Runc . . . 3G 163
PO20: Tang . . . 3A 142
Marston Ct. BN3: Hove . . . 4A 172
Marston Rd. BN14: Broadw . . . 9J 149
Martello Ent. Cen. BN17: Wick . . . 9J 145
Martens Fld. BN7: Rod . . . 4L 157
Martha Gunn Rd. BN2: Brig . . . 4F 154
Martin Cl. RH11: Craw . . . 4F 10
Martineau Cl. PO21: Aldw . . . 2G 180
Martin Rd. BN3: Hove . . . 4F 152
PO9: Hav . . . 1A 136
Martins, The BN10: Tels C . . . 2H 175
RH10: Craw D . . . 4K 13
Martin's La. PO20: Bir . . . 7J 161
Martlet, The BN3: Hove . . . 5M 153
Martlet Cl. PO19: Chich . . . 8C 140
Martlet Ct. *BN2: Brig* . . . 8D 154
(off Hereford St.)
Martlet Ho. BN1: Brig . . . 1E 172 (5B 154)
BN2: Salt . . . 4D 174
Martlet Rd. GU28: Petw . . . 1M 83
Martlets RH20: W Chil . . . 8H 87
Martlets, The BN15: Somp . . . 7N 149
BN16: E Pres . . . 3F 168
BN16: Rust . . . 5N 167
(not continuous)
BN43: Shor S . . . 5J 151
RH10: Craw . . . 6G 10
RH15: Burg H . . . 5B 94
Martlets Cl. RH12: Hors . . . 6N 25
Martlets Ct. BN18: Arun . . . 3H 145
Martlets Trad. Est. BN12: Gor S . . . 1A 170
Martlets Way BN12: Gor S . . . 1A 170
Martletts Cnr. RH12: Rudg . . . 4J 23
Martlet Way PO21: Pag . . . 4B 180
Marts, The RH12: Rudg . . . 4J 23
Martyn Cl. BN5: Henf . . . 2H 111
Martyns Cl. BN2: O'dean . . . 9M 155
Martyns Pl. RH19: E Grin . . . 4F 14
Martyrs Av. RH11: Craw . . . 3E 10
Marvell Cl. RH10: Craw . . . 4L 11
Mary Coombs Ct. PO11: Hay I . . . 9A 158
Marylands RH16: Hay H . . . 4G 73
Marylands Cres. PO22: Bog R . . . 7F 164
Masefield Rd. RH11: Craw . . . 9A 10
Mash Barn La. BN15: Lan . . . 5D 150
Mason Cl. RH19: E Grin . . . 2E 14
Mason Rd. RH10: Craw . . . 8G 10
Masons Fld. RH13: Mann H . . . 4F 46
Masons Way RH20: Pulb . . . 3B 86
Massetts Rd. RH6: Horl . . . 3H 5
Matform Bus. Cen. PO19: Chich . . . 8A 140
Matlock Rd. BN1: Brig . . . 4M 153
Matthew Ho. *BN3: Hove* . . . 7J 153
(off Miles Wlk.)
Matthews Dr. RH10: Craw . . . 1K 29
Matthey Pl. RH10: Craw . . . 3M 11
MAUDLIN . . . 4H 141
Maudlin La. BN44: Bramb . . . 4A 130
Maudlyn Cl. BN44: Bramb . . . 5B 130
Maudlyn Pk. BN44: Bramb . . . 5A 130
Maudlyn Parkway BN44: Bramb . . . 5A 130
Mauldmare Cl. PO21: Aldw . . . 1H 181
Maunsell Pk. RH10: Craw . . . 6K 11
Max Millers Wlk. BN2: Brig . . . 9C 154
Maxton Wlk. RH11: Craw . . . 2D 28
Maxwell Rd. BN17: L'ton . . . 3J 167
BN18: Arun . . . 4F 144
Maxwell Way RH10: Craw . . . 3J 11
Maybridge Cres. BN12: Gor S . . . 1A 170
Maybridge Sq. BN12: Gor S . . . 9A 148
Maybush Dr. PO18: Chid'm . . . 6A 138
May Cl. BN12: Gor S . . . 9A 148
BN17: Climp . . . 3D 166
PO20: Sidle . . . 3J 179
PO22: Bog R . . . 7E 164
May Cotts. BN2: Brig . . . 5D 154
Maydwell Av. RH13: Slinf . . . 9N 23
Mayes Cl. RH10: Craw . . . 7L 11
MAYES GREEN . . . 1C 6
Mayes La. RH12: Warnh . . . 1J 25
Mayfair Ct. PO19: Chich . . . 6B 140
Mayfield BN16: E Pres . . . 1F 168
RH10: Worth . . . 6M 11
Mayfield Av. BN10: Peace . . . 6K 175
(not continuous)
Mayfield Cl. BN1: Brig . . . 9A 134
BN14: Fin V . . . 4E 148
PO21: Pag . . . 9K 163
Mayfield Ct. BN2: Salt . . . 2C 174
RH15: Burg H . . . 5C 94
Mayfield Cres. BN1: Brig . . . 9A 134
Mayfield Pl. PO20: Huns . . . 3C 162
Mayfield Rd. PO21: Bog R . . . 8B 164
Mayfields RH17: Bol . . . 5E 70
Mayflower Cl. RH10: Craw . . . 7M 11
Mayflower Ct. *BN43: Shor B* . . . 7K 151
(off Emerald Quay)
RH16: Hay H . . . 5G 72
Mayflower Rd. RH16: Hay H . . . 5G 72
Mayflower Sq. BN1: Brig . . . 4E 172 (6B 154)
Mayflower Way BN16: Ang . . . 1F 168
Mayhouse Rd. RH15: Burg H . . . 7A 94
Maynard Cl. RH10: Copt . . . 1D 12
Maynards Caravan & Camping Site
BN18: Cross . . . 4K 145
Mayo Ct. BN2: Brig . . . 5C 154
Mayo Rd. BN2: Brig . . . 5C 154
Maypole La. BN18: Yap . . . 8N 143
Maypole La. Caravan Site BN18: Yap . . . 8N 143
Maypole Rd. RH19: Ash W . . . 6L 15
RH19: E Grin . . . 2D 14
Mayridge PO20: Sel . . . 2F 182
May Rd. BN2: Brig . . . 6E 154
Maytree Av. BN14: Fin V . . . 1D 148
Maytree Cl. *BN3: Hove* . . . 5F 152
(off Dorothy Rd.)
BN15: Somp . . . 7M 149
BN16: Ang . . . 9E 146
Maytree Wlk. BN3: Hove . . . 4G 152
Maytree Way PO20: N Mun . . . 9F 140
Mead, The GU32: Peters . . . 7D 54
Mead Ct. PO22: Bog R . . . 8E 164
Meadend Cl. PO9: Hav . . . 9B 116
Meaden Way PO22: Felp . . . 6J 165
Mead La. GU31: Buri . . . 4E 76
PO21: Bog R . . . 8E 164
PO22: Bog R . . . 8E 164
RH20: Storr . . . 5K 107
Meadow, The RH10: Copt . . . 1B 12
Meadow App. RH10: Copt . . . 1B 12
Meadowbank RH14: Wisb . . . 1A 64
RH20: Pulb . . . 4B 86
Meadowbrook Ind. Cen. RH10: Craw . . . 3J 11
Meadow Cl. BN2: Rott . . . 1M 173
BN3: Hove . . . 2K 153
BN11: Wor . . . 1M 171
BN41: Ports . . . 3D 152
BN42: S'wck . . . 5B 152
PO11: Hay I . . . 1A 158
PO18: Mid L . . . 9B 120
PO20: Huns . . . 4C 162
RH10: Copt . . . 1B 12
RH12: Hors . . . 6D 26
RH17: Bal . . . 1B 50
Meadow Ct. PO10: Ems . . . 5F 136
PO22: Midd S . . . 6L 165
RH19: E Grin . . . 2E 14
Meadow Ct. Est. BN11: Wor . . . 1M 171
Meadow Cres. BN11: Wor . . . 1L 171
Meadowcroft Cl. RH6: Horl . . . 5L 5
RH11: Craw . . . 7B 10
RH19: E Grin . . . 2C 14
Meadow Dr. BN5: Henf . . . 1H 111
RH16: Hay H . . . 3J 73
Meadow Farm La. RH12: Hors . . . 4C 26
Meadowfield Dr. PO19: Chich . . . 6D 140
Meadowgate *RH12: Hors* . . . 4C 26
(off Giblets La.)
Meadowland PO20: Sel . . . 4H 183
Meadow Lands GU32: Peters . . . 7E 54
Meadowlands PO9: Row C . . . 3C 116
PO9: Warbl . . . 4A 136
RH11: Craw . . . 6E 10
Meadowlands Dr. GU27: Has . . . 5K 17
Meadow La. BN15: Lan . . . 8B 150
PO20: W Witt . . . 1G 177
RH15: Burg H . . . 7A 94
RH16: Lind . . . 3J 73
Meadow Pde. BN2: Rott . . . 1N 173
Meadow Pk. BN16: E Pres . . . 3G 168
Meadow Rd. BN11: Wor . . . 1L 171
Meadow Rd. Ind. Est. BN11: Wor . . . 9M 149
Meadows BN6: Hass . . . 2N 113
Meadows, The BN3: Hove . . . 2F 152
BN18: Walb . . . 5L 143
PO19: Chich . . . 1A 162
RH13: Southw . . . 2K 67
RH15: Ditch . . . 4G 95
Meadowside BN16: Ang . . . 7F 146
RH6: Horl . . . 1K 5
RH20: Storr . . . 6J 107
Meadowside Ct. BN12: Gor S . . . 2M 169
Meadowside Wlk. PO20: Tang . . . 3M 141
Meadows Rd. PO20: E Witt . . . 4L 177
Meadow Sweet Cl. BN13: Durr . . . 8M 147
Meadow Ter. RH17: Bal . . . 1B 50
Meadow Va. GU27: Has . . . 5J 17
Meadow Vw. BN6: Say C . . . 7E 92
Meadowview BN2: Brig . . . 4F 154
Meadowview Rd. BN15: Somp . . . 5N 149
Meadow Wlk. PO22: Midd S . . . 7A 166
Meadow Way BN12: Fer . . . 2K 169
BN17: L'ton . . . 3M 167
GU28: Petw . . . 1M 83
PO20: Tang . . . 4L 141
PO20: Westg . . . 7E 142
PO21: Aldw . . . 3D 180
PO22: Bers . . . 6B 164
Mead Rd. RH10: Craw . . . 5H 11
Meads, The BN1: Brig . . . 9E 134
GU27: Has . . . 5H 17
RH19: E Grin . . . 5E 14
Meads Av. BN3: Hove . . . 2E 152
Meads Cl. BN3: Hove . . . 2E 152
Meadsway BN18: Slind . . . 1L 143
Meadvale RH12: Hors . . . 9K 25
Mead Way GU29: Midh . . . 2G 80
Meadway BN16: Rust . . . 3C 168
GU27: Has . . . 5H 17
Meadway, The BN2: Brig . . . 8G 154
BN43: Shor B . . . 7J 151
RH6: Horl . . . 2L 5
Meadway Ct. BN13: Wor . . . 9C 148
BN42: S'wck . . . 5N 151
Meadway Cres. BN3: Hove . . . 3H 153
Measham Cl. BN12: Fer . . . 3L 169
Meath Gdns. RH6: Horl . . . 1G 5
MEATH GREEN . . . 1H 5

Monterey Pines—Nolan Rd.

Monterey Pines PO22: Felp .8H 165
Montes Hill RH16: Hay H .1N 73
Monteswood La. RH16: Hay H .9N 51
RH17: Hay H, Hors K .9N 51
Montford Cl. BN43: Shor S .5N 151
Montgomeri Dr. BN16: Rust .1A 168
Montgomery Dr. PO22: Midd S .6L 165
Montgomery Rd. PO9: Hav .4A 136
Montgomery St. BN3: Hove .6H 153
Montgomery Ter. *BN3: Hove .6J 153*
(off Montgomery St.)
Montier Ter. *GU28: Petw .9N 61*
(off Angel St.)
Montpelier Apartments BN1: Brig .7A 172
Montpelier Cres. BN1: Brig .5B 172 (7N 153)
Montpelier Gdns. RH20: Wash .7C 108
Montpelier Pl. BN1: Brig .6A 172 (7N 153)
Montpelier Rd. BN1: Brig .8A 172 (8N 153)
BN16: E Pres .3F 168
Montpelier St. BN1: Brig .6B 172 (7N 153)
Montpelier Ter. BN1: Brig .6B 172 (7N 153)
Montpelier Vs. BN1: Brig .6B 172 (7N 153)
Montpellier Lodge BN1: Brig .6B 172
Montreal Cl. BN10: Peace .5L 175
Montreal Rd. BN2: Brig .7C 154
Montreal Way BN13: Durr .7A 148
Montreux Ct. RH11: Craw .6D 10
Montrose Cl. BN12: Gor S .2A 170
Montrose Ct. BN12: Gor S .1A 170
Monument La. PO18: Wald .6L 117
Monument Vw. BN2: Brig .7E 154
Monxton Grn. PO9: Hav .8B 116
Moons La. RH13: Hors .1B 46
Moorcroft Cl. RH11: Craw .5D 10
Moore Cl. BN13: Durr .7N 147
Moore Ct. RH12: Hors .1L 45
Moore Pl. *PO21: Bog R .8D 164*
(off Victoria Dr.)
Moorfield GU27: Has .6H 17
Moorfoot Rd. BN13: Durr .6D 148
Moorgreen Rd. PO9: Hav .9A 116
Moorhead Rd. RH12: Hors .6E 26
Moorhead Rdbt. RH12: Hors .4E 26
Moorhen Way PO22: Bers .6C 164
Moorhouse La. GU29: Ipin, Mill .3M 57
GU30: Mill .4M 57
GU31: Chit, Mill .4M 57
Moorings, The BN15: N Lan .5C 150
BN17: L'ton .2N 167
BN18: Amb .2K 125
BN43: Shor B .7M 151
RH19: E Grin .1A 14
Moorland Rd. RH10: Craw .9L 11
Moor Pk. *RH6: Horl .3K 5*
(off Aurum Cl.)
Moor Pk. Cres. RH11: Ifield .7N 9
Moor Pl. RH19: E Grin .2D 14
Moor Rd. GU27: Has .6E 16
GU33: Long C .1A 34
Morants Cl. PO19: Chich .5E 140
Moraunt Dr. PO22: Midd S .6L 165
Morcumb Pk. Homes PO10: S'brne .5H 137
Morecambe Cl. RH11: Craw .8B 10
Morecambe Rd. BN1: Brig .8B 134
Morestead BN10: Peace .3K 175
Moreton Rd. PO18: Bosh .8E 138
Morgan Ho. *RH10: Craw .5K 11*
(off Trafalgar Gdns.)
MORGAN'S GREEN .9G 22
Morland Av. BN14: Broadw .6J 149
Morley Lodge BN2: Brig .6C 154
Morleys RH20: A'ton .3E 108
Morley St. BN2: Brig .6F 172 (7B 154)
Mornington Cres. BN3: Hove .6F 152
PO22: Felp .7H 165
Mornington Mans. BN3: Hove .7F 152
Morrell Av. RH12: Hors .6C 26
Morrells Wlk. PO21: Bers .5A 164
Morris Dr. RH14: Bill .2G 65
Morrison Ct. RH11: Craw .2D 28
Morris Way RH20: W Chil .9H 87
Morth Gdns. RH12: Hors .1N 45
Mortimer M. BN3: Hove .5H 153
Mortimer Rd. BN3: Hove .5H 153
Morton Cl. RH11: Craw .3D 28
Morton Ct. BN41: Ports .5D 152
Morton Rd. RH19: E Grin .5E 14
Mosdell Rd. PO10: S'brne .5L 137
Mosse Gdns. PO19: Fish .6L 139
MOULSECOOMB .3E 154
Moulsecoomb Community Leisure Cen. .2F 154
Moulsecoomb Pl. BN2: Brig .3E 154
Moulsecoomb Station (Rail) .3E 154
Moulsecoomb Way BN2: Brig .2F 154
Moulsecoomb Wild Pk. (Local Nature Reserve) .1E 154
Mount, The GU27: G'wd .1A 18
RH11: Ifield .4L 9
Mountbatten Cl. RH11: Craw .1E 28
Mountbatten Ct. BN3: Hove .5G 152
BN17: L'ton .2N 167
(off Ensign Way)
PO21: Bog R .1M 181
Mt. Caburn Cres. BN10: Peace .2J 175
Mount Cl. RH10: Craw .5M 11
Mount Cotts. RH11: Ifield .5M 9
Mount Dr. BN2: Salt .2D 174
Mountfields BN1: Brig .3D 154
Mount La. PO19: Chich .7B 140
RH10: Turn H .8H 13
Mount Noddy .2E 14
Mt. Noddy RH17: Ans .6L 71
Mount Pk. BN44: Stey .5A 130
Mt. Pleasant BN2: Brig .8C 154
BN18: Arun .2G 145
Mountview Rd. BN15: Somp .5N 149
Mount Way BN15: N Lan .4B 150
Mountwood Rd. PO10: S'brne .4K 137
PO20: Sel .2K 183
Mt. Zion Pl. BN1: Brig .6D 172 (7A 154)
Mouse La. BN44: Wis, Stey .1L 129
Moutheys La. PO18: E Ash .4G 139
Mowatt Rd. GU26: Gray .1F 16
Mowbray Dr. RH11: Craw .8B 10
Moyne Cl. BN3: Hove .4G 153
Moyne Rd. RH11: Craw .1E 28
M'Tongue Av. PO18: Bosh .6F 138
Muccleshell Cl. PO9: Hav .1A 136
Mudberry La. PO18: Bosh .5D 138
Muddleswood Rd.
BN6: Alb, Newt, Poyn .6D 112
Mudland Rd. PO20: Sidle .4L 179
Muggeridges Hill RH12: Capel .4B 8
Muir Ct. *BN14: Broadw .8G 149*
(off Rectory Gdns.)
Muirfield Cl. BN13: Durr .7C 148
RH11: Ifield .7N 9
Muirfield Ct. *RH16: Hay H .5F 72*
(off Caxton Way)
Muirfield Rd. BN13: Durr .7B 148
Mulberry Cl. BN1: Brig .2A 154
BN12: Fer .2K 169
BN12: Gor S .1A 170
BN15: Lan .7B 150
BN43: Shor S .4N 151
RH12: Hors .6N 25
Mulberry Ct. BN12: Gor S .2A 170
GU28: Petw .1M 83
(off Meadow Way)
PO20: Sel .3H 183
(off East St.)
PO21: Pag .4C 180
Mulberry Gdns. BN12: Gor S .2A 170
RH12: Broadb H .8J 25
Mulberry Ga. RH19: Felb .1A 14
Mulberry Hollow BN16: Ang .9C 146
Mulberry La. BN6: Ditch .4E 114
BN12: Gor S .1A 170
Mulberry La. Trad. Est. BN12: Gor S .1A 170
Mulberry Lodge *BN16: Rust .3B 168*
(off Cudlow Gdn.)
PO10: Ems .3F 136
Mulberry Rd. RH11: Craw .3D 10
Mulberry Wlk. RH15: Ditch .5G 95
Mullein Wlk. RH11: Craw .1C 28
Mumford Pl. PO19: Chich .8D 140
Munmere Way BN16: Rust .2D 168
Munnion Rd. RH17: Ard .3J 51
Munns Dr. RH15: Burg H .4C 94
MUNTHAM .6C 44
Muntham Dr. RH13: B Grn .7C 44
Murial Ho. BN3: Hove .5G 152
Murina Av. PO21: Bog R .7D 164
Murray Ct. RH11: Craw .2C 28
RH13: Hors .7E 26
Murray Rd. PO20: Sel .4G 183
Murrell Gdns. PO22: Barn .6H 143
Muscliffe Ct. PO9: Hav .9B 116
Museum Hill GU27: Has .5M 17
Musgrave Av. RH19: E Grin .5E 14
Mustang Cl. BN18: Ford .2B 166
Muster Ct. RH16: Hay H .5E 72
Muster Grn. Nth. RH16: Hay H .4E 72
Muster Grn. Sth. RH16: Hay H .5E 72
Mutton's La. RH20: A'ton .4B 108
My Lord's La. PO11: Hay I .9B 158
Myra M. RH16: Hay H .4G 72
Myrtle Copse PO22: Felp .6J 165
Myrtle Cres. BN15: Lan .8A 150
MYRTLE GROVE .8J 127
Myrtle Gro. BN16: E Pres .3E 168
Myrtle La. RH14: Bill .2J 65
Myrtle Rd. BN15: Lan .8A 150
Myrtle Ter. *BN5: Henf .3H 111*
(off Weavers La.)
Mytten Bank RH17: Cuck .3A 72
Mytten Cl. RH17: Cuck .3A 72
Mytten Twitten RH17: Cuck .3A 72

N

Nab Tower La. PO20: Sel .2E 182
Nab Wlk. PO20: E Witt .5K 177
Nagels Cl. PO20: E Witt .5L 177
Naiad Gdns. PO22: Felp .7L 165
Naldrett Cl. RH12: Hors .7C 26
Naldretts La. RH12: Rudg .6J 23
Namrik M. BN3: Hove .7J 153
Nanson Rd. BN1: Brig .8E 134
Napier Ho. BN2: Brig .6D 154
Napier Way RH10: Craw .3H 11
Nappers Wood GU27: Fern .4J 37
Nashlands Cotts. RH17: Hand .9E 28
Nash La. RH17: Scay H .5A 74
Nash Rd. RH10: Craw .9G 10
Nash Way BN18: Walb .4L 143
Natal Rd. BN2: Brig .4E 154
Natts La. RH14: Bill .2H 65
Naunton Rd. PO19: Chich .3C 140
Nautilus BN11: Wor .3H 171
Navarino Rd. BN11: Wor .2L 171
Neale Cl. RH19: E Grin .1B 14
Nectar Way PO10: Ems .1G 136
Needlemakers PO19: Chich .7D 140
Needles Cl. RH12: Hors .1M 45
Need's Hill RH13: Part G .2B 90
Nell Ball RH14: Plais .9E 20
(not continuous)
Nelson Cl. BN15: Somp .5N 149
PO10: S'brne .5G 137
PO20: Tang .3M 141
RH10: Craw .7L 11
Nelson Ct. BN43: Shor B .8G 151
Nelson Dr. GU31: Peters .4G 54
Nelson Pl. BN2: Brig .6G 172
BN11: Wor .2H 171
Nelson Rd. BN12: Gor S .9B 148
PO21: Bog R .9B 164
RH12: Hors .8M 25
Nelson Row BN2: Brig .7G 172 (8C 154)
BN18: Ford .1E 166
Nep Cl. BN5: Henf .3H 111
NEPCOTE .9D 128
Nepcote BN14: Fin .9D 128
Nepcote La. BN14: Fin .8C 128
Nepcote Pde. *BN14: Fin .8C 128*
(off Nepcote La.)
Nepfield Cl. BN14: Fin .9C 128
Nep Town Rd. BN5: Henf .3H 111
Neptune Cl. RH11: Craw .8A 10
Neptune Ct. BN2: Brig .8K 173
PO22: Felp .8L 165
Neptune Way
BN17: L'ton, Rust .4N 167
Nesbit Ct. RH11: Craw .9A 10
Nesbitt Rd. BN2: Brig .4E 154
Nest Bus. Pk. PO9: Hav .1B 136
Nestor Ct. BN1: Brig .1B 172
Netherfield Cl. PO9: Warbl .4A 136
Netherfield Grn. BN2: W'dean .5N 155
Netherton Cl. PO20: Sel .3J 183
RH13: Southw .6K 45
Netherwood RH11: Craw .8D 10
Netley Cl. RH11: Craw .3E 28
Netley Ct. BN17: L'ton .3K 167
Nettleton Av. PO20: Tang .3L 141
Nettleton Ct. BN1: Brig .1G 172 (4C 154)
Nevile Cl. RH11: Craw .9C 10
Nevill Av. BN3: Hove .3G 153
Nevill Bungs. BN6: Ditch .5D 114
Nevill Cl. BN3: Hove .3J 153
Nevill Cotts. BN6: Ditch .5E 114
Nevill Ct. BN3: Hove .4J 153
Neville Duke Way PO20: Tang .3M 141
Neville Gdns. PO10: Ems .2E 136
Neville Rd. BN10: Peace .6K 175
PO19: Chich .6N 139
PO22: Bog R .8E 164
Nevill Gdns. BN3: Hove .3J 153
Nevill Pl. BN3: Hove .3J 153
Nevill Rd. BN2: Rott .3N 173
BN3: Hove .3J 153
Nevill Way BN3: Hove .3J 153
Newark Pl. BN2: Brig .7C 154
Newark Rd. RH10: Craw .4H 11
New Barn RH14: Kird .8G 41
New Barn Cl. BN41: Ports .3D 152
BN43: Shor S .4L 151
New Barn Farm La. PO8: Blend .6A 96
New Barn Hill PO18: Box, Good, Hal .9J 121
New Barn La. BN5: Henf .6J 111
GU31: Buri .7C 76
PO21: Bers .5A 164
PO22: Felp .6J 165
RH5: Ock .1E 6
RH20: W Chil .8G 87
Newbarn La. PO18: Wald .6L 117
New Barn Rd. BN2: Rott .1M 173
BN18: Amb .1K 125
BN43: Shor S .4L 151
NEWBRIDGE .1F 64
Newbridge Cl. RH12: Broadb H .8G 25
Newbridge Rd. RH14: Bill .1F 64
Newbridge Rd. E. RH14: Bill .1H 65
Newbridge Rd. W. RH14: Bill .1G 64
New Bridge Rdbt.
RH12: Broadb H .8G 25
NEW BRIGHTON .2F 136
New Brighton Rd. PO10: Ems .4F 136
New Broadway BN11: Wor .1E 170
Newbury La. RH17: Cuck .4N 71
Newbury Rd. RH10: Craw .6M 11
New Church Rd. BN3: Hove .6E 152
New Cotts. RH10: Turn H .8H 13
New Courtwick La. BN17: Wick .9J 145
New Cut PO11: Hay I .1A 158
Newdigate Rd. RH12: Rusp .4F 8
New Dorset St. BN1: Brig .6D 172 (7A 154)
(not continuous)
Newells Cl. BN2: W'dean .4M 155
Newells La. PO18: Bosh, W Ash .6D 138
RH13: Lwr Bee .2F 68
New England Ho. BN1: Brig .3E 172
New England Ri. BN41: Ports .1C 152
New England Rd.
BN1: Brig .3C 172 (6A 154)
RH16: Hay H .5F 72
New England St. BN1: Brig .3E 172 (6B 154)
Newfield Ho. *RH11: Craw .2E 28*
(off Kensington Rd.)
Newfield Rd. PO20: Sel .2L 183
NEWFOUND OUT .6M 45
New Gdns. BN15: Somp .6K 149
Newhall Cl. PO21: Bog R .9A 164
New Hall La. BN5: Small D .8G 111
Newham Cl. BN44: Stey .3N 129
Newham La. BN44: Stey .5M 129
Newhaven Rd. BN7: Rod .5K 157
Newhaven St. BN2: Brig .7C 154
New Heritage Way BN8: N Cha .8E 74
Newhouse Bus. Cen. RH12: Fay .4F 26
Newhouse La. PO18: E Dean .8M 101
RH20: Storr .4A 108
NEWICK .9K 75
Newick Hill BN8: Flet, Newick .9J 75
Newick Rd. BN1: Brig .1F 154
Newland Gdns. BN18: Amb .8L 105
Newland Rd. BN11: Wor .1H 171
BN44: Up B .4E 130
Newlands RH17: Bal .1A 50
Newlands Cl. BN6: Key .4B 114
Newlands Cres. RH19: E Grin .2D 14
Newlands La. PO19: Chich .5A 140
Newlands Pk. RH10: Copt .1F 12
Newlands Pk. Way BN8: Newick .9J 75
Newlands Pl. RH18: F Row .9M 15
Newlands Rd. BN2: Rott .3A 174
RH11: Craw .7E 10
RH12: Hors .7N 25
Newland St. BN11: Wor .1H 171
New La. GU31: S Hart .5A 78
PO9: Hav .3A 136
Newling Way BN13: High S .4C 148
Newman Cl. RH10: Craw .8L 11
Newman Rd. RH6: Horl .1L 5
Newmans Gdns. BN15: Somp .6M 149
BN44: Stey .3A 130
(off Tanyard La.)
Newmarket Rd. BN2: Brig .5D 154
RH10: Craw .9J 11
Newmarket Ter. BN2: Brig .5D 154
New Mill Cotts. GU27: Has .5F 16
New Moorhead Dr. RH12: Hors .5F 26
Newnham Ct. PO9: Hav .9B 116
New Pde. BN11: Wor .2K 171
PO20: Sel .3H 183
PO20: W Witt .4J 177
(off Cakeham Rd.)
New Pk. Rd. PO19: Chich .6C 140
New Pl. Rd. RH20: Pulb .5B 86
Newport *BN43: Shor B .7L 151*
(off Britannia Av.)
Newport Dr. PO19: Fish .6L 139
Newport M. BN11: Wor .1M 171
Newport Rd. RH15: Burg H .5A 94
Newport St. BN2: Brig .6C 154
Newpound RH14: Wisb .6B 42
NEWPOUND COMMON .7D 42
Newpound La. RH14: Wisb .9B 42
New Rd. BN1: Brig .8E 172 (8B 154)
BN6: Clay, Ditch, Key .6N 113
BN13: Durr .7A 148
BN16: Ang, Rust .1C 168
BN17: L'ton .4K 167
BN43: Shor S .6J 151
BN44: Up B .5E 130
GU27: Has .6H 17
GU28: Till .9H 61
GU29: Graff, Hey, S Amb .2A 82
GU29: Midh .1G 80
PO10: S'brne .5L 137
PO10: W'brne .2H 137
PO18: E Dean .8M 101
PO18: E Lav, Good .9D 120
RH13: Southw .6K 45
RH14: Bill .8K 43
New Row BN44: Stey .3A 130
New Salts Farm Rd. BN43: Shor S .7F 150
Newstead *BN1: Brig .4D 172*
(off Howard Pl.)
Newstead Hall RH6: Horl .3M 5
RH14: Adv .6F 64
New Steine BN2: Brig .9C 154
New Steine Mans. *BN2: Brig .8C 154*
(off Devonshire Pl.)
New Steine M. BN2: Brig .8C 154
New St. BN11: Wor .3H 171
GU28: Petw .9N 61
RH10: Craw .5J 11
RH13: Hors .1A 46
New Ter. BN18: Poling .5B 146
NEWTIMBER .7F 112
Newtimber Av. BN12: Gor S .1N 169
Newtimber Dr. BN41: Ports .4C 152
Newtimber Gdns. BN43: Shor S .4J 151
Newtimber Hill .9G 112
Newtimber Place .7F 112
Newtimber Pl. La. BN6: Newt .7F 112
Newton Av. RH19: E Grin .6F 14
Newton Cl. RH16: Lind .2J 73
Newton Ct. RH16: Hay H .4F 72
Newton Rd. BN10: Peace .5J 175
RH10: Craw .2H 11
RH16: Lind .2J 73
NEW TOWN .1A 46
New Town PO19: Chich .7C 140
RH10: Copt .1C 12
Newtown Av. PO21: Bers .6B 164
Newtown Ct. RH13: Hors .1A 46
New Town Rd.
RH20: Coot, Storr .6G 106
Newtown Rd. BN3: Hove .5K 153
New Venture Theatre .7A 172
New Way La. BN6: Clay, Hurst .3K 113
Nicholsfield RH14: Lox .7M 21
Nicolson Cl. PO20: Tang .3L 141
Nicolson Dr. BN43: Shor S .5J 151
Nightingale Cl. GU27: Fern .4J 37
PO9: Row C .5A 116
RH11: Craw .4E 10
RH16: Hay H .5G 73
RH19: E Grin .5D 14
RH20: Storr .6K 107
Nightingale Ct. PO10: W'brne .1H 137
PO22: Midd S .7N 165
Nightingale Ho. RH20: Pulb .7C 86
Nightingale Ind. Est. RH12: Hors .8A 26
Nightingale La. PO18: Hamb .2N 137
RH10: Turn H .7K 13
RH15: Burg H .7A 94
RH20: Storr .6K 107
Nightingale Pk. PO9: Warbl .4B 136
RH20: Storr .6K 107
Nightingale Rd. GU32: Peters .7E 54
RH12: Hors .8A 26
Nightingales BN14: Fin .7C 128
RH20: W Chil .9J 87
Nightingales Cl. RH13: Hors .9C 26
Nightingale Wlk. RH14: Bill .1J 65
Nightingale Way PO20: Sel .1H 183
Nile Ho. BN1: Brig .8E 172
Nile St. BN1: Brig .8E 172
PO10: Ems .5F 136
Nimbus Cl. BN17: L'ton .2N 167
Nimrod Ct. *RH10: Craw .3M 11*
(off Wakehams Grn. Dr.)
Nine Acres GU29: Midh .8G 58
GU32: Steep .1H 55
Nineveh Shipyard BN18: Arun .3H 145
Ninfield Ct. RH11: Craw .1B 28
Ninfield Pl. BN2: Brig .6F 154
Niven Cl. RH10: Craw .7M 11
Nizells Av. BN3: Hove .4A 172 (6M 153)
Nizells La. BN3: Hove .4A 172 (6M 153)
Noah's Ark La. RH16: Lind .2K 73
Noah's Ct. RH10: Turn H .8H 13
Noble Ct. BN3: Hove .6G 153
Noel Grn. RH15: Burg H .4C 94
Noel Ri. RH15: Burg H .4C 94
Nokes Ct. RH10: Craw .7H 11
Nolan Rd. BN2: W'dean .6M 155

No Man's Land—Oakley Gdns.

NO MAN'S LAND .2C 148
Nonnington La. GU28: Graff .7C 82
Nook, The BN6: Say C .7F 92
Nook Caravan Park, The
  PO20: Sel .2G 183
Nookery, The BN16: E Pres .3F 168
Nor'bren Av. PO21: Bers .7B 164
Norbury Cl. BN15: N Lan .5C 150
Norbury Dr. BN15: N Lan .5B 150
Nordseter Lodge *BN16: Rust* .4A 168
  (off Sea La.)
Nore Cres. PO10: Ems .4D 136
Noredown Way PO18: Mard .7L 97
Nore Farm Av. PO10: Ems .4D 136
Nore Rd. BN9: Newh .6N 175
Noreuil Rd. GU32: Peters .6D 54
Norfolk Bri. BN43: Shor S .6H 151
Norfolk Bldgs. BN1: Brig .7A 172
Norfolk Cl. PO21: Bog R .1K 181
  RH6: Horl .3J 5
  RH11: Craw .1A 28
Norfolk Cotts. BN18: Burp .8N 125
  BN44: Stey .3A 130
  (off High St.)
Norfolk Ct. *BN1: Brig* .7A 172
  (off Norfolk Sq.)
  BN11: Wor .1G 170
  (off Victoria Pk. Gdns.)
  BN16: Rust .4A 168
  (off Chanctonbury Rd.)
  RH12: Hors .6E 26
Norfolk Gdns. BN17: L'ton .4M 167
Norfolk Ho. BN11: Wor .1H 171
  PO9: Hav .4A 136
Norfolk M. BN1: Brig .7A 172 (8N 153)
  BN17: L'ton .4M 167
  (off Norfolk Pl.)
Norfolk Pl. BN1: Brig .7A 172
  BN17: L'ton .4M 167
Norfolk Rd. BN1: Brig .6A 172 (7N 153)
  BN17: L'ton .5M 167
  RH12: Hors .9A 26
Norfolk Sq. BN1: Brig .7A 172 (8N 153)
  PO21: Bog R .1K 181
Norfolk St. BN1: Brig .8A 172 (8N 153)
  BN11: Wor .1G 170
  PO21: Bog R .1M 181
Norfolk Ter. BN1: Brig .6A 172 (7N 153)
  RH12: Hors .9A 26
Norfolk Way PO22: Midd S .7A 166
Norman Cl. BN17: L'ton .3M 167
  RH14: Bill .9K 43
Norman Cres. BN43: Shor S .4J 151
Normandy RH12: Hors .1N 45
Normandy Cl. RH10: Craw .8K 11
  RH19: E Grin .4F 14
Normandy Ct. BN11: Wor .3F 170
  PO19: Chich .6D 140
  (off Joys Cft.)
Normandy Dr. BN16: E Pres .4F 168
Normandy Gdns. RH12: Hors .1N 45
Normandy Ho. BN3: Hove .7L 153
Normandy La. BN16: E Pres .4F 168
Normandy Rd. BN14: Broadw .9G 149
Normanhurst *BN2: Brig* .7C 154
  (off Grove Hill)
Normanhurst Cl. BN16: Rust .4B 168
  RH10: Craw .6H 11
Norman Rd. BN3: Hove .7G 152
  PO11: Hay I .9B 158
  RH15: Burg H .5A 94
Normanscourt BN43: Shor S .4J 151
Norman's Dr. PO22: Felp .6J 165
Normans Gdns. RH19: E Grin .3E 14
Normanton Av. PO21: Bog R .9C 164
Normanton St. BN2: Brig .6D 154
Norman Way BN44: Stey .2A 130
  PO22: Midd S .7N 165
Norris Gdns. PO9: Warbl .5A 136
North Ash RH12: Hors .7N 25
North Av. BN12: Gor S .3C 170
  PO22: Midd S .7N 165
North Av. E. PO22: Midd S .7N 165
North Av. Sth. PO22: Midd S .7N 165
North Bank BN6: Hass .3N 113
Nth. Barnes La. BN7: E Chil, Plump G .2M 115
North Bay PO10: Tho I .1G 159
NORTH BERSTED .6B 164
Nth. Bersted St. PO22: Bers .6B 164
Northbourne Cl. BN43: Shor S .5J 151
Northbrook Bus. Pk. BN14: Broadw .7J 149
Northbrook Cl. BN14: Broadw .7J 149
Northbrook Ct. *RH12: Hors* .7N 25
  (off Hurst Rd.)
Northbrook Farm Caravan Club Site
  BN13: Gor S .7M 147
Northbrook Rd. BN14: Broadw .7J 149
Northbrook Trad. Est. BN14: Broadw .7J 149
NORTHCHAPEL .3H 39
Northcliffe Rd. PO22: Bog R .8F 164
North Cl. BN41: Ports .3C 152
  PO9: Hav .5A 136
  PO19: Chich .7C 140
  RH10: Craw .5H 11
North Comn. Rd.
  BN8: N Cha, Wivel G .4K 95
  RH17: Wivel G .4K 95
Northcote Gdns. PO10: S'brne .5L 137
Northcote La. BN10: Tels C .3G 175
Northcote Rd. PO21: Bog R .8B 164
North Ct. BN6: Hass .3N 113
North Ct. Cl. BN16: Rust .2C 168
Northcourt Rd. BN14: Broadw .9G 149
North Cres. PO11: Hay I .9B 158
Northcroft BN5: Henf .2G 111
Northdown Cl. RH12: Hors .7C 26
Northdown Ter. RH19: E Grin .1D 14
North Dr. BN2: Brig .7D 154
  BN16: Ang .9E 146
Northease Cl. BN3: Hove .3F 152
Northease Dr. BN3: Hove .3F 152
Northease Gdns. BN3: Hove .2G 152
Northease Wall BN7: Rod .3J 157
NORTH END
  BN14 .6C 128
  BN18 .8A 144
  RH19 .1B 14
North End BN6: Ditch .4E 114
  RH19: E Grin .1B 14
Northend Cl. GU28: Petw .8N 61
Northend La. BN6: Hurst .5H 93
North End Rd. BN18: Yap .1N 165
Northerlea *BN41: Ports* .4C 152
  (off Drove Rd.)
Northern Cres. PO20: E Witt .4K 177
Nth. Farm Cotts. *BN41: Ports* .3C 152
  (off North Rd.)
Nth. Farm Ct. BN15: Lan .7B 150
Nth. Farm Rd. BN15: Lan .7B 150
North Fld. PO20: W Witt .1G 176
Northfield PO20: Sel .3K 183
Northfield Ri. BN2: Rott .2A 174
  BN3: Hove .1F 152
Northfield Rd. BN13: W Tar .7E 148
Northfields La. PO20: Westg .5E 142
Northfield Way BN1: Brig .1B 154
Nth. Gdns. BN1: Brig .6D 172 (7A 154)
NORTHGATE .5G 11
Northgate PO19: Chich .6C 140
Northgate Av. RH10: Craw .6G 11
Northgate Cl. BN2: Rott .2N 173
  BN15: Somp .7M 149
Northgate Gyratory
  PO19: Chich .6C 140
  (off Northgate)
Northgate M. *GU29: Midh* .9H 59
  (off North St.)
Northgate Pl. RH10: Craw .5G 11
Northgate Rd. *RH6: Gatw* .5H 5
  (off Racecourse Rd.)
  RH10: Craw .6F 10
North Hall La. TN22: Flet .3J 75
North Ham Rd. BN17: L'ton .2K 167
NORTH HAYLING .1C 158
NORTH HEATH .1E 86
Nth. Heath Cl. RH12: Hors .6A 26
Nth. Heath Est. RH12: Hors .5A 26
Nth. Heath La. RH12: Hors .7A 26
Nth. Holmes Cl. RH12: Hors .6E 26
NORTH LAINE .6E 172 (7B 154)
NORTH LANCING .5B 150
Northlands Av. RH16: Hay H .6H 73
Northlands Bus. Pk. RH12: Warnh .8G 7
Northlands Cotts. RH12: Warnh .8H 7
Northlands La. RH20: Storr .4K 107
Northlands Rd. RH12: Hors .4B 26
  RH12: Warnh .9H 7
North La. BN16: E Pres .2G 168
  BN16: Rust .2A 168
  BN41: Ports .2C 152
  BN44: Wis .5G 109
  GU31: Buri .3D 76
  GU31: S Hart .4A 78
  PO8: Chalt .2C 96
  PO18: Charlt, Sing .8H 101
  RH19: W Hoa .6M 31
  RH20: A'ton, Wis .5G 109
North Lodge BN8: Newick .9K 75
NORTH MARDEN .2E 98
North Mead BN5: Henf .1H 111
  GU28: Petw .8N 61
  RH10: Craw .4G 11
NORTH MOULSECOOMB .1F 154
NORTH MUNDHAM .3F 162
NORTHNEY .9C 136
Northney La. PO11: Hay I .9C 136
Northney Marina .8B 136
Northney Rd. PO11: Hay I .8A 136
North Pallant PO19: Chich .7C 140
North Pde. RH12: Hors .6N 25
North Pk. BN17: L'ton .3J 167
Nth. Perimeter Rd. *RH6: Gatw* .7F 4
  (off Old Control Tower Rd.)
North Pl. BN1: Brig .7F 172 (8B 154)
  BN17: L'ton .4L 167
North Point BN43: Shor B .7K 151
North Pound BN18: Walb .4L 143
North Rd. BN1: Brig .4N 153
  (Middle Rd.)
  BN1: Brig .6D 172 (7A 154)
  (North Gdns.)
  BN15: Lan .7B 150
  BN41: Ports .3C 152
  GU32: Peters .5F 54
  PO18: Bosh .6F 138
  PO20: Sel .3J 183
  PO22: Felp .6H 165
  RH10: Craw .4J 11
  RH16: Hay H .5H 73
Northside PO18: Mid L .7A 120
Nth. South Rd. BN1: Falm .7J 135
NORTH STOKE .4J 125
North St. BN1: Brig .7D 172 (8A 154)
  BN11: Wor .1H 171
  BN17: Wick .1K 167
  BN41: Ports .6D 152
  BN43: Shor S .6H 151
  GU28: Petw .8N 61
  GU29: Midh .9H 59
  GU31: Rog .5E 56
  PO10: Ems .4F 136
  PO10: W'brne .9H 117
  PO19: Chich .7C 140
  (not continuous)
  RH10: Turn H .8H 13
  RH12: Hors .9A 26
  RH13: Hors .9A 26
  RH20: Storr .6J 107
North St. Quad. BN1: Brig .7D 172
Nth. Stroud La. GU32: Rams, Stro .6A 54
Nth. Terminal App. RH6: Gatw .5H 5
North Vw. Ter. BN14: Fin .8C 128
North Walls PO19: Chich .6B 140
  (not continuous)
North Way GU28: Petw .1M 83
  PO22: Felp .8G 164
Northway RH6: Gatw .5H 5
  RH15: Burg H .4D 94
Northway Rd. BN17: Wick .9K 145
Northwood Av. BN2: Salt .3E 174
Northwood Ct. BN14: Broadw .7G 149
Northwood La. PO11: Hay I .3A 158
Northwood Pk. RH10: Craw .2J 11
Northwyke Cl. PO22: Felp .7K 165
Northwyke Rd. PO22: Felp .7K 165
NORTON
  PO20, Westergate .4C 142
  PO20, Selsey .8K 179
Norton Cl. BN3: Hove .7K 153
Norton Dr. BN2: W'dean .4L 155
Norton La. PO18: Nort .4C 142
  PO20: Nort .4C 142
Norton Rd. BN3: Hove .7K 153
  BN15: Lan .8A 150
Norton Wall BN7: Ifrd .2H 157
Norway La. BN17: L'ton .9N 145
  (Rustington By-Pass)
  BN17: L'ton .1M 167
  (The Poplars)
Norway St. BN41: Ports .6E 152
Norwich Cl. BN2: Brig .3H 155
Norwich Ct. *BN11: Wor* .3E 170
  (off Pevensey Gdn.)
Norwich Cres. BN2: Brig .3G 155
Norwich Dr. BN2: Brig .3G 155
Norwich Ho. Rd. BN1: Falm .7J 135
Norwich Rd. PO19: Chich .5B 140
  RH10: Craw .8K 11
Norwood BN1: Brig .1B 154
NORWOOD HILL .2A 4
Norwood Hill RH6: Nor H .2A 4
Norwood Hill Rd. RH6: Charlw, Nor H .2A 4
Norwood La. GU28: Graff .7E 82
Norwood La. Sth. GU28: Graff .2F 102
Novium Museum, The .7B 140
Nowhurst Bus. Pk. RH12: Broadb H .5E 24
Nowhurst La. RH12: Broadb H .6E 24
Nuffield Cl. PO21: Aldw .9N 163
Nuffield Health Club
  Chichester .8B 140
  Crawley .5A 12
Nunnington Farm Caravan & Camping Pk.
  PO20: W Witt .1H 177
Nurseries, The PO21: Aldw .9L 163
  RH17: Bal .1B 50
Nursery, The RH15: Burg H .4D 94
Nursery Cl. BN6: Hurst .9H 93
  BN15: N Lan .5A 150
  BN16: E Pres .4F 168
  BN41: Ports .1A 152
  BN43: Shor S .5L 151
  PO10: Ems .2F 136
  PO22: Barn .7J 143
  RH16: Hay H .4E 72
Nursery Gdns. BN17: Wick .1K 167
  PO19: Chich .8D 140
Nurserylands RH11: Craw .6C 10
Nursery La. BN11: Wor .3G 170
  PO19: Fish .6L 139
  RH6: Hookw .3F 4
  RH17: Wivel G .3K 95
Nursery Rd. BN16: Ang .9F 146
Nursling Cres. PO9: Hav .9A 116
NURSTED .1J 77
NUTBOURNE
  PO18 .6M 137
  RH20 .6F 86
NUTBOURNE COMMON .7F 86
Nutbourne Ct. *RH12: Hors* .6A 26
  (off Woodstock Cl.)
Nutbourne La. RH20: N Hth, Pulb .2F 86
Nutbourne Marshes Nature Reserve .9M 137
Nutbourne Pk. PO18: Nutb .6N 137
Nutbourne Rd. BN14: Wor .9F 148
  RH20: Pulb .6F 86
Nutbourne Station (Rail) .5A 138
Nutbourne Vineyards .6G 86
NUTCOMBE .1G 16
Nutcombe La. GU26: Hind .3G 16
Nutcroft RH20: Pulb .6B 86
Nutham La. RH13: Southw .9L 45
Nuthatch Cl. PO9: Row C .5B 116
Nuthatch Way RH10: Turn H .7K 13
  RH12: Hors .4A 26
NUTHURST .9D 46
Nuthurst Cl. BN2: Brig .7G 154
  RH11: Craw .5C 10
Nuthurst Pl. BN2: Brig .7G 154
Nuthurst Rd. RH13: Map, N'hrst .4C 68
  RH13: Monks G .7E 46
Nuthurst St. RH13: N'hrst .2D 68
Nutley Av. BN2: Salt .3C 174
  BN12: Gor S .3A 170
Nutley Cl. BN3: Hove .2H 153
  BN12: Gor S .3A 170
Nutley Cres. BN12: Gor S .3A 170
Nutley Dr. BN12: Gor S .3A 170
Nutwick Rd. PO9: Hav .2B 136
Nuyuu Fitness
  East Grinstead .3E 14
Nye La. BN6: Ditch .5F 114
  (not continuous)
Nye Rd. RH15: Burg H .5C 94
Nyes Cl. BN5: Henf .2J 111
Nye's Hill RH17: Bol .8A 70
Nyes La. RH13: Southw .7K 45
NYETIMBER .2C 180
Nyetimber Cl. PO21: Aldw .1D 180
Nyetimber Copse RH20: W Chil .9H 87
Nyetimber Cres. PO21: Pag .1D 180
Nyetimber Hill BN2: Brig .3F 154
Nyetimber La. PO21: Aldw, Pag .1C 180
  RH20: W Chil .9G 87
Nyetimber Mill PO21: Pag .1C 180
Nyetimbers, The PO21: Pag .1C 180
NYEWOOD .9D 56
Nyewood Gdns. PO21: Bog R .9C 164
Nyewood Industries GU31: N'wd .9D 56
Nyewood Lane .9B 164
Nyewood La. PO21: Aldw, Bog R .8C 164
Nyewood Pl. PO21: Bog R .1K 181
Nymans Cl. RH12: Hors .4D 26
Nymans Ct. RH10: Craw .9K 11
Nymans Gdns. .3F 48
NYTON .5D 142
Nyton Rd. PO18: Tang .3B 142
  PO20: E'gate, Westg .5F 142

O

Oak Apple Cl. RH13: Cow .8H 69
Oakapple Cl. RH11: Craw .2D 28
Oakapple Rd. BN42: S'wck .3A 152
Oak Av. PO19: Chich .6A 140
  RH20: Storr .4N 107
Oak Bank RH16: Lind .2G 73
Oak Cl. BN1: Brig .2N 153
  BN13: High S .4C 148
  PO19: Chich .6A 140
  PO22: Bers .6D 164
  RH10: Copt .1B 12
  RH13: Southw .2K 67
  RH20: Storr .5L 107
Oak Cotts. GU27: Has .5G 16
  (not continuous)
  RH17: Hand .8E 28
  TN22: Flet .5M 75
Oak Ct. RH10: Craw .2F 10
  RH19: E Grin .2D 14
  (off Newlands Cres.)
Oak Cft. RH19: E Grin .4G 14
Oakcroft Gdns. BN17: L'ton .1M 167
Oakdale Rd. RH16: Hay H .6G 73
Oak Dell RH10: Craw .5L 11
Oakdene RH16: Hay H .4E 72
Oakdene Av. BN41: Ports .2A 152
Oakdene Cl. BN41: Ports .2B 152
Oakdene Cres. BN41: Ports .2A 152
Oakdene Gdns. BN41: Ports .2A 152
Oakdene Pl. RH14: Ifol .8K 21
Oakdene Ri. BN41: Ports .1A 152
Oakdene Way BN41: Ports .1A 152
Oak Dr. GU31: Peters .8E 54
Oak End BN18: Arun .3E 144
  RH20: Storr .5L 107
  RH20: W Chil .9J 87
Oakendene BN2: Brig .1G 154
Oakendene Ind. Est. RH13: Cow .8L 69
Oakenfield RH15: Burg H .3A 94
Oak Farm Pl. RH19: Felb .1N 13
Oakfield GU28: Lods .6C 60
  (not continuous)
  RH14: Plais .9E 20
Oakfield Av. PO20: E Witt .4K 177
Oakfield Cl. RH16: Lind .2H 73
Oakfield Cotts. GU27: Has .1C 38
Oakfield Ct. PO9: Hav .9B 116
  RH6: Horl .2J 5
  (off Consort Way)
Oakfield Rd. PO20: E Witt .4K 177
  RH13: Cow .8H 69
Oakfields RH5: Wall .4B 6
  RH10: Craw .4M 11
Oakfield Way RH19: E Grin .1F 14
Oakford Pk. PO18: Box .9N 121
Oak Gro. PO22: Bog R .6D 164
  RH14: Lox .7N 21
Oak Hall Pk. RH15: Burg H .7C 94
Oakhaven RH10: Craw .8F 10
OAKHILL .1B 46
Oakhill Chase RH10: Craw .5M 11
Oakhill Cotts. RH5: Oak .4D 6
Oakhill Rd. RH13: Hors .9B 26
Oak Ho. RH10: Craw .2F 10
Oakhurst BN5: Henf .1H 111
  BN6: Say C .7F 92
  GU26: Gray .1F 16
  GU29: Midh .9F 58
  RH16: Hay H .1E 72
Oakhurst Bus. Pk. RH13: Southw .6L 45
Oakhurst Gdns. BN16: Rust .2D 168
  RH19: E Grin .2C 14
Oakhurst La. RH14: Lox .5L 21
  RH16: Hay H .1E 72
Oakhurst M. RH13: Hors .7D 26
Oakland Cl. RH13: Hors .2B 46
Oakland Ct. BN11: Wor .2G 171
  BN12: Gor S .2M 169
  BN17: L'ton .4L 167
  BN43: Shor S .6J 151
  PO21: Pag .1C 180
  (off Nyetimber La.)
Oaklands BN12: Fer .2L 169
  BN15: S Lan .8B 150
  GU27: Has .4L 17
  RH6: Horl .2L 5
  RH12: Hors .6M 25
  RH13: Hors .9B 26
  RH14: Bill .2J 65
  RH17: Ard .2J 51
Oaklands Av. BN2: Salt .3C 174
Oaklands Bus. Cen. BN11: Wor .1D 170
Oaklands Ct. *PO19: Chich* .5C 140
  (off Somerstown)
Oaklands La. GU29: W Lav .4G 81
Oaklands Pk. .5C 140
Oaklands Rd. GU32: Peters .5E 54
  PO9: Hav .4A 136
  RH16: Hay H .4E 72
Oaklands Way PO19: Chich .6C 140
  PO20: N Mun .9F 140
Oak La. GU8: Plais .7N 19
  PO20: Apul .3M 161
  RH12: Broadb H .8J 25
Oaklee RH16: Lind .1J 73
Oakleigh Cl. BN11: Wor .9L 149
Oakleigh Ct. BN11: Wor .9L 149
Oakleigh Rd. BN11: Wor .9L 149
  RH12: Hors .7C 26
Oakley Cl. RH19: E Grin .5H 15
Oakley Gdns. BN16: E Pres .3F 168

Owletts—Pelham Sq.

Owletts RH10: Craw . . . 5M 11
Owlscastle Cl. RH12: Hors . . . 6A 26
Oxen Av. BN43: Shor S . . . 5J 151
Oxford Cl. PO20: W Witt . . . 4K 177
Oxford Ct. BN1: Brig . . . 4F 172 (6B 154)
GU29: Midh . . . 1G 81
Oxford Dr. PO21: Aldw . . . 8N 163
Oxford M. BN3: Hove . . . 6L 153
Oxford Pl. BN1: Brig . . . 4F 172 (6B 154)
Oxford Rd. BN11: Wor . . . 1G 171
RH10: Craw . . . 1G 29
RH13: Hors . . . 9A 26
Oxford St. BN1: Brig . . . 4F 172 (6B 154)
PO21: Bog R . . . 1K 181
Oxford Ter. *BN44: Stey* . . . *3A 130*
(off Jarvis La.)
Oxmarket Centre of Arts . . . *7C 140*
(off East St.)
Oxon Ct. BN43: Shor S . . . 5J 151

P

Pacific Ct. BN43: Shor B . . . 7J 151
Pacific Hgts. *BN2: Salt* . . . *3C 174*
(off Suez Way)
Pacific Ho. *BN16: Rust* . . . *4A 168*
(off Harsfold Cl.)
Pacific Way PO20: Sel . . . 4J 183
Packer Cl. RH19: E Grin . . . 1G 14
Packham Way RH15: Burg H . . . 4A 94
Paddock, The BN3: Hove . . . 4L 153
BN17: Lym . . . 7J 145
BN43: Shor S . . . 4G 151
GU27: Has . . . 3J 17
PO20: E Witt . . . 5M 177
PO22: Bog R . . . 7D 164
RH10: Craw . . . 5M 11
Paddock Cl. *BN14: Wor* . . . *9F 148*
(off Haynes Rd.)
GU27: Fern . . . 5J 37
Paddock Ct. BN41: Ports . . . 2B 152
Paddock Fld. BN1: Falm . . . 9J 135
Paddock Gdns. RH19: E Grin . . . 5E 14
Paddock Grn. BN16: Rust . . . 2D 168
Paddockhall Rd. RH16: Hay H . . . 4E 72
Paddockhurst La. RH17: Ard, Bal . . . 6E 30
Paddockhurst Rd. RH10: Turn H . . . 3A 30
RH11: Craw . . . 7C 10
RH17: Turn H . . . 3A 30
Paddock La. PO20: Sel . . . 3H 183
Paddocks PO22: Barn . . . 7J 143
Paddocks, The BN7: Plump G . . . 1M 115
BN7: Rod . . . 5K 157
BN15: S Lan . . . 8C 150
BN44: Up B . . . 3E 130
RH16: Hay H . . . 6D 72
Paddock Way BN14: Fin . . . 8C 128
GU27: G'wd . . . 1B 18
GU32: Peters . . . 7D 54
Padstow Wlk. RH11: Craw . . . 8A 10
Padua Ho. BN2: W'dean . . . 5N 155
Padua Ho. Flats BN2: W'dean . . . 5M 155
Padwick Rd. RH13: Hors . . . 9D 26
Padwicks Fld. RH20: Fitt . . . 5G 85
Page Ct. RH10: Craw . . . 7H 11
RH13: Hors . . . 1A 46
Pages La. BN11: Wor . . . 9L 149
Paget Cl. RH13: Hors . . . 2B 46
Pagets, The BN8: Newick . . . 9K 75
Pagewood Cl. RH10: Craw . . . 8M 11
PAGHAM . . . 4C 180
Pagham Cl. PO10: S'brne . . . 5G 137
Pagham Ct. PO21: Bog R . . . 9B 164
Pagham Harbour Nature Reserve . . . 5M 179
Pagham Harbour Nature Reserve Info. Cen. . . . 5J 179
Pagham La. PO20: Lag . . . 4J 163
Pagham Rd. PO20: Lag . . . 3B 180
PO21: Lag, Pag . . . 3B 180
Pains Flat RH15: Burg H . . . 9M 71
RH17: Ans . . . 9M 71
Pakyns Ct. BN6: Hurst . . . 1G 112
Palace of Fun . . . 9F 172 (9B 154)
Palace Pl. BN1: Brig . . . 8F 172 (8B 154)
Palatine Rd. BN12: Gor S . . . 9A 148
Palings Way GU27: Fern . . . 5J 37
Pallant, The BN12: Gor S . . . 9N 147
PO9: Hav . . . 4A 136
Pallant House Gallery . . . 7C 140
Pallingham Dr. RH10: Craw . . . 9L 11
Pallingham Rd. RH14: Wisb . . . 6M 63
Palm Ct. BN3: Hove . . . 7M 153
BN13: Durr . . . 6C 148
BN16: E Pres . . . 4F 168
Palm Dr. BN2: Brig . . . 8K 173
Palmeira Av. BN3: Hove . . . 7L 153
Palmeira Ct. BN3: Hove . . . 8L 153
(not continuous)
Palmeira Grande *BN3: Hove* . . . *7M 153*
(off Holland Rd.)
Palmeira Ho. BN3: Hove . . . 6M 153
Palmeira Mans. *BN3: Hove* . . . *7L 153*
(off Church Rd.)
Palmeira Pl. BN3: Hove . . . 6M 153
Palmeira Sq. BN3: Hove . . . 8L 153
(not continuous)
Palmer Cl. RH20: Storr . . . 5L 107
Palmer Pl. PO20: N Mun . . . 3F 162
Palmer Rd. BN16: Ang . . . 7E 146
RH10: Craw . . . 9L 11
Palmers Fld. Av. PO19: Chich . . . 5D 140
Palmer's Rd. PO10: Ems . . . 4F 136
Palmers Rd. Ind. Est. PO10: Ems . . . 4F 136
Palmerston Av. BN12: Gor S . . . 2A 170
Palmerston Ho. *RH16: Hay H* . . . *3F 72*
(off Sydney Rd.)
Palmerston Rd. PO11: Hay I . . . 8A 158
Palmers Way BN13: High S . . . 4B 148
Pangdean La. BN6: God G, Hurst . . . 4L 93
Pangdene Cl. RH15: Burg H . . . 7N 93
Pankhurst Av. BN2: Brig . . . 7D 154
Pankhurst Ct. RH11: Craw . . . 2D 28
Pannell Cl. RH19: E Grin . . . 4D 14
Pannells Ash RH14: Ifol . . . 8J 21
Panners Dr. RH20: Pulb . . . 9F 86
Pannett RH15: Burg H . . . 4N 93
Pannett Ho. *RH16: Hay H* . . . *7E 72*
(off Pinewood Way)
Pantiles, The BN12: Fer . . . 3K 169
Panton Cl. PO10: Ems . . . 2E 136
Parade, The BN1: Brig . . . 1L 153
BN3: Hove . . . 3G 152
BN16: E Pres . . . 4F 168
PO20: E Witt . . . *4K 177*
(off Cakeham Rd.)
PO21: Pag . . . 4C 180
RH10: Craw . . . 5G 11
RH12: Hors . . . *8L 25*
(off Cootes Av.)
RH19: E Grin . . . 1B 14
Parade Mans. *BN16: E Pres* . . . *4F 168*
(off Willowhayne Cres.)
Paradise La. PO10: W'brne . . . 1H 137
PARBROOK . . . 2H 65
Parchment St. PO19: Chich . . . 6B 140
Parham . . . 6C 106
Parham Cl. BN2: Brig . . . 8E 154
BN14: Fin V . . . 4D 148
BN16: Rust . . . 4A 168
BN17: L'ton . . . 2K 167
PO19: Chich . . . 8E 140
Parham Ct. BN11: Wor . . . 2E 170
Parham Ho. *BN3: Hove* . . . *6M 153*
(off Chatsworth Sq.)
PARHAM PARK . . . 6C 106
Parham Rd. BN14: Fin V . . . 4D 148
RH11: Craw . . . 5B 10
Parish Ho. RH11: Craw . . . 7F 10
Parish La. RH10: Pease P . . . 4E 28
Park, The BN2: Rott . . . 3A 174
Park & Ride
Hop Oast (Horsham) . . . 4L 45
Withdean . . . 1M 153
Park Av. BN3: Hove . . . 6G 153
BN6: Key . . . 5B 114
BN10: Tels C . . . 4G 175
BN11: Wor . . . 1J 171
BN43: Shor S . . . 5K 151
PO20: Sel . . . 3K 183
PARK BOTTOM . . . 2F 144
Park Cl. BN1: Brig . . . 8N 133
(Park Ct.)
BN1: Brig . . . 9F 134
(Park Rd.)
BN3: Hove . . . 2G 153
BN6: Hurst . . . 1J 113
BN14: Salv . . . 6E 148
BN41: Ports . . . 4D 152
GU27: G'wd . . . 2A 18
RH15: Burg H . . . 5A 94
Park Copse PO20: Sel . . . 1M 183
Park Ct. BN1: Brig . . . 8N 133
(Park Cl.)
BN1: Brig . . . 4A 154
(Whistler Ct.)
BN2: Brig . . . *7D 154*
(off Southover St.)
BN3: Hove . . . *6M 153*
(off Davigdor Rd.)
BN10: Peace . . . *5H 175*
(off Roderick Av.)
RH15: Burg H . . . 5B 94
RH16: Hay H . . . *5F 72*
(off Church Rd.)
Park Cres. BN2: Brig . . . 3G 172 (6C 154)
BN2: Rott . . . 3N 173
(not continuous)
BN11: Wor . . . 2G 171
BN41: Ports . . . 5C 152
GU29: Midh . . . 9G 59
PO10: Ems . . . 4D 136
PO20: Sel . . . 2L 183
RH18: F Row . . . 1N 33
Park Cres. Pl. BN2: Brig . . . 6C 154
Park Cres. Rd. BN2: Brig . . . 6C 154
Park Cres. Ter. BN2: Brig . . . 3G 172 (6C 154)
Park Dr. BN12: Fer . . . 2L 169
BN16: Rust . . . 2C 168
BN18: Yap . . . 2A 166
PO22: Felp . . . 7L 165
Park East RH16: Hay H . . . 7G 73
Parker Cl. RH10: Craw . . . 7M 11
Parker Ct. BN41: Ports . . . 3D 152
Parkers RH13: B Grn . . . 7D 44
Parker's Cotts. PO18: E Lav . . . 8C 120
Parkers Trade Pk. GU32: Peters . . . 6D 54
Park Farm Cl. RH12: Hors . . . 4A 26
Park Farm Rd. RH12: Hors . . . 4A 26
Parkfield RH12: Hors . . . 8N 25
Parkfield Av. PO21: Aldw . . . 9M 163
Parkfield Cl. RH11: Craw . . . 7B 10
Parkfield Ct. BN13: W Tar . . . 9E 148
Parkfield Rd. BN13: W Tar . . . 9E 148
Parkfield Way RH16: Hay H . . . 6C 72
Park Gate BN3: Hove . . . 7M 153
Park Hill BN2: Brig . . . 8C 154
Park Ho. BN11: Wor . . . 1M 171
Parkhurst Gro. RH6: Horl . . . 1G 5
Parkhurst Rd. RH6: Horl . . . 1G 4
Parkland Bus. Cen. BN15: Lan . . . 9A 150
Parklands BN43: Shor S . . . 5M 151
Parklands Av. BN12: Gor S . . . 3B 170
PO21: Bog R . . . 8C 164
Parklands Ct. BN12: Gor S . . . 2B 170
Parklands Rd. BN6: Key . . . 4A 114
PO19: Chich . . . 7A 140
Park La. BN18: Slind . . . 2J 143
BN42: S'wck . . . 6N 151
GU27: Fern . . . 4K 37
PO10: Row C . . . 6H 117
PO18: Hal . . . 9M 121
PO18: Mid L . . . 1N 139
PO18: Row C . . . 6J 117
PO20: Ald . . . 7C 142
PO20: Sel . . . 1K 183
Park La. RH13: Map . . . 3D 68
RH13: W Grin . . . 1A 90
RH16: Lind . . . 9K 51
RH19: Ash W, E Grin . . . 6K 15
RH20: A'ton . . . 1B 108
RH20: Big, Sutt . . . 4A 104
Park Lodge BN3: Hove . . . 5M 153
BN11: Wor . . . 2J 171
Park Mnr. BN1: Brig . . . 2M 153
Parkmead BN2: Brig . . . 6C 154
Park Mews, The *BN1: Brig* . . . *1M 153*
(off London Rd.)
Parkmore Ter. BN1: Brig . . . 2D 172 (5A 154)
Park Pde. *RH16: Hay H* . . . *5F 72*
(off South Rd.)
Park Pl. BN18: Arun . . . 2G 145
RH12: Hors . . . 1N 45
Park Ri. BN3: Hove . . . 2G 152
GU28: Petw . . . 1M 83
RH12: Hors . . . 7M 25
Park Rd. BN1: Brig . . . 9F 134
BN2: Rott . . . 3N 173
BN5: Henf . . . 3H 111
BN10: Peace . . . 6M 175
BN11: Wor . . . 1J 171
BN18: Yap . . . 2A 166
BN43: Shor S . . . 5K 151
GU27: Has . . . 5L 17
GU28: Petw . . . 9N 61
GU31: S Hart . . . 6N 77
GU32: Peters . . . 6F 54
PO10: S'brne . . . 4K 137
PO18: Good . . . 4H 121
PO20: Sel . . . 2L 183
PO21: Bog R . . . 1K 181
PO22: Barn . . . 7L 143
RH12: Fay . . . 2J 27
RH13: Slinf . . . 8B 24
RH15: Burg H . . . 5A 94
RH16: Hay H . . . 5F 72
RH17: Hand, Slau . . . 5D 48
RH18: F Row . . . 1N 33
RH19: E Grin . . . 3D 14
Park Rd. Ter. BN2: Brig . . . 8C 154
Park Royal
BN1: Brig . . . 6A 172 (7N 153)
Parks, The BN41: Ports . . . 2D 152
Parkside BN6: Key . . . 3B 114
BN11: Wor . . . 1J 171
BN43: Shor S . . . 4K 151
PO21: Bog R . . . *8E 164*
(off Up. Bognor Rd.)
RH10: Craw . . . 6G 10
RH15: Burg H . . . 5A 94
RH19: E Grin . . . 3C 14
Parkside Av. BN17: L'ton . . . 3M 167
Parkside Ct. BN17: L'ton . . . 3M 167
Parkside M. RH12: Hors . . . 9A 26
Park Sq. BN2: Brig . . . 8K 173
PARK STREET . . . 8A 24
Park St. BN1: Falm . . . 7K 135
(not continuous)
BN2: Brig . . . 8C 154
RH12: Hors . . . 9A 26
RH13: Slinf . . . 8A 24
Park St. La. RH13: Slinf . . . 8L 23
Parks Vw. *BN2: Brig* . . . *8C 154*
(off Up. Park Pl.)
Park Ter. *BN2: Rott* . . . *3N 173*
(off West St.)
GU28: Till . . . 8K 61
PO21: Bog R . . . 1K 181
Park Ter. Courtyard *RH12: Hors* . . . *1A 46*
(off Park Ter. E.)
Park Ter. E. RH13: Hors . . . 1A 46
Park Ter. W. RH12: Hors . . . 1A 46
Park Vw. BN1: Brig . . . 1B 172 (5N 153)
BN2: Brig . . . 7D 154
PO9: Row C . . . 6B 116
RH6: Horl . . . 2J 5
RH11: Craw . . . 7E 10
RH16: Hay H . . . 3F 72
Park Vw. Cl. BN10: Tels C . . . 3G 175
Park Vw. Ct. BN16: Rust . . . 2B 168
Park Vw. Gdns. RH19: E Grin . . . 1D 14
Park Vw. Ri. BN10: Tels C . . . 4G 175
Park Vw. Rd. BN3: Hove . . . 4K 153
Park Vw. Ter. BN1: Brig . . . 1B 172
Park Village, The BN1: Falm . . . 6H 135
Pk. Village Rd. BN1: Falm . . . 6H 135
Park Way BN42: S'wck . . . 5B 152
GU29: Ease . . . 7K 59
RH6: Horl . . . 2J 5
RH10: Craw . . . 4L 11
RH12: Hors . . . 9N 25
Parkway PO21: Bog R . . . 9B 164
Parkway, The BN16: Rust . . . 3C 168
Park Way Cl. BN42: S'wck . . . 5B 152
Park West RH16: Hay H . . . 7G 72
Parnell Cl. RH10: Craw . . . 8M 11
Parnell Ct. BN3: Hove . . . 7K 153
Parochial M. BN2: Brig . . . 8F 172
Parochial Ter. *BN2: Brig* . . . *8F 172*
(off Steine Gdns.)
Parry Cl. RH13: Hors . . . 7F 26
Parry Dr. BN16: Rust . . . 3A 168
Parsonage Bus. Pk. RH12: Hors . . . 7B 26
Parsonage Cl. GU32: Peters . . . 4H 55
Parsonage Est. GU31: Rog . . . 5E 56
Parsonage Farm Ind. Est. RH12: Hors . . . 6B 26
Parsonage Rd. BN5: Henf . . . 2H 111
RH12: Hors . . . 7A 26
Parsonage Way RH12: Hors . . . 7B 26
Parsons Cl. BN16: Ang . . . 9F 146
GU27: Has . . . 3L 17
RH6: Horl . . . 1G 5
Parsons Grn. GU27: Has . . . 3L 17
Parson's Hill BN18: Arun . . . 2H 145
Parsons Wlk. BN18: Walb . . . 5M 143
RH12: Hors . . . 2K 45
Parthings La. RH13: Hors . . . 3J 45
PARTRIDGE GREEN . . . 5D 90
Partridge Grn. Rd. RH13: Sherm . . . 5F 90
Partridge La. RH5: Newd . . . 2G 9
RH12: Newd, Rusp . . . 2G 9
Partridge Pl. RH10: Turn H . . . 6K 13
Pashley Ct. BN43: Shor S . . . 6J 151
Passfield Wlk. PO9: Hav . . . 9B 116
Paston Pl. BN2: Brig . . . 9E 154
Pasture, The RH10: Craw . . . 6L 11
Pasture Hill Rd. RH16: Hay H . . . 3E 72
PATCHAM . . . 8N 133
Patcham By-Pass BN1: Brig . . . 8N 133
Patcham Grange BN1: Brig . . . 9N 133
Patchdean BN1: Brig . . . 9A 134
(not continuous)
PATCHING . . . 4J 147
Patching Cl. BN12: Gor S . . . 9N 147
RH11: Craw . . . 5B 10
Patching Lodge BN2: Brig . . . 8D 154
Patchings RH13: Hors . . . 8C 26
Paterson Rd. GU33: Long C . . . 1B 34
Paterson Wilson Rd. BN17: L'ton . . . 3L 167
Pathfield Cl. RH12: Rudg . . . 4J 23
Pathfield Rd. RH12: Rudg . . . 4J 23
Pathfields GU27: Has . . . 4L 17
Pathfields Cl. GU27: Has . . . 4L 17
Path Link RH10: Craw . . . 5G 11
Patricia Av. BN12: Gor S . . . 3B 170
Patricia Cl. BN12: Gor S . . . 3B 170
Patrick's Cl. GU33: Liss . . . 6A 34
Patrington Cl. RH11: Craw . . . 9C 10
Patterdale Cl. RH11: Craw . . . 8D 10
Patterson's Wlk. BN12: Fer . . . 4K 169
Pavement, The RH10: Craw . . . 6G 10
Pavilion Bldgs. BN1: Brig . . . 8E 172 (8B 154)
Pavilion Cl. BN6: Hass . . . 2N 113
Pavilion Ct. BN2: Brig . . . 7F 172
BN3: Hove . . . 4B 172
Pavilion M. BN1: Brig . . . 7E 172 (8B 154)
Pavilion Pde. BN2: Brig . . . 8F 172 (8B 154)
Pavilion Retail Pk. BN2: Brig . . . 4D 154
Pavilion Rd. BN1: Falm . . . 7K 135
BN14: Wor . . . 1F 170
Pavilions, The RH10: Worth . . . 5N 11
RH11: Pease P . . . 5E 28
Pavilions in the Park, The . . . 8A 26
Pavilion St. BN2: Brig . . . 8F 172 (8B 154)
Pavilion Theatre
Brighton . . . 7E 172 (8B 154)
Worthing . . . 3H 171
Pavilion Way RH19: E Grin . . . 4E 14
Pax Cl. RH11: Craw . . . 8A 10
Paxmead Cres. BN14: Broadw . . . 7K 149
Pay Gate RH20: Wash . . . 8C 108
Payne Av. BN3: Hove . . . 5H 153
Payne Cl. PO21: Pag . . . 3C 180
RH10: Craw . . . 4M 11
Paynesfield RH17: Bol . . . 6E 70
PAYNES GREEN . . . 4H 7
Payne Ter. BN1: Brig . . . 4C 154
Paythorne Cl. BN42: S'wck . . . 4N 151
Paythorne Drove BN5: Fulk . . . 1N 131
Payton Dr. RH15: Burg H . . . 6A 94
Payton Ho. *RH15: Burg H* . . . *5E 94*
(off Kings Way)
Peace Cl. BN1: Brig . . . 4D 154
PEACEHAVEN . . . 5J 175
Peacehaven Golf Course . . . 6N 175
PEACEHAVEN HEIGHTS . . . 7M 175
Peacehaven Leisure Cen. . . . 5J 175
Peacemaker Cl. RH11: Craw . . . 8A 10
Peace Rd. GU29: Hey . . . 6J 81
Peacheries, The PO19: Chich . . . 8E 140
Peachey Rd. PO20: Sel . . . 4H 183
Peacock Cl. PO19: Chich . . . 4D 140
Peacock Ind. Est. BN3: Hove . . . 3A 172 (6M 153)
Peacock La. BN1: Brig . . . 1N 153
Peacock's Hill RH13: Lwr Bee . . . 3F 68
Peacocks La. RH20: G Grn . . . 6A 88
Peacock Wlk. RH11: Craw . . . 9C 10
Peak, The PO9: Row C . . . 3C 116
Peak La. BN16: King G . . . 4H 169
Pearman St. PO18: Sing . . . 8F 100
Pears Gro. PO10: S'brne . . . 5K 137
Pearson Rd. BN18: Arun . . . 3F 144
RH10: Craw . . . 5L 11
Pearsons Retreat BN11: Wor . . . 1M 171
Pear Tree Cl. RH15: Burg H . . . 5N 93
Peary Cl. RH12: Hors . . . 5A 26
Pease Cft. GU31: S Hart . . . 5A 78
PEASE POTTAGE . . . 5D 28
Pease Pottage Golf Course . . . 5C 28
Pease Pottage Hill RH11: Craw . . . 2E 28
PEASE POTTAGE SERVICE AREA . . . 4E 28
Pebble Wlk. BN17: L'ton . . . 1N 167
Pebble Way BN43: Shor S . . . 5M 151
Peckhams Copse La. PO20: N Mun . . . 2F 162
Peckham's Copse Trout Fishery . . . 1E 162
Peeks Brook La. RH6: Ship B, Horl . . . 7N 5
Peel Cl. BN17: Wick . . . 2J 167
Peele Ho. *RH13: Hors* . . . *4H 45*
(off The Avenue)
Peel Rd. BN2: Brig . . . 9G 154
Peerley Cl. PO20: E Witt . . . 5L 177
Peerley Rd. PO20: E Witt . . . 5L 177
Pegasus Cl. GU27: Has . . . 6F 16
Pegasus Ct. *BN11: Wor* . . . *2G 170*
(off Shelley Rd.)
RH11: Craw . . . 8A 10
RH14: Bill . . . 9J 43
Pegasus Way RH19: E Grin . . . 1H 15
Pegler Ct. *RH10: Craw* . . . *6F 10*
(off Pegler Way)
Pegler Way RH11: Craw . . . 6F 10
Pegwell Cl. RH11: Craw . . . 8B 10
Pelham Cl. BN10: Peace . . . 3K 175
Pelham Ct. BN13: W Tar . . . 8E 148
RH11: Craw . . . 1D 28
RH12: Hors . . . 9M 25
Pelham Dr. RH11: Craw . . . 1C 28
Pelham Pl. RH11: Craw . . . 1D 28
Pelham Ri. BN10: Peace . . . 3J 175
Pelham Rd. BN13: W Tar . . . 8D 148
RH16: Lind . . . 3H 73
Pelham Sq. BN1: Brig . . . 5F 172 (7B 154)

Pelham St.—Potnore

Pelham St. BN1: Brig 5F 172 (7B 154)
Pelham Ter. BN2: Brig 4D 154
PO10: Ems 5G 136
Pelleys La. PO20: Donn 3B 162
Pemberton Cl. BN15: Lan 6B 150
Pembley Grn. RH10: Copt 1E 12
Pembroke Av. BN3: Hove 7J 153
BN11: Wor 2D 170
Pembroke Ct. BN3: Hove 7J 153
(off New Church Rd.)
Pembroke Cres. BN3: Hove 6J 153
Pembroke Gdns. BN3: Hove 7J 153
Pembroke Rd. RH10: Craw 3L 11
Pembroke Way PO21: Aldw 8N 163
Pembury Cl. BN14: Broadw 9H 149
RH16: Hay H 6J 73
Pembury Rd. BN14: Broadw 9H 149
PO9: Warbl 5A 136
Penarth Gdns. BN17: Wick 8J 145
Penbridge La. RH13: Ship 1F 88
Pendarvis Ct. GU26: Gray 1E 16
PENDEAN 4H 81
Pendean RH15: Burg H 7D 94
Pende Cl. BN15: Somp 5A 150
Pendine Av. BN11: Wor 1L 171
Pendragon Ct. BN3: Hove 5J 153
Penfold La. BN16: Rust 1A 168
Penfold Mnr. GU27: Has 5M 17
Penfold Rd. BN14: Broadw 7J 149
RH10: Craw 1K 29
Penfolds Pl. BN18: Arun 3G 144
Penfold Way BN44: Stey 4A 130
Penhill Ct. BN15: S Lan 8C 150
Penhill Rd. BN15: S Lan 8B 150
Penhurst Pl. BN2: Brig 7G 154
BN13: Durr 8N 147
(off Ashburnham Cl.)
Penland Cl. RH16: Hay H 2E 72
Penland Rd. RH16: Hay H 1E 72
Penlands Cl. BN44: Stey 4A 130
Penlands Ct. BN44: Stey 4A 130
Penlands Ri. BN44: Stey 4N 129
Penlands Va. BN44: Stey 4N 129
Penlands Way BN44: Stey 4A 130
Penleigh Cl. BN15: S Lan 8C 150
Penn Cl. PO22: Midd S 7M 165
RH11: Craw 3F 10
Penn Ct. RH11: Craw 6B 10
Penn Cres. RH16: Hay H 4H 73
Pennels Cl. GU30: Mill 8L 35
Penn Gdns. RH20: A'ton 2C 108
Pennicott Rd. PO21: Bers 5A 164
Pennine Cl. RH11: Craw 6D 10
Pennington Ho. RH16: Hay H 6H 73
Penns Ct. BN44: Stey 2N 129
Penns Pl. GU31: Peters 5K 55
Penns Rd. GU32: Peters 5E 54
Pennycord Cl. PO20: Sel 5J 183
Pennycress Av. BN13: Durr 8M 147
Pennyfields PO22: Felp 7K 165
Penny La. PO10: S'brne 5H 137
Penrith Ct. BN14: Broadw 8H 149
Pensfold La. RH12: Rudg 6K 23
Penshurst Cl. RH10: Craw 5M 11
Penstone Cl. BN15: Lan 7A 150
Penstone Ct. BN43: Shor S 5M 151
Penstone Pk. BN15: Lan 7A 150
Pentland Rd. BN13: Durr 6C 148
Penton Ct. PO9: Hav 8B 116
Penwarden Way PO18: Bosh 6F 138
Penwith Dr. GU27: Has 7F 16
Penwood Grn. PO9: Hav 9B 116
Pen-y-Bos Track GU27: Has 8A 18
Peperham Ho. GU27: Has 4L 17
Peperham Rd. GU27: Has 3L 17
Peppard Rd. RH10: Craw 8M 11
Pepper Cl. PO11: Hay I 7A 158
Pepper Ct. BN17: L'ton 3J 167
(off Terminus Rd.)
Pepper Dr. RH15: Burg H 7A 94
PEPPERING 7M 125
Peppering La. BN18: Burp 6N 125
Pepperscoombe La. BN44: Up B 3D 130
Peppersgate RH13: Lwr Bee 2K 69
Peppersgreen La. BN44: A'hst, Wis 3M 109
Pepper's La. BN44: A'hst 2N 109
Peppers Yd. RH12: Hors 8A 26
Perceval Cl. GU29: Ease 8J 59
(off Lutener Rd.)
Perche Ct. GU29: Midh 2F 80
Perching Drove BN5: Fulk 1A 132
Percival Mans. BN2: Brig 9E 154
(off Percival Ter.)
Percival Ter. BN2: Brig 9E 154
Percy & Wagner Almshouses BN2: Brig 6C 154
(off Hanover M.)
Percy Rd. RH12: Hors 8M 25
Percy Ter. GU28: Petw 9N 61
Peregrine Rd. BN17: L'ton 2M 167
Perimeter Rd. RH6: Gatw 6K 5
Perimeter Rd. E. RH6: Gatw 8J 5
Perimeter Rd. Nth. RH6: Gatw 5F 4
Perimeter Rd. Sth. RH6: Gatw 8E 4
Perkstead Ct. RH11: Craw 9C 10
(off Kingsley Rd.)
Perrots La. BN44: Stey 4N 129
Perry Av. RH19: E Grin 1E 14
Perryfield Ho. RH11: Craw 7F 10
(off Perryfield Rd.)
Perryfield La. RH13: Cow, Lwr Bee 3L 69
Perryfield Rd. RH11: Craw 7E 10
Perryfields RH15: Burg H 4N 93
Perry Hill BN2: Salt 1C 174
Perrylands RH6: Charlw 6B 4
Perryman's Hill TN22: Fur G 7K 53
Perryman's La. TN22: Fur G 6K 53
Perrymount Rd. RH16: Hay H 4F 72
Perth Cl. RH11: Craw 3F 10
Perth Ho. GU29: Midh 2G 81
(off The Fairway)
Perth Way RH12: Hors 7C 26
Pescotts Cl. PO20: Bir 7H 161
Peskett Cl. RH13: B Grn 8D 44
Peterborough Rd. RH10: Craw 1G 29
Peterhouse Cl. PO21: Aldw 8A 164
Peterhouse Pde. RH10: Craw 3L 11
Peterlee Wlk. RH11: Craw 1E 28
Peter Rd. BN15: Lan 9N 149
Peters Barn Gallery 2N 81
Peters Cl. RH13: Southw 1L 67
PETERSFIELD 6F 54
Petersfield Bus. Pk. GU32: Peters 6D 54
Petersfield Golf Course 1J 55
Petersfield Mus. 6F 54
Petersfield (Old) Golf Course 8G 55
Petersfield Rd.
GU29: Midh, S'ham 9C 58
GU31: Buri 3D 76
PO9: Hav 2A 136
Petersfield Station (Rail) 5E 54
Petersfield Swimming Pool 6G 54
Petersfield Town FC 5G 55
Peter's Pl. PO20: Sel 2E 182
Peter Weston Pl. PO19: Chich 7D 140
Petlands Gdns. RH16: Hay H 6G 72
Petlands Rd. RH16: Hay H 6F 72
Pett Cl. BN2: Brig 7G 154
Petts Cl. PO20: Sel 1J 183
PETWORTH 9N 61
Petworth Av. BN12: Gor S 4A 170
Petworth Cottage Mus. 9N 61
(off High St.)
Petworth Ct. GU27: Has 5M 17
PO22: Felp 8H 165
(off Felpham Rd.)
RH11: Craw 9B 10
RH14: Bill 2K 65
(off Brooker's Rd.)
Petworth Dr. RH12: Hors 4C 26
RH15: Burg H 3B 94
Petworth House 9M 61
Petworth Ho. BN3: Hove 6M 153
(off Davigdor Rd.)
Petworth Park 7K 61
Petworth Rd. BN1: Brig 8C 134
GU8: Chidd 5G 18
(not continuous)
GU8: Has 6E 18
GU27: Has 5M 17
GU29: Midh 8K 59
RH14: Kird 7G 41
RH14: Wisb 1N 63
Pevensey Cl. RH10: Craw 7L 11
Pevensey Gdn. BN11: Wor 3E 170
Pevensey Rd. BN2: Brig 5D 154
BN9: Newh 7N 175
BN11: Wor 3D 170
PO21: Bog R 8A 164
RH13: Southw 8K 45
Peverel Rd. BN14: W Tar 9E 148
RH11: Ifield 7A 10
Peveril Cl. BN15: Somp 7L 149
Peveril Dr. BN15: Somp 7L 149
Pharos Quay BN17: L'ton 3J 167
(off River Rd.)
Philip Ct. BN3: Hove 6L 153
Phillips Cl. RH10: Craw 2K 29
Philliswood La.
PO18: Chil, Mard 3G 99
Phoebe M. PO18: Nutb 5N 137
Phoenix Brewery Student Residences
BN2: Brig 7C 154
(off Southover St.)
Phoenix Cl. BN17: Wick 1H 167
PO19: Chich 8C 140
Phoenix Cres. BN42: S'wck 5N 151
Phoenix Ho. BN11: Wor 1H 171
(off Chapel Rd.)
Phoenix La. RH19: Ash W 6L 15
Phoenix Pl. BN2: Brig 5G 172
Phoenix Ri. BN2: Brig 5G 172 (7C 154)
Phoenix Way BN42: S'wck 5N 151
Phrosso Rd. BN11: Wor 3D 170
Phyllis Av. BN10: Peace 3H 175
(Heathy Brow)
BN10: Peace 5G 175
(Margaret Ct., not continuous)
Physic Garden, The 6F 54
Pickers Grn. RH16: Lind 1H 73
Pickett's La. RH6: Gatw 7M 5
PICKHURST 1N 85
Pickhurst La. RH20: Pulb 1N 85
Pickhurst Rd. GU8: Chidd 1L 19
Pickwell La. RH17: Ans, Bol 5G 71
Picton St. BN2: Brig 6D 154
Picts Hill RH13: Hors 3L 45
Picts La. RH13: Cow 4J 69
Picturedrome Cinema 9D 164
PIDDINGHOE 2N 175
Piddinghoe Av. BN10: Peace 6K 175
(not continuous)
Piddinghoe Cl. BN10: Peace 5K 175
Piddinghoe Mead BN9: Newh 4N 175
Pierces La. RH16: Hay H 7D 72
Pierpoint Cl. BN6: Hurst 1H 113
Pier Point Rd. PO20: Itchen 5D 160
Pier Rd. BN17: L'ton 4K 167
Piers Secomb Cl. RH20: Cold 2J 105
Pigbush La. RH14: Lox 4M 21
Pigeonhouse La. BN16: Rust 4D 168
Pigeon Pass RH10: Turn H 7K 13
Piggery Hall La.
PO20: W Witt 2K 177
Piggott Pl. GU31: Peters 4H 55
Pig Pound Wlk. RH17: Hand 9D 28
Pike, The RH20: Wash 8C 108
Pilgrim Ct. RH16: Hay H 4H 73
Pilgrims Cl. BN14: Wor 9E 148
Pilgrims Ter. BN13: Wor 1E 170
Pilgrims Wlk. BN13: Wor 1E 170
Pilgrims Way PO21: Pag 2D 180
Pilot Ho. BN2: Brig 8C 154
Pilsey Island Nature Reserve 6L 159
Piltdown Rd. BN2: Brig 7G 154
Pimms Gdns. BN1: Brig 6E 172
(off Orange Row)
Pine Cl. GU29: W Lav 3H 81
PO20: Westg 7E 142
RH11: Craw 3E 10
RH14: Bill 9H 43
RH20: Storr 4N 107
Pine Ct. PO10: Ems 1F 136
Pine Gdns. RH6: Horl 3J 5
Pine Gro. PO9: Hav 4A 136
PO19: W Bro 4M 139
RH19: E Grin 1B 14
Pineham Copse RH16: Hay H 5G 72
Pinehurst RH12: Hors 7N 25
RH15: Burg H 7B 94
Pinehurst Pk. PO21: Aldw 8M 163
Pines, The BN2: Brig 3G 172
BN3: Hove 5A 172 (7N 153)
BN6: Hurst 9H 93
BN16: Ang 9E 146
BN18: Yap 1N 165
RH10: Worth 6M 11
RH12: Hors 6F 26
RH16: Hay H 5J 73
Pines Av. BN14: Char D 6H 149
Pine Shaw RH10: Craw 5M 11
Pines Ridge RH12: Hors 9K 25
Pinetops RH12: Hors 6F 26
Pine Tree Cl. BN6: Hurst 2K 113
Pine Trees BN6: Hass 3M 113
Pine Trees Cl. BN16: Ang 6E 146
Pinetrees Cl. RH10: Copt 1C 12
Pine Vw. Cl. GU27: Has 3L 17
Pine Wlk. PO21: Aldw 8M 163
Pine Way Cl. RH19: E Grin 5E 14
Pinewood BN1: Brig 2N 153
Pinewood Cl. BN1: Brig 3N 153
BN16: E Pres 2F 168
RH12: Broadb H 8H 25
Pinewood Ct. GU29: W Lav 2J 81
RH16: Hay H 7E 72
Pinewood Gdns. PO21: Bog R 9B 164
Pinewood Way GU29: Midh 3G 81
RH16: Hay H 7E 72
Pinfold RH16: Hay H 3E 72
(off Great Heathmead)
Pinfold Cl. BN2: W'dean 7M 155
Pinkhurst La. RH13: Slinf 9E 24
Pinks La. PO20: Bir 9G 161
Pinland Rd. RH13: Part G 7B 90
Pinova Cl. RH11: Ifield 3C 10
Pipers Cl. BN3: Hove 2E 152
RH13: Southw 9K 45
Pipers End RH13: Slinf 8C 24
Pipers La. GU28: N'chpl 2H 39
Pipers Mead PO20: Bir 9G 161
Pippin Link RH11: Ifield 3C 10
Piries Pl. RH12: Hors 9N 25
(off Carfax)
Pitcroft, The PO19: Chich 5E 140
Pitcroft La. GU31: Buri 3F 76
Pitfold Av. GU27: Has 5F 16
Pitfold Cl. GU27: Has 5G 16
Pitsham La. GU29: Bep, Midh 2F 80
(not continuous)
Pitsham Wood GU29: Midh 2F 80
Pitt Ct. BN6: Hurst 2J 113
(off High St.)
Pitt Gdns. BN2: W'dean 5L 155
Pitt La. BN6: Hurst 2J 113
Place St Maur des Fosses
PO21: Bog R 1M 181
(off Belmont St.)
Plainfields Av. BN1: Brig 7B 134
Plainwood Cl. PO19: Chich 3B 140
PLAISTOW 9E 20
Plaistow Cl. BN2: Brig 7G 154
Plaistow Rd. GU8: Chidd 7G 19
GU8: Duns 4C 20
RH14: Kird 2H 41
RH14: Plais, Lox 8H 21
Plantain Cres. RH11: Craw 1C 28
Plantation, The BN13: Salv 6D 148
BN16: E Pres 3F 168
RH20: Storr 6G 107
Plantation Cl. BN13: Salv 6D 148
Plantation Ri. BN13: Salv 6E 148
Plantation Rd. GU33: Hill B 9A 34
Plantation Way BN13: Salv 6D 148
RH20: Storr 6H 107
Plat, The RH12: Hors 8L 25
Platt, The RH16: Hay H 4J 73
PLATT'S GREEN 6J 89
Platts Mdw. RH14: Bill 1H 65
Platts Rdbt. RH14: Bill 1H 65
Plawhatch La.
RH19: F Row, Sharp 5C 32
Playden Cl. BN2: Brig 9F 154
Playden Ct. RH11: Craw 9B 10
Playing Fld. Cl. GU27: Has 3L 17
Plaza Ho. BN1: Brig 6E 172
Pleasant La. PO10: Tho I 3J 159
Plough Cl. RH11: Ifield 4B 10
Plough La. RH12: Hors 6B 26
Plover Cl. PO20: E Witt 5L 177
PO22: Bers 5C 164
RH11: Craw 4E 10
Plovers Rd. RH13: Hors 8C 26
Plummerden La. RH16: Lind 8M 51
PLUMMERS PLAIN 6L 47
PLUMPTON 8M 115
Plumpton Bostall BN7: Plump 9L 115
PLUMPTON CROSSWAYS 7M 95
PLUMPTON GREEN 1M 115
Plumpton Health & Fitness Club 3M 115
Plumpton La. BN7: Plump 4M 115
Plumpton Race Course 3M 115
Plumpton Rd. BN2: Brig 7E 154
Plumpton Station (Rail) 2M 115
Plumtree Cross La. RH13: Itch 6E 44
Plymouth Av. BN2: Brig 4F 154
Poels Ct. RH19: E Grin 2E 14
POLECAT 2H 17
Polecat Hill GU26: Hind 2H 17
GU27: Has 2H 17
Polecat La. RH13: Cops, Southw 2N 67
Polecat Valley GU26: Hind 2H 17
Poles La. RH11: Lowf H 9E 4
Polestub La. RH17: Cuck 2A 72
Policemans La. BN6: Hurst 1H 113
POLING 7A 146
Poling Cl. BN12: Gor S 9N 147
POLING CORNER 5A 146
Poling St. BN18: Poling 7N 145
Pollard Ct. BN11: Wor 2E 170
Pollards RH11: Craw 7C 10
Pollards Dr. RH13: Hors 8B 26
Pollard's Hill RH13: Southw 4L 67
Pollocks Path GU26: Hind 1F 16
Polperro Cl. BN12: Fer 3K 169
Pomper La. BN6: Hurst 5J 93
Pond Cl. RH14: Bill 1H 65
RH14: Lox 7M 21
Pond Copse La. RH14: Lox 6M 21
Pondcroft Rd. RH16: Lind 2J 73
Pond Farm Cl. RH13: Southw 7K 45
Pondfield Rd. RH12: Rudg 3K 23
Pond Head La. RH5: For G, Ock 1B 6
Pond La. BN13: Durr 7B 148
Pond M. BN13: Durr 7B 148
Pond Ri. RH20: W Chil 7K 87
Pond Rd. BN43: Shor S 6J 151
PO20: Brac 6M 177
Pondside RH16: Hay H 6D 72
Pondtail Cl. RH12: Hors 5A 26
Pondtail Copse RH12: Hors 5A 26
Pondtail Dr. RH12: Hors 4A 26
Pondtail Pk. RH12: Hors 5A 26
Pondtail Rd. RH12: Hors 6N 25
Pond Way RH19: E Grin 3H 15
Pond Wood Rd. RH10: Craw 4J 11
Pony Farm BN14: Fin 8D 128
Pookbourne La. BN6: Hick, Hurst 3G 93
Pook Hill GU8: Chidd, Has 1F 18
Pook La. PO9: Warbl 6A 136
(not continuous)
PO18: E Lav, Mid L 9B 120
RH14: Kird 2H 63
Pool Bar Wall BN7: Ifrd 1M 157
Pool Pas. BN1: Brig 9E 172
Pool Valley BN1: Brig 9E 172 (9B 154)
Popes Folly BN2: Brig 4D 154
Pope's La. RH20: Pulb 6D 106
Popes Mead GU27: Has 4L 17
Poplar Av. BN3: Hove 2G 152
Poplar Cl. BN1: Brig 3A 154
BN3: Hove 2G 152
RH11: Craw 3E 10
Poplar Gro. PO11: Hay I 8A 158
Poplar La. RH18: F Row 2L 33
Poplar M. RH16: Hay H 7D 72
Poplar Rd. BN13: Durr 8A 148
RH20: Pulb 6N 85
(off Station Rd.)
Poplars, The BN2: Brig 2G 172
BN6: Key 4B 114
BN12: Fer 4K 169
BN17: L'ton 1M 167
BN18: Yap 1A 166
RH13: Hors 8B 26
Poplars Caravan Park, The PO22: Bers 6E 164
Poplars Cl. RH15: Burg H 5N 93
Poplar Wlk. GU31: Peters 8E 54
Poplar Way GU29: Midh 3G 81
Poppy Cl. BN17: L'ton 1N 167
RH13: Southw 7L 45
Porchester Cl. RH13: Southw 8L 45
Portal Cl. PO18: W Ash 2F 138
PORTFIELD 6E 140
Portfield Av. BN1: Brig 8B 134
Portfield Cl. PO19: Chich 6E 140
Portfield Retail Pk. PO19: Chich 6F 140
Portfield Trad. Est. PO19: Chich 8F 140
Portfield Way PO19: Chich 5F 140
Port Hall Av. BN1: Brig 1B 172 (5N 153)
Port Hall M. BN1: Brig 2A 172 (5N 153)
Port Hall Pl. BN1: Brig 1B 172 (5N 153)
Port Hall Rd. BN1: Brig 2B 172 (5N 153)
Port Hall St. BN1: Brig 1B 172 (5N 153)
Portland Av. BN3: Hove 6G 152
Portland Bus. Pk. BN3: Hove 5G 152
Portland Cl. BN17: L'ton 2N 167
GU32: Peters 4H 55
RH16: Hay H 4H 73
Portland La. BN3: Hove 6F 152
Portland M. BN2: Brig 9D 154
Portland Pl. BN2: Brig 9D 154
Portland Rd. BN3: Hove 5F 152
BN11: Wor 2H 171
RH15: Burg H 5A 94
RH19: E Grin 4E 14
Portland Rd. Trad. Est. BN3: Hove 5F 152
Portland Sq. BN11: Wor 2H 171
Portland St. BN1: Brig 7D 172 (8A 154)
Portland Vs. BN3: Hove 6F 152
Portside BN2: Brig 8K 173
PORTSLADE 4C 152
PORTSLADE-BY-SEA 6E 152
Portslade Sports Cen. 2C 152
Portslade Station (Rail) 5F 152
Portsmouth La. RH16: Hay H 2G 73
Portsmouth Rd. GU26: Brams, Hind, Lip 5A 16
(not continuous)
GU30: Brams, Lip 5A 16
GU30: Lip, Mill 5F 34
GU33: Rake 5F 34
Portsmouth Wood RH16: Lind 1G 73
Portsmouth Wood Cl. RH16: Lind 1G 73
Portsmouth Wood Dr. RH16: Lind 1G 73
Portway BN44: Stey 4N 129
Post Horn Cl. RH18: F Row 2N 33
Post Horn La. RH18: F Row 2N 33
Posthorses RH20: A'ton 3E 108
Post Office La. PO20: N Mun 3F 162
Post Vw. RH20: Storr 7K 107
Pot La. BN12: Fer, Pat 6K 147
BN13: Pat 6K 147
Potnore PO18: Mid L 7A 120

Potteries, The—Reba Ct.

Potteries, The BN6: Ditch 7H 95
Potters Cnr. PO18: Hamb 4B 138
Potter's Cft. RH13: Hors 9B 26
Pottersfield RH10: Craw 5F 10
Potters Grn. PO18: Westh 4G 141
RH13: Cow 7H 69
Potters La. RH15: Burg H 7A 94
Potters Mead BN17: Wick 1J 167
Potters Pl. RH12: Hors 9N 25
Pottery Ho. *RH19: E Grin* *2D 14*
(off Fosters Pl.)
Pottery La. PO18: Nutb 5A 138
Potts La. RH20: Pulb 6B 86
Poulner Cl. PO22: Felp 7H 165
Poulter's La. BN14: Wor 7E 148
Pound, The PO21: Aldw 1G 181
RH15: Burg H 4A 94
Pound Cl. GU28: Petw 1N 83
RH14: Lox 6M 21
Pound Farm Rd. PO19: Chich 7E 140
Poundfield La. RH14: Plais 7H 21
Pound Ga. BN6: Hass 4M 113
POUND HILL 6L 11
Pound Hill Pde. RH10: Craw 5L 11
Pound Hill Pl. RH10: Craw 6L 11
Pound La. BN44: Up B 4E 130
RH13: Cow 9G 68
RH13: Mann H 4F 46
RH13: Ship 1H 89
Pound Lea PO11: Hay I 7A 158
Pound Pl. *GU28: Petw* *9N 61*
(off Pound St.)
Pound Rd. BN18: Walb 4L 143
PO20: W Witt 2F 176
Pound St. GU28: Petw 9N 61
Pound Way BN16: Ang 8F 146
POVEY CROSS 4F 4
Povey Cross Rd. RH6: Horl 4F 4
Poveys Cl. RH15: Burg H 5M 93
Powell Cl. RH6: Horl 1G 5
Powis Gro. BN1: Brig 6C 172 (7A 154)
Powis Rd. BN1: Brig 6B 172 (7N 153)
Powis Sq. BN1: Brig 5B 172 (7N 153)
Powis Vs. BN1: Brig 6C 172 (7A 154)
POYNINGS 1E 132
Poynings Ct. BN14: Fin V 2D 148
Poynings Dr. BN3: Hove 2H 153
Poynings Rd.
BN5: Fulk, Poyn 3B 132
BN45: Poyn 9E 112
(Mill Cl.)
BN45: Poyn 3B 132
(The Street)
RH11: Ifield 7N 9
Poynter Rd. BN3: Hove 5J 153
Poyntz Cl. PO19: Chich 1B 162
Pratton Av. BN15: Lan 6A 150
Prawn Cl. PO20: Sel 2G 182
Precinct, The PO11: Hay I 9A 158
PO21: Aldw 8A 164
Premier Ho. RH10: Craw 2F 10
Premier Pde. *RH6: Horl* *2K 5*
(off High St.)
Prescott Gdns. RH15: Burg H 5A 94
Prescott Ho. *RH15: Burg H* *4B 94*
(off Up. St John's Rd.)
PRESTON 4N 153
Preston Av. BN16: Rust 3C 168
Preston Cir. BN1: Brig 3E 172 (6B 154)
Preston Drove BN1: Brig 3N 153
Preston Grange BN1: Brig 1B 172 (4N 153)
Preston Hall M. *BN16: E Pres* *2E 168*
(off The Street)
Preston Indoor Bowls Club 4N 153
Preston Manor 4N 153
Preston Mans. BN1: Brig 1D 172 (5A 154)
Preston Paddock
BN16: Rust 3D 168
Preston Pk. Av. BN1: Brig 1D 172 (3A 154)
Preston Park Station (Rail) 3M 153
Preston Rd. BN1: Brig 1B 172 (3N 153)
Preston St. BN1: Brig 8B 172 (8N 153)
Preston Village M.
BN1: Brig *4N 153*
(off Middle Rd.)
Prestonville Ct. BN1: Brig 3B 172
Prestonville Rd. BN1: Brig 3C 172 (6A 154)
Prestonville Ter. BN1: Brig 3C 172
Prestwick Cl. RH11: Ifield 7N 9
Prestwick La. GU8: Chidd 1B 18
GU27: G'wd, Chidd 1B 18
Prestwood Cl. RH11: Craw 3D 10
Prestwood La. RH11: Ifield 3M 9
RH12: Rusp 3K 9
Pretoria Av. GU29: Midh 1G 80
Pretoria Cl. GU33: Long C 1C 34
Pretoria Rd. GU29: Midh 1G 80
Prewetts Mill RH12: Hors 1M 45
Priceholme RH17: Ard 3J 51
Price Way RH17: Ard 3J 51
Priestcroft Cl. RH11: Craw 6C 10
Priest House 5M 31
Priestlands Cl. RH6: Horl 1H 5
Priestley Way PO22: Felp, Midd S 7L 165
RH10: Craw 2J 11
Prime Cl. BN18: Walb 5M 143
Primrose Av. RH6: Horl 4K 5
Primrose Cl. BN17: L'ton 1N 167
RH11: Craw 9D 10
RH15: Burg H 4M 93
Primrose Copse RH12: Hors 4A 26
Primrose Ct. BN44: Stey 4A 130
Primrose La. GU33: Rake 5C 34
RH18: F Row 2N 33
Prince Albert St. BN1: Brig 8E 172 (8B 154)
Prince Av. BN15: S Lan 8E 150
Prince Charles Cl.
BN42: S'wck 4B 152
Prince George St. PO9: Hav 4A 136
Prince of Wales Ct. *BN3: Hove* *7H 153*
(off Kingsway)
Prince Regent's Cl. BN2: Brig 9F 154
Prince Regents Ct. BN2: Brig 8F 154
Prince Regent Swimming Complex
7E 172 (8B 154)
Princes Av. BN3: Hove 7J 153
Princes Ct. BN3: Hove 7J 153
BN43: Shor B 7G 151
Princes Cres. BN2: Brig 2G 172 (5C 154)
BN3: Hove 7J 153
Princes Cft. PO21: Pag 2C 180
Prince's Dr. PO18: Good 7G 121
Princes Ga. BN11: Wor 2D 170
Princes Ho. BN1: Brig 8E 172
Princes Marina Ho. BN16: Rust 5B 168
Prince's Pl. BN1: Brig 8E 172 (8B 154)
Princes Rd. BN2: Brig 1G 172 (5C 154)
GU32: Peters 5D 54
Princess Anne Rd. RH12: Rudg 4J 23
Princess Av. BN13: Wor 1D 170
PO21: Aldw 1J 181
Princess Ct. BN13: Wor 1D 170
RH16: Hay H 3G 72
Princess Margaret Rd.
RH12: Rudg 4J 23
Princess Pct. *RH6: Horl* *2J 5*
(off High St.)
Princes Sq. BN3: Hove 7J 153
Princess Rd. RH11: Craw 6E 10
Prince's St. BN2: Brig 8F 172 (8B 154)
Princes Ter. BN2: Brig 9F 154
Prince William Cl.
BN14: Fin V 5E 148
Prings La. RH13: Lwr Bee 1F 68
Prinsep Rd. BN3: Hove 5J 153
Prinstead Ct. PO10: S'brne 5K 137
PRINSTED 6K 137
Prinsted La. PO10: S'brne 5J 137
Prior Pl. PO19: Chich 5E 140
Priors Acre PO18: Box 2M 141
Priors Cl. BN44: Up B 4D 130
PO10: S'brne 4L 137
Priors Leaze La. PO18: Nutb, Hamb 4M 137
Priors Wlk. RH10: Craw 5E 10
Priors Waye PO21: Pag 1C 180
Priors Wood GU27: Has 5H 17
Priory, The BN1: Brig 9M 133
BN3: Hove 8K 153
RH16: Hay H 5G 72
Priory Cl. BN14: W Tar 9E 148
BN15: Somp 6M 149
PO18: Box 2M 141
PO21: Aldw 3D 180
RH6: Horl 1H 5
Priory Ct. BN1: Brig 1D 172
Priory Fld. BN44: Up B 4D 130
Priory Ga. *BN15: Lan* *7B 150*
(off North Rd.)
Priory La. PO19: Chich 6C 140
Priory M. RH16: Hay H 6F 72
Priory Park 6C 140
Priory Rd. BN6: Hass 2N 113
BN16: Rust 2A 168
BN18: Arun 4F 144
PO19: Chich 6C 140
RH15: Burg H 7B 94
RH18: F Row 5G 33
Priory Way RH16: Hay H 6G 72
Private Rd. RH17: Bal 7L 29
Privett Way GU32: Peters 7E 54
Proctor Cl. RH10: Craw 8L 11
Progress Ho. *BN17: L'ton* *3K 167*
(off Arundel Rd.)
Promenade PO21: Aldw, Bog R 1J 181
PO22: Felp, Midd S 9H 165
Promenade, The BN10: Peace 5G 174
(not continuous)
BN17: L'ton 5K 167
PO10: Ems 6F 136
Prospect La. PO9: Hav, Row C 9B 116
Prospect Pl. BN11: Wor 3H 171
RH11: Craw 6E 10
Providence, The PO19: Chich 7B 140
Providence Pl. BN1: Brig 3E 172 (6B 154)
(not continuous)
PO19: Chich *7B 140*
(off Chapel St.)
Providence Ter. BN11: Wor 1J 171
RH10: Turn H 8H 13
Pruetts La. GU31: Liss, Peters 1M 55
Pryors Grn. PO21: Aldw 1E 180
Pryors La. PO21: Aldw 2E 180
Pryors Wood RH12: King 6N 7
Puckshott Way GU27: Has 3M 17
Pudding La. RH6: Charlw 5A 4
Puffin Hill RH10: Turn H 7K 13
Puffin Rd. RH11: Ifield 7N 9
PULBOROUGH 6B 86
Pulborough Brooks Nature Reserve 9B 86
Pulborough Brooks Nature Reserve Vis. Cen.
2C 106
Pulborough Cl. BN2: Brig 6G 154
Pulborough Rd.
RH20: Coot, Storr 5F 106
Pulborough Station (Rail) 6N 85
Pulborough Way PO22: Felp 6L 165
Pulens Cres. GU31: Peters 5J 55
Pulens La. GU31: Peters 4H 55
Pump House, The BN3: Hove 5F 152
Punch Copse Rd. RH10: Craw 5H 11
Punches La. PO20: S Mun 7F 162
Punnetts Ct. RH11: Craw 9B 10
Purbeck Ho. BN2: Brig 8G 172
Purbeck Pl. BN17: L'ton 3J 167
Purcell Rd. RH11: Craw 9B 10
Purley Cl. RH10: Craw 9M 11
Purrocks, The GU32: Peters 4F 54
Purton Rd. RH12: Hors 7M 25
Putmans La. RH20: S Hart 2M 77
Puttick Cl. RH20: Storr 5K 107
Puttocks Cl. GU27: Has 6F 16
Pycroft Cl. PO11: Hay I 1C 158
PYECOMBE 9L 113
Pyecombe Ct. RH11: Craw 9B 10
Pyecombe Golf Course 9M 113
Pyecombe St. BN45: Pye 9J 113
Pyrford Cl. PO21: Pag 1D 180
PYTHINGDEAN 2N 85

Q

Q Leisure 4F 112
Quadrangle, The BN14: Fin 1C 148
RH6: Horl 2J 5
Quadrant, The BN6: Key 3B 114
BN12: Gor S 1A 170
QUAGS CORNER 1C 80
Quail Cl. RH12: Hors 4A 26
Quakers La. RH16: Hay H 4H 73
Quantock Cl. BN13: Durr 5D 148
RH11: Craw 6D 10
Quantock Rd. BN13: Durr 5D 148
Quantocks, The *BN17: L'ton* *2K 167*
(off Arundel Rd.)
Quarries, The RH13: Mann H 4G 47
Quarry Bank Rd. BN1: Brig 3C 154
Quarry Cl. RH12: Hors 5C 26
RH15: Burg H 5E 94
Quarry Hill RH16: Hay H 3D 72
Quarry La. PO19: Chich 8E 140
Quarry La. Ind. Est. PO19: Chich 8E 140
Quarry Ri. RH19: E Grin 1G 14
Quarry Way RH13: Southw 8K 45
Quarterbrass Farm Rd.
RH12: Hors 4A 26
Quashetts, The BN14: Broadw 8H 149
(not continuous)
Quay, The BN43: Shor B 7K 151
Quay Ct. BN43: Shor B 7L 151
Quay Mdw. PO18: Bosh 9D 138
Quayside BN17: L'ton 3H 167
Quayside, The BN43: Shor B 7K 151
QUEBEC 1M 77
Quebec St. BN2: Brig 7C 154
Queen Alexandra Av. BN3: Hove 2J 153
Queen Caroline Cl. BN3: Hove 2J 153
Queen Elizabeth Av.
RH15: Burg H 6A 94
Queen Elizabeth Country Pk. 4B 76
Queen Elizabeth Country Park Cen. 7A 76
Queen Elizabeth Rd. RH12: Rudg 4J 23
Queen Mary Av. BN3: Hove 2J 153
Queen's Av. PO19: Chich 9B 140
Queensborough Ct. BN11: Wor 1E 170
Queensbury M. BN1: Brig 8B 172 (8N 153)
QUEEN'S CORNER 1A 58
Queens Ct. *BN11: Wor* *3D 170*
(off Aglaia Rd.)
RH6: Horl 2J 5
RH16: Hay H 3G 72
Queens Cres. RH15: Burg H 6B 94
Queensdown School Rd.
BN1: Brig 2D 154
BN2: Brig 2D 154
Queens Dr. BN6: Key 3A 114
Queens Flds. E. PO21: Aldw 8A 164
Queens Flds. W. PO21: Aldw 8N 163
Queens Fld. Wlk.
PO21: Aldw 8A 164
Queen's Gdns. BN1: Brig 6E 172 (7B 154)
BN3: Hove 8L 153
PO19: Chich 9B 140
Queen's Ga. RH6: Gatw 6J 5
QUEENS HILL 1N 57
Queens La. BN18: Arun 3H 145
Queen's Mans. *BN11: Wor* *3G 170*
(off Wordsworth Rd.)
Queensmead PO21: Pag 3B 180
Queens Pde. BN3: Hove 3G 153
BN15: Lan *7B 150*
(off North Rd.)
RH13: Hors *1A 46*
(off Queen St.)
Queen's Pk. M. BN2: Brig 7D 154
Queen's Pk. Ri. BN2: Brig 7D 154
Queen's Pk. Rd. BN2: Brig 8C 154
Queen's Pk. Ter. BN2: Brig 7D 154
Queen's Pl. BN1: Brig 4F 172 (6B 154)
BN3: Hove 7L 153
BN43: Shor S 6J 151
Queen Sq. BN1: Brig 7D 172 (8A 154)
Queens Rd. BN1: Brig 7D 172 (8A 154)
BN11: Wor 3G 170
BN15: S Lan 8C 150
BN42: S'wck 4A 152
GU32: Peters 5D 54
RH6: Horl 2J 5
RH16: Hay H 3F 72
RH19: E Grin 4E 14
Queen's Rd. Quad.
BN1: Brig 6D 172 (7A 154)
Queen's Sq. PO21: Bog R 9E 164
RH10: Craw 6F 10
Queens St. GU29: S'ham 7C 58
Queen St. BN14: Broadw 8G 149
BN17: L'ton 3K 167
BN18: Arun 2H 145
PO10: Ems 5G 136
RH13: Hors 1A 46
Queens Wlk. RH19: E Grin 3E 14
Queensway BN2: Brig 7E 154
BN15: Lan 7B 150
PO11: Hay I 1A 158
PO21: Aldw 2G 180
PO21: Bog R 9D 164
RH10: Craw 6G 10
RH13: Hors 1N 45
RH19: E Grin 3E 14
Queen Victoria Av. BN3: Hove 2J 153
QUELL, THE 4C 38
Quell Farm Ind. Est. RH20: Great 3L 105
Quell La. GU27: Has 3B 38
Querneby Cl. BN43: Shor S 6N 151
Quest Cl. PO19: Chich 7D 140
Questen M. RH10: Craw 4M 11
Quinta Carmen *BN11: Wor* *3F 170*
(off Seaview Rd.)
Quinta M. RH11: Pease P 4D 28
Quinton Flds. PO10: Ems 2G 136
Quoin Estate, The BN15: Lan 9A 150

R

Race, The GU29: Ease 7K 59
Racecourse Rd. RH6: Gatw 5H 5
Racecourse Way *RH6: Gatw* *5H 5*
(off Nth. Terminal App.)
RACE HILL 6G 154
Rackfield GU27: Has 4F 16
RACKHAM 7A 106
Rackham Cl. BN13: Wor 8D 148
RH11: Craw 8F 10
Rackham Rd. BN13: Wor 8C 148
BN16: Rust 5A 168
BN18: Amb 8M 105
RH20: Amb, Pulb 8M 105
Rackham St. RH20: Pulb 8B 106
RACTON 7M 117
Racton Rd. PO10: Ems 2F 136
Radbone Cl. BN14: Broadw 7J 149
Radford Rd. PO21: Bog R 7C 164
RH10: Craw 9K 5
Radinden Dr. BN3: Hove 4M 153
Radinden Mnr. Rd. BN3: Hove 5L 153
Radnor Cl. BN13: Wor 9D 148
Radnor Rd. BN13: Wor 9D 148
Raglan Av. BN13: Durr 8C 148
Raglan Ct. *BN1: Brig* *7D 172*
(off Portland St.)
BN11: Wor 2E 170
Raglan Ter. PO10: Ems 4G 136
Railey Rd. RH10: Craw 5G 11
Rails La. PO11: Hay I 9B 158
Railway App. BN11: Wor 1G 171
RH19: E Grin 3E 14
Railway Cotts. RH17: Hors K 2A 52
Railway St. BN1: Brig 5D 172 (7A 154)
Railway Ter. GU29: Midh 1F 80
Rainbow Cl. RH6: Horl 1K 5
Rainbow Sq. BN43: Shor S 5L 151
Rainbow Way RH20: Storr 4L 107
RAKE 6D 34
Rake Bus. Pk. GU33: Rake 6D 34
Rake Industries GU31: Rake 7F 34
Rake Rd. GU30: Mill 9H 35
GU33: Liss 6A 34
Rakers Ridge RH12: Hors 6A 26
Raleigh Cl. BN43: Shor B 7H 151
Raleigh Ct. RH10: Craw 1J 11
Raleigh Cres. BN12: Gor S 1B 170
Raleigh Rd. PO21: Aldw 9K 163
Raleigh Wlk. RH10: Craw 8G 11
Raleigh Way BN12: Gor S 9A 148
Rambledown La. RH20: W Chil 1H 107
Ramblers Way RH11: Craw 3D 28
Ramillies Gdns. PO22: Felp 7K 165
Rampling Ct. RH10: Craw 7H 11
Ramsay Ct. RH11: Craw 2D 28
Ramscote GU31: Peters 5G 54
Ramsdean La. GU32: West 1B 76
Ramsdean Rd. GU32: Rams, Stro 7A 54
Ramsey Cl. RH6: Horl 2H 5
RH12: Hors 6A 26
Ramsey Rd. PO11: Hay I 9A 158
Ramshill GU31: Peters 5G 54
Rams La. GU8: Duns 1G 20
RAMSNEST COMMON 4H 19
Ramster Cotts. GU8: Chidd 4G 19
Rams Wlk. GU32: Peters 6F 54
Randall Scholfield Ct. RH10: Craw 5J 11
Randiddles Cl. BN6: Hurst 3K 113
Ranelagh Vs. BN3: Hove 5K 153
Ranmore Cl. RH11: Craw 3E 28
Ransome Cl. RH11: Craw 9A 10
Ranville Cl. GU28: Petw 1M 83
Ranworth Cl. PO22: Felp 7G 165
Rapeland Hill RH12: Hors 1C 26
Raphael Rd. BN3: Hove 6H 153
Rapley Av. RH20: Storr 5G 107
Rapley Ct. RH16: Hay H 5G 72
Rascals Cl. RH13: Southw 2K 67
Rastrick Cl. RH15: Burg H 7A 94
Ratham La. PO18: Bosh, W Ash 5F 138
(not continuous)
Rathbone Ct. RH20: Pulb 6B 86
Rathbone Ho. RH11: Craw 2D 28
Rathlin Rd. RH11: Craw 9D 10
Raughmere Ct. PO18: Mid L 9C 120
Raughmere Dr. PO18: Mid L 1B 140
Raven Cl. RH10: Turn H 7K 13
RH12: Hors 5B 26
Ravendene Ct. RH11: Craw 7F 10
Raven La. RH11: Craw 4E 10
Ravensbourne Av. BN43: Shor S 4J 151
Ravensbourne Cl. BN43: Shor S 4J 151
Ravenscroft *BN16: Rust* *4B 168*
(off Sutton Av.)
RH20: Storr 7J 107
Ravenscroft Ct. RH12: Hors 8N 25
Ravensdale Cotts. GU26: Hind 3E 16
Raven's Rd. BN43: Shor S 6J 151
Ravens Way PO22: Bers 6C 164
Ravenswood BN6: Hass 3N 113
Ravenswood Ct. BN13: W Tar 8D 148
Ravenswood Dr. BN2: W'dean 7N 155
Ravenswood Rd. RH15: Burg H 5C 94
Rawlinson Rd. RH10: Craw 8M 11
Raworth Cl. RH10: Craw 8K 11
Rawson Vs. BN16: Rust 2B 168
Ray Cl. GU31: Peters 4G 54
Raycroft Cl. PO21: Aldw 1H 181
Rayden Cl. BN17: L'ton 3L 167
Rayford Cl. BN10: Peace 5J 175
Raylands Pk. RH13: Southw 8M 45
Raymer Wlk. RH6: Horl 1L 5
Reading Rd. BN2: Brig 9G 154
Readon Cl. GU31: Peters 5G 54
Read's Wlk. BN44: Stey 1A 130
Reapers Cl. RH12: Hors 6A 26
Reba Ct. BN2: Salt 4D 174

Record Rd.—Rosemary Cl.

Record Rd. PO10: Ems .4E 136
Rectory Cl. BN3: Hove .6F 152
BN43: Shor S .6N 151
RH5: Ock .1G 7
RH20: A'ton .2E 108
RH20: Pulb .6B 86
RH20: Storr .6J 107
Rectory Ct. BN43: Shor S .5M 151
(off Pebble Way)
Rectory Farm Rd. BN15: Somp .6M 149
Rectory Flats RH11: Ifield .4B 10
Rectory Gdns. BN14: Broadw .7G 149
Rectory La. BN13: Clap .4K 147
BN16: Ang .8E 146
GU28: Petw .9N 61
GU30: Brams .4A 16
PO20: Sel .9K 179
RH6: Charlw .6A 4
RH11: Ifield .4B 10
RH20: A'ton .1B 108
RH20: Pulb .6B 86
Rectory Pl. RH20: A'ton .2D 108
Rectory Rd. BN14: W Tar .9E 148
BN43: Shor S .6M 151
RH20: Storr .6J 107
Rectory Wlk. BN15: Somp .6N 149
RH20: Storr .6J 107
Red Admiral St. RH12: Hors .5B 26
Red Barn Cres. PO22: Felp .6H 165
Redbridge La. RH17: Bal .9N 29
Red Cotts. GU27: G'wd .1N 17
Redcotts BN11: Wor .1F 170
Redcross St. BN1: Brig .5F 172
Red Deer Cl. RH13: Hors .8E 26
Redditch Cl. RH11: Craw .1A 28
REDFORD .9C 36
Redford Av. RH12: Hors .7M 25
Redgarth Ct. RH19: E Grin .1B 14
Redgill La. BN8: Newick, N Cha .9G 75
Redgrave Dr. RH10: Craw .7M 11
RED HILL .5B 116
Redhill Cl. BN1: Brig .9L 133
Redhill Dr. BN1: Brig .9L 133
Redhill Rd. PO9: Row C .6B 116
Red Ho. Ct. GU31: Rog .5E 56
Redhouse Farm Caravan Site
PO20: Earn .2A 178
Redkiln Cl. RH13: Hors .8C 26
Redkiln Cl. Ind. Est. RH13: Hors .7C 26
Redkiln Way RH13: Hors .7C 26
Redlands La. PO10: Ems .1F 136
PO20: W Witt .9C 160
Red La. RH13: Ship .9G 67
Red Lion St. GU29: Midh .1H 81
Redlynch Cl. PO9: Hav .1B 136
Red Oak Ct. GU29: Ease .7J 59
(off Egmont Rd.)
Red Ridges PO21: Aldw .1J 181
(off King's Pde.)
Red River Ct. RH12: Hors .6M 25
Redshank Ct. RH11: Ifield .7N 9
(off Stoneycroft Wlk.)
Redvers Rd. BN2: Brig .4E 154
Redwing Cl. BN17: Wick .9J 145
RH13: Hors .8C 26
Redwing Ct. PO10: Ems .1G 136
Redwood Cl. BN13: Durr .8A 148
RH10: Craw .4G 10
Redwood Ct. BN17: L'ton .3L 167
Redwood Dr. RH16: Hay H .6E 72
Redwood Gro. PO9: Hav .1A 136
Redwood Mnr. GU27: Has .4L 17
Redwood Pl. PO21: Aldw .1G 181
Reed Cl. PO20: Huns .4C 162
RH20: Storr .6H 107
Reedings RH11: Ifield .8N 9
Reed Pond Wlk. RH16: Hay H .5H 73
Reeds La. BN6: Say C .9C 92
GU33: Liss .4C 34
RH13: Part G .4D 90
RH13: Southw .7M 45
Reef Cl. BN17: L'ton .4M 167
Rees Cl. BN13: Durr .7N 147
Reeves Hill BN1: Brig .9E 134
Reeves Ho. RH10: Craw .6K 11
(off Trafalgar Gdns.)
Refectory Rd. BN1: Falm .6J 135
Regal Dr. RH19: E Grin .4F 14
Regency Apartments BN11: Wor .3G 171
(off Crescent Rd.)
Regency Ct. BN1: Brig .2M 153
BN12: Fer .2L 169
BN13: Salv .7E 148
Regency M. BN1: Brig .7B 172 (8N 153)
RH16: Hay H .3G 72
Regency Rd. BN1: Brig .8C 172 (8A 154)
(not continuous)
Regency Sq. BN1: Brig .7B 172 (8N 153)
Regency Town House .8M 153
Regent Arc. BN1: Brig .8E 172
Regent Bus. Cen. RH15: Burg H .6N 93
Regent Cl. BN15: S Lan .7E 150
Regent Hill BN1: Brig .7C 172 (8A 154)
Regent Row BN1: Brig .7C 172 (8A 154)
Regents Cl. RH11: Craw .1E 28
Regents M. GU32: Peters .5D 54
RH6: Horl .2J 5
Regent St. BN1: Brig .7E 172 (8B 154)
Regents Way PO21: Aldw .8A 164
Regis Av. PO21: Aldw .3D 180
Regis Bus. Cen. PO22: Bers .6E 164
Regis Ct. BN11: Wor .3E 170
PO21: Bog R .9E 164
Regis Gate PO21: Bog R .8D 164
Reigate Cl. RH10: Craw .3M 11
Reigate Ct. BN11: Wor .2D 170
(off Reigate Rd.)
Reigate Rd. BN1: Brig .1A 172 (4M 153)
BN11: Wor .2D 170
RH6: Hookw, Horl .1E 4
Renfields RH16: Hay H .6D 72
Renoir Ct. PO22: Bers .6B 164
Renoir M. PO22: Bers .6B 164
Renton Cl. RH14: Bill .1H 65
Reservoir La. GU32: Peters .4F 54
Rest-a-Wyle Av. PO11: Hay I .7A 158
Rew La. PO19: Chich .2B 140
Rex Ct. GU27: Has .5H 17
Reynard Cl. RH12: Hors .6E 26
Reynolds La. BN18: Slind .1L 143
Reynolds Pl. RH11: Craw .5E 10
Reynolds Rd. BN3: Hove .6H 153
RH11: Craw .5E 10
Rhodes Way RH10: Craw .9H 11
Ribbetts Ho. BN6: Hurst .2J 113
Rices Hill RH19: E Grin .3F 14
Richard Allen Ct. BN1: Brig .4D 154
Richardson Ct. BN3: Hove .6H 153
RH11: Craw .2D 28
Richardson Rd. BN3: Hove .6H 153
Richborough Ct. RH11: Craw .6E 10
Richmond Av. PO19: Chich .4C 140
PO21: Bog R .9B 164
Richmond Av. W. PO21: Bog R .1J 181
Richmond Cl. BN16: Rust .2D 168
Richmond Ct. BN3: Hove .4A 172
BN11: Wor .2G 170
BN16: Rust .3A 168
RH10: Craw .7G 10
Richmond Gdns.
BN2: Brig .5G 172 (7C 154)
Richmond Hgts. BN2: Brig .7C 154
Richmond Ho. PO19: Chich .7C 140
(off Church Sq.)
PO21: Bog R .9D 164
(off Queensway)
Richmond M. PO22: Shrip .4E 164
Richmond Pde. BN2: Brig .6G 172 (7B 154)
Richmond Pl. BN2: Brig .5F 172 (7B 154)
Richmond Rd. BN2: Brig .5C 154
BN11: Wor .2F 170
PO18: Good .2G 141
PO21: Bog R .9D 164
RH12: Hors .7N 25
Richmond Rd. Nth. PO21: Bog R .8E 164
Richmond Sq. RH19: E Grin .2C 14
Richmond St. BN2: Brig .7C 154
Richmond Ter. BN2: Brig .5G 172
Richmond Way RH19: E Grin .4F 14
Rickfield RH11: Craw .7C 10
RICKMANS GREEN .1M 11
Rickman's La. RH14: Plais, Kird .9F 20
Rickwood RH6: Horl .1K 5
Riddens, The BN7: Plump G .2M 115
Riddens Cl. BN7: Plump G .2M 115
Riddens La. BN7: Plump G .1M 115
Ride, The BN1: Brig .1D 172 (4A 154)
RH14: Ifol .8H 21
Ridge, The RH12: Rudg .3K 23
Ridge Cl. BN41: Ports .1C 152
RIDGE COMMON .3C 54
Ridge Comn. La. GU32: Steep, Stro .5B 54
Ridgehurst Dr. RH12: Hors .1K 45
Ridge Rd. BN1: Falm .6K 135
Ridgeside RH10: Craw .6H 11
(not continuous)
Ridgeside Av. BN1: Brig .9N 133
Ridge Top La. GU32: Frox, Steep, Stro .2A 54
Ridge Vw. BN1: Brig .9F 134
Ridge Way RH17: Hay H .7J 73
Ridgeway BN42: S'wck .4B 152
RH19: E Grin .5E 14
Ridgeway, The GU27: Fern .4K 37
PO19: Chich .6A 140
(off Oliver Whitby Rd.)
RH6: Horl .4J 5
RH12: Hors .7M 25
RH15: Burg H .4C 94
Ridgeway Cl. BN42: S'wck .4B 152
Ridgeway Gdns. BN2: W'dean .6M 155
Ridgeway Ho. RH6: Horl .4J 5
(off The Crescent)
Ridgeway Office Pk. GU32: Peters .7D 54
Ridgewood Av. BN2: Salt .1C 174
Ridgway, The BN2: W'dean .5L 155
PO22: Felp .8J 165
Ridgway Cl. BN2: W'dean .5L 155
Ridings, The BN2: O'dean .9K 155
BN10: Tels C .3H 175
BN16: E Pres .4E 168
BN18: Font .3H 143
BN44: Bramb .5A 130
GU33: Liss .6A 34
PO21: Aldw .2E 180
RH10: Craw .5M 11
RH15: Burg H .6D 94
RH17: Hay H .6J 73
Ridley Ct. RH10: Craw .3M 11
Ridleys RH19: W Hoa .5M 31
Ridleys Cnr. Rdbt. RH10: Craw .4M 11
Rife La. PO20: Sel .2F 182
Rifeside Gdns. BN12: Fer .1K 169
Rife Way BN12: Fer .2K 169
PO22: Felp .8G 164
Rigden Rd. BN3: Hove .5L 153
Riley Rd. BN2: Brig .5D 154
Rillside RH10: Craw .9J 11
Rill Wlk. RH19: E Grin .3H 15
Rimmer Cl. RH11: Craw .3D 28
Ringley Av. RH6: Horl .2J 5
Ringley Oak RH12: Hors .7C 26
Ringley Rd. RH12: Hors .7B 26
Ringmer Cl. BN1: Brig .1F 154
Ringmer Dr. BN1: Brig .1G 154
Ringmer Rd. BN1: Brig .1F 154
BN9: Newh .6N 175
BN13: Wor .8C 148
Ring Rd. BN15: N Lan .4B 150
Ring Rd. Nth. RH6: Gatw .5K 5
Ring Rd. Sth. RH6: Gatw .6L 5
Ringwood Cl. RH10: Craw .8G 11
Ripley Rd. BN11: Wor .2D 170
Ripon Ct. BN11: Wor .2E 170
(off Pevensey Gdns.)
Ripon Gdns. PO21: Aldw .9N 163
Riptide .9C 172 (9A 154)
Rise, The BN41: Ports .3B 152
RH10: Craw .6L 11
RH13: Part G .4D 90
RH16: Hay H .4J 73
RH19: E Grin .4E 14
Rissom Ct. BN1: Brig .3N 153
Ritchie Cl. PO11: Hay I .9A 158
RH10: Craw .1L 29
Rival Moor Rd. GU31: Peters .6J 55
RIVER .7E 60
Riverbank BN43: Shor B .7H 151
Riverbank Bus. Cen. BN43: Shor S .6H 151
River Cl. BN43: Shor B .7H 151
RIVER COMMON .5F 60
RIVERHILL .1E 84
Riverhill La. RH20: Petw .9E 62
River La. GU28: Lods, Riv, Till .5D 60
RH20: Cold .3G 105
River Mead RH11: Ifield .3C 10
RH12: Hors .1M 45
Rivermead RH20: Pulb .6C 86
Rivermead Ct. PO10: Ems .2G 137
River Rd. BN17: L'ton .3J 167
BN18: Arun .3H 145
(not continuous)
Riversdale Gdns. PO9: Hav .3A 136
Riverside BN42: S'wck .7A 152
BN43: Shor B .7J 151
BN44: Up B .4D 130
PO19: Chich .6D 140
RH6: Horl .4J 5
RH12: Hors .9L 25
RH18: F Row .9L 15
RH20: Pulb .4B 86
RH20: Storr .5J 107
Riverside Bus. Cen. BN43: Shor S .6J 151
Riverside Caravan Cen. PO22: Bers .5E 164
Riverside Caravan Pk. BN44: Up B .4D 130
Riverside Ct. RH20: Pulb .6N 85
(off Station Rd.)
Riverside Ind. Est. BN17: L'ton .3H 167
Riverside Pk. BN18: Amb .2K 125
Riverside Rd. BN43: Shor B .7J 151
Riverside Ter. PO10: Ems .5G 136
Riverside Wlk. GU31: Peters .6G 55
(not continuous)
River's Rd. RH16: Hay H .7E 50
River St. PO10: W'brne .1H 137
River Wlk. RH12: Hors .1K 45
River Way PO9: Hav .2A 136
Rixons Cl. RH17: Hors K .5C 52
Rixons Orchard RH17: Hors K .5C 52
Robell Way RH20: Storr .4K 107
Robert Lodge BN2: Brig .9G 154
Roberts Cl. RH13: Southw .6K 45
Roberts Marine Mans. BN11: Wor .3D 170
(off West Pde.)
Robertson Rd. BN1: Brig .3M 153
Roberts Rd. BN15: S Lan .9B 150
Robert St. BN1: Brig .6E 172 (7B 154)
Robert Way RH12: Hors .4C 26
Robin Cl. BN17: Wick .9J 145
RH11: Craw .4E 10
RH13: Southw .8L 45
RH19: E Grin .2F 14
Robin Davis Cl. BN2: Brig .5F 154
Robin Dene BN2: Brig .9F 154
Robin Hood La. RH12: Warnh .6J 25
Robin Hood Rdbt. RH12: Warnh .6M 25
Robinia Lodge BN1: Brig .3N 153
Robin Rise RH16: Hay H .6G 73
Robin Rd. RH15: Burg H .6M 93
Robin Row RH10: Turn H .7K 13
Robins Cl. PO20: Sel .2J 183
Robins Dr. PO21: Aldw .9M 163
Robins La. GU29: Ipin .2N 57
Robinson Cl. BN15: Lan .7B 150
PO20: Sel .1J 183
Robinson Ho. RH11: Craw .7F 10
Robinson Way PO20: E Witt .5M 177
Robins Row BN41: Ports .4C 152
Robinswood Ct. RH12: Hors .7C 26
Robson Ct. BN12: Gor S .1C 170
Robson Rd. BN12: Gor S .2C 170
Rochester Cl. BN3: Hove .7M 153
BN13: Durr .8N 147
PO19: Chich .4B 140
Rochester Ct. BN3: Hove .7M 153
(off Rochester Gdns.)
BN11: Wor .2E 170
(off Pevensey Gdns.)
Rochester Gdns. BN3: Hove .7M 153
Rochester St. BN2: Brig .8E 154
Rochester Way PO21: Aldw .9N 163
ROCK .6C 108
Rockall Cl. BN17: L'ton .1N 167
Rockall Way PO18: Bosh .6G 138
Rock Cl. BN42: S'wck .6A 152
(off Whiterock Pl.)
Rockdene Cl. RH19: E Grin .3G 14
Rockeries, The GU29: Midh .1G 81
(off Cobden Rd.)
Rock Gdns. PO21: Bog R .1L 181
(not continuous)
Rock Gro. BN2: Brig .9E 154
Rockingham Cl. BN13: Durr .7C 148
Rockingham Ct. BN13: Durr .7C 148
Rock La. RH20: Wash .6C 108
Rock Pl. BN2: Brig .9C 154
Rock Rd. RH20: Storr, Wash .4M 107
Rocks, The RH19: Ash W .6J 15
Rocks La. RH17: Bal .2N 49
Rock St. BN2: Brig .9F 154
Rockwood Ct. PO10: Ems .4F 136
ROCKWOOD PARK .7C 14
Rocky La. RH16: Hay H .9D 72
Roderick Av. BN10: Peace .6H 175
(Cavell Av., not continuous)
BN10: Peace .4J 175
(Southview Rd., not continuous)
Roderick Av. Nth. BN10: Peace .1J 175
Roderick Ct. BN10: Peace .4J 175
(off Roderick Av.)
Rodgate La. GU27: Has .6E 18
RODMELL .4L 157
Rodmell Av. BN2: Salt .3D 174
Rodmell Pl. BN1: Brig .8B 134
Rodmell Rd. BN13: Wor .8C 148
Rodney Cl. PO21: Aldw .9L 163
Rodney Cres. BN18: Ford .9D 144
Roebuck Cl. RH13: Hors .7E 26
Roedale Rd. BN1: Brig .4C 154
ROEDEAN .1J 173
Roedean Cl. BN2: Brig .9G 154
Roedean Cres. BN2: Brig .9H 155
Roedean Hgts. BN2: Brig .9H 155
Roedean Path BN2: Brig .1J 173
Roedean Rd. BN2: Brig .9G 154
BN13: Durr .7C 148
Roedean Ter. BN2: Brig .1J 173
Roedean Va. BN2: Brig .1J 173
Roedean Way BN2: Brig .8L 173
Roedeer Copse GU27: Has .5G 17
ROFFEY .7D 26
Roffey Cl. RH6: Horl .2H 5
ROFFEY PARK .5J 27
Roffey Pk. RH12: Colg .5H 27
Roffey's Cl. RH10: Copt .1B 12
Roffey Social and Sports Club .6D 26
(off Leith Vw. Rd.)
Roffye Ct. RH12: Hors .7D 26
ROGATE .5E 56
Rogate Cl. BN13: Salv .7E 148
BN15: Somp .6M 149
Rogate Rd. BN13: Salv .7D 148
GU33: Hill B .9A 34
Roger's La. BN14: Fin .9C 128
Rogers Mead PO11: Hay I .1A 158
Rokewood Dr. RH11: Ifield .3C 10
Rolfe Dr. RH15: Burg H .5E 94
Rollaston Pk. BN18: Ford .2B 166
Rolston Ho. GU27: Has .5H 17
Romaine Cl. RH15: Burg H .3E 94
Roman Acre BN17: Wick .2J 167
Roman Amphitheatre
Chichester .7D 140
Roman Av. BN16: Ang .9F 146
Roman Ct. PO10: S'brne .4K 137
RH15: Burg H .5B 94
Roman Cres. BN42: S'wck .5A 152
Roman Flds. PO21: Bog R .8B 164
Roman Landing PO20: W Witt .1F 176
Roman Rd. BN3: Hove .7F 152
BN42: S'wck .5A 152
BN44: Stey .4B 130
Roman Wlk. BN15: Somp .6M 149
Roman Way BN42: S'wck .5A 152
PO19: Fish .7L 139
RH14: Bill .9J 43
Romany Cl. BN41: Ports .5D 152
Romany Rd. BN13: Durr .8N 147
Romney Broadwalk PO22: Bers .6C 164
Romney Ct. BN11: Wor .3D 170
Romney Gth. PO20: Sel .3K 183
Romney Rd. BN2: Rott .3A 174
BN11: Wor .3D 170
Romsey Cl. BN1: Brig .3C 154
Rona Cl. RH11: Craw .9D 10
Rondle Wood GU30: Mill .2H 57
Ronuk Ho. BN41: Ports .5E 152
(off Carlton Ter.)
Rookcross La. RH13: W Grin .3L 89
Rookery, The PO10: S'brne .4G 136
PO20: Sel .2K 183
Rookery Cl. BN1: Brig .4N 153
Rookery La. PO20: Sidle .2J 179
Rookery Way RH16: Hay H .8F 72
Rookes M. GU31: Peters .5G 54
Rook Farm Way PO11: Hay I .8A 158
Rooksbury Cft. PO9: Hav .9A 116
Rook Way RH12: Hors .5C 26
ROOKWOOD .9A 160
Rookwood Golf Course .7L 25
Rookwood La. PO20: W Witt .8N 159
Rookwood Pk. RH12: Hors .8K 25
Rookwood Rd. PO20: W Witt .1G 176
Roosthole Hill RH13: Colg .2G 46
Ropeland Way RH12: Hors .4B 26
Ropes La. GU27: Fern .5L 37
Ropetackle BN43: Shor S .6H 151
Rope Wlk. BN17: L'ton .3J 167
BN43: Shor S .6H 151
Ropley Rd. PO9: Hav .9B 116
Rosamund Rd. RH10: Craw .8K 11
Rosary, The RH13: Part G .5C 90
Rose Av. PO22: Midd S .7N 165
Rosebarn Cl. RH15: Burg H .7D 94
Rosebery Av. BN2: W'dean .5K 155
BN12: Gor S .2C 170
Rose Cott. La. RH17: S'fld .6J 49
Rose Cotts. RH12: Fay .3M 27
RH18: F Row .9L 15
Rose Ct. BN11: Wor .1M 171
BN17: L'ton .3K 167
(off Gloucester Rd.)
BN43: Shor S .4L 151
PO21: Aldw .9M 163
Rosecroft Cl. BN15: Lan .8B 150
Rosedale Cl. RH11: Craw .8C 10
Rosedene Cl. BN2: W'dean .7M 155
ROSE GREEN .9M 163
Rose Green Art & Craft Cen. .9M 163
(off Rose Grn. Rd.)
Rose Grn. Rd. PO21: Aldw .9L 163
Rose Hill BN2: Brig .3G 172 (6C 154)
Rosehill RH14: Bill .9J 43
Rose Hill Cl. BN1: Brig .3F 172 (6B 154)
Rose Hill Ct. BN1: Brig .3F 172
Rose Hill Ter. BN1: Brig .3E 172 (6B 154)
Rosehill Ter. M. BN1: Brig .3F 172
Roseleigh Gdns. RH17: Scay H .6N 73
Rosemary Av. BN44: Stey .3B 130
Rosemary Cl. BN10: Peace .3J 175
BN44: Stey .3B 130
GU28: Petw .9N 61
PO21: Aldw .9L 163

Rosemary Cl.—St James's Av.

Rosemary Cl. RH16: Hay H . . . 3C 72
RH20: Storr . . . 6J 107
Rosemary Ct. GU27: Has . . . 4L 17
RH6: Horl . . . 1G 4
Rosemary Dr. BN43: Shor S . . . 4L 151
Rosemary La. GU6: Alf . . . 3J 21
GU28: Petw . . . 9N 61
RH6: Charlw . . . 6A 4
RH6: Horl . . . 3K 5
Rosemead BN17: L'ton . . . 3L 167
Rosemead Gdns. RH10: Craw . . . 7G 10
(off Richmond Ct.)
Rose Pl. BN17: L'ton . . . 1A 168
Rose Wlk. BN12: Gor S . . . 2C 170
RH11: Craw . . . 8D 10
RH15: Burg H . . . 1D 94
Rosier Commercial Cen. RH14: Bill . . . 2K 65
Rosier Way RH14: Bill . . . 3K 65
Roslan Ct. RH6: Horl . . . 3K 5
Rossalyn Cl. PO21: Aldw . . . 9K 163
Ross Cl. PO21: Pag . . . 1D 180
RH10: Craw . . . 9H 11
Ross Ct. RH6: Horl . . . 2K 5
Rossiter Rd. BN15: N Lan . . . 5B 150
Rosslyn Av. BN43: Shor S . . . 6K 151
Rosslyn Ct. BN43: Shor S . . . 5J 151
Rosslyn Rd. BN43: Shor S . . . 6J 151
Rossmore Cl. RH10: Craw . . . 2M 11
Rosvara Av. PO20: Westg . . . 6E 142
Rotary Ho. BN15: S Lan . . . 9B 150
Rotary Lodge BN1: Brig . . . 8F 134
BN11: Wor . . . 1F 170
Rotary Point BN41: Ports . . . 4C 152
Rothbury Rd. BN3: Hove . . . 6F 152
Rotherbridge La. GU28: Petw . . . 3L 83
Rotherbrook Ct. GU32: Peters . . . 7D 54
Rother Cl. GU31: Peters . . . 5J 55
RH20: Storr . . . 4L 107
Rothercombe La. GU32: Stro . . . 5A 54
Rother Cres. RH11: Craw . . . 7B 10
Rotherfield Cl. BN1: Brig . . . 8C 134
Rotherfield Cres. BN1: Brig . . . 9C 134
Rother La. GU31: Trot . . . 8K 57
Rothermead GU28: Petw . . . 1M 83
Rotherwick Cl. PO9: Hav . . . 9B 116
Rothesay Cl. BN13: Wor . . . 9C 148
Rothley Chase RH16: Hay H . . . 5G 72
Rothwell Ct. BN9: Newh . . . 5N 175
Rotten Row PO20: Sidle . . . 1F 178
ROTTINGDEAN . . . 3A 174
Rottingdean Pl. BN2: Rott . . . 9N 155
Rotyngs, The BN2: Rott . . . 2N 173
Rough Fld. RH19: E Grin . . . 1D 14
Rough Way RH12: Hors . . . 6C 26
Roundabout Copse RH20: W Chil . . . 2J 107
Roundabout La. RH20: W Chil . . . 2J 107
Roundabout Rd. RH10: Copt . . . 1E 12
Roundhay Av. BN10: Peace . . . 6L 175
ROUND HILL . . . 1G 172 (5C 154)
Roundhill Cres. BN2: Brig . . . 5C 154
Round Hill Rd. BN2: Brig . . . 2G 172 (5C 154)
Round Hill St. BN2: Brig . . . 2G 172 (5C 154)
Roundhouse Cres. BN10: Peace . . . 5K 175
Roundhouse Mdw. PO10: S'brne . . . 6G 137
ROUNDHURST . . . 1C 38
Roundle Av. PO22: Felp . . . 6J 165
Roundle Rd. PO22: Felp . . . 7K 165
Roundle Sq. PO22: Felp . . . 7J 165
Roundle Sq. Rd. PO22: Felp . . . 7J 165
Round Piece PO20: Sel . . . 2G 182
Round Piece La. PO20: Sel . . . 2F 182
Roundstone By-Pass BN16: Ang . . . 1E 168
Roundstone Cres. BN16: E Pres . . . 2E 168
Roundstone Dr. BN16: E Pres . . . 2F 168
Roundstone Ho. Caravan Pk.
BN16: E Pres . . . 1F 168
(off Old Worthing Rd.)
Roundstone La. BN16: Ang . . . 8F 146
Roundstone Pk. RH13: Southw . . . 7K 45
Roundstone Way PO20: Sel . . . 2K 183
ROUNDSTREET COMMON . . . 4B 42
Roundway BN1: Brig . . . 9F 134
RH16: Hay H . . . 8D 72
Roundway, The BN16: Rust . . . 4C 168
Roundway Ct. RH10: Craw . . . 4F 10
Roundwood BN13: High S . . . 5D 148
Roundwood La. RH16: Hay H . . . 9F 50
Rowan Av. BN3: Hove . . . 4G 152
Rowan Cl. BN41: Ports . . . 4C 152
RH10: Craw . . . 6H 11
RH12: Hors . . . 6E 26
RH16: Hay H . . . 5J 73
RH20: Storr . . . 5L 107
Rowan Ct. RH14: Bill . . . 9J 43
Rowan Dr. RH14: Bill . . . 9H 43
Rowan Ho. BN2: Brig . . . 3G 172
BN12: Gor S . . . 9M 147
(off Goring Chase)
Rowan Rd. PO9: Hav . . . 2B 136
Rowans, The BN6: Hurst . . . 9J 93
(off Cuckfield Rd.)
BN11: Wor . . . 2E 170
BN43: Shor S . . . 5H 151
GU26: Hind . . . 1F 16
RH15: Burg H . . . 4M 93
Rowan Wlk. RH10: Craw D . . . 4K 13
Rowan Way BN2: Rott . . . 9M 155
BN16: Ang . . . 9F 146
PO22: Bers . . . 5B 164
RH12: Hors . . . 6E 26
Rowe Av. BN10: Peace . . . 6H 175
(not continuous)
Rowe Av. Nth. BN10: Peace . . . 4H 175
Rowena Ho. RH11: Craw . . . 3F 10
(off Dobson Rd.)
Rowenden Ct. BN2: Salt . . . 3C 174
ROWFANT . . . 5E 12
Rowfant Bus. Cen. RH10: Rowf . . . 6E 12
Rowfant Cl. RH10: Worth . . . 6N 11
ROWFOLD . . . 2M 65
Rowhill Copse Local Nature Reserve . . . 2N 49
Rowhill La. RH17: Bal . . . 3N 49
ROWHOOK . . . 2C 24
Rowhook Hill RH12: R'hook . . . 2C 24
Rowhook Rd. RH12: R'hook, Broadb H . . . 3D 24
(not continuous)
ROWLANDS CASTLE . . . 4C 116
Rowlands Castle Golf Course . . . 4B 116
Rowlands Castle Rd.
PO8: Horn, Ids . . . 9A 96
Rowlands Castle Station (Rail) . . . 4C 116
Rowlands Rd. BN11: Wor . . . 3E 170
RH12: Hors . . . 5D 26
Rowlands Sq. GU32: Peters . . . 7E 54
Rowner Rd. RH14: Bill . . . 1F 64
Rowplatt La. RH19: Felb . . . 1M 13
Roxburgh Cl. BN13: Durr . . . 6D 148
Royal Arc. BN11: Wor . . . 3H 171
(off South St.)
Royal Ashdown Forest Golf Course . . . 2N 33
Royal Bldgs. BN15: Lan . . . 9N 149
Royal Cl. PO19: Chich . . . 7E 140
Royal Cres. BN2: Brig . . . 9D 154
Royal Cres. Mans. BN2: Brig . . . 9D 154
(off Marine Pde.)
Royal Cres. M. BN2: Brig . . . 9D 154
Royal Gdns. PO9: Row C . . . 5A 116
Royal George Pde. BN43: Shor S . . . 4M 151
Royal George Rd. RH15: Burg H . . . 4N 93
Royal Norfolk M. PO21: Bog R . . . 1L 181
(off Norfolk Sq.)
Royal Oak Ho. RH10: Craw D . . . 5J 13
Royal Pde. PO21: Bers . . . 6B 164
Royal Pavilion . . . 8F 172 (8B 154)
Royal Vw. BN2: Brig . . . 7F 172
Royce Cl. PO20: W Witt . . . 2G 176
Royce Rd. RH10: Craw . . . 1J 11
Royce Way PO20: W Witt . . . 2G 176
Royles Cl. BN2: Rott . . . 2A 174
Royston Cl. RH10: Craw . . . 2J 11
Roystons, The BN16: E Pres . . . 4E 168
Ruckmans La. RH5: Oak . . . 6E 6
Rucrofts Cl. PO21: Aldw . . . 9A 164
Rudd Ho. BN13: Durr . . . 6C 148
Rudford Ind. Est. BN18: Ford . . . 2E 166
Rudge Ho. RH19: E Grin . . . 3F 14
(off Cantelupe Rd.)
RUDGWICK . . . 3J 23
Rudgwick Av. BN12: Gor S . . . 2M 169
Rudgwick Cl. BN16: Rust . . . 4A 168
Rudgwick Keep RH6: Horl . . . 1L 5
(off Langshott La.)
Rudgwick Rd. RH11: Ifield . . . 5B 10
Rudkin Pl. PO18: Fish . . . 5K 139
Rudwick's Cl. PO22: Felp . . . 8K 165
Rudwick's Way PO22: Felp . . . 8K 165
Rudyard Cl. BN2: W'dean . . . 5M 155
Rudyard Rd. BN2: W'dean . . . 5M 155
Rufwood RH10: Craw D . . . 4H 13
Rugby Ct. BN2: Brig . . . 9F 154
BN11: Wor . . . 1E 170
(off Rugby Rd.)
Rugby Pl. BN2: Brig . . . 9F 154
Rugby Rd. BN1: Brig . . . 1E 172 (4B 154)
BN11: Wor . . . 1D 170
Ruislip Gdns. PO21: Aldw . . . 1E 180
Rumbolds Cl. PO19: Chich . . . 8E 140
Rumbolds Hill GU29: Midh . . . 9H 59
Rumbolds La. RH16: Hay H . . . 7E 72
Rummers, The PO19: Chich . . . 3B 140
Runcorn Cl. RH11: Craw . . . 1A 28
RUNCTON . . . 3G 163
Runcton La. PO20: Runc, S Mun . . . 3G 163
Runnymede Ct. PO21: Bog R . . . 7A 164
Runshooke Ct. RH11: Craw . . . 9C 10
Runway Pk. RH11: Lowf H . . . 8G 5
Rusbridge Cl. PO21: Aldw . . . 8M 163
Rushams Rd. RH12: Hors . . . 9M 25
Rushes, The RH16: Hay H . . . 5K 73
Rushes Farm GU32: Peters . . . 5E 54
Rushes Rd. GU32: Peters . . . 5E 54
Rushetts Pl. RH11: Craw . . . 3E 10
Rushetts Rd. RH11: Craw . . . 3D 10
Rushey Hill Caravan Pk. BN10: Peace . . . 6M 175
Rushlake Cl. BN1: Brig . . . 9F 134
Rushlake Rd. BN1: Brig . . . 8F 134
Rushwood Cl. RH16: Hay H . . . 5J 73
Ruskin Av. PO21: Bers . . . 5B 164
Ruskin Cl. PO20: Sel . . . 3K 183
RH10: Craw . . . 3L 11
Ruskin Pl. BN3: Hove . . . 5H 153
Ruskin Rd. BN3: Hove . . . 5H 153
BN14: Broadw . . . 9K 149
RUSPER . . . 5G 8
Rusper Ct. Cotts. RH12: Rusp . . . 6H 9
Rusper Golf Course . . . 1E 8
Rusper Rd. BN1: Brig . . . 8E 134
BN13: Wor . . . 8C 148
RH5: Capel . . . 1N 7
RH5: Newd . . . 1F 8
RH11: Ifield . . . 5M 9
RH12: Hors, Rusp . . . 7C 26
RH12: Ifield . . . 5K 9
RH12: Newd, Rusp . . . 1F 8
Rusper Rd. Rdbt. RH12: Hors . . . 4C 26
Rusper Rd. Sth. BN13: Wor . . . 8D 148
Ruspers RH15: Burg H . . . 6E 94
Ruspers Keep RH11: Ifield . . . 5B 10
Russell Cl. BN14: Broadw . . . 8J 149
Russell Ct. BN15: S Lan . . . 8B 150
GU29: Midh . . . 1G 81
(off Bepton Rd.)
Russell Cres. BN1: Brig . . . 3C 172 (6N 153)
Russell M. BN1: Brig . . . 7B 172
Russell Pl. BN1: Brig . . . 8C 172 (8A 154)
Russell Rd. BN1: Brig . . . 8C 172 (8A 154)
PO9: Hav . . . 2A 136
PO20: W Witt . . . 4J 177
Russell's Cl. BN16: E Pres . . . 2G 168
Russells Cres. RH6: Horl . . . 3J 5
Russells Dr. BN15: S Lan . . . 8B 150
Russell Sq. BN1: Brig . . . 7C 172 (8A 154)
Russell St. PO19: Chich . . . 7E 140
Russell Way GU31: Peters . . . 7G 55
RH10: Craw . . . 7J 11
Russet Cl. RH6: Horl . . . 2L 5
Russet Ct. GU27: Fern . . . 4K 37
(off Vann Rd.)
RH13: Hors . . . 7D 26
Russet Gdns. PO10: S'brne . . . 5H 137
Russett Pl. RH14: Kird . . . 7G 41
Rustic Cl. BN10: Peace . . . 3H 175
Rustic Pk. BN10: Tels C . . . 2H 175
(off Rustic Rd.)
Rustic Rd. BN10: Peace . . . 2H 175
RUSTINGTON . . . 3B 168
Rustington By-Pass
BN16: Ang, Rust, L'ton . . . 9A 146
BN17: L'ton . . . 1M 167
Rustington Golf Cen. . . . 9B 146
Rustington Mus. . . . 3B 168
Rustington Retail Pk. BN16: Rust . . . 1C 168
Rustington Rd. BN1: Brig . . . 9B 134
Rustington Trad. Est. BN16: Rust . . . 1B 168
Rustlings Cl. RH16: Hay H . . . 4J 73
Ruston Av. BN16: Rust . . . 3C 168
Ruston Bri. Rd. TN22: Flet, Pilt . . . 6N 75
Ruston Cl. RH10: Craw . . . 9L 11
Ruston Pk. BN16: Rust . . . 3D 168
Rutherford Way RH10: Craw . . . 1J 11
Rutherford Way Ind. Est.
RH10: Craw . . . 1J 11
Rutherwick Cl. RH6: Horl . . . 2H 5
Rutherwick Twr. RH6: Horl . . . 2H 5
Ruthven Cl. RH17: Cuck . . . 2A 72
Rutland Ct. BN3: Hove . . . 6H 153
Rutland Gdns. BN3: Hove . . . 7H 153
Rutland Rd. BN3: Hove . . . 6J 153
Rutland Way PO19: Westh . . . 5F 140
Rydal Cl. BN17: L'ton . . . 2N 167
RH11: Ifield . . . 8N 9
Ryde Ct. BN3: Hove . . . 4F 152
(off Hangleton Gdns.)
Ryde Rd. BN2: Brig . . . 6E 154
Ryders Way RH12: Hors . . . 4C 26
Rye Ash RH10: Craw . . . 5J 11
(not continuous)
Ryebank Caravan Site BN18: Bils . . . 5N 165
Rye Cl. BN2: Salt . . . 2E 174
BN11: Wor . . . 3E 170
Ryecroft BN2: Brig . . . 8G 154
PO9: Warbl . . . 4B 136
RH16: Hay H . . . 6F 72
Ryecroft Cl. BN12: Gor S . . . 3A 170
Ryecroft Dr. RH12: Hors . . . 8L 25
Ryecroft Gdns. BN12: Gor S . . . 2A 170
Ryecroft La. RH20: Storr . . . 6J 107
Ryecroft Mdw. RH13: Mann H . . . 4F 46
Ryecroft Rd. RH17: Bol . . . 6E 70
Rye Farm La. RH13: B Grn . . . 8E 44
Ryefield Cl. GU31: Peters . . . 6J 55
Ryefield Rd. PO21: Bers . . . 5A 164
Ryelands RH6: Horl . . . 1L 5
RH11: Craw . . . 7C 10
Ryelands Dr. BN2: Brig . . . 2E 154

S

Sabre Rd. PO10: Tho I . . . 1G 158
Sachel Ct. Dr. GU6: Alf . . . 1M 21
Sachel Ct. M. GU6: Alf . . . 1L 21
Sachel Ct. Rd. GU6: Alf . . . 1L 21
Sachel Hill La. GU6: Alf . . . 1K 21
Sack La. PO22: Shrip . . . 2E 164
Sackville Cl. RH19: E Grin . . . 1C 14
Sackville College . . . 3F 14
Sackville Ct. RH19: E Grin . . . 4F 14
Sackville Cres. BN14: Broadw . . . 9J 149
Sackville Gdns. BN3: Hove . . . 7H 153
RH19: E Grin . . . 1C 14
(not continuous)
Sackville La. RH19: E Grin . . . 1B 14
Sackville Rd. BN3: Hove . . . 7J 153
BN14: Broadw . . . 9J 149
Sackville Trad. Est. BN3: Hove . . . 5J 153
Sackville Way BN14: Broadw . . . 9J 149
Saddle La. PO20: Sel . . . 3H 183
Saddler Row RH10: Craw . . . 9F 10
Saddlers Cl. RH14: Bill . . . 1H 65
RH15: Burg H . . . 7E 94
Saddler's Row GU28: Petw . . . 9N 61
SADDLESCOMBE . . . 3G 132
Saddlescombe Farm Cotts.
BN45: Brig . . . 2G 133
Saddlescombe Rd. BN1: Brig . . . 3G 133
BN45: Brig, Newt, Poyn . . . 9F 112
Sadlers, The PO18: Westh . . . 4F 140
Sadler St. PO21: Bog R . . . 1L 181
Sadlers Wlk. PO10: S'brne . . . 5G 137
PO19: Chich . . . 7C 140
Sadlers Way GU27: Has . . . 4M 17
Sadler Way BN2: Brig . . . 7G 154
Saffron Cl. BN43: Shor S . . . 4M 151
RH11: Craw . . . 9C 10
Saffron Ga. BN3: Hove . . . 6L 153
Saffrons, The RH15: Burg H . . . 3N 93
Saffrons Ct. BN11: Wor . . . 1E 170
St Agnes Pl. PO19: Chich . . . 7D 140
St Agnes Rd. RH19: E Grin . . . 2E 14
St Aidan Cl. RH11: Craw . . . 8D 10
St Alban's Rd. PO9: Hav . . . 1A 136
St Andrews RH6: Horl . . . 3K 5
(off Aurum Cl.)
St Andrews Cl. BN12: Fer . . . 2K 169
GU27: Has . . . 5K 17
PO20: Oving . . . 7L 141
St Andrews Ct. PO19: Chich . . . 7C 140
(off East St.)
St Andrew's Gdns. BN13: W Tar . . . 9E 148
St Andrews La. PO20: Tang . . . 4L 141
St Andrews Rd. BN1: Brig . . . 4B 154
BN13: W Tar . . . 8D 148
BN41: Ports . . . 6D 152
PO11: Hay I . . . 9B 158
RH11: Ifield . . . 7N 9
RH15: Burg H . . . 4D 94
St Anne's Ct. BN1: Brig . . . 4D 172
(off Howard Pl.)
St Anne's Ct. BN2: Brig . . . 9D 154
(off Burlington St.)
PO20: E Witt . . . 4K 177
St Anne's Gdns. BN6: Key . . . 4B 114
St Anne's Hill GU29: Midh . . . 9H 59
St Anne's Ho. BN1: Brig . . . 4D 172
(off Buckingham Pl.)
St Annes Rd. RH10: Craw . . . 3L 11
St Annes Well Ho. BN3: Hove . . . 7M 153
St Anns Ct. BN3: Hove . . . 6M 153
GU29: Midh . . . 1H 81
(off The Wharf)
St Anns Mans. BN3: Hove . . . 4A 172
St Ann's Well Gdns. . . . 5A 172 (6M 153)
St Anselm's Rd. BN14: Wor . . . 9F 148
St Anthony's Wlk. PO21: Aldw . . . 9M 163
St Anthonys Way BN16: Rust . . . 2C 168
St Aubin Cl. RH11: Craw . . . 1B 28
St Aubins Ct. BN12: Fer . . . 4L 169
St Aubins Rd. BN12: Fer . . . 4L 169
St Aubyns BN3: Hove . . . 7J 153
St Aubyn's Cres. BN41: Ports . . . 6D 152
St Aubyn's Gdns. BN3: Hove . . . 7J 153
St Aubyn's Mans. BN3: Hove . . . 8J 153
(off King's Esplanade)
St Aubyn's Mead BN2: Rott . . . 3A 174
St Aubyn's Rd. BN41: Ports . . . 6C 152
(Gordon Rd.)
BN41: Ports . . . 6E 152
(Norway St.)
St Aubyn's Sth. BN3: Hove . . . 8J 153
St Augustine Rd. BN17: L'ton . . . 4L 167
RH11: Craw . . . 7D 10
St Augustines Cl. RH17: Scay H . . . 6N 73
St Austins GU26: Gray . . . 1F 16
St Barnabas Ct. RH10: Craw . . . 5L 11
St Bartholomews Cl. PO19: Chich . . . 7A 140
St Bernard's Ct. BN15: Lan . . . 8B 150
St Blaises Rd. PO18: Box . . . 2L 141
St Botolph's Ct. BN11: Wor . . . 1F 170
St Botolph's Rd. BN11: Wor . . . 1F 170
St Brelades Rd. RH11: Craw . . . 1B 28
St Catherines Ct. BN17: L'ton . . . 4K 167
RH19: E Grin . . . 2D 14
St Catherines Rd. BN17: L'ton . . . 4K 167
RH10: Craw . . . 3L 11
St Catherine's Ter. BN3: Hove . . . 8J 153
St Christopher's Cl. GU27: Has . . . 5J 17
PO19: Chich . . . 7M 139
RH12: Hors . . . 7N 25
St Christopher's Grn. GU27: Has . . . 5J 17
St Christopher's Rd. BN6: Hurst . . . 1J 113
GU27: Has . . . 5J 17
St Claire Ter. PO21: Bog R . . . 9D 164
St Clares Gdns. PO21: Bers . . . 6B 164
St Clare's M. PO22: Felp . . . 8G 165
St Clement Rd. RH11: Craw . . . 1B 28
St Cuthman's Cl. BN2: Brig . . . 7F 154
St Cuthmans Rd. BN44: Stey . . . 2A 130
St Cyriacs PO19: Chich . . . 6C 140
St David's Ct. BN10: Peace . . . 4H 175
St David's Ga. BN15: Lan . . . 7A 150
St Dunstan's Rd. BN13: Wor . . . 1E 170
St Edmunds Cl. RH11: Craw . . . 3F 10
St Edmund's Rd. RH16: Hay H . . . 6F 72
St Edward's Cl. RH19: E Grin . . . 3C 14
St Elmo Rd. BN14: Wor . . . 9F 148
St Flora's Cl. BN17: L'ton . . . 3M 167
St Flora's Rd. BN17: L'ton . . . 3M 167
St Francis Cl. RH16: Hay H . . . 7G 72
St Francis Gdns. RH10: Copt . . . 1C 12
St Francis Wlk. RH11: Craw . . . 8A 10
St Gabriels Rd. RH14: Bill . . . 1J 65
St Georges BN8: N Cha . . . 9D 74
RH6: Horl . . . 3K 5
St Georges Av. PO9: Warbl . . . 4B 136
St Georges Cl. PO20: Sel . . . 2K 183
RH6: Horl . . . 2K 5
St Georges Ct. RH10: Craw . . . 5F 10
RH19: E Grin . . . 1C 14
St George's Dr. PO19: Chich . . . 1B 162
St George's Gdns. BN11: Wor . . . 2K 171
RH13: Hors . . . 7B 26
St George's La. BN6: Hurst . . . 2K 113
St George's M. BN1: Brig . . . 6F 172 (7B 154)
St George's Pl. BN1: Brig . . . 5F 172 (7B 154)
BN6: Hurst . . . 2K 113
St Georges Rd. BN2: Brig . . . 9D 154
BN11: Wor . . . 1K 171
RH13: Part G . . . 5C 90
St George's Ter. BN2: Brig . . . 9D 154
St George's Wlk. PO20: E'gate . . . 6G 142
St Giles Cl. BN43: Shor S . . . 5L 151
St Helena La. BN6: Streat . . . 8K 95
BN7: Plump G . . . 8K 95
St Helen's Cres. BN3: Hove . . . 2F 152
St Helen's Dr. BN3: Hove . . . 2F 152
St Helen's Rd. BN2: Brig . . . 6E 154
St Helier Cl. RH11: Craw . . . 1C 28
St Helier Ct. BN12: Fer . . . 4L 169
St Helier Rd. BN12: Fer . . . 4L 169
St Heliers Av. BN3: Hove . . . 6G 153
St Hildas Cl. PO20: Sel . . . 4H 183
RH6: Horl . . . 2K 5
RH10: Craw . . . 3L 11
SAINT HILL . . . 8C 14
St Hill Grn. RH19: E Grin . . . 8D 14
Saint Hill Manor . . . 8C 14
St Hill Rd. RH19: E Grin . . . 6B 14
St Hughs Cl. RH10: Craw . . . 3L 11
St Itha Cl. PO20: Sel . . . 4J 183
St Itha Rd. PO20: Sel . . . 4J 183
St Ives RH10: Craw . . . 5L 11
St James Av. BN15: N Lan . . . 5B 150
St James Cl. RH19: E Grin . . . 3D 14
St James Ho. BN2: Brig . . . 8C 154
(off High St.)
RH19: E Grin . . . 3E 14
St James Ind. Est. PO19: Chich . . . 6E 140
St James Rd. PO10: Ems . . . 4F 136
PO19: Chich . . . 6E 140
RH19: E Grin . . . 3D 14
St James's Av. BN2: Brig . . . 8C 154

Seafield Cl.—Silverston Av.

Seafield Cl. BN16: Rust 4B 168
PO20: E Witt 5L 177
Seafield Rd. BN3: Hove 7K 153
BN16: E Pres 4E 168
BN16: Rust 4B 168
Seafields BN43: Shor S 5J 151
PO10: Ems 5E 136
PO20: Brac 6M 177
Seafield Way PO20: E Witt 5L 177
Seaford Rd. BN3: Hove 7E 152
RH11: Craw 2C 28
Seaford Way BN43: Shor B 7L 151
Sea Front PO11: Hay I 9A 158
Sea Front Est. PO11: Hay I 9B 158
Seagate Ct. PO20: E Witt 5J 177
Seagate Wlk. BN17: L'ton 4N 167
Sea Gro. PO20: Sel 4G 182
Sea Gro. Av. PO11: Hay I 9A 158
Seagull Cl. PO20: Sel 1F 182
Seagull La. PO10: Ems 4F 136
(not continuous)
Seahaven Gdns. BN43: Shor B 8G 150
Sea Ho. BN42: S'wck 6A 152
Sea La. BN12: Fer 2L 169
BN12: Gor S 2A 170
BN16: E Pres 4E 168
BN16: King G 4H 169
BN16: Rust 4A 168
PO21: Pag 3B 180
PO22: Midd S 7M 165
Sea La. Cl. BN12: Fer 2L 169
BN16: E Pres 3E 168
Sea La. Gdns BN12: Fer 3L 169
Sea Life
Brighton 9F 172 (9B 154)
Seal Rd. PO20: Sel 4H 183
Seal Sq. PO20: Sel 5H 183
Seamill Ct. BN11: Wor 1M 171
Seamill Pk. Av. BN11: Wor 1M 171
Seamill Pk. Cres. BN11: Wor 1M 171
Seamill Way BN11: Wor 1M 171
Sea Pl. BN12: Gor S 2C 170
Searle Av. BN10: Peace 6L 175
Searle's Vw. RH12: Hors 6B 26
Sea Rd. BN16: E Pres 3F 168
BN16: L'ton, Rust 5M 167
BN17: L'ton 5M 167
PO22: Felp 9G 165
Sea-Saw Way BN2: Brig 6G 155
Seaside Av. BN15: S Lan 8C 150
Seaside Cl. BN15: S Lan 8C 150
Seaside Rd. BN15: S Lan 8C 150
Sea Spray Av. BN43: Shor B 7L 151
Seaton Cl. BN17: Wick 9K 145
Seaton La. BN17: Wick 9K 145
Seaton Pk. BN17: Wick 9K 145
Seaton Rd. BN17: Wick 9K 145
SEA VIEW 9A 158
Seaview Av. BN10: Peace 6L 175
(not continuous)
BN16: E Pres 4F 168
BN16: King G 4J 169
Seaview Ct. BN11: Wor 3F 170
BN15: Lan 9A 150
PO20: Sel 4H 183
Seaview Est. BN42: S'wck 6B 152
Seaview Gdns. BN16: Rust 4B 168
Sea Vw. Rd. PO11: Hay I 9C 158
Seaview Rd. BN2: W'dean 5J 155
BN10: Peace 7L 175
BN11: Wor 3F 170
BN16: E Pres 4F 168
Sea Vw. Way BN2: W'dean 4L 155
Seaward Dr. PO20: W Witt 2G 176
Seawaves Cl. BN16: E Pres 3F 168
Sea Way PO21: Pag 3B 180
PO22: Midd S 7B 166
(Alleyne Way)
PO22: Midd S 8L 165
(Sea La.)
Seawood Ho. *PO20: E Witt* 4K 177
(off Stocks La.)
Second Av. BN3: Hove 8L 153
BN14: Char D 6H 149
BN15: Lan 6B 150
PO9: Hav 3B 136
PO10: S'brne 5K 137
PO20: Brac 6M 177
PO20: Earn 2B 178
PO22: Felp 8J 165
Second Rd. BN10: Peace 5G 175
Sedbury Rd. BN15: Somp 5N 149
Seddon Cl. PO19: Chich 5E 140
Seddon Ct. RH11: Craw 2D 28
Sedgefield Cl. RH10: Craw 5N 11
Sedgewick Cl. RH10: Craw 6L 11
Sedgwick La. RH13: Hors 6B 46
Sedgwick Park 8B 46
Sefter Rd. PO21: Pag 8K 163
Sefton Av. PO21: Aldw 9M 163
Sefton Cl. BN13: Durr 7B 148
Sefton Rd. BN41: Ports 2B 152
Selangor Av. PO10: Ems 4C 136
Selba Dr. BN2: Brig 3F 154
Selborne Cl. GU32: Peters 4F 54
Selborne Pl. BN3: Hove 6L 153
BN17: L'ton 4L 167
(off Selborne Rd.)
Selborne Rd. BN3: Hove 7L 153
BN11: Wor 1K 171
BN17: L'ton 4L 167
Selborne Way BN16: E Pres 3E 168
Selbourne Cl. RH10: Craw 2M 11
Selby Cl. RH15: Burg H 7N 93
Selby Ct. RH16: Hay H 6F 72
Selden La. BN11: Wor 2K 171
BN13: Pat 4G 146
Selden Pde. *BN13: Salv* 6D 148
(off Salvington Rd.)
Selden Rd. BN11: Wor 1K 171
Seldens M. BN13: Salv 7D 148
Selden's Way BN13: Salv 7D 148
Sele Gdns. BN44: Up B 4E 130
SELHAM 2D 82
Selham Cl. BN1: Brig 8F 134
PO19: Chich 2C 140
RH11: Craw 5C 10
Selham Dr. BN1: Brig 8E 134
Selham Pl. *BN1: Brig* 8E 134
(off Beatty Av.)
Selham Rd. GU29: Midh, W Lav, S Amb 1H 81
Selhurst Cl. BN16: E Pres 3D 168
SELHURST PARK 3B 122
Selhurstpark Rd.
PO18: Hal, E Dean, Upw, Eart 2M 121
Selhurst Rd. BN2: W'dean 7M 155
Selkirk Cl. BN13: Wor 9C 148
Selmeston Pl. BN2: Brig 7G 154
SELSEY 3H 183
Selsey Av. PO21: Aldw 1J 181
Selsey Bill 5J 183
Selsey Bus. Cen. *PO20: Sel* 3H 183
(off The Bridle Way)
Selsey Cl. BN1: Brig 8F 134
BN13: Wor 8D 148
Selsey Country Club PO20: Sel 9H 179
Selsey Ct. RH11: Craw 1D 28
Selsey Golf Course 9H 179
Selsey Rd. PO19: Chich 1A 162
PO20: Donn, Sidle 7A 162
PO20: Sidle 1H 179
RH11: Craw 1C 28
SELSFIELD COMMON 2J 31
Selsfield Dr. BN2: Brig 2E 154
Selsfield Rd. RH10: Turn H, W Hoa 9H 13
RH17: Ard, W Hoa 9H 31
RH19: W Hoa 2J 31
SELSMORE 9C 158
Selsmore Av. PO11: Hay I 9C 158
Selsmore Rd. PO11: Hay I 9A 158
Selway La. BN17: L'ton 2M 167
Selwyn Av. BN17: Wick 1K 167
Selwyn Cl. PO21: Aldw 8A 164
RH10: Craw 3L 11
Semley Lodge BN6: Hass 3N 113
Semley Rd. BN1: Brig 4B 154
BN6: Hass 3N 113
Senator Gdns. PO19: Fish 6L 139
Sequoia Pk. RH11: Craw 8F 10
Sergison Cl. RH16: Hay H 4D 72
Sergison Rd. RH16: Hay H 4E 72
Serrin Way RH12: Hors 6B 26
Servite Cl. PO21: Bog R 8C 164
Sett, The BN41: Ports 3D 152
Sevelands Cl. BN2: Brig 6G 154
Seven Dials BN1: Brig 4C 172 (6A 154)
Sevenfields RH15: Burg H 4L 93
Seventh Av. BN15: N Lan 5B 150
Seven Thorns La. GU26: Lip 3D 16
Severals, The GU29: Midh 9E 58
Severals Rd. GU29: Bep, Midh 9D 58
Severn Lodge *BN2: Brig* 8C 154
(off Mt. Pleasant)
Severn Rd. RH10: Craw 7L 11
Seville St. BN2: Brig 6D 154
Sewill Cl. RH6: Charlw 6B 4
Sextant Ct. BN17: L'ton 2N 167
Seymour Ho. *BN2: Brig* 9E 154
(off Seymour Sq.)
Seymour Pl. *PO21: Bog R* 9D 164
(off Queensway)
Seymour Rd. RH11: Craw 1C 28
Seymour Sq. BN2: Brig 9E 154
Seymour St. BN2: Brig 9E 154
Shackleton Rd. RH10: Craw 9G 11
Shadwells Cl. BN15: Lan 6C 150
Shadwells Ct. BN15: Lan 6C 150
Shadwells Rd. BN15: Lan 6C 150
Shaftesbury Av. BN12: Gor S 1C 170
Shaftesbury Ct. *BN16: Rust* 4B 168
(off Shaftesbury Rd.)
Shaftesbury Pl. BN1: Brig 1F 172 (5B 154)
BN16: Rust 4B 168
Shaftesbury Rd. BN1: Brig 2F 172 (5B 154)
BN16: Rust 4B 168
RH10: Craw 8M 11
Shakespeare Rd. BN11: Wor 1F 170
Shakespeare St. BN3: Hove 5J 153
Shalbourne Cres. PO20: Brac 6N 177
Shaldon Rd. PO9: Hav 8B 116
Shalesbrook La. RH18: F Row 2M 33
Shalford Hill GU27: K Grn 2L 37
Shamrock Cl. PO18: Bosh 8F 138
PO19: Chich 5D 140
Shandon Gdns. BN14: Broadw 7H 149
Shandon Rd. BN14: Broadw 6H 149
Shandon Way BN14: Broadw 7H 149
Shands BN6: Key 4A 114
Shandys Cl. RH12: Hors 1L 45
Shanklin Ct. BN2: Brig 5D 154
BN3: Hove 4C 152
(off Hangleton Rd.)
Shanklin Rd. BN2: Brig 5D 154
Shannon Cl. BN10: Tels C 3G 175
BN17: L'ton 4N 167
Shannon Ct. Rd. GU26: Hind 2E 16
Shardeloes Rd. BN16: Ang 7E 146
Sharon Cl. RH10: Craw 9J 11
Sharpenhurst La. RH13: Itch 6F 44
Sharps Rd. PO9: Hav 9B 116
SHARPTHORNE 5A 32
Sharpthorne Cl. RH11: Ifield 6B 10
Sharpthorne Ct. BN1: Brig 4E 172
Sharpthorne Cres. BN41: Ports 3E 152
Sharpthorne Rd. RH19: Sharp 6A 32
Sharrow Cl. RH16: Hay H 4F 72
Sharver's La. GU29: Ipin 3A 58
Shaves Wood La. BN6: Alb 3B 112
Shaw Cl. PO22: Midd S 7A 166
Shawcross Ho. BN1: Brig 3N 153
Shawfield Rd. PO9: Hav 4A 136
Shaw Gdns. PO21: Bers 5B 164
Shaw's La. RH13: Southw 9H 45
Shaws Rd. RH10: Craw 5H 11
Shear Hill GU31: Peters 4H 55
Shearing Dr. RH15: Burg H 7C 94
Shearwater Ct. *RH11: Ifield* 7N 9
(off Stoneycroft Wlk.)
Shearwater Dr. PO22: Bers 6D 164
Sheddingdean Bus. Cen. RH15: Burg H 3A 94
Sheddingdean Cl. RH15: Burg H 4B 94
Sheddingdean Ct. RH15: Burg H 4A 94
Sheddingdean Ind. Est.
RH15: Burg H 3B 94
Sheepbell Cl. BN41: Ports 2D 152
Sheepcote Valley Camping & Caravan Site
BN2: Brig 8H 155
Sheepdown Cl. GU28: Petw 1A 84
Sheepdown Dr. GU28: Petw 9N 61
Sheepfold, The BN10: Peace 3J 175
Sheep Fold Av. BN16: Rust 2D 168
Sheep La. GU29: Midh 9H 59
Sheep Pen La. BN44: Stey 3A 130
Sheep St. GU32: Peters 6F 54
Sheep Wlk. BN2: Rott 1M 173
Sheepwash La. PO18: Mid L 9B 120
PO20: W Witt 9A 160
SHEET 3H 55
Sheffield Cl. RH10: Craw 8K 11
Sheffield Ct. BN1: Brig 4E 172
SHEFFIELD GREEN 3J 75
Sheffield Grn. TN22: Flet, Fur G, Shef P 1H 75
Sheffield Mill La. TN22: Fur G 1J 75
Sheffield Pk. TN22: Shef P 4H 75
Sheffield Pk. Gdns. 4K 75
Sheffield Pk. Ho. TN22: Shef P 4J 75
Sheffield Park Station
Bluebell Railway 5G 75
Shelby Rd. BN13: Durr 7A 148
Sheldon Cl. RH10: Craw 7M 11
Sheldon Ct. BN11: Wor 3F 170
Shellbridge Rd. BN18: Slind 1M 143
Shelldale Av. BN41: Ports 6D 152
Shelldale Cres. BN41: Ports 6D 152
Shelldale Rd. BN41: Ports 5D 152
Shelley Cl. RH10: Craw 4L 11
Shelley Ct. BN11: Wor 2G 170
RH16: Hay H 4E 72
(off Winnals Pk.)
Shelley Dr. RH12: Broadb H 8G 25
Shelley Lodge BN17: L'ton 4M 167
Shelley Rd. BN3: Hove 6H 153
BN11: Wor 2F 170
PO21: Bog R 9C 164
RH12: Hors 8M 25
RH19: E Grin 3C 14
Shelleys Ct. RH13: Hors 7D 26
Shelley Wood RH15: Burg H 4M 93
Shell La. RH17: Bal 1D 50
Shenfield Way BN1: Brig 2C 154
Shenstone RH16: Lind 1J 73
Shepham Av. BN2: Salt 3C 174
Shepherd Cl. RH10: Craw 9G 10
Shepherds Cl. BN9: Pidd 2N 175
PO18: Hamb 3A 138
RH17: Wivel G 4K 95
Shepherds Cot BN10: Peace 2K 175
Shepherds Cft. BN1: Brig 1L 153
BN14: Fin 8C 128
(off Southview Rd.)
Shepherds Gro. La. RH19: Hamm 1N 15
Shepherd's Hill GU27: Has 5L 17
Shepherd's Hill Bungs. *GU27: Has* 5L 17
(off Shepherd's Hill)
Shepherds La. GU28: Lods 6C 60
Shepherds Mead BN14: Fin V 2E 148
RH15: Burg H 4A 94
Shepherds Wlk. BN6: Hass 2N 113
Shepherds Way RH12: Hors 6D 26
Sheppard Way BN41: Ports 2C 152
Sheppey Cl. RH11: Craw 9D 10
Sheppeys RH16: Hay H 7E 72
Sheraton Wlk. RH11: Craw 2D 28
Sherborne Rd. PO19: Chich 7A 140
Sherbourne Cl. BN3: Hove 2F 152
Sherbourne La. PO20: Sel 2F 182
Sherbourne Lodge BN11: Wor 1E 170
Sherbourne Rd. BN3: Hove 3F 152
Sherbourne Way BN3: Hove 2F 152
Sherbrooke Cl. BN13: Durr 7B 148
Sherfield Av. PO9: Hav 9A 116
Sheridan Mans. BN3: Hove 5J 153
Sheridan Pl. RH19: E Grin 3C 14
Sheridan Rd. BN14: Broadw 8J 149
Sheridan Ter. BN3: Hove 5J 153
Sherlock Av. PO19: Chich 6A 140
SHERMANBURY 5F 90
Shermanbury Ct. BN15: Somp 8N 149
RH12: Hors 7A 26
(off Blenheim Rd.)
Shermanbury Dr. RH20: Storr 5H 107
Shermanbury Grange RH13: Sherm 5F 90
Shermanbury Rd. BN14: Wor 9F 148
RH13: Part G 5E 90
Sherrington M. PO20: Sel 2K 183
Sherrington Rd. BN2: W'dean 5N 155
Sherston Cl. *RH20: Storr* 5K 107
(off Windmill Copse)
Sherwood Cl. PO22: Bers 6C 164
Sherwood Dr. RH16: Hay H 4D 72
Sherwood Rd. PO22: Bers 6C 164
Sherwood Wlk. RH10: Craw 9H 11
Shetland Cl. RH10: Craw 5N 11
Shetland Ct. BN13: Durr 8N 147
SHILLINGLEE 6L 19
Shillinglee Pk. Rd. GU8: Chidd 5L 19
Shillinglee Rd.
GU8: Chidd, Plais 7L 19
RH14: Plais 7L 19
SHIMMINGS 9A 62
Shingle Rd. BN43: Shor B 7K 151
Shingle Wlk. PO20: E Witt 5K 177
Shinwell Wlk. RH11: Craw 2D 28
Ship & Anchor Marina Camping Site
BN18: Ford 9E 144
Shipfield PO21: Aldw 1H 181
SHIPLEY 8G 67
SHIPLEY BRIDGE 7N 5
Shipley Bri. La. RH10: Ship B, Copt 1A 12
Shipley Rd. BN2: W'dean 6M 155
RH11: Craw 5C 10
RH13: Southw, Ship 7J 67
Shippam St. *PO19: Chich* 7C 140
(off East Walls)
Ship St. BN1: Brig 9D 172 (9A 154)
BN43: Shor S 6H 151
RH19: E Grin 4E 14
Ship St. Ct. BN1: Brig 8E 172
Ship St. Gdns. BN1: Brig 8D 172 (8A 154)
SHIPTON GREEN 9E 160
Shipton Grn. La. PO20: Itchen 8D 160
Shire Pde. RH10: Craw 5M 11
Shire Pl. *RH10: Craw* 5M 11
(off Byerley Way)
Shirley Av. BN3: Hove 3K 153
Shirley Cl. BN14: Salv 6F 148
BN16: Rust 4C 168
BN43: Shor S 5M 151
PO21: Pag 3C 180
RH11: Craw 1N 27
Shirley Dr. BN3: Hove 2K 153
BN14: Salv 6F 148
PO22: Felp 6H 165
Shirley M. BN3: Hove 6K 153
Shirley Rd. BN3: Hove 5L 153
Shirleys BN6: Ditch 5F 114
Shirleys Gdn. PO22: Felp 7J 165
Shirley St. BN3: Hove 6K 153
Shooting Fld. BN44: Stey 2A 130
Shopfield Cl. BN16: Rust 2B 168
Shop La. PO18: E Lav 9C 120
Shopsdam Rd. BN15: S Lan 9C 150
Shopwhyke Ind. Cen. PO19: Oving 6F 140
Shopwhyke Rd. PO20: Oving 6G 140
SHOPWYKE 6H 141
Shorecroft PO21: Aldw 2H 181
SHOREHAM BEACH 7J 151
Shoreham Beach Local Nature Reserve 8J 151
Shoreham By-Pass BN15: Shor S 4F 150
BN43: Shor S 4F 150
SHOREHAM-BY-SEA 6J 151
Shoreham-by-Sea Station (Rail) 6J 151
Shoreham Ct. BN43: Shor S 5J 151
Shoreham Rd. BN5: Henf, Small D 4J 111
BN43: Up B 6E 130
BN44: Up B 5E 130
RH10: Craw 9L 11
Shore Rd. PO18: Bosh 9E 138
(not continuous)
PO20: E Witt 5J 177
Shoreside Wlk. PO20: E Witt 5K 177
Short Cl. RH11: Craw 3F 10
Short Furlong BN17: L'ton 3M 167
Short Gallop RH10: Craw 5M 11
Shortgate Rd. BN2: Brig 1G 154
Shorts Cl. RH16: Hay H 6F 72
Shortsfield Cl. RH12: Hors 6N 25
SHOTTERMILL 4H 17
Shottermill RH12: Hors 4D 26
Shottermill Pk. GU27: Has 4G 17
Shottermill Pond GU27: Has 6G 17
Shottermill Rd. GU27: Has 6G 16
Shotters RH15: Burg H 6N 93
Shovelstrode La. RH19: Ash W, E Grin 4N 15
Shrewsbury Ct. BN11: Wor 3F 170
SHRIPNEY 3E 164
Shripney Garden Caravan Site
PO22: Shrip 3D 164
Shripney La. PO22: Bers, Shrip 4C 164
(not continuous)
Shripney Rd. PO22: Bers, Bog R, Shrip 7E 164
(not continuous)
Shripney Trade Pk. PO22: Bers 6F 164
Shrubbs Dr. PO22: Midd S 7M 165
Sickle Rd. GU27: Has 6H 17
Sidehill Dr. BN41: Ports 3B 152
Sidengreen La. PO18: Good, Westh 2G 141
Sideways La. RH6: Hookw 4E 4
Sidings, The RH12: Rudg 4J 23
Sidlaw Ter. *PO21: Bog R* 9E 164
(off Clarence Rd.)
SIDLESHAM 3J 179
SIDLESHAM COMMON 7A 162
Sidlesham La. PO20: Bir 7K 161
Sidlesham Salt Marshes 8K 139
Sidney Tidy Ho. *BN2: Brig* 7D 154
(off Queen's Pk. Rd.)
Siena Dr. RH10: Craw 2M 11
Siggs Ct. PO19: Chich 8E 140
Silchester Dr. RH11: Craw 9D 10
Silkin Wlk. RH11: Craw 2C 28
Sillwood Ct. BN1: Brig 7A 172
Sillwood Hall BN1: Brig 7A 172
Sillwood M. BN1: Brig 7A 172
Sillwood Pl. BN1: Brig 7A 172 (8N 153)
Sillwood Rd. BN1: Brig 7B 172 (8N 153)
Sillwood St. BN1: Brig 7A 172 (8N 153)
Sillwood Ter. BN1: Brig 7B 172 (8N 153)
Silver Birch Dr. BN13: Durr 8N 147
PO22: Midd S 6M 165
Silver Birches BN1: Brig 4N 153
BN5: Small D 8J 111
RH16: Hay H 5H 73
Silver Birch Ho. RH11: Craw 2E 28
Silver Ct. RH19: E Grin 2C 14
Silverdale BN6: Key 4C 114
BN11: Wor 1M 171
RH20: Cold 2J 105
Silverdale Av. BN3: Hove 6M 153
Silverdale Cl. PO21: Pag 3C 180
Silverdale Ct. BN3: Hove 6M 153
Silverdale Dr. BN15: Somp 8N 149
Silverdale Rd. BN3: Hove 6M 153
RH15: Burg H 6C 94
Silver Glade RH20: W Chil 1K 107
Silver Lakes PO20: Oving 9J 141
Silver La. RH14: Bill 2J 65
Silverlea Gdns. RH6: Horl 3L 5
Silverlock Cl. PO19: Chich 5E 140
Silverlock Pl. PO10: W'brne 9H 117
Silver Sands Gdns. PO11: Hay I 9B 158
Silverston Av. PO21: Aldw 1J 181

Springfields Farm Ind. Est.—Street, The

Springfields Farm Ind. Est.
RH17: Burg H . . . 3G 95
Springfield Shaw RH17: Bal . . . 1A 50
Spring Gdns. BN1: Brig . . . 7D 172 (8B 154)
BN42: S'wck . . . 6A 152
PO10: Ems . . . 5F 136
RH10: Copt . . . 1D 12
RH12: Hors . . . 8N 25
RH20: Wash . . . 5C 108
SPRINGHEAD . . . 6G 17
Springhills BN5: Henf . . . 3H 111
Springlands La. BN5: Henf . . . 4G 111
Spring La. BN6: Clay . . . 7N 113
RH13: Slinf . . . 8A 24
RH16: Lind . . . 9J 51
Springmead Ct. GU27: Has . . . 6F 16
(off Copse Rd.)
Spring Mdw. RH18: F Row . . . 2M 33
Spring Mdws. GU29: Midh . . . 2G 81
Spring Plat RH10: Craw . . . 6L 11
Spring Plat Ct. RH10: Craw . . . 6L 11
Spring St.
BN1: Brig . . . 7B 172 (8N 153)
Spring Vale GU32: Stro . . . 5B 54
Spring Wlk. RH6: Horl . . . 2H 5
Spronketts La. RH17: Bol, W'lid . . . 3N 69
Sproule Cl. BN18: Ford . . . 2B 166
Sproutes La. RH13: Cool . . . 9A 66
Spruce Pl. RH19: E Grin . . . 1G 15
Spurgeon Cl. RH11: Craw . . . 5E 10
Spur Rd. PO19: Chich . . . 8F 140
Spy La. RH14: Lox . . . 6M 21
Squadron Dr. BN13: Durr . . . 7N 147
Square, The BN1: Brig . . . 8N 133
BN14: Fin . . . 8C 128
BN16: Ang . . . 8E 146
BN18: Amb . . . 8L 105
GU31: S Hart . . . 4A 78
GU32: Peters . . . 6F 54
PO10: W'brne . . . 2H 137
PO18: Comp . . . 5M 97
PO22: Barn . . . 7J 143
RH10: Craw . . . 6F 10
RH20: Storr . . . 6J 107
Square Dr. GU27: K Grn . . . 1K 37
Squires, The RH11: Pease P . . . 5D 28
Squires Cl. RH10: Craw D . . . 4H 13
Squire Way BN5: Henf . . . 3H 111
Squirrel Cl. RH11: Craw . . . 3D 10
Squirrel Ridge RH10: Craw D . . . 5J 13
Squirrels Copse RH20: Storr . . . 4A 108
Stable Cl. RH10: Craw . . . 9M 11
Stable Cotts. RH11: Pease P . . . 3C 28
Stable Fld. PO22: Midd S . . . 7B 166
Stable Flats RH11: Pease P . . . 3C 28
Stable La. BN14: Fin . . . 8C 128
GU31: Peters . . . 6F 54
(off Bowen La.)
Stace Way RH10: Craw . . . 4N 11
Stackfield Rd. RH11: Ifield . . . 7A 10
Stafford Ct. BN2: Brig . . . 8C 154
(off Up. Rock Gdns.)
Stafford Rd. BN1: Brig . . . 2B 172 (5N 153)
GU32: Peters . . . 4F 54
RH11: Craw . . . 3C 10
Staffords Cl. BN16: Rust . . . 2A 168
Staffords Pl. RH6: Horl . . . 4K 5
Stafford Way BN6: Key . . . 4B 114
Stag Cl. BN5: Henf . . . 1H 111
Stagelands RH11: Craw . . . 4D 10
Stagelands Ct. RH11: Craw . . . 4E 10
Stairbridge Ct. RH17: Bol . . . 2H 93
Stairbridge La. RH17: Bol, Hick . . . 8G 70
Stakers La. RH13: Southw . . . 9L 45
(not continuous)
Stalham Way PO22: Felp . . . 6H 165
Stallard Cl. PO10: Ems . . . 4E 136
Stall Ho. La. RH20: N Hth . . . 1E 86
Stamford RH16: Hay H . . . 3E 72
(off Great Heathmead)
Stamford Lodge BN1: Brig . . . 3N 153
(off Cumberland Rd.)
Stammer Ct. BN17: Wick . . . 9M 145
(off Stammer Rd.)
Stammerham Bus. Cen. RH12: Rusp . . . 5B 8
Stammer Rd. BN17: Wick . . . 9L 145
Stammers Hill BN5: Fulk . . . 3B 132
Stanbridge Cl. RH11: Ifield . . . 6A 10
Stanbridge Rd. PO9: Hav . . . 2B 136
Stanbridge Way RH17: Ard . . . 3H 51
Stanbrok Cl. PO21: Aldw . . . 9N 163
Stanbury Cl. PO18: Bosh . . . 6F 138
STANDEAN . . . 5A 134
Standean Cl. BN1: Brig . . . 8E 134
Standen . . . 8D 14
Standen Cl. RH19: E Grin . . . 1A 14
Standen Ct. BN44: Up B . . . 5E 130
(off Downscroft)
Standen Pl. RH12: Hors . . . 4D 26
Stand Gro. Pl. RH17: Ard . . . 4H 51
Standinghall La. RH10: Turn H . . . 9B 12
Standon Cotts. RH5: Ock . . . 1F 6
Standon La. RH5: Ock . . . 2C 6
Stane St. PO18: Westh . . . 4F 140
RH5: Ock . . . 3F 6
RH13: Slinf . . . 4L 43
RH14: Adv, Bill, N Hth . . . 6G 64
RH14: Bill . . . 8K 43
RH20: Pulb, N Hth . . . 5B 86
Stane St. Cl. RH20: Pulb . . . 4B 86
Stane St. Cotts. RH12: R'hook . . . 2C 24
Stanford Av. BN1: Brig . . . 1D 172 (5A 154)
BN6: Hass . . . 3N 113
Stanford Cl. BN3: Hove . . . 4L 153
BN6: Hass . . . 3N 113
PO22: Bog R . . . 7F 164
Stanford Ct. BN1: Brig . . . 2D 172
PO9: Hav . . . 9B 116
RH10: Craw . . . 8L 11
(off Maidenbower Pl.)
Stanford Orchard RH12: Warnh . . . 3K 25
Stanford Rd. BN1: Brig . . . 1B 172 (5N 153)
Stanford Sq. BN11: Wor . . . 2J 171
Stanford Ter. BN6: Hass . . . 3N 113
(off Station App. W.)
Stanford Way RH12: Broadb H . . . 8H 25
Stan Hill RH6: Charlw . . . 5A 4
Stanhope Rd. BN11: Wor . . . 1H 171
BN17: L'ton . . . 2L 167
Stanhorn Gro. PO22: Felp . . . 5H 165
Stanier Cl. RH10: Craw . . . 7K 11
Stanley Av. BN41: Ports . . . 1B 152
Stanley Av. Sth. BN41: Ports . . . 2B 152
Stanley Cen. RH10: Craw . . . 3H 11
Stanley Cl. PO21: Bog R . . . 8E 164
RH10: Craw . . . 8G 11
Stanley Ct. PO22: Midd S . . . 6L 165
Stanley Deason Leisure Cen. . . . 8G 155
Stanley Rd. BN1: Brig . . . 3E 172 (6B 154)
BN10: Peace . . . 3H 175
BN11: Wor . . . 1H 171
BN17: Wick . . . 1K 167
BN41: Ports . . . 5C 152
PO10: Ems . . . 5G 136
Stanley St. BN2: Brig . . . 8C 154
Stanley Wlk. RH13: Hors . . . 9A 26
STANMER . . . 6G 134
Stanmer Av. BN2: Salt . . . 1D 174
Stanmer Ct. BN1: Brig . . . 3B 154
(off Stanmer Pk. Rd.)
BN1: Falm . . . 8H 135
STANMER HEIGHTS . . . 8C 134
Stanmer House . . . 7G 134
Stanmer Ho. BN1: Brig . . . 3B 154
(off Stanmer Pk. Rd.)
Stanmer Pk. (Local Nature Reserve) . . . 7G 135
Stanmer Pk. Rd. BN1: Brig . . . 3B 154
Stanmer Rural Mus. . . . 7G 134
Stanmer St. BN1: Brig . . . 3C 154
Stanmer Vs. BN1: Brig . . . 2C 154
Stanmore Gdns. PO21: Aldw . . . 1G 180
Stanover La. PO22: Flan . . . 5G 165
(not continuous)
Stansfield Ct. BN16: Rust . . . 2C 168
(off Mill La.)
Stanstead Cres. BN2: W'dean . . . 7N 155
STANSTED . . . 6G 116
Stansted Cl. PO9: Row C . . . 4C 116
Stansted Cres. PO9: Hav . . . 8B 116
Stansted House . . . 5J 117
STANSTED PARK . . . 5J 117
Stan's Way RH12: Hors . . . 9N 25
Stanton Dr. PO19: Chich . . . 2B 140
Stanton Rd. GU32: Peters . . . 5E 54
Stanwater La. GU29: Ipin, S'ham . . . 5A 58
Staplecross Ct. RH11: Craw . . . 9C 10
STAPLEFIELD . . . 5H 49
Staplefield Dr. BN2: Brig . . . 2G 154
Staplefield La. RH17: S'fld, W'lid . . . 9F 48
Staplefield Rd. RH17: Cuck . . . 1K 71
RH17: Hand . . . 2E 48
Staple La. PO18: E Lav . . . 6B 120
Staples Barn BN5: Henf . . . 2G 110
Staples Barn La. BN5: Henf . . . 2G 110
STAPLES HILL . . . 7F 40
Staples Hill RH13: Part G . . . 4C 90
Stapleton Ct. PO21: Aldw . . . 1F 180
Stapley Ct. BN3: Hove . . . 5F 152
Stapley Rd. BN3: Hove . . . 5F 152
Starboard Ct. BN2: Brig . . . 8K 173
Starboard Wlk. BN17: L'ton . . . 4M 167
Star Cl. RH13: Hors . . . 7D 26
Starling Cl. RH15: Burg H . . . 5L 93
Star Rd. RH13: Part G . . . 6D 90
Star Rd. Ind. Est. RH13: Part G . . . 5D 90
Station App. BN1: Falm . . . 8J 135
BN3: Hove . . . 5K 153
BN43: Shor S . . . 6J 151
(off Brunswick Rd.)
PO10: Ems . . . 4F 136
PO19: Chich . . . 8B 140
PO21: Bog R . . . 9D 164
(off Longford Rd.)
RH6: Horl . . . 2K 5
RH17: Ard, Hors K . . . 4L 51
RH20: Pulb . . . 6N 85
Station App. E. BN6: Hass . . . 3N 113
Station App. Ind. Est. RH20: Pulb . . . 6N 85
Station App. Rd. RH6: Gatw . . . 5K 5
Station App. W. BN6: Hass . . . 3N 113
Station Cl. BN7: Plump G . . . 2M 115
RH13: Hors . . . 9A 26
Station Cotts. BN6: Hass . . . 3N 113
RH13: Hors . . . 3H 45
Station Goods Yd. BN6: Hass . . . 4N 113
Station Hill RH10: Craw . . . 5K 11
Station Pde. BN11: Wor . . . 1E 170
BN15: Lan . . . 8B 150
BN16: E Pres . . . 2D 168
Station Rd. BN1: Brig . . . 2M 153
BN5: Henf . . . 2G 110
BN7: Plump G . . . 1M 115
BN11: Wor . . . 1H 171
BN16: Ang, E Pres, Rust . . . 2C 168
BN18: Amb . . . 2K 125
BN18: Cross . . . 4J 145
BN18: Ford . . . 9E 144
BN41: Ports . . . 7E 152
BN42: S'wck . . . 6A 152
BN44: Stey . . . 3B 130
GU28: Petw . . . 6L 83
GU29: Midh . . . 1F 80
GU31: Peters . . . 5F 54
GU32: Peters . . . 5E 54
PO18: Bosh . . . 6F 138
PO21: Bog R . . . 9D 164
RH6: Horl . . . 2K 5
RH10: Craw . . . 7F 10
RH10: Craw D . . . 4J 13
RH12: Rudg . . . 4J 23
(Thurne Way)
RH12: Rudg . . . 1G 22
(Cox Grn. Rd.)
RH12: Warnh . . . 3L 25
RH13: Cow . . . 7E 68
(not continuous)
Station Rd. RH13: Hors . . . 4H 45
(Christ's Hospital Rd.)
RH13: Hors . . . 9A 26
(Station Cl.)
RH13: Southw . . . 9K 45
RH14: Bill . . . 1J 65
RH14: Lox . . . 8M 21
RH15: Burg H . . . 6A 94
(not continuous)
RH17: Hors K . . . 5C 52
RH18: F Row . . . 9M 15
RH19: E Grin . . . 3D 14
RH19: Sharp . . . 5A 32
RH20: Pulb . . . 6N 85
Station Rd. Sth. RH13: Southw . . . 9K 45
Station St. BN1: Brig . . . 5E 172 (7B 154)
Station Vs. RH20: Pulb . . . 6N 85
Station Way RH10: Craw . . . 7F 10
Staunton Country Pk. . . . 6A 116
Staunton Country Pk. Vis. Cen. . . . 8A 116
Stavely Gdns. PO19: Chich . . . 2B 140
Stead Cl. PO11: Hay I . . . 9B 158
Stean Furlong BN17: Wick . . . 1J 167
STEDHAM . . . 8C 58
Stedham La. GU29: S'ham, Wool . . . 6C 58
Steele Cl. RH20: W Chil . . . 7K 87
Steele Cres. BN17: Wick . . . 9L 145
Steels La. PO18: Chid'm . . . 8B 138
STEEP . . . 2E 54
Steep Cl. BN14: Fin . . . 9C 128
Steepdown Rd. BN15: Somp . . . 5N 149
Steep La. BN14: Fin . . . 9C 128
Steeple Vw. BN13: W Tar . . . 8E 148
STEEP MARSH . . . 1G 55
Steepwood La. RH14: Adv, N Hth . . . 8G 65
RH20: Bill, N Hth . . . 9G 64
Steeres Hill RH12: Rusp . . . 6F 8
Steers La. RH10: Craw . . . 9L 5
Steine Gdns. . . . 9F 172
Steine Gdns. BN2: Brig . . . 8F 172 (8B 154)
Steine La. BN1: Brig . . . 8E 172
Steine St. BN2: Brig . . . 9F 172 (9B 154)
Stein Rd. PO10: S'brne . . . 3K 137
Stemp Dr. RH14: Bill . . . 1H 65
Stempswood Way PO22: Barn . . . 7J 143
Stennings, The RH19: E Grin . . . 2C 14
Stephen Cl. RH11: Craw . . . 3F 10
Stephens Cl. PO19: Chich . . . 6E 140
Stephenson Dr. RH19: E Grin . . . 5F 14
Stephenson Pl. RH10: Craw . . . 6K 11
Stephenson Way RH10: Craw . . . 6J 11
Stephenson Way Ind. Est. RH10: Craw . . . 6K 11
Stephens Rd. BN1: Brig . . . 3C 154
Stepney Cl. RH10: Craw . . . 8L 11
Stepney Ct. BN1: Brig . . . 4E 172
Sterling Bldgs. RH12: Hors . . . 9N 25
(off Carfax)
Sterling Pde. BN16: Rust . . . 3B 168
Sterling Pk. RH10: Craw . . . 1K 11
Sternway BN17: L'ton . . . 3N 167
Stevenage Rd. RH11: Craw . . . 9A 10
Stevens Ct. BN3: Hove . . . 6G 152
Stevenson Rd. BN2: Brig . . . 8D 154
Stewards Ri. BN18: Arun . . . 4F 144
Stewarts Mdw. GU28: Graff . . . 8D 82
Steyne, The BN11: Wor . . . 2J 171
PO21: Bog R . . . 1L 181
Steyne Gdns. BN11: Wor . . . 2J 171
Steyne St. PO21: Bog R . . . 9D 164
STEYNING . . . 3A 130
Steyning Av. BN3: Hove . . . 2H 153
BN10: Peace . . . 6J 175
(not continuous)
Steyning By-Pass
BN44: Bramb, Stey, Up B . . . 1N 129
Steyning Cl. BN12: Gor S . . . 1A 170
BN15: Somp . . . 5A 150
RH10: Craw . . . 4G 11
Steyning Ct. BN3: Hove . . . 6K 153
Steyning Cres. RH20: Storr . . . 5H 107
Steyning Ho. BN14: Broadw . . . 8H 149
Steyning Leisure Cen. . . . 2N 129
Steyning Mus. . . . 3A 130
Steyning Rd. BN2: Rott . . . 3N 173
BN43: Shor S . . . 9E 130
BN44: A'hst . . . 3A 110
BN44: Wash, Wis . . . 8E 108
RH13: W Grin . . . 1M 89
Steyning Way PO22: Bers . . . 5F 164
Stildon M. RH19: E Grin . . . 1C 14
Stile Gdns. GU27: Has . . . 5H 17
Stipenhoke BN5: Henf . . . 3J 111
Stirling Cl. RH10: Craw . . . 7K 11
RH15: Burg H . . . 4D 94
Stirling Ct. BN3: Hove . . . 6L 153
Stirling Ct. Rd. RH15: Burg H . . . 4D 94
Stirling Pl. BN3: Hove . . . 6J 153
RH12: Broadb H . . . 8H 25
Stirling Rd. PO19: Chich . . . 7C 140
Stirling Way PO21: Aldw . . . 1G 180
RH13: Hors . . . 9B 26
RH19: E Grin . . . 1H 15
Stirrup Way RH10: Craw . . . 5M 11
Stoat Ho. RH11: Craw . . . 3D 10
Stoatley Hollow GU27: Has . . . 3J 17
Stoatley Ri. GU27: Has . . . 3J 17
STOCKBRIDGE . . . 9B 140
Stockbridge Cl. PO9: Hav . . . 9B 116
Stockbridge Gdns. PO19: Chich . . . 1A 162
Stockbridge Pl. PO19: Chich . . . 9B 140
(off Stockbridge Rd.)
Stockbridge Rd. PO19: Chich . . . 9B 140
Stockbridge Rdbt. PO19: Chich . . . 9B 140
Stockcroft Rd. RH17: Bal . . . 9A 30
Stocker Rd. PO21: Bog R . . . 1K 181
Stockfield RH6: Horl . . . 1K 5
Stockheath Rd. PO9: Hav . . . 1A 136
Stockheath Way PO9: Hav . . . 1A 136
Stocklands Cl. RH17: Cuck . . . 1A 72
Stocks Cl. RH6: Horl . . . 3K 5
Stocks Flds. BN44: Wis . . . 6H 109
Stocks La. PO18: E Lav, Westh . . . 1D 140
PO20: E Witt . . . 4K 177
Stocks Mead RH20: Wash . . . 9C 108
Stockwell Cen. RH10: Craw . . . 6J 11
Stockwell Ct. RH15: Burg H . . . 5A 94
RH16: Hay H . . . 6F 72
(off Gower Rd.)
Stockwell Rd. RH19: E Grin . . . 6E 14
Stodham La. GU31: Liss, Peters . . . 1L 55
GU33: Hill B, Liss . . . 1L 55
STOKE . . . 3A 158
Stoke Abbott Ct. BN11: Wor . . . 2H 171
(off Stoke Abbott Rd.)
Stoke Abbott Rd. BN11: Wor . . . 2H 171
Stoke Clump PO20: Sel . . . 1J 183
Stoke Rd. BN18: Amb . . . 4J 125
Stokers Cl. RH6: Gatw . . . 5G 4
Stokes Cl. RH10: Craw . . . 8L 11
Stoneage Cl. PO22: Bers . . . 5D 164
Stonebridge Ct. RH11: Craw . . . 1E 28
RH12: Hors . . . 9L 25
Stonechat Cl. GU31: Peters . . . 7J 55
Stone Cl. BN13: Durr . . . 7D 148
Stone Ct. GU29: Midh . . . 9F 58
RH10: Worth . . . 6M 11
Stonecourt Cl. RH6: Horl . . . 2L 5
Stonecroft BN44: Stey . . . 3A 130
Stonecroft Cl. BN3: Hove . . . 1G 152
Stonecrop Cl. RH11: Craw . . . 9D 10
STONE CROSS . . . 7L 51
Stonecross La. RH16: Lind . . . 7L 51
Stonecross Rd. BN2: Brig . . . 1G 155
Stonedene Cl. RH18: F Row . . . 1N 33
Stonefield Cl. RH10: Craw . . . 7F 10
Stonefields BN16: Rust . . . 3C 168
Stonefield Way RH15: Burg H . . . 3A 94
Stonehall La. RH17: Bal . . . 3C 50
Stoneham Cl. GU32: Peters . . . 5D 54
Stoneham Pk. GU32: Peters . . . 5D 54
Stoneham Rd. BN3: Hove . . . 6H 153
Stone Hatch GU6: Alf . . . 1N 21
Stone Hill RH19: E Grin . . . 1C 32
Stonehill Cres. PO21: Pag . . . 9K 163
Stonehouse La. RH13: Cow . . . 9E 68
Stonehouse Rd. GU30: Lip . . . 7A 16
Stonehurst Ct. BN2: Brig . . . 7D 154
Stonehurst Rd. BN13: W Tar . . . 8D 148
Stone La. BN13: Salv . . . 7D 148
Stoneleigh Av. BN1: Brig . . . 8A 134
Stoneleigh Cl. BN1: Brig . . . 8A 134
RH19: E Grin . . . 3F 14
Stonepark Dr. RH18: F Row . . . 1N 33
Stonepit La. BN5: Henf . . . 2E 110
Stonepound Rd. BN6: Hass . . . 3N 113
Stone Quarry Rd. RH17: Chel C, Chel G . . . 4J 53
STONER HILL . . . 1B 54
Stoner Hill Rd. GU32: Frox . . . 1B 54
Stonery Cl. BN41: Ports . . . 3C 152
(not continuous)
Stonery Rd. BN41: Ports . . . 3C 152
Stone St. BN1: Brig . . . 7B 172 (8N 153)
Stoney Bottom GU26: Gray . . . 1E 16
Stoneybrook RH12: Hors . . . 1K 45
Stoneycroft Wlk. RH11: Ifield . . . 7N 9
Stoney La. BN43: Shor S . . . 6M 151
PO20: Earn . . . 7A 178
RH17: Bal . . . 6B 30
Stoney Stile Cl. PO21: Aldw . . . 1E 180
Stoney Stile La. PO21: Aldw . . . 2E 180
Stoneywish Nature Reserve . . . 4F 114
Stony Mere Way BN1: Brig, Stan . . . 9H 135
STOPHAM . . . 6K 85
Stopham Cl. BN14: Wor . . . 8F 148
Stopham Rd. RH10: Craw . . . 9L 11
RH20: Pulb . . . 7L 85
Stor Mdw. RH20: Storr . . . 5J 107
STORRINGTON . . . 6J 107
Storrington & District Mus. . . . 6H 107
Storrington Cl. BN3: Hove . . . 3G 153
PO19: Fish . . . 5L 139
Storrington Ct. RH11: Craw . . . 5C 10
Storrington Ri. BN14: Fin V . . . 1D 148
Storrington Rd. RH20: Storr, Thake . . . 4M 107
RH20: Wash . . . 7N 107
Story Rd. PO19: Chich . . . 6E 140
STOUGHTON . . . 2D 118
Stour Cl. BN13: Durr . . . 5A 148
GU31: Peters . . . 7E 54
Stour Rd. BN13: Durr . . . 5A 148
Strachey Ct. RH11: Craw . . . 2D 28
Strand, The BN2: Brig . . . 8K 173
BN12: Fer . . . 4K 169
BN12: Gor S . . . 1N 169
Strand Cl. RH10: Craw . . . 8M 11
Strand Ct. BN16: Rust . . . 5A 168
(off Harsfold Rd.)
Strand Pde. BN12: Gor S . . . 9B 148
Strand Pde. Rdbt. BN12: Wor . . . 1C 170
(off The Boulevard)
Strand Way PO22: Felp . . . 8J 165
Strange Gdn. PO21: Aldw . . . 2G 181
Stratford Pl. PO21: Bog R . . . 9D 164
(off Victoria Dr.)
Strathfield Cl. RH16: Hay H . . . 5G 72
Strathmoor Gdns. GU29: Ease . . . 8H 59
Strathmore Cl. BN13: Wor . . . 9C 148
Strathmore Rd. BN13: Wor . . . 9C 148
RH11: Ifield . . . 3C 10
Stratton Ct. PO22: Bog R . . . 7F 164
Strawberry Fld. RH20: Pulb . . . 5B 86
Strawberry La. RH20: Thake . . . 2N 107
Strawlands BN7: Plump G . . . 1M 115
Strawson Ct. RH6: Horl . . . 1H 5
Stream Cl. PO18: Bosh . . . 8E 138
Stream La. RH20: Pulb, W Chil . . . 7G 86
Stream Pk. RH19: E Grin . . . 1A 14
STREAT . . . 4K 115
Streat Bostall BN6: Streat . . . 8K 115
Streatleigh Ct. PO21: Aldw . . . 1J 181
(off King's Pde.)
Streat La. BN6: Streat . . . 8K 95
Streel's La. GU28: Eber . . . 6L 39
Street, The BN5: Fulk . . . 3B 132
BN6: Alb . . . 1E 112
BN6: W'ton . . . 7G 115

Truro Ct.—Vinnetrow Rd.

Truro Ct. BN11: Wor .3E 170
(off Pevensey Gdn.)
Truro Cres. PO21: Aldw .9N 163
Truslers Hill La. BN6: Alb .9B 92
Tryndel Way PO22: Felp .8J 165
Tudor Av. PO10: Ems .1E 136
Tudor Cl. BN2: Rott .2A 174
BN3: Hove .3H 153
BN14: Fin .8C 128
BN15: S Lan .7E 150
GU26: Gray .1F 16
PO11: Hay I .9A 158
PO19: Chich .3B 140
PO22: Midd S .7L 165
RH10: Craw .7M 11
RH19: E Grin .4F 14
RH20: Pulb .7E 86
Tudor Dr. BN44: Up B .3D 130
PO20: Westg .5E 142
Tudor Gdns. RH15: Burg H .4A 94
Tudor Rose Pk. BN10: Peace .6M 175
Tudors, The BN3: Hove .4H 153
(off Wayfield Av.)
Tudor Village RH20: Storr .4A 108
Tufts Fld. GU29: Midh .2G 80
Tufts Mdw. GU29: Midh .2G 80
Tuggles Plat RH12: Warnh .4J 25
Tulip Ct. RH12: Hors .7N 25
Tullett Rd. RH10: Craw .1K 29
Tumulus Rd. BN2: Salt .2C 174
Tunnel Rd. RH6: Gatw .5G 5
Tunnmeade RH11: Ifield .7A 10
Tunsgate BN44: Stey .3A 130
Tunworth Ct. PO9: Hav .9B 116
Tuppenny La. PO10: S'brne .5J 137
Tupper Gdns. PO22: Felp .6H 165
Turkey La. RH15: Burg H .5C 94
Turnberry Ct. RH16: Hay H .5F 72
(off Iona Way)
Turnbull Rd. PO19: Chich .6D 140
Turner Av. RH14: Bill .2H 65
Turner Ct. RH19: E Grin .1G 14
Turner Ho. BN41: Ports .6E 152
(off Gordon Cl.)
Turner Rd. BN14: Broadw .7J 149
Turners Cl. RH13: Southw .1L 67
TURNERS HILL .8H 13
Turners Hill Pk. RH10: Turn H .7K 13
Turners Hill Rd. RH10: Craw D, Turn H .1G 12
RH10: Craw, Worth .6M 11
RH19: E Grin .7N 13
Turners Mead GU8: Chidd .1K 19
RH20: Storr .5G 107
Turners Mill Cl. RH16: Hay H .2E 72
Turners Mill Rd. RH16: Hay H .2E 72
Turners Way RH15: Burg H .4A 94
Turner Wlk. RH10: Craw .9H 11
Turner Way PO20: Sel .3K 183
Turnpike Cl. BN10: Peace .3J 175
PO19: Chich .1A 162
Turnpike Ct. RH17: Ard .2J 51
Turnpike Pl. RH11: Craw .4F 10
Turnpike Rd. BN18: Amb, Pulb .9L 105
RH20: Pulb .9L 105
Turnpike Way RH20: A'ton .2E 108
Turret Ct. RH19: E Grin .1C 14
Turret Ho. PO22: Felp .8H 165
(off Limmer La.)
Turret Ho. M. PO22: Felp .8H 165
(off Limmer La.)
Turtledove Av. RH10: Turn H .7K 13
Turton Cl. BN2: Brig .8E 154
Tuscan Av. PO22: Midd S .7N 165
Tuscan Ct. BN10: Tels C .5F 174
Tuscany Gdns. RH10: Craw .3G 10
Tushmore Av. RH10: Craw .3G 10
Tushmore Ct. RH10: Craw .4G 10
Tushmore Cres. RH10: Craw .3F 10
Tushmore La. RH10: Craw .4G 10
Tushmore Rdbt. RH10: Craw .4F 10
Tussock Cl. RH11: Craw .8C 10
Tuxford Cl. RH10: Craw .8L 11
Tweed La. RH11: Ifield .3B 10
TWINEHAM .4C 92
Twineham Cl. BN2: Brig .6G 154
TWINEHAM GREEN .2C 92
Twineham La. BN6: Alb, Say C .9C 92
RH17: Twine .9C 92
Twitten, The BN2: Rott .3A 174
BN6: Alb .1E 112
BN6: Ditch .4E 114
BN42: S'wck .6A 152
BN44: Up B .5E 130
RH11: Craw .6E 10
RH15: Burg H .4C 94
Twitten Cl. BN42: S'wck .6A 152
Twitten La. RH19: Felb .1M 13
Twittenside BN44: Stey .4A 130
Twittens Way PO9: Hav .4A 136
Twitten Way BN14: Wor .9E 148
Two Barns La. PO18: Mid L .7N 119
TWO MILE ASH .7G 45
Two Mile Ash Rd.
RH13: B Grn, Hors, Southw .7D 44
Two Ways RH14: Lox .7N 21
TWYFORD .8F 32
Twyford Cl. BN13: Durr .7C 148
Twyford Gdns. BN13: Durr .7C 148
Twyford La. RH17: F Row, Hors K .9G 32
RH18: F Row, Hors K .9G 32
Twyford Rd. BN1: Brig .8F 134
BN13: Durr .7C 148
Twyhurst Ct. RH19: E Grin .1D 14
Twyne Cl. RH11: Craw .8B 10
Twyner Cl. RH6: Horl .1M 5
TYE .3C 158
Tye Cl. BN2: Salt .4D 174
Tyedean Rd. BN10: Tels C .4F 174
Tye La. BN18: Walb .4M 143
TYES CROSS .6C 32
Tye Vw. BN10: Tels C .3G 174
Tylden Way RH12: Hors .5C 26
Tyler Rd. RH10: Craw .9F 10
Tyler's Grn. RH16: Cuck, Hay H .4B 72
RH17: Cuck .4B 72
Tymperley Ct. RH13: Hors .8B 26
(off Kings Rd.)
Tyne Cl. BN13: Durr .6A 148
RH10: Craw .7L 11
Tyne Way PO21: Aldw .8M 163
Tynings, The BN15: Lan .8A 150
Tyson Pl. BN2: Brig .8C 154
(off Grosvenor St.)
Tythe Barn RH17: Bol .6E 70
Tythe Barn Rd. PO20: Sel .4J 183
Tytherley Grn. PO9: Hav .8B 116

U

Uckfield Cl. BN2: Brig .7G 154
Ullswater Dr. BN17: L'ton .1N 167
Ullswater Gro. PO22: Felp .6J 165
Ullswater Rd. BN15: Somp .8M 149
Undercliff Wlk.
BN2: Brig, O'dean, Rott, Salt .1J 173
Underdown Rd. BN42: S'wck .5A 152
Underhill La.
BN6: Clay, Ditch, Key, W'ton .7M 113
Undermill Rd. BN44: Up B .4E 130
Underwood Cl. RH10: Craw D .4J 13
Underwood Rd. GU27: Has .4H 17
Unicorn Trad. Est. GU27: Has .4K 17
Union Pl. BN11: Wor .2H 171
Union Rd. BN2: Brig .3G 172 (6C 154)
Union St. BN1: Brig .8E 172
University of Brighton
Circus St. Annexe .7F 172
Falmer Campus .9J 135
Grand Pde. .7F 172
Mithras House .4D 154
Moulsecoomb Campus .3D 154
Prince's St. Annexe .8F 172
University of Chichester
Bishop Otter Campus .5D 140
Bognor Regis Campus .8F 164
University of Sussex .7J 135
University of Sussex Sports Cen. .8J 135
University Way BN1: Falm .8H 135
Updown Hill RH16: Hay H .7D 72
Upfield RH6: Horl .3J 5
Upfield Cl. RH6: Horl .4J 5
Uphill Way PO20: Huns .4B 162
Uplands Av. BN13: High S .4D 148
Uplands Cl. GU27: Has .3M 17
Uplands Rd. BN1: Brig .3D 154
PO9: Row C .4C 116
UP MARDEN .6C 98
Uppark .8N 77
Uppark Gdns. RH12: Hors .5C 26
Uppark Way PO22: Felp .6L 165
Up. Abbey Rd. BN2: Brig .9E 154
Up. Adhurst Ind. Pk. GU31: Peters .2L 55
Up. Bannings Rd. BN2: Salt .1E 174
Up. Beacon Rd. BN6: Ditch .7E 114
Up. Bedford St. BN2: Brig .9D 154
UPPER BEEDING .4D 130
Upper Beeding Sports & Youth Cen. .4D 130
UPPER BEVENDEAN .4K 155
Up. Bevendean Av. BN2: Brig .4F 154
Up. Bognor Rd. PO21: Bog R, Felp .8E 164
Up. Boundstone La. BN15: Lan, Somp .6A 150
(not continuous)
Up. Brighton Rd. BN14: Broadw, Char D .7G 148
BN15: N Lan, Somp .6K 149
Up. Chalvington Pl. BN2: Brig .8F 154
Upper Cl. RH18: F Row .1M 33
UPPER COKEHAM .6N 149
Upper Cotts. BN2: O'dean .9L 155
Upper Dr. BN16: E Pres .4G 168
Upper Drive, The BN3: Hove .1A 172 (5L 153)
UPPER EASEBOURNE .6K 59
Upperfield GU29: Ease .6H 59
Up. Gardner St. BN1: Brig .6E 172 (7B 154)
Up. Gloucester Rd. BN1: Brig .5D 172 (7A 154)
Up. Hamilton Rd. BN1: Brig .2B 172 (5N 153)
Up. Hammer La. GU26: Has, Hind .2E 16
Upper Heyshott GU31: Peters .6G 54
Up. High St. BN11: Wor .1J 171
Up. Hollingdean Rd. BN1: Brig .4C 154
UPPER IFOLD .4F 20
Up. Kingston La. BN42: S'wck .4N 151
BN43: Shor S .4N 151
Up. Lewes Rd. BN2: Brig .3G 172 (6C 154)
Upper Mkt. St. BN3: Hove .8M 153
Upper Mt. GU27: G'wd .2A 18
Upper Nth. St. BN1: Brig .6B 172 (7N 153)
UPPER NORWOOD .7E 82
Up. Park Pl. BN2: Brig .8C 154
Up. Rock Gdns. BN2: Brig .8C 154
Up. Roedale Cotts. BN1: Brig .1B 154
Up. St James's St. BN2: Brig .9C 154
Up. St John's Rd. RH15: Burg H .4B 94
Up. School Dr. GU27: Has .6H 17
Up. Shoreham Rd.
BN43: Shor S .5G 151
Upper Sq. RH18: F Row .9M 15
Upper Stables RH16: Hay H .6D 72
Up. Station Rd. BN5: Henf .2G 110
Upper St. RH20: Fitt .5G 84
Up. Sudeley St. BN2: Brig .9E 154
UPPERTON .7J 61
Upperton Rd. GU28: Till .7J 61
Up. Valley Rd. BN9: Newh .6N 175
Upper Wardley GU30: Mill .5M 35
Upper Wardown GU31: Peters .5H 55
Up. Wellington Rd. BN2: Brig .6D 154
Up. West Dr. BN12: Fer .3K 169
Up. West La. BN15: N Lan .5B 150
Up. Winfield Av. BN1: Brig .8A 134
Upton Av. BN42: S'wck .4A 152
Upton Ct. BN13: Wor .1D 170
Upton Gdns. BN13: Wor .9D 148
Upton Rd. BN13: Wor .9D 148
PO19: Chich .9B 140
UPWALTHAM .7F 102
Upways Cl. PO20: Sel .1J 183
Ursula Av. PO20: Sel .4H 183
(not continuous)
Ursula Av. Nth. PO20: Sel .4H 183
Ursula Sq. PO20: Sel .5H 183

V

Valdoe Trundle PO20: Sel .1J 183
VALE, THE .1C 148
Vale, The BN2: O'dean .8M 155
Vale Av. BN1: Brig .7N 133
BN14: Fin V .3D 148
Valebridge Cl. RH15: Burg H .2D 94
Valebridge Dr. RH15: Burg H .3D 94
Valebridge Rd. RH15: Burg H .3D 94
RH16: Burg H .3D 94
Vale Ct. BN41: Ports .6D 152
RH16: Hay H .7F 72
Vale Dr. BN14: Fin V .3D 148
RH12: Hors .9M 25
Vale Gdns. BN41: Ports .6D 152
Valencia Rd. BN11: Wor .1E 170
Valentine Cl. BN14: Salv .6F 148
BN43: Shor S .4G 151
(off Steyning Rd.)
Valentine Ct. BN3: Hove .6L 153
Valentine Dr. RH15: Burg H .4N 93
Valentines RH14: Plais .6D 20
Valentines Gdns. PO21: Aldw .1E 180
Valentines Lea GU28: N'chpl .2H 39
Valerie Cl. BN41: Ports .3D 152
Vale Rd. BN2: Salt .1D 174
BN41: Ports .6D 152
RH16: Hay H .7E 72
Valetta Pk. PO10: Ems .5E 136
Valetta Rd. PO10: Tho I .3K 159
Vale Wlk. BN14: Fin V .4D 148
Valewood Cl. RH13: Bill .9B 44
Valewood La. RH13: B Grn, Bill .9A 44
Valewood Rd. GU27: Has .7L 17
Valiant Rd. PO10: Tho I .3K 159
Vallance By-Ways Gatwick RH6: Charlw .7B 4
Vallance Cl. RH15: Burg H .4N 93
Vallance Ct. BN3: Hove .7J 153
(off Hove St.)
Vallance Gdns. BN3: Hove .7J 153
Vallance Rd. BN3: Hove .7J 153
Vallensdean Cotts. BN41: Ports .3E 152
Valley Cl. BN1: Brig .1L 153
Valley Dr. BN1: Brig .1K 153
Valley Fld. Ct. BN14: Fin V .2D 148
Valley Gdns. BN14: Fin V .4E 148
Valley Rd. BN9: Newh .5N 175
BN10: Peace .2J 175
BN15: Somp .5N 149
BN41: Ports .2B 152
Valley Vw. TN22: Fur G .1G 75
Valverde Ho. BN3: Hove .6L 153
Van Alen Building, The BN2: Brig .9G 172
Van Alen M. BN2: Brig .9G 172
Vanbrugh Cl. RH11: Craw .9A 10
Vanburgh Ct. BN3: Hove .6K 153
Vancouver Cl. BN13: Durr .7B 148
Vancouver Dr. RH11: Craw .3F 10
Vancouver Rd. BN13: Durr .7A 148
Van Dyck Pl. PO22: Bers .6B 164
Van Gogh Pl. PO22: Bers .6C 164
Vann Bri. Cl. GU27: Fern .4J 37
VANN COMMON .3J 37
Vanners RH10: Craw .5G 10
Vann Lake RH5: Ock .1K 7
Vann Lake Rd. RH5: Capel, Ock .1K 7
Vann Rd. GU27: Fern .4J 37
Vantage Point BN1: Brig .3E 172
(off New England Rd.)
Vanzell Rd. GU29: Ease .8J 59
Varey Rd. BN13: Durr .7N 147
Varndean Cl. BN1: Brig .2N 153
Varndean Dr. BN1: Brig .2N 153
Varndean Gdns. BN1: Brig .2N 153
Varndean Holt BN1: Brig .2A 154
Varndean Rd. BN1: Brig .2N 153
Varsity Rd. PO10: Tho I .3K 159
Vauxhall Way GU32: Peters .6E 54
Vector Point RH10: Craw .2H 11
Velyn Av. PO19: Chich .7D 140
Ventnor Vs. BN3: Hove .7K 153
Ventura PO22: Bers .6D 164
Venus La. PO21: Pag .4A 180
Veras Wlk. RH20: Storr .6A 108
Verbania Way RH19: E Grin .3H 15
Verdley Pl. GU27: Fern .7L 37
Vere Rd. BN1: Brig .2F 172 (5B 154)
Veric BN3: Hove .6L 153
Verica Ct. PO19: Fish .6L 139
Vermont Dr. BN16: E Pres .3F 168
Vermont Way BN16: E Pres .3F 168
Vernon Av. BN2: W'dean .4K 155
BN10: Peace .6K 175
(not continuous)
Vernon Cl. BN16: Rust .3B 168
RH12: Hors .7D 26
Vernon Ct. BN1: Brig .5B 172
Vernon Gdns. BN1: Brig .5B 172
Vernon Ter. BN1: Brig .5B 172 (7N 153)
Veronica Cl. BN16: E Pres .4F 168
Veronica Way BN2: Brig .9C 154
Verwood Rd. PO9: Hav .8B 116
Viaduct Lofts BN2: Brig .5D 154
(off Melbourne St.)
Viaduct Rd. BN1: Brig .3E 172 (6B 154)
Viaduct Ter. BN1: Brig .3F 172
Via Ravenna PO19: Chich .7A 140
Via Ravenna Rdbt. PO19: Chich .8B 140
Vicarage Cl. RH12: Colg .5M 27
Vicarage Flds. BN13: Durr .6B 148
Vicarage Hill RH14: Lox .8N 21
Vicarage La. BN2: Rott .3N 173
BN16: E Pres .3E 168
BN44: Stey .3A 130
GU27: Has .5H 17
Vicarage La. GU28: Lods .7C 60
PO22: Felp .8G 165
RH6: Horl .1H 5
RH17: Scay H .6N 73
Vicarage Rd.
RH10: Craw D .5H 13
Vicarage Ter. BN2: Rott .3N 173
Vicarage Wlk. RH19: E Grin .3F 14
Vicars Cl. PO19: Chich .7C 140
Viceroy Ct. BN12: Fer .3K 169
Viceroy Lodge BN3: Hove .7J 153
Victor Ct. RH10: Craw .3M 11
Victoria Av. BN10: Peace .6J 175
(not continuous)
GU29: Ease .8J 59
RH15: Burg H .5N 93
Victoria Cl. GU29: Midh .1G 80
RH6: Horl .2J 5
RH15: Burg H .6A 94
Victoria Cotts. BN3: Hove .8K 153
(off Sussex Rd.)
Victoria Ct. BN3: Hove .7K 153
BN11: Wor .1G 171
(Victoria Pk. Gdns.)
BN11: Wor .1G 171
(Victoria Rd.)
BN15: Lan .9B 150
BN41: Ports .5E 152
BN43: Shor S .6H 151
(off Victoria Rd.)
RH13: Hors .9A 26
Victoria Dr. PO21: Bog R .1K 181
Victoria Gdns. BN17: L'ton .4K 167
(off Clifton Rd.)
PO20: Westg .6E 142
RH15: Burg H .6A 94
Victoria Gro. BN3: Hove .7L 153
Victoria Ind. Est. RH15: Burg H .6N 93
(not continuous)
Victoria M. BN2: Rott .3N 173
(off West St.)
PO21: Bog R .8D 164
(off Victoria Dr.)
RH11: Craw .6F 10
Victorian Bus. Cen.
BN18: Ford .9D 144
Victoria Park .5F 72
Victoria Pk. Gdns. BN11: Wor .1G 170
BN41: Ports .5E 152
(off Old Shoreham Rd.)
Victoria Pl. BN1: Brig .6B 172 (7N 153)
GU30: Lip .2A 36
PO21: Bog R .1K 181
Victoria Rd. BN1: Brig .6B 172 (7N 153)
BN11: Wor .1G 171
BN41: Ports .5D 152
BN42: S'wck .6N 151
BN43: Shor S .6H 151
PO10: Ems .4E 136
PO11: Hay I .2A 158
PO19: Chich .7E 140
PO21: Bog R .1K 181
RH6: Horl .2J 5
RH11: Craw .6E 10
RH15: Burg H .5N 93
RH16: Hay H .6G 73
RH17: Bal .1B 50
Victoria Rd. Sth.
PO21: Bog R .1K 181
Victoria Sq. RH6: Horl .2J 5
(off Consort Way)
Victoria St. BN1: Brig .6B 172 (7N 153)
RH13: Hors .9A 26
Victoria Ter. BN3: Hove .8K 153
PO10: Ems .4G 136
PO10: S'brne .5J 137
RH19: E Grin .1E 14
Victoria Vs. BN18: Yap .2A 166
Victoria Way RH15: Burg H .6A 94
RH19: E Grin .5F 14
Victor Rd. PO10: Tho I .3K 159
Victory Ct. PO21: Bog R .1K 181
(off Aldwick Rd.)
Victory M. BN2: Brig .8L 173
Victory Rd. RH12: Hors .8M 25
View, The PO21: Pag .3C 180
View Rd. BN10: Peace .4J 175
Views Path RH16: Hay H .5J 73
Viking Ct. BN17: L'ton .4K 167
(off Surrey St.)
Viking Ho. RH6: Lowf H .8F 4
Viking Way PO18: Bosh .8E 138
Village, The BN44: A'hst .2A 110
Village Barn, The
BN1: Brig .7N 133
Village Cl. BN41: Ports .3D 152
Village Grn. BN9: Pidd .1N 175
Village Sq. BN2: Brig .8K 173
Village St. GU32: Peters .3H 55
Village Way BN1: Falm .8K 135
Villa Pl. PO22: Midd S .7A 166
Villiers Cl. BN2: W'dean .5M 155
Villiers Ct. BN1: Brig .5E 172
Vinall Gdns. RH12: Broadb H .7H 25
Vinalls Bus. Cen. BN5: Henf .3H 111
Vincent Cl. BN15: Lan .7A 150
RH13: Hors .9C 26
Vincent Rd. PO20: Sel .4G 183
Vincent's Ct. BN2: Brig .8L 173
Vine Cotts. GU28: N'chpl .2H 39
Vine Pl. BN1: Brig .6C 172 (7A 154)
Vineries, The
BN3: Hove .4A 172 (7N 153)
RH15: Burg H .5E 94
Vineries Cl. BN13: Salv .7E 148
Vinery, The BN18: Poling .5B 146
Vinery Ct. BN13: Salv .7E 148
Vines Cross Rd. BN2: Brig .6G 155
Vine St.
BN1: Brig .6F 172 (7B 154)
Viney Cl. RH20: A'ton .2D 108
Vinnetrow Bus. Pk. PO20: Runc .1G 162
Vinnetrow Rd. PO20: Runc .8F 140

A-Z West Sussex Atlas 227

Vinson Rd.—W. Ashling Rd.

Vinson Rd. GU33: Liss 6A 34
Virgin Active
Crawley 5F 10
Virginia Gdns. PO22: Felp 6K 165
Viscount Dr. PO21: Pag 3D 180
Vivienne Cl. RH11: Craw 3F 10
Vogue Gyratory BN2: Brig 5D 154
Volk's Electric Railway 9C 154 & 8H 173
Vowels La. RH19: E Grin 2K 31
Vulcan Cl. RH11: Craw 1E 28
Vulcan Rd. PO10: Tho I 3K 159

W

Wad, The PO20: W Witt 2F 176
Waddington Cl. RH11: Craw 9C 10
Wade Ct. Rd. PO9: Hav 5A 136
Wade End PO20: Sel 2G 182
Wade La. PO9: Hav 6A 136
Wadeway, The PO20: Sel 2G 182
Wadeys, The RH14: Bill 1H 65
Wadham Cl. RH10: Craw 3L 11
Wadhurst Cl. PO21: Bog R 8C 164
Wadhurst Ct. BN11: Wor 1E 170
Wadhurst Dr. BN12: Gor S 2N 169
Wadhurst Ri. BN2: Brig 8G 154
Wadurs Swimming Pool 4N 151
Wagg Cl. RH19: E Grin 3G 14
Waggoners Wells La. GU26: Gray 1C 16
Wagstaff Cotts. RH13: Sherm 5F 90
Wagtail Cl. RH12: Hors 4A 26
Wain End RH12: Hors 6A 26
Wainwrights RH10: Craw 9F 10
Wakefield Ct. RH12: Hors 9M 25
Wakefield Pl. *BN2: Brig* 5C 154
(off Wakefield Rd.)
Wakefield Rd. BN2: Brig 5C 154
Wakefield Way PO21: Aldw 8N 163
Wakefords Way PO9: Hav 8A 116
Wakehams Grn. Dr. RH10: Craw 3M 11
Wakehurst Ct. BN11: Wor 1K 171
Wakehurst Dr. RH10: Craw 9F 10
Wakehurst La. RH17: Ard 2H 51
Wakehurst M. RH12: Hors 1K 45
Wakehurst Place 8G 31
Wakehurst Pl. BN16: Rust 2B 168
Wakestone La. RH20: Fitt, Kird, Wisb 6G 63
WALBERTON 5M 143
Walberton Cl. PO22: Felp 7H 165
Walberton Ct. BN11: Wor 3D 170
WALBERTON GREEN 4K 143
Waldby Ct. RH11: Craw 9C 10
Waldegrave Ct. *BN2: Salt* 1D 174
(off Westfield Av.)
Waldegrave Rd. BN1: Brig 3A 154
Walders Rd. BN16: Rust 2A 168
WALDERTON 4A 118
Waldron Av. BN1: Brig 8E 134
Waldron Pl. BN1: Brig 8E 134
Walesbeech RH10: Craw 7J 11
Walesbeech Rd. BN2: Salt 4D 174
Wales Farm La. BN7: Plump 7K 115
Waley's La. RH5: Ock 2G 6
Walhatch Cl. RH18: F Row 1M 33
Walker Rd. RH10: Craw 8K 11
Walkestone La. RH20: Fitt 2F 84
Walk Ho. BN1: Brig 6F 172
Walkway, The BN16: Ang 9F 146
Wallace Av. BN11: Wor 2D 170
Wallace Ct. BN11: Wor 2D 170
Wallace M. BN11: Wor 3D 170
Wallace Pde. *BN12: Wor* 2D 170
(off Goring Rd.)
Wallace Rd. BN16: Rust 1B 168
Wallage La. RH10: Craw D, Rowf 6D 12
Wall Cott. Dr. PO19: Chich 7B 140
Walled Garden, The RH14: Lox 4M 21
Wallfield PO21: Aldw 2H 181
WALL HILL 8L 15
Wall Hill Rd. RH19: Ash W, F Row 7K 15
Wallis Ct. RH10: Craw 2H 11
Wallis Ho. *RH19: E Grin* 3E 14
(off Orchard Way)
Wallis Way RH13: Hors 7D 26
RH15: Burg H 4M 93
WALLISWOOD 3B 6
Wallis Wood Nature Reserve 2C 6
Wallner Cres. PO22: Felp 7K 165
Wallrock Wlk. PO10: Ems 1F 136
Walls Wlk. *PO19: Chich* 7C 140
(off Friary La.)
Walmer Cl. BN2: Brig 4J 155
RH13: Southw 8L 45
Walmer Cres. BN2: Brig 4J 155
Walmsleys Way PO20: Brac 6N 177
Walnut Av. BN16: Rust 3A 168
PO19: Chich 5A 140
Walnut Cl. BN1: Brig 2N 153
Walnut Ct. *BN13: Salv* 7E 148
(off Offington La.)
RH13: Hors 1B 46
Walnut La. RH11: Craw 3D 10
Walnut Lodge BN14: Wor 9G 148
Walnut Pk. RH16: Hay H 5J 73
Walnuts, The RH12: Hors 7N 25
Walnut Tree Caravan Pk. PO20: W Witt 9N 159
Walnut Tree Cl. PO11: Hay I 9A 158
Walnut Tree Dr. PO10: W'cote 2L 137
Walnut Tree Way BN13: Durr 8N 147
Walpole Av. BN12: Gor S 2B 170
Walpole Rd. BN2: Brig 8D 154
Walpole Ter. BN2: Brig 8E 154
Walsham Cl. PO22: Felp 6G 165
Walsingham Rd. BN3: Hove 7H 153
WALSTEAD 3L 73
Walstead Ct. RH10: Craw 7F 10
Walstead Ho. RH10: Craw 7F 10
Walstead Lodge *RH16: Hay H* 6G 72
(off Whitelands)
Walter May Ho. *BN2: Brig* 8G 154
(off Whitehawk Rd.)
Walters Grn. BN17: Wick 8J 145
Waltham Pk. Rd. RH20: Cold 9F 84
Walthurst La. RH14: Wisb 3L 41
Walton Av. PO21: Bog R 9F 164
Walton Bank BN1: Brig 9F 134
Walton Cl. BN13: Durr 7D 148
Walton Dr. RH13: Hors 7E 26
Walton Heath RH10: Craw 4M 11
Walton La. PO18: Bosh 8F 138
Walton Lodge BN13: Durr 7D 148
Walton Rd. PO21: Bog R 9E 164
Walwyn Cl. PO20: Bir 8H 161
Wanderdown Cl. BN2: O'dean 9M 155
Wanderdown Dr. BN2: O'dean 9M 155
Wanderdown Rd. BN2: O'dean 9L 155
Wanderdown Way BN2: O'dean 9M 155
Wandle Cl. RH10: Craw 7L 11
Wandleys Caravan Pk. PO20: E'gate 4G 143
Wandleys Cl. PO20: E'gate 4G 143
Wandleys Dr. PO20: E'gate 4G 143
Wandleys La. BN18: E'gate, Walb 4G 143
PO20: E'gate, Walb 4G 143
Wansford Way PO22: Felp 8K 165
Wantage Cl. RH10: Craw 9L 11
Wantley Hill Est. BN5: Henf 1J 111
Wantley La. RH20: Storr 5K 107
Wantley Rd. BN14: Fin V 4E 148
Wappingthorn Farm La. BN44: Stey 8M 109
Wapple Way BN6: Streat, W'ton 5G 115
Warbleheath Cl. PO18: Mid L 8B 120
Warblers Way PO22: Bers 5C 164
Warbleton Cl. BN2: Brig 8F 154
Warbleton Ho. *RH11: Craw* 9B 10
(off Breezehurst Dr.)
WARBLINGTON 4B 136
Warblington Av. PO9: Warbl 4B 136
Warblington Rd. PO10: Ems 6E 136
Warblington Station (Rail) 3B 136
Warbrook Ct. PO9: Hav 9B 116
Warburton Cl. RH19: E Grin 3G 14
Ward Cres. PO10: Ems 2G 136
Warden Ct. RH17: Cuck 3A 72
WARDLEY 5M 35
Wardley Grn. GU30: Mill 6M 35
Wardley La. GU30: Mill 5M 35
Ware Ct. *RH15: Burg H* 5E 94
(off Kings Way)
Wareland Ho. *RH19: E Grin* 3E 14
(off Railway App.)
Warelands RH15: Burg H 7A 94
Warenne Rd. BN3: Hove 2E 152
Warleigh Rd. BN1: Brig 2F 172 (5B 154)
Waltersville Way RH6: Horl 4L 5
Warmdene Av. BN1: Brig 8A 134
Warmdene Cl. BN1: Brig 9A 134
Warmdene Rd. BN1: Brig 8A 134
Warmdene Way BN1: Brig 8A 134
WARMINGHURST 1B 108
Warminghurst Cl. RH20: A'ton 2D 108
Warnborough Ct. PO9: Hav 8B 116
Warner Cl. RH10: Craw 1L 29
Warner Ct. RH15: Burg H 5B 94
Warner Farm Touring Pk. PO20: Sel 1G 182
Warner La. PO20: Sel 2F 182
Warner Rd. BN14: Broadw 9K 149
PO20: Sel 4G 183
Warners Pde. *BN11: Wor* 1G 171
(off Orme Rd.)
Warnes BN11: Wor 2J 171
WARNHAM 3K 25
Warnham Cl. BN12: Gor S 3B 170
Warnham Ct. BN3: Hove 7K 153
RH12: Warnh 4K 25
Warnham Ct. M. RH12: Warnh 4K 25
Warnham Mnr. RH12: Warnh 4G 25
Warnham M. BN12: Gor S 2B 170
Warnham Nature Reserve 6M 25
Warnham Park 5K 25
Warnham Ri. BN1: Brig 9B 134
Warnham Rd. BN12: Gor S 2B 170
RH10: Craw 8J 11
RH12: Broadb H 7H 25
RH12: Warnh, Hors 6M 25
Warnham Station (Rail) 3N 25
WARNINGCAMP 2L 145
Warningcamp La. BN18: W'camp 2L 145
WARNINGLID 9B 48
Warninglid La. RH13: Plum P 6M 47
RH17: Plum P, W'lid 6M 47
Warninglid Rd. RH17: S'fld 5G 49
WARREN, THE 9A 100
Warren, The BN12: Fer 4L 169
RH15: Burg H 7D 94
Warren Av. BN2: W'dean 4K 155
Warren Chase RH20: Storr 5K 107
Warren Cl. BN2: W'dean 5J 155
BN14: Salv 6F 148
RH19: Felb 1M 13
Warren Cotts. RH17: Hand 2D 48
Warren Ct. BN14: Salv 6F 148
BN15: Lan 8A 150
BN42: S'wck 4A 152
Warren Cres. BN16: E Pres 2E 168
Warren Cft. RH20: Coot 6G 106
Warren Dr. RH11: Craw 5C 10
RH13: Southw 7K 45
Warren Farm La. PO19: Chich 3B 140
Warren Farm Pl. BN14: Fin V 5E 148
Warren Gdns. BN14: Salv 6F 148
Warren La. BN8: N Cha 9E 74
Warren Lodge BN10: Tels C 3G 175
Warren Ri. BN2: W'dean 5J 155
Warren Rd. BN2: Brig, W'dean 6F 154
BN14: Salv 5E 148
GU33: Liss 3A 34
Warren Side GU31: S Hart 5A 78
Warren Way BN2: W'dean 5L 155
BN8: N Cha 9F 74
BN10: Tels C 3G 174
PO22: Barn 7J 143
Warren Wood BN8: N Cha 8G 74
Warrington Cl. RH11: Craw 1A 28
Warrior Cl. BN41: Ports 3D 152
Warrs Hill Rd. BN8: N Cha 8E 74
Warwick Cl. PO21: Pag 1D 180
Warwick Ct. BN3: Hove 4A 172
BN18: Arun 3G 144
PO10: Ems 5F 136
(off High St.)
Warwick Gdns. BN11: Wor 2J 171
Warwick La. *BN11: Wor* 2J 171
(off Warwick St.)
Warwick Mt. *BN2: Brig* 9D 154
(off Montague St.)
Warwick Pl. BN11: Wor 2J 171
PO22: Felp 7L 165
Warwick Rd. BN11: Wor 2J 171
Warwick St. BN11: Wor 2H 171
Warwick Wlk. BN43: Shor S 4J 151
Washbrooks Family Farm 2H 113
WASHINGTON 9C 108
Washington Bostal RH20: Wash 2B 128
Washington Pk. RH20: Wash 8C 108
Washington Rd. BN44: Stey, Wis 8K 109
PO10: Ems 4F 136
RH11: Craw 9A 10
RH16: Hay H 4G 73
RH20: Storr 6K 107
Washington Rdbt. RH20: Wash 8C 108
Washington St. BN2: Brig 7C 154
PO19: Chich 6B 140
Wassand Cl. RH10: Craw 6J 11
WATERBEACH 9J 121
Waterbury Hill RH17: Hors K 5B 52
Watercress Pl. RH13: Hors 8C 26
Watercress Ter. PO10: Ems 1G 136
Waterdyke Av. BN42: S'wck 6A 152
Waterfield Cl. RH13: Hors 8B 26
Water Fld. Gdns. PO19: Chich 7M 139
Waterfield Gdns. RH11: Craw 8A 10
Waterford Cl. BN10: Peace 2J 175
Waterford Gdns. BN17: Climp 3D 166
Waterfront, The BN2: Brig 8K 173
BN12: Gor S 4C 170
WATERGATE 2N 117
WATERHALL 8K 133
Waterhall Golf Course 8J 133
Waterhall Rd. BN1: Brig 8K 133
Waterhouse Sq. RH17: Cuck 2N 71
Waterlands La. RH12: R'hook 3C 24
Water La. BN13: Ang 8E 146
BN16: Ang 8E 146
BN17: Wick 2K 167
BN44: Wis 7G 109
RH20: Storr 4K 107
Water La. Ind. Est. RH20: Storr 4K 107
Waterlea RH10: Craw 7J 11
Waterloo Pl. BN2: Brig 5F 172 (7C 154)
Waterloo Rd. PO9: Hav 3A 136
PO22: Felp 8H 165
Waterloo Sq. PO21: Bog R 1L 181
Waterloo St. BN3: Hove 7A 172 (8M 153)
Waterplat, The PO19: Chich 5E 140
Waters Edge PO21: Aldw 2G 181
RH20: Pulb 7N 85
Watersedge Gdns. PO10: Ems 5F 136
PO20: W Witt 5J 177
WATERSFIELD 3G 105
Watersfield Rd. BN14: Wor 8F 148
Waterside RH6: Horl 1J 5
RH19: E Grin 3H 15
Waterside, The *BN17: L'ton* 3J 167
(off River Rd.)
Waterside Cl. RH11: Craw 8A 10
Waterside Dr. PO19: Chich 1B 162
Watersmead Bus. Pk. BN17: L'ton 9M 145
Watersmead Cl. BN17: L'ton 1N 167
Watersmead Dr. BN17: L'ton 1N 167
Watersmeet PO19: Chich 7M 139
Waterstone Cl. PO20: Itchen 5C 160
Water Vw. RH6: Horl 2M 5
Waterworks Cl. RH18: F Row 8M 15
Waterworks Rd. GU32: Peters 2G 54
Watery La. PO18: Funt 9D 118
PO19: Huns 1C 162
(not continuous)
Watling Cl. BN42: S'wck 6A 152
Watling Ct. *BN42: S'wck* 6A 152
(off Watling Rd.)
Watling Rd. BN42: S'wck 6A 152
Watson Cl. RH10: Craw 8L 11
Watson Way PO20: Westg 6E 142
Wattlehurst Farm 5M 7
Watts Lodge *RH15: Burg H* 5E 94
(off Kings Way)
Waveney Wlk. RH10: Craw 8K 11
Waverley Ct. BN11: Wor 3F 170
RH12: Hors 9M 25
Waverley Cres. BN1: Brig 4D 154
Waverley Rd. BN16: Rust 3B 168
PO21: Bog R 8B 164
Wavertree Ct. *RH6: Horl* 3H 5
(off Massetts Rd.)
Wavertree Rd. BN12: Gor S 1B 170
Way, The BN16: E Pres 4F 168
Wayfield Av. BN3: Hove 4G 153
Wayfield Cl. BN3: Hove 4H 153
Wayland Av. BN1: Brig 1L 153
Wayland Hgts. BN1: Brig 1L 153
Wayside BN1: Brig 8M 133
BN15: Lan 8N 149
RH11: Ifield 8A 10
Wayside Av. BN13: Durr 6B 148
Wayside Cotts. RH20: Great 2M 105
Wayside Rd. BN16: Ang 9F 146
Weald, The RH19: E Grin 1F 14
Weald & Downland Open Air Mus. 9E 100
Weald Av. BN3: Hove 4H 153
Weald Cl. BN6: Hurst 1H 113
RH13: Hors 2B 46
Weald Ct. Rd. RH14: Bill 2J 65
Weald Dr. RH10: Craw 7J 11
Weald Dyke BN43: Shor B 7J 151
Wealden Dr. PO18: Westh 4G 141
Wealden Ho. RH19: E Grin 6J 15
Wealden Way RH16: Hay H 5E 72
Wealdon Cl. RH13: Southw 1K 67
Weald Ri. RH16: Hay H 8F 72
Weald Rd. RH15: Burg H 5N 93
Wear Cl. BN13: Durr 6A 148
Weare St. RH5: Capel, Ock 1L 7
Wear Rd. BN13: Durr 6A 148
Weaver Cl. RH11: Ifield 7A 10
Weavers Cl. GU29: Ease 7H 59
RH15: Burg H 7E 94
Weavers Ct. *BN43: Shor S* 6H 151
(off Ropetackle)
Weavers Grn. PO9: Hav 2C 136
Weavers Hill BN16: Ang 8F 146
Weavers La. BN5: Henf 3H 111
Weavers Mead RH16: Hay H 7D 72
Weavers Ring BN16: Ang 8F 146
Webb Cl. PO21: Pag 4C 180
RH11: Craw 2D 28
Webb La. PO11: Hay I 9A 158
Weddell Rd. RH10: Craw 9H 11
Wedges, The RH13: Itch 5B 44
Wedglen Ind. Est. GU29: Midh 1F 80
Wedgwood Rd. PO22: Felp 8H 165
Weirbrook RH10: Craw 9J 11
WEIR WOOD 1H 33
Weir Wood Reservoir 1F 32
Weir Wood Reservoir Nature Reserve 2C 32
Weir Wood Sailing Club 9H 15
Welbeck Av. BN3: Hove 7G 153
Welbeck Cl. RH15: Burg H 4E 94
Welbeck Ct. BN3: Hove 7G 153
Welbeck Dr. RH15: Burg H 3D 94
Welbeck Mans. *BN3: Hove* 7G 153
(off Welbeck Av.)
Welesmere Rd. BN2: Rott 1A 174
Welkin, The RH16: Lind 1H 73
Welland Cl. BN13: Durr 5B 148
Welland Rd. BN13: Durr 5B 148
Wellcroft Cotts. BN6: Alb 2E 112
Wellend Vs. BN1: Brig 1D 172 (5A 154)
Weller Cl. RH10: Worth 7M 11
Wellers Cl. PO22: Felp 6H 165
Wellesley Av. BN12: Gor S 2B 170
Wellesley Ct. BN11: Wor 3D 170
Wellfield RH19: E Grin 5J 15
Wellfield Cotts. *GU31: S Hart* 5A 78
(off Tipper La.)
Wellhouse La. RH15: Key 9C 94
Well Ho. Rd. RH20: A'ton 2E 108
Wellingham La. BN13: High S 4C 148
Wellingham Way RH12: Fay 1M 27
Wellington Cl. RH10: Craw 3N 11
Wellington Ct. *BN2: Brig* 6C 154
(off Wellington Rd.)
BN2: Brig 8L 173
BN11: Wor 2E 170
PO9: Hav 3A 136
Wellington Gdns. PO20: Sel 2J 183
Wellington Ga. RH19: E Grin 1G 14
Wellingtonia Ct. *BN1: Brig* 2N 153
(off Laine Cl.)
Wellington Pl. PO20: Tang 3M 141
Wellington Rd. BN2: Brig 6C 154
BN10: Peace 6L 175
BN41: Ports 7D 152
PO19: Chich 4C 140
PO21: Bog R 9C 164
RH12: Hors 9A 26
Wellington St. BN2: Brig 6D 154
Wellington Town Rd. RH19: E Grin 2D 14
Wellington Way RH6: Horl 1H 5
Well La. GU27: Has 5M 17
GU29: Midh 4G 81
Well Rd. PO21: Pag 4B 180
Wellsbourne *BN2: Brig* 8G 154
(off Findon Rd.)
Wells Cl. BN7: Plump G 1M 115
RH12: Hors 9K 25
Wells Ct. *BN11: Wor* 3E 170
(off Pevensey Gdn.)
Wells Cres. PO19: Chich 4A 140
PO21: Aldw 9M 163
Wellsfield PO20: W Witt 2G 177
Wells Ho. *GU29: Midh* 2G 80
(off Bridgefield Cl.)
Wells Lea RH19: E Grin 1D 14
Wells Mdw. RH19: E Grin 1D 14
Wells Rd. RH10: Craw 1G 29
Wellswood RH16: Hay H 6G 72
Wellswood Gdns. PO9: Row C 3C 116
Wellsworth La. PO9: Ids, Row C 3C 116
Wellwood Cl. RH13: Hors 7E 26
Welwyn Cl. RH11: Craw 1A 28
Wembley Av. BN15: Lan 7A 150
Wembley Gdns. BN15: Lan 7A 150
Wenban Pas. *BN11: Wor* 1H 171
(off Wenban Rd.)
Wenban Rd. BN11: Wor 1H 171
Wenceling Cotts. BN15: S Lan 8F 150
Wendale Dr. BN10: Peace 2K 175
Wendover Grange BN3: Hove 7J 153
Wendy Ridge BN16: Rust 2A 168
Wenlock Cl. RH11: Craw 8C 10
Wensleydale RH11: Craw 9E 10
Wensley Gdns. PO10: Ems 2F 136
Wentworth Cl. BN13: Durr 5D 148
PO22: Barn 6J 143
Wentworth Ct. BN11: Wor 2F 170
BN16: E Pres 4F 168
(off The Nookery)
Wentworth Dr. PO10: S'brne 3L 137
RH10: Craw 5M 11
Wentworth St. BN2: Brig 9C 154
WEPHAM 9N 125
Weppons BN43: Shor S 6J 151
Wesley Cl. RH6: Horl 1J 5
RH11: Craw 9A 10
Wessex Av. PO20: E Witt 4L 177
PO21: Aldw 1J 181
Wessex Ct. BN11: Wor 2G 171
Wessex Wlk. BN43: Shor S 4J 151
WEST ASHLING 2E 138
W. Ashling Rd. PO18: Hamb 2A 138
(not continuous)

West Av.—Widewater Ct.

West Av. BN11: Wor .2E 170
BN15: S Lan .8D 150
PO21: Aldw .9A 164
PO22: Midd S .6N 165
RH10: Craw .4J 11
West Bank BN18: Yap .8A 144
West Beach BN43: Shor B .8G 150
PO20: W Witt .4H 177
West Beach Local Nature Reserve .5J 167
W. Beach Rd. PO20: W Witt .4H 177
WEST BLATCHINGTON .3H 153
West Blatchington Windmill .3H 153
WESTBOURNE .2H 137
Westbourne Av. BN14: Broadw .9H 149
PO10: Ems .3F 136
Westbourne Caravan Pk. PO10: W'brne .1K 137
Westbourne Cl. PO10: Ems .3G 136
Westbourne Gdns. BN3: Hove .7J 153
Westbourne Gro. BN3: Hove .6J 153
Westbourne Pl. BN3: Hove .7J 153
Westbourne Rd. PO10: Ems, W'brne .2G 136
Westbourne St. BN3: Hove .6J 153
Westbourne Vs. BN3: Hove .7H 153
W. Bracklesham Dr. PO20: E Witt .5L 177
Westbridge Path PO18: Mid L .1A 140
Westbrook BN2: Salt .2C 174
RH18: F Row .9L 15
Westbrook Cl. PO18: Bosh .8E 138
Westbrooke BN11: Wor .2H 171
Westbrooke Ct. *BN11: Wor* .*2G 171*
(off Crescent Rd.)
Westbrook Fld. PO18: Bosh .8D 138
West Brook Way PO22: Felp .6K 165
Westbrook Way BN42: S'wck .6B 152
WEST BROYLE .3M 139
W. Broyle Dr. PO19: W Bro .3M 139
West Bldgs. BN11: Wor .3G 171
WEST BURTON .6D 104
Westburton La. RH20: Bury .7D 104
W. Burton Rd. RH20: Bury .7D 104
Westbury Ct. BN11: Wor .2F 170
WEST CHILTINGTON .7K 87
WEST CHILTINGTON COMMON .9H 87
West Chiltington Golf Course .6J 87
W. Chiltington La. RH13: Bill, Itch .4M 65
RH14: Bill .9L 65
(not continuous)
West Chiltington Mus. .7J 87
W. Chiltington Rd. RH20: Pulb .7E 86
RH20: Storr .3J 107
RH20: W Chil .7L 87
West Cl. GU27: Fern .4K 37
PO22: Felp .8J 165
PO22: Midd S .7L 165
Westcombe BN1: Brig .3B 172
West Comn. RH16: Hay H, Lind .3G 72
West Comn. Dr. RH16: Lind .2H 73
Westcott Cl. RH11: Craw .3E 28
Westcott Keep *RH6: Horl* .*1L 5*
(off Langshott La.)
West Ct. *BN43: Shor S* .*6H 151*
(off West St.)
Westcourt Pl. BN14: Broadw .9G 149
Westcourt Rd. BN14: Broadw .1G 171
Westcroft BN7: Plump .6M 115
WEST DEAN .9C 100
Westdean Av. BN9: Newh .7N 175
West Dean Gdns. .9C 100
WEST DEAN PARK .1C 120
Westdean Rd. BN14: Wor .8F 148
WESTDENE .9L 133
Westdene Dr. BN1: Brig .9L 133
Westdene Woods Local Nature Reserve .9M 133
Westdown Ct. BN11: Wor .1E 170
West Dr. BN2: Brig .8C 154
BN12: Fer .4K 169
BN16: Ang .9C 146
PO21: Aldw .2D 180
PO22: Midd S .7A 166
WEST END .2F 110
West End La. BN5: Henf .3D 110
GU27: Has .3E 18
West End Way BN15: Lan .9A 150 & 1N 171
WESTERGATE .6E 142
Westergate Cl. BN12: Fer .2L 169
Westergate M. PO20: Westg .5E 142
Westergate Rd. BN2: Brig .1F 154
Westergate St. PO20: Westg .8E 142
Westerley Gdns. *PO20: E Witt* .*5M 177*
(off Plover Cl.)
Westerman Complex BN3: Hove .5H 153
Western Av. PO10: Ems .5D 136
Western Cl. BN15: Lan .9N 149
Western Concourse BN2: Brig .9K 173
Western Esplanade BN3: Hove .7F 152
BN41: Ports .7F 152
Western Lodge *BN15: Somp* .*6N 149*
(off Cokeham Rd.)
Western Pde. PO10: Ems .6E 136
Western Pl. BN11: Wor .3G 171
Western Rd. BN1: Brig .7A 172 (7M 153)
BN3: Hove .7L 153
BN6: Hurst .1H 113
BN8: Newick .9J 75
BN15: Lan, Somp .8M 149
BN17: L'ton .4L 167
BN43: Shor S .6J 151
PO20: Sel .4J 183
RH15: Burg H .5N 93
RH16: Hay H .6G 72
Western Rd. Nth. BN15: Somp .7N 149
Western Row BN11: Wor .3G 171
Western St. BN1: Brig .8A 172 (8M 153)
Western Ter. BN1: Brig .7A 172 (8N 153)
BN15: Somp .6K 149
WESTERTON .2H 141
WESTFIELD .9A 158
Westfield PO22: Bers .5C 164
Westfield Av. BN2: Salt .1D 174
BN16: E Pres .4F 168
Westfield Av. Nth. BN2: Salt .1D 174
Westfield Av. Sth. BN2: Salt .1D 174
Westfield Cl. BN1: Brig .1B 154
Westfield Cres. BN1: Brig .9B 134
Westfield Ri. BN2: Salt .1D 174
Westfield Rd. RH11: Craw .6D 10
W. Front Rd. PO21: Pag .5B 180
W. Furlong Ct. *BN6: Hurst* .*2J 113*
(off W. Furlong La.)
W. Furlong La. BN6: Hurst .2J 113
West Gate BN7: Plump G .1M 115
Westgate PO19: Chich .7N 139
Westgate Leisure Cen. .7B 140
Westgate Link Rdbt. PO19: Chich .7N 139
Westgate Rdbt. PO19: Chich .7B 140
WEST GREEN .5E 10
West Green Dr. RH11: Craw .5E 10
West Green Pk. .5E 10
WEST GRINSTEAD .2N 89
West Gun Copse RH13: Hors .5H 45
Westham BN2: Brig .8G 154
WESTHAMPNETT .4G 141
Westhampnett Rd. PO19: Chich .6E 140
WEST HARTING .2N 77
West Head BN17: L'ton .4M 167
WEST HILL .1E 50
West Hill BN13: High S .3C 148
RH17: Ard, Bal .1E 50
RH19: E Grin .4D 14
West Hill Cl. BN13: High S .3C 148
Westhill Dr. RH15: Burg H .5N 93
West Hill Pl. BN1: Brig .5D 172 (7A 154)
West Hill Rd. BN1: Brig .5C 172 (7A 154)
West Hill St. BN1: Brig .5C 172 (7A 154)
WEST HOATHLY .5M 31
W. Hoathly Rd. RH19: E Grin .7D 14
(not continuous)
West Hove Golf Course .9E 132
Westingway PO21: Bog R .9B 164
West Jetty BN2: Brig .9K 173
WEST KINGSTON .4H 169
Westlake Cl. BN13: Wor .8D 148
Westlake Gdns. BN13: Wor .8D 148
Westland Av. BN14: Wor .9E 148
Westland Ct. *BN41: Ports* .*6C 152*
(off West Rd.)
Westlands BN12: Fer .3K 169
BN16: Rust .2N 167
PO20: Bir .6G 161
RH13: Hors .8B 26
Westland's Copse La. GU28: Riv .5G 60
Westlands La. PO20: Bir .7G 160
Westlands Rd. PO20: Huns .4C 162
RH16: Hay H .4J 73
West La. BN15: Lan .6B 150
PO11: Hay I .3A 158
RH19: E Grin .4D 14
WEST LAVANT .9N 119
WEST LAVINGTON .2J 81
Westleas RH6: Horl .1G 4
WEST LEIGH .9A 116
West Leigh RH19: E Grin .5E 14
West Leigh Pk. .1A 136
Westloats Gdns. PO21: Bog R .7C 164
Westloats La. PO21: Bog R .7B 164
West Mallion *RH16: Hay H* .*6G 73*
(off Colwell Cl.)
West Mans. BN11: Wor .3F 170
WEST MARDEN .7L 97
W. Mare La. RH20: Pulb .7D 86
West Mead BN16: E Pres .4D 168
West Meade GU30: Mill .8L 35
Westmead Gdns. BN11: Wor .2D 170
Westmead Rd. PO19: Chich .7M 139
West Meads RH6: Horl .2L 5
W. Meads Dr.
PO21: Aldw, Bers, Bog R .7A 164
WESTMESTON .7G 115
Westmeston Av. BN2: Salt .2B 174
Westmeston Bostall BN6: W'ton .8G 115
West Mill La. BN5: Small D .7F 110
Westminster Ct. BN11: Wor .2K 171
Westminster Dr. PO21: Aldw .9M 163
Westminster Rd. RH10: Craw .7L 11
Westmoreland Wlk. BN43: Shor S .4H 151
Westmorland Ct. BN3: Hove .4B 172
Westmorland Dr. PO22: Felp .6J 165
Westmount BN2: Brig .7D 154
Westmount Caravan Pk. PO20: Sel .2H 183
Westmount Cl. BN42: S'wck .5N 151
WESTON .9B 54
Weston Ho. GU32: Peters .6E 54
Weston La. GU32: West .9B 54
PO18: Funt .9C 118
Weston Rd. GU31: Peters .6G 54
Westons Cl. RH12: Hors .4A 26
W. Onslow Cl. BN12: Fer .1K 169
West Pallant PO19: Chich .7C 140
West Pde. BN11: Wor .4D 170
RH12: Hors .7N 25
West Pk. Cres. RH15: Burg H .4M 93
West Pk. La. BN12: Gor S .2C 170
West Pk. Rd. RH10: Copt .1F 12
RH17: Hand .3D 48
West Point BN43: Shor B .7K 151
WEST PRESTON .2D 168
W. Preston M. *BN16: Rust* .*3D 168*
(off Station Rd.)
West Quay BN2: Brig .9K 173
West Ridings BN16: E Pres .4D 168
West Rd. BN41: Ports .6C 152
BN45: Newt .9F 112
PO10: Ems .5D 136
W. Sands Caravan Pk. PO20: Sel .2E 182
(not continuous)
W. Sands La. PO20: Sel .2F 182
Westside GU28: Till .9J 61
WEST STOKE .8K 119
W. Stoke Rd.
PO18: W Sto, Mid L .9K 119
PO19: W Bro .9K 119
West Strand PO20: W Witt .3E 176
West St. BN1: Brig .8D 172 (8A 154)
BN2: Rott .3N 173
BN6: Ditch .4D 114
BN11: Wor .3G 171
West St. BN15: Somp .6K 149
BN41: Ports .6E 152
BN43: Shor S .6H 151
GU27: Has .4L 17
GU29: Midh .1H 81
GU31: Rog .5D 56
PO10: Ems .5F 136
PO19: Chich .7B 140
PO20: Sel .4G 182
PO21: Bog R .1L 181
RH11: Craw .7F 10
RH12: Hors .9N 25
RH14: Bill .1H 65
RH15: Burg H .4N 93
RH19: E Grin .4E 14
RH20: Storr .6J 107
West Sussex Golf Course .1F 106
WEST TARRING .8E 148
WEST THORNEY .3K 159
WEST TOWN .1H 113
West Tyne BN13: Durr .7B 148
Westup Rd. RH17: Bal .1N 49
West Vw. BN3: Hove .6L 153
RH16: Lind .3J 73
West Vw. Cl. BN2: W'dean .5L 155
Westview Cl. BN10: Peace .5L 175
West Vw. Cotts. PO10: S'brne .3L 137
West Vw. Dr. BN18: Yap .2N 165
West Vw. Gdns. BN18: Yap .3N 165
RH19: E Grin .4E 14
Westview Ter. *BN14: Fin* .*8C 128*
(off North Vw. Ter.)
W. Walberton La.
BN18: Walb .3J 143
West Wlk. BN16: E Pres .4D 168
Westward Cl. PO18: Bosh .8F 138
Westward Ho. *PO19: Chich* .*7M 139*
(off Fishbourne Rd. (East))
Westward La. RH20: W Chil .1H 107
West Way BN3: Hove .3F 152
BN13: High S .4B 148
BN15: S Lan .8D 150
PO19: Fish .7L 139
PO19: W Bro .4M 139
RH10: Craw .5J 11
RH13: Slinf .8B 24
Westway BN17: Wick .1J 167
PO22: Bog R .7E 164
RH6: Gatw .6K 5
RH10: Copt .1A 12
Westway Cl. BN41: Ports .1A 152
Westway Gdns. BN41: Ports .1A 152
WEST WITTERING .1G 176
Westwood Cl. PO10: Ems .3G 137
WEST WORTHING .2D 170
West Worthing Station (Rail) .1E 170
West Worthing Tennis & Squash Club .7M 147
Wetherdown GU31: Peters .6G 55
Wey and Arun Junction Canal .8N 63
Weycombe Rd. GU27: Has .4L 17
Weydown Cotts. GU27: Has .2L 17
Weydown Ct. GU27: Has .4K 17
Weydown Ind. Est. GU27: Has .4K 17
Weydown Rd. GU27: Has .5K 17
Weydown Rd. Ind. Est. GU27: Has .5K 17
Wey Gdns. GU27: Has .6H 17
Wey Hill GU27: Has .5J 17
Wey Lodge Cl. GU30: Lip .7A 16
Weysprings GU27: Has .4H 17
Whapple, The BN17: L'ton .4N 167
Wharf, The GU29: Midh .1H 81
Wharf Rd. BN17: L'ton .3J 167
BN41: Ports .7F 152
Wheatcroft BN17: Wick .1J 167
Wheatear Dr. GU31: Peters .6J 55
Wheatfield Rd. PO20: Sel .2K 183
Wheatfield Way BN2: Brig .2G 154
RH6: Horl .1K 5
Wheatlands Cl. BN10: Tels C .2H 175
Wheatsheaf Cl. RH12: Hors .6B 26
RH15: Burg H .3N 93
WHEATSHEAF COMMON .2K 35
WHEATSHEAF ENCLOSURE .2L 35
Wheatsheaf La. RH17: Cuck .3B 72
Wheatsheaf Rd. BN5: Henf, W'cote .9J 91
Wheatstone Cl. RH10: Craw .1K 11
Wheelbarrow Castle GU29: Ease .7J 59
Wheeler Ct. RH16: Hay H .7G 72
Wheeler Rd. RH10: Craw .8K 11
Wheelers Way RH19: Felb .1M 13
Wheelwright La. RH15: Burg H .7E 94
Wheelwright Lodge *BN15: Somp* .*6N 149*
(off West St.)
Wheelwrights RH20: W Chil .7K 87
Wheelwrights Cl. BN18: Arun .3G 145
GU27: Fern .*4K 37*
(off Haslemere Rd.)
Wherwell Ct. PO9: Hav .9B 116
Whichelo Pl. BN2: Brig .7D 154
Whichers Cl. PO9: Row C .6B 116
Whichers Ga. Rd. PO9: Row C .6B 116
Whippingham Rd. BN2: Brig .5D 154
Whippingham St. BN2: Brig .5D 154
Whipping Post La. BN2: Rott .3N 173
Whistler Av. PO19: Chich .4C 140
Whistler Cl. RH10: Craw .9H 11
Whistler Ct. BN1: Brig .4A 154
Whitaker Pl. PO20: Oving .6K 141
White Acre BN17: Wick .1J 167
White Av. GU33: Long C .1B 34
Whitebeam Ct. RH16: Hay H .7E 72
Whitebeam M. RH16: Hay H .7D 72
Whitebeam Rd. BN13: Durr .8A 148
White Beam Way PO20: Tang .4M 141
Whitebeam Way PO22: Midd S .6M 165
Whitechimney Row PO10: W'brne .2H 137
White City GU29: Midh .1G 81
Whitecroft BN16: Rust .3B 168
RH6: Horl .1K 5
Whitecross St. BN1: Brig .5E 172 (7B 154)
Whitegate Cl. RH10: Copt .1B 12
WHITEHALL .1F 88
Whitehall Dr. RH11: Ifield .6A 10
Whitehall Pde. *RH19: E Grin* .*3E 14*
(off London Rd.)
White Hart Ct. RH12: Hors .7N 25
WHITEHAWK .7G 154
Whitehawk Cl. BN2: Brig .8F 154
Whitehawk Cres. BN2: Brig .8F 154
Whitehawk FC .8H 155
Whitehawk Hill Rd. BN2: Brig .8E 154
Whitehawk Race Hill Local Nature Reserve
.6F 154
Whitehawk Rd. BN2: Brig .7F 154
Whitehawk Way BN2: Brig .7G 154
White Horse Caravan Pk. PO20: Sel .2H 183
White Horse Ct. *RH20: Storr* .*6J 107*
(off High St.)
Whitehorse Rd. RH12: Hors .5E 26
White Horse Sq. BN44: Stey .3A 130
White Horses Way BN17: L'ton .3N 167
White Horse Yd. *RH20: Storr* .*6J 107*
(off High St.)
White House, The RH10: Craw .1F 10
White Ho. Gdns. GU32: Peters .4E 54
White Ho. Pl. BN13: Durr .5C 148
White Ladies Cl. PO9: Hav .4A 136
Whitelands PO22: Felp .6H 165
RH16: Hay H .6G 72
Whitelea Rd. BN17: Wick .2K 167
White Lion Ct. *BN43: Shor S* .*6H 151*
(off Ship St.)
White Lodge BN3: Hove .5L 153
BN17: L'ton .3L 167
Whitelot Cl. BN42: S'wck .3A 152
Whitelot Way BN42: S'wck .3A 152
WHITELY HILL .2A 30
Whitely Hill RH10: Worth .2A 30
Whiteman's Cl. RH17: Cuck .1N 71
WHITEMANS GREEN .1N 71
Whitemans Grn. RH17: Cuck .1M 71
White Oak Wlk. PO9: Hav .9B 116
White Rd. GU28: Graff .3B 102
PO18: E Dean .9B 102
(not continuous)
PO18: E Dean, Graff .5A 102
Whiterock Pl. BN42: S'wck .6A 152
Whites Cl. BN6: Hurst .9J 93
Whiteside Cl. PO19: Chich .6D 140
Whites La. GU27: Fern, Henl .6E 36
White St. BN2: Brig .8C 154
White Styles Rd. BN15: Somp .6M 149
White Styles Ter. BN15: Somp .6M 149
Whitethorn Dr. BN1: Brig .9K 133
Whitethorn Rd. PO11: Hay I .9B 158
Whitethroat La. RH17: Bal .4K 49
Whitewalls *RH11: Craw* .*6B 10*
(off Rusper Rd.)
Whiteway La. BN2: Rott .2A 174
BN7: Rod .5H 157
Whiteways PO22: Bers .6B 164
Whiteways Cl. BN17: L'ton .2K 167
PO22: Bers .6B 164
Whiteways Lodge Rdbt. BN18: Houg .4E 124
Whitfield Cl. BN16: Ang .9F 146
GU27: Has .2L 17
PO22: Bog R .7F 164
Whitfield Rd. GU27: Has .3L 17
Whitgift Wlk. RH10: Craw .9F 10
Whitley Cl. PO10: W'brne .9H 117
Whitmore Way RH6: Horl .1F 4
Whitsbury Rd. PO9: Hav .9A 116
Whittingehame Gdns. BN1: Brig .2A 154
Whittington Ct. PO10: Ems .5F 136
Whittington Rd. RH10: Craw .9F 10
Whittle Way RH10: Craw .9J 5
Whitwell Hatch GU27: Has .6M 17
Whitworth Ho. *BN11: Wor* .*1F 170*
(off St Botolph's Rd.)
Whitworth Rd. RH11: Craw .2F 10
WHYKE .7D 140
Whyke Cl. PO19: Chich .9D 140
Whyke Ct. PO19: Chich .9D 140
Whyke La. PO19: Chich .7D 140
Whyke Marsh PO19: Chich .9D 140
Whyke Rd. PO19: Chich .7D 140
Whyke Rdbt. PO19: Chich .9D 140
Whylands Av. BN13: Durr .5B 148
Whylands Cl. BN13: Durr .5B 148
Whylands Cres. BN13: Durr .5B 148
Whytings RH13: Mann H .4F 46
WICK .1K 167
Wickbourne Ho. *BN17: Wick* .*2J 167*
(off Clun Rd.)
Wick Cl. PO22: Felp .7J 165
Wick Ct. *BN17: Wick* .*1H 167*
(off Phoenix Cl.)
Wickenden La. RH19: Sharp .7C 32
Wickens Ct. RH16: Hay H .7D 72
Wickets, The RH15: Burg H .3A 94
Wick Farm Rd. BN17: Wick .2J 167
Wick Hall BN3: Hove .5A 172 (7M 153)
Wickham Cl. RH6: Horl .1H 5
RH16: Hay H .2F 72
Wickham Dr. BN6: Hurst .2K 113
Wickham Hill BN6: Hurst .3L 113
Wickham Way RH16: Hay H .2F 72
Wickhurst Cl. BN41: Ports .3B 152
Wickhurst Gdns. RH12: Broadb H .8J 25
Wickhurst La. RH12: Broadb H .8J 25
Wickhurst Ri. BN41: Ports .2B 152
Wickhurst Rd. BN41: Ports .3B 152
Wickland Ct. RH10: Craw .9F 10
Wicklands Av. BN2: Salt .3C 174
Wick La. GU29: Ease .5K 59
PO22: Felp .7J 165
Wickor Cl. PO10: Ems .3G 136
Wickor Way PO10: Ems .2G 136
Wick Pde. BN17: Wick .1K 167
Wicks Farm Caravan Pk. PO20: W Witt .9B 160
Wicks Rd. RH14: Bill .1H 65
Wick St. BN17: Wick .2K 167
Wickwoods Health Club & Spa .5B 112
Widdicombe Way BN2: Brig .3F 154
Widewater Cl. BN15: S Lan .8F 150
Widewater Ct. BN43: Shor B .8F 150

A-Z West Sussex Atlas 229

MIX
Paper from
responsible sources
FSC® C005461
www.fsc.org

SAFETY CAMERA INFORMATION

PocketGPSWorld.com's CamerAlert is a self-contained speed and red light camera warning system for SatNavs and Android or Apple iOS smartphones/tablets. Visit www.cameralert.co.uk to download.

Safety camera locations are publicised by the Safer Roads Partnership which operates them in order to encourage drivers to comply with speed limits at these sites. It is the driver's absolute responsibility to be aware of and to adhere to speed limits at all times.

By showing this safety camera information it is the intention of Geographers' A-Z Map Company Ltd., to encourage safe driving and greater awareness of speed limits and vehicle speed. Data accurate at time of printing.

HOSPITALS, HOSPICES and selected HEALTHCARE FACILITIES covered by this atlas.

N.B. Where it is not possible to name these facilities on the map, the reference given is for the road in which they are situated.

ACRE DAY HOSPITAL 3G **170**
29 Wordsworth Road
WORTHING
BN11 3NJ
Tel: 01903 216807

ALDRINGTON HOUSE 6H **153**
35 New Church Road
HOVE
BN3 4AG
Tel: 01273 778383

ARUNDEL & DISTRICT HOSPITAL 2G **144**
Chichester Road
ARUNDEL
BN18 0AB
Tel: 01903 882543

BOGNOR REGIS WAR MEMORIAL HOSPITAL 7D **164**
Shripney Road
BOGNOR REGIS
PO22 9PP
Tel: 01243 865418

BRIGHTON GENERAL HOSPITAL 6E **154**
Elm Grove
BRIGHTON
BN2 3EW
Tel: 01273 696011

BRIGHTON NUFFIELD HEALTH HOSPITAL 5K **155**
Warren Road
BRIGHTON
BN2 6DX
Tel: 01273 624488

CHALKHILL 6G **73**
Lewes Road
HAYWARDS HEATH
RH16 4BQ
Tel: 01444 472 672

CHESTNUT TREE HOUSE (CHILDREN'S HOSPICE) 5C **146**
Dover Lane
Poling
ARUNDEL
BN18 9PX
Tel: 0845 4505820

CHICHESTER CENTRE, THE .5D **140**
Graylingwell Drive
CHICHESTER
PO19 6GS
Tel: 01243 791900

CHICHESTER NUFFIELD HEALTH HOSPITAL 4B **140**
78 Broyle Road
CHICHESTER
PO19 6WB
Tel: 01243 887663

CRAWLEY HOSPITAL 6E **10**
West Green Drive
CRAWLEY
RH11 7DH
Tel: 01293 600300

EMSWORTH VICTORIA HOSPITAL 5F **136**
North Street
EMSWORTH
PO10 7DD
Tel: 01243 376041

GATWICK PARK SPIRE HOSPITAL 3G **4**
Povey Cross Road
HORLEY
RH6 0BB
Tel: 01293 785511

GORING HALL BMI HOSPITAL 2N **169**
Bodiam Avenue
Goring-by-Sea
WORTHING
BN12 5AT
Tel: 01903 506699

HASLEMERE COMMUNITY HOSPITAL 4M **17**
Church Lane
HASLEMERE
GU27 2BJ
Tel: 01483 782334

HAYWARDS HEATH NUFFIELD HEALTH HOSPITAL 3E **72**
Burrell Road
HAYWARDS HEATH
RH16 1UD
Tel: 01444 4847916

HOLY CROSS HOSPITAL 4H **17**
Hindhead Road
HASLEMERE
GU27 1NQ
Tel: 01428 643311

HORSHAM HOSPITAL 8N **25**
Hurst Road
HORSHAM
RH12 2DR
Tel: 01403 227000

HOVE POLYCLINIC 4H **153**
Nevill Avenue
HOVE
BN3 7HY
Tel: 01273 696011

HURSTWOOD PARK NEUROLOGICAL CENTRE 7H **73**
Lewes Road
HAYWARDS HEATH
RH16 4EX
Tel: 01444 441881

LANGLEY GREEN HOSPITAL 2F **10**
Martyrs Avenue
CRAWLEY
RH11 7EJ
Tel: 01293 590400

MARTLETS HOSPICE 4H **153**
Wayfield Avenue
HOVE
BN3 7LW
Tel: 01273 273400

MCINDOE SURGICAL CENTRE 1F **14**
Holtye Road
EAST GRINSTEAD
RH19 3EB
Tel: 01342 330300

MEADOWFIELD 5B **148**
Arundel Road
WORTHING
BN13 3EP
Tel: 01903 843200

MIDHURST COMMUNITY HOSPITAL 8H **59**
Dodsley Lane
Easebourne
MIDHURST
GU29 9AW
Tel: 01730 819100

MILL VIEW HOSPITAL 4G **153**
Nevill Avenue
HOVE
BN3 7HZ
Tel: 01273 696011

MONTEFIORE HOSPITAL, THE
. . . . .4A **172** (6M **153**)
Montefiore Road
BRIGHTON
BN3 6EP

NEVILL HOSPITAL 4G **153**
Laburnum Avenue
HOVE
BN3 7JW
Tel: 01273 821680

NHS WALK-IN CENTRE (BRIGHTON) 5E **172**
84-87 Queens Road
BRIGHTON
BN1 3XE
Tel: 01273 203146

NHS WALK-IN CENTRE (CRAWLEY) 6E **10**
Crawley Hospital
West Green Drive
CRAWLEY
RH11 7DH
Tel: 01293 600300

PETERSFIELD HOSPITAL 6E **54**
Swan Street
PETERSFIELD
GU32 3LB
Tel: 01730 263221

PORTSMOUTH SPIRE HOSPITAL 9D **116**
Bartons Road
HAVANT
PO9 5NP
Tel: 02392 456000

PRINCESS ROYAL HOSPITAL 6H **73**
Lewes Road
HAYWARDS HEATH
RH16 4EX
Tel: 01444 441881

QUEEN VICTORIA HOSPITAL 1F **14**
Holtye Road
EAST GRINSTEAD
RH19 3DZ
Tel: 01342 414000

ROYAL ALEXANDRA CHILDREN'S HOSPITAL 9E **154**
Eastern Road
BRIGHTON
BN2 5BE
Tel: 01273 696955

ROYAL SUSSEX COUNTY HOSPITAL 9E **154**
Eastern Road
BRIGHTON
BN2 5BE
Tel: 01273 696955

ST BARNABAS HOUSE HOSPICE 8M **147**
2 Titnore Lane
WORTHING
BN12 6NZ
Tel: 01903 706398

ST CATHERINE'S HOSPICE (CRAWLEY) 8F **10**
Malthouse Road
CRAWLEY
RH10 6BH
Tel: 01293 447333

ST PETER & ST JAMES HOSPICE 4M **95**
North Common Road
North Chailey
LEWES
BN8 4ED
Tel: 01444 471598

ST RICHARD'S HOSPITAL 5D **140**
Spitalfield Lane
CHICHESTER
PO19 6SE
Tel: 01243 788122

ST WILFRID'S HOSPICE 9B **140**
Grosvenor Road
CHICHESTER
PO19 8FP
Tel: 01243 775302

SALVINGTON LODGE 5B **148**
Salvington Hill
WORTHING
BN13 3BW
Tel: 01903 266399

SOUTHLANDS HOSPITAL 5L **151**
Upper Shoreham Road
SHOREHAM-BY-SEA
BN43 6TQ
Tel: 01903 205111

SUSSEX BEACON (HOSPICE) 4F **154**
10 Bevendean Road
BRIGHTON
BN2 4DE
Tel: 01273 694222

SUSSEX EYE HOSPITAL 9E **154**
Eastern Road
BRIGHTON
BN2 5BF
Tel: 01273 606126

SUSSEX ORTHOPAEDIC NHS TREATMENT CENTRE 6G **73**
Lewes Road
HAYWARDS HEATH
RH16 4EY
Tel: 0333 200 1728

WORTHING HOSPITAL 1J **171**
Lyndhurst Road
WORTHING
BN11 2DZ
Tel: 01903 286754

ZACHARY MERTON HOSPITAL 4C **168**
Glenville Road
Rustington
LITTLEHAMPTON
BN16 2EB
Tel: 01903 858100

NOTES